"大学堂" 开放给所有向往知识、崇尚科学，对宇宙和人生有所追问的人。

"大学堂" 中展开一本本书，阐明各种传统和新兴的学科，导向真理和智慧。既有接引之台阶，又具深化之门径。无论何时，无论何地，请你把它翻开……

大学堂 026

The Technique
of Translation

翻译的技巧

钱歌川 著

Chien Gochuen

目　录

序 1

第一编　汉译英与英文句型 1

　壹　由要素来分的造句 2
　　(1) 汉文易写英文难通 2
　　(2) 动词的种类和变化 2
　　(3) 动词与五种句型 8
　　(4) 第一句型的自动构造 9
　　(5) 第二句型的不完全自动构造 12
　　(6) 第三句型的他动构造 17
　　(7) 第四句型的授与构造 25
　　(8) 第五句型的不完全他动构造 30

　贰　由构造来分的造句 37
　　(1) 用单句来翻译 37
　　(2) 用合句来翻译 48
　　(3) 用复句来翻译 52

　叁　由内容来分的造句 63
　　(1) 用平叙句来翻译 63
　　(2) 用疑问句来翻译 69
　　(3) 用命令句来翻译 75
　　(4) 用感叹句来翻译 81

第二编　英文惯用法及其翻译 ·· 89

Ⅰ. It 的造句 ··· 90

(1) it... 不定词 ·· 90

(2) it... for... 不定词 ··· 91

(3) it... 动名词 ·· 93

(4) it... 子句 ··· 94

(5) it is... 子句 ·· 95

(6) it... 名词 ··· 97

Ⅱ. 名词的造句 ·· 98

(7) "all + 抽象名词"或"抽象名词 + itself" = very + 形容词 ········ 98

(8) "the + 单数名词"的特殊用法 ································ 98

(9) 无生物的主语 ·· 99

(10) something (much) of, nothing (little) of ···················· 100

(11) 属格的主格作用和宾格作用 ································ 102

(12) 名词(A) + of + a + 名词(B) ································ 104

(13) 名词 + of + 属格 + 名词 ··································· 105

(14) of + 抽象名词 = 形容词,of 从略 + 普通名词 ················ 105

(15) one's own + 名词,of one's own + 动名词 ··················· 106

(16) have + the + 抽象名词 + 不定词 ···························· 107

(17) that(those) + 先行词 + 关系代名词 ························· 108

(18) one thing ... another ······································· 109

Ⅲ. As 的造句 ··· 109

(19) "as... as"的三种用法 ····································· 109

(20) as... as any,as... as ever ································· 110

(21) as... as... can be ··· 111

(22) as... , so... ·· 112

(23) It is in (or with)... as in (or with) ························· 112

(24) as much, as many, like so many ···························· 113

(25) as good as, as well as ······································ 114

(26) 句首的"as it is",句尾的"as it is" ························· 115

(27) 过去分词 + as it is,现在分词 + as it does ·················· 116

(28) 名词等 + as + 主语 + 动词等 ······························ 117

Ⅳ. 动词的造句 ·· 118

(29) may well + 动词, and well + 主语 + may ·············· 118

(30) may as well…as, might as well…as ·············· 119

(31) so that…may, lest…should ·············· 120

(32) cannot help + 动名词, cannot but + 原形不定词 ·············· 121

(33) have + 宾语(物) + 过去分词 ·············· 122

(34) have + 宾语(人) + 原形不定词 ·············· 123

(35) have + 宾语 + 副词(地点,方向等) ·············· 125

(36) have + 宾语 + 现在分词 ·············· 125

(37) find oneself ·············· 126

(38) find…in ·············· 127

(39) "do" 的两种用法 ·············· 127

(40) "depend on" 的两种用法 ·············· 129

(41) know…from ·············· 130

(42) had better + 原形不定词, would rather + 原形不定词 ·············· 130

(43) make…of ·············· 131

(44) make one's way ·············· 132

(45) rob…of ·············· 133

(46) seize…by the… ·············· 135

(47) see if…, see that… ·············· 135

(48) take…for granted ·············· 136

(49) used to + 原形不定词, be used to + 动名词 ·············· 137

(50) be + 自动词的过去分词 ·············· 140

(51) 否定 + fail + 不定词 ·············· 141

(52) 动词 + 原形不定词 ·············· 142

(53) leave + much(nothing) + to be desired ·············· 143

(54) be + 不定词 ·············· 143

(55) have + 不定词 + 宾语, have + 宾语 + 不定词 ·············· 145

(56) prevent + 宾语 + from + 动名词 ·············· 146

(57) persuade + 宾语 + into + 动名词, dissuade + 宾语 + from + 动名词 ·············· 147

Ⅴ. 不定词的造句 ·· 148

(58) 表目的、原因、结果等的不定词 ·············· 148

(59) so as + 不定词, so...as + 不定词 ·················· 150

(60) too... + 不定词, not too... + 不定词, too...not + 不定词 ·················· 151

(61) only too... + 不定词, too ready + 不定词 ·················· 152

(62) 不定词的感叹用法 ·················· 153

(63) not to speak of, not to say ·················· 154

Ⅵ. 动名词的造句 ·················· 155

(64) There is no + 动名词 ·················· 155

(65) for + the + 动名词 ·················· 155

(66) above + 动名词 ·················· 156

(67) worth + 动名词 ·················· 156

(68) far from + 动名词 ·················· 158

(69) busy + 动名词 ·················· 159

(70) on + 动名词, in + 动名词 ·················· 159

Ⅶ. 否定词的造句 ·················· 160

(71) no more...than ·················· 160

(72) no less...than ·················· 162

(73) not so much...as, not so much as ·················· 163

(74) Nothing is more...than, Nothing is so...as ·················· 164

(75) cannot...too ·················· 165

(76) 否定 + without ·················· 166

(77) 否定 + but ·················· 167

(78) 否定 + until(till) ·················· 168

(79) not so...but, not such a...but ·················· 168

(80) "not A but B", "B, (and) not A" ·················· 169

(81) 否定 + because ·················· 170

(82) not because...but because ·················· 171

(83) not that...but that ·················· 171

(84) 否定 + every(all, both, always, quite) ·················· 172

Ⅷ. what, who 的造句 ·················· 174

(85) what he is, what he has ·················· 174

(86) what + 名词, what little + 名词 ·················· 174

(87) what with...and what with, what by...and what by ·················· 175

(88) what is + 比较级 ·· 176

(89) A is to B what X is to Y ·· 177

(90) who + 肯定, who + 否定 ··· 177

(91) 疑问词 + should...but ··· 178

(92) Who knows but (that) ·· 179

Ⅸ. 条件及让步的造句 ··· 179

(93) 省略 if 的句法 ··· 179

(94) If it were not for (= Were it not for) + 名词, If it had not been for
(= Had it not been for) + 名词, But for + 名词, But that + 名词子句 ········ 181

(95) 命令句 + and, 命令句 + or ··· 182

(96) 名词 + and ·· 183

(97) 动词 + 疑问词 ··· 184

(98) no matter + 间接疑问句, 疑问词 – ever + may ························ 185

(99) 动词 + as + 主语 + 助动词 ··· 186

(100) if any ··· 186

(101) be it ever (或 never) so, let it be ever (或 never) so ················· 187

(102) once ··· 188

(103) were to ·· 188

(104) 含有条件意味的字眼 ··· 189

Ⅹ. 形容词副词的造句 ··· 190

(105) "the + 形容词" 的两种用法 ······································· 190

(106) 最上级形容词含有 even 之意 ······································ 192

(107) the + 比较级...the + 比较级 ······································ 192

(108) the + 比较级 + 理由 ·· 193

(109) the last... + 不定词, the last... + 形容词子句 ······················· 194

(110) so + 形容词 (副词) + that, so + 动词 + that ·························· 195

(111) so that ··· 196

(112) so much so that ··· 197

(113) such...as, such...that ·· 198

(114) 比较级 + than, more + 原级 + than ································· 200

(115) more...than + can ··· 201

(116) more than + 动词 ·· 202

(117)less...than 202
(118)much more,much less 203
(119)would sooner(rather)...than,would as soon...as 204
(120)no sooner...than,hardly...when 205
(121)anything but,nothing but,all but 206
(122)short of,be short of,nothing short of 207
(123)ever so 208
(124)good and 的副词用法 209
(125)to one's + 感情名词,to the + 感情名词 + of 210
(126)so far,so far as,so far as...is concerned 211

Ⅺ.连词的造句 212
(127)and that 212
(128)at once...and 213
(129)in that 213
(130)It is true...but 214

Ⅻ.其他的造句 215
(131)one,as such 215
(132)one thing...another 216
(133)in + 人物 216
(134)before 的四种译法 217

第三编　疑难句法及文章译例 219

壹　英文类似句辨异 220

贰　常易译错的文句 245
　Ⅰ　中译英 245
　Ⅱ　英译中 263

叁　翻译实例 283
　Ⅰ　中译英 283
　　(1)郑燮致弟书 283
　　(2)中国的山水画 284
　　(3)为学 284
　　(4)光与色 286
　　(5)教学相长 286

(6) 翻译文欠通顺 ……………………………………………… 287

(7) 学无所用 ………………………………………………… 288

(8) 画蛇添足 ………………………………………………… 288

(9) 嗟来食 …………………………………………………… 289

(10) 老与少 ………………………………………………… 290

(11) 雕刻奇技 ……………………………………………… 291

(12) 狐疑 …………………………………………………… 292

(13) 怕伞的姑娘 …………………………………………… 294

(14) 偷窃狂 ………………………………………………… 296

(15) 狐假虎威 ……………………………………………… 298

(16) 习惯说 ………………………………………………… 298

(17) 黔之驴 ………………………………………………… 299

(18) 少年孔融的机智 ……………………………………… 300

(19) 绝妙好辞 ……………………………………………… 301

(20) 韩信忍受袴下辱 ……………………………………… 302

Ⅱ 英译中 ……………………………………………………… 304

(1) Too Clever Not to See ………………………………… 304

(2) The Busy Broker ………………………………………… 305

(3) Speculation on Important Subjects …………………… 305

(4) A Feeling of Eternity …………………………………… 306

(5) The Spirit of Fair-Play ………………………………… 307

(6) On D. H. Lawrence …………………………………… 307

(7) On Books ……………………………………………… 308

(8) Arguments against Smoking ………………………… 308

(9) The Definition of a Gentleman ……………………… 309

(10) The Law of the Jungle ……………………………… 309

(11) Some well-informed People ………………………… 310

(12) The English Humour ………………………………… 311

(13) The Trouble with Translation ……………………… 312

(14) Too Distinguished to be a Personality ……………… 313

(15) Schadenfreude ……………………………………… 314

(16) Aloneness is Worse than Failure …………………… 315

7

（17）Being One's True Self ……………………………………… 316
（18）Happiness Consists in Love …………………………………… 317
（19）The Cosy Fire of Affection ……………………………………… 318
（20）Irrational Man ……………………………………………………… 320

附录　当代英美名作摘译 ……………………………………………… 323

（1）William Plomer：On Not Answering the Telephone ………… 324
（2）Louis Kronenberger：A Note on Privacy …………………… 325
（3）Lawrence George Durrel：Justine …………………………… 327
（4）Lawrence George Durrel：Mountolive ……………………… 329
（5）P. H. Newby：A Parcel for Alexandria ……………………… 331
（6）Muriel Spark：The Girls of Slender Means ………………… 332
（7）J. D. Salinger：The Long Debut of Lots Taggett …………… 334
（8）J. D. Salinger：The Catcher in the Rye ……………………… 336
（9）Iris Murdoch：The Bell ………………………………………… 337
（10）Iris Murdoch：The Flight from the Enchanter ……………… 339
（11）Truman Capote：Breakfast at Tiffany's ……………………… 341
（12）Truman Capote：Breakfast at Tiffany's ……………………… 342
（13）James Baldwin：Notes of a Native Son ……………………… 344
（14）William Styron：Lie Down in Darkness …………………… 346
（15）William Styron：The Confessions of Nat Turner …………… 348
（16）Stan Barstow：Gamblers Never Win ………………………… 350

习题解答 …………………………………………………………………… 353

出版后记 …………………………………………………………………… 402

序

  这本小著前后写了十年之久，在我七十生辰的当月，总算全部脱稿，可以付诸剞劂了。

  我开始在大学里教翻译课，是在台湾大学，后来因移砚他校，停了一个相当长久的时期，直到一九六四年应聘南来星洲，先在义安学院，继在新加坡大学，今在南洋大学，每年都教翻译，而且成了我的专科。在海外和在国内，教翻译是不同的。因为国内的大学，是把这门课开设在外文系里，而且是高年级才有的，可是在星洲，翻译是中文系的课程，各年级都有，这当然是为配合当地需要的缘故。国内把这门课开设在外文系，教的人比较不大吃力，星洲因为是中文系的课程，教时就比较要困难些。大家都知道在我国或星洲，谈到翻译，大抵是指中英对译。中文是我们的母语，无论如何，总比英文要好得多，所以学生到了外文系三、四年级时，英文也学到了相当的程度。可以自由表达了，这时来学翻译，无论是中译英或英译中，都能写出通顺的文字来，问题只在对内容的含义，可能有译得不恰当的地方。在星洲的情形可不同了，因为读中文系的同学，英文好的不多，教翻译的人，先得讲解英文，事倍功半。

  本书除第三编的一小部分外，其余都是在星洲写成的。九年来不断地加以增补修订，始有今日的面貌。当然我不敢自诩内容已臻完善，不过我已尽了最大的努力，使之切合学生的需要，可以作为翻译教本。第一编教学生用各种各样的英文句型来翻译，使之熟悉英文的写法，以补救英文较差的缺憾。如每周三小时，两小时讲解，一小时练习，本编是足够一年之用的，第一编所注重的是中译英，而第二编则把重点移到英译中的上面，分门别类的介绍英文的惯用句，各种特殊的表现法，除加上适当的汉译外，并详为解说，每种句法皆附有习题，以供练习之用。学生学完一种表现法后，即进行习题翻译，如此一再实验，定能有所心得。第二编的内容也超过可供每周三小时用一年的教材。以上两个年度的教程，仍不外是奠定基础的准备工作，要到第三年才正式进入实际翻译的阶段。

  第三编的主体为长篇的中译英和英译中，这便是我们通常所遇到的翻译材料。除此以外，另备一些可供讲解的教材，以助学习。在第三编的头上，有英文类似句的研究，又有容易译错的文句及其正确译法，这些都是极有用的资料，不易搜集到的。在长篇翻译的教材中，中文方面有浅近的白话，和艰深的文言。在翻译文言文的时候，必须有一番准备工夫，译者得先把文言译成白话，然后才好译成英文，否则难免差误。在英译中方面，则未采用古文，完全选的近代人的作品，内容也不限于文艺方面，而包含哲学，政治，语文，人生问题，原子弹的恐怖，甚至局外人对越战的看法等各方面,以便译者可接触到英文表现的各种面貌。书末附录现在生存的英美名家代表作的节译,更可看出现代英文的趋势,并得以此为踏脚石,进而直接阅读现代文学名著。

  过去出版的有关翻译的书,无论中外,大都是讲理论的,偶有谈实际的也只是举出几个例子而已。像本书这样有系统,有方法,来研究翻译的书,似乎还不多见,也可说是破天荒之举,如能对初学者有所裨益,该编者多年的辛劳就得到酬报,而感到满足了。书中错误,在所不免,仍希读者,不吝指正。

一九七二年春　歌川识于南洋大学

第一编　汉译英与英文句型

壹　由要素来分的造句

(1) 汉文易写英文难通

汉译英必须采用英文的句法,来表达汉文的意念,不可照汉文直译,如照汉文的句法直译,则译出来的不像英文。为避免写成中国式的英文,首先就要把英文的一些基本句型学会,而且要记在心上,当我们动手翻译时,便能运用自如,随便采用哪种句型,都合乎英文的惯用句法了。

我们既能说中国话,又能读中国文,在翻译上对于汉文方面是不会有很多困难的,问题只有英文这一方面,因此我们在汉译英的时候,还是要从英文着手,要把写作英文的基本句型,来作为翻译的工具。

现在我们先来学会以要素为主的五种英文的句型,作为学习翻译的第一步。因为任何英文句子,总不外是这五种句型当中的一种,现代英文是没有第六种句型的。这五种句型是由动词的不同而分别出来的,所以我们在研究五种句型之前,要先把英文动词的种类搞清楚一下。

五种句型是以要素(element)来分的,那么在英文句子中有些什么要素呢? 那一共有四个要素,即主语(Subject)、述语(Predicate)、宾语(Object)、补语(Complement)。任何一个句子,必须有主语和述语。另外一些句子,除主语述语外,还有宾语或补语,或宾语补语同时都有。决定一个句子是不是要有宾语补语的,就在动词,而且动词是两个基本要素当中的一个。所谓述语,原是叙述一件事物的动作或状态的,结局就是动词。这是任何一个句子非有不可的基本因素。学英文把动词的用法学会了,英文就学通了十分之八九了。

(2) 动词的种类和变化

一个英文动词本身虽只有现在形、过去形、过去分词形和现在分词形四种形式,例如"看见"这个动词,则有 see,saw,seen,seeing 四个不同的变化,但这四种形式运用起来,也可变出十六种不同的时态,即

1. He sees(现在)
2. He saw(过去)
3. He has seen (现在完成)
4. He had seen (过去完成)
5. He is seeing(现在进行)
6. He was seeing (过去进行)
7. He will see(现在推量)
8. He would see (过去推量)
9. He has been seeing (现在完成进行)
10. He had been seeing (过去完成进行)

11. He will have seen（现在完成推量）

12. He would have seen（过去完成推量）

13. He will be seeing（现在进行推量）

14. He would be seeing（过去进行推量）

15. He will have been seeing（现在完成进行推量）

16. He would have been seeing（过去完成进行推量）

这便是英文动词的变化和用法。奇数是现在，偶数是过去。所谓"完成"是英文特有的动词时态，它本身又有现在、过去、未来之分，现在完成所代表的时态，是从过去到现在，过去完成是指过去的过去，未来完成是说未来的过去。所谓"进行"是真正的现在，即正在进行中的动作，英文的现在时态，只是一种经常的现象而已。所谓"推量"即指未来的事现在加以预测，并不怎样确实的。

所谓现在、过去、未来三种基本的时态，每种又包含得有单纯的，以前的，以后的三个时期，现举例说明如下：

Ⅰ. PRESENT

1. Simple present：

   I take three meals a day.

2. Before – present：

   I have finished my meal.

3. After – present：

   I am about to start my meal.

Ⅱ. PAST

1. Simple past：

   Last Wednesday at two o'clock my plane left.

2. Before – past：

   Last Wednesday at two o'clock I had just returned from London.

3. After – past：

   Last Wednesday at two o'clock I was about to give my speech.

Ⅲ. FUTURE

1. Simple future：

   Next Wednesday at two o'clock I will land at New York.

2. Before – future：

   Next Wednesday by two o'clock I will have landed at New York.

3. After – future：

   Next Wednesday at two o'clock I will be about to land at New York。

再就性质来说，英文动词又可大别为两类：自动词（Intransitive Verb）和他动词（Transitive Verb）。**自动词**是说明主语的动作或状态的，它自身已能完成一个意念，不必要补足什么要素，而成为一个完整的动作。例如唐诗人贾岛的名句：

鸟宿池边树，僧敲月下门。

译成英文时，便是

Birds dwell in a tree by the pond.
A *monk knocks* at the door under the moon.

又如，

皓月当空。
The *moon shines* brightly.
凉风起天末。
A cool *breeze sprang* up in the sky.
日出于东而落于西。
The *sun rises* in the east and *sets* in the west.
到了春天美丽的花朵开遍原野。
In spring beautiful *flowers bloom* in the open country.
我今天觉得好多了。
I feel much better today.
我对他那贵重的援助非常感谢。
I am deeply indebted to him for his valuable assistance.

在以上例句中有主语 Birds 及其述语 dwell
在以上例句中有主语 monk 及其述语 knocks
在以上例句中有主语 moon 及其述语 shines
在以上例句中有主语 breeze 及其述语 sprang
在以上例句中有主语 sun 及其述语 rises
在以上例句中有主语 sun 及其述语 sets
在以上例句中有主语 flowers 及其述语 bloom
在以上例句中有主语 I 及其述语 feel
在以上例句中有主语 I 及其述语 am

前七例是说明主语的动作的，后二例是说明主语的状态的。

他动词就不同了，若单说 have, make 等字时，意念是不完全的，必得再加上宾语，才能表出一个完全的意念，例如：

我在新加坡有许多熟人。
I have many *acquaintances* in Singapore.
我早已跟他结识了。
I made his *acquaintance* long ago.
我害了重伤风。
I have taken a bad *cold*.

我带着照相机到槟城去玩了一星期。
I made a week's *trip* to Penang with my camera.

所有的他动词都要有宾语，否则不成句，因为他动词没有宾语就不能表示出一个完全的意念来，上举四例：

主语	述语	宾语
I	have	acquaintances
I	made	acquaintance
I	have taken	cold
I	made	trip

这两种动词又可以再细分为四种，即：完全自动词（Complete Intransitive Verb）与不完全自动词（Incomplete Intransitive Verb）；完全他动词（Complete Transitive Verb）与不完全他动词（Incomplete Transitive Verb）。现在分别举例说明如下：

完全自动词本身已能表示一个完全的意念，无须再加补语，例如

昨夜下了大雨。
It rained heavily last night.
一轮明月在东方升起。
A beautiful *moon has risen* in the eastern sky.
在晴天众鸟欢鸣。
In fine weather *birds sing* merrily.

在以上各例句中除主语和述语外，便没有其他的要素了，那就是说，没有宾语或补语，有的只是无关重要的形容词，副词，或形容词片语，副词片语之类罢了。如第一句中的 heavily 是副词，last night 是副词片语。第二句中的 a 和 beautiful 是形容词，in the eastern sky 是副词片语。第三句中的 in fine weather 是副词片语，merrily 是副词。这些都是修饰语，不是文句不可缺少的要素。所以这种完全自动词的句子，在语言学上称为 favourite sentence（最普通的句子），因为它只需要"动作者＋动作"就行了。

不完全自动词本身不能表出一个完全的意念，必须补上另外的字才能成句。你单说 He is，即"他是"，听者必然要问"他是什么"？又如你说 He becomes，即"他变得"，听者必然要问"他变得怎样了"？我们如果在这两种说法的后面，加上 rich 一字，意念便完全了。即变成 He is rich. "他是有钱人"。He becomes rich. "他变得有钱了"。这个 rich 的字，在文法上就叫做补语。又因为这是补足主语的意味的，所以称为**主格补语**（Subjective Complement）。加上补语的不完全自动词，便能表示出一个完全的意念来了。

他是一位教师。
He is a *teacher*.
他好像很诚实的样子。
He seems quite *honest*.
他直到最后都是很忠实的。

He remained faithful to the last.

天气变得很热了。

It has become much *warmer*.

她渐入老境。

She is growing (or *getting*) *old*.

那谣言证实了。

The *rumour proved true*.

霜叶红于二月花。

The frosted maple *leaves have turned red*, much redder than the flowers in spring.

在上面的例句中,有三个要素,举出如下:

主语	述语	补语
He	is	teacher
He	seems	honest
He	remained	faithful
It	has become	warmer
She	is growing	old
rumour	proved	true
leaves	have turned	red

完全他动词是不要补语的,但它非有**宾语**不可。有时采用一个宾语,有时采用两个宾语。先看采用一个宾语的造句。这是任何他动词都可以用的,只要有宾语,就可造出一个句子来,别的字多也无用。

树大招风。

Tall *trees catch* much *wind*.

我们每天学英语。

We study English every day.

我昨天在理发店遇见他。

I met him at the barber's yesterday.

他的法国话比英语说得好。

He speaks French better than *English*.

在上面的例句中,有三个要素,举出如下:

主语	述语	宾语
trees	catch	wind
We	study	English
I	met	him
He	speaks	French;English

采用两个宾语的完全他动词,又叫做**授与动词**(Dative Verb)。这是由"授物与人"(give

something to a person)或"授人以物"(give a person something)的基本观念而产生的。这个"人"与"物",都是句子当中的宾语,所以就变成一个句子有两个宾语了。通常"物"是直接宾语(Direct Object),"人"是间接宾语(Indirect Object),因为真正给的是物,接受那物的才是人。

把货物交给我,我就会付你钱。
Give *me* the *goods*, and I will give *you* the *money*.
她问那孩子叫什么名字。
She asked the *boy* his *name*.
医生不许他的病人喝酒。
The doctor forbade his *patient wine*.
我羡慕你的健康。
I envy *you* your good *health*.
请你帮我一个忙好吗?。
Will you do *me* a *favour*?
付一块钱给车夫。
Pay the *driver* one *dollar*.
他们对我们并无恶意。
They meant *us* no *harm*.

通常是把间接宾语放在直接宾语之前,如果为加强语气等原因而把直接宾语放到前面去的话,就要在间接宾语前加介词 to,for,of 等而做成一个片语,例如:

我寄了一封信给她。
I sent *her* a *letter*. = I sent a letter *to* her.
我为她买了一袭新衣。
I bought *her* a new *dress*. = I bought a new dress *for* her.
我想求你一件事。
I wish to ask *you* a *favour*. = I wish to ask a favour *of* you.

这样一来,采用两个宾语的授与动词,就变成采用一个宾语的普通动词了。句中的 to her, for her, of you,都是介词的片语,等于一个形容词的作用。不过有人还是把它视为两个宾语的句子。

单有宾语还不能表示一个完全的意念,必得再加以补语的,便是**不完全他动词**。这种动词含有使动的作用,是有所作为的,所以又称为**作为动词**(Factitive Verb)。例如:

他使父母快乐。
He *made* his *parents happy*.
总统任命他为将官。
The president *made him* a *general*.

结果是父母感到快乐(His parents were [*or* became] happy.),那人成为将军(He was [*or* became] a general.),这都不外是那动词有所作为的结果。第一句中的 happy 是形容词补语(Adjective Complement),第二句中的 general 是名词补语(Noun Complement),二者都是补足句中的宾语的,所以

就叫作**宾格补语**(Objective Complement),跟上面说过的主格补语不同。

英文的动词,自动或他动,完全或不完全,都不是固定不移的,任何一个动词,常有变化发生,一定要看它用在什么句子中,才能确定它的性质乃至它的意义。例如:

(a)鸵鸟不能飞。

The ostrich cannot *fly*.(这个 fly 是自动词)。

(b)我会放风筝。

I can *fly* a kite.(这个 fly 是他动词)。

同是一个自动词,也有完全及不完全两种用法,例如:

(a)车轮徐转。

The wheels are *turning* slowly.(这个 turn 是完全自动词)。

(b)树叶转黄。

The leaves are *turning* yellow.(这个 turn 是不完全自动词)。

同是一个他动词,也有完全及不完全两种用法,如

(a)我们用葡萄造酒。

We *make* wine from grapes.(这个 make 是完全他动词)。

(b)把你的故事说得有趣一点。

Make your story interesting.(这个 make 是不完全他动词)。

又如

(a)I *think* it is right.(完全他动词)。

(b)I *think* it right.(不完全他动词)。

英文的自动词照规矩是不能接上一个宾语的,不过有时用一个介词为媒介,也可以接用宾语,如

人人都笑我。

Everybody laughed *at* me.

思君令人老。

To think *of* you makes me old.

(3)动词与五种句型

所有的英文句子,归纳起来,不过五种句型构造,即是

1. 第一句型的自动构造(Intransitive Construction)。

这需要用四种要素中的两种基本要素:

Subject + Predicate

例句:车轮转动。

Wheels *turn*.

2. 第二句型的不完全自动构造(Neuter Construction)。
这需要用四种要素中的三种要素：

  Subject + Predicate + Complement

  例句：牛奶变酸了。

    Milk *turns* sour.

3. 第三句型的他动构造(Transitive Construction)。
这也需要用四种要素中的三种要素：

  Subject + Predicate + Object

  例句：人们转动车轮。

    Men *turn* wheels.

4. 第四句型的授与构造(Dative Construction)。
这虽则只用到三种要素，但宾语这个要素，得分为间接与直接两个：

  Subject + Predicate + Indirect Object + Direct Object

  例句：母牛给我们牛奶。

    Cows *give* us milk.

5. 第五句型的不完全他动构造(Factitive Construction)。
这是要动用四种要素的：

  Subject + Predicate + Object + Complement

  例句：打雷使牛奶变酸。

    Thunder *turns* milk sour.

而这五种句型，如下表所示，又都是由动词出发的，可见动词对英文造句是何等的重要呀。

动词 { 自动词 { 完全自动词……………………(第一句型)
     不完全自动词 + 补语……………(第二句型)
  他动词 { 完全他动词 { + 一个宾语………(第三句型)
         + 两个宾语………(第四句型)
    不完全他动词 + 宾语 + 补语…………(第五句型)

(4) 第一句型的自动构造

  主语 + 述语

  从英文的造句法(Syntax)上来看，每个句子都必须具备主语和述语两个部分。表示思想主题的是**主语**，述说动作、状态、性质等的是**述语**。

  这两个部分是任何英文句子不可或缺的，如果在句中不见了这两个部分，或其中的一个部分，那只是在字面上临时把它省略了，并不是原来就不存在的。例如：

  "走开！"Go away!——这个命令句译成英文时是把主语的 you 省略了，原应作 You go away！

的。又如

　　一个多么漂亮的姑娘！
　　What a pretty girl!

这个惊叹句译成英文时,是把主语的 she 和述语的 is 省略了。原应作 What a pretty girl she is! 的。

　　我很快就会再写信给你的。
　　Write you soon again.

这个平叙句译成英文时,是省略了主语的 I 和助动词的 will 的,原应作 I will write you soon again. 的。根据以上的例子,就可知道没有主语述语的句子,只是临时省略,原来的句子是非有不可的。主语述语对文句既有这般重要,我们决不可加以忽视,在阅读时找出文句,尤其是长的文句的主语述语,对我们了解文义,是有极大的帮助的。

对于第一句型的句子*,普通都是把它分做两个部分,例如 These pretty little birds sing very merrily. 一句,普通把 These pretty little birds 四字看作主部的 Subject,把 sing very merrily 三字看作述部的 Predicate. 主部的中心一定是一个名词,或名词同等语,所以那个名词才是主部的本体,英文叫作 Subject‑word（主语本字）。在上例中的 Subject‑word 是 birds,这便是我们读书时第一个要找出来的字。同样地述部的中心,一定是一个动词,所以这个动词才是述部的本体,英文叫作 Predicate‑verb（述语动词）。在上例中的 Predicate‑verb 是 sing。我们读书时第二个要找出来的字就是它。把一句长文的主语和述语找出来,无异提纲挈领,抓住要点,对文句的主动者及其动作,已经有所了解,整个句子的含义,便可掌握到十之七八了,因为其余的大都是修饰语,在文法上是无关重要的。

在第一句型的构造中,常见的有下列三种形式：

1. S. + Vi：
   Birds sing.

2. S. + Vi. + Adverb(Adverb Phrase)：
   Birds sing merrily (in the tree).

3. S. + Vi. + Adverb Infinitive：
   John has gone to buy books.

现在我们再举出一些第一句型的例子,来看它是怎样发展的。

　　在量上有所得,在质上必有所失。
　　If *anything gains* in quantity, *it* must *lose* in quality.
　　勿做得不偿失的事。
　　Do not *pay* too dear for your whistle.
　　在教室里上课时不要讲话。

---

* 当然不限于第一句型,任何句型,任何复杂的文句,都可分成两个部分,例如 The boy who just came in, the one in the blue suit, I studied English in Canada for two years when he was a child.

You must not *talk* in class.

你来此有何贵干？

What have *you come* here for?

昨夜发生火灾。

A *fire broke* out last night.

当我到车站时正下大雨。

It rained heavily when *I arrived* at the station.

他的弟弟考取了南洋大学。

His *brother succeeded* in the examination of Nanyang University.

他为着转地疗养昨天到金马仑去了。

He went to the Camelon highland yesterday for a change.

我想考取所以拼命用功。

I studied with might and main not to fail in the examination.

因为战争的缘故物价天天上涨。

The *prices go* up every day owing to the war.

这些果树明年就要开始结果子了。

These *trees* will *begin* to bear next year.

对人客气是不会吃亏的。

It pays to be polite.

我明天午后三时到四时之间来看你。

I will *come* to see you between three and four tomorrow afternoon.

只有人类会说话。

Man alone can *speak*.

我通常是早上七时起床。

I generally *get* up at seven in the morning.

王君不久即将出洋研读数学。

Mr. Wang will shortly *go* abroad to study mathematics.

习题 1

试将下列各句译成英文，句中须用完全自动词。

1. 健全的思想寓于健全的人格。
2. 我们不是为食而生，乃是为生而食。
3. 合则留，不合则去。
4. 说话不要支吾其词。
5. 在中国学年为八月一日起到七月三十一日止。
6. 我兄弟前天由此放洋，下月半前后可抵伦敦。
7. 他可能很快回来，不过我不能说一定。
8. 猫在黑暗中也能看见。

9. 这把小刀好切得很。
10. 那工作做了不合算。
11. 这些鸡已经开始生蛋了。
12. 我的朋友是站在我一边的。
13. 太阳好像是围绕着地球在走。
14. 因为太暗我看不清楚。
15. 走了约摸一个钟头,我们到达了目的地。
16. 勤则不匮。(《左传》)
17. 卧不安席,食不甘味,心摇摇如悬旌。(《国策》)
18. 下乔入幽。(《孟子》)
19. 东风解冻。
20. 臣无祖母,无以至今日;祖母无臣,无以终余年;祖孙二人,相依为命。(李密)

(5) 第二句型的不完全自动构造

主语 + 述语 + 补语

第二句型的造句和第一句型不同的地方,就是句中多了一个补语的因素。这是与不完全自动词有连带关系的。凡是遇到不完全自动词的时候,就有加上补语的必要。补语主要是由形容词或名词构成的,但用别的词类也未尝不可,关键是在动词,如果那动词是不完全的自动词,则在其后接上的任何字都是补语。

不完全自动词的代表动词是"be",说 I am, you are, he is 等,意念都是不完全的,必须加上一个表示身份或状态或性质的字眼上去,才能成为完整的句子。这个表示身份或状态或性质的字眼,便叫作补语。华文也是一样,单说"他是"是不能成为一个句子的,必须加上表示身份的名词,或是表示状态或性质的形容词才行。例如说"他是一个什么人",后面就要接上名词的补语,若说"他是什么状态或性质",便不能接名词,而要接形容词的补语了。到底要接名词或是要接形容词,在下笔之先必须想想才不会弄错,因为"他是一个学生"(He is a student.)是说明他的身份的,用上一个名词,当然简单明了,没有问题。至于"他在生病",是说他的状态的,可就不能用名词了。如果用名词而译成 He is illness. 就是错的,必须改说为 He is ill. 才通,因为 illness 是名词,ill 才是形容词。表示状态或性质必须用形容词作补语,表示身份才用名词。用名词作补语的,我们可以说"他是学生",同样也可以说"学生就是他"。但用形容词作补语时,我们却不能说"他是病",当然"病也不是他",用公式表出时,He = student. He ≠ illness. 中国语在形容词的尾上用一个"的"字,等于形容词的尾缀,这是很重要的。"他是勤快的",或简单地说"他勤快",英文译成 He is diligent. 中英文都是通顺的。如果说"他是勤快",中文句子就不完善了,因为"勤快"是一个抽象名词,不是一个形容词,如果"他是勤快",那么,岂不"勤快就是他"了。需知他并不等于勤快,一方是人,一方是一种性质,二者是不能相等的。英文也是一样,我们不能说 He is dligence. 因为 he 并不是 diligence,所以不可以用名词,中英文都要用形容词,中文用"勤快的",英文要用 diligent 才对。

现在我们再举一例,来作进一步的说明。

(a)他是诚实的。(He is honest.)

(b)他是一个诚实的人。(He is an honest man.)

(a)句的补语是形容词(honest),(b)句的补语是名词(man)。(a)句是答复"他是怎样"的,所以说,他是诚实的;(b)句是答复"他是什么"的,所以说,他是人。因此,(a)句必须用形容词,如果说成 He is honesty. 就错了,因为他并不是诚实那回事。(b)句中的 honest 一字,只是用来修饰 man 的,不是主要的因素。(a)句中的 honest,便是补语,为四种要素之一。附带要注意的一点,man 是一个普通名词,依照文法的规定,普通名词如非用复数,就必须加冠词,所以,如果说成 He is man. 或 He is honest man. 就错了。一定要说 He is a man. 或 He is an honest man. 才行。如果补语的名词变成复数的话,这个冠词就用不着了,如:

(a)他是聪明的。(He is clever.)

(b)他是一个聪明的孩子。(He is a clever boy.)

(a)他们是聪明的。(They are clever.)

(b)他们是一些聪明的孩子。(They are clever boys.)

以上用作形容词或名词的补语,是与句中的主语有关的,所以又称主格补语。

上面已经说过,补语并不限于名词和形容词,其他的词类,都可以用作补语,只要那动词是不完全的。任何一个不完全的动词,都需要加上补语,不管那补语是一个怎样形式的字眼,其他词类用在补语的地位上即变成补语了。不过名词和形容词,仍是补语的两大因素,其他只能算是同等语。Noun – Element = Noun and Noun Equivalent. Adjective – Element = Adjective and Adjective Equivalent.

兹将可构成主格补语的字眼分类举出如下:

1. 名　词：He is a *teacher*.(他是教师。)
2. 代名词：It's *me*.(是我。)
3. 形容词：We are *ready*.(我们准备好了。)
4. 副　词：He is *out*.(他出去了。)
5. 不定词：He seems *to be* honest.(他好像是诚实的。)
6. 分　词：I got *hurt*.(我受伤了。)
   It is *interesting*.(这很有趣。)
7. 动名词：Seeing is *believing*.(看见才相信。)
8. 片　语：He is *at home* in history.(他精通历史。)
   It is *of no use* to try further.(不用再干下去了。)
9. 子　句：The pen is *where it was*.(笔在原来的地方。)

上面说过 He is diligence. 一句是不通的,应说 He is diligent. 才可以,因为非用形容词不可,但英文的形容词,常可用"of + 名词"所构成的形容词片语来代替,如 useful 可用 of use 来代替,useless 可用 of no use 来代替,故上举第八项中的第二例,也可以说成 It is useless to try further. 所以上面说的 He is diligence. 那个不通的句子,只消加上一个"of",而说成 He is of diligence. 也就通了。这个"of + 名词" = 形容词,也是常用的一种补语,再举数例如下:

这本杂志是很有用的。
This magazine is *of great use*. (= very useful)
这些书对我毫无价值。
These books are *of no value* to me. (= valueless)

有些没有形容词的名词，当然更要用 of – phrase 了，如

这些东西都是同样的价钱。
These articles are (*of*) *the same price*.
这两个茶杯是同样大小的。
These two cups are (*of*) *the same size*.

兹再将需要有主格补语的不完全自动词分别举例说明如下。需要主格补语的代表动词是"be"，此字原作"存在"解，用作动词时本身几乎没有什么意思，而只担承把主语和补语联系起来的任务罢了，从他这种任务来看，用方法上的专门术语说，叫做 Copula = linking verb（联系词）。在"be"以外的动词，也多少带着 Copula 的任务的，所以这样的动词，也都要有补语才行。例如 lie，意为"用某种状态躺着"，引申为"在某种状态中"；seem 意为"好像在某种状态中"；remain 意为"维持某种状态不变"。此外还有由变化而成为某种状态之意的自动词 become，grow 等，也可以作为需要补语的动词来用。

（一）用属于 be 一类的动词来翻译：

这朵玫瑰花很香。
This rose *smells* sweet.
这纸很粗糙。
This paper *feels* rough.
他那时看去好像耽于回想似的。
He *looked* reflective for a few moments.
他的声音听来好像很愤恨的样子。
His voice *sounded* resentful.
他好像不是寻常的乞丐。
He *seemed* no ordinary mendicant.
也像一切羞怯的人一样，他有时显得傲慢。
Like all shy men he sometimes *appeared* arrogant.
他直到四十岁都还没有结婚。
He *remained* unmarried till forty years old.
他醒来躺着很久才起床。
He *lay* awake a long time before getting up.
我很敬重他。
He *stands* high in my estimation.
他生为圣徒，死为烈士。
He *lived* a saint, and *died* a martyr.

(二)用属于 become 一类的动词来翻译：

那两个人一天天变得更亲密了。
The two were *becoming* more intimate every day.
我的预言成为事实了。
My prediction *has come* true.
那棵树长得越来越高了。
The tree *grew* taller and taller.
我希望他很快康复。
I hope he will *get* better (or recovered) soon.
他在不久的将来就会成为一个优秀的工人的。
He will *make* a capital workman one of these days.
于是他突然变得严肃了。
Then he suddenly *fell* grave.
我的头发变白了。
My hair *has turned* grey.
那狗发狂了。
The dog *has run* mad.
这个新发明会成为对全人类有用的吧。
This new invention will *prove* useful to all humanity.
一听那话她脸色登时变得苍白，直白到嘴唇了。
On hearing that, her face *went* white to the lips.

(三)为着要显示 seem 等字中所潜在的 Copula 的意味，不妨加上 to be 的字样进去。

鸟鸣山更幽。
It *seems to be* more lonesome in the mountains when birds are singing.
他显得很年轻。
He *appears to be* young.
那终会成功的。
It will *prove* to be successful.
那谣言变成事实了。
The rumour has *turned out to be* true.
如果你继续这样懒惰下去，你总有一天要后悔的。
If you *continue to be* idle, you will be sorry for it some day.

这类的自动词是可以反映出说话者的心情的，如 He seems to be ill. 一句话，是表示说话的人不愿直接肯定地说出 He is ill，而只是用 seems to be(好像是)作为推测之辞。

在第二句型的构造中，有下列十二种形式：

1. S. + be – V. + Noun：

Jack is a schoolboy.

2. S. ＋ be－V. ＋ Pronoun：

   The umbrella is mine.

3. S. ＋ be－V. ＋ Adjective：

   He is kind.

   Your story is interesting.

4. S. ＋ be－V. ＋ to－Infinitive：

   I am to start tomorrow.

5. S. ＋ be－V. ＋ －ed＋to－Infinitive：

   I am pleased to meet you.

6. S. ＋ Vi. ＋ Noun：

   He became a merchant.

7. S. ＋ Vi. ＋ Adjective：

   He got angry.

   He looks happy.

8. S. ＋ Vi. ＋ －ing：

   The boy came running.

   He stood waiting for me.

9. S. ＋ Vi. ＋ －ed：

   He looked pleased.

   He went home disappointed.

10. S. ＋ Vi. ＋ Prep. ＋ －ing：

    The prices go on rising.

11. S. ＋ Vi. ＋ Adjective ＋ to－Infinitive：

    He felt very happy to see me elected.

    It remains much to be done.

12. S. ＋ Vi. ＋ Adjective ＋ that（if,whether,where,when,why,etc.）Clause：

    I feel certain that he is coming with me.

    Are you sure if (whether) John is going with us?

    He looked blank when he was informed of his dismissal.

习题 2

试将下列各句译成英文,句中须采用不完全自动词。

1. 我们选择朋友时非十分谨慎不可。
2. 美国人好活动而富于独立精神。
3. 那大学的入学试题很难,我不知能否考取。
4. 她觉得有点窘,不知如何是好。
5. 良药苦口利于病。

6. 他立志坚定不移。

7. 他始终都用心在听讲。

8. 这个办法并不一定永远有效。

9. 真价常不能被人认识。

10. 世事尚待证明。

11. 他依然怏怏不乐,一声不响。

12. 她坐着沉思了好几分钟。

13. 他似乎知道那个事实。

14. 那以后他们就满足了。

15. 中国人的态度是对西方行为的一种反感。

16. 在世界上相距最远的东西两端的地方,经过多少世纪,实际上完全不知道彼此的存在。

17. 他的游记是一种非常有趣味的记录。

18. 很少旅行家的记录有马可·波罗写的那样生动,那样有内容的。

19. 似乎有稍加说明的必要。

20. 不做时代落伍的学生,对当前的出版物是不能忽视的。

(6) 第三句型的他动构造

主语 + 述语 + 宾语

这是用完全他动词加上一个宾语而构成的句子。在这个句型中新出现的一个因素,就是宾语。构成宾语的,都是名词或名词同等语,例如:

1. Do you know *Mr. Chang*?（Noun）
2. I like *him* very much.（Pronoun）
3. I like *to read*.（Non Infinitive）
4. I like *reading*.（Gerund）
5. I know *how to swim*.（Noun Phrase）
6. I know *that he is an honest man*.（Noun Clause）

主语和宾语一定是非名词莫办的,因此我们可以说,任何字句一登上主语或宾语的宝座,它就变成名词了。

宾语并不一定是在动词后面的,有时也会跑到动词的前面去,如 What did Jack build? This is the *ship* that Jack built. 并不一定每次都如 Jack built a *ship*. 一样在动词后面。

他动词的宾语从意义上看,有三种不同的字汇。即:

一、为表示结果的宾语,如我们分明是在纸上写字,结果却写成了一封信,因而我们就说写信（write a letter）。再如我们挖土,结果挖成了一个洞,我们就说挖洞（dig a hole）。

二、为表示一般意义的宾语,有 things, matters 等,例如 If she is really bad, it simplifies *things* very much.（Galsworthy: *Fraternity*）（她要是真的坏,那事情倒简单多了。）

三、为模拟宾语（sham object）"it"。这是英文的一种惯用法,它本身根本没有什么意思,也不是专指一件什么事物,如 He lords *it* over his inferiors.（他对部下如君临一般高傲不堪。）If you are found out, you will catch *it*. (如果你被他们看到,你就要挨骂的。)

有些句子我们中文是要用自动词的,而英文则惯用他动词来说,因为我们很少用事物来作他动词的主语的,英文为说话求简起见,常爱以事物为主动者,这类造句很多和我们说法不同,宜加注意,例如:

你来此何事?
What has *brought* you here? = What have you *come* here for?
从这条路去,就可以到火车站。
This road will *take* you to the station. = If you follow this road, you will *get* to the station.
什么事使他这样生气?
What *made* him so angry? = Why did he *get* so angry?
你肯帮助我的话,我就一定会成功的。
Your assistance will *make* my success certain. = If you assist me, my success will *be* certain.
看到这个使我想起以前的好日子。
This *reminds* me of the good old days. = When I see this, I think of the good old days.
我们靠希望而生存。
Hope *keeps* us alive. = We *live on* by hope.
衣食足而后知礼仪。
Wealth *enables* men to be courteous. = If men have wealth, they *are* able to be courteous.
因为天气坏,我们未能动身。
Bad weather *prevented* us from starting. = We *could* not start because of the bad weather.

他动词后面所接用的宾语,中英两种语文的表现法也有不同的地方。现分五项将英文特异之处说明如下:

(一)具有"夺取"意义的动词

凡被夺取的目标,在中文的说法应该是"物",而在英文则要说"人"。在被夺取的物品之前加一个"of"的介词,造成一个片语接在"人"的后面。

强盗抢了他的钱。
A highwayman *robbed* him of his money.

同样的用法还有下列种种情形。

他把海上的强盗一扫而光。
He *cleared* the sea of those robbers.
忧烦的习惯夺去了我们的和平和安乐。
The habit of worrying *robs* us of peace and comfort.
我学了很多,足以诊好我从前的好幻想的毛病。
I have learned enough to *cure* me of my old fancies. (Stevenson)
我将永远无法完全放弃这种感觉。
I shall never be able entirely to *divest* myself of this feeling.

国王剥夺了他一切的荣誉。

The king *stripped* him of all his honours.

他忘不了过去那种痛苦的回忆。

He could not *rid* himself of the painful memories.

你来了省得我去麻烦写一封长信。

Your coming *relieves* me of the bother of writing a long letter.

他只求自己获得享乐,不管是从谁夺取得来。

He does not care whom he *deprives* of enjoyment, so that he can obtain it.

(二)具有"供给"意义的动词

在英文的表现法中,不能直接把所供给的事物作为宾语,必须以介词 with 为媒介,才能说出那事物来。同时只有受到供给的人才能成为宾语。如"供给某人金钱"为 supply him with money,"车上载草"为 load a cart with straw,"在玻璃杯中倒满清水"为 fill the glass with water."给人食物"为 provide a person with food,"供给我许多消息"为 furnish me with a lot of information,"把那本书呈献给他"为 present him with the book,"赐予接见"为 favour me with an interview,"把秘密告诉她"为 trust her with a secret 等等。

(三)具有"作成"意义的动词。那时句中的"of"所引出的名词,便是作成什么的材料,如"愚弄他",英文说 make a fool of him,便是把他当作材料,作成一个愚人。又如"专攻英文"为 make a special study of English. 意即把英文当作材料来作出一种专门的研究。

(四)不把直接接受动作的人身上某一部分作为宾语,而要把那个人当作对象来说,是大处着眼的意思。

他轻拍我的背。

He *patted* me on the back.

他抓住我的衣领。

He *seized* me by the collar.

他命在旦夕。

Death *stared* him in the face.

他紧紧握着我的手,不让我走。

He *held* me by the hand firmly and would not let me go.

我抓住了他的胳膊。

I *caught* him by the arm.

他拖着我的衣袖。

He *pulled* me by the sleeve.

她打他一记耳光。

She *strikes* him across the face.

在受到动作的人体上某一部分的前面,一般只用冠词 the,不用人称所有格的形容词,如 my, his 等,但有时也可以用,不过用法稍古,如"她吻了他的面颊"说 She kissed him on his cheek. "他敢于用最温柔的态度执了她的手"说 He presumed in the gentlest manner to take her by her hand.

(Lamb, Tales from Shakespeare)说 I caught him by the hand,英文的味道特别浓厚,若照中文的说法,改为 I caught his hand,也未尝不通,不过两者之间是有 nuance 的不同的。

（五）有许多动词我们中文都是作自动词用的,而英文却是他动词,后面要接宾语,例如：

不幸降临到他身上。
A misfortune *befell* him.
这种式样的衣服对你很适合。
This style of dress *becomes* you well.
二者大小相似。
They *resemble* each other in size.
半小时内我们就到槟城了。
We can *reach* Penang in half an hour.
据说那屋子有鬼。
They say ghosts *haunt* that house.
不要走进这房门去。
Don't *enter* this room.

英文的自动词在下列四种情形中,便可当作他动词用,后面直接接上宾语:1. 接用同系宾语(Cognate Object),如"他过了幸福的一生"(He *lived* a happy *life*.) 2. 具有使动的意味(Causative Sense),如"农人种稻"(The farmer *grows* rice.) 3. 接用介词(Preposition),如"你在看什么?"(What are you looking *at*?) 4. 伴有补足字(Complement),如"我们时常谈一通夜"(We often talked the night *away*.)

1. **同系宾语**

   我做了一个奇怪的梦。
   I *dreamed* a strange *dream*.
   他一睡不醒。
   He *slept* the *sleep* that knows no waking.
   我打了一场好仗。
   I have *fought* a good *fight*. (Bible)
   他吐了一口气,才来念了祈祷文。
   He *sighed* a *sigh* and *prayed* a *prayer*. (Scott)

不但自动词如此,他动词有时也可接用同系宾语,例如 tell a tale, sing a song, see a sight 等等。

在同系宾语上附有修饰形容词时,通例可换成态度副词(Adverb of Manner),如 live a long life = live long; live a happy life = live happily; die a natural death = die naturally; die a violent death = die by violence 等等。

有的宾语与动词不同语源,但意义相通,也可视为同类,如 run a race; run a course; run one's career; fight a battle; blow a gale; strike a blow; ring a peal; wreak one's vengeance 等等。

漠然无所指的宾语"it",也可看做一种同系宾语,如

我决心奋斗到底。
I am determined to fight *it* out. (= fight to the end)
安哲罗勋爵很有爵爷的神气。
Lord Angelo dukes *it* (= plays the part of duke) well. (Shakespeare)
我已惯于栉风沐雨。
I am used to roughing *it*.
白人对土人如君临一般。
The whites lord *it* over the natives.
我们是生来为君王效犬马之劳的。
We are born to slave *it* for our lord. (Thackeray)
他到各地巡回演出。
He is starring *it* in the provinces.
我们不得不冒雨而行。
We had to walk *it* in the rain.
你能游泳过去吗?
Can't you swim *it*?

在某些熟语中可将同系宾语略去,如 look thanks 为 look a look of thanks 之略。

他眼中现出言语无法表达的感谢。
He looked the thanks he could not express.
她以短剑相刺的目光望看我,而走出房间去了。
She left the room, looking daggers at me.
我问他是否满意,他点头表示首肯。
I asked if he was satisfied, and he nodded assent.
那人的字写得好吗?
Does the man write a good hand?

用最上级形容词时,多半也要把同系宾语略去。

那妇人在那个时候看去最美。
The lady was looking her best (look).
她唱出她最好听的歌声来取悦他。
She sang her sweetest (song) to please him.

其他如 do one's best (or utmost) = do all one can do(尽全力);see the last of anything = see it no more (再也不见了); hear the last of anything = hear of it no more (再无消息);breathe one's last = expire (呼出最后一口气,即死去)。

2. 含使动意

她把蜡烛竖在地板上。

She *stood* the candle on the floor. (Dickens)

我慢慢地带马走上小山。

I slowly *walked* my horse up the hill.

他们把船开到滩上去了。

They *ran* the ship aground.

他们使马泅水渡河。

They *swam* their horses across the river.

那船上挂出降旗。

The ship *was flying* the flag of truce.

下次满潮时船就可以浮起来了。

The next tide will *float* the ship.

巡洋舰把那运输船击沉了。

The cruiser *sank* the transport.

他们过分地酷使了那些马。

They *work* the horses too hard.

我躺下来好让两条疲惫的腿子休息一下。

I laid myself down to *rest* my wearied limbs.

3. 接用分词

怎样得到那个结果的呀？

How was the result *brought about*?

她在年轻的时候，追她的人很多。

She was much *run after* in her youth.

顽皮的孩子人人皱眉。

Everybody *frowns at* a naughty child.

越有越是想要。

Possession makes one *wish for* more.

愚人才不认错。

Fools *persist in* their error.

我不知道真有这样的人。

I do not *know of* any such man.

我不会把这问题一直讲下去的。

I shall not *dwell on* the subject at any length.

你最好有空的时候把那事情仔细想一下。

You had better *think over* the matter at your leisure.

我的母亲反对这门亲事。

My mother *objects to* the match.

娱乐不能妨害正事。

Pleasure must not *interfere with* duty.

4. 加补足字

做人不可醉生梦死。

One must not sleep or dream one's life *away*.

睡眠能恢复疲劳。

You can sleep *off* your fatigue.

别的客人都走光了他还不走。

He sits *out* the other guests.

他能说服别人听从他的意见。

He can talk people *over* to his own views.

你自己去查字典吧。

Look *up* the word for yourself in the dictionary.

他们大叫把演讲者轰下台来。

They shouted *down* the orator.

他使我厌烦死了。

He bored me *to* death.

他向我说出种种道理,使我非答应不可。

He has reasoned me *into* compliance.

我说得他把原来的决定推翻了。

I have talked him *out of* his resolution.

在第三句型的构造中也有下列十一种形式:

1. S. + Vt. + Noun:

    I keep a diary every day.

2. S. + Vt. + Pronoun:

    They know us very well.

3. S. + Vt. + – ing:

    I like playing tennis.

    I do not advise your seeing him at this time.

4. S. + Vt. + Prep. + – ing:

    Mrs Smith objected to our riding across the lawn.

    The girl insists on going to the movies.

    He persists in doing something in his own way.

5. S. + Vt. + to – Infinitive:

    I like to play tennis with them.

6. S. + Vt. + what (whom, which) + to-Infinitive:

    I don't know what to do.

    I don't know what book to read.

    We must know whom to choose.

I don't know whom to go to.

Do you know which to choose?

Do you know which way to take?

7. S. ＋Vt. ＋how（when,where）＋to-Infinitive：

You must learn how to swim.

We must decide when to start.

She will show where to sit.

8. S. ＋Vt. ＋that Clause：

I hear that he is in Singapore now.

9. S. ＋Vt. ＋what（who,whom,which）Clause：

I know what his name is.

I know what I must do.

Do you know what answer he made?

Do you know who he is?

Do you know whom we chose?

I cannot see which（which way）is better.

We don't know which（which way）he took.

10. S. ＋Vt. ＋how（when,where,why）Clause：

I wonder how old that man is.

I know when（where）you were born.

No one knows why he did such a thing.

11. S. ＋Vt. ＋if（whether）Clause：

I wonder if it will rain tomorrow.

I don't know whether the news is true or not.

习题 3

试将下列各句译成英文,句中须采用完全他动词。

1. 昨天的迎新会你出席了没有?
2. 苏君顺利地进了牛津大学。
3. 王君文官考试优等及第。
4. 我们要奋斗的话,就要奋斗到底。
5. 在印尼他们剥夺了华侨一切的财产。
6. 他把我所要的一切都给我了。
7. 他抓住我的手,不让我走。
8. 她假装对我朋友说话,实际是说给我听的。
9. 勤能补拙。
10. 我一定想要你来。

11. 他不用功,在学校里又混过了一年。
12. 我旅行时总是坐的三等。
13. 他讲演完毕时,听众大声喝采。
14. 他在夜里十一时十分钟断气。
15. 你能像那老人一样游过长江吗?
16. 我给了那可怜的孩子一点钱去买东西吃。
17. 她写了一封长信给我,谈到她的将来。
18. 我们讨论那个问题直到夜深。
19. 他承认她是对的。
20. 她提议我们应从头来过一次。

(7) 第四句型的授与构造

主语 + 述语 + 间接宾语 + 直接宾语

这是在一句当中用两个宾语的造句法。普通的他动词只要有一个宾语就行了,但这种他动词却需要两个宾语,即除了直接的宾语外,还需要有一个间接的宾语。那个间接宾语,在拉丁文中称为与格(Dative Case),Dative 意为英文的 giving. 因此对于要有间接宾语的这一类的动词,就称为授与动词(Dative Verb)。英文与拉丁文不同,间接宾语与直接宾语并没有各自不同的形态,所以间接宾语并无所谓授与格的名称,不过形态虽同,在意味上却是有这种授与格的存在的,因此在英文中也仍然保留着 Dative 这个名称。

间接宾语通常是人,而直接宾语则通常是说的事物,如 That will save *me* a lot of *trouble*.(那将省我不少的麻烦。)但偶然也有间接宾语不是说人的,如 He allowed his *imagination* full play.(他任意胡思乱想。)

通常是把间接宾语放在直接宾语的前面的,但有时为着加强语气,或使意义更为明白起见,也可以把间接宾语移到直接宾语的后面去,不过在那时候,就得在间接宾语前加上"to","for","of"等介词,而把它做成介词片语,使之完全失去宾语的性质了,例如:

He gave me a book. = He gave a book *to* me.
He will buy me a knife. = He will buy a knife *for* me.
I wish to ask you a favour. = I wish to ask a favour *of* you.
He played our master a dirty trick. = He played a dirty trick *on* our master.

但两个宾语如果都是简短的代名词时,间接宾语即令移到直接宾语的后面去,也不要加用介词,如:

Her mother did not give it her.(她母亲并未把那个给她。)
We rather shrank back when she proffered it us. (Caskell, Cranford)(当她提出那个来的时候,我们都退缩了。)

间接宾语移到了直接宾语的后面仍不加介词,是因为省略掉了,而且只有在简短的代名词如 it, me, her, him 等时才可省略,不省当然是可以的,如说 Please give it *to* her.(美国说法)。省略后便成为 Please give it her.（英国说法）。凡遇到间接与直接二者全是短字,也可以说成 Please give her it. 但如直接宾语不是代名词而是名词时,要前后调动就非加介词不可,那时我们必须说：

  Please give the book *to* her.

若照平常的次序说 Please give her the book. 当然是可以的。应该注意的是,我们不可以说 Please give the book her. 因为直接宾语不是代名词,故"to"不能略去。间接宾语为名词,而不是代名词时,也不能把"to"略去,如

  I gave it *to* the beggar.

不能说 I gave the beggar it. 但可以说 I gave the beggar a coin. 或是 I gave a coin to the beggar.

  如果间接与直接两种宾语的音价（phonetic value）相等,或直接的更轻,那么,还是要维持原来的次序的,如

  I grudge him you. (Shaw)（我不肯把你交给他。）
  Do not send me those. (Onions)（不要把那些东西送给我。）
  Bring me him down like a ripe apple. (Stevenson)（把他当作一个熟透了的苹果一般,小心地带到我这儿来。）
  Tell him this. (Onions)（把这件事告诉他。）

间接宾语多半是人,而且是受惠者:（a）他是获得什么东西,看到什么东西,或听到什么东西的人（the person to whom something is given, shown or told）；或是（b）别人为他做了什么的人（the person for whom something is done）。这便是间接宾语为数最多的两大类。间接宾语如果不是受惠者,如

  He asked me a few questions.（他问了我几个问题。）
  I can forgive him anything and everything.（一切我都可以赦免他。）

等句中的间接宾语,是不能得到任何利益的。这时节我们就不妨把两个宾语都看作直接宾语。

  授与动词可以细分为四类,即授与（give）东西,告知（tell）事情,贡献（render）服务,及施行（perform）恩惠（有关得失的）。前三类中的间接宾语都可以加"to"改成介词片语,即 to-phrase, for-phrase（有的文法家将此视为一个间接宾语）等,如：

  Give me the book. = Give the book *to* me.
  Tell us a story. = Tell a story *to* us.
  Do me a favour. = Do a favour *to* me.

唯有最后一类不能用"to",要用表示目的的介词"for"来把间接宾语改写为介词片语,如

  Get me a glass of water. = Get a glass of water *for* me.

这种用法的动词在现代英语中为数极少,如果在古代的话,则几乎任何动词上都可以加一个恩惠的授与格（Dative of Favour）,如 Open me the door. 今则说 Open the door for me. 他如 Shakespeare 说的：Heat me these irons hot.（趁热为我打铁）等等都是的。

  只有授与动词如 give, bring, teach, show, ask, send, make, lend, owe, tell, sell, cost, read, write, offer, pass, pay, promise, choose, find, leave, get, play, reach, sing 等,才能接用两个宾语,其他的他动词则只能接用一个宾语。今就同义的动词举例比较如下：

(a) We *gave* him a watch. (= gave a watch to him)

(b) We *presented* him with a watch. (presented a watch to him)

(a) A litle was *given* him.

(b) A litle was *conferred* on him.

(a) He *teaches* us English.

(b) He *instructs* us in English.

(a) He *asked* me a question.

(b) He *put* a question to me.

1. 有授与意味的授与动词——兹就其惯用句法例示如下：

我在一个月前通知他解职。
I have *given* him a month's warning (notice).

我当面责备他是撒谎。
I *gave* him the lie in his throat.

公平地说,敌人是勇敢的。
To *give* the devil his due, the enemy are quite brave.

接到来函使我大为高兴。
Your letter has *afforded* me much pleasure.

他每月给他儿子五百元。
He *allows* his son five hundred dollars a month.

我在他头上给以重重的一击。
I *struck* him a hard blow on the head.

我将尽量给你帮助。
I'll *lend* you all the assistance in my power.

他传言说要来。
He has *sent* us word that he is coming.

如果有什么信件寄来请转给我。
Please *forward* me any letter that may come.

他答应给我职务。
He has *promised* me an appointment.

我去烹点茶来给你喝。
I will *make* you some tea. (= I will make some tea for you.)

她自制了一袭新衣。
She *made* herself a new dress. (= She made a new dress for herself.)

她为他做一个好妻子。
She *made* him a good wife. (*cf.* 她会成为一个好妻子的。译成 She will make a good wife. 句中的 make = become. 此句为第二句型,即"主语 + 述语 + 补语"。)

2. 有告知意味的授与动词：

> 王先生教我们的英文。
> Mr. Wang *teaches* us English.
> 请你告诉我去车站的路好吗？
> Will you please *show* me the way to the station?
> 孩子们要我讲故事给他们听。
> The children *want* me to tell them a story.
> 你唱支歌给我听吧，在我离去之前。
> *Sing* me a song before I leave.
> 让我把他刚来的信念给你听。
> Let me *read* you his letter just received.

3. 有贡献意味的授与动词：

> 运动是对你有益的。
> Exercise will *do* you good.
> 喝少量的酒是无害的。
> A little wine will *do* you no harm.
> 公平地说一句，他并不是坏人。
> To *do* him justice, he is not a bad man.
> 请你帮我一个忙好吗？
> Will you *do* me a favour?
> 在我贫困时，他给了我不少的帮助。
> He has *rendered* me great help in time of need.

4. 有得失意味的授与动词：

> 我去替你买张戏票来。
> I will *get* you a ticket.
> 你有了这张票即可入场。
> This ticket will *gain* you admission.
> 我要尽量使你获得好的条件。
> I will try to *procure* you the best terms I can.
> 那本书使他出了名。
> The book *won* him a reputation.
> 他太迟钝了，以致失掉了那个机会。
> His slowness *lost* him the chance.

5. 还有一种变则的授与动词，是只有间接宾语而无直接宾语的，与文法原则相反，故称变则。

> 这件衣服你穿了很合适。

The dress *becomes* you very well.

年轻人宜彬彬有礼。

Modesty *becomes* a young man.

我已有准备来应付可能到来的最坏的情形。

I am prepared for the worst that can *befall* me.

这幢房子花了我三万元。

This house *cost* me thirty thousand dollars.

你多久才把英文学好的？

How loog did it *take* you to master English?

这件衣我穿了五年。

This coat has *lasted* me five years.

我的英文知识给了我很大的用场。

My knowledge of English *stood* me in good stead.

在第四句型的构造中有下列三种形式：

1. S．＋Vt．＋Noun（Pronoun）＋Noun：

   I gave John（him）the book.

   I bought John（him）the book.

   I asked John（him）the question.

2. S．＋Vt．＋Noun（pronoun）＋how（when，where，what，which）＋to‐Infinitive：

   I taught John（him）how to drive a car.

   Did he tell you when to start?

   Please show me where to find them.

   He told me what to do next.

   He showed me which（which way）to choose.

3. S．＋Vt．＋Noun（pronoun）＋that（what，which，who，how，when，where，why，if，whether）Clause：

   He told me that he did not know it.

   He asked me what was the right way to do it.

   Will you tell me which（which book）you have read?

   He does not tell me who is going with us.

   He does not tell us whom he is going to bring.

   He asked me how（where，when，why）I was going to do it.

   Will you ask him if（whether）he is coming with us?

习题 4

试将下列各句译成英文，句中须采用授与动词。

1. 只有人类有天赋的说话才能。

2. 他让了座位给她。
3. 他父亲留给他一大笔遗产。
4. 我把那钱付给他了。
5. 我来把信念给你听。
6. 你给我唱一支中国歌好吗?
7. 我很羡慕你运气好。
8. 我很恭维了他。
9. 敬祝成功愉快。
10. 我很抱歉给你许多麻烦。
11. 他们甚至连极微薄的报酬都不给我。
12. 我希望你不至拒绝我的请求。
13. 旅客只许带三十磅的行李。
14. 中国古话说,女子无才便是德。
15. 他们对自己的国家没有一点责任感。
16. 她要不是为着对她孩子的爱她就愿意死去。
17. 我并不羡慕阔人的财富,那使他们非常忧烦。
18. 公平地说一句,他一直是一个好丈夫,也是一个好父亲。
19. 那个恶棍长久逃避追捕终于落网。
20. 微物请赐哂纳为幸。

(8) 第五句型的不完全他动构造

主语 + 述语 + 宾语 + 补语

这是英文造句中四种要素具备的句型。句中的他动词是不完全的,所以有了宾语,还是不能使意念完全,必得再加上一个补语才行。例如:

他使父母快乐。

He made his parents happy.

句中的 he 是主语,made 是述语,his parents 是宾语,happy 是补语。因为这个述语是不完全他动词,所以单有宾语不够,还得加上补语。这种动词英文又称 Factitive Verb(作为动词)。这个 factitive 意为 making 因为它是有所作为的。照普通的话说,它能使人做什么,使人变得怎样,比方说"人们选举他为市长",就是使他做市长。"儿子使父母快乐",就是使父母变得快乐。"我们叫他傻瓜",就是使他成为傻瓜。诸如此类,都是表示作为、使成、变得等的意思。

We named him John. (= He was named John.)

They call him Jack. (= He is usually called Jack.)

They appointed him governor. (= He was appointed governor.)

They elected Washington president. (= Washington was elected president.)

They crowned William king. (= William was crowned king.)

由于上面的这些例子,可见在"作为动词"后的宾语,都含有被动的意思,这就是"作为"的结果。使动是可以包括在被动中的,如云 He made his parents happy. = His parents were made happy. 意即他的父母被使快乐,被儿子使他们快乐。

我们还记得在第二句型的不完全自动构造中,也是需要采用补语的,即是说不完全自动词与不完全他动词,都需要有补语以完全文句的意念,不过前者为主格补语,后者为宾格补语,比较如下:

不完全自动与主格补语	不完全他动与宾格补语
She became (was made) his wife.	He made her his wife.
She became (was made) happy.	He made her happy.

宾格补语也和主格补语一样,可分 Noun – Element(名词及其同等语)和 Adjective – Element(形容词及其同等语)两大类。还可细分如下九项:

1. They appointed Nelson *admiral*. (Noun)
2. I believed it *him*. (Pronoun)*
3. He painted the house *green*. (Adjective)
4. What time do you expect her *back*? (Adverb)
5. I have always found him *to be* a true friend. (Infinitive)
6. I kept him *waiting*. (Present Participle)
7. We call such a way of life "*eating* the bread of idleness". (Gerund)
8. I found everything *in good condition*. (Phrase)
9. We have made him *what he is*. (Clause)

他动词中可作"作为动词"用的有 make, elect, think, have, keep, find, leave, create, show, appoint, name, suppose, call, prove, believe, imagine 等字,而某些形容词或名词前后加"en"时,也可作成具有作为意味的动词,如

To enable = to make able

To enfeeble = to make feeble

To weaken = to make weak

To strengthen = to make strong

To lengthen = to make longer

To shorten = to make shorter

To widen = to make wider

To harden = to make hard

To soften = to make soft

---

* I believed it (to be) him. 的 to be him 为 believed 的 Objective Complement,而 him 又是 be 的 Complement,用的 Objective Case. 其 Passive Voice 的 It was believed to be he. 中的 to be he,是 was believed 的 Subjective Complement,而 he 又是 be 的 Complement,用的 Nominative Case. 他例如:We suspected the intruders to be them. The intruders were suspected to be they. 在 be 的后面是主格和宾格都可以接用的。

To broaden = to make broad or broader

上举的"作为动词"中有些字如 find, think, show, prove 等，实际原来是不定词构造（Infinitive Construction）的省略形，即：

We supposed him [to be] dead.
We found him [to be] alive.
You must show yourself [to be] a gentleman.
He has proved himself [to be] worthy of confidence.

在这种句型中有时因声调的关系，常要在宾语地位上用"it"来代替不定词，而将不定词移到别处去，因为 to be 作补语用固可，作宾语用就有些拗口，应加用一个代名词的"it"进去，才合乎惯用语法，如

我觉得这样做是我的义务。

一句，如译为 I think *to do* so my duty. 则不顺口，应改为

I think *it* my duty to do so.

才妥。又加

我认为那个要实行很难。

一句，如译为 I found *to put* it in practice very difficult 则不顺口，应译为

I found *it* very difficult to put it in practice.

才合乎英语的惯用法（usage）。

同是一个他动词可用作完全他动，也可用作不完全他动，如

(a) I found the book *easily*.
(b) I found the book *easy*.

在(a)句中的 found 为完全他动词，easily 为修饰动词的副词，全句意为"很容易地找到了那本书"。在(b)句中的 found 为不完全他动词，在宾语外，还得加一个补语，意念才能完全。第二句意为"这本书我读了觉得很容易"，即容易读懂的意思。easy 是修饰 book 的，原是说 I found the book was easy, 略去了 was 便成此型，而那主格补语便成为宾格补语了。比较：

(a) I believed the untrue report.（完全他动词）
(b) I believed the report untrue.（不完全他动词）
(a) I make a point of siding with the weaker party.（完全）
(b) I make it a rule to side with the weaker party.（不完全）
(a) I made a workbox out of it.（完全）
(b) I made it into a workbox.（不完全）

英文还可以说成这样的妙语：She made him a good husband because she made him a good wife.（因为她成为他的好妻子，所以也把他做成了好丈夫）。前面一个 made 是作为动词，后面一个

made 是授与动词。

1. 认识动词,即有心灵感觉(mental perception)的动词,其宾格补语主要是表示性质的,如 think, consider, call, believe, imagine, find, prove 等。在那宾格与补语之间,有时可以加上"to be"的字眼,例如:

我素来认为他是诚实的。
I have always thought him honest.
军队觉得在酷热下进军几不可能。
The troops found it almost impossible to march in the great heat.
那孩子走出学校进入社会时,并不以为统治是荒诞的,权威是可笑的。
When he leaves school and enters the world, the boy is not disposed to consider rule absurd and authority ridiculous.
他确实不是邪恶的,不过人们易于想像他的性格是柔弱的。
Vicious he could assuredly not be, but one easily imagined him weak in character.
从那种娱乐的形式看来,好像可以判明他的诚实。
Such a form of pastime seems to prove him sincere.

2. 感觉动词,即有身体感觉(physical perception)的动词,有 see, hear, feel, want, wish, like, hold, keep, leave, have, wear 等。

现今我觉得我的生活有说不出的空虚。
Now I feel my life unspeakably empty.
他们都指望我死,想得我的钱。
They all want me dead, and are hankering for my money. (Thackeray, *Vanity Fair*)
她回答说她完全满足于现况,不再想望别的什么。
She replied that she was quite contented and wished nothing different.
她披头散发。
She wore her hair loose.
那消息使得我漠然地感到不安。
The news left me vaguely uneasy.
她请医生替她检查了眼睛。
She had her eyes examined by the doctor.

3. 有些作为动词,在宾格补语之前,有加上一个"as"的必要。这个"as"是专为那动词而添附的,并无特殊意义。

她认为从那个根源可以产生任何好的事情出来,并非寻常的现象。
She regarded it as extraordinary that anything good could come from that source. (Gissing, *Life's Morning*)
他们认为已经绝望,就把他放弃了。
They gave him up as hopeless.
我认为他是一个很诚实的人。

I esteem him as a very honest man.

有人解释说,这个是有伤达克夫人的人格的。

Some persons understood this as an imputation on Mrs Ducker.

从许多随笔家及杂文家中,选出这些人作为最能代表维多利亚朝的特征的。

These were selected, from among many essayists and miscellaneous writers, as most typical of the Victorian Age.

在谈论她的时候,巴氏夫妇说她羞怯那是不错的。

The Boxendales were not wrong in discussing her as shy. (Gissing, *Life's Morning*)

4. 有些宾格补语是表示由那动作的结果而产生的状态。这类动词多半有使动意味(make, render, set, drive 等),或表示一般的动作(strike, beat, shoot, fold 等)。

我要解除他的一切困难。

I will set all his troubles right.

我在那种地方看到她,真使我惊讶得哑口无言。

I was struck dumb with astonishment at the sight of her in such a place.

休士那个家伙是可以做出很卑鄙的行为的。

That fellow Hughs could make himself quite nasty. (Galsworthy, *Fraternity*)

他决心对公众开放他那美丽的花园。

He decided to throw open his own beautiful gardens to the people.

你那感恩戴德之心,使你不可能对你的恩人做出这种事来。

Your gratitude should have rendered you incapable of such conduct towards your benefactor.

5. 反身自动词如要宾格补语时,也像作为动词时一样,那补语是表示动作的结果所产生的状态的。

他说话把声音都说哑了。

He talked himself hoarse.

大多数的人在那种情形中是欲罢不能的——他们都喝得烂醉如泥。

Most people in that state can't stop—they drank themselves dead drunk. (Galsworthy, *Motley*)

他们谈得睡着了。

They talked themselves asleep.

我们必须摆脱这种古老的伤感的想法。

We have got to shake ourselves free of the old sentimental notions.

"啊,我只是要求一点——请你清醒过来听我说话。"

"Why, this is what I want—and just shake yourself sober and listen, will you?" (Eliot, *Silas Marner*)

6. 在采取宾格补语的他动词中,如 see,原是指"看到的状态",现在却变成指"看到的时候",而在状态上加有时间的意味了。

我还会再见到他活着的人吗?

Shall I see him again alive?

我记得他年轻的时候。

I remember him young. (Lawrence, *White Peacock*)

她看到他的时候,他是年轻、骄傲、而又强壮的,现在他已年老,疲惫不堪,样子可怕,而已经死了。

She saw him young, and proud, and strong, and now he was old, and worn, and horrible, and dead. (Bennett, *Old Wives' Tale*)

在第五句型的构造中有下列九种形式。

1. S. + Vt. + Noun (Pronoun) + Noun (Pronoun):

   I thought him an honest man.

   I thought your brother you.

2. S. + Vt. + Noun (Pronoun) + Adjective:

   Her words made the man (him) angry.

3. S. + Vt. + Noun (Pronoun) + –ing:

   I saw John (him) entering the room.

4. S. + Vt. + Noun (Pronoun) + –ed:

   This word made his master (him) very pleased.

5. S. + Vt. + Noun (Pronoun) + to–Infinitive:

   I want John (him) to come here at once.

6. S. + Vt. + Noun (Pronoun) + zero–Infinitive:

   No one can make John (him) do the work.

   Will you please let me go in his place?

   I did not see anyone (him) enter the room.

7. S. + Vt. + Noun (Pronoun) + as + Adjective (Noun):

   They represented him as reliable.

   We will consider *Hamlet* as an example of a Shakespearian tragedy.

8. S. + Vt. + Noun (Pronoun) + Prep. + Noun:

   He put his affairs in order.

   I found him in good health.

   We consider this of the essence of the English character.

   I thought it of no use.

   He has set a new scheme on foot.

   I mistook him for my brother.

   Please make yourself at home.

9. S. + Vt. + Noun (Pronoun) + Clause:

   He has made the company what it is today.

   Call it what you will.

这五种句型只是一些不同的表达方式而已,所以我们可以用来表达同样的一个意思,如战争使我们的生意萧条。

(1st pattern) Our business has suffered not a little through the war.

(2nd pattern) The effect upon our business of the war has been striking.

(3rd pattern) The war has affected our buisiness to a remarkable extent.

(4th pattern) The war has done our business much harm.

(5th pattern) The war has rendered our business dull.

习题 5

1. 美国人民决不会选举一个黑人做总统的。
2. 他们选举王君为议员。
3. 户外运动使我们心身强健。
4. 世人都以为他正直,实则他是一个骗子。
5. 我吃过晚饭照例出去散步一回。
6. 在别人没有注意的时候,他走出那房间去了。
7. 我换了一张新牌照,又有三年好用。
8. 我们发现他躺在马路边上。
9. 他们正在我园里偷水果,我把他们抓住了。
10. 我们的身体和衣服都要保持清洁,以免生病。
11. 那叫作所答非所问。
11. 我认为他说的不适切。
13. 我感觉到那问题很难解决。
14. 我认为把那件事情守秘密是贤明的。
15. 荀爽以御李(膺)为荣。
16. 我把他看做我的恩人。
17. 他把国家的情形说得十分令人慨叹。
18. 他们把她描写成天仙一般的美女。
19. 他的英文极好。
20. 我国向来尊重学问。

贰　由构造来分的造句

(1) 用单句来翻译

所谓单句,英文叫作 Simple Sentence,是在一个句子中,只包含得有一个主语和一个述语的,例如

    Birds sing.（鸟鸣。）

    What have you been doing?（你在做什么?）

    What beautiful hair that little girl has!（那小女孩有多么美丽的头发呀!）

单句并不一定是很短的,有时因为修饰语加多了,也可以把句子拉得很长,现举几个例子如下：

    Nearly all the boys in this class go somewhere for the summer.（几乎班上所有的学生都要到什么地方去过暑假。）

    They saw a burning house, standing a little distance from the road, with some stately fir-trees in the foreground.（他们见到离开大路不远的地方,有一幢房子起火了。在那房子前面长得有一排森森的枞树。）

    Caught in a shower on his way to his house in Lloyd Road, a tall English gentleman, a teacher of English in one of the most flourshing private schools in Singapore, began running, with some books under his arm, in order to catch a bus going at full speed about twenty yards ahead of him.（一个身材高大的英国人,是新加坡顶发达的一间私立学校的英文教员,在回返劳益路他的住宅去的途中,遇到了骤雨,他手臂下夹着几本书,开始向前跑,想去搭乘在他二十码光景前面以全速力在开行的那辆巴士车。）

我们由中文翻译英文的时候,应运用英文各种惯用的句法,采取各种不同的方式,即以单句而论,也是有许多方式可以用来把句子扩大的：（一）用补语的,（二）用宾语的,（三）用形容词或副词的,（四）用动词片语的,（五）用独立片语的,（六）用副词片语的,（七）用介词片语的,（八）用名词片语的,（九）用代名词片语的,（十）用分词片语的。所以在主语和述语以外,还可以增加许许多多的字句,因为上述十种方式,并不限于一句只许用一种,我们同时可以用上好几种,如上举最后的一个例句,caught in a shower 是分词片语,a tall English 是形容词,a teacher of English 是同格名词,running 是宾语,with some books under his arm 是副词片语,in order to catch a bus 是介词片语,going at full speed 是形容词片语等等,所以原来只有主语 gentleman 和述语 began 两个字,现却拉长到五十五个字了。

(一) 用补语的

不完全的动词必须有补语,才能使句子表达出一个完全的意念来。自动词用主格补语,他动词用宾格补语。

（a）主格补语

他看去很年轻。

He looks *young*.

华盛顿小时是一个好孩子。

Washington was *a good boy*.

中国是要养儿防老的。

In China a son should be *the staff* of his parents' old age.

（b）宾格补语

人民选举他做总统。

People elected him *president*.

他使国家富强了。

He made his country *wealthy and powerful*.

（二）用宾语的

英文的他动词是要加上宾语才能成句的。用宾语的句子可分下列六种译法：

（a）用一个宾语

除你以外我没有朋友。

I have no *friend* but *you*.

天生丽质。

Nature has molded *her form* and *features* with masterly touch.

（b）用两个宾语

那老人讲一些有趣的故事给我们听。

That old man tells *us* amusing *stories*.

一磅烟丝只够他吸两个礼拜。

A pound of tobacco only lasts *him* a *fortnight*.

（c）用表结果的宾语（Object of Result）

她点燃了一把火。

She lights a *fire*.

他在木板上钻了一个洞。

He bores a *hole* in the plank.

我在那上面画了一朵花。

I painted a *flower* on it.

（d）用同系宾语（Cognate Object）

他发出了一声短促的苦笑。

He laughed a little short ugly *laugh*.

他过着一种凄凉寂寞的生活。

He is living a sad and lonely *life*.

(e) 用反身宾语(Reflexive Object)

他在晚会上感到很快乐。

He *enjoyed himself* at the party.

你应利用图书馆的书。

You should *avail yourself* of the books in the library.

(f) 用保留宾语(Retained Object)

凡有间接和直接两个宾语的文句,如由主动改为被动时,通常有两种说法,即每次只能用一个宾语,间接的或直接的,作为主语,其未用作主语的,就称为保留宾语,如

我给了那孩子一支自来水笔。

I gave the *boy* a fountain *pen*.

如将上句改为被动时态,则有下列两种形式:

The *boy* was given a fountain pen by me.

A fountain *pen* was given the boy by me.

(三) 用形容词或副词的

(A) 用形容词的,又可分为(a)叙述的用法,(b)限定的用法,(c)名词的用法,(d)副词的用法,(e)同格的用法五种译法。

(a) 叙述的用法(Predicative Use)

这朵玫瑰花是红的。

This rose is *red*.

他对那结果感到满意。

He was *content* with the result. (*cf.* contented)

这不值得那样麻烦。

It is not *worth* the trouble. (*cf.* worthy)

专限于叙述用法的形容词有:ill(*cf.* sick), well(*cf.* healthy), glad, sorry, exempt 等,其他还有以 "a-" 开头的字,如 alone, asleep, awake, afraid, alike, ashamed, akin 等,例如:He was fast asleep. (熟睡) 也多半只有叙述用法。

(b) 限定的用法(Attributive Use)

这是一朵红玫瑰花。

This is a *red* rose.

知足常乐。

A *contented* person is happy with his status quo.

他找到一个敢于和他相抗的敌人。

He found a *worthy* enemy.

儿童教育必须由所能聘到的最好的教师来施行。

The education of children must be conducted by the best *attainable* instructors.

没有一件伟大的事不是由热忱来做成的。

Nothing *great* was ever achieved without enthusiasm. (Emerson)

(c) 名词的用法(Noun Use)

他有审美的眼光。

He has an eye for *the beautiful*.

阔人也有他们的苦恼。

The rich have their troubles too.

级长阻止强者欺侮弱者。

The monitors hinder *the strong* from bullying *the weak*.

她是一个俗气的富婆。

She's one of *the vulgar rich*. (Gissing)

他对周围老少的人群投以一瞥。

He cast a look at the crowd of *old and young* about him. (对称时可略去冠词)

(d) 副词的用法(Adverbial Use)

他们平安到达了。

They arrived *safe*. (= They were safe when they arrived. 句中的 safe 为补语)

红颜薄命。

He died *young*. (= He was young when he died. 句中的 young 为补语)

我很想对你做得诚实一点。

I want to act *honest* with you.

看得轻松一点吧。

Take it *easy*.

我大为吓到了。

I'm *awful* frightened.

那会很合我的式。

That will suit me *fine*.

(e) 同格的用法(Appositive Use)

一个饥饿疲惫的猎户睡在床上。

A hunter, *hungry and exhausted*, slept on the bed.

他又忧伤又疲倦,慢慢地走回家去了。

Sad and weary, he slowly walked home.

他老是神经过敏,这时尤其如此。

Always sensitive, he was especially so at this moment. (Gissing)

她的面貌虽不难看却很平凡。

Her features, though not *plain*, were insignificant. (Austen)

仍然是绿的叶子被风吹得从灌木篱笆上飘落下来。

The leaves, *still green*, were tossed off the hedgerow trees by the wind.

（B）用副词的，又可分为(a)修饰动词、形容词或其他副词，(b)修饰名词或代名词，(c)修饰副词片语，(d)修饰全句，(e)作形容词用，(f)作名词用，(g)作补语用七种译法。

(a) 修饰动词、形容词或其他副词：

她听了那笑话开心地大笑。
She laughed *heartily* at the joke.
我现在已准备好了。
I am ready *now*.
她英语说得非常好。
She speaks English remarkably *well*.

(b) 修饰名词或代名词：

这事小孩子也能做。
Even a child can do it.
圣人也不免有过。
Even Homer sometimes nods.
只有你能猜。
Only you can guess.
已有大批人聚集在那里了。
Quite a crowd had already gathered there.
唯有约翰知道这事。
John *alone* knows about it.
你还要什么？
What *else* do you want?
我也有烦心的事。
I, *too*, have troubles.

(c) 修饰副词片语：

我们及时到达。
We arrived *just* in time.
我在战争结束后随即来到新加坡。
I came to Singapore *soon* after the war.
正十时关大门。
The gate is shut *exactly* at 10 o'clock.
他差不多快渡过河去了。
He is *almost* across the river.
他旅行了世界一周。
He has traveled *entirely* around the world.

(d) 修饰全句：

简单地说，事实就是这样。

Briefly the facts are these.

很幸运地我去时他正在家。

Fortunately I found him at home.

确实你是错了。

Certainly you are in the wrong.

他愚笨地把那鹅杀了。

He *foolishly* killed the goose.

那真是一个好计划。

That is an excellent plan *indeed*.

(e)作形容词用：

这是下行车吗？

Is this a *down* train?

在那边那位绅士是他的父亲。

That gentleman *there* is his father.

我在归途中遇到了他。

I met him on my way *back*.

从这件事产生的不愉快情形，和吃了大肉的早餐，可能就是他对一般世界失去希望的原因吧。

The unpleasant circumstances resulting from this together with heavy meat breakfasts, may probably have contributed to his desponding views of the world *generally*. (Eliot)

他一切都完了。

All is *over* with him.

我们一定要想办法赶走这些苍蝇。

We must do something to keep the flies *off*.

他把袜子穿反了。

He put on his socks wrong side *out*.

(f)作名词用：

从这儿去有多远？

How far is it from *here*?

今天是我生日。

Today is my birthday.

那个描写了人生的浮沉。

It described the *ups and downs* of life.

(g)作补语用：

火熄灭了。

The fire is *out*.

战争结束了。

The war is *over*.

蔷薇开了。

The roses are *out*. (= open)

幕已揭开。

The curtain was *up*.

(四)用动词片语的

英文动词除单字(如 come 等)及群字(如 will come 或 will have come 等)外,还有动词片语(verb phrase),那是动词和其他词类,尤其是名词,结合而成的一种片语,常另具特殊意义,所以我们特别列成一项,来供翻译时采用。

你不应该拿你小弟弟们来开玩笑。
You should not *make fun of* your little brothers.

明天市公会堂要举行音乐会。
A concert is to *take place* at the town hall tomorrow.

我们没有钱就生活不了。
We cannot *get along* without money.

他赶不上班。
He couldn't *keep up with* the class.

我期待着你的回信。
I *look forward to* receiving your reply.

你必得把所作的决定重新加以考虑。
You must *think better of* your resolution.

我规定在晚饭前出外散步一回。
I *make a point of* taking a walk before supper.

我不作弄天真老实的人。
I don't *play a trick on* innocent people.

他的脚有什么毛病。
He *has something the matter with* his foot.

我和那件事没有关系。
I *have nothing to do with* the matter.

(五)用独立片语的

独立片语有三种,有用独立不定词构成的,有用独立分词构成的,有用独立介词构成的。兹分别采用翻译如下:

(a)独立不定词。这是用来修饰全句的。从文法上讲,它和主句毫无联系。

老实说,我并不喜欢他。
To tell the truth, I do not like him.

他可谓一部活辞典。
He is, *so to speak*, a walking dictionary.

使事情更糟的,天又下起雨来了。

To make the matter worse, it began to rain.

此外还有 to speak candidly, to be frank with you, to be sue, to return to the subject, to be brief, to make a long story short, strange to say, needless to say 等等。

(b) 独立分词。这个与主语无任何文法上的关系,其形式有下列三种:

1. 分词前带有意味上的主语的

太阳落山,孩子们回家去了。
The sun having set, the children went home.
有他在此,便无危险。
He being here, there is no danger.
工作做完,他们就回家了。
The work done, they left for home.
春天来了,我们到公园去散步。
Spring coming on, we go to gardens to take a walk.
他是我的长辈,我应当尊敬他。
He being my elder, I should respect him.

2. 无人称的独立分词

严格地说,他并不算一个爱国者。
Strictly speaking, he is not a patriot.
以他的年龄而论,他是够聪明的了。
Considering his age, he is very clever.
从各方面来考虑,他的命运是幸福的。
Taking all things into consideration, his lot is a happy one.

其他如 judging from, talking of, 等皆是。

3. 由 with 引导的独立分词

那小妇人慢慢前进,眼睛恶意地盯在那张粉红色的纸上。
The little woman advanced slowly *with her eyes fixed malevolently on the pink paper*. (Wells)
这个小村庄是位于平坦雄伟的牧场和麦田的中央,前有一列白杨树在风中摇曳。
This little village was set midst flat breadths of pasture and corn-lands, *with long lines of poplars on the foreground bending in the wind*.

(c) 由表感情上之结果(resulting emotion)的"to"所引导的独立片语。

使我喜慰的,我发觉他还活着。
To my joy, I found him alive.
使我吃惊的,他居然把一切都说出来了。
To my surprise, he confessed everything.
使我失望的,他竟不同意我的计划。
To my disappointment, he did not consent to my plan.

使我满意的,是他终于解决了那个问题。
To my satisfaction, he has solved the problem at last.
使他悲伤的,他知道他父亲去世了。
To his sorrow, he learned that his father was dead.

(六)用副词片语的

当心地写。
Write it *with care*.
天黑了,我们才回家。
We came home *after dark*.
他现在住在本村。
He lives *in this village at present*.
亲切地对待他。
Treat him *with kindness*. (= kindly)
我出外散步去了。
I went out *for a walk*.
他们匆匆回家了。
They went home *in a hurry*.
我们努力用功以求考取。
We work hard *to pass the examination*.
这本书太难懂。
This book is too difficult *to understand*.

(七)用介词片语的

介词片语有两种形式皆可用来翻译。一种是介词片语(preposition phrase),另一种是介词的片语(prepositional phrase)。所谓介词片语是一个名词或形容词前后都有介词而构成的片语,如 by means of, on account of, at the mercy of, for the purpose of, in return for, in respect to, in love with 等等,而所谓介词的片语,则为介词加名词。其中的名词实为那个介词的宾语,如 of diligence, in my hand, with pleasure 等等,其功用可修饰名词,有时也可修饰动词。

(a)介词片语

他因生病,所以没有来。
He did not come *on account of* illness.
他们远赴台湾。
They went *as far as* Formosa.
贾克由于不屈不挠的精神而获得成功。
Jack succeeded *by dint of* perseverance.
思想由言语表达。
Thoughts are expressed *by means of* words.

旅人以驴代马。

The traveller is using an ass *as a substitute for* a horse.

他和她结婚是看上了她的财产。

He married her *with an eye* to her fortune.

我喜欢小黑(狗名),是因为它的头脑好。

I love Blackie *for the sake of* his sense.

他想要建房子,所以买了一块地皮。

He has bought a piece of land *with a view to* building a house.

(b)介词的片语

一个品行优良的人受人尊敬。

A man *of good character* is to be respected.

凡 of + abstract noun = adjective, of use = useful, of diligence = diligent, of freedom = free, of security = secure, of importance = important, of wisdom = wise, of kindness = kind, of beauty = beautiful 等等。

苹果放在篮子里。

The apples are *in the basket*.

国王死后政府改变了很多。

After the king's death, many changed were made *in the government*.

玛丽对他那样不客气使我感到羞辱。

I am mortified *by Mary's treating him so unkindly*.

那个大建筑工程已经开始五年了。

The great structure has been *under construction about five years*.

他的语言教授法是最新式的。

He is very *up to date in his methods of language teaching*.

我们吃点鹿肉换个口味。

Let us have venison *for a change*.

一个健康的人一般都是乐天的。

A healthy man, *as a general rule*, is optimistic.

(八)用名词片语的

凡作名词用的片语,便是名词片语,例如:

他是一个诚实的人。

He is *an honest man*.

狮为万兽之王。

The lion is *the king of beasts*.

我喜欢打网球。

I like *to play tennis*.

我不晓得要怎样办。

I did not know *what to do*.

教育部批准了他出国深造。

The Ministry of Education has ratified his going abroad for higher studies.

母亲很高兴,他这样快回家。

Mother rejoiced at his *coming home so soon*.

(九) 用代名词片语的

夫妻应当互助。

Husband and wife should help *each other*.

人们喜欢互殴。

People like to fight *one another*.

(十) 用分词片语的

(a) 用现在分词的

在路上走着,我遇见了一个老朋友。

Walking along the street, I met an old friend.

因为疲倦了,他躺下睡一会儿。

Being tired, he lay down to sleep.

用趾尖行走,我蹑足走到了他的背后。

Walking on tiptoe, I approached him behind.

说完这个他递了一封信给我。

Saying this, he handed a letter to me.

向右转弯,你就可看到你要找的屋子。

Turning to the right, you will find the house you are looking for.

他说英语,时常说错。

He often makes mistakes when *speaking English*.

情侣的时间是很长的,虽则感觉很短。

For lovers' hours are long, though *seeming short*.

(b) 用过去分词的

划船划得疲倦了,我一定要休息一下。

Fatigued with rowing, I must have a rest.

极其细心建筑出来的这些庙宇,是不容许加以冒渎的。

Built with infinite care, the temples are not allowed to desecrate.

习题 6

试用英文单句译出下列各句:

1. 太阳落山了,我们回家去。

2. 忙中有错。
3. 我两年前才认识他的。
4. 请代我谢谢他的礼物。
5. 言归正传,他们当天便结婚了。
6. 以貌取人,失之子羽。
7. 贪爱钱财是万恶之源。
8. 他来看我目的在借钱。
9. 同盟国家互相猜忌。
10. 名誉与金钱无关。
11. 他赚了一大笔钱,他母亲高兴极了。
12. 写完了那封信,我就出去散步了。
13. 他易于满足。
14. 早起三朝当一天。
15. 病从口入。
16. 一寸黄金买不到一寸光阴。
17. 知人知面不知心。
18. 破帽之下多好人。
19. 智慧就在认识机会。
20. 人谁无过。

(2) 用合句来翻译

所谓合句,英文叫作 Compound Sentence,是由两个或两个以上的独立子句(Independent Clause)所构成的。采用这种句型来翻译的时候,实比采用单句还要来得简单,但要注意一点,子句与子句间要用对等连词(Coordinate Conjunction)来结合成为合句才是。对等连词约可分为下列四种:

(一)累积连词(Cumulative Conjunction):有 and, both……and, not only……but also, no less than, as well as, furthermore, besides, moreover 等。

(二)选择连词(Alternative Conjunction):有 or, either……or, nor, neither……nor, otherwise, or else 等。

(三)反意连词(Adversative Conjunction):有 but, yet, while, nevertheless, still, however, whereas, only, notwithstanding 等。

(四)推论连词(Illative Conjunction):有 for, therefore, so, thus, hence, wherefore, consequently, accordingly 等。

在以上的对等连词中,有的并不是真正的连词,而是接续副词(Conjunctive Adverb),又称关系副词(Relative Adverb),拿来用作对等连词的,例如:

那里没有一个人,所以我也就走了。
There was no one there, *so* I went away.

我们在那里呆了一个钟头就回家了。
We stayed there an hour; *then* we went home.

你一旦露出任何恐惧的迹象,他就会攻击你。
Once you show any sign of fear, he will attack you.

她是留学美国的,所以她英语说得好。
She is an American returned student, *therefore* she speaks good English.

这书一脱稿,我马上和出版家订好了出版合约。
Immediately this was done, I completed an arrangement with my publishers.

我很想去,不过我却不愿冒着雨去。
I want to go very much; *still* I do not care to go through the rain.

他是一个聪明人,而仍不免常犯错误。
He is a wise man, *nevertheless*(或 none the less 或 and yet)he often makes mistakes.

我很愿意做,只是我太忙了。
I would do it with pleasure, *only*(= except that) I am too busy.

我正要说话,铃子就响了。
I was just going to speak, *when* the bell rang.

此外还有原是不对等的连词,如 as,until,while,when 等,有时也可拿来作对等连词用,例如:

他是一个美国人,我听他说话就知道。
He is an American, *as* I know from his accent.

在此他又犯了一般以貌取人的通病,那过后就可以证明的。
Here he fell into the common error of judging by appearances, *as* will be proved hereafter.

那个婴孩变得越来越虚弱,终于不久就死了。
The little baby grew more and more sickly, *until* presently it died.

一条轮船正用全速力在走,突然一下驶入浅水而触礁了。
A steamer was going along at full speed, *when* it suddenly got into shallow water and ran aground.

他正想要用脚后跟践碎那株小草,而一个新的念头使他停下来了。
He was about to crush the plant with his heel, *when* a new thought made him stop.

某种习惯一直在形成而牢固起来,终至变得牢不可破。
All the while a certain habit is forming and hardening, *until* at last we find ourselves helpless.

有的人富,有的人穷。
Some men are rich, *while*(= whereas) others are poor.

当我在纽约的时候,我见过他好几次。
I saw him several times *while* I was in New York.

我弟弟发了财,而我还依旧穷困。
I have remained poor, *while* my brother has made a fortune.

那帽子的颜色我虽则很喜欢,但形式我不爱。
While(= Though) I like the colour of the hat, I do not like its shape.

上面最后两例是由其前一例的基本用法逐渐引申出来的。

现将真正的对等连词的用法,例示如下:

小红低唱我吹箫。
I played on the flute, *and* Hsiao Hung sang to it.

他开始说话,全体肃静。
He began to speak, *and* all was still.

过几分钟他就睡熟了。
A few minutes more, *and* he lay sound asleep.

赶快,那么你就可以赶上火车。
Make haste, *and* you will catch the train.

他在恐怖中从家中逃走了,从那以后我再没有见到他。
He fled from the house in terror, *and* I have never seen him since.

你一定要把文书归档,否则你就不会受到信赖。
You must have your papers on file, *or* no credit will be given.

穿上你的外套,否则你会着凉的。
Put on your overcoat, *or* you will catch cold.

要么进来,要么出去。
Either come in *or* go out.

你必须说实话,或者什么也不说。
You must *either* tell the truth *or* say nothing.

强使污物留下的话,不是引起皮肤病,就是伤害血液。
Either the skin will become diseased, *or* the blood will be injured by being forced to retain its impurities.

赶快,否则你就要迟了。
Hurry up *or else* you'll be late.

我没有钱,我也不想有钱。
I am not rich, *nor* do I wish to be.

既非他错,也非我错。
Neither he is mistaken *nor* I am.

约翰和我都没有到会。
Neither John *nor* I attended the meeting.

他是一个能干的人,但这问题对他也嫌太难了。
He is an able man, *but* the problem was too hard for him.

他的身体虚弱,但他仍要工作。
He is not in good health, *but* he still wants to work.

你现在必得离去,但下回你可以再来。
You must go now, *but* you may come again.

他不可能懒惰,因为他有很大的进步。
He cannot be idle, *for* he makes remarkable progress.

油完了,因为灯已熄灭。

The oil must be out, *for* the lamp has gone out.

林肯不但是黑人的朋友,也是弱者和无告者的朋友。

Lincoln was *not only* a friend of the negroes, *but* a friend of the weak and the helpless.

他不但给了我钱,还给了我一个装钱的皮包。

He gave me *not only* the money, *but also* a purse to put it in.

事业的成功,不但要有精力,还得有耐性。

Not only energy, *but* patience is necessary to success in life.

你须听话,否则你将受罚。

Do what you are told; *otherwise* you will be punished.

抓住那个机会,不然你将后悔。

Seize the chance, *otherwise* you will regret it.

有人喜欢吃肥肉,而另有人就讨厌它。

Some people like fat meat, *whereas* others hate it.

他很聪明而他的妹妹就有点愚笨。

He is clever *whereas* his sister is foolish.

总督看了请愿书,但他仍然拒绝赦免那孩子。

The governor read the petition; *nevertheless* he refused to pardon the boy.

他有学问又有经验。

He has experience *as well as* knowledge.

合句有时不用连词而用标点也是可以的,尤其在古文中常有见到,例如:

Cowards die many times before their death; The valiant never taste of death but once. (Shakespeare, *Jul. Caes.* II, ii, 32f.)(对照意味)

John Told had drunk a large quantity of liquor, he was both merry and tipsy. (Powys)(因果关系)

Shakespeare was born in 1564; he died in 1616. (罗列一起)

A writer wants something more than money for his work: he wants permanence. (继续谈论)

而《圣经》上的合句则连词和标点都用得很多:

And the rain descended, and the floods came, and the winds blew, and beat upon that house; and it fell; and great was the fall of it. (Matt. vii. 27)

合句有时既可借用复句的不对等连词,则合句与复句岂不变得一样的而没有分别了,须知二者的分别并不全在连词,还有其他重要的因素。凡用有限制用法的关系词(Relative)的文句就是复句,用有非限制用法即继续用法的关系词(通例在其前有 Comma)的文句便是合句,如:

He is the man *whom* I met in the train. (复)

I met Mr. A, *who* (= and he) told me the news. (合)

This is the place *where* I was born. (复)

Then my parents went to America, *where* (= and there) I was born. (合)

Then I went to Rome, *where* (= and there) I stopped for a week. (合)

This book, *which* (= though it) appeared about a month ago, has already gone through several editions. (复)

When at home, he shuts himself up in his study. (复)

在合句中连词的位置多半是放在两个子句之间,如:

He is young, *and yet* he is prudent.

I was ill, *so* I did not go.

I knew it was him *the minute* I saw him.

但是复句的连词就多半是放在附属子句之前,如:

Let us go to bed, *as* it is late.

Though he is poor, he is honest.

Brave *as* she was (= *Though* she was brave), she trembled.

Brave *as* she was (= *Because* she was brave), she attacked.

习题 7

试用英文合句译出下列各句:

1. 日暮途远。
2. 不自由毋宁死。
3. 聪明人为求知而读书,愚人则为文凭。
4. 天将下雨,因为晴雨表渐见降低。
5. 几家欢乐几家愁。
6. 他自己家里有很多事要做,而他却来帮我的忙。
7. 他硬不肯听,要我怎样去说服他。
8. 他分明知道打扰我们,他还要说个不停。
9. 他借我五千元,只还来两千。
10. 当我对你说话的时候,请你不要作声。
11. 他有钱无处用,而我无钱可用。
12. 他是唯一的候选人,因此他当选了。
13. 他是很孚众望的候选人,结果他是会当选的。
14. 我憎恨他,而你只是不喜欢他而已。
15. 人生不满百,常怀千岁忧。
16. 我必须把他的一份给他,因我已答应两人平分。
17. 我到达车站的时候,火车已经开走了。
18. 他口中高谈和平,而实际却带给我们战争。
19. 我接受了他善意的劝告,所以我现在并不觉得新生活徒劳无功。
20. 这种工作也许别人可以,我是不能做的。

(3) 用复句来翻译

所谓复句,英文叫作 Complex Sentence,是由两个或两个以上的独立子句所构成的。构成合句的子句一定是对立的,而构成复句的子句,其中只有一个是主要子句(Principal Clause),其余的都是附属子句(Dependent Clause)。在复句中所用的连词,不是对等连词,而是不对等连词(Subordinate Conjunction)。这种不对等连词,多半是放在附属子句前面的。

依照外形分类,不对等连词可分为下列四种:

(一)单纯连词(Simple Conjunction):as,if,than,that,though,lest,when,since,while,etc.

(二)复合连词(Compound Conjunction):although,because,unless,whereas,etc.

(三)关联连词(Correlative Conjunction):as……as,as……so,so……as,so……that,whether……or,etc.

(四)片语连词(Phrase Conjunction):as soon as,as (or so) long as,as if,as though,in case,in order that,in that,for fear (that),the moment,etc.

英文连词常用其他词类来充任,如:

1. 名词:*Next time* I see you,I will lend you the book.(下次我看见你的时候,我就把那本书借给你。)

   I'll tell him *the moment* he gets in.(他一来我就告诉他。)

2. 代名词:*Whichever* you choose,I'll give it to you.(随便你选择哪一个,我都可以给你。)

3. 动词:*Suppose* I were going away,should you be sorry?(我如离去,你会觉得难过吗?)

4. 副词:*Now* (that) you are here,you'd better stay.(既来之,则安之。)

5. 介词:You will not have better health *without* you take better care of yourself.(你要是不更加讲究卫生,你就不会有更好的健康。)

   For all (that) you say,I still like him.(不管你怎样说,我还是喜欢他。)

用介词 without 作连词,是古文或方言的用法,现代英文,多用 unless.

依照内容分类,不对等连词可分为下列三种:

(一)用于形容词子句的:who,whose,whom,that,which,when,where,why,etc.

(二)用于副词子句的:

1. 时间:before,after,as,since,till,until,when,while,as soon as,as (or so) long as,no sooner……than,scarcely (or hardly)……when,etc.

2. 地点:where,whence,whither,wherever,etc.

3. 方式:as,as if,as though,etc.

4. 比较:as,when,the,than,etc.

5. 原因:as,because,since,etc.

6. 目的:that,so that,in order that,lest,for fear,etc.

7. 结果:that,so that,so (or such)……that,so……but that,etc.

8. 条件:if,unless,provided (that),in case (that),on condition (that),in the event (that),supposing (that),suppose(that),etc.

9. 让步:although,though,as,if,even if,notwithstanding (that),whether,etc.

(三)用于名词子句的 that,whether,if,who,which,how,when,where,why,etc.

(一) 用于形容词子句的译例

敬人者人恒敬之。
He *who* respects others is constantly respected.

昨天我们在戏院里遇见的那人是我的老师。
The man *whom* we met in the theatre yesterday is my teacher.

作品获奖的女孩是全班中年纪最小的。
The girl *whose* work got the prize is the youngest in the class.

我现在写的这封信是一封英文信。
The letter *that* I am writing is an English letter.

这就是我所选定的书。
This is the book *which* I chose.

礼拜天是我最清闲的时候。
Sunday is the day *when* I am least busy.

我不知道你到底要到哪里去。
I don't know the exact place *where* you want to go.

那就是我喜欢读中文的理由。
That is the reason *why* I like to study Chinese.

他在英国时，专门从事古堡的研究。
While he was staying in England, he made a study of old castles.

三尺童子无不识之。
There is no child *but* knows him (= who does not know him).

人孰无过。
No man *but* errs (= who does not err).

彼纵下愚，犹能知此。
He is not such a fool *but that* he knows it.

彼虽下愚，尚不至认敌为友。
He is not such a fool *but what* (= but that) he can tell a friend from a foe.

(二) 用于副词子句的译例

1. 时间：

你买东西，非钱不可。
When you buy things, you must have money.

你不肯听我怎能对你说明呢？
How can I explain it to you *when* you won't listen?

有生命就有希望。
While there is life, there is hope.

当我生病的时候，他代替了我的位置。

He took my place *while* I was ill.

在我写这个的时候，你可以做点别的事情。

While I am writing this, you can be doing something else.

他还没有到我就离开了。

I left *before* he arrived.

我离开了以后他才到来。

He arrived *after* I left.

我没等待好久他就来了。

I had not waited long *before* he arrived.

等雨停了再说。

Let's wait *until* (or till) the rain stops.

我到新加坡差不多五年了。

It is almost five years *since* I came to Singapore.

我正要走的时候他回家来了。

He returned home *as* I was leaving.

一息尚存，奋斗到底。

So long as I live, I must fight it out.

你现在已经很大了，应该学点礼貌。

Now (that) (= As) you are a big boy, you must behave better.

我一做完就发现错了。

Immediately (或 Directly 或 The moment) (= As soon as) I had done it, I knew I had made a mistake.

他一见到那个，就动身回家去了。

He started back home *as soon as* he saw it.

He had *no sooner* seen it *than* he started back home.

He had *scarcely* seen it *when* he started back home.

He had *hardly* seen it *before* he started back home.

2. 地点：

精神一到，何事不成。（有志竟成。）

Where there is a will, there is a way.

谁也不去的地方，他也不喜欢去。

He does not like to go *where* nobody is going. (Lynd)

谁也不晓得她是从何处来的。

No one knows *whence* she came.

他随遇而安。

He will be happy *wherever* he lives.

无论何处有口角，总有他在场。

Wherever there is a quarrel, there he is sure to be.

3. 方式：

入乡问俗。

When in Rome, do *as* the Romans do.

他说英语好像他父亲一样。

He speaks English *as* his father does.

我就是这样去(不换衣服)。

I'll go *just as* I am.

他的行动好像很怕的样子。

He acted just *as if* (or as though) he were afraid.

他对待我好像对待下属一样。

He treats me *as if* I were his subordinate.

种瓜得瓜,种豆得豆。(因果报应,丝毫不爽)。

As yon sow, *so* you shall reap. (Proverb)

有其父必有其子。

As is the father, *so* is the son.

珊瑚非树,犹鲸非鱼。

Just as a coral grove is not a tree, *so* a whale is not a fish.

4. 比较：

那太太和她丈夫一样高。

The wife is as tall *as* the husband (is).

太太没有丈夫高。

The wife is not so tall *as* the husband (is).

她比她丈夫高。

She is taller *than* her husband (is).

他像他妹妹一样亲切。

He is as kind *as* his sister (is).

他又诚实又亲切。

He is as kind *as* (he is) honest.

他妹妹诚实,而他就亲切。

He is as kind *as* his sister is honest.

他像死人一样。

He is as good *as* dead.

她与其说是漂亮,不如说是可爱。

She is more attractive *than* pretty.

与其说他不好交际,不如说他羞怯。

He is more shy *than* unsocial. (= He is shy rather than unsocial.)

与其说他是活着,不如说他是死了。

He was more dead *than* alive.

我们登得越高,气候越冷。

The higher up we go, the colder it becomes.

多多益善。

The more, the better.

越近骨头的肉,味道越美。

The nearer the bone, the sweeter the meat.

欲速则不达。

More haste, worse speed.

他半闭着眼睛,好像在回想什么。

He half-closed his eyes *as though* trying to recall something.

他说英语好像说自己的母语一样地熟练。

He can speak English with the same ease *as if* it were his mother tongue.

我现在确信眼下这个样子最好。

I am now quite certain that things are for the best *as* they are.

她聪明的程度远不及他的邪恶。

She was not nearly so clever *as* he was wicked.

你说你只有几本书,但你这儿的书就比我的要多上五倍。

You said you had a few books; but there must be five times as many here *as* I have. (Gissing)

我们必须接受事物的现状。

We must take things *as* we find them in the world.

他有一点过分爱好杯中物,正如水手们常有的现象。

As is often the case with sailors, he was a little too fond of liquors.

有急流一般的大的澎湃的声音。

There was a loud roaring *as* of rushing waters.

5. 原因:

因为我们没有钱,所以用不着去想度假的事。

Since we have no money, it is no good thinking about a holiday.

既然你要去,我就陪你去吧。

Since (或 As) you are going, I will accompany you.

因为他诚实,所以大家都喜欢他。

He is beloved of all *because* he is honest. (原因)

Cf. He must be honest, *for* he is beloved of all. (理由)

合句用 for,复句用 because,但 for 不用于会话体(conversational style),例如:"They ate their food uncooked, *for* the use of fire was unknown."一句,到会话中则变成"Why did they eat their food uncooked?" "*Because* the use of fire was unknown."不可用 for。

因为下雨,我就没有出门。

I did not go out *because* it rained.

在否定后接用的 because 如作 though 解,翻译时绝无问题,如 You should not despise a man because he is poor. 译为"虽则他穷,你也不要轻蔑他。"或译为"不要因别人穷就轻蔑他。"都是一样,错不了的。但如遇到不作 though 解的否定后接的 because,就得特别当心了。因为它可能有两种解释,例如:I didn't go because I was afraid. =（1）I didn't go, and the reason was fear.（我怕所以我没有去。）=（2）I went, but the reason was not fear.（我不是因为怕才去的。）一义说"去了",另一义说"没有去",竟发生完全相反的含义了。

因为他成绩好,所以薪水高。
He was well paid, *as* he had done the work well.
你疲倦了,最好去休息吧。
As you are tired, you had better rest.

6. 目的:

他们因为怕赶不上火车,急急忙忙地走了。
They hurried *that*（或 so that, in order that）they might not（说话时美国常用 wouldn't）miss the train.
要想动手搞另外的,你就得先把这个做完。
Finish this *that*（或 so that, in order that）you can start another.
当心以免从树上掉下来。
Be careful *lest*（或 for fear〔that〕）you should fall from the tree.（lest 用于写作,说话时则用 for fear）。
为着要去早晨的新鲜空气中把那问题仔细考虑一番,所以我出外散步了。
I went out for a walk, *so that* I might think the matter over in the fresh morning air.
为节省时间,队长亲自装上了马鞍。
The captain, *in order that* there might be no time lost, saddled his horse himself.
我们通常只是为求得别人的称赞而称赞别人。
We usually praise others *only that* we may be praised.

7. 结果:

我太疲倦,随即上床去睡了。
I was so tired *that* I went to bed at once.
那使他大为震惊,登时脸都白了。
It gave him such a shock *that* his face turned white.
他是那样的一个撒谎者,所以没有人喜欢他。
He is such a liar *that* no one likes him.
那是一个非常愚笨的计划,谁也不赞成。
It was a plan so stupid *that* no one approved of it.
我们经过长时间一直走得很快,所以十分疲倦了。
We walked very fast for a long time, *so that* we got quite tired.
他去得很早,所以占了一个好位子。

He went early *so* he got a good seat.

他说得那般清楚,我们每个字都听得见。

He spoke so clearly *that* we could hear every word.

你站近些使我可以看清楚你的面孔。

Draw nearer *so that* I can see your face.

她说的话那般有趣,使我既不知道也未注意时间的流逝。

She interested me so much *that* I neither knew nor heeled how time passed. (Caskell, *Cranford*)

我微不足道,无可效劳。

I am such a tiny thing *that* I am little use to you.

没有一个人老得不能学的。

No man is so old *but that* he may learn. (However old a man may be, he may learn.)

无论怎样的难事久练自易。

Nothing is so hard *but that* it becomes easy by practice.

不雨则已,雨必滂沱。(重重不幸,祸每两临。)

It never rains *but* it pours. (= It never rains without pouring.)

裁判虽属公平,仍然有人不服。

Justice is never done *but* some people will be found to complain.

一定有事要发生的。

It can not be *but that* something will happen. (= Something must happen.)

人谁能免于过失。

It is impossible *but that* a man will make some mistakes.

8. 条件:

你如果明天有空,请来我家坐坐。

If (you are) free tomorrow, please come to see me.

只要你一年内还我,我是可以把那笔钱借给你的。

I don't mind lending you the money *provided* (that) you pay it back within a year.

你要不是一个完全的笨蛋,你就不会那样对待你叔叔的。

Unless you are a perfect fool you will behave properly to your uncle.

只要有二十个人肯捐一百元,我也就照捐不误。

I will subscribe a hundred *provided* twenty others will do the same.

即令发生最坏的情形,至少她也就有一个安全的地方可作退步的。

At least there will be a retreat secured for her *in case* the worst should ensue. (Thackeray, *Vanity Fair*)

非我喝酒,他不罢休。

Nothing will content him *but* I must drink.

若非贫穷,我是决意要出洋去的。

I would go abroad *but that* (= but for the fact that) I am poor. (but for my poverty.)

无论如何必须达到我的目的。(不达目的,事必棘手。)

It shall go hard *but* (= unless) I will accomplish my purpose.

9. 让步：

虽则天气很冷，他并没有升火。

(*Al*)*though* it was cold, he did not light the fire.

不问他成败如何，我们都要尽力帮忙。

Whether he succeed(s) or fail(s), we should have to do our best.

即令他穷，他看去很快乐。

If he is poor, he looks happy. (if = even if)

哪怕我有钱，我也要工作。

Even if I were rich, I would work.

姑认这是真的，又将怎样？

Granting（或 Granted）*that* this is true, what follows?

天虽则黑了，我们还是找到了回家的路。

Dark *as* it was (= Though it was so dark), we found our way back.（注意 as 前如用名词，也要将冠词略去，如 Poor piper as I am. = Though I am a poor piper.）

他虽然吓坏了，但并没有倒下。

Startled *though* he was, he did not lose his balance.

糖虽是一种主要的食料，我们却不能以之为生。

Important *as* sugar is as an article of food, we cannot live upon it.

哪怕牺牲性命，他也要干到底的。

He will go through with it *if* it costs him his life.

即令你向他提出，他也不会接受的。

Even if you offer it to him, he won't accept it.

他虽有时感受风寒，然其身体极为强健。

He is extremely strong—not *but that* (= though) he will catch a cold at times.

（三）用于名词子句的译例

他曾到此是确实的。

That he was here is true.

Cf. It is true *that* he was here.（副词子句）

我想他在城里。

I think (*that*) he is in town.

他说他要来的。

He said (*that*) he would come.

你不能来使我感到遗憾。

I am sorry (*that*) you can't come.

不晓得他在不在家。

I wonder *if* (或 whether) he is at home (or not).

我相信他说的不错，而到现在为止谁也没有讲过这岛上的状况。

I believe (*that*) he was really right, and *that* nobody had told the situation of the island. (Stevenson)

我不知道我能不能进大学。

I don't know *whether* I shall be able to go to college or not.

问他是不是到动身的时候了。

Ask him *if* it is time to start.

我不清楚是他要打梅先生呢,还是梅先生要打他。

I am not clear *whether* he was going to strike Mr. Mell, or Mr. Mell was going to strike him. (Dickens, *David Copperfield*)

他问我是不是有什么要他做的事情。

He asked me *if* I had any business he could arrange for me.

他一再地问我在那里我是不是有什么事情要办。

He repeated the inquiry *if* I had any business there.

他做出这样的愚行来真是遗憾。

It is to be regretted *that* he should have committed this foolish act.

他完全相信他父亲会替他还债的。

He had a perfect belief *that* his father would pay his debt for him.

谁是下届美国总统尚未决定。

Who will be the president of the U.S.A. next time is undecided.

我问你在这三者之中最喜欢哪一个。

I ask you *which* of the three you like best.

我要用你所喜欢的名字来叫你。

I will name you *what* you like.

我不知道他怎样完成那工作的。

I know nothing as to *how* he has finished his work.

他要何时回家,连他太太都不知道。

When he will come home is not known to his wife.

我要把这个送给任何需要它的人。

I will give this to *whoever* wants it.

听说他要来,我们都高兴。

The news, *that* he will come, gives us much pleasure.

我确信他必成功。

I do not doubt (but) *that* he will succeed. (这个来自法兰西语的否定后的 but 是无意义的,下同。)

我不否认他是勤快的。

I do not deny (but) *that* he is diligent.

他的年轻并不妨碍他教书。

His youth hinders not *but that* he may teach. (= His youth does not hinder him from teaching.)

没有什么事可以妨碍我完成目的的。

Nothing shall hinder *but that* I will accomplish my purpose. (= Nothing shall hinder me from accomplishing my purpose.)

或者如此,亦未可知。
Who knows *but* it may be so?

习题 8

试用英文复句译出下列各句:

1. 我们都晓得时间就是金钱。
2. 我不知道这是真的还是假的。
3. 这就是昨天对我狂吠的那条狗。
4. 我亟想知道他这个时候在不在家。
5. 自从他去年离开这里以来我还没有见到过他。
6. 他说话的神气就好像什么都懂得似的。
7. 你越用功,进步越快。
8. 你既然这样讲,我就得相信呀。
9. 我们读书是为了求知。
10. 我打开窗子邀明月进来。
11. 他太狡猾所以没有人和他做朋友。
12. 豹死留皮,人死留名。
13. 如果合算的话,我就接受那个工作。
14. 没有人比不要听的人更聋的了。
15. 如果你是上等人,你就要像个上等人的样子。
16. 听来也许觉得奇怪,我太有钱反买不起它。
17. 我并不羡慕他富有,那使他非常烦恼。
18. 忧愁使他变成这个样子。
19. 在我们愉快地玩着的时候,时间过得很快。
20. 没有互敬是不能有友谊的。

叁 由内容来分的造句

(1) 用平叙句来翻译

平叙句(Declarative 或 Assertive Sentence)是叙述事实的文句,我们日常讲话,大部分都是用的这种句子。如我在本书前面讲过的,英文的句型共有五种,其用字的排列次序为:

1. "主语 + 自动词",如 Birds sing. (鸟鸣。)
2. "主语 + 自动词 + 补语",如 The rose smells sweet. (玫瑰花香。)
3. "主语 + 他动词 + 宾语",如 He has plenty of sense. (他富有见识。)
4. "主语 + 他动词 + 间接宾语 + 直接宾语",如 He teaches us English. (他教我们英文。)
5. "主语 + 他动词 + 宾语 + 补语",如 You must keep it a secret. (你必须保守秘密。)

英文句中用字的排列次序常有变化,并不一定照这五种句型的规矩来说。兹就惯用法找出一些变化的形式,来作为平叙句的译法;至于普通五种句型所表现的平叙句法,因为前面已经详细讲过了,所以这儿不拟再说。

(一) There + 动词 + 主语

凡说到事物或人的有无时,在主语所含文字较长的情形下,为引起听者对主语的注意起见,在应说主语的地位上,用 there 一字充数,而将真正的主语移到后面去说,如

桌子上有一本书。
There is a book on the desk.
后来他确知悔悟了。
There came a time when he did repent.
人们看到了一个奇异的光景。
There was seen a strange sight.
从前有一位大王名叫亚菲来德。
Once there lived a great king whose name was Alfred.
一切寂静无声。
There fell a deep silence.

(二) 把条件句中的连词省略,而将助动词放在主语的前面去,本动词的 be 及 have,也有这种助动词同样的用法。例如:

如果你找到了,请告诉我。
Should you find them, kindly let me know.
她要有一个小孩的话,她就快乐了。
Had she a child, she would be happy.
他要是还在世,他会怎样说呀!

Were he alive, what would he say?

我要是见到了他,我会责备他的。

Did I see him, I would blame him for it.

(三)副词(片语) + 动词 + 主语

为着引起读者的注意或好奇心起见,又为着保持字数较多的主语和动词的密切结合起见,常把动词放到主语的前面去。在这种情况下,也有采用 there 的时候。

一个女郎和一条狗来到街头了。

Down the street came a girl and a dog.

名单上还可加入下列的名字。

To the list may be added the following names.

在房间的当中,枝形吊灯下面,站着老家长乔戎。

In the centre of the room, under the chandelier, stood the head of the family, old Jolyon.

在他后面走进来一个身材高大的女人,体态丰腴,容仪端正,头发还是棕色的——那就是瓦丽斯夫人。

Behind him had come in a tall woman, of full figure and fine presence, With hair still brown—Lady Valleys herself.

(四)为着加强副词(片语)、补语、宾语或本动词起见,常将这种字放在一句的头上。

1. 惊叹词变来的副词及介词,与同形的副词及 here, there。

副词 + 动词 + 名词
代名词 + 动词

(a) 枪声砰的一响,那鸟就掉下来了。

Bang went the gun, and the bird fell.

砰的一下又是一声枪声。

Bang came another shot.

皮鞭重重地抽去。

Crack goes the whip!

(b) 天花板掉下来了。

Down came the ceiling.

他走下去了。

Down he went.

老鼠都跳进去了。

In plunged the rats.

我们像一阵风似的走了。

Off we went like the wind.

笛声一再高扬。

On and on went the puper.

行行复行行。

On and on they went.

那对夫妇一下就冲出去了。

Out rushed the man and his wife.

他们冲出去了。

Out they rushed.

马车驰过去了。

Over went the carriage.

他拿着盘子走过去了。

Over he went with the dish.

蜻蜓轰然上升。

Up went this roaring dragonfly.

他们上去了。

Up they went.

(c) 托孟来了。

Here comes Tom.

他来了。

Here he comes.

这是你的上衣。

Here is your coat.

这就是的。

Here it is.

那是你的手套。

There are your gloves.

那就是的。

There they are.

注意：here, there 如做"在这里"，"在那里"解时，仍可放在句首，但字的排列要照普通的顺序，如 *Here* the game keeper found the dead body.（猎场看守人在这里找到了那尸体。）*There* Scott wrote all his works.（史各特就在那里写出了他全部的著作。）

2. 上述 1. 项以外的副词及副词片语。

副词（片语）+ 助动词 + 主语 + 本动词

我们对于这个决定深为后悔。

Bitterly did we repent our decision.

那情景我记得很清楚。

Well do I remember the scene.

我曾指出时间是过得很快的，但是徒然。

In vain did I point out how time was getting on.

我们再也见不到他的面了。

Never shall we see his face again.

我做梦也未曾想到这样的事。
Never had I even dreamed of such a thing.
对于这个使命我决不再向前移动一步。
Not another step will I budge on this errand.
直到那个时侯我才实感到形势的危险。
Not till then did I realize the danger of the situation.
他不但从来没有踏进大门来过,甚至连在窗口也没有露过面。
Not only did he never cross the threshold, but he never so much as showed his face at a window.
为着闲人去游荡,世界上再没有比伦敦更好的地方了。
Nowhere in the world is there such a place for an idle man as London.
我们没有想到会再也见不到他的。
Little did we think that we should never see him again.
他一进房来就破口大骂。
Scarcely had he entered the room when he broke out in insuits.
那对他们最没有兴趣的了。
Least of all is it to their interest.
我看见过他好多次。
Many a time have I seen him.
这种光景我以前只见到过一次。
Only once before have I seen such a sight.
他只有一次对我说过话。
Only on one occasion did he speak to me.
迟迟地他才明白那火灾是发生在他自己家里。
Only slowly did he understand that the fire was in his own house.

3. 补语：

   补语 + 主语 + 动词

   (a) 罗杰始终是一个坏脾气的家伙。
   Cantankerous chap Roger always was.
   他们非常感谢我要援助他们。
   Very grateful they were for my offer of help.
   幸而我们知道她的名字。
   Lucky it is that we know her name.
   (b) 我的懊悔是痛苦而无益的。
   Bitter but unavailing were my regrets.
   我采取正当措施极为有效。
   So effective it is that I have taken the right measures.

4. 宾语：

   宾语 + 主语 + 动词

宾语+助动词+主语+本动词

(a) 我们虽然能够知道过去,但对未来却只能推测。

The past one can know, but *the future* one can only feel.

我们高兴地记得许多事情,也高兴地忘却许多事情。

Many things we gladly remember, *others* we gladly forget.

金银我都没有,我所有的只有这些,现在都给你好了。

Silver and gold have I none, but *such as I have* give I thee.

(b) 他没有给她说一句好话。

Not a word did he say in her favour.

不到最后一张纸印好,他们谁也不会有一分钟休息的。

Not a moment's rest will any of the men enjoy until the last paper is printed.

只有两个人死去了,没有继续受苦。

Only two had merciful death released from their sufferings.

5. 本动词:

你抱怨也得去。

Growl you will and *go* you must.

他说我们必须赶上她。

He says *overtake* her we must.

因为我们必须找到那个解毒剂,不然就得发现民主政治是欺诈的。

For *find* that antidote we must, or *discover* democracy to be fraudulent.

"如果你马上打电报去,他是可以阻止的。"而他就是这样被阻止了。

"If you telegraph at once, he can be stopped." And *stopped* he was.

(五) 为着和上文联系,某些字眼要放在句首。

这种威胁他简直无法实行。

This threat he was quite unable to carry out.

这到底是什么我说不出来。

What it is I cannot tell.

这个议论的全程有赖于此。

On this depends the whole course of the argument.

我相信那些话是有预言意味的。在那些话中间有着劳工阶级成功地进行斗争的秘密。

I believe those words are prophetic. *In them* is the secret of a successful prosecution of the struggle of the working class.

随后就吹起逆风来了。

Then came unfavourable winds.

其次就是付款的问题。

Next comes the question of pay.

这便是此人的生平与性格。

Such are the life and character of this man!

医生在他的(创办医院的)计划书上这样说。

So the physician said in his prospectus.

他加速了他的步伐,我也如此。

He quickened his pace, and *so* did I.

你们错了,我们也错了。

You were wrong, *so* were we.

"你现在一定要去睡觉呀。""正是。你也是呀。"

"You must go to bed now." "*So* I must. *So* must you."

树倒下来了,一定会死的。

As the tree falls, *so* must it die.

种瓜得瓜,种豆得豆。

As a man soweth, *so* shall he reap.

自作自受。

As you make your bed, *so* you must lie on it.

那件事他什么也不知道。他的妻子也和他一样。

He knew nothing about it. *No more* did his wife.

试想想田野的百合是怎样生长;它们既不劳动,也不纺织。

Consider the lilies of the field, how they grow; they toil not, *neither* do they spin. (Matt. 6:28)

我也不必告诉你,我做这些事是凭什么职权。

Neither do I tell you by what authority I do these things.

那一切都是真的,我们不可忘记。

All that is true, *nor* must we forget.

我不知道,我也猜不出来。

I know not, *nor* can I guess.

我不告你虚伪,更不告你欺诈。

I do not accuse you of falsehood, *still less* (do I accuse you) of dishonesty.

习题 9

1. 笨人无药可医。
2. 她每星期写一封信回家。
3. 他把钱都花在买书上面了。
4. 阔人也和穷人一样烦恼。
5. 这个礼拜下了不少的雨。
6. 现在是到了要思索的时候。
7. 她的缝纫机原来就是放在这里的。
8. 在他后面接着来了长蛇似的兵马。
9. 一按机关地雷立刻爆炸。

10. 在蒙茅斯要塞陆军通讯队所养的鸽子是最有代表性的。
11. 人们最喜欢的就是名利。
12. 杯中只有一点水。
13. 罕有比这更为忙乱的。
14. 他要看到了我,立刻就会认识的。
15. 他甫发言,听众就阻碍他。
16. 关于此事我们意见不同的地方就在此。
17. 他们得看护病伤的人。
18. 他不会成功的,虽则他从未这样努力试过。
19. 知足的人是幸福的。
20. 那演说家如是说。

(2) 用疑问句来翻译

疑问句(Interrogative Sentence)是发出疑问的文句,正好像肯定形(Affirmative Form)的句子大都可以变成否定形(Negative Form)的句子一样,一般的叙述句也是大都可以变成疑问句的。例如"他礼拜天上教堂。"译成:

He goes to church on Sunday. 是肯定平叙句,而

He does not go to church on Sunday. 是否定平叙句。

Does he go to church on Sunday? 才是疑问句。

感叹句有时也勉强可改成否定,不过只能改为相反的意思,例如"这朵花多么美呀!" How beautiful this flower is! 改为否定时便成为"这朵花多么丑呀!" How ugly this flower is! 改为疑问句则成为 Is this flower beautiful? 意为"这朵花美吗?"和感叹句的含义(对此花之美大为惊叹)大不相同了。

英文的疑问句,从用字的排列上看,有三种基本的构成形式。

1. 最普通的字序(word-order)为:

Predicate – Verb + Subject

(a)在下列动词的场合,不用 Do – Form:Be(was;were),have(Past Tense 时偶然也可用 Do – Form),shall(should),will(would),can(could),may(might),must,ought to,need(v. aux.),dare(v. aux.),used to.

你好吗?
Are you well?

他来了吗?
Has he come?

我们赶得上火车吗?
Shall we be in time for the train?

你明天要来吗?

Will you come tomorrow?

你能读中文吗?

Can you read Chinese?

我可以回家去了吗?

May I go home?

你一定这样快就要走吗?

Must you go so soon?

我应该做这事吗?

Ought I to do this?

他非急不可吗?

Need he hurry?

你敢从那高墙上跳下来吗?

Dare you jump from the top of that high wall?

他曾经住在这里吗?

Used he to live here?

(b) 在其他的动词的场合,就要用 Do – Form:

你喜欢他吗?

Do you like him?

你昨天看见他吗?

Did you see him yesterday?

2. 主语为疑问词或含有疑问词时的字序为:
Subject + Predicate – Verb

什么风把你吹来的?

What brought you here?

《哈姆雷特》是谁作的?

Who wrote *Hamlet*?

昨天有谁来了?

Who came yesterday?

什么人(哪一个)这样说的?

What (Which) man said so?

要做什么?

What is to be done?

如果在 1. 型上再加疑问词时,则仍依照 1 型的字序,不必改变。

他说什么?

What did he say? (句中 what 为 say 的宾语)

你有多少孩子?

How many children have you?

他是哪里来的？

Where has he come from? （句中的 where 为 from 的宾语，from where 为 Predicate – Verb 的 Modifier.）

你讲的是谁？

Whom are you talking of?

你何时从英国回来的？

When did you return from England? （句中的 when 为 Predicate – Verb 的 Modifier.）

3. 全照平叙句的字序，只消在句尾加上一个 Interrogation Mark（疑问号），以表示疑问的意思就行了。说的时候，句尾稍加扬起。

你还没有去吗？

You are not going yet?

上面这三种疑问句的造型，还可以补充说明一下。属于 1 型的疑问句，都是可以回答 Yes 或 No 的，在说话时，这类问话都要在句尾用升调（Rising Intonation）。至于 2 型的疑问句，就不能回答 Yes 或 No，因为它所问的不是是非的问题，而是"是什么"，"为什么"，"怎么样"，"哪一个"，"何时"，"何地"，"何人"等的问题。这类问话都是要在句尾用降调（Falling Intonation）的。至于 3 型已如上述，在说话时句尾要用升调，而文字的排列次序，完全和平叙句一模一样，只在句尾多了一个问号而已。这一类型的疑问句，也可再细分为下列两类：

(a) 对于说话的人原是用不着要问的，不过为慎重起见，再来问一下，例如：

我想，你有钱吧？

You have some money, I suppose? （Stevenson）

这个我可以看吧？

I may read this? （Dickens）

情形与此类似，而将疑问句的省略式附于平叙句之后，也是口语中经常见的。英文把它叫做 Tag-question，通常那附加的疑问句是不要译出的。

你不喜欢读小说吧？

You don't like to read novels, do you?

他去了美国吧？

He has gone to America, hasn't he?

你每个礼拜五都有英文课吧？

You have English lessons every Friday, don't you?

他们早餐吃茶点的吧？

They have tea for breakfast, don't they?

天气很好呀。

It's a fine day, isn't it? （J. K. Jerome）

(b) 凡表惊讶或怪异的时候，也可以用这种形式。

你不想去？

You don't wish to go?
我的父亲死了?
My father is dead?

上面这种形式的句子,普通常用不定词的造句来表达,例如:

他欺骗我?
He to deceive me?（=To think that he should deceive me!）
一个英国人叛国?
An Englishman betray his country?
路易士跟布兰芝结婚?
Lewis marry Blanche?（Shakespeare）
怎可放弃真理的大义?
How relinquish the cause of truth?（Goldsmith）

这三种疑问句的基本构成形式,Harold E. Palmer 把 1 型叫作 General Question(一般疑问),2 型叫作 Special Question(特殊疑问);而 Otto Jespersen 又把 1 型叫作 Nexus Question(叙述关系的疑问)。2 型叫作 X–question(含有未知数的疑问)。至于 3 型就被 Onions 及 Curme 称为 Deliberative Question(深思熟虑的疑问)。

除此三种而外,还有一种所谓 Rhetorical Question(修辞的疑问),是指那些表面上是疑问句,实则什么都不要问,而只是作为一种反语来表示自己的相反的意见,好使对方接受而已。这种表现法实较平叙句更为有力,更要充满感情,例如:

有什么用?
What is the use?（=It is no use.）
谁不晓得?
Who does not know?（=Everyone knows.）
有人写过这样没有意义的东西吗?
Was ever such nonsense written?（=Never was such nonsense written.）

在这种修辞的疑问中,肯定的疑问句相等于否定的平叙句,例如:

黑人能够改变他的肤色,豹子能够改变它的斑纹吗?
Can the Ethiopian change his skin, or the leopard his spots? 如用平叙句说时,当然就变成 cannot 了。

否定疑问句相当于肯定平叙句,例如:

这不好笑吗?
Isn't it funny?（= It is very funny.）

有时连句尾的问号都可以省去:

Yet, *are we not* like spoilt children who have so many new toys to play with that we have ceased to wonder at anything.（可是,我们真好像是不断地给与许多新玩具的惯坏了的孩子似的,对任何东西都不感到新奇了。）

有时加上一个否定字的 not，也和没有此字的句子一样，结果变成同样的意思，例如：

    他发现这个时极为惊异。

    What was hit astonishment on finding it?　= How great was his astonishment on finding it!（感叹句）

    What was *not* his astonishment on finding it?（修辞的疑问）= No astonishment could be greater than his was on finding it.

兹就四种疑问句分别举例译出如下：

(一)一般疑问句

    今夜月亮圆了没有？
    Is the moon full tonight?

    公众不是最好的批评家吗？
    Is the public not the best judge?

    你知道猫有九条命吗？
    Do you know the cat has nine lives?

    英国人喜欢户外运动吗？
    Are the English fond of outdoor sports?

    他坚持要一意孤行吗？
    Will he have his own way?

    她的眼睛是蓝色的还是棕色的？
    Has she blue eyes or brown eyes?

    你从前认得他吗？
    Used you to know him?

    他应该马上动身吗？
    Ought he to start at once?

    衣服穿得太脏是对人的一种无礼。
    Isn't untidy dress a form of discourtesy?

    他这样愚笨真令人吃惊？
    Isn't it surprising that he should be so foolish?

    你的意思是拒绝吗？
    Am I to understand that you refused?

(二)特殊疑问句

    谁会想到这样呀？
    Who would have thought so?

    一部车子里能够坐多少人？
    How many passengers can ride in one carriage?

    你手里是什么？
    What have you in your hand?

    从这里到车站哪条路最近？

Which is the shortest way from here to the railway station?

那本书你在哪里找到的?

Where did you find the book?

她为什么要这样说?

Why did she say so?

她何时起生病的?

Since when has she been ill?

你对于中国电影觉得怎样?

How do you like Chinese movies?

假期何时开始?

When will the holidays begin?

(三)熟虑疑问句

他还没有来吗?

He is not coming yet?

那房间里什么也没有?

Nothing was found in the room?

我并不感兴趣。

We were not amused, were we? (Queen Elizabeth)

那真奇怪呀。

That's queer, isn't it?

我要尊敬你吗?

I honour thee?

他不会说英语?

He doesn't speak English?

你不吃蛋糕?

You don't eat cakes?

再不要了吗?

No more?

他把约会忘记了?

He to forget the appointment?

他是一个君子?

He a gentleman? (= He is not a gentleman.)

你不去开会吗?

You are not going to the meeting?

(四)修辞疑问句

这有什么麻烦?

What is the trouble? (= It is no trouble.)

谁不喜欢名利?

Who does not care for fame and wealth? (= Everybody likes fame and wealth.)

你能忘记那可怕的光景吗?

Can you forget that terrible scene? (= You cannot forget that terrible scene.)

本性难移。

Can man change his nature?

世界上有这样的事吗?

Has ever such a thing happened in the world?

我不应该留我兄弟在此。

Am I my brother's keeper? (= It is not my duty to keep my brother.)

我不在乎。

What do I care? (= I don't care.)

我有足够的钱吗?

Have I money enough? (= I haven't enough money.)

习题 10

1. 这有什么关系?
2. 你那支手杖是哪里买的?
3. 难道你不以儿子为荣吗?
4. 他是干什么的?
5. 这本书你花了多少钱?
6. 你打算雇用哪一位?
7. 有什么你要的东西我可以替你找来吗?
8. 有谁不犯过失?
9. 有很会游泳的女子吗?
10. 发生了什么事情吗?
11. 你喝点啤酒好吗?
12. 你有些英文书吗?
13. 给我一点葡萄酒好吗?
14. 你说莎丽要跟谁结婚?
15. 你知道空中楼阁是怎样一回事?
16. 明天我要去讲些什么呢?
17. 附近有公共汽车吗?
18. 你想她什么时候可以回来?
19. 他在英国住上十年之久还不懂英文?
20. 如果我坐三点半的车去,可以赶上吗?

(3) 用命令句来翻译

命令句(Imperative Sentence)是表示命令、请求、忠告、愿望、禁止等的文句,普通是对第二人

称说的,所以常把对方的主语 you 省去。中国话也一样不说"你",单说动词就行,例如:

> 进来!
> Come in.
> 不要闹。
> Be quiet.
> 把门关上!
> Shut the door!
> 快说!
> Speak!
> 过来!
> Come here!
> 快走,玛丽,快走!
> Run, Mary, run!

有时为着要和别人区别,特别有指明对方的必要时,也可以把主语说出来,例如:

> 你同我到车站去。
> You go with me to the station.

兹就命令句的各种形式,逐条例解如下:

1. 最普通的形式是略去第二人称的主语。

   > 把握时机。
   > Make hay while the sun shines. (Proverb)
   > 回去照我吩咐你的去做好了。
   > Go home and do what you are told.
   > 请把面包递给我。
   > Pass me the bread, please.
   > 要诚实呀!要诚实呀!要诚实呀!
   > Be true! Be true! Be true! (Hawthorne)
   > 把书拿出来看。
   > Show the book. (C. Brontë)

2. 否定的命令句常要加用助动词的 do,有时也可保留主语。普通是表示禁止的意思。

   > 不要这样大声说话。
   > Don't talk so loud!
   > 孩子们,不要懒惰。
   > Don't be idle, my boys.
   > 你不要去把这个秘密告诉他呀。
   > Don't (you) go and tell him the secret!
   > 你不要就开始。

Don't you begin it.

决不要撒谎。

Never tell a lie.

你不要管我。

Never do you bother yourself about me. (Eliot)

不要怕。

Fear nothing.

不要动。

Don't you stir!

不要为他着急。

Don't you worry about him.

不要为我难过。

Don't you go feeling sorry for me.

不要为一吻所欺骗而自寻苦恼。

Suffer not yourselves to be deceived by a kiss. (Patrick Henry)

在古文中或诗中虽有否定词仍然可以不加 do,如美国诗人 Longfellow 的诗句:

Tell me not, in mournful numbers,

Life is but an empty dream!

(毋作悲哀语,谓人生若梦。)

3. 肯定的命令句常加上一个助动词的 do 字,以加强语气,表示恳请。

务请你到这里来。

Do come here!

请不要吵闹。

Do be quiet!

务请你去。

Do go, please.

求你赏一文钱吧。

Do give me just one penny!

求你坐一会儿吧。

Sit down for a moment, pray, do!

4. 命令句法在古时是不略去第二人称的主语的,不过那时常把主语放在动词后面,例如 Go and do thou likewise. (你去照样做吧。) Enter ye in at the strait gate. (你们要进窄门。) So speak ye, and do so. (你们就该照这律法说话行事。) 以上这些引用的句子都是《圣经》上的,由于这种用法遗留下来,现代英文中便有 mind you, look you, mark you, speak you 等等惯用语句:

你要当心,他还没有付款。

Mind you, he hasn't paid the money yet.

赞美主。

Praise you the Lord!

5. 在现代英文中为加强语气或代表对照起见,也还是可以保留第二人称的主语的。特别提出对方来说,以便唤起对方的注意。

我不晓得要怎样说,诺拉,你去吧。
I don't know what to say, Nora, you go!

"你在此看守她,"医生对他的助手说,"我要八点钟才能回来。"
"You watch her," the doctor said to his assistant, "I shan't be back before eight."

你注意我说的话。
You mark my words!

你不要惹那条狗。
You let that dog alone!

你坐下来吃你的早餐好了。
You sit down and get your breakfast!

你听我的劝告,不要去。
You follow my advice and don't you go! (Emphasis)

你要当心呀,你听到了吗?
You be careful, you hear? (Emphasis)

这个我搞不好,你来试试看。
I cannot manage this; you try. (Contrast)

约翰,你先坐下吧,有人会再去拿些椅子来的。
You take that seat, John, and someone (= one of you present) fetch a few more chairs. (Contrast)

啊,请你们那个进去告诉她一声吧。
Oh, please, someone (= someone of you) go in and tell her.

6. 对于第一人称和第三人称的命令句,就要加用 let 一字,而把主语变成宾语。

让我看看。
Let me see!

让我们走吧。
Let us go!

让他进来。
Let him come in!

让他们向前走。
Let them walk on.

我们在这里停留一个礼拜吧。
Let us stay here a week.

如果是恳求的话,还可以在 let us 前加 do 或 don't 的字样,如:

啊,请让我们吧。
Oh, do let's!

不要让我们那样做呀。

Don't let us do that!

Compare：

  Let's〔lets〕go.（我们去吧。）

  Let us〔lets〕go.（＝Set us free）（让我们走吧。）

  Let us〔lets〕know（＝Tell us）the time of your arrival。（告诉我们你到达的时间。）

  Let's let him go.（＝Let's allow him to go.）（让我们允许他去吧。）

  Let it be distinctly understood（＝Understand〔it〕distinctly）that I will stand no nonsense.（要明白我是不会容忍胡闹的。）

  Let me see! What is the name of that man?（让我想想看他姓什么。）

  Let me not hear of it any more.（我不要再听到这个了。）

  Let's not do what is wrong.（让我们不要做错事。）

  Let's go for a walk, shall we?（我们去散散步吧。）

以下则形式(Form)上为间接命令，而意味(Sense)上却是直接命令：

  Let the pupils beware of bad company.（Boys, beware of bad company.）（学生不要交坏朋友。）

  Let any one of you, who can answer this question, hold up his hand.（你们任何人，谁能回答这问题的举手。）

  Now let's every one go to bed that we may rise early.（Walton）（大家早早去睡，我们明天好早早起身。）

7. 命令句中的假设语气的用法：

在 Older English 中命令句的主语如系第一人称或第三人称的时候，就用假设语气现在(Subjunctive Present)来表示。今日在诗中极少数惯用语句中，还有这种用法的遗留。

  他们说我做错了。让它去吧。

  They say I have done wrong. Be it (Let it be) so.

  让我们向前进吧。

  Move we (＝Let us move) on. (Scott)

  不要爬得太高，以免跌得太重。

  Climb we not (＝Let us not climb) too high,／Lest we should fall too low. (Coleridge)

  我们的路在那边；让我们蜿蜒爬上高处。

  Thither our path lies; wind we (＝let us wind) up the heights. (Robert Browning)

这种形式在现代口语中也有遗留下来的痕迹可寻。那些带有命令形(Imperative Form)的假设语气现在(Subjunctive Present)，可用作让步的意思。

  不管天气如何，我都要去。

  I will go, be the weather what it may (＝whatever the weather may be).

  不管花多少钱，我都要买。

  Cost what it may (＝Whatever it may cost), I will buy it.

不管你怎样说,他都不听。

Say what you will (= Whatever you may say), he does not mind us.

无论他们怎样努力去干,也决不会成功的。

Try as they may (= However had they may try), they will never succeed.

无论它们怎样挣扎,钓钩已钩牢在它们鳃上了。

Do what they might (= Whatever they might do), the hook was in their gills. (George Meredith)

可以说强盗已被击溃了。

Suffice it to say that the robbers were defeated. (Farley)

金窝银窝,不如自己的狗窝。

Be it ever so humble, there is no place like home.

不管是什么事情,始终都要说实话。

Be the matter what it may, always speak the truth.

8. 命令句法的时态在性质上原是现在,不过偶然也有用完成式的,那当然是为着加强语气而用的。

算了吧。

Be gone!

够了,不要再这样胡说了。

Have done with such nonsense!

9. 命令句的特殊用法。

(a) 为表示条件有时也可以用命令语气:

只要你看管小钱,大钱就会看管自己的。

Take care of the pence, and the pounds will take care of themselves. (= If you take care of the pence, the pounds will take care of themselves.)

只要你敢走近我一步,我就要打碎你的嘴。

Take a step near me, and I'll smash your mouth.

你说呀! 不说我就开枪啦。

Speak! or I fire. (= If you do not speak, I [will] fire.)

(b) 表示假设等。

假如你有了一笔钱,例如一千镑吧,你会用来做点什么?

Suppose (= If) you had a sum of money—say (= for instance) a thousand pounds—what would you do with it?

下星期休假一天何如?

Suppose we take a holiday next week.

他连日常必需品都没有,遑说什么奢侈品。

He lacks the bare necessaries of life, let alone (= not to mention) luxuries.

(c) 命令句又可用作副词同等语(Adverb – Equivalent)。

毕竟,他那样的人是不会再度遇见的吧。

Take him for all in all (= After all), we shall not look upon his like again. (A. Huxley)

确实,马克爵士和那事毫无关系。

Rest assured (= Assuredly) Sir Mark had nothing to do with the matter.

习题 11

1. 我们不要做不诚实的事。
2. 我不想再听到这件事了。
3. 你要勤快点才好呀。
4. 不要懒惰呀。
5. 不要急急离去呀。
6. 拿把椅子来让你叔叔坐。
7. 那只猫你让它去吧。
8. 胡兰芝,现在你读。
9. 务请赏光。
10. 你不要挂意。
11. 不要忘记你的功课。
12. 不要过分依赖别人的帮助。
13. 你告诉他这是紧急的事。
14. 不要胡说八道。
15. 请大家安静下来。
16. 不要担心。
17. 你戒了酒,健康就会好些。
18. 永不要说别人的坏话。
19. 不要像许多人一样,只为娱乐而读书。
20. 请等一会,我马上就来。

(4) 用感叹句来翻译

感叹句(Exclamatory Sentence)是表示惊愕、苦痛、欢喜等感情或加强说出某种事实、希望、命令、疑问等的文句。在这种句子的尾上,常要加上一个惊叹号(Exclamation Mark),以代替句点(Period);在句首则常有 How 或 What 的字眼。How 常用于形容词的前面,而 What 则用于名词的前面,例如:

How lucky you are!(你多么幸运呀!)

What a lucky girl you are!(你是一个多么幸运的女子呀!)

但不用 how 或 what 也是可以构成感叹句的。那是形式不完备的感叹句。

一般的文法家多是将平叙句、疑问句、命令句、感叹句并列,把感叹句作为由内容来分的四种句型之一,但也有人,如荷兰的英文学者 Hendrik Poutsma(1857—1937),在他著的 *A Grammar of*

Late Modern English 一书中,便把感叹句看做平叙句的一种。

因为人类是感情的动物,常要表现出各种各样的感情来。《礼记·礼运》上说:"何谓人情?喜怒哀惧爱恶欲七者,弗学而能。"因而被认为在语言中,这种感叹句是起源最古的文句。它是感情激发时的叫声,因而保存着朴素的形式。它常将主语和动词全部略去,有时甚至只有一个字。兹分别举例说明如下:

普通在句首用 what 或 how 的,可分三类,即

1. 将 how 用作 Exclamatory Adverb 的:

> 今夜的月光何等明亮!
>
> How bright the moon shines tonight!
>
> 这花多么的美呀!
>
> How beautiful this flower is!
>
> 我们快乐的日子多么短促呀!
>
> How short our happy days appear!
>
> 那狗跑得好快!
>
> How fast the dog runs!
>
> 你多么亲切!
>
> How kind of you!
>
> 雷打得多么响!
>
> How it thunders!
>
> 他的决心唱得多么高调!
>
> How high a pitch his resolution soars!

2. 将 what 用作 Exclamatory Adjective 的:

> 那女子具有多么美丽的头发!
>
> What beautiful hair that girl has!
>
> 他的房子好大!
>
> What a big house he has!
>
> 人是多么渺小呀!
>
> What paltry creatures we are!
>
> 这年头充满着幻想的色彩!
>
> What visionary tints the year puts on!(Lowell)
>
> 啊,我的国人呀,那儿的秋天多好呀!
>
> Oh, what a fall was there, my countrymen!(Shakespeare)

3. 将 what 用作 Exclamatory Pronoun 的:

> 他们不晓得是怎样想像的呀!
>
> What might they not have imagined!
>
> 他发现那个时不胜诧异。
>
> What was his surprise when he found it!

上面说，Poutsma 认为感叹句是一种平叙句，其实我觉得感叹句和疑问句更为接近，在形式上，在意义上，都有很深的关系。主语与动词的排列次序，感叹句确是和平叙句一样的，但除开这一点，感叹句就更像疑问句了。试比较如下：

  { 疑问句：How old is he？（他几岁？）
    感叹句：How old he is！（他好老！）

  { 疑问句：What man？（什么人？）
    感叹句：What a man！（何等了不起的人！）

  { 疑问句：What book is it？（这是什么书？）
    感叹句：What a good book it is！（多么一本好书！）

  { 疑问句：What act was it？（那是什么行为？）
    感叹句：What an act it was！（那算什么行为！）

  { 疑问句：What dreadful act has he committed？（他做了什么可怕的事？）
    感叹句：What a dreadful act he has committed！（他做了一件多么可怕的事！）

由上面的例句我们可以看得出来，感叹句用了 what 一字，又在其后接有单数普通名词时，便要加上一个不定冠词，这是在疑问句中所不需要的。

感叹句并不老是照平叙句一样，先说主语后说动词的，有时也可以照疑问句的次序，先说动词，再说主语。这是为要对主语加重的说法，尤其是移到句尾的字眼，说来特别响亮。

  我做了一件多么愚笨的事呀！
  What a poor fool was I！
  我们真希望上天没有赋予我们说话的能力！
  How would we wish that Heaven had left us still！
  在石头上流动的水波，多么的光耀！
  How bright are its waters, playing over the stones！（避免把修饰语的 playing，说成动词的 are playing 的关系而倒装。）
  他的话多么动听呀！
  How persuasive are his words！（Sheridan）
  我在儿童时代老是在这些树下玩耍的。
  How often have I played under these trees as a boy！（Irving）
  啊，那是多么奇怪的光景！
  Oh, what a sight was that！（H. R. Haggard）
  人是(上帝)多么巧妙的作品呀！
  What a piece of work is man！（Shakespeare）
  人是多么奇怪的东西！
  What a strange thing is man！（H. S. Merriman）
  裘蒂斯，裘蒂斯，你多么可爱呀！
  Judith, Judith, how lovely are you！（Curme）
  从这小山开始路就宽了，这地方多么使人愉快呀！

> How pleasant is this hill where the road widens. (Curme)

也有让疑问句一点不改来作感叹句用的。那称为 Exclamatory Question,例如:

> 她多么可爱呀!
> Isn't she a sweet girl!
> 谁会想到这样的事!
> Who would have thought of such a thing!
> 啊,那真好玩!
> Oh, wouldn't it be fun! (Dickens)
> 多少次她没有坐在那里了!
> How many times had she not sat there! (Galsworthy)

还有就照平叙句一模一样来说,只在句尾附加一个惊叹号,以表示确说的形式,也可以当作感叹句用:

> 这座桥绝对是危险的!
> The bridge is absolutely unsafe!
> 那绝对不可以做!
> It simply cannot be done!

在感叹句中有时可以将补语置于句首:

> 你们英国人是多么的冷血呀!
> Cold-blooded people you Britishers are!
> 你圆满地达成了使命!
> Well hast thou fulfilled thy mission!

此外感叹句还有种种破格的形式:

1. 省略句。

> 看呀!
> Look!
> 蚀呀!
> An eclipse!
> 啊,坏蛋!
> O, the wretch!
> 幸运儿!
> Fortunate man!
> 何等愚笨!
> What folly!
> 何其无礼!
> What impertinence!
> 好大的鼻子!

What a nose!

多么可惜!

What a pity (it is)! 或 What a shame!

他真笨!

How foolish (it is) of him!

真是厚颜!

What impudence!

想得真妙!

What an idea!

这是多么的客气呀!

Wonderful civility this! (C. Brontë)

多么不像从前他们白家的爷们呀!

How unlike their Belgic sirs of old. (Goldsmith)

如果我有这种愿望,我就要快乐十倍了!

This wish I have (＝If I have this wish), then ten times happy me! (Shakespeare)

一个多么了不起的女人——啊,一个多么了不起的女人!

What a woman—oh, what a woman! (Doyle)

2. 抗议句

什么? 说我爱! 说我求婚! 说我找老婆!

What? I love! I sue! I seek a wife!

说我对肯医生讲了什么不礼貌的话? 天不会允许的!

I say anything disrespectful of Dr. Kenn? Heaven forbid! (George Eliot)

他的祖父怎么会是一个商人! 他是一位绅士呀!

Why, his grandfather was a tradesman! He a gentleman! (Defoe)

她要算是美人的话,她的母亲也就可以算是才子了!

She a beauty! I should as soon call her mother a wit. (Austen)

说他傲慢吗! 啊,他决不会的!

He arrogant! No, never!

3. 将补语放在句首。

你居然笑,真是可怕呀!

How horrid of you to smile!

对于一个情夫,这样是颇有鼓励的呀!

Pretty encouragement this for a lover!

4. 将宾语放在句首。

但那正是这些女孩子们要说的话呀!

But the things these girls would say!

当他说这话时,他自己也觉得是伪君子的行为!

The hypocrite that he felt himself as he said this!

5. 加用 to think, fancy, O that 等字在句首。

他会在这次危机中拆我的烂污真不堪设想!
To think that he should fail me in this crisis!

啊,这样壮丽的王宫里,居然会有欺诈的行为!
O, that deceit should dwell
In such a gorgeous palace! (Shakespeare)

他居然相信呀!
Fancy his believing it!

竟至要等待整个下午!
Fancy having to wait all afternoon!

试想他对那件事竟一无所知!
To think of his not knowing anything about it?

从未听到这样的事!
If ever I heard the like! (= I never heard the like.)

祈愿句(Optative Sentence)通常是看作感叹句的一种的:

共和国万岁!
Long live the Republic! 或 May the Republic live long!

愿你的国降临。愿你的旨意行在地上,如同行在天上。
Thy kingdom come, thy will be done. (Matt. 6:10)

有你这样的好心肠,上帝是会保佑你的。
God bless and reward you for all your kindness! (Stowe)

愿上帝原恕我!
God forgive me! (Miss Mulock)

啊,女王,但愿如此!
So be it, O Queen! (H. R. Haggard)

愿我的房子是山边的茅屋!
Mine be a cot beside the hill! (Rogers)

愿上帝帮助我!
So help me God!

愿我再也不会见到他的面孔!
May I never see his face again!

愿今夜没有噩梦来打扰我的睡眠!
May no evil dream disturb my rest! (Evening Hymn)

愿他安息!
May he rest in peace! (Irving)

我要是在那里就好了!
Would that I were there! 或 Oh were I but there!

雷白卡,你要能多留一下就好了!

Oh that you could stay longer, dear Rebecca! (Thackeray)

但愿我行事坚定,得以遵守你的律例!

O that my ways were directed to keep thy statute. (Psalm)

愿我能够把这一切铸成一顶皇冠!

Would I could coin it all into a crown! (Lord Lytton)

我要是没有遇到它就好了!

Wish to God that I had never seen it! (Doyle)

啊,愿我能够再见到他一次!

Oh, that I could have seen him once again! (Watts-Dunton)

但愿我有这种精神,而不是我孩子的。

I would that it had been my soul and not my boy's. (H. R. Haggard)

啊,要是这样就好了!

Oh had it been so!

那时我要在巴黎就好了!

Oh to have been in Paris then!

愿他安乐地长生不老!

May he live long in peace!

但愿是由那纯洁的火焰点燃的火把!

O for a kindling touch from that pure flame. (Wordsworth)

愿你有一个光明的前途!

Bright be the future that lieth before thee! (Scott)

愿那秋天是阴暗的!

Black be its fall. (Stevenson)

愿你的树林是绿的,花是美的!

Green be your woods, and fair your flowers! (Byron)

祈愿句的反面便成为咒骂了,如

我碰了鬼!

Devil take me! (Lamb)

该死的文法!

Grammar be hanged!

愿上帝使你瞎眼。

May God strike you blind.

习题 12

1. 雪多么洁白呀!
2. 这落日真是光辉灿烂呀!
3. 这花多美呀!
4. 你好迟呀!

5. 这机器的声音真大呀!
6. 我们玩得多么有趣。
7. 他真是傻瓜。
8. 人的头脑真是太巧妙了。
9. 一个多么卑鄙的流氓!
10. 愿他有好的运道!
11. 每年真不知有多少人到耶路撒冷朝圣。
12. 我要能够去那音乐会就好了!
13. 他的鼾声多大!
14. 他口若悬河!
15. 在这里遇到你,我真高兴!
16. 愿她婚后幸福!
17. 朋友们再会!
18. 好呀,她来了!
19. 哎呀,我完了!
20. 愿天下有情人都成眷属!

第二编　英文惯用法及其翻译

Ⅰ．It 的造句

(1) it...不定词

  (a) *It* is wrong *to tell* a lie.
   撒谎是不对的。
  (b) He does not think *it* wrong *to tell* a lie.
   他不认为撒谎是不对的。

  这种形式上的主语或宾语,是中文表现法中所没有的。这些句子的真正的主语或宾语移到后面去了,而不在原来的地位上,于是那里就产生一个空缺,只得用"it"填补上去,所以这个"it",英文就叫做填补词(expletive)。

  如果把(a)例真正的主语恢复它原来的地位时,便成为:

   To tell a lie is wrong.

这正是中国话的表现法,但英文除极少数的文句外(如 To teach is to learn. To eat is to live.)一般都不喜欢用不定词作主语,而要改用形式上的"it"来作主语,把它说成:

   It is wrong to tell a lie.

  英文用不定词作主语虽不流行,但至少文句是通的。用不定词作宾语,则有背英文的惯用法,成为不通的了。如说成,He does not think to tell a lie wrong. 或说成,He does not think wrong to tell a lie. 都要不得,必须加用形式上的宾语"it"进去,而把它说成:

   He does not think it wrong to tell a lie.

才合乎英文惯用的语法。因为惯用法不允许拿不定词作宾语,所以凡遇到不定词要用作宾语时,就采用形式上的"it"来代替它。

  不定词虽不能用作宾语,但可用作补语,如 We found him to be alive. (我们发觉他还活着。)这种作补语用的不定词,有时可以略去,单说 We found him alive. 意思也是一样,而且更加简明有力。

  形式上的宾语,在某些常说的文句中,可以省略不用,尤其是后接不定词的时候为然,如:

   Your father thought 〔it〕 fit to leave me guardian. (你父亲认为请我做监护人最为适合。)
   If God sees 〔it〕 fit that I should marry, he would provide me with a worthy husband. (如果上帝认为我应该结婚,他就会供给我一个如意郎君的。)
   And are you sure of all this, are you sure 〔of it〕 that nothing ill has befallen my boy? (Goldsmith) (这一切都是真的吗,你确实知道我儿子没有遭遇任何不顺利的事吗?)
   I am sorry 〔for it〕 that you are going away. (你要走我很难过。)
   Men differ from brutes in 〔it〕 that they can think and speak. (人之所以异于禽兽,就在能思想能

说话。)

He forgot everything but [it] that he was near her. (Galsworthy)(他跟她在一块儿就把一切都忘了。)

It is easy to learn English, but it is difficult to attain perfection in it. (英文易学难精。)
It is much easier to read French than read Greek. (学法文比学希腊文容易多了。)
It may be advisable to wait till they come back. (最好是等他们转来。)
She had said what it was necessary to say. (要说的她都说了。)
It needs no great sagacity to see that the writer is a novice at his task. (很容易看得出来那作家是一位生手,刚从事写作的。)
I found it very difficult to put it in practice. (我觉得实行很难。)
He took it upon himself to pay off the debt. (他自愿负责还清债务。)
I know it to be the established custom of your sex to reject a man on the first application. (Jane Austen)(我知道拒绝男子的第一次求婚是你们女性的固定的习惯。)
Fortunately I have it in my power to introduce you to very superior society. (幸而我还有能力可以介绍你给非常上流的社会。)
If you take it into your head to go on refusing every offer of marriage in this way, you will never get a husband at all. (如果你执意要继续这样来拒绝所有的求婚,你就永远得不到一个丈夫了。)
Make it the first object to be able to fix and hold your attention upon your studies. (把专心致志于学业,持久不懈,作为第一目标。)
The fog made it difficult to calculate the distance. (雾迷了眼,看不出距离来。)

1. It was glorious to acquire a place by justice, yet more glorious to prefer justice before a place.
2. I have my own views about learning a language. I think it waste of time to acquire a greater knowledge than suffices me to read fluently and talk enough for the ordinary affairs of life. (Maugham)
3. How far cards might have helped him here it is difficult to say. (Hugh Walpole)

(2) it...for...不定词

(a) *It* is difficult *for* him *to do* so.
　　要他这样做是有困难的。

(b) I think *it* dfficult *for* him *to do* so.
　　我想要他这样做是有困难的。

这是属于"it...不定词"同一形式的,"it"仍然是代表不定词的形式上的主语或宾语。翻译时必须把句中的不定词看作主动词,因为介词"for"的宾语是不定词的意味上的主语(sense subject),即宾语的"him"应译成主语才。如果我们把填补词的"it"去掉,恢复原来应有的形式时,便成 To do so is difficult for him. 这个"for him",也可译成中文的"在他",全句译为"要这样做,在他是有困难的"。但不如把"him"当作主语来译更加利落。

这个"for"有时可以换为"of",如 It was brave indeed, of you to attempt it.(你真大胆敢于去尝试一下。)何时要用"for",何时要用"of",依前面的那个形容词而定。如果那个形容词是指的一种行为的性质(the nature of an action),就要用"for";如果那形容词是指的行为的性质,同时又指行为的人(the doer of an action),就要用"of"了。换句话说,单说行为的用"for",说行为及行为者的用"of",前者以"necessary"为例,后者以"kind"为例,造成句子,便是:

(a) It is necessary for you to do so.

(b) It is kind of you to do so.

句中说的"kind of you",可译为"你的行为是亲切的",也就是说"行为者的你是亲切的"。句中说的"necessary for you",可译为"你的行为是必要的",却不能说什么"行为者的你",即是:

(a)"必要的"(necessary)是指"行为",不是指"行为者"。

(b)"亲切的"(kind)既是指"行为",又是指"行为者"。

(b)句的意思是"他这样做是亲切的",同时也是"这样做的人是亲切的",但(a)句则只能说"这样做是必要的",却不能说"这样做的人是必要的",因为这样一来,变成必要的是"人",而不是"事"了。我们只能改说成 You are kind to do so. 不能改说成 You are necessary to do so. 其理甚明。再举一例,以资比较:

(a) It was impossible for him to go alone.

(b) It was foolish of him to go alone.

(a)句中的"impossible",也和"necessary"一样,是指"事"而不是指"人",所以要用非人称的"it"做主语,但(b)句中的"foolish"则和"kind"一样,既可指"事",又可指"人",说 It is foolish 既可以,说 You are foolish 也可以,不过我们却不能说 It is foolish to do so. 也不能说 It is foolish for you to do so. 一定要说 It is foolish of you to do so.

It is no time for me to hide anything. (Doyle)(什么东西都来不及藏起来。)

It is time for us to start. (= that we should start)(现在是我们动身的时候了。)

It is an evil thing for a man to have suspicion. (Caxton)(人要怀疑是一件坏事。)

It is not common for him to receive letters. (Doyle)(他接信是不平常的。)

It is enough for me to say that some of its circumstances passed before my own eyes. (Dickens)(关于我亲眼看见许多这样的情形的事,我已经说得够了。)

It is easier for a camel to go through a needle's eye than for a rich man to enter into the kingdom of God. (Luke, xviii, 25)(骆驼穿过针的眼,比财主进上帝的国,还容易呢。)

How was it possible for so great a commerce to flourish? (Gissing)(这样大的贸易怎么可以兴隆呢。)

1. It is so very difficult for a sick man not to be a scoundrel. (Dr Johnson)

2. It is not supposed to be easy for women to rise to the height of taking the large free view of anything—anything which calls for action.

3. It is foolish of him to set himself to perform an impossibility.

4. It is not good for a man to be alone.

5. It was wrong of you to borrow his bicycle without asking his permission.

6. I think it wise of him not to accept their offer.

(3) it... 动名词

(a) *It* is no use *talking* about it.

空谈无益。

(b) I think *it* rather dangerous your *venturing* out to sea.

我想你冒险出海是相当危险的。

"It is no use + Gerund" = "It is of no use + Infinitive",可译作"无益"或"无用"。这个形式上的主语是和代表不定词一样,是代表后面的动名词的。二者所不同的,就是后接不定词的前面要用形容词,后接动名词的前面才用名词。因为依照惯用语法,只能说 It is useless (= of no use) to protest. 不能说 It is no use to protest. 所以我们如果要把例句中的"talking"改为"to talk"时,前面说的"no use"那个名词,就得改为"of no use"的形容词才行。It is no use doing. = It is no good doing. *Cf.* There is no doing. = It is impossible to do. 例如

There is no knowing what may happen. (未来的事是不可能知道的。)

It is no use crying over spilt milk. (覆水难收。)
It was very odd and amusing seeing her friends on the stage. (见到她的朋友登台表演,她觉得奇怪有趣。)
It's not worth while your going. (你不值得去。)
It is very funny his going without saying goodbye to anyone. (他一声不响地走了,真是奇怪。)
It is no good talking of his domestic matters. (不要谈论他的家事。)
It is useless your trying to evade the question. (你用不着环顾左右而言他。)
It was no use men being angry with them for damaging the links. (他们把高尔夫球场弄坏,人们也不必生气。)
It is useless your saying anything. (你说也没有用。)
It is no use hoping for or expecting anything now. (现在用不着希望或期待什么。)
It is no use your trying to deceive me. (你别想欺骗我。)
It is no use my arguing with you. (我用不着和你争论。)
Don't you find it very unpleasant walking in the rain? (你不觉得在雨中行走不舒服吗?)
Do you think it odd my having gone to church? (你觉得我去做了礼拜奇怪吧。)

1. It is no good talking about the greatness of our country, unless we do something to make it great.
2. It is worth while asking how far their education contributed to their success.
3. You must find it rather dull living here all by yourself.

(4) it... 子句

(a) *It* is true *that he went there.*
他去了那里是真的。

(b) I think *it* true *that he went there.*
我想他去了那里是真的。

这是"it... 不定词"的一种变形，形式上的主语或宾语所代表的，在此句型中便是后面的子句(that – Clause)。这两种句型差不多都是可以随时变换的，单句变成复句，复句也可以变成单句，例如：

I have some purchases *that I must make.* (*to make*)（我要买些东西。）
There was not an instant *that we could afford to lose.* (*to lose*)（一刻都不能耽误。）
There are many difficulties *that will have to be overcome.* (*to overcome* 或 *to be overcome*)（有许多困难尚待克服。）
Egypt was the first country *that became civilized* (*to become civilized*).（埃及是最早的文明古国。）
I want a hat *that will go* (*to go*) with this dress.（我想要一顶配合这衣服的帽子。）
There is no reason *that she should give me* (*for her to give me*) such a dirty look.（她没有理由要对我做出那样的怪相。）
It is dangerous *that you have* (*to have*) a smattering of superficial knowledge on a subject.（对于任何问题一知半解的知识都是危险的。）

表"目的"的 in order that... may，也可改为 in order to do，比较下列二句：

(a) The teacher explained that passage again and again in order *that* every student *might* understand it.
(b) The teacher explained that passage again and again in order *to make* every student understand it.

可知这种句型在英文中是用得极多的，在口头说的短句中，常将"that"略去，把两个子句连着来说，如 I think (that) you had better go. = It is advisable for you to go. 在主句的"it + 动词"之后，子句之前，可接用形容词、名词、副词，或什么都不接，而直接接上子句也行。

It is clear that you did not want to do the work.（很明显地你不想做那工作。）
It is a blessing that we do not know what is going to happen.（我们不知道未来的事是幸福的。）
It is your own concern whether you believe me or not.（信不信是你自己的事。）
It matters little who does it so long as it is done.（只要事情做了，谁做都行。）

It is amazing what progress the child is making under the new teacher. (在新老师教导之下那孩子的进步神速。)

I think it probable that he may give his assent. (我想他大概会同意的。)

We regarded it as preferable that he should continue in his position with us. (我认为他能继续在我们这里帮忙更好。)

It is a thousand pities that it should have come to this. (那会变成这个样子真是可惜。)

It is probable that he'll come again. (他大概会再来的。)

It often happens that the biter is bit. (请看剃头者,人亦剃其头。)

It seems that there is going to be a change. (好像会有变动。)

How is it that you are late? (你怎么会迟到的?)

It is under such circumstances that one recognizes one's true friends. (患难见交情。)

It occurred to me (that) there was no time to lose. (Stevenson) (我感到事已迫切。)

It was to save them from destruction (that) I parted with your dear person. (Fielding) (为救助他们免于灭亡,我才离开了你。)

He made it clear that the plan was impossible. (他明白地说了那计划行不通。)

Depend upon it (that) there is some mistake. (那一定有错。)

You must see to it that no harm comes to her. (你必须注意不要伤害她。)

I took it for granted that he would not come. (我认为他不会来。)

May I take it that you will sign the document? (我相信你会在文件上签字的吧。)

And publish it that she is dead indeed. (Shakespeare) (公开宣布她已死亡。)

No one wished it to be known that he failed to see the wonderful clothes. (谁也不希望别人知道他没有看见皇帝的新衣。)

Rumour has it that there will be war. (谣言说快要打仗了。)

1. It is true the Chinese attitude is to a large degree a reaction to the behaviour of the West, so that the latter must be taken into account, and will frequently be criticized.

2. It is hoped that men will be honest, but from a higher motive than because honesty is the best policy.

3. It is a rule never to be forgotten, that whatever strikes strongly, should be described while the first impression remains fresh upon the mind. (Dr Johnson)

4. I have heard it remarked by a statesman of high reputation that most great men have died of overeating themselves.

(5) it is... 子句

It is diligence *that makes up for deficiency.*
勤能补拙。

这和上项所说的"it...子句"完全不同,因为这个"it"不是代表后面的子句的。这是一种加重语气的说法。句中关系代名词的先行词,须与后接附属子句中的动词在数、性、人称上保持一致。这种关系代名词是属于限制性的(restrictive),自应以用"that"为宜,不过常被换上"who"、"which"来说,也是可以的,而且甚至有将关系代名词略去的。

上举例句的原句,不是 That makes up for deficiency is diligence. 而是 Diligence makes up for deficiency. 其加重说法便是套上"It is...that..."的形式。说 It is I that am wrong. 比说 I am wrong. 要加强得多。再看两种比较的说法:

$\begin{cases}\text{You are guilty.}(普通说法)\\ \text{It is you that are guilty.}(强调说法)\end{cases}$

$\begin{cases}\text{Edison invented the gramophone.}(普通)\\ \text{It was Edison who invented the gramophone.}(强调)\end{cases}$

$\begin{cases}\text{Stupid pupils do not ask questions.}(普通)\\ \text{It is not stupid pupils who ask questions.}(强调)\end{cases}$

$\begin{cases}\text{We should be grateful to men like Edison.}(普通)\\ \text{It is to men like Edison that we should be grateful.}(强调)\end{cases}$

如果主动词后面接的是一个不定词,就无须要有子句来加强语气,例如:

  SIMPLE:The tough little man's object in life is to avoid work.

  EMPHATIC:It is the tough little man's object in life to avoid work.

为回答 Who is the tough little man? 一问,也有两种不同的方式,一为普通的说法,一为加强的说法。

  SIMPLE:The tough little man is a person whose object in life is to avoid work.

  EMPHATIC:The tough little man is a person whose object in life it is to avoid work.

句中"it"不代表后面子句的例子,还有 It was not that he had plenty of money.(那并不是因为他有很多的钱。)这个"it",意为"the reason"或"what I mean."详见后面的"否定的造句"。

  What is it that you have to sell?(Dickens)(你要出卖的是什么?)

  It is not only bachelors on whom the young ladies confer their affections.(Thackeray)(年轻女子要和他谈情说爱的,不只是单身汉而已。)

  It is not who rules us that is important, but how he rules us.(重要的不是谁统治我们,而是他怎样统治法。)

  It is only shallow people who judge by appearances.(Oscar wilde)(只有浅薄的人才会以貌取人。)

  It is a kind of miracle brought us here.(Bacon)(我们来到这里,简直是一种奇迹。)

  It is I have been stupid.(Wells)(愚笨的是我。)

  I wonder who it was defined man as a rational animal.(Wilde)(人是一种理性的动物,这不知是谁下的定义。)

  It is proud he must be to get you.(Yeats)(= Proud he must be to get you.)(得到了你,他一定是很自负的。)

It was your brother who talked the most.（说话最多的就是你的兄弟。）

It is the first step which is troublesome.（只有初步麻烦一点。）

It is not helps but obstacles that make a man.（使人成功的,不是助力,而是阻力。）

It is only education which will conquer prejudice.（克服偏见唯有教育。）

It was thanks to him that I got well.（要谢谢他把我的病治好了。）

It was with some difficulty that he found the way to his own house.（他费了不少的劲才找到路回家。）

It was not till evening that we got the news.（我们到晚上才得到消息。）

It is a wise father that knows his own child. (*Merchant of Venice*, II, ii)（任何聪明的父亲都不见得完全知道他自己的儿子的。）*

1. It is an ill wind that blows nobody good.
2. Yet it is not he who sings loudest and jokes most that has the lightest heart. (Irving)
3. It is the want of money and need of it that gives most of us activitacy.
4. Reading furnishes the mind only with materials of knowledge; it is thinking that makes what we read ours.
5. Most large companies have trained specialists, called personnel managers, whose job it is to interview and pass judgment on prospective employees.
6. He is an interpreter, one whose duty it is to act as a bridge or channel between the minds of his readers.

(6) it... 名词

It is strange *this Norse view of Nature.*
挪威人对大自然的这种看法是很奇怪的。

这个"it"是代表后面的名词的,在名词的前面,经常伴有"this","that","the"的字样。上例去掉形式上的"it",恢复原来的说法,便是 This Norse view of Nature is strange. 不过一般人说时,都喜欢采用 It is strange... 的形式。我们不可误会这是"it... 子句"型,省略了"that"的,试看下面的类例,便无法把"that"加进去。

It was very funny the way in which the penguins used to waddle.（企鹅走路的那样子真是滑稽。）

His coat it was all of the greenwood hue.（他的上衣完全是绿林的颜色。）

1. It is strange the number of mistakes he always makes.
2. It's so dreadful, her father and mother dead almost at the same time. (Gissing)

---

* 此种句法一不当心即将译错。梁实秋译:"聪明的父亲才能认识他自己的儿子呢。"朱生豪译:"只有聪明的父亲才会知道他自己的儿子。"

3. He wondered if it was true what Mabel had said.

Ⅱ. 名词的造句

(7) $\begin{cases} \text{all} + 抽象名词 \\ 抽象名词 + \text{itself} \end{cases} = \text{very} + 形容词$

(a) He was *all gentleness* to her.
　　他对她非常的温存。
(b) To his superiors, he is *humility itself*.
　　对于长辈他极为谦逊。

"all + 抽象名词" = "抽象名词 + itself" = very + 形容词。这原是表示某种性质到了极点的一种说法,有"非常","只管","一味","尽"之意,有时甚至可以译为"…的化身","…的具体化"。普通名词的复数形用在"all"之后,也是属于这一类型的句子,如 She is all smiles.(她一味笑。) He is all eyes.(他盯着看。)

I am all attention.(我全神贯注地在倾听着。)
I am all anxiety.(我真担心。)
"It's simplicity itself",he remarked,chuckling at my surprise——"so absurdly simple that an explanation is superfluous."(Doyle)("那简直是再简单也没有了",他望着我惊异的表情,咯咯地笑着说,"简直简单到用不着再加说明。")

1. "I am all astonishment," said Nelson, "when I reflect on what we have achieved."
2. Washington was discretion itself in the use of speech, never taking advantage of an opponent, or seeking a short-lived triumph in a debate. (Smiles)
3. While she was waiting for the tinkling of the bell, all nerves, suddenly he stood before her. (Maugham)

(8) "the + 单数名词"的特殊用法

(a) *The horse* is a noble animal.
　　马是高尚的动物。
(b) *The pen* is mightier than *the sword*.
　　文笔比刀剑更要强而有力。(文胜于武)

定冠词的"the"与单数普通名词结合时,有下列五种用法:(1)特定之物(particularizing),(2)

集合复数(collective),(3)代表性的单数(representative),如(a)例,(4)代替抽象名词(abstractive),即指那个名词所有的抽象的观念,如(b)例,(5)定性的用法(qualitative),代替"such"或"so"的字样,用于普通名词或是抽象名词都可以。现在就根据这五种用法举例如下:

Shut the door please.(请把门关上。)(1)
The cabinet has resigned.(内阁辞职了。)(1)
I am going to the station.(我上车站去。)(附近的)(1)
They are the teachers of our school.(他们是本校的教员。)(全体)(2)
The stars are out.(星星出来了。)(常见的)(2)
The cherry trees are in blossom.(樱花开了。)(附近所有的樱花)(2)
The gentleman glories in his honourable poverty.(君子安贫。)(乐于清贫,"the"表其类全体的性质或作用。)(3)
The whale is not a fish, but a mammal.(鲸不是鱼,而是哺乳动物。)(3)
Bitters are good for the stomach.(苦味有益于胃。)(3)
The face is the index of the mind.(面情为心情的表征。)(3)
The child is father of the man.(儿童为成人的胚胎。)(儿童的性情虽长大了也不变。江山易改,本性难移。)(3)
We should give up the sword for the pen.(化干戈为玉帛。)(4)
The heart sees farther than the head.(情有胜于智的先见。)(4)
We must keep the wolf from the door.(= keep hunger away)(我们必须防止饥饿。)(4)
When a man is reduced to want, the beggar (element) comes out.(人穷志短。)(人穷则乞丐的性质俱现。)(4)
When I hear this song, I feel the patriot rise within me.(我听了这支歌便发生爱国的心情。)(闻歌而有故国之思。)(4)
He is not the boy to (= such a boy as will) tell a lie.(他不是说谎的孩子。)(5)
He had the goodness (= was so good as) to grant my request.(他亲切地允许了我的请求。)(5)

1. The bamboo is one of the most wonderful as well as beautiful productions of the tropics.
2. He allowed the father to be overruled by the judge, and declared his own son to be guilty.

(9)无生物的主语

Business took me to the town.
我因事进城去了。

中国话对于每个句子,差不多都是用人作主语,很少用无生物的。英文本也可以用人作主语,但用无生物作主语,却使得英文的气味更加浓厚。上例当然也可以说,I went to the town on business. 不过不及用无生物主语来得漂亮。有时为避免把人转入,用无生物主语则更为含蓄,如不说 We request,而说 It is requested,便觉得是间接的要求了。例如 It is requested that every guest should bring a gift with him for exchange. (每位客人请携带一件礼物以便交换。) Contributions are requested for the refugees. (为难民呼吁捐款救济。) 与无生物主物同用的动词,主要有 make, enable, remind, prevent, show, bring, keep 等字。

This medicine will make you feel better. (= If you take this medicine, you will feel better.)(你吃了这药就会好些。)

His wealth enables him to do anything. (= He can do anything because he is rich.)(他有钱什么都可以做。)

The sight of the orphan always reminds me of her parents. (= Whenever I see the orphan, I remember her parents.)(一见到那孤儿,我就想到她的父母。)

Bad weather prevented us from starting. (= We could not start because of bad weather.)(天气太坏,我们无法动身。)

Careful comparison of them will show you the difference. (= If you compare them carefully, you will see the difference.)(你只消仔细比较一下,就可以发现不同。)

A few steps across the lawn brought me to a large, splendid hotel. (走过草地几步,我就到了一个华丽的大旅馆。)

A bit of knowledge kept me from making a big mistake when an important question was to be decided. (我因稍具知识,所以在决定重要问题的时候,还没有犯大的过错。)

1. His work made it impossible for him to get home oftener than every other weekend.
2. Machinery had made the products of manufactories very much cheaper than formerly.
3. My hunger and the shadows together tell me that the sun has done much travel since I fell asleep.

(10) something (much) of
nothing (little) of

(a) Mr. Li is *something of* a philosopher.
李君略有哲学家的风味。

(b) Mr. Wu is *nothing of* a musician.
吴君全无音乐家的风味。

(c) Mr. Lu is very *much of* a poet.
卢君大有诗人气派。

(d) Mr. Liu is *little of* a scholar.
刘君几无学者风度。

这是表示"程度"的形容词片语,有时可以当作副词来译。"something of" = to some extent (某程度），在问句或条件句中，则说"anything of"，中文可译为"略有"，"多少"。至于"nothing of"，则可译为"全无"，"毫无"。"to be something of + 名词" = "to have something of + 名词 + in + 代名词"，所以 He is something of a philosopher. = He has something of a philosopher in him. 又 He is nothing in ability of an orator. = He has nothing of an orator in his ability.（他毫无演说家的才能。）

英文的"much"一字作名词用时，意为"多量"，"多额"，"许多"（a good deal），"重要的人或物"，"了不起的东西"等。如 How much are eggs?（鸡蛋多少钱？）Much of the time was wasted.（时间大半浪费了。）"much of"可译为"大有"，通常与否定连用，如 He is not much of a scholar.（他算不得一个学者。）意为"不是很好的或重要的学者"。与这"much of"相反的说法，为"little of"，可译为"几无"。至于"much of"的变形则为"a great deal of"，而"little of"的变形则为"a bit of"。这个"much of"又还可以用比较级的形式，如 Oscar Wilde 在 De Profundis（《狱中记》）中说，I am far *more of* an individualist than I ever was.（我现在比以前更是一个个人主义者了。）又如 Conan Doyle 在 The Sign of Four 中说，The truth is that I was never *much of* a credit to the family, and I doubt if they would be so very glad to see me. They were all steady, chapel-going folk, small farmers, well known and respected over the country-side while I was always *a bit of* a rover.（实际那个家族对我是没有什么信誉的，是不会高兴见到我的。他们都是信仰上帝，稳健的小农，在乡下颇有名气，受人尊敬，而我却老是有点流浪儿的味道。）

这一类的名词用法，最好当作副词来译，就容易了，例如 He has seen something of life. 与其译为"他看过了一些人生"，不如译为"他略具阅历"或"他稍阅世"。He is something of a scholar. 也同样地可译为"他略具学识"或"他稍有学问"。

英文的"something of"与"something like"，又有程度的不同。"something like" = something approximating in character or amount，指数量或性质略同的事物，又可作 somewhat（似乎，略微）解。This is something like a pudding.（此物略似布丁）。It shaped something like a cigar.（其形略似雪茄）。

从前北京大学有两位教授（陈源和刘复），感情闹得不好。就是为着"something"一字。当陈通伯在伦敦把刘半农介绍给一位英国学人时，因知刘不大愿意透漏他北大教授的身份，故含糊地说了一句：Mr. Liu is something of a professor or a lecturer. 刘听了大不受用，后来回到北京，刘在《语丝》上为文讥讽陈，故意把"北京大学教授陈源先生，即署名西滢的便是"一句中国话，加注译成英文说："A Teacher of the Peking National University. Something like a Professor or a Lecturer."比陈说的"something of"更降了一级，变成"something like"了。可见"something"不是一个好字眼，不可随便乱用，因此字略等于中国话的"一点儿"，如 to know something of everything，意为什么都知道一点儿，其实什么都不懂。

They say that he had no university education, but he seems to be something of a scholar.（据说他并未受过大学教育，但他看去好像学者的样子。）

He has not much education, but he seems to be very much of a gentleman.（他虽未受过太多的教育，但很有君子风度。）

That's too much of a good thing.（那事好过了头，反而糟了。）

I like warm weather, but with the mercury standing at 95° in the shade, it is a little too much of a good thing. (我喜欢热天,但室内达到九十五度,则未免有点过佳,反而觉得不妙。)

He is very much of a gentleman. (他是一个非常体面的绅士。)

He is more of a scholar than a teacher. (与其说他是教师,不如说他是学者。)

If he is anything of a gentleman, he will keep his promise, I should think. (他如果有一点君子的风度,我想他就会守约的。)

There was only a wooden latch to his door, because he had been too much of a skinflint to pay for one of the new iron locks to be fixed on. (Walter de la Mare)(他家门上只有一个木闩,因为他太吝啬而不肯花钱买一把新的铁锁装上。)

His features were agreeable; his body, though slight of build, had something of athletic outline. (他的面貌令人有愉快之感,他的身体虽很瘦小,但有点运动家的轮廓。)

Although not a strong boy, there was nothing of the coward about him. (他虽不是一个强壮的少年,但却没有一点胆怯的迹象。)

You may have something of a Roosevelt, something of a Newton in yourself; you may have something very much greater than either of these men manifested waiting your help to give it expression. (你也许具有罗斯福的才能,牛顿的智慧,你也许具有比他们两人所显示的更为伟大的本领,在等待着你把它表现出来。)

1. When Waddington left her Kitty thought over what he had so carelessly said. It hadn't been very pleasant to hear and she had had to make something of an effort not to show how much it touched her. (W. S. Maugham)

2. It was the first word of kindness the child had ever heard in her life; and the sweet tone and manner struck strangely on the wild, rude heart, and a sparkle of something like a tear shone in the keen, round, glittering eye. (H. B. Stowe)

3. There was nothing of the student about him, but very much of the miner.

4. As you know, Gurdon, I never was much of a ladies' man. (F. M. White)

(11) 属格的主格作用和宾格作用

(a) No one came to my *mother's rescue*.
    谁也不来救助我的母亲。

(b) *The love of money* is the root of all evil.
    爱财是一切罪恶的根源。

英文属格的用法,都有主格作用和宾格作用的分别,要看文气才能决定是哪一种。由他动词变来的名词,差不多都有这两种用法。

美总统 Lincoln 的名言,"the government of the people, by the people and for the people",便是一个好的例子。句中的"of the people"一语,到底是主格作用呢,还是宾格作用,颇引起意义上的争执,因为它可以解释为(1)"人民治理的"(主格作用),也可以解释为(2)"治理人民的"(宾格作用),到底是何者只好去问林肯本人了。普通把他这句名言译为"人民的,由于人民的,为着人民的政治",把"of"一字含糊地译成一个"的"字,不分宾主,实在是一种过关的办法,但意义是不够明显的。另外一种简单的译法是"民治、民有、民享",这就明白表示出主格作用来了。Austen O'Malley 写有这样的一句 parody(模仿他人的作品而改作的讽刺诗文):The American government is a rule of the people, by the people, for the boss. (美国的政治是人民为着政党的领袖而统治人民的。)这好像是把"of"看作宾格作用了。

上举的(a)(b)两句,都是用为宾格作用的,现再举例比较如下。其中主格作用是通常的意思,宾格作用为偶然的用法。

$\begin{cases} \text{The conquests of Caesar}(主格作用) \\ \text{Caesar's conquest of Britain}(宾格作用) \end{cases}$

$\begin{cases} \text{The writings of Plato}(主) \\ \text{The writing of a book}(宾) \end{cases}$

$\begin{cases} \text{The commands of the general}(主) \\ \text{The command of an army}(宾) \end{cases}$

$\begin{cases} \text{John's fear}(约翰所怀的恐怖) \\ \text{The fear of John }(恐怕约翰的心情) \end{cases}$

$\begin{cases} \text{Your dismissal of him}(主) \\ \text{Your dismissal by him}(宾) \end{cases}$

Nature is not over-merciful in her treatment of delinquents. (主)

Are you satisfied with your treatment? (宾)

She has never recovered her loss. (主)

I have never recovered her loss. (宾)

Thanks to their father's rescue, they could return home safe. (幸获父亲援救,他们才能安然回家。)(主)

They hurried to their father's rescue. (他们赶快去救父亲。)(宾)

The love of Browning for Italy. (白朗宁对意大利的爱。)(主)

A mother's love of children. (母爱。)(宾)

The love of God. (上帝的爱。)(主)

God's love of man. (上帝爱世人。)(宾)

His memory is very bad. (他的记忆力很坏。)(主)

A monument is dedicated to his memory. (为纪念他而立的碑。)(宾)

She doesn't want his praise. (她不要他赞美。)(主)

She has come to sing his praise. (她来赞美他。)(宾)

1. His death was hastened by the shock of her loss.

2. A mother's love for her own child differs essentially from all other affections.

3. Succeeding ages will reverence his memory.

4. There were no legal reason to justify his expulsion.
5. The mere saving of pennies regardlss of the sacrifices we make to save them is not scientific and practical thrift.
6. His greatness was in his perseverance in the pursuit of his project.
7. The loss of these aesthetic tastes is a loss of happiness.

(12) 名词(A) + of + a + 名词(B)

(a) It was *a great mountain of a wave*.
    那是一个像山一样高的大浪。
(b) *That fool of a Tom* did it.
    这是托姆那个笨蛋做的。

这叫作同格的属格(Appositive Possessive),在"of"前后的名词,指同一人或同一物。其中的"名词 + of",构成一个形容词片语,以修饰后来的名词。在这个同格的"of"后出现的名词前面,必须加不定冠词,哪怕是固有名词,这个不定冠词都不能省。

最普通的有"a devil of a man","a rascal of a fellow","to catch a death of a cold"等 idiomatic expressions,可解释为"a devil of"等就像"a kind of","a sort of"一样的表现法,从文法上看,"devil","kind"等是主体(principal),而"of"以下为附属(adjunct),即所谓修饰语(modifier),但从意义上看,则恰相反,"kind of","devil of"的"of",可视为前一字的后缀(suffix),不妨将"a devil of a man"改写为"a devilish man",将"a rascal of a fellow"改写为"a rascally fellow",将"a death of a cold"改写为"a deadly cold"。他如"a brute of a man" = "a brutal man","an awful fool of a woman" = "an awfully foolish woman"。英国名作家 Thackeray 在 *Vanity Fair* 中有所谓"her old sharper of a father"(她那骗子的老父)的说法。

That old cripple of a Henn. (Sean O'Faolain)(那个年老的残废者亨。)
She was much better educated than that fool of a Beatrice. (A. Huxley)(她比那愚笨的比特里斯受过更好的教育。)
This huge lunatic warren of a London. (J. B. Priestley)(这个巨大狂人收容所一般的伦敦。)
Those pigs of girls eat so much. (那些猪一般的女子吃那么多。)
He was a fine figure of a young man. (他是一个翩翩佳公子。)
I've got the devil of a toothache. (我牙痛不堪。)
It would make the deuce of a scandal. (Galsworthy)(这会弄得声名狼藉的。)
Mr. A lives a hell of a long way off. (他住得远哉遥遥。)
She was an angel of a wife. (天仙一般的妻子。)
She gave a party in her baby-house of a dwelling. (她在她那婴儿屋子一般的小住宅中开了一个晚会。)
He was a big clumsy giant of a man with a broad face and small suspicious eyes. (Christie)(他是一个具有大脸孔和多疑的小眼睛的,笨拙如巨人般的男子。)

At Jutland, although I was in the devil of a funk all the time, I was sort of pleased with myself too. (Walpole)
(在遮特兰,虽则我始终都很恐惧,但我却多少还能自得。)

The child is a treasure of a son. (那是一个宝贝儿子。)

He lives in a palace of a house. (他住在一座宫殿似的大屋子里。)

Your fool of a husband said so. (你那愚笨的丈夫说的。)

She is an old blackguard of a woman. (她是一个老毒妇。)

1. He was a brute of a man for all that you may say in his praise. (Nesfield)
2. Down with the Bourbons, and that great pig of a Louis XVIII! (Hugo)
3. They gave Sally this little blue butt-twitcher of a dress to wear. (J. D. Salinger)

(13) 名词 + of + 属格 + 名词

It was beyond expectation for *a man of your taste*.
遇到一位像你这样有风趣的人,真是出乎意外。

在"名词 + of + 属格 + 名词"的形式中,其属格的含义为:"像……那样的"。

He is a man of your experience. (他是一个像你那样经验丰富的人。)

I am not a man of his means. (我不是他那样的资产家。)

You are a lady of her wisdom. († 你是一个像她那样贤慧的淑女。)

1. The watch was by no means low-priced, and was too expensive for a person of my limited means; still it was cheap at the price asked, for as to its action it defied all comparison.
2. Methought he strove to shine more than ordinarily in his talkative way, that he might insult my silence, and distinguish himself before a woman of Arietta's taste and understanding. (Spectator)

(14) of + 抽象名词 = 形容词
of 从略 + 普通名词

(a) It was *of great importance*.
这是非常重要的。

(b) The earth is *the shape* of a pear.
地球是梨子形的。

在(a)例中"of + 抽象名词"的形式,是和形容词同义的。如"of importance" = important. "of use" = useful. "of no use" = useless. 这都是可以译为"…的"的, 如"a man of courage" = a courageous man(勇敢的人;勇士)。"a lady of virtue" = a virtuous lady(贤德的女人,淑女)。他如"a child of fortune"(幸运儿)。"a man of business"(实业家)。用普通名词也是一样,如"a man of family"(名门之子)。"a man of few words"(寡言的人)。"a man of his word"(言行一致的人)。

在(b)例中的"the shape",虽字面上看不见"of"一字,但意味上实等于说"of the shape"一样。凡形状、年龄、大小、色度、价格等有关的字,多有这种用法。如"同一大小"说"of a size",如果加上形容词时,就常要把"of"略去,说成"the same size",如像"age","price","size"等字,是没有形容词的,因此,"of age","of size","of price",就弥补了这个缺憾,而代行形容词的任务了。

Bernard Shaw was an Englishman of letters.(萧伯纳是英国的文人。)
Su Tung-po was a man of parts.(苏东坡是多才多艺的人。)
He is a man of means.(他是资产家。)
Chu Ko-lian was a man of resources.(诸葛亮足智多谋。)
They are all of an age.(他们同年。)
They are all the same age.(他们都是同年的。)
These glasses are of a size.(这些玻璃杯大小一样。)
These glasses are the same size.(这些玻璃杯都是同样大小的。)
Her dress is the colour of grass.(她的衣服是草绿色。)
This shirt is exactly the right size.(这件衬衫大小正好。)
The island is about one-third the size of Singapore.(那岛的大小略等于新加坡三分之一。)

1. The heroic bravery displayed by this officer, in the midst of a hail of bombs from the enemy, was of the highest order.

2. The towers were exactly the same height.(Kruisinga)

3. He must have been almost the same age as was my father when I first met him.

4. Unsuccessful candidates are five times the number of successful ones.

(15) one's own + 名词
of one's own + 动名词

(a) He shines *his own shoes*.
   他自己擦皮鞋。

(b) It is a tree *of his own planting*.
   这是他手栽的树。

英文说的"one's own",除"自己的"一个意思外,还有"为自己"一个意思,即英文"by oneself"的意思,如(a)例 He shines his own shoes. = His shoes are shined by himself. 原来"own"是加强的说法,单说 That is his house.(那是他的家)已经够了,但要加强时便说 That is his own house. 单说 He has a house.(他有一幢房子)也够明白了,但要加强时就说 He has a house of his own.(他自己有一幢房子)。要注意的是:不能说 He has his own house. 因为现代英文不可以把属格代名词和指示代名词连用,即是:不能说"this my (own) house",而要说"this house of mine",或"this house of my own",因此惯用法就要说 He has a house of his own. 尤其是在动词"have"之后。(b)例的"of one's own doing",意为"自己做的"(done by oneself),往往可省略"own"一字,如"a tree of his own planting"也可以说成"a tree of his planting."

She has no children of her own. (她自己没有生孩子。)
The moon has no light of its own. (月亮本身无光)
It is a poem of his own composing. (= It is a poem composed by himself.)(这是他自己做的诗。)
This profession is of my own choosing. (这是我自己选择的专业。)
He lived a colorful life and, in the end, a disastrous one, which is no less moving because much of the disaster was of his own making. (Arthur Mizener)(他过的一种多彩多姿的生活,而最后却是多灾多难的生活,那同样令人感动,因为灾难大半是他自己招致的。)

1. He dressed his own food.
2. Usually that which a man calls fate is a web of his own weaving, from threads of his own spinning. (Doyle)
3. She married him of her own choice against her parents' will.

(16) have + the + 抽象名词 + 不定词

I *had the fortune to succeed.*
我很幸运获得成功。

这个 have = possess,原指肉体上或精神上的特征,作为一种天禀而具有的,比方说,He has a good memory. (他的记性好)。又如 Irishmen have red hair. (爱尔兰人天生是红头发)。进而由普通名词发展为抽象名词,后面接上一个不定词,而成为一种惯用的语法了。例如

She had the cheek (= impudence) to say such a thing. (她厚颜地说出这样的话。)这就等于说:She was so impudent as to say such a thing.
How can you have the heart (= hard-heartedness) to drown such darling little kittens?(你何忍把这些如此可爱的小猫去淹死?)这就等于说:How can you be so hard-hearted as to drown such darling little kittens?
Will you have the goodness (= kindness) to do it for me? (= Will you be so kind as to do it for me?)(请你帮忙替我做一下好吗?)

所以例题的句子也可以说成 I was so fortunate as to succeed. 或 I was fortunate enough to succeed. 而含义完全一样。此外，在抽象名词后的不定词，有时也可变成"of + 动名词"，如 May I have the pleasure of dancing with you?（我可不可以和你跳一回舞？）

I had the luck to find him at home.（我幸运地遇见他正在家里。）
He had the misfortune to break his leg.（他不幸折断了腿。）
Those who have the interest of their country at heart are praiseworthy.（忧国之士值得颂扬。）
He had the courage to express his opinion.（他毫无忌惮地申述了他的意见。）
I had the folly to spend all I earned.（我竟愚笨得丧尽所获。）
That wretch has had the audacity to touch my children's doll.（V. Hugo）（那个小坏蛋竟有狗胆来动我孩子们的玩具。）
He had the kindness to show me round the place.（他亲切地带我参观了一圈。）
He had the imprudence to marry beneath him.（他不谨慎地竟至娶家世寒微的女子为室。）

1. The boy waved the fan to and fro and drove away the buzzing flies whenever they had the impertinence to come near the baby's face.
2. He had the foresight to carry fire insurance.

(17) that (those) + 先行词 + 关系代名词

He lost *that picture which* he had got with much trouble.
他把那费了很大的劲才得来的画丢了。

这是所谓"强烈的限制"（strong restriction）用法，即是为加强限制的意思，在"who"，"which"的先行词（Antecedent）前加用"that"，"those"的字眼。这种表现法和说"such...as"差不多。句中的"that"，不能译为"那个"。

The root is that part of the vegetable which least impresses the eye.（根是植物最不引人注目的部分。）
That virtue which requires to be ever guarded is scarcely worth the sentinel.（= Such virtue as requires…）（需要常常保护的美德是不值得看守的。）
Those rich men are great who do not think themselves great because they are rich.（并不以为他们有钱就是伟大的阔人们，才算伟大。）
Those persons who do most good are least conscious of it.（"Those… who or which" = "only those" or "all those"）（为善最多的人很少感觉到他是在为善。）

A dog will become attached to those members of the family who are kind to it. (家里的人谁对狗好,狗就喜欢跟谁。)

1. Milton had that universality which belongs to the highest order of genius.
2. Education alone can conduct us to that enjoyment which is best in quality and infinite in quantity.

(18) one thing ... another

It is *one thing* to know and *another* to teach.
自己知道是一件事,要教别人又是另外一件事。

这个例句又可简约地说 To know is one thing; to teach is another. (= Knowing and teaching are different.)意即自知和教人是两回事,有的人知道但不能教,虽有一肚子学问却不会教书。"another" = an + other。"one... another"不可与"one... the other"以及"the one... the other"混乱。在二者之中任取其一(one),剩下的便是另外的一个了(the other)。例如 They have two daughters; one is a singer, the other an actress. (他们有两个女儿,一为歌手,一为女伶。)"the one... the other" = the former... the latter. (前者... 后者),例如 Mary has a white and a red rose; the one is lovelier than the other. (玛丽有一株白玫瑰和一株红玫瑰;白玫瑰比红玫瑰好看。)

It is one thing to own a library; it is another to use it wisely. (藏书是一件事,能否善于利用又是另外一件事。)
To have money is one thing, to spend it wisely is quite another. (有钱是一件事,贤明地用钱又是另外一件事。)
It is one thing to know a language, and it is another to know about it. (懂得一种语文是一件事,具有关于那种语文的知识又是另外一件事。)

1. There is no more dangerous experiment than that of undertaking to be one thing before a man's face and another behind his back.
2. Others hold that the essence of art is one thing and the form another.

Ⅲ. As 的造句

(19) "as... as"的三种用法

(a) He is *as* kind *as* his sister (is).
他像他妹妹一样和蔼。
(b) He is *as* kind *as* (he is) honest.
他又诚实又和蔼。
(c) He is *as* kind *as* his sister is honest.

他妹妹诚实而他就和蔼。

英文"as+形容词+as"的形式,是表示程度相同的某种性质的,如(a)例,表示两个不同的人相同的性质,(b)例表示同一人的不同的性质,(c)例表示两个人的不同的性质。句中第一个"as"为指示副词,第二个"as"为连词,因此在第一个"as"后面,只能接用一个形容词或副词,而在第二个"as"后面,便要接上一个子句。如系否定时则第一个"as"改为"not so",例如 He is not so kind as you are.

这个"as...as"是平等比较,高一级的比较则用"-er...than",至于对同一人所有的不同性质的比较,则用"more + positive"的形式,如 She is more attractive than pretty.(与其说她漂亮,不如说她可爱。)She is more shy than unsocial. (= She is shy rather than unsocial.)(与其说她不爱交际,不如说她害羞。)The man was more dead than alive.(那人只剩得奄奄一息了。)

He is as clever as his sister.(他和他姊姊一样聪明。)
She is not so pretty as her sister.(她没有她妹妹好看。)
No country suffered so much as England. (Macaulay)(没有一个国家受过英格兰那样多的痛苦。)
He is as cunning as you are clever.(他的狡猾好似你的聪明。)

1. He is as old as his cousin. (Greene)
2. He was as covetous as cruel. (Wotton)
3. Dobbin looked as pale and grave as his comrade was flushed and jovial. (Thackeray)

(20) as...as any
as...as ever

(a) He is *as* great a statesman *as any*.
(b) He is *as* great a statesman *as* ever lived.
他是一位稀有的大政治家。

英文的"as...as"原为同等比较的意思,加上"any"或"ever"的时候,就变成"不让","不弱",甚至"古今无双的"的意思了。在"as...as any"后面,又可以接上名词,如 He works as hard as anybody.(他勤勉不逊于任何人。)如果在"any"后接物而不接人,则有"as...as anything can be"(= as...as possible)一个表现法,意为"愈…愈佳",如 I will make it as clean as anything can be. (我要尽量把它弄清洁。)这个"as...as ever",另外又有"as...as before"(照旧)的意思,如 He works as hard as ever.(其勤勉不减于以前。)He is as busy as ever.(他照旧忙。)She is as pretty as ever.(她还是一样的漂亮。)这个"ever" = always.(素常。)

His behaviour is as good as ever. (他的行为和过去一样的好。)

His trust in his friend was as firm as ever. (他对其朋友的信任照常坚定。)

He is as diligent a man as ever lived. (其为人勤勉不让古今的人。)

They continued to fish up plate, bullion, and dollar, as plentifully as ever. (他们继续地捞起一些碟子、金块和银元,和以前一样地多。)

The dog was as courageous an animal as ever scoured the woods. (狗的勇敢不逊于到现在为止在森林中跑动的任何动物。)

Then as for active exercise, she could ride on horseback as well as any man in his kingdom. (Hawthorne)(至于说到实际的运动,她的骑术不弱于国内任何男子。)

1. His novels have as good a chance of surviving as any that have been written in the last hundred years. (Maugham)

2. It's not only real, but it's as fine a string of pearls for its size as I've ever seen. (Maugham)

(21) as...as...can be

It is *as* plain *as* plain *can be*.

那是再明白也没有了。

上例单说是 It is plain. 也就够了,现在为要加强"plain"的意思,所以把同一个形容词再说一遍,最后再加上"can be"的字样,表示"明白到不能再明白的程度"。这种表现法有时可将第一个"as"省掉,或将"can be"略去。这个"can be",有时也可说成"may be"的。

You are as wrong as wrong can be. (你大错特错。)

A lot of these boys were green as green can be. (Bob Considine)(这些男孩子许多都是精力充沛无以复加的。)

Gabby yanked him quick as quick. (John Tunis)(加比急急地把他用力猛拉。)

I am as thirsty as thirsty may be. (我口渴得不得了。)

She is as happy as happy can be. (她快乐已极。)

The place is as still as still. (那地方静寂得无以复加。)

1. "Thou'rt wrong, my friend," said good King Hal; "as wrong as wrong can be." (Mackay)

2. The old folks made me welcome; they were as kind as kind could be. (Woolson)

3. Since I have been in prison he has always been coming to see me, and at times he would talk to me, and was as good to me as could be. (Plato's *Death of Socrates*)

(22) as..., so...

As rust eats iron, *so* care eats the heart.
忧能伤人,亦犹锈之蚀铁。

这个"so"的意思是"in the same proportion","in like manner","in the same way"(亦复如此)。为着加强语气,又可在"as"前加用"just"一字。有时在主句中,可将动词置于主语之前。

As you treat me, so I will treat you. (你怎样待我,我也怎样待你。)
As the lion is king of beasts, so is the eagle king of birds. (鹰为鸟中之王,正好像狮为兽中之王一样。)
As fire tries gold, so does adversity try courage. (正如火可以试金一样,逆境也可以试人的勇气。)
As the human body is nourished by the food, so is a nation nourished by its industries. (正像身体要靠食物营养一样,国家要靠工业营养。)

1. Just as no two words are truly synonyms, so no two different expressions, or ways of expression, can mean exactly the same thing. (G. H. Vallins)
2. Just as the chemist draws his deductions from the results of laboratory experiments, so must students of language draw their deductions from an observation of the facts of language. (R. C. Pooley)

(23) It is in (or with)...as in (or with)

It is in life *as in* a journey.
人生好比旅行一样。

这个表现法是由"as...so"(正像)变化而来的,意为"is like",可译作"犹如","正好像"。例句可说成 Life is like a journey.句首的"it",并不指什么,只是一般漠然的用法。

It is in studying as in eating; he who does it gets the benefits, and not he who sees it done. (读书和吃饭一样,得到利益的是实际在吃的人,而不是在旁观看的人。)
It is with women as with flowers. (妇美如花。)
It is with a machine as with a child that must always be taken care of. (机器也和小孩一样,需要时常加以照顾。)
It is in mind as in body which must be nourished by good food. (精神和身体都必须有好的食物来营养。)
It is with one as with the other. (= One is like the other.) (彼此相似。)

1. It is in man as in soils, where sometimes there is a vein of gold which the owner knows not of.
2. It is with words as with sunbeams; the more they are condensed, the deeper they burn. (Southey)

(24) as much
  as many
  like so many

(a) I thought *as much*.
  我亦作如是想。
(b) Those five days seemed to me *as many* years.
  那个五天对我好像五年一样。
(c) They work *like so many* ants.
  那些人就像那么多的蚂蚁一样在做工。

  这个"as much" = as much as that, 具有三种意思：①"the same degree or quantity of", 表同样程度的, 同样分量的, 例如 He has gold as much as silver. (他有与白银同样多的黄金。) ②"as well"; "equally", 表同等或同样的, 例如 He was greatly respected, and his brother as much despised. (他很受人尊敬, 而他的兄弟则很受人鄙视。) ③"the same thing"; "just so", 表同一事; 意为"亦然", 例如 I was not at all vexed at my failure, for I had expected as much. (我对失败一点也不烦恼, 因为我早知道会失败的。)
  至于"as many" = the same number of, 是表同数的, 意为"其数相同", 例如 He made six mistakes in as many paragraphs. (他在六节中犯了六个错误。) 这个"as many"如用在"like"后面"as"就要改变为"so", 说成"like so many", 意也是"好像同样数目的", 又可译成"宛如…似的", 例如 We worked like so many bees. (我们宛如那样多的蜜蜂似的工作了。)

  I was not in the least surprised, for I had expected as much. (我一点也没有吃惊, 因为我早料到会有那样的事。)
  I found ten misprints in as many pages. (我在十页中就发现十个错误。)
  You have made two blunders in as many minutes. (你在两分钟之中就犯了两次大错。)
  It was a truly awful sight, watching the numberless little wooden houses catching fire one after another, and flaming up like so many match-boxes. (那真是一个可怕的光景, 望着无数的小木屋, 一个又一个地着火燃烧, 就像烧着那样多的火柴盒子一样。)

1. "Nay, I told you as much before," said Blount. (Scott)
2. The wall was about fifteen feet high, and as many feet thick.

3. All our streets are lined with trees, and like so many stars among the leaves and branches, the street lamps shed their light.

4. I assembled a number of my play-fellows, and we worked diligently like so many emmets. (Franklin)

(25) as good as
as well as

(a) It is *as good as* done.

这就和做好了一样。

(b) It is broad *as well as* long.

那既长且宽。

英文的"as good as"有两个意思：①"amounting to"；"not falling short of"，意为"等于"，"同样"，"几如"，"不欠缺"，例如 He was as good as his word.（他不爽约。实践其言。）（句中"word"换为"promise"也是一样。）②"virtually"；"essentially"；"in every essential respect"，意为"实际上"，"其实"，"实在"，"在各要点上"，例如 He is as good as dead already.（宛如死人。行尸走肉。名存实亡。他简直和死人一样。）

至于"as well as"则有四个意思：①"no less than"；"equally with"，意为"等于"，"不下于"，"亦"，"一样好"，例如 I have understanding as well as you.（我的理解力和你一样好。）②"both...and"；"one equally with the other"，意为"与"，"及"，"二者皆"，例如 Work in moderation is healthy as well as agreeable to the human constitution.（适度的劳动对身体给与快感，又有益卫生。）③与"not only...but also"有连带关系，如云 He has experience as well as knowledge. = He has not only knowledge, but also experience.（他有学识又有经验。学识自不待言，连经验也很丰富。）注意改写时要把顺序颠倒，如(b)例 It is broad as well as long. = It is not only long, but also broad. ④"as well as"还可以代替"better than"用，例如 As well (= better) be hanged for a sheep as (= than) for a lamb.（与其盗小羊而受绞刑，毋宁盗大羊合算。窃钩不如窃国。）

The sailors did noble duty that day, in the dogged faith that they would "give as good as they got, anyhow."（那些水手们当日尽了高尚的职责，在那顽强的信仰中，一言以蔽之，他们是要以其所受施诸其人的。）

I will let you have a geography that is not new. It is as good as a new one.（我要给你一本旧的地理书。因为那和新的一样。）

She said that he was as good as engaged to a girl out there, and that he had never dreamt of her. (W. D. Howells)（她说那男人在外洋有一个女子等于订了婚一样，而他却从来没有梦想过她。）

The merchant as good as promised the orphan boy, that he would adopt him.（那商人等于是答应了那孤儿要收他为养子。）

This is the case with manufacturing as well as with agricultural interests.（这是对工业有利，对农业也一样好的实例。）

In polity, as well ecclesiastical as civil, there are always evils which no art of man can cure. (Hooker)(在政治形态上,也和在教会组织及国家行政上一样,总有许多坏处是人力无法治好的。)

1. Out of the eight men who had fallen in the action, only three still breathed; and of these two were as good as dead.
2. Men should be gentle as well as brave and women brave as well as gentle.
3. I returned to the den to cook myself a meal, of which I stood in great need, as well as to care for my horse, whom I had somewhat neglected in the morning. (R. L. Stevenson)
4. Doris' musical background stemmed from her father, William, who was an organist, as well as a violin, piano, and voice teacher. (R. G. Hubler)

(26) 句首的"as it is"
句尾的"as it is"

(a) If I were rich, I should do so. *As it is*, I do nothing.
　　如果我有钱的话,我就要这样做。但实在太穷,我什么都不能做。
(b) The painter does not copy nature *as it is*.
　　画家描绘大自然,并不是完全写实的。

英文说的"as it is"(过去时态为"as it was")这个表现法,有两种场合,因用的位置不同,而影响到意义的差别。

(a) 用于句首,接在假设语气之后。例如 If I were a college graduate, I would go abroad. As it is, I cannot go. (如果我是大学毕业生的话,我就要出洋去。但事实上,我可不能去。)这个"as it is" = as it stands; to state the matter as it really stands; as a matter of fact; in reality, 意为"在事实上","就实际的情形而论",简略成为"实际上","事实上"。接在假想之后,作为报告实情时的导言。用过去动词时,意义不变。如 As it is, we cannot help her. 过去时则为 As it was, we could not help her. 如系说人,则要随人称的不同而改变动词,如 Paint me as I am. (照我现在的样子来画。)在许多场合可用其他同样意义的片语来取代,如 *As matters stand*, I do not like to make the plan public. (在目下的状态中,我不想把那计划公开。) *As the case stands*, I don't care to make public the reason for my visit. (在目下的状态中,我还不想公开我访问的理由。) *As things now are*, we cannot put the plan into practice. (以目下的状态,我们还不能把那计划付诸实行。) *As things go*, it is impossible to make a forecast of the development of the peace talk. (以目下的情形而论,和谈的发展如何是未能预测的。)

(b) 用于句尾,接在名词或代名词之后。例如 I take the world as it is. (世界就是这个样子,我并不指望它会变好。) Leave it as it is. (就让它是那样,不要动好了。) You has better take things as they are. (你最好接受事物的现状。)这个"as it is"(复数为"as they are"),意为"照现状","it"指前面的名词,所以那名词如为复数时,就要改为"they",动词也跟着要改为"are"。

If he were not ill, he would go to see the play. As it is, he has to stay at home. (如果他不生病的话,他是要去看戏的。实际上,他只好呆在家里了。)

If I had been rich, I would have bought it. As it was, I missed the chance of getting it. (我有钱早就买了,但实际上我却失去了获得那个的机会。)

We hoped things would go better, but as it is they are getting worse. (我们原指望事态好转,可是实际上却更糟了。)

Please leave the apple-box as it is. (请把苹果箱照原样放着。)

He finds fault with society as it is without having anything better to suggest in its place. (他并没有提出什么替代的良策,只是一味对现实社会加以非难。)

He took the bundle just as it was to the police-station. (他把那包裹原封不动地送到警察局去了。)

I often wish I could read. As it is, I have nothing to do but to think. (我常希望我能阅读。像我现在这样一字不识,我除了思索之外,什么也不能做。)

1. There is no alleviation for the sufferings of mankind except veracity of thought and action and the resolute facing of the world as it is.

2. I should have followed him through the open window if I had been stronger. As it was, I rang the bell and roused the house. (Doyle)

(27) 过去分词 + as it is
现在分词 + as it does

(a) *Hidden as it was* by the trees, the tomb was difficult to find.
深藏在树木中,那坟墓很难找到。

(b) *Standing as it does* on a high hill, the church commands a fine view.
像这样建立在高山上,教堂的眺望很好。

这是上项用法的变形。这个"as it is"(过去用"was")是强调前面的过去分词的,"it"是指主句中的主语,在上例中则指"the tomb",如果不要加强来说,则取消"as it was",说成 Hidden by the trees, the tomb was difficult to find. 意思还是一样。

在过去分词之后所接的"as it is",到了现在分词之后,就要把动词"be"改为"do";这个"as it does"也好,前述的"as it is"也好,都是为加重语气而设的插入句,去掉它也是无妨的,如(b)例改说成 Standing on a high hill, the church commands a fine view. 意思还是一样的。这个在现在分词后接用的"as it does"(或"as he does";"as she did"等),可译为"因为是这样","实际…故"等等。

Written as it is in good English, this book is recommendable to all. (实际是用美好的英文写的,所以这本书

可以向大众推介。)

Burdened as he was, he could not walk fast. (因为负荷太重,所以他不能走快。)

Living as we do in a remote village, we rarely have visitors. (因为是住在这样远离城市的村庄上,我们是很少有客人的。)

Bathing as he did several times a day, he could not get his hair to stay down. (因为是这样一天去游泳好几次,他的头发是不会平伏的。)

1. Published as it was at such a time, his work attracted much attention.

2. This movement, arising as it does among the poor themselves, is likely to have more force than if it was from the upper classes. (Dixon)

3. Coming as it did at a period of exceptional dullness it attracted perhaps rather more attention than it deserved. (Doyle)

(28) 名词等 + as + 主语 + 动词等

(a) *Child as she was*, she was more than a match for him.
她虽是一个小孩,却甚过做他的对手。

(b) *Strange as it may sound*, it is true.
听来虽觉奇怪,却是千真万确的。

(c) *Try as you may*, you will never succeed.
你尽可以试试看,不过你决难成功。

在"名词(形容词) + as + 主语 + 动词"的形式中的"as",如例(a)及(b),多为"though"或"although"的意思,是一种表示让步的句子,上例可改写为 Though she was a child(注意这时要加上冠词)及 Although it may sound strange。至于"动词 + as + 主语 + 助动词"的形式,也是让步的说法。Try as you may = Although you may try. 见(c)例。试比较下举二例:

(1) Clever as he was, he found not a little difficuty in solving the problem which was anything but difficult. (他虽很聪明,也很难来解决那个决非困难的问题。)

(2) Clever as he was, he found little difficulty in solving the problem which was none too easy. (他因为很聪明,所以一点不困难,就把那个决非容易的问题解决了。)

(1) Clever as he was = Although he was clever.
(2) Clever as he was = As he was clever.

(1)意为"虽则",(2)意为"因为"。这个"as"何时作"虽则"解,何时作"因为"解,就要看后面的文句才能决定。这原是由"(as) clever as he is"强调的省略而来,"像他那样聪明",变成"他虽则聪明"。在美国现仍有人用"As clever as"的形式。又(a)例中的名词,因移到句首去,便得将冠词略去,如恢复普通说法时,则非有冠词不可,如 Warrior as he was = Though he was a warrior (他虽为武士)。Woman as I am = Though I am a woman(我虽属女流)。至于(c)例,因前为动词,句法全变,应译为"尽管"。

Young as he is, it is but natural that he should commit such a mistake. (他因为年轻,要犯这种错误也是当然的事。)
Woman as she is, she was brave. (她虽是女流,那时却够勇敢了。)
Poor piper as I am, I won't do anything below contempt. (我虽滥竽,但不做可鄙的事。)
Young as he is, he is able. (他虽年轻,但很能干。)
Teacher as he is, he explains it very clearly. (因为他是教师,所以解释得很清楚。)
The Greeks, eminent as they were in almost every department of human activity, did surprisingly little for the creation of science. (希腊人在人类一切活动的领域虽然都很优越,但对于科学的创造上,却毫无贡献。)

1. Young as he was, and poor as he was, no King's or Lord's son could come up to him in learning.
2. Struggle as we may, we can never be completely satisfied.
3. Dull as a student may be, and difficult as a subject may seem to be at first sight, he will find the study become easier or at least less difficult, if he can persevere and does not neglect it.

IV. 动词的造句

(29) may well + 动词
and well + 主语 + may

(a) He *may well* be proud of his success.
他获得那样的成功是很可以骄傲的。

(b) He is proud of his success, *and well he may*.
他对于自己的成功感到骄傲,也是应该的。

在(a)例中的"may well" = have good reason(其中的"well" = with good reason = reasonably),意为"那样也是有理由的","无怪"。在(b)例中的"well + 主语 + may" = and with reason,附在主句之后,意为"那也是应该的"。这个"well"是修饰整个句子的副词,以表示说话者的意见的。有时不说"may",单用一个"well",也能表达"with good reason"的意思,如 We cannot very well refuse him. (我们没有好的理由来拒绝他。)内容如果是指的过去的话,"may"则可改为过去时态的"might",不过有时候,用过去时态的"might",并不一定是指过去,而是一种客气的说法,用来表现在的,如 She might well ask that. (她这样问一声,也不为无理吧。)还有"may well"的"well",又可作"probably"(大概)解,如 It may well be true. (那大概是真的。)

She may well be proud of her son.(她对她自己的儿子感到骄傲,是有理由的。)
You may well say so.(你很有理由这样说。)
Well he might be proud and glad.(他要感到骄傲而又高兴也是应该的。)
You may well refuse him.(你拒绝他是对的。)
He was proud of his feat, and well he might.(他自夸他的功绩是有理由的。)

1. As regards its climate, Japan does not differ materially from Britain, and in this, the country may well be called "the Britain of the Pacific".

2. The good lady was in an acstasy of delight. And well might she be proud of her boy. (Hawthorne)

3. During this period I met persons who by their rank, fame or position might very well have thought themselves destined to become historical figures. (Maugham)

(30) may as well...as
might as well...as

(a) You *may as well* call a cat a little tiger *as* call a tiger a big cat.
你如把虎叫做大猫,同样也无妨把猫叫做小虎。

(b) You *might as well* throw your money away *as* spend it in gambling.
你要把钱花在赌博上,就不如丢掉的好。

英文说的"may as well...as"和"might as well...as",都是用于现在的,并无现在时和过去时的分别,其所不同的是前者指"可能的事",而后者指"不可能的事"。这种句中的"well",也和上项(29)"may well"中的"well"意思相同,都是作"合理的","理所当然的"(reasonably; with good reason)解,所以"may as well...as" = have as good reason to...as,不过这个表现法中的意义的重点,在"as...as"之间的比较,有时可解释为"与其…做,宁肯…做为佳",如 One *may as well* not know a thing at all *as* know it imperfectly.(与其一知半解,不如完全不知的好。)在第二个"as"以下的句子,是常被省略的,如 I may as well go at once.(我还是马上去的好。)后面省去了 as not(与其不去)的字样。第一人称的 I may as well 与第二人称的 you had better 相当,但较 had better 为弱,所以意为"为宜","还是那样做的好"。如(a)例是"合理的"的意思。

现在再看(b)例。句中 throw your money away(A),是谁也不干的愚行,spend it in gambling(B),也是不弱于(A)的愚行,为要强调(B)的愚笨,故在(A)句中不用"may"而用"might",是假定的说法,表示不可能的事。这种"as...as"的造句,原意为比较,即(B)和(A)一样,可译成"不啻","犹之","可与相等",但由力加否定的关系,有时可采用选择的译法:"与其那样不如这样的好"。在第二个"as"后的字句,常被省略,因为由前面的文字可以想像出来。

You may as well (= had better) begin at once (as not). (你宜早日着手。)因马上着手与不马上着手的理由同样充分，所以还是马上着手的好。

You might as well throw your money into the sea as lend it to him. (你借钱给他，不啻把钱丢在海里。)

I might as well act it as say it. (我那样说就等于那样做。)

I think we may as well set out on our travels. (我想我们最好就出发去旅行。)

You might as well erect a house without bricks and mortar as try to get on in life without education. (不受教育而想立身处世，就像没有砖和灰泥来建造房子一样。)

You may just as well tell me the truth. (你把事实告诉我是为你好。)

One may as well be hanged for a sheep as a lamb. (与其窃钩而诛，毋宁窃国。)

You might as well advice me to give up my fortune as my argument. (你要我放弃议论，还不如要我放弃财产。)二者皆不可能。

1. Friendship is a vase, which, if it is cracked by accident, may as well be broken at once.

2. You might as well expect the sun to rise in the west as expect me to change my opinion.

3. When this lady saw that the magazine was not going to rise, she became a little disgusted with the editor and decided that she might as well get what there was to get while there was still something available. (Hemingway)

(31) so that...may
lest...should

(a) I run fast *so that* I *may* catch the train.
我快跑为的是要赶上火车。

(b) I run fast *lest* I *should* miss the train.
我快跑以免赶不上火车。

这两种表现法，都是表示"目的"的，"lest...should"的说法较古，现今多用"for fear that"来取代了。"that...may"也略带古风，"in order that...may"，则是郑重的表现法。这个表"目的"的"may"，有时也可换用"can"，"shall"等字。(a)例可译作"俾可"，"以求达到"，而(b)例则为"以免"，"以求不至"，又可翻译为"因恐"，"免得"。这个"so that"在会话体中及美国话中，常只用一个"so"字，而不用"that"，在"so that"的前面有时用逗号(Comma)，有时不用，逗号的有无，完全不影响文义。"lest...should"除上述"for fear"外，还可代以"in case"，后面仍接"should"不变。在最近的美国话中，则将"should"略去不说，后接原形动词，如 Take care lest you fall. (当心不要跌倒。)这个"lest...should"的口语表现法为"so as not to"。

We whispered lest he should hear. (怕他听见故细声说。)

Man does not live that he may eat, but eats that he may live. (人非为吃而生,乃为生而吃。)

He spends that he may succeed, and succeeds that he may spend. (他消耗以求成功,成功以便消耗。)

They placed a guard at the door, lest the prisoner should find means of escape. (他们派了一个卫兵来看守房门,以免犯人想办法逃走。)

He tried to shout so that he might be heard all along the street. (他试着大声叫喊,指望沿街有人听到。)

Kindly sign it and return to me, so I can put through a voucher for the $1,000 we agreed on. (请签字后寄回给我,俾可将我们双方议定的一千元顺利完成保证手续。)

I wrote out an itinerary so they could follow us. (Hemingway)(我定出了一个旅程表,以便他们可以追随我们而来。)

1. Science consists in grouping facts so that general laws or conclusions may be drawn from them. (Darwin)
2. When the schoolboys find a nest, they are very careful not to disturb it lest the mother bird should be frightened and desert it.

(32) cannot help + 动名词
cannot but + 原形不定词

(a) I *cannot help admiring* his courage.
(b) I *cannot but admire* his courage.
我对于他的勇气不胜佩服。

在(a)例中的"help"意为"避免",可用"avoid"、"resist"、"forbear"等取代。同义的说法还有"cannot keep (或 refrain, abstain) from - ing",如 We cannot keep from admiring the scenery. (我们不禁大为赞赏那种风景。)至于(b)例的"cannot but",是稍具古风的表现法,其中的"but" = except,意为"除了那样做以外,什么也不能做",最后成为"不得不"了。比较下面三种说法:

Formal: I cannot but feel sorry for him.
Informal: I can't help feeling sorry for him.
Vulgar: I can't help but feel sorry for him.

把最后一例说成卑语的,只是英国的说法,在美国却视为正常的英文,在 *Webster's New World Dictionary of the American Language* 上就举有"cannot help but" = cannot fail to; be compelled or obliged to 的解释。

I cannot help thinking he's wrong. (我不禁认为他错了。)

I cannot but feel thankful that it formed such a material part of my education. (我不禁深为感谢,那竟形成了我教育上重要的一部分。)

I cannot help forming some opinion of a man's character from his dress. (我不得不多少要从一个人穿的衣

服来判断他的性格。)

　　We cannot but believe in the youth who is always trying to improve himself. (常要努力改进自己的青年,我不得不信赖。)

　　I could not but laugh on seeing such a funny sight. (看到这样滑稽的光景,我不禁笑出来了。)

　　The little child was so beautiful, kind, and good, that no one who saw her could help loving her. (那个小孩非常美丽,又亲切,又善良,所以没有人见到她不爱她的。)

　　I cannot help wondering about the child. (关于那个孩子的事,我不禁感到奇怪。)

　　1. She could not help sympathizing with every little helpless thing; her heart was always touched by a bird or beast that had been hurt.

　　2. When I consider the greatness that he afterward achieved I cannot but smile as I remember the fashion in which he was discussed at my uncle's table. (Maugham)

(33) have + 宾语(物) + 过去分词

　　(a) I *had* my watch *mended*.
　　　　我找人把我的表修理好了。

　　(b) I *had* my watch *broken*.
　　　　我把我的表弄破了。

　　(c) We *have* our enemy almost *surrounded*.
　　　　我们差不多把敌人包围起来了。

　　例(a)表主语的意志,例(b)则与主语的意志完全无关,例(a)为使动,例(b)则为被动。例(a)的主语有意去请人修表,而例(b)的主语实无意把表弄破。例(c)为保持那种被动(在例句中为"被包围")的状态。(a)句中的"have",有时可换用"get",以限制其意义。普通受 Passive Form 的动作者为主语,例如 My watch was stolen. (我的表被窃。)一语,其中受动作者为"watch",今若欲说"我被窃去一只表",便是: I had my watch stolen. 此时的主语,间接受到动作,故此种体裁,称为"间接受动态"(Indirect Passive Form)。如果说 He was handed a short note. 听来很不自然,故改说 He had a short note handed to him. (有人交给了他一封短信。)凡 Passive (被动)皆无意志,若加上意志便成为 Causative(使动)之意,例如 I will have (= cause) a new house (to be) built. (我欲使新屋建成。我欲建筑一幢新居。)在用作使动时"have"要读重音,用作被动时则不要,如 He *had* his salary raised. (他使薪水提高了。) I had my *hat* blown off. (我的帽子被风吹落了。)

　　I had my foot severely trodden upon in the bus. (我在公共汽车里被人重重地践踏了脚。)
　　He had his left hand cut off. (他被人砍去了左手。)
　　She has her head turned. (= she has gone mad.) (她发狂了。)

We shall have our rights trampled under foot. (我们的权利将为人所蹂躏。)

I will have a new suit made. (我想制一套新装。)

I will have my photograph taken. (我要去照相。)

No family is too poor to have the table covered with a clean cloth. (没有一个家庭会穷困到连放在餐桌上的干净桌布都没有的程度。)

He had his right leg pierced by a shot. (他的右腿为子弹所贯穿。)

Old ladies in the States will have new novels read to them. (美国的老太太喜欢叫人把新出的小说读给她们听。)

He has his leg pulled. (= He is befooled.) (他受了人家的愚弄。)

Falling from his bicycle, he had his arm sprained. (他从脚踏车上跌下来把胳膊跌断了。)

So I went first to have my wounds dressed. (所以我先去把伤包扎好。)

You must have this fact impressed upon your mind. (你必须把这事实铭记在心上。)

He had a ticket given him. (有人给了他一张票。)

I had my right leg hurt in the accident. (在车祸中我伤了右腿。)

After paying his bill and buying his railway ticket, he had only fifty cents left. (付清了账又买了火车票,他只剩下五角钱了。)

Did he have his hair cut yesterday? (他昨天去理过发了吗?)

I have my revolver loaded. (我把手枪装上子弹了。)

We'd clear away all these cases and have the whole of that wall filled by a heroic fresco of Hector and Andromache. (Huxley) (我们要把这些箱子全部都清理出来,好让墙壁充满描写赫安英雄事迹的壁画。)

Sadie had her hand clapped to her cheek as though she had toothache. (Mansfield) (沙娣好像牙痛似的,把一只手敲着她的面颊。)

This error was particularly magnified by the fact that by the time of Yalta we already had Japan beaten. (*Reader's Digest*) (到雅尔塔协定时,我们算是已经把日本打败了,由这事实看来,那错误尤为显著。)

1. He who wished to read the hearts of this husband and wife who stood at right angles, to have their wounds healed by Law, would have needed to have watched the hundred thousand hours of their wedded life. (Galsworthy)

2. Some are born great, some achieve greatness, and some have greatness thrust upon them.

3. We need to have our liberties taken away from us in order to discover that they are worth dying for. (Gardiner)

4. I had my plans arranged by which I should have the opportunity of making the man who had wronged me understand that his old sin had found him out.

(34) have + 宾语(人) + 原形不定词

(a) I *have* him *mend* my watch.

我请他修理我的表。

(b) He *had* his mother *die*. (= His mother died.)

他遭母丧。

这个"have + 宾语（人）+ 原形不定词"（无"to"的不定词，在此作宾格补语用）的形式，有两种解释：凡在主语无意志之下而发生的事，是用的被动的作用，若加上主语的意志进去，就是用的使动的作用了。何时为被动，何时为使动，要看前后文才能决定，但有时从助动词上也可以看得出来，例如

(a) I will have many people come. （将使许多人来）是有意志的。

(b) I shall have many people come. （将有许多人来）是无意志的。

在(a)句中"will"后的"have"，已成为"make"之意了。这种说法美国人用的颇多。英国人表"请人为某事"之意时，则用"get"，但后面须接用有"to"的不定词，即限于使动时，等于"get + 宾语 + 有 to 的不定词"，如 I get him to mend my watch. （我找他替我修理手表。）I will get some one to translate the letter. （我要找人把这封信译出来。）英国人表"使人为某事"之意时，则用"make"，如 I will make my servant clean your shoes. （我将叫仆人替你擦皮鞋。）在美国"get"和"make"都不用，而一律用的"have". 如 We had a fire break out last night. （昨夜附近有火警。）I had him write the letter. （我使他写那封信。）

至于上举例句的第二例，也是有有意志与无意志之分的，如 His mother died. （他母亲死了。）是无意志的，如加上有意志的成份进去，当做一个人自己的经验来说时，就成为 He had his mother die. （他遭母丧。）

在"have"后接"人"和接"物"的不同，使宾格补语的形式随之而异，即接"人"时用原形不定词，接"物"时用过去分词，比较如下：

Please *have* the porter *carry* this trunk.

Please *have* the trunk *carried* by the porter.

I don't like to have you go. （我不想你走。）

He likes to have people come. （喜有客来。）

I will have someone come and keep me company. （希望有人来为我作伴。）

I wouldn't have you do that. （我不想你那样做。）

I should like to have her meet you. （我希望她能见到你。）

I had them clean the house before your arrival. （使人洒扫以待。）

My wife would have me buy that television set. （我太太只想要我买那架电视机。）

I don't like to have somebody else tell me I ought to do this thing and that. （我不喜欢老是要别人来指挥我做这样做那样。）

If you will have me stay, I shall stay. （必欲留我，我就留下。）

What would you have me do? （有何吩咐？）

The students are afraid of having him become principal. （学生生怕他当校长。）

These little animals seem glad to have people visit them. （这些小动物喜欢有人去看它们。）

1. It is his nature to do to others what he would have others do to him.
2. As we lived near the road, we often had the traveller visit us to taste our gooseberry wine. (Goldsmith)
3. I would rather have lost them twice over than have had this happen. (Hardy)
4. I had a cultivated Englishman ask me if it were true Negroes could not walk on the same sidewalks as white Americans. (*The New York Times*)

(35) have + 宾语 + 副词(地点,方向等)

(a) Let's *have* him *here*.
　要他到这里来吧。
(b) He *had* a tooth *out*.
　他拔了一个牙齿。

这种句法中的"have",也是使动的意思,原则上和前面两项无异,不过翻译时须看前后文的关系,采用适当的字眼,不一定要把使动译出来,如(a)例,便可不必译为"使他来这里",第二句的(b)例,也不必译为"要牙医为他拔牙"。如例句所示,在"have"后,是既可接"人",又可接"物"的。

We'll have the big table here. (把大桌子放在这里吧。)
Let me have Mr. Wong over. (去请王先生来吧。)
I had him there. (在那一点上我把他击败了。)指议论时说的。
He was had up for exceeding the speed limit. (他因开车超速而被起诉。)

1. We shall be having the decorators in next month.
2. He won't stand for it. He'll have you out on Tuesday, so that you may as well make up your mind to it. (Maugham)

(36) have + 宾语 + 现在分词

(a) I can't *have* him *doing* that.
　我不能让他那样做。
(b) I *have* a car *waiting* for me.
　我有汽车在等待着。

这个"have + 宾语 + 现在分词"的表现法,有两种含义,如(a)例为"许可",(b)例为"使动"。动词"have"的原义为"具有",即具有某种情形,如 I have a lot of visitors coming. (我有许多客人要来。)
有时不用现在分词,而改用形容词,也是类似的用法,例如 I can't have you idle. (我不能让你这样懒惰。)

I won't have you going out. (你不要老是跑出去。)
I had it coming. (= I deserve it.) (这是当然的报应。)
I won't have you smoking at your age. (我不想要你这样小就抽烟。)
We told him we had relatives coming. (Hedley Gore) (我们告诉了他说我们有些亲戚要来。)

1. I see that woman downstairs has a couple of sailors sitting there. I wonder how she's gotten acquainted with them. (Maugham)
2. It is generous of me to have you doing nothing.
3. I will not have you talking indecently before the children! (Sinclair Lewis)

(37) find oneself

After half an hour I *found myself* in front of the house.
半小时之后,我就觉得我已经站在那房子的前面了。

英文说的"find oneself"有三个意思:①起居,动定,例如 How do you find yourself this morning? (= How are you this morning?) (你今早觉得身体好吗?) ②自给自足,例如 He works for one hundred dollars a month and finds himself. (他每月有工资一百元足以自给。) ③自觉,自知,发现自己的能力,例如 After trying various jobs he found himself and became a successful reporter. (换了几个职务之后,他发现了自己的能力,成为一个成功的记者。) 最后一解为"感觉到自己在某种特定的场所,地位,或状态中",引申而为"注意一看则身在"或简单地说成"觉得"。这种说法,实含有"意想不到","偶然","竟至"的意思在内。例如 I find myself in a church. (我发觉走进了一个教堂。) I found myself in his company. (注意一看,他陪伴着我。)

She returned to England to find herself famous. (她回到英国发觉自己竟成名了。)
She found herself a mother at fifteen. (她十五岁就做了母亲。)
Moving homeward by a new way, I presently found myself on the side of a little valley, in which lay a farm and an orchard. (Gissing) (从一条新路向着家园走去,我随即就来到了一个小谷的旁边,那里有农场和果木园。)
Otherwise he "found" himself in childish fashion out of the six or seven weekly shillings. (F. Marzials) (不然的话,他就要用小孩子的方式从每周六、七先令中自谋生活。)
In many places the churches are trying to get hold of the neglected strangers and help them to "find themselves" in their unfamiliar surroundings. (James Bryce) (在许多地方教会努力要收容那些无人过问的外来人,帮助他们在不熟悉的环境中发现自己的能力。)
When he awoke, he found himself in jail. (他一醒来,睁开眼睛一看,自己竟在牢狱里了。)

He found himself at last. (他终于发现了自己的天分。)

1. I awoke one morning and found myself famous. (Lord Byron)
2. The hours moved on, and he found himself staring at his small candle, which struggled more and more faintly with the morning light.
3. In about forty-five seconds I found myself again in the waiting room with the compassionate secretary, who made me sign more documents. (Conrad)

(38) find... in

I *found* a true friend *in* him.
我发现他是一个真实的朋友。

在这个动词"find"的后面,除接介词"in"外,还可以接"that"引导的子句或不定词的造句。意为(由经验而)发现,觉悟,知道,(试过之后而)认明,认定,验出。例如 I find that the work pays. (我始知此事合算。) We found that the report was false. (= We found it to be false.) (问明而后知为虚报。) I awoke to find it a dream. (醒来始知为梦) 在"in"前面的动词,并不限于"find",他如 "see","have","behold","lose" 等都可以用。

I found a friend in a supposed enemy. (我在原来以为是敌人的当中得到了一个朋友。)
Columbus found a warm supporter in Queen Isabella. (哥伦布获得伊莎贝拉女王的热心赞助。)
I found an enthusiastic coadjutor in the person of a young fellow named Wong Ming. (我获得一个名叫王明的热心的青年助手。)
Dostoievski finds brothers in thieves and murderers. (陀思妥耶夫斯基把小偷和杀人犯视为兄弟。)
We found victory in defeat. (我们认定失败就是胜利。)
We lost a great scholar in Dr. Hu Shih. (胡适的死使我们失去了一个伟大的学者。)

1. Many on becoming rich have found in wealth not an escape from evil, but a new and worse form of it.
2. It was easy to see in Gladstone the perfect model of the upright—the man whose life had been devoted to the application of high principles to affairs of State.

(39) "do"的两种用法

(a) You know more than I *do*.
你比我知道的多。

(b) I *do* want to know the truth.
我真想要知道真相。

除疑问句和否定句以外所用的"do",有两种用法:一为代替已说过的动词以避免重复,这叫做代动词(pro-verb),如(a)例中的便是以"do"代替"know"的。在英文中除助动词及"be"动词外,其余所有的动词,都可以用"do"来代替。第二种用法是加强动词意味的,这是助动词,如(b)例所示,是加强动词"want"的,普通单说 I want to know the truth. 意思也是一样。加强语气时可译作"真","真正","实在"等。

Do you drink? Yes, I do. (你喝酒吗? 我喝。)

Don't you drink? Nor (或 Neither) do I. (你不喝酒吗? 我也不喝。)

You stammer sometimes; so do I. (你有时口吃,我也是一样。)

You dislike dogs as I do cats. (好像我不喜欢猫一样,你不喜欢狗。)

No father could have loved his children better than he did us. (没有别个父亲有我们的父亲这样爱他的孩子的。)

I do believe you. (我确实相信你说的话。)

I do wish you had seen him. (我真希望你见到了他。)

I did see him. (我确曾见到了他。)

He does work hard, but he often fails. (他确是很用功,但老是考不上。)

I did go, but failed to see him. (我确是去了,但没有见到他。)

Do stay here. (务请留此。)

Do be patient! (务请忍耐。)

Don't be anxious! (勿忧。)

Rarely did she laugh. (她难得笑。)这是倒装法,仍为加强语气的。

He is generally very reserved, but if he does talk, he always speaks to the purpose. (夫人不言,言必有中。)

The area could support a far larger population than it does at present. (那地方可以维持比现在大得多的人口。)

He had bought the home furnished sometime previously from a Lord somebody who needed cash, as so many do these days. (今天有非常多的人也是这样,因为需要现金就把房子卖掉,不久以前他从一个叫什么的勋爵那里买了这幢有家具的房子。)

Magnesium lives well with other metals—and, as in any good marriage, each partner functions better with the other than either does alone. (镁跟其他的金属结合得很好,所以好像很相合的婚姻一样,各金属单独的时候不如与其他结合时更能发生作用。)

1. I have somewhere seen it observed that we should make the same use of a book that the bee does of a flower; she steals sweets from it, but does not injure it.

2. Suppose you think of an important idea. Unless you can write it down, your idea will probably die when you do. Even if you do write it down, it perishes as soon as the mice eat the paper, which they often do and do quickly.

(40)"depend on"的两种用法

(a) He *depends on* his pen for his living.

他靠文笔为生。

(b) Success *depends on* perseverance.

成功恃乎毅力。

英文的"depend on"或"depend upon",由主语不同而发生意义上的差异。如(a)例以"人"为主语时,便有"依靠","信赖"的意思,如(b)例以"物"为主语时,则意为"以⋯为据","凭⋯而定","由⋯为转移","恃乎"。关于"depend"一字,另外还有两个惯用句,即① depend upon it. = You may be certain; I assure you.(你可以相信;请你确信;我可担保。)例如:The school boy is very idle and heedless now; but depent upon it, he will some day regret his idleness.(那学童现在很懒惰又不用心,不过我可以担保将来总有一天他会后悔的。)② That depends (on circumstances).(视情形而定;视情形如何,难以逆料。)

He is not to be depended upon. (他不可靠。)

Chinese varsity men mostly depend on their parents for support, but American college boys are independent of them. (中国大学生依赖父母;美国大学生自己工读。)

We depend on the newspaper for daily news. (我们靠报纸得知每日新闻。)

I shall have to depend on you to do it. (我只得仰仗足下来做。)

He no longer depends on his father. (他早已不靠父亲了。)

I cannot depend on your promise unless you give me the necessary security. (除非你提出必要的保证,否则,我是不能信赖你的诺言的。)

His departure depends on the weather. (他何时动身要凭天气而定。)

The effect depends on the cause. (结果由于原因。有因始有果。)

Everything depends on the amount of money given. (凡事皆凭金钱的多少而定。凡事以财力大小而定。)

The sale depends on the quality. (销路决定于品质。以货色的优劣而决定销路的大小。)

Victory does not always depend on numbers. (精兵不在多。)

1. A man must so train his habit as to rely upon his own powers and depend upon his own courage in moment of pressing necessity.

2. Few realize how much the happiness of life and the formation of character depend on a wise selection of books we read.

3. I am deeply convinced that our peace of mind and the joy we get out of living depend not on where we are, or what we have, or who we are, but solely upon our mental attitude. Outward conditions have very little to do with it. (D. Carnegie)

(41) know...from

He does not *know* an adjective *from* an adverb.

他连形容词和副词都分不清楚。

这个"know...from"是为表示辨别而用的,有时也可以说"tell...from",它的意思是"能加辨别","能够分辨",如 to know right from wrong 为"辨是非",to know a friend from an enemy 是"分敌友"等等。

I do not know the one from the other. (我未能辨别二者之差异。)

I cannot tell the one from the other. (不能区别彼此。)

Is it possible to tell a good book from a bad one? (要判别一本书的好坏是可能的吗?)

They do not know B from a bull's foot-B from a broomstick-B from a battledoor (*or* battledore)-chalk from cheese. (他们一无所知。)

How do you know an Englishman from an American? —By the way he speaks English. (英国人和美国人的区别,听他们说英语就可知道。)

I can tell an Italian from a Frenchman. (我能辨别意大利人和法国人。)

I can tell a crocodile from an alligator (the difference between them). (我能分别普通的鳄鱼和美洲产的鳄鱼。)

1. It is hard to know flatterers from friends, for as a wolf resembles a dog, so a flatterer, a friend.
2. Much as sheep look alike, there is a difference between them, and John knows one from another. (Much as...alike = Though sheep look much alike)

(42) had better + 原形不定词
would rather + 原形不定词

(a) You *had better go* at once.

你最好马上去。

(b) I *would rather go* at once.

我宁肯马上去。

照字面看来,"had","would"虽则是过去形,但在此等惯用句中,决无过去的意思,而只是一种假设语气的说法罢了。(a)例含有劝告的意思,可译为"最好是",(b)例含有选择的意思,可译为"宁肯",二者不可混同。这个"had better"的说法,有时可说成"had best",那就更接近中文的说法了,不过不大通用,例如 I'd best go and settle the score. (Thackeray)(我最好去把债务弄清楚)。I had best start for home.(我最好就动身回家去)。这个"had better"有时还可以用过去形,如 You had better do it. 的过去形便是 You had better have done it.(你最好那样做了就好了)。

有人把"had better"及"would rather"两种说法混为一谈,而形成"would better"及"had rather"的说法,这是不妥的,最好避免不用。例如 I had rather be a doorkeeper in the house of lord than dwell in the tents of wickedness.(我与其住在罪孽的天幕中,宁肯做神殿的司阍)。

我们须注意"had better"是用于劝解或间接命令的,所以有时可能含有"have a duty to"或"have an obligation to"的意思,自然是带有一种命令的口气,说 You had better go away. 含义为 You should do what you are told or else you will suffer rather serious consequences.(你应该照吩咐去做,不然的话,就要遭受严重的后果)。因此对长辈是不宜用"had better"的,对不大熟悉的人须存几分客气也不宜用,与其说 You'd better take a bus. 不如说 I suggest you take a bus. 与其说 You had better wear a blue necktie with that suit. 不如说 It might be better to wear a blue necktie with that suit. 或 It would be better for you to wear...

When he proposed to fly across the Atlantic, I said, "You had better not try!"(Kirkpatrick)(当他打算要飞越大西洋时,我劝说:"你最好不要去尝试。")

We had better not remain here any longer.(我们最好不要在此久留。)

I would rather die than live in dishonour. = I would sooner die than live in dishonour. = I would (just) as soon die as live in dishonour.(与其屈辱而生,宁愿光荣而死。)

I would rather be a poor man in a garret with plenty of books than a king who did not love reading.(我与其做一个不爱读书的国王,宁肯做一个住在屋顶楼上而拥有许多书的穷人。)

He said he would rather have lost both his legs than have seen dishonour brought upon the English nation.(他说与其见到英国民族蒙受耻辱,宁肯自己失去双腿。)

You had better not work after yon have tired yourself.(疲劳之后最好不要用功。)

You had better go back—the risk is great. (Thomas Hardy)(你最好回去,危险太大。)

I really don't think I'd better. (J. D. Salinger)(我想我最好不要去。)

You had better make hotel reservations before you leave here.(你离开此地以前,最好先把旅馆的房间订好。)

1. If you can neither receive nor bestow benefit, you had better leave that company at once.
2. I do not flatter you, young people, when I say I would rather talk to you than to the grown-up people.

(43) make...of

I will *make* a scientist *of* my son.
我要把儿子做成一个科学家。

英文"make...of"的形式,原意为"以之为材料而做成","使之成为"。这个"of"有"from"之意,不改变原料本质的用"of",如 The desk is made of wood.(桌子是木头做的),桌子做成之后还看得出木头的本质。改变原料本质的用"from",如 Paper is made from rags.(纸是破布做的),做成了纸之后,就看不见破布的影子了。同样的情形,葡萄可以造酒,但酒中看不见葡萄,我们说 We make grapes into wine. 或者说 Wine is made from grapes. 又如 Aspirin is made from coaltar.

英文用介词"from"、"of"、"out of"表示原料,用"into"表示制成品。造句的方式为 to make material into object 或 to make object from (或 of 或 out of) material. 这个"out of"中的"out"一字,常可略去不用,尤其是紧接在"made"一字后时为然,如 Many things are made (out) of paper. 成语有 to make a mountain of a molehill(小题大做;言过其实);to make ducks and drakes of one's money(挥霍无度;浪费金钱);to make fun of a person(开玩笑,戏弄)。

She often makes a hero of her husband.(她常把她丈夫当作英雄,推崇备至。)
Don't make a fool of him.(不要愚弄他。)
He made an ass (a fool, a beast) of himself.(他做着愚相。)
I don't want to make a cat's paw of him.(我不想拿他当傀儡。)
She has made a conquest of a man.(她使他成为她在爱情上的被征服者。)
A well-to-do farmer in China cannot make up his mind to make a farmer of his son, unless he deems his son incapable of undertaking any other profession.(一个中国富裕的农夫不能够决心让他的儿子成为农夫,除非他认为他儿子不能够干其他的职业。)
Nothing more makes a coward of a man than to be in the wrong.(没有别的事情比做错事更能使人胆怯的。)
A sea life may be the very thing required to make a strong man of him.(海上生活也许是使他成为一个强壮的人所必要的事。)

1. The artist can within certain limits make what he likes of his life. In other callings, in medicine for instance or the law. you are free to choose whether you will adopt them or not, but having chosen, you are free no longer. (Maugham)

2. Men who have done great things, made stepping stones of their failure.

(44) make one's way

He'll have no difficulty in *making his way* in the world.
他要出人头地是没有什么困难的。

英文的"make one's way"有两个意思:①进行(proceed),例如 make one's way on foot(步行前进),make one's way home(回家)。It rapidly made its way into universal favour.(那个很快地就获得了世人的爱好。)②在事业上的进展(make progress in one's career),如 He has yet his way to make in the world.(他还没有成就。)《综合英汉大辞典》上解释较详：to make one's way (through difficulties—homeward—in life—in one's profession)(排除困难而)进,(向家)行,(生涯)昌盛,(职业)成就。由此看来,我们可以知道,一个人在社会上的成功,并不是轻易得来的,而是由于"努力上进","力争上游"才获致的。上面说的 through difficulties 是历尽艰苦才得到的,正所谓"吃得苦中苦,方为人上人"。

由这个成语而产生出许多类似的表现法,用其他种种动词和"way"(进路)组合起来,差不多都有这种排除万难而得以前进的意思,如 The chick breaks its way out into the world.(鸡雏啄破蛋壳出来进入世间。)cleave one's way through many difficulties to prosperity(排除万难,打开出路,以臻繁荣。)conquer one's way to the higher happiness(克服挡在路上的苦难,而达到更大的幸福。)corkscrew one's way through a crowd(在群众的夹缝中走。)又如 cut one's way 意为排除障碍始得前进,即所谓筚路蓝缕,例如 Great men are those who cut their way to success through difficulties.(伟人都是历尽艰苦而达到成功的。)他如 feel one's way up the stairs(摸上楼梯。)fight one's way out of the seething swaying mob(从沸腾浮动着的群众中打出一条出路来。)fight one's way in life (in the world).(人生奋斗。)A young man must find his own way in the world without props and safeguards.(年轻人必须在没有支持和保护之下自己来打天下。)I had some difficulty in finding my way back.(我很费了劲才找到路回家。)He forced his way from a humble origin to an exalted position.(他从微贱中奋斗而达到高位。)又可说 forge one's own way to success(打开成功之路。)labor one's way with great difficulty(艰苦奋斗。)With no further formal education, he had worked his way to a major position.(他没有受过更多的正式教育,也搞到一个重要的位置了。)He worked his way through college as a waiter.(他半工半读,一面当侍者,一面读完大学。)

The young man will make his way, for he is industrious and economical.(那青年既勤快又节俭是会成功的。)
He (Disraeli) is determined to make his way. (*Edinburgh Review*)(他是决心要成功的。)
Snails are making their way as an article of food.(蜗牛渐渐变成食品了。)
The word is a provincialism, but has made its way into standard speech.(这字原为方言,次第变成标准语了。)
The carp always makes its way up a waterfall.(鲤鱼跳龙门。)
Be active! That's the way to make you way〔up〕in the world.(放活跃些！那就是你出人头地的办法。)

1. So long as you are not a useful, faithful, and truthful man, you can scarcely hope to make your way in the world.
2. He has made his way to presidency step by step.
3. There is scarcely a great truth but has had to fight its way to public recognition in the face of opposition.

(45) rob...of

He *robbed* me *of* my watch.

他抢夺了我的表。

"他动词+宾语(人)+of+宾语(物)"的形式,是英文的特殊语法,和中文大不相同的。英文凡具有"夺取"意义的动词,就要用这种表现法。被夺取的目标分明是"物",英文偏要说"人",而在被夺取的"物"之前,加上一个"of"的介词,把它造成一个片语,接在"人"的后面。这个"of"的意思是表"分离"的。

英文在 rob, deprive, deliver, divest, break, relieve, clear, inform, bereave, cure, strip, rid 等有夺取,除去,减轻,通知等意的动词上,都可以采用这一种表现法。动词 steal(窃)虽与 rob(盗)相类,但用法完全不同,和它同用的介词不是"of"而是"from",即"steal...from",如 A thief stole some cigarettes from that shop.(有贼从那店里偷去一些香烟。)如果是具有"供给"之意的动词,就要用"with"来代替"of",如说 supply him with money(供给他钱), fill the glass with water(倒水入杯), furnish one with information(给他消息), favour one with an interview(赐予接见), trust one with a secret(告以秘密)等。

He does not care whom he deprives of enjoyment, so that he can obtain it.(他只求自己获得享受,不管是从谁夺取得来。)

I don't want to rob him of his inalienable rights.(我不想夺取他做人固有的权利。)注:Life, liberty, and the pursuit of happiness have been called the inalienable rights of man.(生命,自由与追求幸福,被称为人类不可剥夺的权利。)

He cleared the sea of those robbers.(他肃清了海盗。)

I have learned enough to cure me of my old fancies.(Stevenson)(我学到足以诊好我从前好幻想的毛病。)

I shall never be able entirely to divest myself of this feeling.(我将永远无法完全放弃这些感觉的。)

He could not rid himself of the painful memories.(他忘不了过去那种痛苦的回忆。)

Your coming relieves me of the bother of writing a long letter.(你来了省得我去麻烦写一封长信。)

He was determined to break himself of the bad habit of lying in bed late of a morning.(他决心革除睡早觉的恶习。)

Thieves stripped the house of everything valuable.(贼偷去了家中一切贵重的东西。)

Death bereft (or bereaved) him of his son.(他有失明之痛。)

Four years of war drained the country of men and resources.(四年的战争使国家耗尽壮丁和资源。)

1. He informed me of the news so that I got prepared in time.

2. A foolish notion that it is more dignified to be seen in a carriage than on horseback, had deprived all French noblemen of the use of the saddle.

3. It was fortunate for me that I suddenly achieved popularity as a dramatist and so was relieved of the necessity of writing a novel once a year to earn my living.(Maugham)

(46) seize... by the...

He *seized* me *by the* arm.
他抓了我的胳膊。

这是纯粹的英文表现法,和中文不同,其形式为"他动词+宾语+介词+the+名词"。中国话一定用属格,而英文则先把整个的对象说出来,然后再说到那对象身体的局部。这是大处着眼,小处着手的办法。身体的局部接受动作时,不用代名词的属格"one's",而采用"介词+the+名词"的形式。这一类的动词有 seize, catch, take, strike, drag, pat, hit, hold, pull, stare, look 等,而介词则有 by, on, in, over, across, with 等。"他抓了我的胳膊"这句话,依照中文的说法,译成 He seized my arm. 也不为错,不过英语的气味不浓,和说 He seized me by the arm. 二者间的 nuance(细微差异),是很难言传,而只可意会的。但是如"不要让别人牵着你的鼻子走"一句话,则必须译成 Don't let them lead you by the nose. 若说 Don't let them lead your nose. 就不成话了。

He kissed his horse on the forehead. (他在额上吻了他的马一下。)
He struck me on the head. (他打了我的头。)
I caught him by the right hand. (我握住他的右手。)
He pulled me by the sleeve. (他拉住我的衣袖。)
I gave him a blow on the head. (当头一棒。)
He looked me in the face. (他凝视着我。)
He wounded me in the arm. (他扭我的胳膊。)
He slapped me on the shoulder. (他拍我的肩。)
Poverty stared him in the face. (赤贫迫在眼前。)
He presumed in the gentlest manner to take her by her hand. (C. Lamb)(他敢于用最温柔的态度执了她的手。)注:古文可以说 by her hand. 但现代英文则必须说 by the hand.

1. Never hold anybody by the hand in order to be heard out.
2. If that woman crosses my threshold, I shall strike her across the face.
3. The doctor angrily seized him by the collar, and asked him what he meant by such bad behaviour.

(47) see if...
see that...

(a) He came out to *see if* it had begun to rain.
他出来看是不是已经下雨了。

(b) He came out to *see that* the boy did not get hurt.
他出来注意防止小孩受伤。

(a)例的"see if"中的"if",是作"whether"解的,意为"是不是"。在"see"后不一定要接"if",还可接用其他各种各样的疑问词。至于(b)例的"see that"中的"see",则有"take care"之意。这个"see that",实为"see to it that"的省略说法。"see to it" = look well to it; attend; consider; take care(加意及之,留神,注意,当心)。这种句中的"that"有时也可省掉不说。基本句型为"see that something is done"(当心照料,监督)转为"负责担任;保证"之意。

See if he can do it. (看看他是不是能做这个。)
Go and see if there is anything to eat. (去看看有什么吃的东西没有。)
Go and see what is the matter. (去看看发生了什么事。)
Let's see how the land lies. (让我们先来窥探一下形势。)
See how the wind blows. (观看形势;默察大势;观望。)
I will see that they do it. (我当负责要他们做。)
I will see that he pays you. (或 see that you are paid 或 see you paid)(我必令他还钱给你;我保证他一定还你。)
See to it that this does not occur again. (保证不再发生同样的事。)
See to it that you do not offend him. (当心不要冒犯他。)
I will see to it that everything is ready for your departure. (我会注意准备好一切让你起程。)
See to it that the boys learn the lesson well. (请留意使学生熟习功课。)
See to it that the work is done before dark. (你注意天黑前要做好。)
I will see [that] you avenged. (必定使你可以报仇。)
I will see [that] you hanged first. (那里有人肯做这样的事?)

1. Many men do not allow their principles to take root, but pull them up every now and then, as children do flowers they have planted, to see if they are growing.

2. If a captain loves his ship truly, he must not neglect to attend to the smallest defect in her. He must report it and see that it is made good.

3. "I've been here when there's been cholera and I haven't turned a hair. The great thing is not to eat anything uncooked, no raw fruit or salads, or anything like that, and see that your drinking water is boiled." (Maugham)

(48) take...for granted

(a) We *took* it *for granted* that you knew the whole matter.
    我们认为那件事情你当然是完全知道的。
(b) She began to *take* her husband *for granted* until he threatened to leave her.
    她开始有点瞧不起她丈夫的样子,直到她丈夫声称要离家出走,她才改变态度。

英文成语"take...for granted"的形式,等于"assume as true",可译作"认为当然","假定是实",即并无明确的证据,也信以为真的意思。普通的用例为"take it for granted",其中的"it"为形式上的宾语,代表后面的"that-Clause";如果不用"it"而用名词时,则"that-Clause"可以不要。这个"granted",分明是一个分词,在此权充介词"for"的宾语,如果把它看做前面省去了"being"一字也就好解释了。在"take"后面的宾语,一向都只限于"it"或事物的名词,但新近美国《韦氏大辞典》上,却增加了一个新的用法,即在"take"后面接用人的宾语,如(b)例所示,便是那辞典上举出的例句。对这个新义的解释,该辞典作"to pay inadequate attention to or value too lightly (as a possession, right or privilege)",意即对地位、权利或特权,不加重视,或不十分注意,自然是带有瞧不起的神气。

I take it for granted that you will be interested in it, too. (我认为你当然对此也会感兴趣的。)

I just took it for granted that we will close on May Day. (我认为劳动节商店当然是关门的。)

I took it for granted that he would come. (我以为他一定会来的。)

He takes nothing for granted. (他对任何事物都不视为当然。)

I took his qualifications for granted. (我姑认为他的资历是真实可靠的。)

They themselves take their love for granted, and do not care what strangers may think about it. (他们本人认为他们的相爱是理所当然的,别人怎样想法,他毫不介意。)

I took for granted the innumerable little jobs she did for me. (Siegfried Sassoon)(我把她为我做的那些无数的小事视为当然。)

Physical and intellectual miracles we take for granted. (M. B. Johnstone)(我们把心身的奇迹认为是当然的。)

Cf. From your manner I am to take it as true. (Hardy)(从你的态度看来,我得把那个看做真的了。)

1. Of the rural life of England he knew nothing; and he took it for granted that everybody who lived in the country was either stupid or miserable.

2. I take the goodness of the good for granted and I am amused when I discover their defects or their vices; I am touched when I see the goodness of the wicked and I am willing enough to shrug a tolerant shoulder at their wickedness. (Maugham)

3. I went there as a kid and grew up with the place. They took me for granted. (Elizabeth Wilson)

(49) used to + 原形不定词
be used to + 动名词

(a) He *used to do* such a thing.
　　他以前常做这样的事。

(b) He *is used to doing* such a thing.
　　他惯于做这样的事。

在(a)例中说的"used to do",表示过去的习惯,即"以前常那样做",这表示现在已不那样做了。在(b)例中的"be used to doing" = be accustomed to doing,是表示现在的惯常行为,其中的"be",有时可说成"get",比如我们新到一个地方,对于当地的情形陌生,人们就会说:You will soon get used to it.(过些时间你就会习惯的。)又"他惯于登山。"就说 He is used to mountain-climbing. 这个"be used to"和前面的"used to",含义大不相同,试比较下面两句:

(a) I am used to sitting up late at night.
(b) I used to sit up late at night.

(a)句意为"我惯于迟睡。"(b)句意为"我以前总是睡得很迟的。"

英文还有一个"would"字,也和"used to"一样,是表过去习惯的,但二者在用法上略有不同。表示不规则的习惯时用"would",表示有规则的习惯则用"used to"。用"would"时多伴有"always","often","frequently","sometimes","for hours"等副词。比较下面四个句子,不难有所分辨。

(a) He climbs a mountain every Sunday.
（每个礼拜天他都要去爬山。）
(b) He will often climb a mountain of a Sunday.
（他常要在礼拜天去爬山。）
(c) He used to climb a mountain on a Sunday.
（他以前常要在礼拜天去爬山。）
(d) He would often climb a mountain when young.
（他年轻时常去爬山。）

这种"would"具有一种"回想的心情",而"used to"只是表示"过去与现在的对比"而已。再看下例:

He would often sit for hours, book in hand.（他从前常要手里拿一本书,一坐就是好几个钟头。）
Sometimes the boys would play a trick on their teacher.（有时孩子们常要对老师开个玩笑。）

这都是回想着过去而说的,表示以前常要那样做,指过去的反复的动作或习惯。至于"used to",就是拿现在和过去比较,例如:

He used to play tennis before his marriage.
（他在结婚以前常打网球。）现在不打了。

一般是客观地说过去的事用"used to",带有意志时则用"would"。用"would"比"used to"略带文气。第三人称用"will"也可表习惯的行为,如 He will often get up at midnight to jot down something in his notebook.（他常半夜起来在笔记本上记下一些事情）。如用"would"则对所有的人称都可以。有时"would"和"used to"是可以混同的,如

When I was a boy, I would（或 used to）get up early.
（我小时候,总是起身很早的。）

英文的"used to"常和表现状态的动词同用,如:

There used to *be* a church here.

(以前这里有一个教堂。)

When I was a boy, I used to *like* chocolate. (but I don't like it any more). (在小孩子的时候,我爱吃巧克力糖。)意即现在不再爱吃了。这个用法是不可以换用"would"的,因为说 When I was a boy, I would like chocolate 是不通的。I would like chocolate, 意为"我想吃巧克力糖"。如果不想强调现在与过去的对照,就用单纯的过去动词也同样可以达意,如 There *was* a church here. He *played* tennis before his marriage. 至于现在的情形如何,就不在话下了。

People used to think that the sun went round the earth. (从前的人以为太阳是围绕着地球转动的。)现在的人就不这样想了。

He usedn't to answer. (他总是不回答。)

I used to go fishing on Sundays when I lived in Taipei. (我住在台北时礼拜天常去钓鱼。)

I am used to the military life now. (我现在已惯于军队生活了。)

I'm sure it's because she is not used to the new typewriter yet. (那一定是因为她未用惯这架新的打字机。)

I got〔became〕used gradually to the vegetarian diet. (我逐渐习惯于素食了。)

The country inn was as pleasant as it used to be in the old times. (那间乡下客栈还是和从前一样舒服。)

That is how automobiles used to be made. (那就是汽车以前的制造法。)

The book used to belong to you?(Gissing)(这本书是你的吗?)

I used to remonstrate with Laura like a fussy old uncle but she'd only laugh. (Nigel Sligh)(我以前常要像一个讨厌的叔叔似的,老是给罗娜劝告,而她只是笑笑而已。)

There are some kinds of butterflies that used to be quite common, and now they are quite rare; I expect in a few years there will be none left at all. (Sweet)(某些种类的蝴蝶,以前很普通,现在却稀少了;我想再过几年就恐怕完全没有了。)现在、过去、未来的比较。

Sometimes he used to tell us of his expeditions through the woods and fields round his home, and how he explored the solitary brooks and ponds; and then he would describe the curious animals and birds he saw. (Sweet)(以前他时时对我说关于他在他家周围的森林和原野中探险的事,以及他怎样找到一些寂静的溪流和池塘的情形,然后他老要描述他所见到的珍禽异兽。)

"I often used to have a bit of fun with her, in the hold (= old) times!" Mr. Bailey spoke as if he had already had a leg and three-quarters in the grave, and this had happened twenty or thirty years ago. (Dickens)("在很久很久以前,我常要跟她开开玩笑,"倍雷先生说,俨然他已经有一只脚和四分之三进入坟墓了似的,而这已经是二三十年前的事了。)

1. "I care nothing for the world," he declared, "for the future, for what people will say, for any kind of established position, or even for literary fame, which in my early days I used to stay awake so many nights dreaming about." (Lynd)

2. Of course he suggested seeing her home, which she wouldn't hear of at first—she said there was really no

need, she was used to the journey alone and her parents' house was only a few minutes' walk from the station. (Hilton)

3. The air of our island was so genial and balmy that we could have slept quite well without any shelter; but we were so little used to sleeping in the open air, that we did not quite relish the idea of lying down without any covering over us. (R. M. Ballantyne)

(50) be +自动词的过去分词

Spring *is come.*
春满人间。

在动词"be"之后接用自动词的过去分词，不可看做被动语态，而应视为一种完成式才对，因为那是指某自动词的动作在完成后的状态。我们现在所说的完成式（现在）只有"have done"一个形式，但在 OE（古英文）的时代是"have + 宾语 + 过去分词"，例如现在说 I have caught the fish. 古代说 I have the fish caught. 和现代表示使动或被动的形式一样（如被动说的 We have our enemy almost surrounded. 及 Did he have his hair cut yesterday? 及使动说的 I had my watch mended. 等）但用于"have + 宾语 + 过去分词"这个形式的动词主要是他动词，而自动词，尤其是表运动、变化、终止等的自动词，如"come"，"go"，"arrive"，"fall"，"arise"，"become"，"grow"，"change"，"die"，等字，就采用"be + 过去分词"的形式，和用"have"的形式，在意义上毫无分别。但这种自动词的"be + 过去分词"的形式，经由 Middle English（中世英语）到 Modern English（现代英语）而渐渐失势，为"have"的形式所侵蚀，所以我们今日说到 Perfect Tense（完成时态）就只知"have done"一个形式了。

但古代自动词的用法并没有绝迹，现在表示运动和变化的少数自动词如"come"，"go"，"arrive"，"depart"，"fall"，"rise"，"set"，"grow"等，仍保留"be + 过去分词"的形式，在用法上与"have"的形式分庭抗礼，以"have"表完成的动作（action），"be"表完成的状态（state），例如：

　　He has gone.（他已经走了。）重点指动作的完成。
　　He is gone.（他已不在此了。）重点指动作的结果（现状）。

自动词的过去分词用于动词"be"后时，是表示那个自动词的动作完成了的状态，所以 He is gone. = He is no longer here. 说他已不在此，正是那"去"的动作完成后的状态。Spring is come. 其"来"的动作完成后的状态正是莺飞草长，杂花生树的春满人间的情形。The leaves are fallen. 是落叶满地的一片秋天的景象。The weeds are grown. 是杂草丛生的废园的样子。这些用在"be"后自动词的过去分词，最好把它当作形容词看待，以免发生被动的错误观念，而事实上许多过去分词的自动词辞典上也标明是形容词，如"agreed"便是其中的一个字，例：We were agreed on that point.（我们在那一点上意见一致。）I am agreed to accept the offer.（我同意接受那个提议。）如果用在名词前面，更是不含被动意味的形容词了，在此情形如系他动词则有被动意味。比较：a faded flower（已经谢了的花），是自动词过去分词变来的形容词，不含被动意味，只表"已经"之意。a broken promise（被破坏了的诺言），是他动词过去分词变来的形容词，故含有被动意味在内。

We are prepared for the worst.(准备最坏的情形来临。)
He was married.(他结婚了。)
The train was stopped.(火车停了。)
The day for payment is come.(发薪的日子来了。)
All hope is gone.(一切的希望都完了。)
I was determined to go.(我决心去。)
The sun is risen.(= The sun has risen and is now in the sky.)(太阳出来了。)太阳已经升起,现在在天上看见太阳。
The sun is set.(太阳落山了。)
My money is gone.(我的钱花完了。)
She found that her strength was gone.(她发觉她的气力都没有了。)
He is dressed elegantly.(他衣着华丽。)
Here's Mr. Land come all the way from Yorkshire.(这是从约克县远道而来的蓝先生。)在"come"前省略了"who is"二字。
Arrived at the spot, the party lost no time in getting to work.(一到现场,那一行人马上开始工作。)句首略去"being"一字。

1. All the guests are arrived and we'll have dinner served right now.
2. We are gathered here this morning to discuss without any prejudice the question of the day.
3. I'm almost finished with my work, but there are a few odds and ends left to be done.

(51) 否定 + fail + 不定词

He *cannot fail to rise* early.
他一定要很早起身。

英文的"cannot fail to do"和"cannot but do"同义,可译作"一定","必须","不得不"等。这个表现法的基本字"fail",是由自动的"fail in an attempt"(失败,未成)变成他动的"fail do to something"(疏失,忘置,不济,不能,难能),其反对字的"succeed"则只能作自动,不能作他动,即只能说"succeed in doing",不能说"succeed to do"。以"fail"为句中主动词后接不定词时,意即"cannot do"。至于在"fail to do"之意上再加否定时,即成"not fail to do" = be sure to do(certainly)。

I shall not fail to (= certainly) do so.(我必照办。)
He never fails to (= is sure to) accomplish his purpose.(必达目的。)

Never fail to (= be sure to) come to me. (务必相助。)
Don't fail to let me know. (务请相告。)
You will never fail to be moved by the beauty of the sight. (你一定会被那美丽的景象所感动的。)
I cannot fail to save enough money to buy a new watch. (我一定要储蓄足够的钱,好买一只新表。)

1. Nobody can fail to see that they have reached a crisis in their national development.
2. If we love our fellow creatures, as we ought to do, we cannot fail to be courteous to them.

(52) 动词 + 原形不定词

Go bring me my hat.
去把我的帽子拿来。

依照英文的习惯,两个动词不能连用,必得用"and"连接起来,或是把第二个动词改为不定词,即是说"go and bring"或"go to bring"两种形式。但我们现在采用的例句,既不用"and"也不用不定词,把两个动词连用在一起,似乎是不合惯用语法,其实这只是"go to bring"的省略,把后接的不定词的"to"略去,使它成为原形不定词(bare infinitive 或称 zero infinitive)。在表运动的动词如"come","go"之类时,常要将其后的不定词的"to"略去。现在的人以为这是美国人的用法,其实在中世英文时代老早就有了,不过到1890年以后,英国就不用了,仅在方言中还存在罢了。Jespersen 说,"This is pretty frequent in recent American books."(这在美国书中是很常见的。)会话中固不待言,文学作品中亦频频出现。其实这也不是美国人复古,而是十九世纪爱尔兰的大批移民到来以后,受到爱尔兰语影响的结果。在现代爱尔兰的语文中,还不失为一种惯用的语法,如 Go call them here again. (W. B. Yeats) I'll go tell Jack Smith's... (Lady Gregory) 现在美国话中这种用法极多,甚至把"go get"(获得,弄到手)的动词,转为名词的"go-getter"(活动家),如 The thing to do then, as a live bunch of go-getters, is to capitalize Culture. (S. Lewis)(作为一个活泼的活动家随后要做的事,就是把"文化"也资本化起来。

Let's go talk to the other fellows. (John Steinbeck) (我们到别的人们的地方去谈谈吧。)
Won't you go take a look at him? (id) (你不去看他一眼吗?)
I'd better go fetch him before all the fish die of age. (Puss'n Pooch) (我最好去找他来,怕这些鱼因年老而死光。)
I'd better go telephone Dilly first. (电影 *Love Letters*) (我最好先去打个电话给狄莉。)
She's better come get you, anyway. (H. Hamilton) (总而言之,她最好来带你去。)
Better come join us. (S. Lewis) (你跟我们一起去吧。)
Run get the ball for me, Jamie. (B. Tarkington) (詹米,你跑去替我把球拾来吧。)
I like say something if you got a minute. (id) (如果你得空,我想和你说几句话。)

He offered to help carry her basket.(他说要替她提篮子。)
I have heard say he is a miser.(我听说他是一个守财奴。)
Don't leave go until I tell you.(我不说你就不要放手。)
I hear say that there will be an election soon.(Zandvoort)(我听说不久要举行选举。)
I hear tell there's a new arrival six days old.(我听说有一个出生六日的婴孩。)
Let it go hang! (让它去吧。)

1. Go look up the tree and see if there is any ripe fruit on it. (Haggard)
2. If you like not my writing, go read something else. (Burton)

(53) leave + much(nothing) + to be desired

The book *leaves much to be desired*.
这本书写得极不完善。

英文说的"leave much to be desired" = be very imperfect,意为"极不完善","缺点很多"。而"leave nothing to be desired" = be perfect,意为"完善","毫无遗憾","没有缺点"。

Your behaviour leaves much to be desired.(你的行为尚须改进。)
It leaves nothing to be desired.(那毫无缺憾。)
The telephone service at Singapore leaves nothing to be desired.(新加坡的电话服务无复遗憾。)
The system of water supply in the city leaves much to be desired.(本市的自来水供应制度极不完善。)
The system of internal communication in England almost leaves nothing to be desired.(英国的国内交通制度完善得很。)
This steamer leaves nothing to be desired so far as comfort and luxury are concerned.(在舒服和豪华方面这轮船可谓尽善尽美了。)

1. When this disagreeable difference has been removed, the friendly relations between the two Republics, cordial even when one was yet an Empire, will leave nothing to be desired. (Wu Ting Fang)
2. If you will balance it on your finger you will find that it is perfect weight, and as to the finish it leaves nothing to be desired. (Fred M. White)

(54) be + 不定词

He *is to arrive* at seven in the morning.
他预定早晨七时抵埠。

这个"be + 不定词"是不定词的叙述用法,好像形容词一样。英文的这种表现法,有许多不同的含义,如上例便是表"预定"的,除此基本含义之外,它还可以表"可能",表"义务",表"假设",表"目的",表"结果",表"运命"等。但注意不要与名词用法相混,如 To see is to believe. (百闻不如一见。)这句中的动词后虽然也是接的不定词(to believe),但它是名词补语,和我们现在讨论的叙述用法的形容词补语完全不同。

We are to meet him at the airport. (我们要到飞机场去接他。)(预定)
The meeting is to be held on Sunday. (定了礼拜天开会。)(预定)
We are to go to town this afternoon. (我们打算今天下午进城去。)(预定)
In the sky not a cloud was to be seen. (青天无片云。)(可能)
Every misfortune is to be subdued by patience. (一切不幸都可能由忍耐克服。)(可能)
Her feelings as she read the letter were scarcely to be defined. (她看信时的心情不可名状。)(可能)
You are to stay here till I come back. (你得待在此地等我回来。)(命令)
You are always to knock before you enter my room. (在进入我的房间前你要敲门。)(命令)
It was understood that everybody was to pay his own expenses. (听说各人付各人的钱。)(义务)
Let me know everything that I am to know without delay. (我需要知道的事赶快都告诉我吧。)(义务)
She asked him what she was to do. (她问他看她要做点什么。)(义务)
If he were to come, say that I am absent. (他来了,只说我不在家。)(假设)
Certain skills must be learned if one is to use English effectively. (如果想要有效地使用英语,某些技巧是必须学会的。)(假设)
If it is to be done at all, do it well. (如果一定要做的话,就好好地做吧。)(假设)
This house is to be let or sold. (这房子要出租或出售。)(目的)
Not an instant is to be lost. (一秒钟也不要浪费。)(目的)
And the augurs were as clever as are politicians, who also must practise divination, if ever they are to do anything worth the name. (D. H. Lawrence)(现代的政治家也和古代的占兆家一样,不得不实行占兆,如果他们想要做点名副其实的事情的话,所以古代的占兆家也和现代的政治家一样聪明。)(目的)
He was to blame for not locking the door. (没有锁门是他的过错。)(结果)
Am I to understand that you have engaged yourself to this young gentleman? (Shaw)(你是说你已经和这个青年男士订了婚吗?)(结果)
The Prince of Wales has been touring the worldwide dominions of which, some day, he is to be the crown head. (H. G. Wells)(将来命定要做英国领土之王的皇太子,去周游了遍及全世界的领土回来了。)(运命)
The worst is still to come. (还有最坏的要来。)(运命)

1. If you are to understand this strange, rather sad story, you must have an impression at least of the background—the smashed dreary city of Vienna divided up in zones among the four Powers. (G. Greene)

2. The President of the University is to give a speech at the convivial meeting.

3. "I am all astonishment. How long has she been such a favourite? —and pray, when am I to wish you joy?" (Jane Austen)

(55) have + 不定词 + 宾语
have + 宾语 + 不定词

(a) I *have to spend much money*.
我非花许多钱不可。
(b) I *have much money to spend*.
我有许多钱可花。

英文的"have to do"和"have...to do"两种形式,在意味上不一定有区别,大都是同义的,如 I have to write a composition. 和 I have a composition to write. 两句都是作"我非做一篇作文不可。"解,意即 I must write a composition. 但 COD(《简明牛津字典》)的编者特别举出意义不同的例句来证明二者是可能有不同解释的:

(a) I had to do my work.
(b) I had my work to do.

(a)句中的"had to"注明为"be obliged"(不得不,必须)之意。(b)句中的"had to"注明为"be burdened with"(使负担)之意。

美国的 Fries 在他著的 *American English Grammar* 一书中(169页),也举例加以分别:

> Speeches may be broadly divided into two kinds. There is the speech a man makes which he *has something to say*, and the speech he endeavours to make when he *has to say something*. (演说可大别为两类。一类是一个人有话想说的时候而去发表的演说,另一类是他并没有打算说话,而临时被迫演说,只好努力去找些话来说以应付过去。)

他这说法是不错的,我还可以举出日常的用例:

(a) I have something to tell you. (我有话跟你说。)
(b) I have to tell you something. (我必须告诉你一件事。)

可知"have + 宾语"的作"有"解,"have + 不定词"的作"必须"解,但一般的用法二者的分别并不太明显(not always very well marked)。

I have three miles to walk. (有三里路要走。)意为非走不可,无车代步。不能说 I have to walk three miles. 因为并非有走三里路的必要,而是因为路程长达三里的意思。

Whom have I to complain of but myself? (Milton)(我除了自己以外,还能向谁抱怨呢?)
I have only to blame myself. = I have only myself to blame. (我只怪自己。)
As a matter of fact, he's having to sell his house. (事实上,他现在非把房子卖掉不可。)

He has several letters to write. (他有几封信要写。)

He has nothing to eat. (他没有东西吃。)

I have a knife to sharpen my pencil with. (我有削铅笔的小刀。)

The weather has to be good; otherwise, we'll postpone it. (一定要好天气,否则,我们就延期。)

Do I have to go to bed now, mother? (妈,我就要去睡吗?)

Wake them all up, if you have to, but find that paper! (没有办法的时候,只好把他们全部叫醒,那文件无论如何要找出来!)

My doctor says I haven't to (=mustn't) eat meat, but I don't have to (=needn't) take his advice if I don't want to. (医生说我不可以吃肉,不过如果我不想听他的话,我就不一定要服从他。) don't have to 或说 haven't got to 也是一样。

He has to get through work before eight. (八点钟以前他必须把工作做完。)

Everything had to have his approval. (一切都得由他批准。)

You don't have to decide this matter at once. (你不用马上决定。)

1. Some authors write because they have to tell a story rather than they have a story to tell. (Anthony Trollope)
2. I played away a month on account of illness, so I had to work hard to make up for lost time.
3. She has never expressed an opinion, and the inference was that she had no opinion to express.
4. We have some miles to drive, even from the small station.

(56) prevent + 宾语 + from + 动名词

Illness *prevented him from going* there.
他因为生病未能去那里。

英文说的"prevent a person from doing something",意即"hinder him so that he cannot do it",可译作"阻止去做"或"使不能做",是指妨碍一个人去做什么事说的。这个"from"是表示"分离"的。动词"prevent"有时改用"hinder","deter","keep","stop"等字也是一样,如用"restrain"则为"抑制",若用"prohibit"则为"禁止",用法相同,都是后接"from"加动名词或名词的,不过如用与"prohibit"同义的"forbid"时,用法就不同了。在动词"forbid"后不能接介词"from",而要接不定词,才符合英文的惯用法。如"他父亲禁止他抽烟"一句话,译成英文时,用"prohibit"则说 His father prohibited him from smoking. 用"forbid"则说 His father forbade him to smoke. 这两个动词意义虽同,用法上也略有分别:"forbid"指直接或私人下的命令,或定下办法来禁止,并希望他人遵循,而"prohibit"则指当局制定正式规章,如政府的立法禁止之类,并有强迫执行之意,如 Smoking is prohibited in theatres. (戏院中奉令禁止吸烟。) Swimming in the reservoir is prohibited. (禁止在贮水池中游泳。)

This is only to prevent him from going abroad. (这只有妨碍他出洋的。)

He could not keep from the use of tobacco. (他未能停止吸烟。)

What prevented you from coming last night? (昨夜你为何没有来?)

Urgent business prevented me from calling on you. (因有要事,以致未能奉访。)

Bad weather prevented us from starting. = We could not start because of bad weather. (因为天气不好,所以没有能够动身。)

We must prevent the trouble (from) spreading. (我们必须阻止纷争扩大。)

Please refrain from smoking. (请免吸烟。)

Failure in the examination should not deter you from trying again. (这次考试落第,不应妨碍你再试的勇气。)

Tired as I was—exhausted, in fact—I was prevented from sleeping by the pain in my knee. (Jack London) (我虽则疲劳,实际上是筋疲力竭了,我因膝痛未能入眠。)

If he would only keep from bad company, he might yet do well. (只要他不要再交结坏朋友,他还是可以变好的。)

Her lips were set together almost as if she was pinching them tight to prevent words or sounds (from) coming out. (Gaskell) (她的嘴唇为着不让语言或声音出来,几乎好像夹紧了一样完全闭着。)

A man can never be hindered from thinking whatever he chooses so long as he conceals what he thinks. (一个人只要他不把心里所想的事说出来,他高兴怎样想就怎样想,是谁也不能阻止他的。)

1. Society does not in any age prevent a man from being what he can be (= become).
2. If you apply the principles of efficiency to your work, nothing can stop you from achieving your ambitions.

(57) persuade + 宾语 + into + 动名词
dissuade + 宾语 + from + 动名词

(a) I *persuaded him into doing* so.
    我劝说他才这样做的。
(b) I *dissuaded him from doing* so.
    我劝阻他才不这样做的。

某种他动词的后面接"into doing"时,便产生肯定的意思;接"from doing"时,便产生否定的意思。前者的"into"表他动词的"结果",后者的"from"表"制止","抑制"。后面不用动名词而改用名词也可以,如 I dissuaded her from her folly. (我劝她少做蠢事。)他动词"persuade"是劝人去做一件事,而"dissuade"则是劝人不要去做一件事,所以劝告成功,便是去做了(into doing),或是不做了(from doing)。普通在"persuade"后又常接用不定词以代替动名词,如不说 I have persuaded him into doing it. 而改说 I have persuaded him to do it. 也是一样。但反对字的"dissuade"后便一定要接动名词,不可以接不定词,即是我们只能说 I should dissuade you from going. 不可以说 I should dissuade you to go. 不过这个"from"有时也可换用"out of"或"against",如 I tried my best to reason him out of his fears, but it was all in vain. (我尽力劝他不要怕,但毫无效果。) They dissuade people against going to China.（他们劝人不要到中国去。）

The father dissuaded his son from leaving school.（父亲劝他的儿子不要中途辍学。）
He was persuaded into doing it against his own wish.（他被劝服去做他违心的事。）
They dissuaded her from going on the stage.（他们劝她不要去演戏。）
The priests of the old religions used to persuade the people to do all hurt to the Christians.（古宗教的僧人们老是劝说人们对基督徒加以种种危害。）
I could not persuade her to (= into) my way of thinking.（我不能说服他依从我的想法。）
I have convinced her that she needs a holiday, but cannot persuade her to take one.（我已使她相信她需要度假，但不能说服她真去。）
I knew I should study, but he persuaded me to go to the movies.（我知道应该读书，但他劝诱我去看电影。）

1. I honour the man who can neither be bribed nor frightened into doing wrong.
2. Literature serves a human animal struggling to persuade the universal Sphinx to propose a more intelligible riddle. (Santayana)

V. 不定词的造句

(58) 表目的、原因、结果等的不定词

(a) I went *to see* him off.
　　我去送了他的行。
(b) I am glad *to see* you.
　　见到你我真高兴。
(c) He worked only *to fail*.
　　他努力终归失败。

在"动词的造句"中，我们已经涉及一些不定词的用法，但那是以动词为主，不定词只是附属而已。现另辟专栏来研讨不定词的一些特别用法。就不定词而论，最复杂而又最难辨别的，就是它的副词用法。那可以用来表"目的"，"原因"，"结果"，"理由"，"条件"，"让步"等等，一不当心，就会译错。上举(a)例所示，凡用于不表感情的动词之后的不定词，便是表示"目的"的。(b)例中用于表示感情的形容词或自动词之后的不定词，则是表示"原因"的。(c)例中用于无意志动词之后的不定词，便是表示"结果"的，在"only"或"never"后的不定词，多属此类。现将各种副词用法，分别举例说明如下：

We eat to live, (but do) not live to eat.（我们为生而食，不是为食而生。）(目的)

The boy rushed his home work through and went out to play. (那男孩急急忙忙把作业做好,出外玩去了。)(目的)

They are selling red feathers to raise money for crippled children. (他们在卖红羽毛为残废儿童筹募基金。)(目的)

She wept to see him in this condition. (看到他这个样子她不禁哭了。)(原因)

They were delighted to learn of the arrival of our baby. (他们听说我们生了孩子大为高兴。)(原因)

She was hurt to find that no one admired her performance. (她发觉谁也不赏识她的演奏颇为伤心。)(原因)

He awoke to find (= and found) himself famous. (他一觉醒来发现自己出名了。)(结果)

Few live to be a hundred. (活到百岁的人无几。)(结果)

I little thought then that I left it (= the house), never to return. (Dickens)(在当时简直没有想到我离开那个家就再不会回去了。)(结果)

She will grow up to be a fine woman. (她会长成一个漂亮女人的。)(结果)

It is discouraging to tell the truth only to find that we are not believed. (我们说的真话,结果却无人相信,未免使人气馁。)(结果)

One day Mr. Nelson disappeared from town, never to be seen again. (有一天芮先生在城里不见了,以后再没有人看到他。)(结果)

He must be a fool to say so. (说这样的话,他真傻呀。)(理由)

He must have studied hard to have succeeded so splendidly. (他如此高中,一定是很用过功来的。)(理由)

What a fool I was to have expected him to help me! (指望他会帮我的忙,我多么傻。)(理由)

They must be crazy to let him drive their car. He hasn't got a driver's licence. (他没有开车的执照,他们竟糊涂地让他去驾驶他们的车子。)(理由)

To hear you sing, people might take you for a girl. (听你唱歌,人们会以为你是女子。)(条件)

I should be glad for Mary to go. (Curme)(玛丽要能去的话,我真高兴。)(条件)

To look at her you'd never guess she was a university lecturer. (看她的样子你决想不到她原是大学的讲师。)(条件)

You would have done better to have made up with them. (你要跟他们和解了的话,就更好了。)(条件)

To do his best, he could not finish it in a week. (即令尽他的力量去做,一个礼拜也做不好。)(让步)

1. They were shocked to see the state of the bell-rope.

2. I come to bury Caesar, not to praise him. (Shakespeare)

3. He did not live to enjoy the fruits of what he had done.

4. We rushed through it only to find ourselves back again in prison.

5. If modern individuals and modern nations pursue again these crazy competitions, without regard for the dignity of human life, we shall live to see ten millions perish for every million who perished in the war.

6. Many a young person has felt that life was not worth living after a broken love-affair, only to discover a few years later that happiness was waiting, after all.

(59) so as + 不定词
so...as + 不定词

(a) We started early *so as to get* there before noon.

我们为要在正午以前赶到那里,所以很早就动身了。

(b) We started *so* early *as to get* there before noon.

我们因为很早动身,所以在正午以前就到达那里了。

在(a)例中将"so as (not) to do"连用,与用子句的"so that + may"一样,是表示"目的"的,意为"为着(不)要"。如 We started early so as to get there in time. = We started early, so that we might get there in time.(我们早早动身,俾可及时赶到那里。)至于在(b)例中把"so...as to"分开来用,便产生出"结果"之意,表示因果关系,有时也可表"程度",等于用子句的"so...that",可译作"因为…所以",如 We started so early as to get there in time. = We started so early that we got there in time.(我们早早动身,以致及时到达了那里。)表"程度"的如 He was so angry as to be unable to speak. = He was so angry that he could not speak.(他大为生气,连话都说不出来了。)

Come early so as to get a good seat. (= Come early, so that you may get a good seat. = Come early in order to get a good seat.)(早点来可以占到好位子。)

She walked softly so as not to make any noise. (= She walked softly that she might not make any noise. = She walked softly in order not to make any noise.)(她轻移莲步,不使出声。)

Houses should be built so as to admit plenty of light as well as of fresh air. (建筑家屋应使空气流通,阳光直射。)

Books are now so cheap as to be within the reach of almost every one. (书籍现在非常的便宜,几乎任何人都能购读。)

Something fresh and green was springing forth so as to be ready for the summer. (为准备好以便迎接夏季,新绿正在迸发。)

He listened attentively so as not to miss a single word. (他不想漏掉一个字,所以很用心地听了。)

He went so far as to say that she was a liar. (他甚至说她是撒谎。)

In those days ships were sometimes so delayed by contrary wind as to run short of fresh water and provisions. (当时船因遇到逆风而迟误,以致发生淡水和食粮不足的现象。)

Without, the storm drove so fast as to create a snow-mist in the kitchen. (Hardy)(外面暴风雪吹得很急,以致在厨房中造成沉沉的雪雾。)

1. Before we start to investigate that, let us try to realize what we do know, so as to make the most of it, and to separate the essential from the accidental. (Doyle)

2. Vegetables are not produced so abundantly as to suffiee for the wants of the whole country.

(60) too... + 不定词

not too... + 不定词

too... not + 不定词

(a) She is *too* angry *to speak*.
　　她愤怒得说不出话来。

(b) He is *not too* old *to do* it.
　　他不是老人，那个他是可以做的。

(c) He is *too* angry *not to say* it.
　　他在盛怒之下，不免要说出这样的话来。

这三个句子中的不定词，都是表示"限定"的。在(a)句中的"too... to do"，是以不定词来修饰前面的"too"字，因而这个不定词就含有否定的意思在内，可译作"太…而不能"，用英文解释则为 She is so angry that she cannot speak.（她如此愤怒以致不能说出话来。）但是这个表现法如果在前面加上一个"not"的字样，如(b)例所示，便是把(a)句加以否定，意即"并不太…所以能做"，但这个否定的"not"，如果不是加在"too"之前，而是加在不定词的"to do"之前，如(c)例所示，那就是把原有的否定打消了，原为"不能说"变为"不是不能说"也就是"可能说"了。这个"not"是修饰不定词的，以英文解释时便是 He is so angry that he cannot but say it.（他是那般愤怒而忍不住要说出那样的话来。）

The news is too good to be true.（消息太好，恐不可靠。）

The flower is too beautiful to last.（花太美难经久。）

I was too excited to speak.（我兴奋得说不出话来了。）

English is not too difficult to learn.（英文并不太难学。）

The expression is well known to many students of French, but it is far too good not to be requoted here.（这句话是学法文的学生都知道的，不过实在说得太好，这儿不免要再度引用一下。）

This coffee is too hot (for me) to drink.（咖啡太烫我不能喝。）

His income is too small to support his family.（收入微薄无法养家。）

The light was too dim to be used for close work.（灯光太弱不能做细工。）

The change which these years have brought about is too remarkable to be passed over without being noticed, too weighty in its lesson not to be laid to heart.（近年来所发生的变化是极为显著而不容有所忽视，在得到的教训上极为沉痛而不容吾人不深为铭记。）

Elliott was too clever not to see that many of the persons who accepted his invitations did so only to get a free meal and that of these some were stupid and some worthless. (W. S. Maugham)（艾略特是聪明的人必然看得出来，大多数接受他的邀请的人，只是为着要来吃一顿不花钱的饭，他知道他们当中有些是愚笨的，另外有些却是不足轻重的。）

He is too much of a man of the world not to know better. (像他那样精通世故的人,当无做此事的道理。)

1. It is flattering to believe that their thoughts are too profound to be expressed so clearly that all who run may read, and very naturally it does not occur to such writers that the fault is with their own minds which have not the faculty of precise reflection. (Maugham)

2. If we were not too proud to explain ourselves or to ask explanations of others, most of the misunderstandings of life would disappear. (A. G. Gardiner)

3. I had read too many novels and had learned too much at school not to know a good deal about love, but I thought it was a matter hat only concerned young people I could not conceive that a man with a beard, who had sons as old as I, could have any feelings of that sort. (Maugham)

(61) only too... +不定词
too ready +不定词

(a) I am *only too* glad *to do* so.
我非常高兴去做。

(b) She is *too ready* to speak.
她真是爱说话。

凡在"not","only","all","but"等字后面的"too",其句中的不定词是没有否定意义的。"only too"意为"very"或"exceedingly"。这是从字面上来看的说法,如果从构造上来看,不定词如系修饰"too"后面的字,而非修饰"too"时,也不含否定的意思。这种句中的不定词是修饰"too"后面的"ready"一类的字的,也可以说"too"是修饰"ready to speak"的,所以(b)例 She is too ready to speak. = She is too talkative. 这类句子在"too"后常用的字除"ready"以外,还有"apt","eager","easy","inclined","willing"等字。

You know but too well to hold your tongue. (你深知少说的好。)
They are all too satisfied to take the opinions of others without the pain of thought for themselves. (他们都太满意于接受别人的意见,自己懒得去想。)
I shall be only too pleased to do my best in that line of work. (我很高兴尽力于那方面的工作。)
I am only too delighted to accept it. (我很高兴接受那个事情。)
He is too ready to promise. (他轻诺。)
He is too ready to suspect. (他易疑。)
She is too ready to talk. (她多言。)
We are too apt to overlook our own faults. (我们很容易忽视自己的过错。)
People are too apt to do so. (人们常要这样做。)
They are too apt to keep their inferiors at a distance. (他们常要对部下抱敬远态度。)

Beginners are too apt to make mistakes. （初学者容易弄错。）

The political freedom we have today will never be too easy to preserve. （我们今日所有的政治上的自由,是决不容易维持长久的。）

1. I soon perceived that she possessed in combination the qualities which in all other persons whom I had known I had been only too happy to find singly. （J. S. Mill）

2. Philosophers have been too ready to suppose that question of fact can be settled by verbal considerations.

(62) 不定词的感叹用法

To think that he has become a minister!
想不到他居然当了部长。

不定词单独用时往往有感叹的意思,最普通的形式为"To think that..."和"To go..."在这种不定词的前面,可看做是省略了 I am astonished to think that... 或 What a foolish thing it is to go... 或 It surprises me... 等字样。上举的例句前面,即可加上 How astonishing it is 的字样来解释。如译为"真是出乎意外"或"真想不到"时,便可传出原意。这种省略句中所用的不定词（Infinitives in Elliptical Constructions）,都是表示感叹的,其主语为说话的人。例如诗人 Robert Browning 的名句：O to be in England now that April's there! (= Oh how happy I should be, were I in England now that April is there.)（今正值英伦四月,我要在那里就好呀!）有时可将不定词的"to"略去,如 She talk to him! （她跟他说话！〔那是不可能的。〕）

To think that in just a few days we'll be parting! （想不到只有几天我们就要分别了。）

I to marry before my brother, and leave him with none to take care of him! （Blackmore）（要我比哥哥先结婚,而让他失去照顾,那怎使得！）

A gentleman to come to that. （一个上等人竟下流到这样的程度。）

To treat in such a manner the friend of his father! （竟这样对待他父亲的朋友。）

To think that he should fail me in this crisis! （在这危机中想不到他竟一点也不帮我。）

To think that neither of his children should come to help! （试想他的孩子竟然一个也不来帮忙。）

O to have lived (= O how I wish I had lived) in the brave days of old! （啊！但愿我曾生活在从前那样美好的日子里。）

1. To come to sneaking things like that! It's upset me frightfully. （Galsworthy）

2. Foolish fellow! To suppose that he could be pardoned.

3. To think that you, of all persons, should say so!

(63) not to speak of
not to say

(a) He knows Latin, *not to speak of* English.

他懂得拉丁文,英文自不待言。

(b) He knows Latin, *not to say* English.

姑且不说英文,拉丁文他也懂得。

这是不定词的独立用法,两个说法形似而义不同,不可混淆。"not to speak of" = without even speaking of; to say nothing of; not to mention; as well as; in addition. 意即"自不待言","更不必说","犹其余事","何况"等。至于"not to say" = one might almost say; if not. 意为"姑且不说","即不说","姑置不论","甚至","虽未到那种程度","若非"等。

He cannot afford the ordinary comforts of life, not to speak of luxuries. (他连日常生活的舒服都负担不起,哪里还谈得上奢侈。)
Japan is noted for Mt. Fuji, not to speak of its cherry blossoms. (日本樱花出名自不待言,富士山也有名于世。)
The scholar is well versed in Greek and Latin, not to speak of English which is his mother tongue. (那学者精通希腊、拉丁语,他的母语英文更无论了。)
The painter is a little singular, not to say grotesque. (那画家虽不能说是古怪,也可算奇特的了。)
He is very good-natured, not to say foolish. (他老实得几乎有点愚笨。)
He is extremely frugal, not to say stingy. (不说他吝啬也罢,至少他是极其节俭的。)
He is dishonest, to say nothing of his other faults. (他不正直,其余的坏处更不必说了。)
She is a good housekeeper, not to speak of being a good cook. (她不但是一个做菜的能手,而且也很会治家。)
He raised quite large and salable crops of hay and oats, to say nothing of his own vegetables and fruit. (T. Dreiser)(他自己用的蔬菜水果固不待言,他还培植了许多可销售的大量干草和燕麦。)
His speech was very eloquent last night, to say nothing of its having been significant. (昨晚他的演说意味深长自不待言,而且极为动听。)
He is a graduate student, but he cannot speak English, not to mention (= to say nothing of) French. (他是研究所的学生,但法文固不必讲了,连英文都不会说。)
We're too busy to take a long vacation this year, not to mention the fact that we can't afford it. (出外度一个长的假期费用太大自不待言,而时间上也无此余裕。)

1. If there be plenty of traffic, the railway is able to make transportation very economical, not to speak of its regularity, ease, and rapidity.

2. As a matter of fact, all great discoverers worthy of the name have at one time or another been regarded as dreamers, not to say mad.

Ⅵ. 动名词的造句

(64) There is no + 动名词

There is no knowing what may happen.
未来的事无法知道。

这句惯用语法,意为"不可能",或"未可逆料"。There is no doing. = It is impossible to do. = We cannot do. 在动名词后,常接以疑问词开头的子句。Charlotte Brontë 说的 There was no possibility of taking a walk that day.(那天是不可能出去散步的。)也属于这一类的句法。另外有一种句式:"There is no use(或 good) + 动名词",就和"There is no + 动名词"大不相同,如 Oscar Wilde 说的 There's no use staying on.(用不着再呆下去。)这可能是"It is no use + 动名词"的变形,如 There is no good telling any more about it. 改为 It is no good telling any more about it. 似乎更好,因为谚语原是 It is no use crying over spilt milk.(覆水难收。)又有人说正规的表现法在动名词前应该有一个介词,如 Charles Dickens 说的 There is no use in talking.(用不着说。)至于 There is no use our coming here. 一句,也可以在"our coming"前加上一个介词的"in"字。

There is no denying this.(这个无可否认。)
There is no accounting for tastes.(嗜好各有不同,是无法说明的。)
There is no telling what will happen.(Curme)(未来的事未可逆料。)
There is no getting along with him.(id.)(跟他是无法相处的。)
There is no saying how long the war is going to last.(战争还要继续多久是未知数。)
There's no telling when he will arrive.(不晓得他何时到达。)
There is no knowing when we shall meet again.(后会无期。)
There is no going out in this snow-storm.(在这样的大风雪中,是不可能外出的。)*Cf*. It is impossible (for us) to go out in this snow-storm.

1. There was no saying how he might behave upon these occasions.
2. There is no knowing when one's house may come tumbling down about one's ears.
3. He had always been excitable, but now he was beside himself; there was no reasoning with him.

(65) for + the + 动名词

You can have it *for the asking*.
那个你只消索取即可得到。

这个"for + the + 动名词"的形式,意为"for the mere act of doing",或是"if one only + 现在动词",可译作"只消","只要"。句中的"for"有时可换用"with",如 Things which perish with the using. 只要索取即可得到,当然是免费的,所以"for the asking" = for nothing(免费;不取分文)。

It is yours for the asking. (你要就送你。)
It may be had for the asking. (免费奉送。)
You may have it for the asking. (你要就拿去。)
The choicest gold is to be had for the digging. (最上等的黄金只要挖掘就可以得到。)
A lass that may be had for the asking. (Scott) (一个女孩只要你要就是你的。)
Remarkable facts were to be had for the picking up. (T. H. Huxley) (很显著的事实俯拾皆是。)

1. If an individual was not satisfied with his calling or his salary, he could obtain a farm for the asking and begin a new industrial life. (F. W. Blackmar)
2. Who would be satisfied with the success which may be had for the wishing?

(66) above + 动名词

He is not *above asking* questions.
他不耻下问。

一个人为自尊心或道义感而不屑于去做某种事情,英文就说"be above doing",可译为"不屑为","决不肯做","耻于去做"。这个"above"意为"超过……的范围",有时后面接名词也是一样,如 He is above reproach. (他是无可责难的。)

He is above telling a lie. (他不是一个肯说谎话的人。)
Poor as he was, he was above selling his country at any price. (他虽穷苦,无论给他多少钱,他也不肯出卖祖国。)

1. Any one who would profit by experience will never be above asking help.
2. National spirit should be so high as to make a strong power to be above bullying a weak one.

(67) worth + 动名词

Whatever is *worth doing* at all is *worth doing* well.
任何值得做的事,就值得做好。

在"worth"这个形容词后,惯用法要接一个宾语,而这个宾语又通常是动名词构成的。如 This book is worth reading.(此书值得一读。)句中的"reading"是 Active 的形式而含义却是 Passive。本来动名词是没有被动语态的,常以主动语态来表示被动的意思,如说 The garden wants weeding.(花园需要清除杂草。)实为"being weeded"之意,即被人清除杂草。本例说的"worth reading",亦复含有"worth being read"之意,但习惯上不这样说,而把这个被动的形式,让给另外一个同义的形容词"worthy"去专用。故"此书值得一读"可译成下列两种形式:

  This book is worth reading.
  This book is worthy of being read.

这个"worth + 动名词"又可变为"worth-while + 动名词"或"worth one's while + 动名词",不过意义上微有不同罢了。说"worth doing"意为"值得去做",说"worth(one's)while doing"意为"值得花时间去做",例如 It is not worth-while your doing.(这不值得你费神去做。)The museum is worth seeing.(这博物馆值得看。)又 worth-while 在叙述用法时应分为二字,如 All this fussing is hardly worth while.(这一切的大惊小怪是值不得的。)普通常用的形式是"worth doing"或"worthwhile to do",虽则说"worthwhile doing"也不为错。

  It is worthwhile to read this book.
  It is worthwhile reading this book.

以上二句从文句的构造上看,"to read this book"和"reading this book",同样是句中真正的主语,"it"不过是形式上的主语而已。但是如果我们说 It is worth discussing the question further. 就是错误的,因为句中的"it"是形式上的主语,真正的主语应为"discussing the question further"而"worth"的宾语落空了。这变成 Discussing the question further is worth. 所以不通。应改为 The question is worth discussing further. 或 It is worth while to discuss the question further 后一种改正法:"to discuss the question further"与"it"为同格,而"worth"则有"while"一字作为它的宾语。

又我们只能说 Is today's film worth seeing? 不能说 Is today's film worth to see? 因为"worth"后必须接动名词或名词,如 It is not worth a penny.(一文不值。)只有在"worthy"后才可以接不定词,如 He is worthy to lead.(他能做领袖。)

现代英语说的"worth doing",在稍古的用法中则说"worth the doing",例如 The conversation are worth the remembering or recording.(Thackeray)Everything that made a hard life worth the living.(Kipling)Any success you may achieve is not worth the having unless you fight for it. 最后一例中的"worth the having"实为"worth the act of having"加强的说法。

  Venice has many places worth visiting.(威尼斯有许多值得去游玩的地方。)
  It is worth your while to go and see them.(你值得花些时间去游览。)
  A book which is worth reading at all is likely to be read more than once.(一本果真值得我们去读的书,就值

得多读几遍。)

This is worth saying. = To say this is worth while. = It is worth while to say this. (这话值得说。)

He ought to spend his time on some worthwhlie reading. (他应该花时间去读些值得读的书籍。)

This book is worthwhile reading. (这书值得花时间去读。)

It isn't worthwhile going there now. (现在要去那里却是浪费时间。)

1. Nothing worth having can be had without labour.

2. It is far better to do well a bit of work which is well worth doing than to have a large fortune.

(68) far from + 动名词

The noise, *far from abating*, continued to increase.

那声音不但丝毫未停止,反而增大了。

英文说的"far from",意为"not at all",加重时说"so far from"。这成语中的"far",原是表示距离的,转而成为比喻的用法,具有"远未","绝非"之意。有时在"from"后接上一个形容词,也可视为省去了动名词"being"的说法,例如 He is far from happy. 即"from being happy"之略。此外"from"后接名词或代名词,也是常有的事,如 It is far from the truth. (远非真实。) a house far from the town. (远离城市的屋子。)还有成语的"far from it"(决无其事;一点也不),也就是英文"not in the least"的意思。例如:"Mr. Dickson, you say, is not, strictly speaking, handsome!" "Handsome! Oh no; far from it. ——certainly plain". (Jane Austen) ("你说狄克逊先生,严格地讲并不漂亮!""漂亮!啊,不,一点也不——他确是长得很平凡的呀。")最后说的是"其貌不扬"的婉说法。

Far from reading the letter, he did not open it. (哪里谈得上看信,他拆都没有拆开。)

It was far from being good. (一点也不好。)

I am far from blaming him. = I do not blame him at all. (我一点也不怪他。)

His explanation is far from (being) satisfactory. (他的说明决不能令人满意。)

He was a good worker at school and far from stupid. (他在学校时很用功,决不愚笨。)

The room was far from comfortable. (这房间一点也不舒服。)

It's far from well. (= not at all well; a long way from being well.) (这个一点也不好。)

He is far from well. (他一点也不健康。)

His style is far from perfect. (一点都不完善。)

I am far from content. (决非满意。)

1. So far from repenting of his error, he glories in it.

2. Indeed, so far from poverty being a misfortune, it may, by vigorous self-help, be converted even into a blessing.

（69）busy + 动名词

He is *busy preparing* for the examination.
他忙于准备考试。

这个"busy + 动名词"的形式，应视为"busy in doing"的省略，在《牛津大辞典》上也说"busy in doing"的 modern use 便是"busy doing"，所以 He is busy writing letters. 可以说是 He is busy in writing letters. 的现代英语的形式。在形容词"busy"之后只能接动名词，不可以接不定词，即不可以说 He is busy to prepare for the examination. 但可以说 He is too busy to prepare for the examination.

He is busy writing a report.（他忙于写报告。）
The German was busy in washing his hands.（Bulwer）（那德国人忙着洗手。）
Nanny has been busy ironing this evening.（G. Eliot）（南妮今晚一直在忙着烫衣。）
Farmers are busy working in the fields.（农人在田里忙于工作。）
I found him busy packing his trunk.（我看见他正忙于收拾行李。）
Ruth was busy at her desk correcting test papers.（Caldwell）（鲁仕正在桌上忙着批改试卷。）

1. He was then so tremendously busy handling piles of desk work.
2. Mr. A is busy (in) canvassing for the Conservative candidate.

（70）on + 动名词
in + 动名词

(a) *On reaching* Hongkong, I went to see him.
　　一到香港我就去看他了。
(b) *In walking* downtown, I met him.
　　在闹市走着时我遇到了他。

在这用法中的介词"on"有"as soon as"或"when"的意思，而"in"则有"when"或"while"的意思。这种句子如果把动名词前的介词略去，使之由动名词构造（Gerundive Construction）变成分词构造（Participial Construction），即说成 Reaching Hongkong, I went to see him. 及 Walking downtown, I met him. 意思也还是一样，并无任何不同。如果一定要加以区别的话，动名词构造对于时间的观念表现较强而已。现在的倾向，动名词构造比较要占优势些。

On seeing me (= When he saw me) he escaped.（他一见到我就逃走了。）

On entering (= When we entered) his room, we at once perceived that he was a man of taste. (一走进他的房间,我们立刻就看出他是一个趣味丰富的人。)

On arriving (= On his arrival) in Singapore, he received a visit from a college professor. (一到新加坡他就接受了一位大学教授的访问。)

In talking (= When we talk) about imagination we invariably talk of the poet. (谈到想像时我们一定就会谈及诗人的。)

There's no point in doing that. (那样做毫无意义。)

Am I right in thinking that a nuclear war will never happen? (核子战争永不会发生,我这样想对吗?)

He found an outlet for his anger in kicking the dog. (他拿狗来出气。)

They decided on building a theatre. (他们决定建造一座戏院。)

He is intent on pleasing people. (他只想讨好别人。)

He is engaged in collecting stamps. (他从事集邮。)

In making a dictionary he displays a special skill. (编字典他有特殊技能。)

Come, there's no use in crying like that. (Carroll) (喂,那样的大哭大叫也没有用呀。)

I have spent my life in finding that out. (Galsworthy) (我为要找出那个来,花了一生的工夫。)

He was so long in answering a salutation. (Galsworthy) (他没有马上回礼。)

He was drowned in crossing the water. (他渡河时淹死了。)

In crossing (= While I was crossing) the Lozere I had come among new natural features. (Stevenson) (渡过泸哲尔河时,我来到新的自然美景之中了。)

1. We should not be too hasty in condemning all compromise as bad morals.
2. On reaching home we found she had given us up after searching a little while. (Hardy)

VII. 否定词的造句

(71) no more... than

You can *no more* swim *than* I can fly.

你不能游泳跟我不能飞行一样。

这种表现法是为加强"than"前的否定而用的。在"than"以后的文句,表面上看去虽有肯定的形式,然其含义仍属否定。此点在翻译时应特别注意,以免译错。句中的"no more"可换用"not any more",普通是没有什么不同的,意为"not... just as... not"。又"no more than"不可和"not more than"混同,因后者意为"至多"(at most)。

这个作"同样"解的"no more... than"的基本用法是表示普通的比较,如 He has no more money than you have. (他的钱和你一样多。)不过另外还有三种特殊用法,是颇难翻译的。

(1) 为著名的 whale pattern:

A whale is no more a fish than a horse is. (= A whale is not a fish any more than a horse.) (鲸之

非鱼犹马之非鱼也。)马之非鱼显而易见,鲸之非鱼亦同于马。用以将后半句与前半句一同打消,以后者的不可能,来打消前者的可能性。

(2)成语中的"no"不是修饰"more",而是修饰后面的名词的,其"than"也不是连词,而是介词。

"Than whom", said Dupin, "no more sagacious agent could, I suppose, be desired, or even imagined."(E. A. Poe)(别指望有比此人更聪明的侦探,连想都不要想。)

句中的"no"就是修饰"agent"的,改写过一下,便成为 no agent more sagacious than whom 了。在"than"后只有单字无子句,故非连词而为介词。

(3)为"no more than" = only(不过,仅,只),如:

He has no more than $10 = He has only ten dollars. (他只有十块钱。)

He is no more than a puppet. (他只不过是一个傀儡。)

No more than three days = only three days. (只有三天。)

上举的用法(1),可译为"与…同样不是…","跟…一样不是…"(= as little as),如 He is no more a god than we are. (他和我们一样都不是神。)比较:

(a) I am no more mad than (= as little mad as) you are.

(我和你一样并没有发狂。)

(b) I am not more mad than (= not so mad as) you are.

(我发狂没有发得你那样厉害。)

There is no more dependence to be placed on his words than there is on the wind. (= Just as we cannot depend on the wind, so we cannot depend on his words.)(其言之不可信赖,也像风之不足信赖一样。)

It is not easy to give away money any more than it is to make money. (用钱不容易,正如赚钱不容易一样。)

He could no more bear the noise of a child than he could fly. (他决受不了小孩的吵闹。)

There is no more dangerous experiment than that of trying to appear what one is not. (在人前装模作样,是比什么还要危险的尝试了。)

The jest about her (a wife) being able to say no more about his (a husband) occupation than "he is something in the City" is not entirely an absurdity. (P. Carr: *The English Are Like That*)(关于丈夫的职业,妻子只好说"他是金融界的一位大亨",那样的笑话,也不能完全说是荒谬。)

A home without love is no more a home than a body without a soul is a man. (正像没有灵魂的身体不成其为人一样,没有爱情的家庭也不成其为家庭。)

A man has no more right to say an uncivil thing than to act one. (一个人无权说无理的事,就像无权做无理的事一样。)

The gospel of making a fortune is no more true than what I tell you. (你们所说的致富之道跟我讲的一样是靠不住的。)

He cannot effect the impossible any more than we can. (他不能做不可能的事也跟我一样。) "effect" 意为"实现"。

He was no more than skin and bone, was partly paralysed, and wore spectacles of such unusual power, that his eyes appeared through the glasses greatly magnified and distorted in shape. (R. L. Stevenson)(他只剩下皮包骨了,半身不遂,因为戴着非常深度的眼镜,所以在那镜子后面的眼睛,看去扩大得多,而且变了样子。)

1. But Judith did not want or intend to forget John. She could no more have considered marrying another man than she could have accepted some strange new God thrust suddenly upon her. (K. Winsor)
2. Doris gave no sign of good looks, her nose was too long and her figure was lumpy; so that Mrs Garstin could hope no more for her than that she should marry a young man who was well off and in a suitable profession. (W. S. Maugham)
3. John was eight years older than she and for many years he paid her scanty attention, though he took it for granted that eventually they would marry; the betrothal papers had been signed while he was yet a child and Judith no more than a baby. (K. Winsor)

(72) no less...than

A whale is *no less* a mammal *than* a horse is.
鲸是哺乳动物,和马是哺乳动物一样。

这是和前项正相反的一个表现法。在"no more...than"的场合,连词"than"前后都是否定,而在"no less...than"的场合,则连词"than"前后都是肯定。用减少的否定词以加强肯定的意思。可译作"不逊于","不弱于"。在普通的比较级,"no less than" = as many (much) as; just,例如 He owns no less than (= as many as) ten houses. (他拥有的房子达十幢之多。) There were no less than fifty killed and wounded. (死伤达五十人。) 但特别用法的 "no less...than" = quite as...as,例如 She is no less beautiful than her sister. (她美不逊于她的姊姊。) 意即其美正复相等。

比较:(a) The number of the students is not less than (= at least) 1,000. (学生人数至少有一千人。)

(b) The number of the students is no less than (= as many as) 1,000. (学生人数多达一千人。)

(a) He has not less (= perhaps more) than $100 in his pocket. (他口袋里至少有一百元,也许不止此数。)

(b) He has no less than $100 in his pocket. (他口袋里竟有一百元,可算相当多了。)

连用的"no less than" = as many as, as much as, exactly,据 ALD 上说是"expressing surprise at the amount,例如 He won no less than $5,000 in the lottery. 或 He won $5,000, no less, in lottery. (他中了五千元之多。)

比较:(a) He gave me no less than (= as much as) $100.

(b) He gave me no more than (= only) $100.

分开的"no less...than" = quite as...as; the very,具有两个意思:(1)不逊于,如 She is no less (quite as) beautiful than (as) her sister. (貌美不逊其姊。)(2) 不外是，如 He is no less a person than the king. (他正是国王其人。)就等于说 He is the very king.

He was no less a person than the President. (= He was a person no other than the President.)(他正是总统其人。)

The writer is no less a personage than a prince. (那作家的名望正如一个王子。)"no less... than" = of as high a station or rank as, exactly, the very. 意为"身家相若"，"权位相等"，"恰好"，"正是"。

Our soldiers fought with no less daring than skill. (= Their daring equalled their skill.)(我们的军人战斗既勇敢而又熟练。)

Sunlight is no less necessary than fresh air to a healthy condition of body. (日光和新鲜空气同样对身体的健康情形是有必要的。)

He is no less guilty than you. (他和你同样有罪。)

As regards our foreign policy, it is no less our interest than our duty to maintain the most friendly relations with other countries. (关于我国的对外政策，维持和别国的友好关系，是我们的义务，同样地也是我们的利益。)

We hope to invite no less a person than an assistant professor. (我们希望聘请一位助教授阶级的人。)

In Japan he is famous already, a personality no less in the public eye than the Crown Prince or the slugging first baseman of the Tokyo Giants. (在日本他早出了名，在一般人的眼中，他简直像皇太子或是东京巨人队棒球的第一垒击球手一样的名人。)

1. Want of care will not less ruin the good man than the man of lax morals.
2. The technique of writing is no less difficult than that of the other arts and yet, because he can read and write a letter, there is a notion that anyone can write well enough to write a book. (Maugham)

(73) not so much... as
not so much as

(a) His success is *not so much* by talent *as* by energy.
他的成功与其说是由于才能毋宁说是由于精力。

(b) He did *not so much as* turn his face.
他连头也没有回一下。

英文说的"not so much... as" = rather than，其中的"as"有时可以换用"but rather"，可译为"与其说是…毋宁说是"。而"not so much as" = without (或 not) even，可译为"甚至…都没有"，其中的"not"有时可以换用"without"。

The oceans do not so much divide the world as unite it. (与其说陆以洋分，毋宁说陆以洋合。)

He is not so much a scholar as a writer.（与其说他是学者，不如说他是作家。）

The farmer looks wealthy, but he has not so much wealth as people at large think.（那农夫看上去很有钱的样子，但没有一般世人所想象的那样有钱。）

Success in life does not depend so much on one's school record as on one's honesty and diligence.（事业的成功并不靠在学校时的成绩，而要靠为人的诚实和勤勉。）

She is a society woman, but strange to say, she cannot so much as (= even) write her own name.（她是一个社交妇女，但说也奇怪，她甚至连自己的名字都不会写。）

He went away without so much as saying good-bye.（他甚至不辞而去。）

He did not so much as punish one of the murderers, nor did he show the least tenderness to the survivors. (Macaulay)（对于那些杀人犯他甚至一点也没有处罚他们，而对于那些生存者他也没有表示一点亲切。）

Law, in its true notion, is not so much the limitation as the direction of a free and intelligent man to his proper interest.（法律真正的意义，是要把一个自由而有理性的人，导向正当的利益上去，而不是对此加以限制的。）

The window was so narrow that one could not so much as get one's head through.（那窗子小得连头都伸不出去。）

There is nothing in the world that I like so much as music.（世界上再没有别的东西比音乐更要使我爱好的了。）

The great use of a school education is not so much to teach you things as to teach you the art of learning.（学校教育最大的效用，不在教你一些知识，而在教你学习的方法。）

1. It is not men's faults that ruin them so much as the manner in which they conduct themselves after the faults have been committed.

2. The policeman walked through the crowd without so much as turning his face to either side.

3. It is not so much the hours that tell as the way we use them. (Sir J. Lubbock)

(74) Nothing is more...than
Nothing is so...as

(a) *Nothing is more* precious *than* time.
   没有什么比光阴更可贵的东西了。

(b) *Nothing is so* precious *as* time.
   像光阴那样可贵的东西再没有了。

英文形容词的比较，虽有寻常级（positive degree），比较级（comparative degree），最高级（superlative degree）三种不同的形式，但无论是平等的比较或高一级的比较，都可以用来表出最高级比较的意思，例如 He is *as* sympathetic a man *as* ever breathed. = He is *more* sympathetic *than* any other man that ever breathed. = He is *the most* sympathetic man that ever breathed. 第一句为 positive，第二句为 comparative，第三句为 superlative，而全都表出同样的意思来，都可以用"最"字来翻译。"Nothing is more...than"和"Nothing is so...as"两种表现法，都具有最高级比较的意思。句中

"nothing"一字,可换用其他的否定字如"no","nobody","nowhere","little","few","handly","scarcely"等等,"as...as"的否定形通常是"not so...as".

No one is so foolish as to believe that anything happens by chance.(谁也不会愚笨到相信世间有什么偶然发生的事。)

To my mind nothing is more horrible than a hydrogen bomb in the world.(我觉得世间没有什么比氢弹更可怕的了)。

No complaint is more common than that of a scarcity of money.(最普通的抱怨就是说钱不够用。)

Nothing sounds more ridiculous (than this).(没有比这说得更荒谬的了。)

Nothing can be more attractive to the eye.(没有比这更好看的东西了。)

Nothing is more valuable than health.(没有比健康更可宝贵的东西。)

No other animal is so large as a whale.(没有比鲸更大的动物。)

1. Scarcely any part of the world affords so great a variety in so small an area as our own island.
2. Nothing is so uncivil as the habit of smoking in the streetcar.
3. Nothing is more important for the student who loves literature than to become intimately acquainted with great critics.

(75) cannot...too

We *cannot* thank him *too* much.
我们无论怎样感谢他也不为过。

英文说的"cannot...too",意为"it is impossible to overdo...",或"no matter how much more you do,you will never overdo it",或"the more,the better"(无论怎样也不为过)。其中的"can"表可能性,"too"有"over-"之意,可换用"enough"或"sufficient"等字样。不用"not"而用其他的否定字,如"hardly","scarcely"等也是可以的。下列六句意思完全一样:

You cannot be too careful.
You cannot be over careful.
You cannot be careful enough.
You cannot be sufficiently careful.
You cannot take enough care.
You cannot take sufficient care.

下面的句子也相仿佛:

I cannot see enough of him.
We cannot recommend this book too strongly.

We cannot exaggerate his attainments.

This point cannot be over-emphasized.

You cannot be too careful in crossing the street. (过街越当心越好。)

You cannot begin the practice too early. (练习开始得越早越好。)

Good manners cannot be too much valued. (礼貌是值得尽量尊重的。)

This introduces a fact of an importance that cannot be overstressed. (这介绍我们一个事实,其重要性无论怎样强调都不为过。)

That which is good cannot be done too soon. (好事做得越快越好。)

The importance of scientific study cannot be overvalued. (研究科学的重要,估价决不会太高。)

It is impossible to speak in terms of too high praise of his merits. (他的功绩无论怎样赞扬也不为过。)

I cannot be too grateful for his kindness. (对于他的帮忙,无论怎样感谢也不为过。)

1. A man who has received a kindness cannot be too grateful for it.

2. The importance of reading aloud, and of rewriting again and again can hardly be overestimated.

3. A book may be compared to your neighbor; if it be good, it cannot last too long; if bad, you cannot get rid of it too early.

(76) 否定 + without

You *cannot* speak *without* moving your lips.

你不动嘴唇便不能说话。

通常的情形是两个否定构成肯定,但翻译时最好还是保留否定的语气,实比肯定更要强而有力。这种双重否定的用法,变化颇多,分别举例以见一斑。大抵皆可译为"每…必","无…不"。

One cannot succeed without perseverance. (人无毅力不能成事。)

You cannot make omelettes without breaking eggs. (不事耕耘,焉得收获。不打破蛋就不能做煎蛋卷。)

He cannot speak English without making mistakes. (He cannot but make mistakes when he speaks English.) (他说英语每说必错。)

One cannot look at Emerson's picture without feeling that he was not only wise but good. (看到艾默生画像的人,没有不感觉到他的贤明与善良的。)

They never meet without quarrelling. (= They never fail to quarrel when they meet.) (他们每次见面必要吵架。)

It never rains without pouring. (= It never rains but it pours.) (祸不单行。不雨则已,雨必滂沱。)

No one can read it without crying. (无人读此而不下泪。)

No pleasure without pain. (有乐必有苦。)

No gains without pains. (无不劳而获者。)

No roses without thorns. (凡物必有缺憾。)

No one should ever go to London without seeing some of his wonderful creations. (没有一个人到伦敦不去看看他那令人惊奇的几幅油画的。)

Not a day passed without their meeting. (他们无日不相见。)

In India , not a year passes without a number of people falling victims to the ferocity of the tiger. (印度每年必有多人死于虎患。)

1. Just as we cannot understand Chinese literature without any knowledge of the works of Confucius, so all students of English should know something about the English Bible.

2. We cannot pick up even an ordinary book, a magazine or a newspaper without finding in it references to the Bible and quotations from its pages.

(77) 否定 + but

There is *no* rule *but* has exceptions.

条条规则都有例外。

在否定字或准否定字的后面,所有的"but",都是具有"which not","who not","that not"等否定意义的关系代名词或连词,因而构成前后的双重否定,可译成"没有…不是"。上例又可说成 The exception proves the rule.

There is no one but hopes to be rich. (没有人不想发财。)

There is no one but knows that. (无人不知。)

There is scarcely a man but has his weak side. (人皆有缺点。)

There is nothing in the world but teaches us some good lesson. (世界上的一切都能给我们好的教训。)

No leader worthy of the name ever existed but was an optimist. (值得做首领的人都是乐观主义者。)

It was impossible but he should see it. (他一定看到那个的。)

No man is so old but he may learn. (没有老到不能学习的人。)

I never think of summer but I think (= without thinking) of my school days. (想到夏天就想到我的学生时代。)

It never rains but it pours. (祸不单行。破屋又遭连夜雨。)

She would have fallen but that I caught her (= if I had not caught her). (如果不是我抓住她,她早已掉下去了。)

Justice was never done but that (= without the result that) someone complained. (即使是公平裁判也还是有人要抱怨的。)

Scarcely a week passes but she writes to her old parents.(差不多每星期她都要写信给她的父母。)

1. There has not been a statesman of eminence but was a man of industry.
2. There was scarcely a family but had at least one relative among the wounded.
3. No two people can be half an hour together but one shall gain an evident superiority over the other.
4. Never a week passes the whole year round but that, in some part of the world, wheat is being reaped for the British market.

(78) 否定 + until(till)

The value of health is *not* esteemed *until* it is lost.
人要到失去了健康,才知道健康的可贵。

在否定字如"no","not","never","little","few","seldom"等的后面所接用的"until"或"till",与其照字面译为"直到…为止,…不",不如译为"要…才…",把否定译成肯定,才合乎中文的语法。

Nobody knows what he can do till be has tried.(任何人都要试一试,才知道他能做什么。)
He will not come till eight o'clock.(他要八点钟才来。)
He didn't arrive until the meal was over.(他到饭后才来。)
Man in general does not appreciate what he has until he loses it.(一般人要等到失去他的所有才知珍惜。)
I am afraid I cannot finish the work till Friday.(我恐怕要到星期五才能做完。)
He didn't go abroad till he graduated from college.(他到大学毕业后才出洋深造。)
It was not till yesterday that I got the news.(直到昨天我才听到那个消息。)
Do not start till I give the word.(等我下命令才出发。)

1. Some take no thought of money until they come to an end of it, and many do the same with their time.
2. True friendship is like health, the value of it is seldom known until it is lost.
3. The central fact of biology, evolution, was not established until modern science had been in existence for over two hundred years.

(79) not so... but
not such a... but

(a) He is *not so* sick *but* he can come to school.
他并没有病到不能上学。

(b) He is *not such a* fool *but* he knows it.

他并不是连那个都不知道的傻子。

这和(77)项的"否定+but"相似,不过那个"but"多半是关系代名词,而本项中的"but",就是含有"that...not"意味的连词。把句中这个"but"改写为"that...not",和前面的"so"或"such"连起来,即成为"so...that"或"such...that"的形式,更可以看出是表程度的了。又"but"有时可说成"but that"或"but what",意思还是一样,有"without the fact that"(除去那事实外)之意。这个"but"是不对等连词,作用和"that"相似。"否定+so+but"的形式,和"however+may"相同,如 There is nothing so hard but it becomes easy by practice. = However hard anything may be, it becomes easy by practice. 意为"无论怎样…也不是不能"。

There is not such a fool but that he can see it. (没有愚笨到连这个都不懂的人。)
No man is so foolish but he may give another good counsel sometimes. (无论怎样愚笨的人有时也能给别人好的忠告。)
His income is not so small but he can support his family. (他的收入无论怎样少也能维持他一家的生活。)
The current was not so strong but he could swim against it. (激流并未强到他不能逆泳的程度。)
The streets were not so crowded but our car could go through. (街上并不是拥挤得不能通车。)
It was not such a cold night but we could go out. (那天夜里并不是寒冷得不能外出。)
No man is so old but (that) he may learn. (没有人老到不能学习的。)

1. There is nothing so strong but it is in danger from what is weak.
2. The material destruction of the war not so great but that it could by this time have been repaired, had a good peace been made without delay.

(80) not A but B
B, (and) not A

(a) He excels *not* in English, *but* in mathematics.
他擅长的不是英文,而是数学。

(b) He excels in mathematics, *and not* in English.
他长于数学,而非英文。

这是将否定和肯定并举的句法,先说否定须接用"but",先说肯定则接用"and",不过有时也可以将"and"略去不说。

He has in mind not a particular class of readers but men and women in general. (他心中所指望的,不是一个

特殊阶级的读者,而是一般的男女。)
　　He has in mind men and women in general, not a particular class of readers. (他心中所指望的,是一般的男女,而不是一个特殊阶级的读者。)
　　He is not my son, but my nephew. (他不是我的儿子,而是我的侄儿。)
　　He is my nephew, (and) not my son. (他是我的侄儿,不是我的儿子。)
　　The most important thing in the Olympic Games is not to win but to take part. (奥林匹克运动会最要紧的不是优胜而是参加。)
　　It is not work, but overwork, that is hurtful; and it is not hard work that is injurious so much as unwilling work. (有害的不是工作而是过度工作;辛劳的工作并没有不愿意的工作那样有害于健康。)

1. The end of law is not to abolish or restrain, but to preserve and enlarge freedom.
2. It is the monotony of their minds, not of their surroundings, that is chiefly responsible for their weariness.

(81) 否定 + because

　　Don't give up *because* it is difficult.
　　不要因为困难就放弃呀。

　　连词"because"在肯定句中是对主句(main clause)全体说的,如 I was fatigued because I had sat up all night. (我因通宵未眠而感疲惫。)至于在否定句中,则不是指主句全体,而是指句中的一个字,如例句中的"difficult"一字。但"because"与否定同用时,常会发生两种不同的含义,例如:

　　(a) I didn't go because I was afraid.
　　　　= (1) I didn't go, and the reason was fear.
　　　　　　(我怕所以我没有去。)
　　　　= (2) I went, but the reason was not fear.
　　　　　　(我不是因为怕才去的。)而是因为别的原因。
　　(b) I did not marry her because I loved her.
　　　　(1) 我不是因为爱她才和她结婚的。
　　　　(2) 我因为爱她才不和她结婚。

　　如果连词"because"是用作"though"解时,就比较好译,因为译成"因为"或是译成"虽则",都不算错。

　　You should not despise a man because he is poor. (不要因为别人穷就轻蔑他。)或译(虽则他穷你也不应该轻蔑他。)
　　We should not look down upon the man because he is out of employment. (我们不要因为那人失业就瞧不起他。)

Don't be vain because you are good-looking. (不要因为你长得漂亮就虚荣起来。虽则你长得漂亮也不要虚荣。)

He cannot go to school because he is sick. (他因生病不能上学。)

I did not go out because it rained. (我因为下雨没有出门。)

I will not do that because it would be of no avail. (因为没有用我不要做它。)

The seed does not complain because there are stones and turf in its way. (种子并不因为有石头和草皮挡住它的路而抱不平。)

1. He has no reason to think less of himself because he is not dressed in a rich and fashionable manner.
2. Because a lad does not happen to be strong, it does not necessarily follow that a sea-life would not suit him.

(82) not because... but because

A mountain is *not* famous *because* it is high, *but because* it has some spirit dwelling in it.

山不在高,有仙则名。

英文的"not because... but because"可译为"不是因为…而是因为"。这个"because"可用为连词,后接用子句,也可用为副词,后接用片语,如上举例句中的"because"是连词,下例中的"because"便是副词：The ship was delayed not because of the war, but because of a snow-storm. (船的延误非因战争乃因风雪。)

I recommend her not because she is beautiful, but because she has a talent for music. (我推荐她并不是因为她美,而是因为她有音乐天才。)

A mountain is not valuable because it is high, but because it has trees. (山并不因高而有价值,而是因为有树木才贵重的。)

Some women do not buy their new dresses because they like them, but because they do not like to be behind the fashion. (有些女人买新衣并不是因为她们喜欢,而是因为她们不愿落在时髦的后面。)

Religions succeed not because they are true, but because they provide what people want. (宗教的成功并不是因为它们是真理,而是因为它们供给人们所需要的东西。)

1. He is good, not because of any virtue, but because he is too much of a coward to be bad.
2. The difference in your bonus is not because of your efficiency but because of your long absence.

(83) not that... but that

Not that I loved Caesar less, *but that* I loved Rome more.

我并非因爱凯撒浅,而是因爱罗马深。

这个"not that...but that"中的"that"= because,全句可补"it is"来解释,意即 It is not because I loved Caesar less, but because I loved Rome more. 这个"it"实具有"the reason"(其理由为)或"what I mean"(我想说的是)的意思。又"but"后的"that"有时可以省去。这种没有主句(principal clause)的表现法,原是用"not"一字来代表主句的一种省略说法,可解释为 I do not mean that I loved Caesar less, but that I loved Rome more.

Not that I dislike the work, but that I have no time to do it for the time being. (不是因为我不喜欢那工作,而是因为我眼下没时间去做。)

It is not that I am unwilling but that I have no time. (不是因我不愿,而是因没时间。)

No, thank you. I don't want any more, not that I don't like them, but I am just full and cannot eat anything more. (谢谢你,我不要了。我不能再吃了,并不是因为我不喜欢吃,而是因为我吃得太饱,什么也吃不下了。)

Not that I don't want to help you, but that it's beyond my power to do so. (并非我不帮忙,实力有未逮。)

Not that I like a dog but that I dislike a cat. (并不是因为我喜欢狗,只是因为我不喜欢猫。)

1. Our boast is not that we have more ideas, but that our ideas are better sounder.
2. We want to get into good society not that we may have it, but that we may be seen in it, and our notion of its goodness depends primarily on its conspicuousness.
3. If I accidentally had my attention drawn to the fact that some other boy knew less than myself, I concluded, not that I knew much, but that he, for some reason or other, knew little.

(84) 否定 + every(all, both, always, quite)

(a) I do *not* know *every* one of them.
　　我不全认识他们。

(b) *All* that glitters is *not* gold.
　　发光的东西未必都是黄金。

(c) The rich are *not always* happy.
　　富人未必常是幸福的。

不定代名词(the indefinite pronoun)的"every","all","both",以及副词的"always","quite",与否定结合时,不是全部否定(total negation),而是部分否定(partial negation),意即不是"全不是",而是"不全是"。注意"not all"与"not at all"(全部否定)的不同。例如 Both (of them) are not my brothers. = One is not my brother, but the other is. 意即"他们两个当中,只有一个是我的兄弟"。如果要说两个都不是的话,英文应说 Neither (of them) is my brother.

试比较下面三句的含义：

  I know both of them. (他们两人我全认识。)
  I do not know both of them. (他们两人我只认识其中一个。)
  I do not know either of them. (他们两人我全不认识。)

换上"all"一字，也是同样的情形：

  I know all of them. (他们我全认识。)
  I do not know all of them. (他们我不全认识。)
  I do not know any of them. (他们我全不认识。)

由以上的例子看来，我们知道"both"是部分否定，而"either"，"neither"才是全部否定；"all"，"every"是部分否定，而"no"，"any"，"none"等字才是全部否定。

  All that glitters is not gold. (发光的东西未必都是黄金。)
  None (Nothing) that glitters is gold. (发光的东西都不是黄金。)
  Every man cannot be a poet. (不是人人可作诗人。)
  No man can be a poet. (无人可作诗人。)

  You can't fool all the people all the time. (你未必能够老是愚弄所有的人。)
  He is not always so sad. (他并不是经常这样悲伤的。)
  Somehow the old house is not quite what it should be. (Charles Lamb) (不晓得怎样的，那老屋并不十分合乎理想。)
  He did not read every book in his library. (他并没有把他图书室所有的书全部读完。)
  Every man is not polite, and all are not born gentleman. (不见得人人都懂礼貌，而所有的人未见得都是生来的君子。)
  We did not see all the pictures, for it needs many visits to do so properly. (我们并没有看完所有的画，要规规矩矩全部看完必须去参观好多次才可以。)
  Every man cannot be rich, but every man can be a gentleman. (不见得人人都能致富，但人人都能成为君子。)
  Opportunities come to all, but all are not ready for them when they come. (机会是均等的，人人都有，但不见得人人都能准备好去接受它，当机会到来的时候。)
  The biographies of scientists are not always good literature, but they have immense educational value. (科学家的传记并不见得是好的文学作品，但它们都有很大的教育价值。)

  1. All great truths are obvious truths. But not all obvious truths are great truths. (A. Huxley)
  2. As play was forbidden on Sunday, this seemed to me a not quite intolerable way of passing the time away. (Lynd)

Ⅷ. what, who 的造句

(85) what he is
what he has

We honour him for *what he is*, not for *what he has*.
我们尊敬的是他的人品而不是他的财富。

这个"what"是关系代名词,"what" = that which,意为"所","者","…的事物"。"what he is" = his character,是说"他现在的状态",即"他现在的人品(personal character)",或"他所具有的学识品德"。如用过去动词说"what he was"则为"他当时的状态",也就是"他当时的人品"。"he is"可换为"you are"或"I am"等,用法也是一样。至于"what he has" = his property,则意为"他所有的",也就是"他的财产"。

It is not a question how much a man knows, but what use he can make of what he knows; not a question of what he has acquired, and how he has been trained, but of what he is, and what he can do. (问题不在一个人知道多少,而在他能否运用他的知识;问题不在他所学为何,受过怎样的教育,而在他的人品以及他的能力。)

He has made what I am. (我之有今日是他所赐予的。)

Coal and iron have made England what she is. (英国之有今日是由于煤与铁的赐予。)

A man's dignity depends not on what he has but on what he is. (一个人的高贵,不在于他的财富,而在于他的人品。)

What a man is contributes much more to his happiness than what he has. (一个人的品德比他的财富更能够使他幸福。)

1. He is rich or poor according to what he is, not according to what he has. He is rich who values a good name above gold.

2. Half the unhappiness in the world is caused by losing the blessing which would result from the enjoyment of what we have in envying others and longing for what they have.

(86) what + 名词
what little + 名词

(a) He gave me *what money* he had about him.
他把他身上所有的钱都给我了。

(b) I gave him *what little money* I had.
我竭尽绵薄将我仅有的钱都给他了。

这个"what+名词"的形式有"all the...that"或"that...which"的意思,可译作"所有的都"或"所",是将"what"用作关系代名词的。"what money" = all the money that. 在这种"what"后常带有"little","few"一类的形容词,含有"虽少但全都"或"所仅有的"之意。"little"用于数不清的名词上,"few"用于数得清的名词上。

I will use what influence I have with the minister in your behalf. (我当竭尽绵力为君向部长推荐。)
I will lend you what books I can spare. (我所不用的书虽为数不多可悉数借给你。)
He does not read many books, but what books he reads, he reads very carefully. (他读书不多,然所读少数的书皆读得很仔细。)
I have come to render what service is in my power. (我特来为你效一点能力所及的微劳。)
He saves what little he earns. (他储蓄仅有的一点收入。)
She saved what little money she could out of her slim salary to help her brother go to school. (她从她微薄的薪水中留出钱来送她弟弟上学。)
She waited with what patience she could command. (她竭力忍耐在等待。)
The leaves were trembling with what little breeze there was. (微风吹动木叶。)

1. What crops survived the long drought perished in the subsequent inundation. (Brinkley)
2. I shall tell you how in such a situation I acquired what little ability I may be supposed to have in that way. (Franklin)
3. One of the saddest sights is that of a young man who has sacrificed what little health and constitution he had for a college course.

(87) what with... and what with
what by... and what by

(a) *What with* illness *and what with* losses, he is almost ruined.
  半因生病,半因亏损,他几乎整个毁了。
(b) *What by* bribes *and what by* extortions, he made money.
  或由受贿,或由勒索,他发了财。

这是"what"的副词用法,可译作"多少","半","或"(somewhat; partly)。当"what"与"with"结合时,表"原因",与"by"结合时表"手段"或"方法"。普通是在一句中重复地用,但也有把第二次要用的略去不说。

What with teaching and what with writing, my time is wholly taken up. (或因授课,或因写作,以致全无

暇暑。)

What with his studies and what with his sports, the school-boy has no time left for idle thoughts. (半以功课,半以运动,使学生无暇胡思乱想。)

What by policy and what by force, the English made themselves masters of all India in 1876. (英人在1876年用策略或用兵力征服了整个印度。)

What with drink and (what with) fright he did not know much about the facts. (半由酒醉,半由恐怖,他对于那真相知道得很少。)

What with the wind and (what with) the rain, our walk was spoiled. (风风雨雨使得我们的散步全遭破坏。)

What with overwork and under-nourishment he fell ill. (由于过劳,加上营养不足,他终于病倒了。)

Young people cannot be expected to read, what with automobiles, sports and television. (有了汽车、运动和电视,我们还能指望青年人读什么书。)

1. In less than a minute the storm was upon us —in less than two the sky was entirely overcast and what with this and the driving spray, it became suddenly so dark that we could not see each other in the fishing boat.

2. What by threats and what by entreaties, he finally accomplished his purpose.

3. What with tending the sick and wounded and making sandbags, sometimes turning out as many as four dozens of them in a day, her time was fully occupied.

(88) what is + 比较级

It's a good book, and *what is more*, it's quite a cheap one.
这是一本好书,而且,价钱又很便宜。

用在句首的"what"多半有名词的作用,但用在插入句中,则变成带有副词的作用了。如插入句中用为独立语句的"what is more" = moreover; besides, 作"而且"或"更有进者"解。比较级偶也可换用最上级。

We were overtaken by the night on the way, and what was (still) worse, it began to rain. (我们还在路上天就黑了,还有更糟糕的,天又下起雨来了。)

He is a good scholar, and what is better, a good teacher. (他是一个优秀的学者,而且,还是一个优秀的教师。)

She is good-looking, rich, and, what is the best of all, clever. (她美而富,而最了不得的是,她又聪明。)

The rules must be few, and, what is more important, comprehensive. (规则宜简,更重要的在能包括。)

And, what makes the matter worse, he has taken to drinking. (而更糟的是他又喝起酒来了。)

What's more, he was not a very pleasant person. (加之,他又不是一个愉快的人。)

1. Hard work, moreover, tends not only to give us rest for the body, but what is even more important, peace to the mind.

2. Thus the young man of promise broke not only all the promises he had made to himself and others, but, what was worse than all, the heart of his aged father also.

(89) A is to B what X is to Y

The man who cannot be trusted is to society what a bit of rotten timber is to a house.
不能信赖的人对于社会，正如朽木对于家屋一样。

在这种造句中的"what"是一个关系代名词，从文法上来看，这个 what-Clause 是"A is"的补语，即 A is what (= that which) X is to Y to B. 或用括弧把"to B"括开，则更明白，即 A is (to B) what X is to Y. 又"what"放在第一个名词子句的头上也是可以的。又不用动词"be"而改用别的动词如"stand"也未尝不可。介词"to"有时也可换用别的介词如"for"等。句中的 what-Clause 既放在句首，则可再用一个"that"在后来子句的头上，例见后面的〔类例〕中。

What the blueprint is to the builder the outline is to the writer. (作家对于写作的轮廓，就像建筑师对于蓝图一样。)
What the leaves are to the forest,/That to the world are children. (Longfellow) (木叶对于森林，正像小孩对于世界一样。)
Air is to us what water is to fish. (空气对于我们犹水之于鱼。)

1. What Newton was to mechanics and Darwin to biology, Freud was to psychology.
2. He crooked his knee and foot so as to caress the quadruped in a nerve under the angle of the jaw, the stimulation of which... is for a dog what a good cigar is for a man. (G. K. Chesterton)

(90) who + 肯定
who + 否定

(a) *Who can* rely on such a man as to tell a lie?
谁能信任这样一个撒谎的人？(谁也不能信任)
(b) *Who cannot* rely on such an honest man?
谁不能信任这样一个正直的人？(谁都能信任)

这种句子虽有问句的形式，但并不是要问什么，只是加强语气而已。这原是反语的表现法，在文法上就称为修辞的疑问句。因为不是普通的问话，所以不要作答。(a)例"who + 肯定"就等于加强语气来表示"nobody + 肯定"的意思。(b)例"who + 否定"即"everybody + 肯定"的加强说法。在"who"之外还可换用其他的疑问词如"what"，"when"，"where"，"how"等等。

Who knows (= Nobody knows) what will happen tomorrow? (谁晓得明天会发生什么事?)
Where will I not go with you? (和你在一起天涯海角我都要去。)
Who does not love his country? (谁不爱自己的国家?)
Why should you be surprised? (= You should not be surprised at all.) (你用不着惊奇。)
Who shall decide when doctors disagree? (Pope) (学者意见不一致时无人能决定。)
Don't stand as if you were afraid; who is the wiser? (不要怕，谁也不知道的。)
Who does not hope to be good? (人谁不想做好?)
Why can't we kiss and be friends? (Maugham) (我们为什么不能相吻为友呢?)

1. Who wishes to employ anyone who has not enough self-respect?
2. What would I not give to have such a cow?
3. Where are the snows of yesteryear?

(91) 疑问词 + should...but

Who should fail *but* that man?
除那人外还有谁会失败呢?

英文的"疑问词 + should...but"的形式，表示过去的意外的事，是一种反语的说法，意为"none...but"，可译作"岂料"，如上例可意译为"想不到失败了的竟是他"。凡"who"，"why"，"how"等疑问词接上"should"时，都可以表示"意外"，"不可解"，"惊讶"等。

Who should write it but himself? (除他本人以外还有谁会写呢?)
Who should come in but the very man? (进来的正是那人。)
The door opens, and—who should enter but the very man we were talking of? (门开处谁想到走进来的正是我们方才谈论的人。)
Who(m) should I meet but my old friend Tom? (我遇到的原是老朋友托孟。)
Of course he married, and who should be his wife but Barbara? (Dickens) (当然他结婚了，他的妻子是谁呢，就是巴白拉呀。)
Fancy this: last night at about six, who should walk in but Elwin? (Dickens) (试想想：昨夜六时走进来的是谁，竟是艾尔温。)

1. Passing through one of the principal streets, whom should I meet but our cousin to whom you first recommended me? (Goldsmith)

2. This morning he rose very early, and what should he do but take it into his head to wash down the stairs. (Fagazzaro)

(92) Who knows but (that)

Who knows but (*that*) he may go?
他多半会去的。(或者他会去也未可知。)

这表现法照字面解时为"除了他可能去的这件事以外,还有谁知道别的事",是反语的问句,即除此以外别的谁也不知道。反面的说法则为 I do not know but that he may go. 是说谁也不知道那以外的事,意即"除了他可能去以外别的我都不知道"。结果正反两句,意思完全相同,皆可译为"多半"。那"that"可省去,有时也可换用"what"。普通反面的说法用的颇多,"but"在否定后实无任何意义,因为那是从法语转变来的。

Who knows but it may be so? (或者如此,亦未可知。)
I do not doubt (but) that he will succeed. (我确信他必成功。)
I do not deny but that he is diligent. (我不否认他的勤勉。)
He is extremely strong—not but that he will catch a cold at times. (他虽有时感受风寒,然其身体固甚强健。)
He is not such a fool but that he knows it. (他纵下愚犹能知此。)
He is not such a fool but what (＝but that) he can tell a friend from a foe. (彼虽下愚,当不至认敌为友。)

1. Who knows but we may make an agreeable acquaintance with this interesting family? (Hook)
2. Not but what he did his best. (Nesfield)

IX. 条件及让步的造句

(93) 省略 if 的句法

(a) *Were he* alive, what would he say?
他要是还在世的话,他会怎样说呀。

(b) *Had I* been there, I should have said so.
如果我在那里的话,我就会这样说的。

凡有"were"，"had"，"should"，"would"，"could"等〔助〕动词出现在主语前面，而又不是疑问句的时候，便一定是略去了"if"或"though"那种连词，而构成条件或让步的假设语气的造句了。上例"were he"即"If he were"之略；"Had I been"即"If I had been"之略。有时连加重语气的"do"，也可当作普通助动词而同样省略"if"来用。这类句子都可译为"如果…的话"或"即令…"。

Were I rich, I would give you some money. = If I were rich, I would give you some money.（如果我富有的话，我就要给你一些钱的。）

Had you followed her advice, you would have succeeded. = If you had followed her advice,……（如果你听了她的劝告，你就早已成功了。）

Did I see him, I would blame him for it. = If I did see him,……（如果我当时看到了他，我就早已为那件事责备过他了。）

Should he read this book forever, he would not grow wise. = Though he should read this book forever,……（即令他一直不停在读此书，他也不会变得明智的。）

Had I known it, I should have told it to you.（我要知道的话，我早告诉你了。）

They might live quite comfortably were it not for a quarrel with their nextdoor neighbour.（他们如果没有和邻居吵架的话，就会过得很舒服的。）

Had he planted the tree near the road, strangers would have stolen the fruit.（他当时要是把那树种在路边，路人早就盗取果实了。）

Should this vote go (= If this vote should go) against the ministry, it could not carry on the government.（万一这次选举内阁失败的话，现政府就不能继续执政了。）

Many a murderer would have remained innocent had he not possessed (= if he had not possessed) a knife or a gun.（如果当时没有刀枪在手，许多杀人犯都不至犯下大罪了。）

Could he have foreseen (= Even if he could have foreseen) that he was to lose everything, his iron soul must not have been shaken.（如果他预知他会失去一切，他的铁一般的意志就决不会动摇了。）

Had he made an obvious mistake (= Though he had made an obvious mistake), he still refused to admit it.（他虽犯了明显的错误，还是不肯认错。）

以上各例都是假设语气过去及假设语气过去完成，所以动词的时态前后都是一致的，但假设语气现在及假设语气未来，前（条件句）后（归结句）句中动词的时态，就可以不一致了，例如 If this be true（条件句），I am sorry for it.（归结句）。前面的条件句为假设语气现在，后面的归结句为直陈语气现在，前后动词的时态是不一致的。又例如 If it should be true, I shall be very happy. 前面的条件句为假设语气未来，后面的归结句为直陈语气未来，动词时态也不一致。再看下面的类例：

Should the weather be wet (= If the weather should be wet), the meeting will not be held.（如天下雨会议停开。）

Should it rain tomorrow (= If it should rain tomorrow), I shall stay at home.（如果明天下雨，我就呆在家里不出去。）

Should a table stand in the way and unexpectedly cause pain, the child, once recovered from the feeling of surprise, may beat it in anger. (如果有一张桌子妨碍了他,意外地引起痛苦的话,那孩子一旦从惊奇的感觉中恢复过来,他也许就要愤怒地去打击那张桌子的。)

1. Had his abilities been equal to his disposition, he would have made a very good king.
2. Many of the successful men, had they been able to choose for themselves, would have selected some quite different profession from that in which they have made their fortunes.

(94) **If it were not for** (= Were it not for) + 名词
　　If it had not been for (= Had it not been for) + 名词
　　But for + 名词
　　But that + 名词子句

(a) *If it were not for his help*, I should fail.
(b) *If it had not been for his help*, I should have failed.
(c) *But for his help*, I should fail (have failed).
(d) *But that he helps*, I should fail.
　　如果不是他帮忙的话,我就失败了。

这些都是表条件的句子,四句具有同样的意思,但造句法各有不同。(a)句是假设过去,(b)句是假设过去完成,(c)句是上举二者的省略说法,可用作假设过去,也可用作假设过去完成,(d)句后面接名词子句,采用现在时态的动词,但它所表达的意思,却是假设过去。如果条件句是表假设过去完成时,后面主句中的动词当然也可改为过去时态了。(c)句的"but for"有"except because of"的意思。

I would go by steamer but that I am a poor sailor. (假设过去)(我要不是因为晕船,我就坐船去了。)"but that I am" = if I were not.

We should have arrived earlier but that we met with an accident. (= if we had not met with an accident.)(假设过去完成)(我们如果不是途中遭遇事故,我们就早早到达了。)

But for (= Had it not been for) you, I should have been ruined. (如果不是你帮忙,我早已毁了。)

But for (= If it were not for) human selfishness, all might prosper. (如果不是人类的自私,一切就繁荣了。)

All would go well if it were not for losses and want of work. (如果不是损失和失业的话,一切就好了。)

But for his personal example of courage, the battle would have been lost. (如果不是他个人以身作则,勇猛向前的话,恐怕早战败了。)

I should have married her, but that it pleased her father to refuse me. (如果不是她父亲反对这门亲事的话,我早就和她结婚了。)

But that I saw it, I could not have believed it. (我要不是亲眼看见的话,我是不相信的。)

I should think it summer still, but that I see the lanes yellow-purfled with flowers of autumn. (Gissing)(如果不是我看见小路上饰满了秋天的黄花,我还以为仍是夏天呢。)

But for the thick trees, the bitter wind would blow the house to pieces. (如果不是那丛密的树木挡住,强风就会把屋子吹成碎片的。)

But for an unexpected emergency, I could have paid him a visit. (如果不是意外发生的紧急事件,我早已去拜访过他了。)

If it were not for the immense income derived from advertising newspapers could not be sold so cheaply. (如果不是在广告上有莫大的收入,报纸就不能卖得这样便宜的。)

I do not know what I should do for relaxation, were it not for the innumerable detective stories. (如果没有那无数的侦探小说,我真不晓得要怎样消遣。)

What a delightful parent my father would have been, had it not been for his strictness. (如果不是那样的严厉,我父亲就是一个非常令人愉快的人了。)

1. Birds are good friends to man. If it were not for them the world would be overrun with insects.
2. Freedom might have come later in India and in a different form if it had not been for Gandhi.
3. People who have pleasant homes get indoor enjoyments that they would never think of but for the rain.
4. But that he came to my rescue then, I should certainly have died.

(95) 命令句 + and
命令句 + or

(a) *Work* hard, *and* you will succeed.
努力工作,那么,你将成功。

(b) *Work* hard, *or* you will fail.
努力工作,否则,你将失败。

英文的"命令句 + and"等于"if";"命令句 + or"等于"if not"。这合句的前后句为顺意时,就用"and"作连词,如前后句为逆意时,就用"or"作连词。(a)句既有"if"之意,用中文解说,便是"如果那样就会(成功)",(b)句既有"if not"之意,中文可说"如果不是那样,就会(失败)"。所以(a)句改为复句时便是 If you work hard, you will succeed. 而(b)句改为复句时,便是 If you do not work hard, you will fail. 又(a)句中的"and",有时可以略去。这种(a)型的造句,后句中的动词如果用了过去时态的话,前句的命令就变成条件了,用例见下。

Give him an inch, and (= if you give……) he'll take an ell. (得寸进尺。)

Let a man be once a beggar, and he will be a beggar for life. (讨过饭的人永远想讨饭。)

Talk of the devil, and he'll appear. (说到曹操,曹操便到。)

Scratch a Russian, and yon will find a Tartar. (文明人剥去一层皮,就变成野蛮人了。)

Sit back and rest, and you will feel much better. (坐着休息一下就好了。)

Keep away from those high tension wires, or you'll be electrocuted. (不要靠近那高压线,否则你会触电的。)

Write it down, or you'll forget it. (写下来以免忘记。)

Give him time, and he was generally equal to the demands of suburban customers. (如果给他以时间,他大概就可以答应郊区顾客的要求了。)

Hurry or interrupt him, and he showed himself anything but the man for a crisis. (Gissing)(时间太仓促或者对他说话加以阻挠的话,他就会显示出他不是一个能应付危机的人。)

Try and calm yourself, and your mind will be easy again. (镇静一点,你的心就可安定下来。)

Ask a European critic to name the two leading American poets, and in most cases he will reply, "Poe and Whitman". (要一个欧洲的批评家提名两个美国一流诗人的话,他多半会回答,爱伦·坡与惠特曼。)

1. Let a man learn as early as possible honestly to confess his ignorance, and he will be a gainer by it in the long run.

2. Take away from Shakespeare all his bits of natural description, all his casual allusions to the life and aspects of the country, and what a loss were there!

3. Don't go too close to him, or you will be found fault with.

(96) 名词 + and

A few *minutes*, *and* they went away.

再过几分钟,他们就走了。

这种"名词 + and" = 副词子句。因为它可改为由"if"、"when"、"after"等开头的副词子句,如上例的 A few minutes and = When a few minutes had passed. 上项讲过的"命令句 + and",是和这个相类似的造句,因为把命令句中的动词略去,只留下名词时,就成为现在讲的这种句法了。

One more effort, and we shall succeed. (= If we make one more effort, we shall succeed.)(再努力一下,我们就会成功的。)

One foot nearer, and you are a deadman. (再靠近一步,你就没有命了。)

Another month and I'll be ordering you off! (再过一个月,我就会把你赶走的。)

A few minutes more, and he lay sound asleep. (再几分钟他就睡熟了。)

Another half hour, and all the doors would be locked. (再过半个钟头,所有的门都要上锁了。)

A word, and he would lose his temper. (你再说一句他就会生气了。)

A little farther, and (= When they had gone a little farther) they turned off to the left in the direction of an olive orchard. (Wallace)(他们再走得远一点,就要朝着橄榄园的方向左转去了。)

1. A turn of the path and we were in a fairy land, whose existence no one a hundred yards off would have suspected.

2. The bullet lodged in my left shoulder—a little lower, and I should have been in Paradise long ago.

(97) 动词 + 疑问词

Say what you will, I don't like it.
不管你怎么说,那个我总是不喜欢的。

这种"动词 + 疑问词" = 让步句。这是在假设语气中用作副词子句的句法。"动词 + 疑问词 + will",常有"即令"那种让步的意思。上举例句就等于说 Whatever you may say 一样。句中的疑问词除"what"外,还可换用"when","where"等,而"will"也可换用"may"。

Look where I will, I see nothing like him. (Brontë) (= Wherever I may look...)(无论我到哪里去找,都找不到他那样的人。)
Do what he could, the king could neither soothe nor quell the nation as he wished. He was at his wit's end. (那国王无论怎样也不能如愿地把全国的老百姓加以抚慰或是镇压下来。他简直黔驴技穷了。)
Go where I will, I find a house full of peace and cordiality. (Cowper) (= Wherever I may go...)(无论走到哪里,我都会看到一个充满和平与温情的家庭。)
Come what will (或 may), I am prepared for it. (无论变得怎样我都准备好了。)
Let others say what they will, I always speak the truth. (让别人高兴怎么说就怎么说,我是总要说真话的。)
Later writers, say what you will of their genius, have rarely equalled the elaborate beauty of the ancients. (Thoreau)(后世的作家不管你对他们的天才怎样说,是很少有能够与古代作家那种精巧的美匹敌的。)
A man thinking or working is always alone, let him be where he will. (Ibid)(一个思想或工作的人无论到哪里都是孤独的。)
Come what might, they were alone in the world with no one to help them. (Dickens)(无论发生什么,他们在这世上是孤独的,谁也不来扶助。)
Here, wake at what hour I may, early or late, I lie amid gracious stillness. (Gissing)(在这里,我无论在何时醒来,或迟或早,都是躺在可感谢的静寂之中的。)

1. Die in what manner I may, I will die like the son of a brave man.
2. The youth who expects to get on in the world must make up his mind that, come what may, he will succeed.
3. Say what you may about it, it is your father that made you what you are.

(98) no matter + 间接疑问句
疑问词 – ever + may

(a) *No matter how* hard it *may* be, do your best.
(b) *However* hard it *may* be, do your best.
不管那是怎样的难,你还是尽你的全力吧。

(a)(b)两例虽则表现法不同,但都是表让步的,意思相同的句子。据专家解释(a)句是句首省略了"it is"二字,全句应作 It is no matter how hard it may be. 这两种句法中的"may"可以略去不说,也可以换用别的助动词。又在"no matter"之后,接用由"whether"引导的子句也是可以的。这个"how"也可以换用"what","who","which","when","where"等疑问词。至于(b)例中的"however",也可换用"whatever","whoever","whichever","whenever","wherever"等字,不过在" – ever"后的"may",在现今口头英语中多采用直陈语气,例如不说 Whoever it may be,而改说 Whoever it is;不说 Whichever you may choose,而说 Whichever you choose 等等。因为这种让步句的比较古一点的说法,和上项相似,是用动词开头的,不过只限于用"be"一个动词。在这种句法中,又可用"ever so"来代替疑问词。

Whoever (= No matter who) may come, he will be welcome.(无论谁来都欢迎。)
It's a very fine house, whomever (= no matter whom) it belongs to.(这是一幢漂亮的房子,不管它是谁的。)口语说 whoever.
Whatever (= No matter what) you (may) do, do it well.(不管你做什么,都要好好的做。)
Whichever you (may) choose, you will be pleased.(随便你选择一个,你都会满意的。)
I will go, whatever the weather may be (= be the weather what it may).(不管天气如何,我都会去的。)
Forgive her all her sins, be they ever so many. (= however many they may be).(完全赦免她的罪过吧,不管那有多少。)
Be it ever so humble (= However humble it may be), there's no place like home.(无论怎样卑陋,还是自己的家舒服。)
Whatever be our fate, let us not add guilt to our misfortunes. (Goldsmith) (= whatever our fate may be)(不管我们的运命怎样,我们不要在我们的不幸上面再加罪过了。)
The idle, useless man, no matter to what extent his life may be prolonged, merely vegetates.(那懒惰无用的人,不管他寿命多长,也不过是饱食终日,虚度一生。)
There is but one safe way for every young person starting in life, whatever the business may be.(不问是干哪一行的,对于每个开始出来谋生的青年人,只有一条安全的路好走。)

1. He taught all his young gentlemen to box like featherweights, no matter whether they weighed one hundred

and five or two hundred and five pounds. (Hemingway)

2. However experienced you are, however competent, you never entirely conquer the difficulties of technique, and by the time you have learnt to write, it is very likely that you have nothing more to write about. (Maugham)

(99) 动词 + as + 主语 + 助动词

Try as you may, you will not succeed.
无论你怎样去试，你也不会成功的。

这是以假设语气现在动词开始的让步句，与(97)项的表现法一样，也可以不用"as"而用疑问词的"how"，又与上项"no matter + 间接疑问句"的意思相同，故依照上项表现法改写为 No matter how you (may) try 时，意义仍然不变。从属于句中的助动词，常用"may"、"might"、"will"、"would"这种表现法格调很高，是表示感情的。

I couldn't read it, try as I would. (Maugham)（我无论怎样试，也读不懂。）
I followed him, but, search as we would, we could find no trace of... (Christie)（我追踪了他，但是，无论怎样搜寻，我们也找不到他的踪迹。）

1. Choose as I pleased, the roads always ended by turning away from it. (= my destination) (Stevenson)
2. Try as she would, she could never remember a word of what he had said. (A. Huxley)

(100) if any

(a) He despises honour, *if any* one does.
世上果真有人轻视名誉的话，他便是一个。
(b) He has little , *if any*, money.
他即令有钱，也是极少的。

英文说的"if any"、"if ever"，意为"果真有或即令有的话"(if there is [are] any at all)，是为加强语气而用的。如(a)例，意为"如果世界上果真有那种人的话"，如(b)例则可译为"即令有，也"，它通常是伴有"little"、"few"、"seldom"等准否定字的。与此形式相近的还有"if anything"的说法，那意思是"if at all"或"if there is any difference"，可译为"倘有异同"、"如果稍有区别的话"。还有"if a day"的说法，意为"at least"。

Correct errors, if any. (= if there are any)（改错。如果有什么错误的话就改正。）
There are very few trees, if any. （即令有树也是极少的。）

There is little, if any, hope. (希望甚微。)

It occurs seldom, if ever (= seldom or never). (即有其事,亦必不多。)

He is little, if at all, better than a beggar. (= little or no better than a beggar.)(殆与乞丐无异。)

There are few, if any, such men. (if there are any such men) (= few or no such men)(即有其人,亦必不多。)

If anything, he is a little better today. (如果说有什么不同,他比昨天略为好了一点。)

He is, if anything, a shade better today. (他今天略为好了一点。)

The carriages of the German State railways are, if anything, better than those of the large French companies. (德国国营铁路的火车,倘有异同,比法国大公司的火车要好一点。)

If anything, a Judas is worse than a Nero. (如果要加以区别的话,犹大比尼禄更坏。)

True greatness has little, if anything, to do with rank or power. (真正的伟大是几与地位或权力无关的。)

1. Though the French are little, if at all, inferior to the English either in boating or sailing, their taste for these pursuits are extremely limited.

2. If there is anything in the world that a young man should be more grateful for than another, it is the poverty which necessitates starting life under very great disadvantage.

(101) be it ever (或 never) so
   let it be ever (或 never) so

Be it ever so humble, there's no place like home.
无论怎样简陋,还是自己的家好。

这个"be it"中的"be",是古代假设语气的遗留,现在的英语便说"let it be"。至于"ever so"(其古形为"never so",并无否定之意),就是"very"的意思。这两种说法都是表让步的。在"let"后也可接其他的字句。

Let it be ever so humble, home is home. (无论怎样简陋,总是自己的家。)

A man thinking or working is always alone, let him be where he will. Solitude is not measured by the miles of space that intervene between a man and his fellows. The really diligent student in one of the crowded hives of Cambridge College is as solitary as a dervish in the desert. (Thoreau)(一个人在思想和工作时总是孤独的,无论他在什么地方都是一样。孤独是不能用介乎一个人和他朋友之间的空间的里数来测量的。在哈佛大学的丛集如蜂窝的地方,勤读的学生,也和沙漠中托钵僧一样的孤独。)

Let it ever be so weak, there is nobody but loves his country. (无论国家怎样的弱,没有人不爱他的国家的。)

1. There is no living plant or animal, be it ever so common, that will not repay study, and provide, if intelligently observed, quite an interesting story.

2. Let his occupation be what it may, he must devote himself if he is to succeed.

(102) once

Once you hesitate you are lost.

你要踌躇一下,你就完了。

这个"once"是接续副词(Conjunctive Adverb),有"侯门一入深如海,从此萧郎是路人"中的"一"的意思即"一度"(when once),有时又可解释为"as soon as"(随即)或"whenever"(无论何时)之意。

〔When〕once〔it is〕gone, you will never get it back. (一度失去了,再也找不回来。)
Once you begin, you must continue. (一经开始,你就得继续下去。)
Once started, it was hard to stop. (一度开动了,就不容易停下来。)
Once (= If once) within call, we are safe. (一度进入叫喊能听到的范围内,我们就安全了。)
Once you consent you are trapped. (一度你同意了,就上了圈套。)
It is to be explained perhaps by the fear that once foreign affairs become predominant, home affairs take a back place. (要加以说明的也许是担心国外的事情一度占优势令人注意的话,国内的事情就要退居后位了。)

1. But their aloofness might have quite the same opposite result of that which they desire; for once (= when once) the crisis had arrived, home affairs would indeed be swamped.

2. Once you are married, there is nothing left for you, not even suicide, but to be good. (Stevenson)

(103) were to

If the sun *were to* rise in the west, I would not do so.

即令太阳从西边出来,我也不做这样的事。

在条件句中用的"were to",表示与未来的事实相反的假设,含有"万一"之意,稍古一点的说法是用"should",意思一样,不过"were to"比"should"不确实的意思更为强烈,所以现代英语的普通口语,都用"were to"来取代"should"了。又在口语中如主语是单数时,连"were to"有时也更改成直接语气的"was to"了,例如 If this collection was to be sold, it would fetch a lot of money. (D. Sayers)(这些收藏如果出卖的话,就可以得到一大笔钱。)If he was to come in at this moment, I should fall down on my knees in thankfulness. (L. P. Hartley)(他要是在此时走进来,我就会跪下来感谢的。) If I was to be shot for it, I couldn't. (就要杀我,我也不能。)

If he were to come, say that I am absent. (他若来了,只说我不在家。)

If I were to go abroad, I would go to Europe. (如果我有可能出洋的话,我就要到欧洲去。)

If he should (= were to) hear of your marriage, he would be surprised. (他要是听到了你结婚的消息,他一定会惊异的。)

Even if you were to try, you wouldn't be able to do it. (Hornby)(即令你去试试,你也做不到的。)

If you were to start early tomorrow morning, you would (或 could, might, ought to, should) be at your destination by evening. (如果你明天早上早早动身的话,你就会在晚上到达目的地。)

If he were to call, tell him to wait. (如果他来访时,要他等一下。)

He wouldn't do it unless you were to order him to. (除非你命令他做,否则他是不会做的。)

It would be appropriate if they were to blow a siren. (他们只要吹一下号角就对了。)

Supposing I were to die as I sit at this table, what would the difference be? (K. Mansfield)(即令我现在坐在这桌子上就是这样死了,也不会有什么不同呀。)

If anything were to happen to him the family would be left poorly off. (如果他发生了什么事情,那一家人的衣食就成问题了。)

If you were to throw him to the lions, that would no doubt be persecution. (Shaw)(若是你把他投向狮子,那无疑就是迫害呀。)

Would it spoil it if I were to ask his name? (我要是问问他的名字不会坏事吧。)

1. If the sun were to be extinguished, the whole earth would be fast bound in a frost so terrible that every animal would die.

2. If we were to think that Mrs Gerard were right, my dear Judge, then we should quit you judging men and I analysing them, and we should follow her.

(104) 含有条件意味的字眼

(a) A *close* observer would have noticed it.
    如果是一个细心的观察者,就早注意到了。

(b) *With* his aid you would succeed in it.
    有他帮忙,你就可以成功。

(c) You would do well *to write* more distinctly.
    你要是再写得清楚一点就好了。

英文表示假设的方法很多,并不一定要用明显的条件句,如(a)例中用的一个形容词"close",即含有"if the observer had been close"之意。(b)例中的介词"with",也含有"if you had his aid"之意。（c）例中的不定词"to write"，也含有"if you should write"之意。此外其他的字，也都可以用为假设的。

Anybody *who* should do that（= if anybody should do that,he）would be laughed at.（任何人如果那样做，就要被人笑的。）（关系代名词）

I am otherwise engaged,*or*（= if I were not otherwise engaged）I would go myself.（我要不是因为有别的事，我就亲自去了。）（连词）

I would have let you know by letter,*but* there was no time.（= if there had been time）（我要有时间的话，我早就用信通知你了。）（连词）

He said he would have done,*only* you treated him so off-hand.（= if you had not treated him so off-hand）（他说他本打算要做的，只是因为你待他太不客气了。）（副词）

Turning（= If you turn）to the right,you will find the house.（你向右转去，就看见那房子了。）（现在分词）

The book cannot be interesting,*judged*（= if it is judged）by its contents.（从内容上看来，这本书不会有趣的。）（过去分词）

Your *refusal* to come（= If you should refuse to come,you）might give offence.（你要不到会得罪人的。）（名词）

A *Chinese*（If he were a Chinese,he）would not do this.（这种事中国人是不会做的。）（名词）

1. He would have paid more attention to a *pretty* girl.
2. *Without* history we should be at a loss to understand our presence on the earth either as a nation or as individuals.
3. He would be wrong *in* refusing to go.
4. *To hear* him talk,one would take him for a fool.
5. The same thing,*happening* in wartime,would amount to disaster.
6. *Born* in better times,he would have done credit to the profession of letters.

X. 形容词副词的造句

(105)"the + 形容词"的两种用法

(a) *The righteous* are bold as a lion.
    正义之士，其勇如狮。
(b) *The beautiful* lives forever.
    美是不朽的。

英文的"the + 形容词"，可以等于复数普通名词，也可以等于抽象名词，即是单数的名词。二者全看形容词的性质而定，在字面上是看不出来的。如（a）例所示，"the righteous"为"righteous people"之意。说"the righteous"是复数,单数要说"a righteous man"。最常见的这种用法有"the rich" = rich people. "the poor" = poor people. 如(b)例所示,则完全不同了。"the beautiful" = beauty. 是一个抽象名词,这是近乎文言的语法。英诗人 Keats 的名句 A thing of beauty is a joy forever.(美的东西是永远的喜悦),和上举例句意思相近。他例如"the sublime" = sublimity. 这两种用法也可适用于"the + 现在分词"及"the + 过去分词",不过不一定是等于复数普通名词罢了。

现在且把这个"the + 形容词(分词)"的用法分成四类来翻译:(1)"…的人们",如 *The sick are here cared for.* (病人们在这里受到看护。) *The wounded* and *the dying* were rushed to hospital. (受伤的人们和垂死的人们被急送到医院去了。)(2)"…的一个人",如 *The deceased* was a great friend of mine. (死者是我的好朋友。) *The accused* was soon acquitted. (被告随即就宣告无罪了。)(3)"…的一切",如 In the old society many readers loved *the sensational*. (在旧社会里许多读者爱好骇人听闻的一切事情。) He has no eye for *the beautiful*. (他没有审美的眼光。)(4)"…的一件事",如 *The unexpected* always happens. (意料不到的事常会发生。天有不测风云。) *The inevitable* was not long in coming. (那不可避免的事不久就发生了。)

在"the"与形容词之间还可以再加形容词,用法不变,如"the leisured rich"(有闲的阔人们),"the hungry poor"(饥饿的穷人们),"the aged poor"(年老的穷人们),"the bereaved poor"(孤苦无依的穷人们)等等。

The beautiful is higher than the true. (美高于真。)

Confucius did not talk of the supernatural. (子不语怪力乱神。)

The oppressed and the exploited looked forward to their liberation. (被压迫的人们和被剥削的人们盼望得到解放。)

The rich are apt to look down on the poor. (阔人常要轻视穷人。)

The power of fortune is acknowledged by the unhappy; for the happy impute all their success to their merits. (运命的力量为不幸者所承认;因为幸福的人把他们一切的成功都归于他们自己的实力。)

The living may have less to say to us than the dead. (现在活着的人也许没有死去的人那样多的话要对我们说的吧。)

Local government was generally regarded as a hobby of the well-to-do and the retired. (地方政治一般认为是富裕的人和退休的人所有的癖好。)

The deceased was 102 years of age. (死者有一百零二岁。)

The accused held back the names of his partners. (被告不肯说出同谋者的名字来。)

The sublime is in a grain of dust. (一粒尘土之中也有崇高的东西。)

In their education the useful has of late been encroaching on the ornamental. (近来在他们的教育上,有用的东西侵入到装饰的东西当中去了。)

By nature she had a taste for the gorgeously beautiful. (她生性爱好华美。)

We are apt to accept the obvious too easily. (我们容易接受明显的东西。)

Adventure allows the unexpected to happen to us. (冒险引起意外。)

In an attempt to explain the unknown, primitive man fashioned various kinds of superstitions. (为着想要说明

未知的东西,原始人作出各种各样的迷信来。)

The poet had an ardent yearning for the supernatural. (诗人憧憬超自然的东西。)

1. It is generally the idle who complain they cannot find time to do that which they fancy they wish.
2. There is but a step from the sublime to the ridiculous. (Napoleon)

(106) 最上级形容词含有 even 之意

The shortest cut would take us five hours to get there.

即令走捷径也要五小时才能到达。

英文这种"the + 最上级"的形式,不宜只照字面翻译为"最",因为其中包含得有"even"的意味。应译为"即令","哪怕是"等才对。

The best brewer sometimes makes bad beer. (即令是最好的酿造家,有时也不免要造出坏啤酒来。)
The lion's roar will strike terror to the bravest heart. (听到狮吼,哪怕是非常勇敢的人也不免要惊恐。)
There is no smallest doubt about it. (毫无疑惑。)
This does not concern me in the least. (毫无关系。)
It fulfilled every faintest hope. (哪怕是极微的希望都试过了。)

1. By the law of nature the stream will run down, and the strongest man cannot stop it.
2. The industrial arts are necessary arts. The most degraded savage must practise them and the most civilized genius cannot dispense with them.

(107) the + 比较级... the + 比较级

The richer a man is, *the greedier* he gets.

人越有钱越是贪婪。

这是一种复句(Complex Sentence),前为附句,后为主句,故第一个(附句中的)"the" = in whatever degree; to what extent, 为关系副词,而第二个(主句中的)"the" = in that degree; to the extent, 则为指示副词。在主句中有时可用"do"以加重语气,如 The farther we proceed, the more difficulties *do* we meet. (我们越前进,遭遇的困难愈多。)这个"do we meet"是强调,不是倒装。这种复句,常用省略的说法,如 The sooner, the better. (越快越好。)是略去了主语和动词的。The nearer the bone, the sweeter the meat. (越靠近骨头的肉其味越美。)是略去动词的。More haste, worse speed. (欲速则不达。)是略去副词的。有时又可把主句放在附句的前面去,如 I sing the worse, the more I practise. (= The more I practise, the worse I sing.)（越练习越唱得坏。）

The sooner he comes, the happier I shall be.（他越早来,我越高兴。）

The more he gets, the more he wants.（越有越贪。）

The more he flatters, the less I like him.（他越逢迎我越不喜欢他。）

The stone gets the harder, the longer it is exposed to the weather.（越是在空气中暴露得久,石头变得越硬。）

The higher a mountain is, the more people like to climb it; the more dangerous the mountain is, the more they wish to conquer it.（山越高,人越爱爬山;山越危险,人越想克服它。）

My experience has led me, the longer I live, to set the less value upon mere cleverness.（因为经验增长的关系,年龄越大,我对单是聪明越觉得没有什么价值。）

The more things a man is interested in, the more opportunities of happiness he has, since if he loses one thing he can fall back upon another.（人对越多的事物发生兴趣,便越多获得幸福的机会,因为他失去对一件事物的兴趣,又可从另外一件事物上获得兴趣。）

The more complex his material, the greater must be his art.（作家的材料越是复杂,他的技术越要伟大。）

The nearer the train approached the scene, the drearier became the aspect.（火车越接近现场,那光景越加可怕。）

1. Lying on the grass, he looked straight up into the sky. It was very blue, and the longer he looked, the higher it seemed to look.

2. A great part of our lives is occupied in reverie, and the more imaginative we are, the more varied and vivid this will be. (Maugham)

(108) the + 比较级 + 理由

I like him all *the better for* his faults.

因为他有缺点,我更加喜欢他。

这个表现法是只用一个"the + 比较级",后面就接上表理由的"for","because","on account of","owing to"等,具有"更加"的意思。常出现的为"all（或 much）the + 比较级"的形式,这个"all"或"much"是为加强语气而用的,可以不必译出。句中的"the" = to that degree。

成语说的"none the less"（依然。但仍不失为。）如 He has faults, none the less he is the best student of the class.（他有缺点,但仍不失为这班上最好的学生。）实有"虽然如此"（nevertheless）之意,也和本项为同一用法。

有时可将说理由的字句省略,而在别的地方表示出那个理由来,如 I *said nothing*, which made him all the more angry.（我一言不发,使他更为生气。）We are apt to *undervalue the purchase* we can not reach, to conceal our poverty the better. (我们常有将自己买不起的东西过低估价的倾向,借以隐藏我们的贫穷。)

We do not like him the less *because* he has faults. —We like him none the less *for* his faults. —*He has faults*, but we do not like him the less. —We do not like him the less *on that account*. (我们并不因他有缺点,而较少喜欢他。)

If he doesn't understand English, it is all the better for you. (如果他不懂英语,那对你更好呀。)

The danger makes the sports only the pleasanter. (那运动因有危险而更加有趣。)

He is the worse for drink. (他喝醉了。)

We should not think the worse of a man because he is ill-dressed. (我们不应因人衣服褴褛而藐视其人。)

I think none the worse of him because he accepted their offer. (他接受了他们的建议,我并不因此就对他不尊敬了。)

The coat is much the worse for wear. (那上衣穿得很破了。)

He won't come. —So much the better. (他不来更好。)

I am the more inclined to help him, because he is poor. (因为他穷,我更加想要帮助他。)

It is none the less true because it sounds strange. (听来很怪,却是真的。)

It is all the more dangerous for not being generally recognized as snch. (一般不认为危险的,反而更加危险。)

You may be as neat as you please and I shall love you the better for it; but this is not neatness, but frippery. (Goldsmith)(你们照自己的意思弄整洁就好了,那样我会更加爱你们的,但照现在这样,并不是整洁,而只是矫饰〔俗丽〕而已。)

1. Indulged in to excess, reading becomes a vice—a vice all the more dangerous for not being generally recognized.

2. I think one of the most useful discoveries I ever made was how easy it is to say "I don't know". I never noticed that it made anyone think the worse of me. (Maugham)

(109) the last... + 不定词
the last... + 形容词子句

(a) He is *the last* man *to accept* a bribe.
  他决不是受贿赂的人。

(b) He is *the last* man *I wanted to see*.
  他是我最不愿见的一个人。

句中的"last"为"the least likely"的意思,是否定地加以推论的想法。译为"最不大可能的","最不适的"。由原意的"最后去做",变成"决不去做"。

He is the last man to do such a thing.（他决不做这样的事。）

You should be the last man to wish it.（你决无希冀此事之理。）

I should be the last man to speak lightly of the profession of a clergyman.（我决不轻视牧师的职务。）

The very last thing of which man can make his boast is his knowledge.（人类对自己的知识是决难夸口的。）

That is the last thing one would expect.（那是一种最不可能预期到的东西。）

The author should be the last man to talk about his work.（作者最不宜讨论他的作品。）

Money is the last thing he wants, and you won't succeed by offering it.（他决不要钱,你想用钱去买动他是决不会成功的。）

You are the last person I was going to see. Why did you come to see me?（你是我决不想要会见的人。你为什么要来见我?）

Romantic is the last thing I am.（我决不是浪漫的人。）

Certainly the last thing an Englishman should despise is poetry.（一个英国人决不会轻视诗歌的。）

1. He was the last man in the world to suffer his authority to be set at naught.

2. A pretext was the last thing that Hastings was likely to want. (Macaulay)

(110) so + 形容词(副词) + that
so + 动词 + that

(a) This coffee is *so hot that* I cannot drink it.

这咖啡太烫,我不能喝。

(b) He ran *so fast that* nobody could catch him up.

他跑得那样快,谁也赶不上他。

(c) It *so happened that* he was not at home.

他碰巧不在家。

在"so"后接形容词或副词的,是表示因果关系,"so"以下表原因,"that"以下表结果。在"so"后接副词的,多是用来表程度的。在"so"后如接动词,就是表方法、状态、程度或目的的。This coffee is so hot that I cannot drink it. = This coffee is too hot (for me) to drink. 在"so + 形容词(副词)"后不接"that"引导的子句,而接不定词也是可以的,不过要用关系副词连起来,如 He was so angry that he could not speak. 一句可改为 He was so angry *as* to be unable to speak.

The world is probably so made that men are unable to live without loving others.（大概这个世界上的人是非爱他人就不能生活的。）

It is so easy that a boy can learn it.（那非常容易,小孩子都能学会。）

Man is so created that he lives with woman.（男人是被造来和女人共同生活的。）

He so handled that matter that he won（= as to win）over his opponents.（他为着赢得反对者的支持,而把事情那样处理了。）

He spoke so rapidly that we could not clearly understand him.（他说话太快,所以我们没有能够完全听懂。）

Those ponds and streams are so small that they cannot be shown in your maps.（那些池塘和小溪,因为太小,所以地图上没有。）

They were so close (that) I heard every word.（他们很靠近我,所以他们说的每个字我都听到。）美国口语略去"that"一字。

His income is so small that he can not support his family.（他收入太少,不能养家。）

These shoes are so small that I cannot put them on.（这双鞋太小,我不能穿。）

It was so cold that we lost the use of our hands.（太冷,我们手都不能动了。）

He had lived so long in the east that he had got out of English ways.（他在东方住得太久,所以英国的生活习惯都忘记了。）

The orange was so sour (that) I couldn't eat it.（橙太酸我不能吃。）

I was so astonished that I could not utter even a word.（我吃惊得说不出话来了。）

The current was so strong that he could not swim against it.（水流太急,他不能逆泳。）

He spoke English so fluently that everyone was astonished.（他英语说得那样流利,大家都吓倒了。）

The streets were so crowded that our car had to go very slowly.（街上太拥挤,汽车只好慢慢的走。）

Explanations were of no use because he was so prejudiced that he would not listen to reason.（说明对他无用,因为他不肯听从道理。）

1. I do not think anyone writes so well that he cannot learn much from *Fowler's Dictionary*. (Maugham)

2. Many foods are never so cheap that the poorest people can afford to eat them.

3. May we so live that our children's children may look upon us as having set them an example.（"may+主语+原形不定词"是祈愿句法。）

(111) so that

So that it is done, I don't care who does it.
只要做好就行,我不管是谁做的。

这个"so that" = if only, so long as, provided that,是表条件的,有时可将"that"省略。这是略带古风的说法,但在美国语中用的很多,可译为"只要",因系条件句,所以第三人称单数的现在动词上可以不加〔s〕,例如 He can stay long so that he *catch* the train.（只要他能赶上火车,仅可多呆一会。）不过这种表条件的用法,属于古文体,现在我们不宜采用。

除古文体表条件外,现代英文又常用"so that"来表目的和结果。表目的的"so that" = in order that,后常接"may"及"should","would","could"等字,口语则用"can",有时也可用单纯过去代替

"might do"。如表目的时说 Switch the light on so that we can see what it is.（打开电灯,好来看过究竟。）表结果时则说 Nothing more was heard of him, so that people thought he was dead.（再也没有听到他的讯息,因此人们以为他死了。）用单纯过去时态的如 He went early so that he got a good seat.（他早早去所以占到了一个好位子。）比较:

  He spoke clearly, so that everyone could hear.（结果）
  He spoke clearly so that everyone might hear.（目的）

  I'll write to him today so that he may know when to expect us.（我今天要写信给他,为着要使他知道我们何时到达。）
  They are climbing higher so that they may get a better view.（他们爬得更高,以便看得更远。）
  School was closed early in order that the children might go home ahead of the storm.（学校早早下课,以便学生在暴风雨前回家。）
  We put up a fence so that the neighbors should not overlook us.（我们搭一个围墙,以免邻居看见我们。）
  He slammed the door so that his mother would know he was home.（他把门砰的一声关上,好让他母亲知道他回来了。）
  Speak up so that the students sitting in the back of the room can hear you.（把声音放大一点,以便坐在后面的学生可以听到。）
  They are hurrying so that they won't miss the train.（他们匆忙赶去,以免脱车。）
  All precautions have been taken, so that we expect to succeed.（一切准备妥善,因此我们期待成功。）
  You may keep the book, so that you bring it back in good condition.（只要你不弄坏还来,你可以把这本书借去阅读。）
  To find her (= Megan) again he knew he had only... to take train himself and go back to the farm, so that she found (= might found) him there when she returned. (Galsworthy, *The Apple Tree*)（为要找到美冈他知道他只有自己搭火车回农场去,她若回家了,就会到农场来看他的。）
  Put the butter in the icebox, so that it may (will) not get soft.（把牛油放在冰箱中就不会软化。）
  Come early so that you may get a good seat.（早来可以占到好位子。）
  So that it be done, it matters not how.（只要能做成,不管用什么方法。）
  So that it is true, what matters who said it?（只要确实,管它是谁说的。）
  I got up early so that I might be in time for the first train.（我为着要赶上头班车,故特早起。）*Cf.* I got up so early that I was in time for the first train.（因我早起,故赶上了头班车。）前句表有意志的目的,后句表无意志的结果。

 1. I warned him so that he might avoid the danger.
 2. Society is not very particular what a man does, so that it prove him to be a man.
 3. To him it was indifferent who was found guilty so that he could recover his money.

(112) so much so that

  He is very ignorant *so much so that* he cannot read his own name.

他非常无知,甚至连自己的名字都不认识。

在"so much so that"中,第一个"so"是承接"that"以下的,与前面说过的表因果关系的"so that"的用法一样;第二个"so"是为避免重复起见,用来代表前面那个叙述形容词的,在上例中即代表"ignorant"一字。至于"much"便是为免除两个"so"连在一块儿而插入其间,作为缓冲的字眼,所以结局在本句中就等于说"so ignorant that"一样。全句可解释为 He is very ignorant *to that extent or degree so that* he cannot read his own name. 如果后面不接"that"所引导出来的子句,而改用不定词时,则为 He cannot so much as (= even) read his own name. 或整个说出来 He is very ignorant so much as to read his own name.

The invalid was very tired when he returned from the ride; so much so that he could not sit up. (病人坐车回家时非常疲倦,疲倦得甚至不能坐起来。)

Ships were built, and kept thoroughly efficient, so much so that the country remained safe for very many years. (兵舰造起来了,发挥充分的效率,那样,使国家永保太平无事。)

The first born was greatly privileged—so much so that the equal inheritance by two or more offspring was totally denied. (长子被给与很大的特权,至于由两个或更多的儿子来平等地继承遗产的事是完全被否认了。)

He is poor—so much so that he can hardly get enough to live. (他很穷,穷得几乎无以为生。)

All parts of the British Isles are noted for their dampness, and Ireland so much so that the people of Ireland have this saying, "In England, it rains all day; in Scotland, it rains all night; but in Ireland, it rains both day and night." (不列颠群岛各地以潮湿著名,爱尔兰亦复如此,所以爱尔兰人有这样的说法,"在英格兰整天下雨,在苏格兰整夜下雨,但在爱尔兰,日日夜夜都下雨"。)

1. It is very fierce and savage—so much so that the natives dread it more than they do the lion.

2. But is not the fear of death natural to man? So much so, Sir, that the whole of life is but keeping away the thoughts of it. (Dr. Johnson)

(113) such...as

such...that

(a) It is *such* an easy book *as* he can read.

这是他能读的一本容易的书。

(b) It is written in *such* easy English *that* he can read it.

这是用浅易英文写的书,所以他也能读。(结果)

这是用他也能读懂的那样浅易的英文写的。(程度)

英文的"such...as"是表程度的,而"such...that"则可表结果,也可表程度。(a)例中的"as"

是关系代名词,也是"read"的宾语,所以不要说成"read it"。(b)例中的"such...that"与"so...that"同义,所不同的是"such+(形容词)+名词+that"而"so+形容词(副词)+that",这个"that"是连词,所以在"read"后必须有一个宾语"it"。

It was such a cold night that we all kept indoors. (那天夜里冷极了,我们都没有出门。)

The children were having such a good time that their mother hated to call them it. (孩子们玩得非常开心;母亲不忍叫他们回家。)

Let us discuss such things as (= those things which) we can talk of freely. (让我们讨论一些我们可以自由谈论的事吧。)

This book is written in such easy English as beginners can understand. (这本书是用初学者也能读懂的浅易英文写的。)

This book is written in such easy English that beginners can understand it. (这本书是用浅易英文写的,所以初学者也能读懂。)

I don't know whether he is really such a great scholar as people say. (我不晓得他是否真如世人所说的是一个大学者。)

The silkworm is an animal of such acute and delicate sensation that too much care cannot be taken to keep its habitation clean, and to refresh it from time to time with pure air. (蚕是一种感觉敏锐而纤细的生物,要注意尽量地保持它居处的清洁,时时使它获得新鲜空气。)

It was the discovery of this extraordinary fact by generations of people long dead that made the greatness of such works as those of Shakespeare, of Dante, or of Goethe. (L. Hearn)(使莎翁、但丁或歌德的作品变得那样伟大的,是由于老早就死了的多少代的人们,发现了这个异常的事实的原故。)注意:上半句为"the discovery of this fact by people"的加重语气的说法。"made the greatness of"意为"使之变成伟大"。

For the man sound in body and serene of mind there is no such thing as bad weather; every sky has its beauty, and storms which whip the blood do but make it pulse more vigorously. (G. Gissing)(对于一个身体健全,精神平静的人,是没有坏天气的;无论什么天气都有它的美丽,激励血液的暴风雨,只会使脉膊跳动得更加活泼。)"do but make" = only make.

He was no more than skin and bone, was partly paralysed, and wore spectacles of such unusual power, that his eyes appeared through the glasses greatly magnified and distorted in shape. (R. L. Stevenson)(他只剩下皮包骨,半身不遂,戴着非常深度的眼镜,使他的眼睛经过镜子看去,大为扩大,且变得奇形怪状。)

1. My father, I do not know why unless he was drawn by some such restlessness for the unknown as has consumed his son, went to Paris and became solicitor to the British Embassy. (Maugham)

2. Books did not much attract him; when he opened one he was sure to come upon something or other which took such possession of his thoughts, or so affected his imagination, that he went off into dreaminess, and for that day he read no more. (G. Gissing)

(114) 比较级 + than
more + 原级 + than

(a) He is *bolder than* his brother.
   他比他的兄弟要大胆些。
(b) He is *more bold than* strong.
   与其说他刚强,不如说他大胆。

(a)例的"bolder than"是形容词的普通比较级,对同一性质来比较其不同的程度或大小,至于(b)例,则是将不同性质加以比较,其中的"more"有"rather"(毋宁)的意思。普通比较级的形式虽为"-er than",但有时只用"-er"也就够了,试看下面四句:

(1) This cord is strong*er than* that one.
(2) This cord is *a* strong*er one*.
(3) This cord is *the* strong*er one* of the two.
(4) This cord is *the* strong*er* (of the two).

注意不用"than"时冠词的用法。当"more"用作"rather"之意时,就是比较同一人或同一物的两种不同的性质,在"than"后可接形容词,副词,名词,片语或子句等。

It is more than probable that he will fail. (十之八九,他会失败。)
He has more than 10,000 dollars—more than enough. (他有万元以上,绰有余裕。)
He is more shy than unsocial. (他是害羞,不是不爱社交。)
His mother is more kind than intelligent. (他母亲不是聪慧,而是和蔼。不是智者,而是仁人。)
He is more witty than wise. (与其说他聪明,不如说他机智。)
He is more dead than alive. (与其说他活着,不如说他死了。)
He is more knave than fool. (与其说他蠢,不如说他坏。)
Li Yu was more of a poet than a king. (李煜与其说是一位国君,不如说是一位词人。)
She was dressed more than simply. (他穿得岂只是朴素,简直近乎破烂。)
I prayed to heaven in my heart that my boy, my more than son, might live. (Haggard) (我私自心里祷告,求上苍让我的儿子,我那心肝儿子,活下去吧。)
Oh, great Sciolto! Oh, my more than father. (啊,伟大的西奥图!啊,我那单说是父亲还嫌不足的亲爱的人。)
Friend of my bosom, thou more than a brother, /Why wert not thou born in my father's dwelling? (Charles Lamb)(我的知交,你胜过亲兄弟,你为何不生在我父亲的家里?)
During the last fifty years the short story has developed in scope and variety more rapidly than during the preceding five centuries. (J. Hadfield)(在过去五十年中,短篇小说的视野和变化,比以前五百年都要更迅速地发达了。)

Public opinion is always more tyrannical towards those who obviously fear it than towards those who feel indifferent to it. A dog will bark more loudly and bite more readily when people are afraid of him than when they treat him with contempt, and the human herd has something of this same characteristic. (B. Russell)(舆论常是对于显明地怕它的人比毫不介意它的人更要残暴。狗对于怕它的人要大吠并随时准备来咬,对于轻蔑它的人,它就没有这样,人类也多少具有这同样的特质。)

1. Smike, more dead than alive, was brought in and locked up in a cellar. (Dickens)
2. He did not taken the fever, after all; he was more frightened than hurt.
3. I have noticed that when someone asks for you on the telephone and, finding you out, leaves a message begging you to call him up the moment you come in, and it's important, the matter is more often important to him than to you.

(115) more... than + can

He earns *more* money *than* he *can* spend.
他赚的钱,他用不完。

这个表现法是不能照字面来翻译的。在"more than"以后的文句,英文虽是肯定,但中文必须翻为否定。这和其他接子句或接单字、片语的有所不同。注意在后接的子句中常用"can"的助动词,当然也有不用"can"而用别的动词的。在"more... than... can"时,意为"达到不可能的程度";在"more than... can"时,意为"简直不可能"。

He has more books than he can read. (= He cannot read all his books.)(他藏书多到他不可能读完的程度。)
That is more than I can tell. (= I cannot tell that.)(那我简直不懂。)
How he manages to live is more than I can tell. (= above my comprehension)(他怎样生活的,我简直猜不透。)
It is more than flesh and blood can bear. (这非血肉之躯所能忍受。)
His insolence is more than I can stand. (他的无礼我受不了。)
The beauty of the place is more than I can describe. (那地方景色之美,非笔墨所能形容。)
I don't do more than I can help. (能够不做的我便不做。)

1. So many mothers and fathers died that there were more Orphans than the asylum could possibly take care of.
2. We all complain of the shortness of time, and yet we have more than we know what to do with.

(116) more than + 动词

This *more than satisfied* me.
这使我十二分的满意。

这是在文法上破格的造句法,把"more than"放在动词之前,是表示就用更强意的动词也无妨,用英文说时则为"to do more than to",可译为"深为"、"岂特"、"十二分的"等。

He more than hesitated to promise that. (他对于答应那件事,岂特是踌躇而已〔简直是拒绝了〕。)
More is meant than meets the ear. (Milton) (有言外之意。)
Rose's cheeks were more than touched by the sun. (Gissing) (露丝的面颊深受太阳的伤害。)
He has more than repaid my kindness. (他岂只是报答了我的帮助而已。)
She was more than pleased with her daughter's performance. (她对女儿的演奏十二分的高兴。)
I prefer autumn to spring. What we lose in flowers we more than gain in fruits. (比春天我更要喜欢秋天。我们失去春花而以秋果补偿绰绰有余。)

1. He more than smiled, he laughed outright. (Rowe)
2. He is more than pleased with the result.

(117) less...than

During the week he saw *less* of her *than* usual.
在那一星期内,他比平常要少见到她。

英文的"less...than"是低一级的比较,意为"较少"、"较差"、"不及"、"不如"。"A is less...than B"略等于"A is not so...as B"的说法。这个"less"作形容词用时较为易译,作副词用时,则较难译。下面是"less"与"more"用法的比较:

Proof-reading is *not interesting*, still *less* so when it is one's own work.
Proof-reading is *uninteresting*, still *more* so when it is one's own work.

He was less hurt than frightened. (他受的伤不如吓的厉害。)
I regard him less as my teacher than as my friend. (我把他看做朋友,甚过我把他看做老师。)
You're more of a scholar than he is, but you've got less common sense. (作为一个学者你在他以上,就常识而论则你不如他。)
She eats less than a bird. (她吃得太少。)

He'll be back in less than no time. (他将马上回来。)

His lecture left me less than satisfactory. (他的演讲怎也不能使我满意。)

This razor runs less of a chance of getting cut. (这把剃刀差不多不可能割破脸。)

Father understood less of money matter than a child. (父亲对钱的事比小孩还要不懂。)

If you smoke cigars or a pipe, you're still risking cancer. But a good deal less than you are if you stick to cigarettes. (你抽雪茄或烟斗,还是有得癌症的危险,不过比抽纸烟的危险性少得多了。)

He observed with interest the errors of her face and figure, the thin underlip, too heavily penciled eyebrows, and her legs less than slim although not actually skinny. (他颇感兴趣地望着她面孔和身体上的一些缺点,那太薄的下嘴唇,画得太浓的眉毛,和她那瘦弱的双腿,虽然没有达到皮包骨的程度。)

1. A man less thick-witted than the skipper might have been forgiven if he were bewildered by Neilson's words. (Maugham)
2. Learning is, in too many cases, but a foil to common sense, a substitute for true knowledge. Books are less often made use of as "spectacles" to look at nature with, than as blinds to keep out its strong light and shifting scenery from weak eyes and indolent dispositions. (W. Hazlitt)

(118) much more
much less

(a) He likes a child, *much more* a baby.
他喜欢小孩,更加喜欢婴孩。

(b) He does not like a child, *much less* a baby.
他不喜欢小孩,更加不喜欢婴孩。

例句中(a)(b)两种表现法,都有"更加"的意思,不过用法不同罢了。(a)是用于肯定句之后,表程度的增加,(b)是用于否定句之后,表程度的减少。(a)表更多,(b)表更少。"much"改为"still"还是一样。(a)可译为"更加","当更"。(b)可译为"遑论","何况"。所谓否定后接"much less",肯定后接"much more"的说法,也不过是最基本的用法罢了。在文人笔下,即令是肯定句,如含有否定意时,也可接"much less";至于在否定的陈述之后,用"much more"的也不是没有。这个"much less"普通有"not to speak of"之意,故上面把它译作"遑论"。在"it is impossible"后不接"much less",而要接"much more",即有"much more impossible"之意。

It would be impossible for any American much more an American who was stupid and provincial to gain their confidence. (Whitford) (任何美国人,尤其是愚笨而粗俗的美国人,更不可能获得信任。)

It is scarcely imaginable how great a force is required to stretch, still more break, this ligament. (Curme) (要把这条韧带拉长,尤其是要把它拉断,需要多大的力量,简直不可想象。)

I like music, much more dancing. (我喜欢音乐,更加喜欢跳舞。)

I don't like music, much less dancing.（我不喜欢音乐,更不喜欢跳舞。）

I do not even suggest that he is negligent, much less that he is dishonest.（我甚至没有暗示说他怠忽,更没有说他欺诈。）

If you must work so hard, how much more must I?（你尚且如此刻苦,我一定要更加努力才行。）

No other country accepted the proposal, much less acted upon it.（没有别的国家接受那个提案,更没有哪个国家采取行动的。）

Every one has a right to enjoy his liberty, still more his life.（人人都有享受自由的权利,生命更加如此。）

Not all verse is poetry; not all prose about the past is history, nor is all literary work literature. The discrimination is habitually applied to other subjects, and clearly it is the quality which is decisive, not the quantity, scope or subject-matter, still less the popularity, of the work.（并非所有的韵文都是诗,并非所有关于过去的散文都是史,并非所有的著作都是文学。这种辨别常可应用到别的科目上,很明显的,有决定性的,是那作品的质,而不是量,也不是它的范围或题材,更不是它的声望。）

1. One would not wish to visit the white mountains in winter, still less would he be willing to live there in that season.

2. If worship even of a star had some meaning in it, how much more might that of a Hero.（Carlyle）

（119）would sooner（rather）...than
would as soon...as

(a) I *would sooner* (rather) die *than* disgrace myself.

(b) I *would as soon* die *as* disgrace myself.

我宁死不受辱。

这表现法中的"would"是表愿望的,与"wish〔to〕"相同。句中的"soon"也不作"早","快"解,而是"愿意地","高兴地"（readily, willingly）的意思,（a）例中的"sooner"为比较级,结局与"rather"同义。英文的"rather"原来是"rathe(＝early, soon)"的比较级,不过现在只剩下"rather"一字,但仍保持它比较级的作用。（b）例中的"would as soon die as",是用的平等比较,一般的情形谁也不希望死,所以这句话的意思是希望与那同样的程度,结局也是"would sooner...than"的意思。"would sooner（rather）"可译为"宁愿","than"以下便要译成否定。"rather than"＝might as well...as.

He would sooner die than consent to such a plan.（他宁死也不肯同意这个计划。）

The brave soldier would as soon die as yield to such an enemy.（那个英勇的军人宁死也不肯屈服于这样的敌人。）

What strikes me most is that here are three thousand young men, every one of whom would rather lose a game than play it unfairly.（最使我感动的是这里的三千个青年,人人都宁肯比赛失败,而不愿作弊取胜。）

I would sooner die at once than live in this agony.（与其生存在这种苦痛中我宁肯早死的好。）

I would rather you came tomorrow than today.（我宁愿你明天来。）

I would rather be deaf than blind〔if I were to be either of them〕.（我宁愿聋不愿瞎。）

He would rather resign than take part in such dishonest business deals.（他宁肯辞职而不愿参加这种不正当的勾当。）

I would just as soon stay at home〔as go〕.（我宁愿呆在家里。）

I would rather you remained here.（Dickens）（我宁愿你留下不走。）

I would rather never allude to the past for it is very painful to me.（C. Doyle）（我不愿再提到过去,因那使人痛苦。）

1. I asked if she would like a taxi. "No, I'd sooner walk, it's such a lovely day," she answered.（Maugham）

2. I'd as soon put that little canary into the park on a winter's day, as recommend you to bestow your heart on him!（Brontë）

(120) no sooner... than
hardly... when

(a) He had *no sooner* seen me *than* he ran off.

(b) He had *hardly* seen me *when* he ran off.

他一看到我就跑掉了。

这两种表现法都是"随即"的意思,表示两种动作跟着发生,几乎是同时的现象。我们要注意的是不可把两个意义相同的表现法混乱,英美未受教育的人每每说成"no sooner... when",其实只需看"sooner"是比较级,当然是要接上"than"才通。这个"hardly"有时说成"scarcely"也是一样,后接的"when"稍古的说法为"before",意思不变。如用稍古的说法,将"no sooner"或"hardly（scarcely）"置于句首时,就要把主语和动词颠倒过来,如 No sooner had he seen me 及 Hardly had he seen me. 这种说法在意义上没有什么不同,只是语气上有些加强而已。与此同义的还有"as soon as + 主语 + 动词","the moment（或 the instant）+ 主语 + 动词",及"directly（或 immediately）+ 主语 + 动词"。例如 As soon as（或 the moment 等）he saw me, he ran off. 还有在动名词项下说过的"on + 动名词"也有"as soon as"的意味,如 On arriving home he wired me.（他一到家就打电报给我了。）

No sooner had I started than it began to rain. = Scarcely (Hardly) had I started when (before) it began to rain.（我一动身天就下雨了。）

Let me know directly (immediately) he comes.（他一来就请通知我。）

He ran away the moment (the instant) I came in.（我一进来他就逃了。）

I had scarcely started before a man came up to me and asked me if he was right in thinking my name was so-

and-so. (Maugham)(我甫出门就有一个人走过来问我是不是姓什么的。)

Directly he had gone, she burst into great sobs. (他一走她就啜泣起来。)

The instant that we heard the sound, Holmes sprang from the bed, struck a match, and lashed furiously with his cane at the bell-pull. (Doyle)(我们一听到有声音,福尔摩斯就立刻从床上跳将起来,擦燃一根火柴,用手杖去猛击那钟绳。)

I had no sooner opened the cage than out flew the little bird. (我一开笼小鸟就飞出去了。)

No sooner had I glanced at this letter than I concluded it to be the one of which I was in search. (我一见那信便知道正是我找寻的一封。)

No sooner had I come into contact with him than I determined to get to know him well. (我一接近他,马上我就决心要和他做好朋友。)

1. No sooner had the thief perceived that than he sprang to his feet and took to flight.
2. Hardly had he started when the sky became overcast and down came the rain again.
3. The moment the door was opened, the dog flew to the chest.
4. As soon as a man begins to love his work then he will begin to make progress.

(121) anything but
nothing but
all but

(a) He is *anything but* a scholar.
他决非一个学者。

(b) He is *nothing but* a scholar.
他不过是一个学者。

(c) The boy *all but* fell into the well.
那孩子几乎掉到井里去了。

英文的"anything but" = never. "nothing but" = only. "all but" = almost, nearly 在这三种表现法中的"but",都有"except"(除开)之意。"anything but"意即"除此之外别的都是",是表强调的否定的。"否定字 + anything but" = "nothing but",意即"除此之外别的都不是"。至于"all but"是指"everything short of",所以结局是和"almost","nearly"同义了。

He is anything but a scientist. (他决非科学家。)

I'm nothing but a student. (我不过是一个书生而已。)

A trouble of the eye all but drove me mad with fear of blindness. (Gissing)(我的眼痛使我生怕要瞎几乎为之发狂。)

Famous as the actress may be, her manners are anything but gracious. (那女伶虽很有名然举止欠佳。)

Strange to say, man is nothing but a bundle of habits.(说来奇怪,人不过是一堆习惯而已。)

If nothing but plain common sense were admitted, we should have had little or no great poetry.(R. Lynd)(如果是普通常识以外什么都不认可的话,那么,我们就不会有伟大的诗篇了。)

The house was all but completed when he was drafted and sent to the East.(那房子几乎快落成了,而他便受到征召,送往东方去了。)

It is anything but pure.(不纯。)

His English is anything but correct.(他的英文错误百出。)

His English is all but correct.(他的英文几乎是正确的。)

His English is nothing but correct.(他的英文只是不错而已。)

He is anything but a fool.(他决不是傻子。)

He is all but a fool.(他几乎可说是傻子。)

1. He wandered up and down among the crowd in anything but a calm frame of mind.

2. Science is, I believe, nothing but trained and organized common sense.

3. Physical labour carried beyond a certain point is atrocious torture, and it has very frequently been carried so far as to make life all but unbearable.(Russell)

(122) short of
be short of
nothing short of

(a) *Short of* theft, I will do anything I can for you.
除了偷窃之外,我什么都愿为你效劳。

(b) We *are short of* hands at present.
我们眼下人手不够。

(c) His conduct was *nothing short of* madness.
他的行为简直是发了狂。

英文的"short of"=except,是副词的用法。在这前面常用的动词有"come","fall","run"等,有"不足","欠缺"的意思,其"of"作"from"解。至于"be short of"及"nothing(或 little) short of"中的"short of"则为形容词,在"be short of"时意为"不足"或"离开",在"nothing short of"时意为"完全",用法仍有如副词一般。

The result fell short of my expectation.(那结果出乎我所预料。)

The result was nothing short of my expectation.(那结果正如我所预料。)

Short of some tremendous accident or untoward event it could not be anything else.(除了是一件重大事件或不幸事件外,这不可能是别的事情。)

They were short of money.（他们缺少钱。）
They were still five miles short of their destination.（他们距目的地还差五英里。）
It was little（或 nothing）short of miraculous（或 a miracle）.（这几乎是奇迹。）
The arrow fell short of the mark.（矢未中的。）
We have run short of tea.（我们的茶叶不够了。）
He committed every crime short of murder.（他只差没有杀人，什么罪都犯了。）
We have reason to believe that our education falls short of what we should wish it to be.（我们有充分的理由相信，我国的教育还未达到我们所理想的境地。）

1. In this instance fame has fallen short of the truth.
2. Sleep was out of the question; for even if they dared to stay, they knew that to lie down on the ground was little short of certain death.
3. To impose a new civilization on an ancient culture is naturally a gigantic undertaking; and Japan can only be admired for attempting it, and having so well succeeded in accomplishing it. Could the achievement have been realized without losing some of the virtues of either civilization, it would be nothing short of a miracle.

(123) ever so

(a) There are *ever so* many schools in Taiwan.
　　台湾的学校非常的多。
(b) Be a man *ever so* rich, he ought not to be idle.
　　人无论怎样有钱，也不可以懒惰。

在（a）例中的"ever so" = very; exceedingly，可译作"非常"，在（b）例中的"ever so"，便有让步的意思，等于说"however"，有"in or to whatever conceivable degree or extent"的意思。可译作"无论怎样的"。这个"ever so"的古写法是"never so"，从字面看去好像意思相反，其实完全同义，例如英文名歌中有一句脍炙人口的句子，便是用的古文说法：Home is home, be it never so humble.（= however humble it may be）。（无论怎样卑陋，家总是自己的好。）我们由下面三个句子可以看出文字演变的迹象来：(1) He looked never before so healthy〔as then〕,—(2) He looked never so healthy.—(3) He looked ever so healthy.

He is ever so strong.（他非常强壮。）
The patient is ever so much better.（病人好得多了。）
Betide what may, we will not despair, were the world never so unfriendly.（Carlyle）（无论发生什么事情，我们也不会绝望，即令世界变得非常冷酷无情。）
I like it ever so much.（我非常喜欢它。）
Thank you ever so much for you kindness.（真谢谢你的帮忙。）

No one will be vexed or uneasy, linger I ever so late. (无论我呆到好晚,也没有人讨厌的。)

She's got ever so many books. (他有非常多的书。)

Let him be ever so bad, he has some good points. (Curme)(他虽很坏,却也有他的好处。)

He was ever so tired. (= He was as tired as he could possibly be.)(他非常疲倦。)

There is no place like home, be it never so homely. (即令很鄙陋,还是自己的家好。)

Such a mean fellow, though never so rich, should not be admitted into society. (这样卑鄙的人,虽则有钱,也不应允许他进入社交界。)

1. There be heard ever so many more voices, and it was noiser than ever.

2. If my life's journey is to be along an easy road to success, I shall have no objection; if it is to be along a hard one, let it be ever so rough, I will make it smooth and gain my object nevertheless.

3. He is in error, though never so wise.

(124) good and 的副词用法

The apples are *good and* ripe.

这些苹果完全成熟了。

普通用"and"来连结两个形容词时,是表示两个形容词的对等作用,但第一个形容词如果是"good","nice","fine"等字的话,当它和"and"结合起来时,便构成"well"或是"nicely"意味的副词同等语了。在美国口语中,这种表现法用得很多,是作为强意语(intensifier)用的,例如"good and sweet","good and cold","good and plenty"等皆是,意为"very"或"thoroughly",翻译时应特别注意,不可把"good and ripe"译成"又好又熟",它的原意实为"well ripe"(熟透)罢了。这个表现法普通都可改为副词,如"nice and cool" = nicely cool(凉爽),"snug and warm" = snugly warm(暖适)。在 COD 上将"nice and"解释为"satisfactorily"。他例还有"fine and","lovely and","bright and","rare and","big and"等等。"lovely and warm" = dilightedly warm(温暖)是女性用语。

I am good and tired. (我很疲倦。)

It's good and cold out. (外面很冷。)

When it was good and dark I slid out from shore before moonrise. (Mark Twain)(天完全黑了,我就在月亮出来以前从河岸上溜出去了。)

The boy was bad. Yes! He was good and bad. (那孩子坏呀。是的!他真是很坏。)

The house stands nice and high. (那房子位置很高。)

The room was nice and cool. (房间凉爽。)

He's good and dead, he is. (Stevenson)(那家伙死僵了。)

You're fine and strong, aren't you? (G. Eliot)(你孔武有力。)

You'll make yourself fine and beholden to Aaron. (G. Eliot)(你对爱伦要很感激才是。)

The place is nice and healthy. (那地方对健康很好。)
The dish is nice and warm. (菜热的好吃。)
I was rare and hungry. (Stevenson)(我很饥饿。)
She would make thee rare and happy, Seth. (G. Eliot)(塞司,她会使你幸福的。)

1. The car is going nice and fast.
2. I wish your eyes would always flash like that, for it looks so nice and manly. (Doyle)

(125) to one's + 感情名词
to the + 感情名词 + of

(a) *To my* joy, he was quite free from danger.
　　使我高兴的是他已脱险了。
(b) He has recovered, much *to the delight of* his friends.
　　他病好了,使得他的朋友们大为欢喜。

这是表结果的副词片语,句中的"to"就是表结果的介词。这两种形式和表感情的抽象名词结合时,意为"令人(喜、怒、哀、乐)的"。

I found to my horror that the man was mad. (我发觉那人已发了疯大吃一惊。)
To my shame I must confess that I wronged you. (实在可羞耻,然我必得自认错怪了你。)
I found to my joy (= was rejoiced to find) that he was alive. (令人可喜的是他还活着。)
To our surprise (或 astonishment) he has succeeded. (他的成功使我们感到惊异。)
To my disappointment, I found that he had left this country. (听说他已出国使我怅惘。)
So the matter has ended to the unspeakable relief of everybody. (事情如此了结,大家都非常安心了。)
She revenged herself to her heart's content. (她尽情报复了。)
The little animal, to the astonishment of the spectators, expired without showing any signs of pain. (使观众大吃一惊的是那个小动物竟一点痛苦的样子也没有就气绝了。)
To her horror she saw clouds of smoke issuing from her master's nose! (使她大为恐怖的是她看到一阵阵的烟从她主人的鼻孔中冒出来!)

1. And to his great surprise and sorrow, he saw that his dear old mother was seriously ill in bed, looking very pale and almost without consciousness.
2. One of the commonest faults of writing is the use of long and many-syllabed words when short, simple words would do as well. The greatest writers often do this, to their shame.

(126) so far
so far as
so far as... is concerned

(a) *So far* so good. (= Up to this point everything is satisfactory.)
到目前为止一切良好。

(b) He isn't dead *so far as* I know.
据我所知他并未死。

(c) *So far as* his eyes *were concerned*, he was already an old man.
单就视力来说，他已经是一个老人了。

英文的"so far" = so far forth = thus far，意为"到目前为止"。"so far as"与"as far as"同，照字面译时为"像……那样远"，如 We did not go so far as the bridge.（我们没有走到桥那样远去），引申为"就……而论"，如 So far as I know, he has not much money.（就我所知，他没有很多的钱。）至于"so far as... is concerned"，意为"就关于……来说"，"别的不说，单就……来说"。"so far as I am concerned" = as for me.（就我个人来说）。"as far as"由"距离"而变成"范围"，"as far as"是一个介词片语（Preposition Phrase），而"so far as"一般用作连词片语（Conjunction Phrase），表程度或界限的"in so far as"，则常用作连词，如作介词用是不合文法的（ungrammatical）（MEU）。"so far as"虽与"as far as"通用，但"so far"却与"as for"不同，"as for"与"as to"一样，是再提到已说过的事时用的，意为"关于"，如 As for me, I think I'd rather stay at home.（至于我呢，则宁留在家里。）As for news, I have little to say.（关于报导，无可奉告。）

So far you have been successful.（到目前为止，你是成功了。）

In as far as it is an inspiration, it is a gift from Heaven.（A. A. Milne）（只要是灵感，就是天赐。）

If I understand your brother, he only means so far as your having some thoughts of marrying.（J. Austen）（就我所理解的来说，你的兄弟不过是说，只有你想着结婚的事。）

So far you are right.（到此为止你是对的。）

Now that we have come so far, we may as well go all the way.（已经走了这么远，我们不难走完全程的。）

But so far there is no certainty as to the main starting grounds of the locusts.（Henry Jackson）（但是到现在为止，我们还不知道蝗虫主要的出发点在哪里。）

No casualties were reported thus far.（至今为止还未接到死伤的报告。）

Very wisely, he did as she ordered, for as far as he knew the revolver might be loaded.（H. Horn）（很聪明地他照她吩咐的做了，因为就他所知，那手枪也许是上了子弹的。）

Man is a rational animal—so at least I have been told. Throughout a long life, I have looked diligently for evidence in favour of this statement, but so far I have not had the good fortune to come across it.（人是理性的动物——至少我听说的是如此。在很长的时间里，我一直勤勉地在搜寻支持此说的证据，但至今为止我没有那

般好运找到它。)

So far as the style is concerned (= as regards the style), it leaves very little to be desired. (仅就文章来说,几乎无可指摘。)

The sun appears to take his daily course over the earth, while it is really the earth which moves. The sun, at least, so far as we are concerned, is standing still. (太阳好像是每天围绕地球在走,而实际走动的却是地球。至少就我们地球上的人来说,太阳是屹立不动的。)

1. The man who enjoys watching football is so far superior to the man who does not.
2. As far back as history goes men have always had some knowledge of the facts of nature; and those nations, like the Egyptians and Chinese, which long ago had become highly civilized, had learnt a great deal, and must probably have known some things of which we are still ignorant.
3. So far as people who have no ear for music are concerned, it would be a waste of time and money for them to try to learn music.
4. The literature of the past is only of value in so far as it has significance today, just as history is only of use if it can throw a light upon the contemporary scene.

XI. 连词的造句

(127) and that

Return to your work, *and that* at once.
回去工作,而且要马上去。

这个"and that"应译为"而且",是加强语气的省略说法,如 You must tell him at once. 一句普通的话,加强语气说时,便是 You must tell him, and tell him at once. 再简略地说,便成为 You must tell him, and that at once. 了。可知这个"that"是代表"tell him"的。一般都是将这个指示代名词的"that",用来代表上文的全部或一部分,如例题的句子便是以"that"代表"return to your work."整个句子的。OED 上说,"Used emphatically, instead of repeating previous words or phrase. Preceded by *and* (rarely *but*), and referring, to something in the previous cluse". 一般都是用"and that"的形式,不过如指前面的复数名词时,也可说成"and those",例如 I have only three rings, and those not of the best. (and those = and those three rings)。又如 With very short intervals of sleep, and those entirely filled with dream. (Fielding)

The snow began to come down and that in earnest. (开始下雪了,而且下得很大。)
He makes mistakes, and that very often. (他弄错,而且常常弄错。)
He will come, and that soon. (他要来,而且马上要来。)

I studied Greek and Latin, when I was young, and that at Oxford. (我年轻时学过希腊语拉丁文,而且是在牛津大学学的。)

All men seek after happiness, and that without any exception. (所有的人都要追求幸福,且无例外。)

Every moment may be put to some use, and that with much more pleasure than if unemployed. (时时刻刻都是可加利用来做点什么事的,而且比不做事更为快乐。)

He speaks English, and that very well. (他会说英语,而且说得很好。)

The ostrich swallowed a stone, and that a considerably big one. (鸵鸟吞下了一块石头,而且是一块相当大的石头。)

1. They alone have the right to change it, and that only in a particular way. (James Bryce)

2. I have tried in vain to account for the fact that with their absurd habits of eating and indolence, the German students can study so many hours and that to extreme old age.

(128) at once... and

The novel is *at once* pleasing *and* instructive.

那部小说既有趣又有益。

普通说"at once"的意思是"立刻"(immediately),如 She told him to leave the room at once. (她要他立刻离开那房间。)但这个"at once"也可作"同时"(at the same time)解,尤其是后面跟得有"and"时为然,例如 Do not all speak at once. (不要大家同时说话。)英文的"at once A and B"与"both A and B"同义,都是所谓相关连词(Correlative Conjunction)。

I was at once (= both) comforted and terrified by this thought. (这样一想既安心而又恐惧。)

His father was at once strict and kindly. (他父亲又严厉又仁慈。)

The expression was at once grand and sweet. (Hawthorne)(那表情既威风而又温和。)

He was at once detested and despised. (他既可恨又可鄙。)

The story he told us was at once interesting and instructive. (他讲给我们听的故事,既有趣,又有益。)

1. Very few will doubt that it is science which has at once quickened the demand for general education in modern times and the education itself effective.

2. Accustomed to play the host in the highest circles, he charmed and dominated all whom he approached; there was something at once winning and authoritative in his address (= personal bearing); and his extraordinary coolness gave him yet another distinction in this half maniacal society. (R. L. Stevenson)

(129) in that

Men differ from brutes *in that* they can think and speak.

人之所以异于兽类,就在能说话又能想事。

这是一种近乎文言的表现法,意思由"在那样的一点上",而变成"因为"(since;because)了。有时也可以说"in this",二者都是很庄重的文体,在正式的论述中常见的用法。

The budget is unrealistic in that it disregards increased costs. (这预算不符实际,因为忽视了增加的费用。)
Vinyl is similar to cellophane in that it is transparent. (乙烯基在透明的一点上,与玻璃纸相似。)
He didn't think the better of her in that she had a lot of imagination. (因为她的想像力丰富,他对她的评价不高。)
There is not a war in the world, no, nor an injustice, but you women are answerable for it, not in that you have provoked, but in that you have not hindered. (世界上任何一次战争,不,任何一次不讲道义的行为,都应由你们女人来负责,并不是因为那是你们鼓励起来的,而是因为你们没有去加以阻止。)

1. Some things they do in that they are men...some things in that they are men misled and blinded with error. (Hooker)
2. The scheme differs from the common method of accounting for the origin of our affections in this, that it supposes what is personal or selfish in our affections to be the growth of time and habit. (Hazlitt)

(130) It is true...but

It is true I went there, *but* I saw none.
我诚然去过那里,但我没有见到一个人。

这种"It is true...but"的形式,意为"诚然是…不过"。"It is true"有时可换用"I admit","It is admitted","no doubt","indeed","to be sure"等字样,"but"也可换用"yet","still"等字,"it is"也可以略去,意思都是一样。

It is true he is young, but he is prudent for his age. (诚然他是年轻,但以他的年龄,他是谨慎明智的。)
It is true he is old, but he is still strong. (老则老矣,然其体力犹健。)
A good method, to be sure—but hard to practice. (诚属妙策,然不易实行。)
For me, indeed, there is no labour at any time, but nevertheless does Sunday bring me repose. (对我来说,诚然是任何时候都没有劳动,不过到了礼拜天才真正获得心神的安静。)
Life is indeed a tragedy at times and a comedy very often, but as a rule it is what we choose to make it. (诚然人生有时是悲剧,而常常是喜剧,不过一般说来,还是看我们自己要它是什么就是什么。)
It is true that he did his best, but on this occasion he was careless. (诚然他是尽了全力,但在这个场合,他

却不免疏忽了。)

His music was not classical indeed, but was good of its kind. (他的音乐诚非古典,但是在那一类中还算是好的。)

It is hot, no doubt, but then the heat is dry. (确是很热,但没有湿气。)

1. It is true that road travel in the old days was difficult, tedious, and uncomfortable, but it was comparatively safe.
2. Those who are born in the purple have indeed many advantages, but they pay dearly for them.

XII. 其他的造句

(131) one
as such

(a) If you want a watch, I will give you *one*.
  如果你想要一只表,我就给你一只。
(b) He is a student, and must be treated *as such*.
  他是一个学生,我们一定要以学生待他。

为避免反复使用同一个名词,我们常要采用代名词,如果是同名同物时用"it",如果是同名异物时则用"one",如:

(1) If you want *the* watch, you can have *it*.
(2) If you want *a* watch, you can have *one*.

第一句是代表同名同物,故用"it";第二句是代表同名异物,故用"one",我们也可以说,"it"是指特定的东西,而"one"则是指不定的东西。作为反复代名词用的"such",只有"as such"一个用法。换句话说,反复代名词普通是用"one",如在"as"后就换用"such",即不说"as one",而说"as such"。英文的"as such"含义有二,其一为"照其资格"(in that capacity),另一为"其本身"(in itself 或 in themselves)。

I have lost my umbrella; I think I must buy one. (我把雨伞丢了,我想要另买一把。)
When the telephone was invented and was ready to use, hardly anybody cared to install one. (当电话发明了,且可供实用时,却很少的人要装置它。) the telephone 指一般的电话,故不用"it"而用"one"。
He is a child, and must be treated as such. (他是一个小孩,必须把他作小孩看待。)
He is the master, and as such must be obeyed. (他是主人,因此必须服从他。)
He was a foreigner and was treated as such. (他是一个外国人,所以被当作外国人看待。)
It was as a physician that he presented himself, and as such was cordially received. (Hawthorne) (他以医师的身份在这里出现,而大家便热诚地把他当作医师来接待他。)
History as such is too often neglected. (历史本身常被忽视。)

Wealth, as such, doesn't matter much. (单是有钱算不得什么。)

In country places strangers are welcome as such. (在乡下外来的人就因为这个理由而大受欢迎。)

1. He had not been bred a soldier, and had no inclination to bocome one.

2. New-year resolutions are good enough as such, but unless they are got into heart and life, as well as down in neat lines on papers, they will amount to little.

3. Witty men are apt to imagine they are agreeable as such. (Steele)

(132) one thing... another

It is *one thing* to speak and *another* to act.
说是一件事，做又是另外一件事。

在"one thing... another (thing)"的表现法中，"one"和"another"是对立的，正好像"some... other"是对立的一样，不可把这两个同义的表现法混淆起来。"one thing"有时可以略去，有时又可将"thing"字换用别的名词。这可翻译为"…是一事…又是一事"，表示二者判然不同，不可混为一谈。

Theory is one thing and practice (is) another, so they don't necessarily go together. (理论和实际判然不同，不一定能达到一致。)

For one reason or another (或 For some reason or other) he resigned his post. (不晓得什么理由他辞职了。)

To know is one thing, and to teach is another. (自己懂得是一件事情，要教人又是另外一件事情。)

That's quite another thing. (那是另外一件事。)

One man's meat is another man's poison. (施于甲为肉，施于乙为毒。利于甲者未必利于乙。)

1. It is one thing to own a library; it is quite another to use it wisely.

2. There is no more dangerous experiment than that of undertaking to be one thing before a man's face and another behind his back.

(133) in + 人物

They have an enemy *in him*.
他才是他们的敌人。

这个"in" = in the person of (在那人身上)，表一个人身上所有的性质、资格、能力等，原是由于形状(与形状有关的用"in"，如"in a circle"，"in print"，"in couples"，"in a heap"，"in human shape","in ruins"等)所转来,而有"即…是也","就是"的译法。这种"in"多出现在"have","find","see","behold","lose"等动词的后面。

We found a true friend in (the person of) him. (他才是我们真正的朋友。)
I have a good companion in (the shape of) a dog. (我有良朋,即犬是也。)
We have lost a good teacher in Mr. Wong. (王先生之死,使我们痛失良师。)
They see a great man in every Chinese. (他们见到中国人都认为是伟大的。)
He had something of the hero in him. (或 in his nature)(他有英雄气概。)
The love of beauty is inherent in poets. (爱美乃诗人之天性。)
I didn't suspect she had it in her. (我想她没有那种气质。)
I will defend him as far as in me lies. (我要尽力为他辩护。)
China lost a great artist in (the death of) Chi Pai-shih. (齐白石之死,使中国失去了一个伟大的艺术家。)

1. If ever thou wanted a friend, thou shalt have one in Richard Steele. (Thackeray)
2. You behold in me one who has slain the monster.
3. I recognized an old friend in the star actor.

(134) before 的四种译法

(a) *Before* he came here, he was in America.
他来此以前是在美国。(以前)
(b) You must not count your chickens *before* they are hatched.
小鸡尚未孵出不可作数。(尚未)
(c) It was long *before* he came.
他过了许久以后才来。(以后)
(d) It was not long *before* he came.
他不久就来了。("before"不要译出)

这个连词的"before",不可只照字面译为"以前",因为由句子的不同,还有其他各种译法,甚至译成相反的意思,或根本不去理它。我们翻译成中文时,必须注意中文的语法,不可死抱着英文原文的意思不放,如"before they are hatched"一句话,常被人译成"未孵出前",又是"未",又是"前",不免重复,不如译成"未孵出时"或"在孵出前"。

He went away before I could reply. (或 before I had time to reply). (我未及作答他已离去。)
She became a mother before she had attained her fifteenth year. (她不到十五岁已做了母亲了。)

It was midnight before he returned.（他在夜半以后才回来。）

I had not waited long before he came.（稍候即至。）

I had not gone a mile before I felt tired.（没有走到一英里路,我已经疲倦了。）

They had not been married a month before they quarrelled.（结婚未足月,夫妻已反目。）

My father died before I was born.（父亲在我出生以前就去世了。）

He arrived there before it began to rain.（他到达那里的时候,天还没有下雨。）

1. He had gone some distance before he missed the book.
2. They had not proceeded far before they perceived a bear making toward them with great rage.

第三编　疑难句法及文章译例

壹　英文类似句辨异

英文中常常有些句子,看去很是相似,其实总有一点不同,而那一点不同,就使得意义大为悬殊。这些句子最易使初学者难于觉察,而把意义弄错。读书误解,译书谬误,大都是由于这些地方有欠仔细所致,所以不要以为是小处,其实大有细心研究的必要。所谓差之毫厘,失之千里,正是像这样的。有时只因为在句子中多加了一个小小的冠词,而使得意义大变;有时两个成语,除有的多了一个不定冠词外,别无差异,而意义也就大不相同。有时因一个形容词或副词的地位不同,也会使句子产生不同的意义。诸如此类,不胜枚举,兹就见闻所及,采集一百二十例,除附译文外,又多加以注释,俾使研习翻译的学生,有所了解,而获助益。

1. (a) *A number* of members *are* absent.

    (b) *The number* of members *is* alarming.

    (a) 多数的会员没有到会。

    (b) 会员人数多得可惊。

    注　英文的 number 一字,有两个主要的含义:一为"数目"或"总数",如(b)例,故为单数。一为"许多"或"多数",如(a)例,故为复数。他例如 The number of fools is infinite. (愚人的数目是无穷尽的。) He owns a number of houses in this street. (他在这街上有许多屋子。)

2. (a) They are *the students* of our school.

    (b) They are *students* of our school.

    (a) 他们是本校的全体学生。

    (b) 他们是本校的一部分学生。

    注　有定冠词的复数名词代表全体,无定冠词的复数名词,代表一部分。他例如 The Americans are an active people. (美国人是活跃的民族。) Americans think that they can win the war in Vietnam. (美国人以为他们可在越南战胜。)

3. (a) His success is *out of question*.

    (b) His success is *out of the question*.

    (a) 他必成功。

    (b) 他必失败。

    注　out of question = beyond question. 无疑;不待言。out of the question = not to be thought of; quite impossible. 决不可能;无讨论的价值。

4. (a) The enemy is *in possession of* the fortress.

    (b) The fortress is *in the possession of* the enemy.

    (a) 那炮台一时为敌人所占领。

    (b) 那炮台的主权为敌人所有。

    注　in possession of = having in one's possession. 保持在某人手中,但主权并非某人所有。in the possession of = held by; possessed of. 为某人所有, 即主权属于某人。前者为一时占有, 后者为主权所有。前者以人为主语, 后者以物为主语。

5. (a) She was *with a child*.

    (b) She was *with child*.

    (a) 她带了一个孩子。

    (b) 她身怀六甲。

    注 be with child = be pregnant. 怀孕。

6. (a) She *kept the house*.

    (b) She *kept house*.

    (a) 她守在家里。

    (b) 她管理家务。

    注 keep house = manage the affairs of a household. 还可以再加形容词, 如 keep a good house = provide good food and plenty of comfort. 治家有条。所以管家婆就叫 housekeeper。

7. (a) A lawyer would *make a better statesman than a soldier*.

    (b) A lawyer would *make a better statesman than soldier*.

    (a) 律师比军人更易成为好政治家。

    (b) 律师改做政治家比改做军人更易成功。

    注 (a)句的 than a soldier = than a soldier would make a statesman. 两人相比, 应重复 that 后的冠词。(b)句的 than soldier = than he would make a soldier. 两职相比, 便在 than 后不要重复冠词。

8. (a) He is *rather a foolish fellow*.

    (b) He is *a rather foolish fellow*.

    (a) 说他是一个愚笨的人更为恰当。

    (b) 他是一个有点愚笨的人。

    注 (a)句中的 rather 是修饰 a foolish fellow 的, (b)句中的 rather 只是修饰 foolish 一字的。他例如 We have come rather a long way. (way = distance)(我们是从相当的远距离来的。) We have come a rather long way. (way = route)(我们来自颇远的路程。)

9. (a) Miss Taylor was *in charge of* the children.

    (b) The children were *in the charge of* Miss Taylor.

    (a) 戴小姐负责管理孩子。

    (b) 孩子由戴小姐照顾。

    注 如果把受照顾者作主语时, 就应在 charge 前加一个定冠词。他例如 The patient is in the charge of the nurse. 或 The nurse is in charge of the patient.

10. (a) The new harbour is *in course of* construction.

    (b) Fossils were found *in the course of* the work.

    (a) 新码头正在兴建中。

    (b) 在工事中发现了化石。

    注 in course of = in process of. 正在。in the course of = during or before the end of. 在…中; 在…时间之内。

11. (a) The maid of honour had grey *hair*.

(b) The maid of honour had grey *hairs*.

(a) 白头宫女。

(b) 二毛宫女。

注 (a) 句中的 hair 是一个集合名词,代表整体,即全部的头发,如说 She has golden hair. (满头金发。) 这是一个不可数的(uncountable)名词,不能加〔s〕使它变成复数的。但(b)句中的 hairs,便是一个可数的(countable)普通名词,指一部分而言,如说 grey hairs,意为头发花白,两色相间,故中文称为"二毛",通例指老年,如《左传》上说的"不擒二毛",《圣经》上说的 bring down a person's grey hairs in sorrow to the grave. (使老年忧愁促其早死。)

12. (a) He is *a child of ten*.

    (b) He is *a father of ten*.

    (a) 他是一个十岁大的孩子。

    (b) 他是一个有十个孩子的父亲。

    注 (b) 句的表现法,可以看出语言的经济。

13. (a) She served me with *a kind of coffee*.

    (b) She served me with *coffee of a kind*.

    (a) 她请我喝一种咖啡。

    (b) 她给我一杯说是咖啡而非咖啡的东西。

    注 (b) 句是表现出一种轻蔑的说法。意为徒有其名,实则太无味了。参考 a kind of gentleman 虽不能说很标准,总算是一种绅士。a gentleman of a kind 也称为绅士,实在是冒充的,强调 non-typical position of the individual,非典型的,算不了什么绅士。

14. (a) You have offended the girl as deeply *as I*.

    (b) You have offended the girl as deeply *as me*.

    (a) 你触犯了那女子之深和我一样。

    (b) 你触犯了那女子和触犯了我一样的深。

    注 (b) 句中的 me 为 offended 的宾语,而非 as 的宾语。as me = as you have offended me.

15. (a) You love me better *than he*.

    (b) You love me better *than him*.

    (a) 你爱我比他爱我更甚。

    (b) 你爱我比爱他更甚。

    注 (a) than he = than he loves me.

    (b) than him = than you love him.

16. (a) *This is no place* for me to go to.

    (b) *There is no place* for me to go to.

    (a) 那不是我去的地方。

    (b) 我没有地方好去。

    注 there is 为"有",there is no 为"没有"。

17. (a) Under the Mongol Dynasty Chinese men of letters stood *at the foot of* the social ladder.

    (b) He lay the money and treasures *at the feet of* the beautiful lady.

    (a) 在元朝统治之下,中国的文人社会地位最低。

(b)他把财宝献给那个美妇。

注 （a）at the foot of 在底层，在基部，如 the foot of a mountain 山脚。at the foot of the page 在页底。My house stands at the foot of a hill. 我家位于山麓。Notes are given at the foot of every page. 每页下端有注。（b）at the feet of 在脚跟前，在足下，如 They fell down at the feet of their enemy. 他们降服了。屈伏在敌人的足下。

18. (a) This is *my portrait*.

    (b) This is *a portrait of me*.

    (c) This is *a portrait of mine*.

    (a)这是我画的肖像画。

    (b)这是我的肖像。

    (c)这是我所藏的肖像画。

    注 除(b)意为 representing me（画的是我的像）以外，其余二句都不十分肯定，如(c)除 my property（所藏）一义外，还有 painted by me（所绘）的意思。(a)更是几乎三个意思都有，既有所绘意，也有所藏意，还有画我的肖像的意思。

19. (a) They are *an industrious people*.

    (b) They are *industrious people*.

    (a)他们是一种勤励的国民。

    (b)他们是一些勤励的人们。

    注 a people = a nation 国民。people = men 人们。

20. (a) You will find *some cigars of mine* in the drawer.

    (b) You will find *some of my cigars* in the drawer.

    (a)在那抽屉里你可以找到我的雪茄烟。

    (b)在那抽屉里你可以找到我有些雪茄烟在那里。

    注 （a）表示全部，(b)表示一部分。又如说 three of my sisters 意为我许多姊妹中的三个；说 three sisters of mine 则表示三个以外再没有姊妹了。

21. (a) *No one* appeared from *anywhere*.

    (b) They appeared from *nowhere*.

    (a)任何地方都不见人影。

    (b)他们不知是从哪里来的。

    注 （a）句中的 anywhere 和(b)句中的 nowhere 都是名词。(b)句中的 nowhere = no place（无论哪里都不是的地方。）The rumor came from nowhere.（那谣言不晓得是从哪里来的。）如说"他逃到不知哪里去了"英文就说 He has escaped nobody knows where.（= He has escaped God knows where.）

22. (a) We met *nobody*.

    (b) We did*n't* meet *anybody*.

    (a)阒无一人。

    (b)我们一个人也没有看见。

    注 （a）句带点文言的味道，(b)句才是口语的说法。

23. (a) He is *not a fool*.

    (b) He is *no fool*.

(a) 他不是傻子。

(b) 他不但不傻, 而且聪明。

注　一般的情形是 No sound was to be heard = Not a sound was to be heard. He has *no* money. = He has *not any* money. 但这个 no 又可以表示与它后接的字相反的意思, 如上举例句说的 He is *no fool*. = He is a *clever* man. 及 He showed *no great* skill. = He showed very *little* skill. 上举的 (a) 句为普通的否定句, 意即 He is not foolish. (他并不傻。) (b) 句意为 He is nobody's fool. 昔日国王豢养的小丑或弄臣叫做 fool, 是供人愚弄的, 现在说他不受任何人的愚弄, 可见他不傻, 而且是很聪明的。

24. (a) He has *no more than* ten books.

(b) He has *not more than* ten books.

(a) 他只有十本书。

(b) 他至多不过十本书。

注　no more than = only. 仅只。

not more than = at most. 至多; 或不足。

25. (a) It is *not always good* to live alone.

(b) It is *not good always* to live alone.

(a) 离群索居不一定好。

(b) 老是离群索居是不好的。

注　(a) 是部分否定。(b) 是全部否定。

26. (a) He is *not a little* afraid of it.

(b) He is *not a bit* afraid of it.

(a) 他非常怕。

(b) 他一点也不怕。

注　not a little = much. not a bit = not at all. 二者皆系副词片语。

27. (a) He has *not a little* experience.

(b) He has *not the least* experience.

(a) 他很有经验。

(b) 他毫无经验。

注　not a little = much. not the least = no. 二者皆系形容词片语。

28. (a) He is *not quite* so diligent as she.

(b) He is *not nearly* so diligent as she.

(a) 他没有她那样勤学。

(b) 他决无她那样勤学。

注　not quite = a little less... than 稍稍不及 (不足), 稍劣。not nearly = far from 大为不及 (不足), 大劣。

29. (a) I *ask you nothing*.

(b) I *ask nothing of you*.

(c) I *ask you for nothing*.

(a) 我没有什么要问你的。

(b) 我没有什么要求你的。

(c) 我没有什么要请求你的。

注　（b）有时也可以说成（a），因为这个 of 是 out of 的意思。（c）ask for 意为 demand（要求，请求），如 ask for a loan of money.（请求告贷。）

30. （a）We *hadn't anything* to eat.

   （b）We *didn't have anything* to eat.

   （a）我们家里一点吃的东西也没有了。

   （b）我们什么也没有吃。

   注　（a）句意为 We had no food in our possession.（b）句意为 We did not partake of any food.

31. （a）Write and tell me *whether* I am to come.

   （b）Write and tell me *if* I am to come.

   （a）请写信通知我看我有去的必要没有。

   （b）如果我没有去的必要你就不必回信了。

   注　表示"要不要"或"是不是"等意时，英文常用 whether 一字，有时在口语中则用 if 代 whether，二者原是没有什么分别的。不过把两句话比较研究时，也多少可以发现有些歧异，据 Palmer 的说法，用 if 时，等于说 Send me a letter if I am to come, but if I am not to come, don't trouble to send me a letter.

32. （a）This is *the same* knife *as* I have lost.

   （b）This is *the same* knife *that* I have lost.

   （a）这把小刀和我失掉的一把完全一样。

   （b）这就是我失掉的那把小刀。

   注　the same...as 同类物。the same...that 同一物。

33. （a）Ask him *when he comes back*.

   （b）Ask him *when he will come back*.

   （a）他回来的时候你就问他。

   （b）你问他要什么时候回来。

   注　（a）句中的 when he comes back 是副词子句，故要用现在时态代未来时态；（b）句中的 when he will come back 是名词子句，故仍保留未来时态。

34. （a）I *have to spend much money*.

   （b）I *have much money to spend*.

   （a）我非花许多钱不可。

   （b）我有许多钱可花。

   注　（a）句中的 have to = be obliged to，不得不，必须。（b）句中 have much money = am rich enough. 他例如：（a）I have to tell you something.（我必须告诉你一件事）（b）I have something to tell you.（我有话要跟你说。）可见 have to 分开和连续，意思是可能发生歧异的。

35. （a）*Whoever says so* is a liar.

   （b）*Whoever may say so*, he is a liar.

   （a）说那种话的人，不问是谁，都是撒谎。

   （b）谁说那种话，也就是撒谎。

   注　在（a）中的 whoever = the person that. 在（b）中的 whoever = though any person.

36. （a）They say Joe is mad, and *so he is*.

   （b）She is mad, and *so is he*.

(a)人们说乔发狂了,他真是那样的。

(b)她发狂了,他也是一样。

注 "so + 主语 + 动词"中的 so,意为 yes(正是)。"so + 动词 + 主语"中的 so,意为 also(也是)。

37. (a)*I am sorry* to disturb you.

(b)*I should be sorry* to disturb you.

(a)打扰你真对不起。

(b)如果会打扰你的话,那就真对不起啦。

注 (a)句意为事实上是在打扰。(b)句意为还不晓得是不是会打扰,如果是的话。类例如:(a)I think it is not true.(我想这不会是真的。)(b)I should think it is not true.(我看这恐怕不会是真的。)

38. (a)She wrote she *was coming*.

(b)She wrote (for) me *to come*.

(a)她写信说要来。

(b)她写信要我去。

注 (b)句中的 for,说话时可省略。英文说的 write for 是写信去要什么,如 I will write for a copy.(我就写信去买一部。)句中的 to come,是宾格补语,即是说要我到她那里去。"去"的意思而用"来"表示的,是主观的说法。

39. (a)It *makes* him *fear*.

(b)It *makes* him *feared*.

(a)那使他怕起来。

(b)那使他受吓不小。

注 (a)句指自己怕;(b)句指别人使他怕。

40. (a)I *left* the window *open*.

(b)I *kept* the window *open*.

(a)我让窗子开着。

(b)我故意开着窗。

注 (a)意为让它去,不在乎。(b)意指故意的动作。

41. (a)I had money enough *to buy it*.

(b)I had money enough *to have bought it*.

(a)我曾有足够买那东西的钱。

(b)如果我要买那东西的话,我是有足够的钱的。

注 (b)句中实含有 I had money enough,but I did not buy it. 的意思,用 to have bought,是表示与过去的事实相反的情形,在本句中即是说"未买"。有的文法家把它看作假设语气。

42. (a)Did you say *what* he wanted?

(b)*What* did you say he wanted?

(a)你曾说他要什么是不是?

(b)你曾问他要的是什么?

注 (a)句的答案是 Yes,I did. 或 No,I didn't. (b)句的答案是 I said he wanted some paper. 之类,(b)句中的 did you say 是插入句。

43. (a)Did you do *any work* last evening?

(b) Did yuu do *some work* last evening?

(a) 昨天晚上你做了点什么事吗?

(b) 你要做的事昨天晚上又做了一点吗?

注 (a)句的说法是对别人做的事或没有做,完全不知道的时候发问的,而(b)句则是知道对方有事要做(每晚),问他进行的情形如何时而说的。

44. (a) He is *as good as dead*.

(b) His brain is *as good as ever*.

(a) 他简直像死了一样。

(b) 他的头脑还是和从前一样的好。

注 (a)句中的 as good as 是一个成语,意为"几乎等于","简直一样",(b)句中的 good 作"好"的本意解释,照字面译即可。

45. (a) *Which train* are you going by?

(b) *What train* are you going by?

(a) 你坐哪一班车去?

(b) 你坐几点钟的车去?

注 (a)句中的 which 是指"哪一个?",即在许多当中指定一个。(b)句中的 what,作疑问形容词用,意为"什么?"问什么火车,即指几点钟开的火车。

46. (a) He is afraid to die.

(b) He is afraid that he will die.

(c) He is afraid of death.

(d) He is afraid of dying.

(e) He is afraid of being killed.

(a) 他怕死。

(b) 他惧怕他会死。

(c) 他怕死亡。

(d) 他担心会死。

(e) 他担心被杀。

注 在 be afraid 后,可自成段落,不必接任何字,也可以接 that 引导出来的子句,或不定词或 of 片语。这比说 fear,更为口语化。(a)句的 He is afraid to die. = He dare not die. 因为恐怖那种结果而不敢尝试。又如说 He is afraid to swim,是说他怕而不敢下水去游泳。如说 He is afraid of drowning. 就是他生怕淹死。前者是未下水,后者是已下水。(d)句的 He is afraid of dying. = He is afraid lest he should die. 意为他担心他会死。这个 lest,用于 fear 或 be afraid 后意为 that. 至于在 afraid of 之后,可接动名词或名词,而(e)句的 afraid of being killed,还是一样,只是加了一个被动进去而已。(c)句的 He is afraid of death. = He is afraid to die. 在 afraid 后接子句时(如 lest...should,that...might 等),不问是假设语气或直陈语气,都是指不希望有的事,所谓 unpleasant probability,担心有那样的事发生。他例如 I am afraid lest I should (= that I might) hurt his feelings. (生怕使他不高兴。) I am afraid (that) we are not in time. (我恐怕我们迟到了。) I am afraid (that) it will rain. (= lest it should rain). (怕会下雨。) 普通"afraid + 子句",表遗憾或抱歉的意思,如 I am afraid (that) I cannot lend you $1,000. (对不起,我恐怕不能够借给你一千元。)

47. (a) He is *certain of returning*.

(b) He is *certain to return*.

(a) 他自信一定要回来的。

(b) 他一定会回来的。

注 (a) 句是表示其主语的"他",对他自己将要回来的事毫无疑惑;(b) 句是说别人对他将要回来的那回事没有疑惑。同样地 He is sure of success. (他自认一定成功。) He is sure to succeed. (我想他一定成功。)

48. (a) It has been raining *continually* for two days.

(b) It has been raining *continuously* for two days.

(a) 断续地下了两天的雨。

(b) 不停地下了两天的雨。

注 (a) continual = frequently or closely repeated 表断断续续,即是间歇的。(b) continuous = without interruption 表继续不断的。

49. (a) Have you finished your homework *yet*?

(b) Have you finished your homework *already*?

(a) 你的课外作业做好了吗? (还是没有?)

(b) 你的课外作业就已经做好了? (真快!)

注 (a) 句是普通情形"问对方是否已经做好"。(b) 句则知道对方已经做好,而不免觉得惊奇对方何以如此的快,already 一字要念得重一点。

52. (a) *Happily* he did not die.

(b) He did not die *happily*.

(a) 他幸免于死。

(b) 他未死于安乐。

注 (a) 句中的副词 happily,是修饰整句的,而 (b) 句中的副词 happily 则是修饰动词 die 的。

51. (a) *Any* doctor will say *something* to please his patients.

(b) *Some* doctor will say *anything* to please his patients.

(a) 任何医生都会对他的病人说点安慰的话的。

(b) 有的医生会对他的病人说点安慰的话的。

52. (a) He is *the only son* of a poor man.

(b) He is *only a son* of a poor man.

(a) 他是一个穷人的独子。

(b) 他不过是一个穷人的儿子。

注 在 (a) 句中,only 作形容词用,比较简单。在 (b) 句中,only 作副词用时就复杂多了。作副词用的 only,最好是尽可能接近它所修饰的字,否则意义就变了。随着一个句子的语词的多少,而使 only 一语变动其地位,因而产生同数含义不同的句子出来,如由 only, the English, love, sports 四语构成的句子,则产生下列四种不同的句子:(1) Only the English love sports. (只有英国人爱好运动。) 意指没有别的人。(2) The English only love sports. (英国人只是爱好运动而已。) 而并不实际去运动。(3) The English love sports only. (英国人只爱好运动。) 别的都不爱好。(4) The English love their only sports. (英国人爱好他们唯一的运动。) 并没有别的运动。

53. (a) *By trimming* the sails, he tided over the crisis.

(b) *Trimming* the sails, he tided over the crisis.

(a) 临机应变,度过危机。

(b) 见风转舵,他得以渡过难关。

注 (a)句是普通的表现法,(b)句则为生动(vivid)的表现,因句中加上了一个 by 字,就显得语调太硬了。trim the sails = set sails to suit the wind,引申为 change one's opinion, views, etc. to suit circumstances.

54. (a) It was *the second year* of the Republic.

(b) It was *in the second year* of the Republic.

(a) 时在共和二年。

(b) 那是共和二年发生的事。

注 (a)句中的 it 是代表"时"的,(b)句中的 it 是代表"事"的。

55. (a) He *agreed to* the plan.

(b) He *agreed with* the plan.

(a) 他赞成那计划。

(b) 他认为那计划很好。

注 (a)句的 agree to = give consent to,而(b)句的 agree with = regard...with approval.

56. (a) He was *familiar to* me.

(b) He was *familiar with* me.

(a) 他是我很熟悉的人。

(b) 他跟我太亲密了。

注 (a)句中的 familiar to = well known to; accustomed to. 如 His face is familiar to me.(很是面善。)(b)句中的 familiar with 如对事物说时,意为"精通"(well versed in),如对人来说,则含有轻蔑之意,表示超越身份,交情等不当的亲密。他例如 He made himself much too familiar with my wife.(他对我的太太过分亲密太冒失了。)I am familiar with the countryside.(对这乡间我很熟悉。)

57. (a) I have a *friendship for* him.

(b) I have a *friendship with* him.

(a) 我跟他有交情。

(b) 我和他交游。

注 (a)句的 have friendship for somebody,意为对某人具有好感,例如 His friendship for Byron began in the same year.(他和拜伦的交谊也是同一年开始的。)(b)句的 have friendship with somebody,意为"与之交游",即和某人交际,彼此有往来,但不一定有交情。

58. (a) *At the beginning* of the term, our teacher addressed us in an eloquent speech.

(b) *In the beginning* God created the heaven and the earth.

(a) 在学期开始的时候,我们的老师洋洋洒洒地向我们说了许多话。

(b) 起初上帝创造了天和地。

注 (a)句的 at the beginning = at the start,意为"在开始的时候",(b)句的 in the beginning = at first,意为"起初"。同类的句子还有 at the end = at last,意为"最后",如 At the end of the term we shall have examinations(在学期结束时,我们有考试。) in the end = after all; finally,意为"毕竟","终于",如 In the end he found out all the secret. (他终于发觉了所有的秘密。) 还有 at the middle = between beginning and end, 意为"在半途", 如 The novelist was born at the middle of the 19th century. (那小说家生于十九世纪中叶。) I entered the school at the middle of April. (我是四月半入校的。) in the middle = in the centre or heart 意为"在中央", 如 The boy stretched himself at full length in the middle of the room. (那男孩伸长手脚睡在房间的中央。) In the middle of the night, there was a fire near my house. (在夜半我家附近起了火。)

59. (a) I am busy *at the moment*.

(b) Let's set aside *for the moment* the question of expense.

(c) Try to be calm and sensitive *in the moment* of danger.

(d) He is one of the men *of the moment*.

(e) She burst out crying *on the moment*.

(f) The clock is timed *to the moment*.

(a) 我眼下很忙。

(b) 我们暂时不妨把费用问题搁在一边。

(c) 危险当头, 必须镇定灵敏。

(d) 他是当今风云人物之一。

(e) 她当场就哭出来了。

(f) 那时钟报时绝对准确。

注 at the moment = just now. for the moment = temporarily. in the moment = in case. of the moment = important at the present time. on the moment = all at once; on the spot. to the moment = with absolute punctuality.

60. (a) I have to be *at business* by nine.

(b) I have been pressed *by business*.

(c) He has a good head *for business*.

(d) He is *in business* with his father.

(e) Are you in London for pleasure or *on business*?

(f) In my daily walk *to business* I frequently meet a certain gentleman.

(a) 我九点钟就要到店里去营业。

(b) 我一直非常繁忙。

(c) 他有经商之才。

(d) 他们开一爿父子商店。

(e) 你来伦敦是为游玩还是因公?

(f) 我每天走去店里的时候, 常遇到一位绅士。

注 at business 到店里去营业, 出差, 在执行任务。by business 由于事务, 例如 I was prevented by business. (为事所阻。) for business 为着事务, 为经商。in business. 从商, 从事实业, 如 a man in business (实业家)。This firm is now more than 60 years in business. (那店已经开办六十年了。) on business 因商务, 因公, 有事。No admittance except on business. (非公免进。) to business 办公, 上班。At what time do you go to business every morning? (每天早晨你何时去上班?)

61. (a) The animal likes to live *by itself*.

(b) The bird builds its nest *for itself*.

(c) The door opened *of itself*.

(d) It is a small thing *in itself*.

(e) He was *beside himself* in joy.

(f) He had the room all *to himself*.

(a) 那动物爱独居。

(b) 那鸟自力营巢。

(c) 那门自开。

(d) 这本来是小事。

(e) 他得意忘形。

(f) 那房间归他专用。

注　by oneself = alone,意为"独自","离群索居",但往往用作"自力","自然地"的意思。for oneself = independently,意为"独立","自力","不依赖他人",但往往有 for its own sake(为自己)的意思。of oneself = spontaneously(出于自动,自然而然),但往往用作"独自","不假外力"的意思。in oneself = absolutely 意为"原来","本来"。beside oneself = wildly excited;mad;out of one's sense,意为"神经错乱","忘形","疯狂"。to oneself = for one's use solely. 意为"专用","限于自己一人"。

62. (a) He went to Taipei *for pleasure*.

(b) He went to Taipei *with pleasure*.

(c) He went to Taipei *at pleasure*.

(a) 他往台北游玩去了。

(b) 他高兴地到台北去了。

(c) 他随心所欲地到台北去了。

注　for pleasure,意为"寻乐","行乐"。with pleasure,意为"乐意地","愿意地"。at pleasure,意为"随意地","恣意地"。他例如 He likes traved for pleasure. I will do it with pleasure. Will you come with us? Yes, with pleasure. You may come or go at pleasure.

63. (a) He spoke nothing *on purpose*.

(b) He spoke nothing *to the purpose*.

(c) He spoke nothing *to no purpose*.

(a) 他什么也没有故意说。

(b) 他说的一点也不得要领。

(c) 他所言无不生效。

注　on purpose 故意。to the purpose 中肯。to no purpose 无效,毫无结果。例如 People sometimes work to no purpose. 人们有时辛苦工作而无收获。

64. (a) He presented a pistol *to me*.

(b) He presented a pistol *at me*.

(a) 他送了我一支手枪。

(b) 他以手枪向我。

注　(a) 为好意的馈赠,(b) 为敌意的威胁,at 在此表目标。

65. (a) The boat was *under the bridge*.

(b) The boat was *below the bridge*.

(a) 船在桥拱下面。

(b) 船在桥的下流。

66. (a) I shall be here *till* three o'clock.

(b) I shall be here *by* three o'clock.

(a) 一直到三点钟,我都在这里。

(b) 至迟三点钟,我会到这里来。

注　till = as late as, up to, 至, 直到。by = not later than, as soon as, before, 迄, 到…为止。by 可以不到指定的时候, till 则一定要到指定的时候。二字都是表示时间的限度,即"为止",(a)句说的是人已经在此,(b)句说的是人还未来。

67. (a) *With this* he went away.

(b) *On this* he said so.

(c) *At this* he got angry.

(a) 他一面这样说,一面就走了。

(b) 他随即这样说了。

(c) 他一见到这个就生气了。

注　with this = as saying 这样说着。on this = hereupon 于此,随即,随后。at this = at seeing (或 hearing) this 见到这个,听到这话。

68. (a) I am quite *at fault*.

(b) You are much *in fault*.

(c) He is faithful *to a fault*.

(a) 我十分迷惑。

(b) 你咎有应得。

(c) 他非常忠实。

注　at fault = at a loss, in a puzzled or ignorant state, 不知所措,昏乱,迷惑。in fault = guilty, to blame. 有过失,应尸其咎。to a fault = excessively, too (much). 太,过于,非常。

69. (a) *In a word*, he is only a student.

(b) He calmed them *at a word*.

(a) 一言以蔽之,他不过一介书生而已。

(b) 他一句话,就把他们镇定下来了。

70. (a) He *sticks to* nothing.

(b) He *sticks at* nothing.

(a) 他对任何事都无恒心。

(b) 他无所踌躇。

注　stick to,意为"坚持"。stick at,意为"犹豫"。

71. (a) He has *as much as* she.

(b) He has *half as much as* she.

(c) He has *as much again as* she.

(d) He has *half as much again as* she.

(a)他有她一样多(的钱)。

(b)他只有她一半那样多(的钱)。

(c)他有她两倍那样多(的钱)。

(d)他有她一倍半那样多(的钱)。

72. (a) He will love his books *as long as* he lives.

(b) He will love his books *so long as* they are instructive.

(a)在他有生之日,他总是爱书的。

(b)只要那些书对人有益,他总是爱的。

注 as long as = while,当…之间,so long as = if only,provided that,on condition that 只要。但二者也常混用。

73. (a) I run away *for my life*.

(b) I cannot run *for the life of me*.

(c) I never ran so fast *in my life*.

(a)我拼命地逃跑。

(b)要我的命我也跑不动。

(c)我一生中从来没有跑过这样快的。

注 for one's life,意为"拼命","无论如何"。for the life of one,意为"怎也不能","要命也不能"。in one's life,意为"一生当中",多用于否定句中。

74. (a) His English is *anything but* correct.

(b) His English is *nothing but* correct.

(c) His English is *all but* correct.

(a)他的英文错误百出。

(b)他的英文只是不错而已。

(c)他的英文差不多没有错误。

注 anything but = far from,not at all,决非,并不。nothing but = only,只,不过。all but = almost,差不多。

75. (a) The portrait *is drawn from* 〔*the*〕 *life*.

(b) The portrait *is drawn to the life*.

(c) The portrait *is drawn as large as life*.

(a)这张肖像是写生的。

(b)这张肖像栩栩如生。

(c)这张肖像和真人一样大。

注 draw from life,意为"写生",只表画的过程,而不问画的结果。至于 draw to the life,即意为"逼真","和活的一样",只提画的结果,不管画的过程。其中 from 指由来,to 指结果。as large as life,是说画的大小,和真人一般大。

76. (a) They *inquired about* the matter.

(b) They *inquired into* the matter.

(c) They *inquired after* me.

(d) They *inquired for* me.

(a)他们曾询及此事。

(b)他们曾查究此事。

(c)他们曾来问我的安。

(d)他们来问我在不在。

注　inquire about = ask to tell about 问及,问到。inquire into = investigate 调查。inquire after = ask about a person's health or welfare 请安,问候。inquire for = try to learn where a person is. 探问某人的行踪。

77. (a)He was *at home in* English.

(b)He was *at home* wherever he was.

(a)他精通英文。

(b)他随遇而安。

注　英文的 at home 一个片语,有很多意思。其基本含义为"在家里",因为人在自己家里很是随便而感到舒适,所以又有"无拘束","安祥","舒适"之意。第三有接见客人的意思,at home 为"会客",not at home 为"不会客","不接见客人",如云 He is not at home to anyone except relatives.(他除亲人外不见客。)在 at home 后接上介词 in 时,则有"精通"之意,如 He is quite at home in modern history.(他精通现代史。)

78. (a)I have no opinion *as to* the result.

(b)*As for* me, I have no opinion at all.

(a)关于那结果我没有意见。

(b)至于我个人,是毫无意见的。

注　as to 及 as for,都有"关于"的意思,不过 as for,则有"别人(物)怎样我不知道,至于我(这个)……"之意。

79. (a)They are all *of age*.

(b)They are all *of an age*.

(a)他们都已成年。

(b)他们都是同年的。

注　of an age 中的 an,有 the same 的意思。

80. (a)Speak to him *as soon as* you can.

(b)Speak to him *as fast as* you can.

(a)你马上就去对他说的。

(b)你对他说话越快越好。

注　(a)句意为"立刻",指时间的迟早。(b)句意为"尽快地",指动作的速度。

81. (a)He is *a man of family*.

(b)He is *a family man*.

(a)他是世家子弟。

(b)他是有家室的人。

注　(a)句中的 of family = nobly born,出身名门。(b)句中的 family man = man with family,即 domestic person,有妻室儿女的人,或爱好呆在家里的人。说 family marriage,意为生有儿女的婚姻。类似的表现法有 a man of the world(劳苦的人),a worldly man(俗物)。a teacher of English(英文教师),an English teacher(英国教师,不一定是教英文的)。

82. (a)We must get it *at any price*.

（b）We must get it *at any cost*.

（a）无论要多少钱，我们都得买来。

（b）无论任何代价，我们都得把它弄到手。

注 price 是专指关于金钱的，cost 则与劳瘁，努力，健康，甚至生命，都有关系。

83. （a）He *has an eye for* pictures.

（b）He *has an eye to* pictures.

（c）He *has kept an eye on* this picture long before he bought it.

（a）他有识别画的眼力。

（b）他只注意那些画。

（c）他购此画之前，久已注意及之。

注 （a）have an eye for = be able to see well or quickly, 有鉴别力。（b）have an eye to = have as one's object, 着眼，作为注视之的。（c）keep an eye on = have one's eye on, keep watch on（lit. & fig.），watch carefully, 目不离的注意，留心照拂。

84. （a）He is *too* glad *to do* so.

（b）He is *only too* glad *to do* so.

（a）他高兴得不能去这样做。

（b）他极高兴去这样做。

注 （a）too...to do, 意为"太…而不能"，他例如 She is too young to understand such things. = She is so young that she cannot understand such things.（她太年轻不懂得那样的事。）The news is too good to be true.（消息太好恐不足信。）（b）only too...to do, 意为"正是所愿"，"甚为"，无否定意。他例如 I am only too willing to serve you.（极愿效劳。）I am only too pleased to help you.（我极高兴来帮助你。）

85. （a）He knows German, *to say nothing of* English.

（b）He knows German, *not to say* English.

（a）他懂得德文，英文自不待言。

（b）即不说英文，德文他也懂得。

注 to say nothing of, 自不待言，更不必说。not to say, 姑且不说，即使不说。他例如 He is dishonest, to say nothing of his other faults.（他不正直，其余的坏处更不必说。）He is very good-natured, not to say foolish.（他老实得几乎有点愚笨。）

86. （a）Won't you *go* to the concert this evening?

（b）Won't you *come* to the concert this evening?

（a）今天晚上的音乐会你去不去听？

（b）今天晚上的音乐会你也去听听好吗？

注 在逻辑上应当说"去"的时候，常改说为"来"，是客气的表现，因为是拿对方做主体，以他的立场来说话。我去你家，你来我家云云，是以"我"为主体的说法，如说，"明天我来看你"代替"去看你"，就是以"你"为主体的。上举的（a）例是漠不相干的问法，而（b）例用上 come 一字，则含有"我也将去听"的意思在内，因为不是去到对方的家，所以用不着客气，而只是表"我当然是要去的"含义，因此在译文中用了一个"也"字，来表示此种内涵。

87. （a）I *hate to lie*.

（b）I *hate lying*.

(a)我不能撒谎。

(b)我素来不喜欢撒谎。

注 (a)句是说临时的,指现在,指在这场合。(b)句则含有"素来","一向"的意思,语气较强。在 hate 一个动词后面,接用不定词或动名词皆可,含义微有不同。

88. (a) I *remembered mailing* the letter.

(b) I *remembered to mail* the letter.

(a)我记得发有那信的。

(b)我记起要发信。

注 (a)句在 remember 后接动名词,是说过去的事,有 remember having done 的含义,(b)句在 remember 后接不定词是说未来的事,有 not to forget to do 的含义。相反的字 forget 用法也是一样。

89. (a) She *stopped talking*.

(b) She *stopped to talk*.

(a)她停止说话了。

(b)她停下来说话。

注 (a)句中的 talking 为动名词,是动词 stop 的宾语。(b)句中的 stop 为自动词,to talk 为不定词的副词用法。

90. (a) I *saw* him only once.

(b) I *have seen* him only once.

(a)我只见过他一次。

(b)我生平只见过他一次。

注 (a)句的意思是指"他在这里的时候",而(b)句则可在句尾加入 in the whole of my life 来解释,即"在我一生之中,先后只有一次"。

91. (a) I *have not looked* at the paper this morning.

(b) I *did not look* at the paper this morning.

(a)我今天还没有看报。

(b)今天的报都没有工夫看。

注 (a)句是上午说的。(b)句是下午或晚上说的。

92. (a) *Have you ever seen* such a picture?

(b) *Did you ever see* such a picture?

(a)你看到过这样的画没有?

(b)你恐怕没有见过这样的画吧?

注 (a)句是平常 colourless 的问句,而(b)句则含有"我想你是没有的"的意味在内。要加上 ever 一字时才有此意。

93. (a) You *must not* play here.

(b) You *will not* play here.

(a)你们不可以在这里玩。

(b)你们不要在这里玩。

注 (b)句的说法虽同是禁止之辞,但比(a)句来说委婉而又优雅。

94. (a) I *soon informed* them of the affair.

(b)I *had soon informed* them of the affair.

(a)我马上把那事情通知他们了。

(b)我随即就把那事情尽快通知他们了。

注 (b)句是生动的(vivid)表现法。

95．(a)This book *is* worth reading.

(b)This book *should be* worth reading.

(a)这本书值得一读。

(b)这本书确是值得一读。

注 (b)句是加强语气的说法。

96．(a)Let'*s go*.

(b)Let *us go*.

(a)我们去吧。

(b)你让我们走吧。

注 (a)句的意思为 shall we go? (b)句的意思为 Set us free. 如果是一个人则说 me 以代 us. 如 Let me go! = Take your hands off me. 或 Don't hold or keep me.

97．(a)He *doesn't need* to be told.

(b)He *needn't be* told.

(a)(他已经知道)用不着告诉他。

(b)(他知道怎样去做的)用不着告诉他。

注 (a)强调现状。(b)强调今后的行为。

98．(a)If you *want anything*, let me know.

(b)If you *want for anything*, let me know.

(a)假使你要什么，告诉我好了。

(b)假使你需要什么而得不到的话，告诉我好了。

注 (a)句中的 want 为他动词，意为"想要"或"需要"。(b)句中的 want 为自动词，所以后接用介词 for，意为"欠缺"或"不足"。英国话说的 I want you to come. 美国话则说 I want for you to come.

99．(a)The surgeon *consulted* the orthopedist in reaching his decision.

(b)The surgeon *consulted with* the orthopedist in reaching his decision.

(a)那外科医生请教过整形医生之后才作决定。

(b)那外科医生与整形医生商量之后才作决定。

注 (a)句中的 consult 是他动词，意为 seek advice or an opinion from a qualified source(请教，咨询)。(b)句中的 consult 为自动词，所以后接 with，意为 confer with(商量)。

100．(a)I *know* him.

(b)I *know of* him.

(a)我认识他。

(b)我知道他。

注 (a)句意为 I have made his acquaintance, 认识，彼此有接触，有往来，也可称为朋友。(b)句意为 I know about him. 或 I know him by reputation. 或 I have been told about him, but probably have not met him personally. 只知其名，如在报上每天见到的大人物，也知其身份，地位，或品德学问，但多半从

101. (a) He *had trouble* on my account.

(b) He *took trouble* on my account.

(a) 他为得我而惹了麻烦。

(b) 他为得我而不辞劳苦。

注　have trouble 含有讨厌之意。take trouble 有不惮烦之意。

102. (a) He *must needs* go at once.

(b) He *needs must* go at once.

(a) 他坚持立刻要去。

(b) 他必须立刻就去。

注　needs 在此是副词,由于放在 must 的前后不同,而意义有别。must needs = insist on doing,意即主张一定要怎样,而 needs must = cannot help doing,意即不得不。

103. (a) He *was proved* to be a swindler.

(b) He *proved* to be a swindler.

(a) 业已证明他是一个骗子。

(b) 后来判明他是一个骗子。

注　(a) 句中的 prove 是他动词,他例如 His guilt was clearly proved. (他的罪已明白地证明了。) (b) 句中的 prove 是自动词,有 turn out (后来判明) 之意。他例如 Our reference books proved (to be) insufficient. (我们的参考书显得不够。)

104. (a) I *can but* read the book.

(b) I *cannot but* read the book.

(c) I *do nothing but* read the book.

(a) 我只好读那本书。

(b) 我不得不读那本书。

(c) 我一味读那本书。

注　can but = can only 唯有。cannot but = am compelled to,为加强 must 的说法,意即"不得不"。至于 do nothing but,意为别的什么都不做,就只是…。

105. (a) I *hope* he *will* do it.

(b) I *wish* he *would* do it.

(a) 我希望他会做。

(b) 他要肯做就好了。

注　(a) 句的 I hope,表可能实现的希望。(b) 句的 I wish,表不可能实现的希望。所以在 hope 后接直陈语气 (Indicative)。而在 wish 后就要接假设语气 (Subjunctive)。

106. (a) He writes *well*.

(b) He writes *a good hand*.

(a) 他的文章做得好。

(b) 他的字写得好。

107. (a) He has no one *help him*.

(b) He has no one *to help*.

(c) He has no one *to help him*.

(a)他不要人帮他的忙。

(b)他没有人要帮忙。

(c)他没有人帮他的忙。

 注 (a)句"have+人+原形不定词",有"令","使"之意。他例如:Please *have* the boy *bring* the books to my house. (b)句中 help 的宾语为 no one. (c)句中 help 的宾语为 him.

108. (a) He *made me a teacher*.

(b) He *made a teacher of me*.

(a)他派我去做了一个教师。

(b)他把我培养成了一个教师。

 注 (a)是任命我为教师。(b)是使我受必要的师范教育而成为教师。

109. (a) You *had better make it* at once.

(b) You *had it made better* at once.

(a)你最好马上去做。

(b)你马上把它改好。

 注 (a)句中的 you had better,是一种假设语气的说法,含有劝告的意思,可译为"最好是"。(b)句中的 had it made better,为"have+宾语+过去分词"的句法,在此为使动。它又可作被动用,其主语可分有意志与无意志两种,例如 I had my watch mended. 是有意志的,而 I had my watch stolen. 便是无意志的了。

110. (a) I *sent* a maid *to the doctor*.

(b) I *sent* a maid *to the doctor's*.

(c) I *sent* a maid *for the doctor*.

(a)我已派女仆到医生那里去了。

(b)我已派女仆到医生家里去了。

(c)我已派女仆去请医生来了。

 注 在中国话(a)(b)两句很容易相混,不过内容还是有分别的,即(a)是有事直接去找医生商量,到他家里也行,到他诊所也行,只要能找到他本人即可。而(b)的意思,就专限于到医生家里或送礼或取物,不一定要找到医生本人。(a)句注重在人,(b)句注重在地。至于(c)句,则意为请医生来。说 send for 是英文的惯用句,send for him = tell him to come(请他来)。send for the book = order it as purchase(定购)。

111. (a) He *may be* a good man.

(b) He *may possibly* be a good man.

(a)他也许是一个好人。

(b)他是一个好人也未可知。

 注 (a)充满可能性(possibility),好人的成分多。(b)缺乏可能性,外表虽则像是好人,骨子里怎样却不知道。possibly = perhaps. (或许,可能)。

112. (a) He *cannot be* a good man.

(b) He *cannot possibly be* a good man.

(a)他不会是好人。

(b)他决不会是好人。

注 在 cannot 上加一个 possibly,意为绝对不会,绝对不能。如 How can I possibly do it? (我如何能做这事?)

113. (a) I will *allow* him to do so.

(b) I will *permit* him to do so.

(a)我将让他去那样做。

(b)我将允许他去那样做。

注 allow 表默认。permit 表许可。

114. (a) You *may well say* so.

(b) You *may as well say* so.

(a)你说的有理。

(b)你也可以这样说。

注 两个 well 都是副词,而具有 with reason, justice or fairness 之意,至于 as well 则意为 with equal reason, advantage, etc.

115. (a) He *used to go* out at night.

(b) He *was used to going* out at night.

(a)他以前常在晚上出去。

(b)他曾习惯于晚上出去。

116. (a) He *kept smoking* all the while.

(b) He still *kept on smoking*.

(a)他在那个时间中始终在抽着烟。

(b)他至今还是抽烟如故(尚未戒除)。

注 "keep + 动名词"表继续不断的动作,"keep on + 现在分词",表保持某种状态不变。

117. (a) I must *have this coat ironed*.

(b) I must *have ironed this coat*.

(a)我必得把这件上衣拿去烫一下。

(b)我一定是烫过了这件上衣。

注 (a)句为"have + 宾语 + 过去分词"的形式,是表未来要做的。(b)句为"must have + 过去分词"的形式,是表过去推量的。

118. (a) I *saw* him *enter* the room.

(b) I *saw* him *entering* the room.

(a)我看见他走进那房间里去了。

(b)我看见他正走进那房间里去了。

注 (a)句意为 He entered the room and I saw it. (b)句意为 He was entering the room when I saw him. (a)句是叙述那件事实的,而(b)句则是说明那种动作的。

119. (a) He *guessed my age*.

(b) He *guessed at my age*.

(a)他猜出了我的年龄。

(b)他试猜着我的年龄。

注　同一动词常有他动自动两种用法,用于他动的意思比较确实的,用于自动的意思就表示不可靠了。如 catch a ball(接球)是表示确实可以抓到它的,这是用的他动词,但 catch at a ball(抢球)是表示大家争夺去抓那球,不一定抓得到手,这是用的自动词。guess 用作他动词时,意为"猜想","猜出",例如 You guesssd right.(你猜对了。)I should guess his age at 50. 或 I should guess him to be 50.(我猜想他有五十岁了。)作自动词用时,含有"猜猜看"的意思,如 Can't you even guess at her age?(你猜猜她的年龄看。)I cannot even guess at her age.(我对她的年龄甚至连猜都猜不出来。)

120. (a) He *proceeded to* the question.

(b) He *proceeded with* the question.

(a) 他已开始研究那问题了。

(b) 他继续去研究那问题了。

注　(a)句中的 proceed = begin, go forward (to do),开始进行。(b)句中的 proceed = continue, go on (with, in),(停止后)继续进行。

习　题

试就(a),(b)不同的含义译成中文:

1. (a) I met a young *man* in the street.

(b) I met a young *person* in the street.

2. (a) He came *to the town* in the evening.

(b) He came *to town* in the evening.

3. (a) You can tell me your opinion *while we eat*.

(b) You can tell me your opinion *while we are eating*.

4. (a) They *will be* coming.

(b) They *are* coming.

5. (a) It *seems* he is rather slow-witted.

(b) It *would seem* he is rather slow-witted.

6. (a) They *live* in Singapore.

(b) They *are living* in Singapore.

7. (a) He *pushed* the door.

(b) He *pushed at* the door.

8. (a) He went out *on a fine day*.

(b) *One fine day* he went out.

9. (a) She *sat up for* her husband all night.

(b) She *sat up with* her husband all night.

10. (a) We are sure *that man is mortal*.

(b) We are sure *that man is dead*.

11. (a) *The* cause of John's anxiety was his failure to pass the examination.

(b) *A* cause of John's anxiety was his failure to pass the examination.

12. (a) The prime minister appeared *on television*.

(b) The prime minister's address was broadcast *by television*.

13. (a) This is a *credible* story.

    (b) This is a *creditable* achievement.

14. (a) He is *not a teacher*.

    (b) He is *no teacher*.

15. (a) What do you *want from* me?

    (b) What do you *want with* me?

16. (a) He has *no less than* ten books.

    (b) He has *not less than* ten books.

17. (a) I have been *wired to* from home.

    (b) I have been *wired for* from home.

18. (a) This is a flash of humour *which surpasses Lin Yutang*.

    (b) This is a flash of humour *which Lin Yutang surpasses*.

19. (a) He is *sure of success*.

    (b) He is *sure to succeed*.

20. (a) *Few* of us know the truth.

    (b) *A few* of us know the truth.

    (c) *Not a few* of us know the truth.

21. (a) *On the contrary* he said nothing.

    (b) He said nothing *to the contrary*.

22. (a) *It is a pity* you did not go.

    (b) *It is a mercy* you did not go.

23. (a) I *wonder that* it is so.

    (b) I *wonder how* it is so.

24. (a) It *may* be done.

    (b) It *might* be done.

25. (a) I *wish I were* as rich as he.

    (b) I *wish to be* as rich as he.

26. (a) Let us *repair* our house.

    (b) Let us *repair* to our house.

27. (a) He wrote a letter *to me*.

    (b) He wrote a letter *for me*.

28. (a) He threw a bone *to the dog*.

    (b) He threw a bone *at the dog*.

29. (a) The lamp is *on* the table.

    (b) The lamp is *over* the table.

30. (a) He *is possessed of* great wealth.

    (b) He *is possessed with* dangerous ideas.

31. (a) I *doubt if* he is guilty.

(b) I *suspect that* he is guilty.

32. (a) He always *interferes in* my business.

    (b) He always *interferes with* my business.

33. (a) He *passed by* a scholar.

    (b) He *passed for* a scholar.

34. (a) Air *consists of* oxygen and nitrogen.

    (b) Hapiness *consists in* contentment.

    (c) His action *consists with* his words.

35. (a) What is he *about to speak*?

    (b) What is he *to speak about*?

36. (a) I saw *a great many men* there.

    (b) I saw *many a great man* there.

37. (a) I never *heard her sing*.

    (b) I never *heard her song*.

38. (a) We hired the boat *by the hour*.

    (b) We hired the boat *for an hour*.

39. (a) Whose brothers *take you* to the park?

    (b) Whose brothers *do you take* to the park?

40. (a) *Many* of the jewels were stolen.

    (b) *Most* of the jewels were stolen.

41. (a) He was *looked upon as* a genius.

    (b) He was *looked up to as* a genius.

42. (a) I must *look to* the matter.

    (b) I must *look into* the matter.

43. (a) I *don't care* to go abroad.

    (b) I *don't mind* going abroad.

44. (a) I *shall* have some people come tomorrow.

    (b) I *will* have some people come tomorrow.

45. (a) The island is five miles *around*.

    (b) The island is five miles *across*.

46. (a) I *have studied* English for five years.

    (b) I *have been studying* English for five years.

47. (a) He *has been to* New York.

    (b) He *has gone to* New York.

48. (a) They are *at play* in the garden.

    (b) They said so only *in play*.

49. (a) He did it *in haste*.

    (b) He did it *in a hurry*.

50. (a) I have nothing *to write*.

(b) I have nothing *to write with*.

(c) I have nothing *to write on*.

51. (a) There is nothing *to see*.

(b) There is nothing *to be seen*.

52. (a) Such men are *hard to find*.

(b) Such men are *hard to be found*.

53. (a) I am *anxious about* the result.

(b) I am *anxious to know* the result.

54. (a) I *did not notice* him.

(b) I *took no notice of* him.

55. (a) She *met* a friend in the street.

(b) She *met with* an accident in the street.

56. (a) Is there *any* difficulty in this?

(b) Is there *some* difficulty in this?

57. (a) I admire her as much *as he*.

(b) I admire her as much *as him*.

58. (a) I will pay at the end of *the* month.

(b) I will pay at the end of *a* month.

59. (a) I came to the meeting *in time*.

(b) I came to the meeting *on time*.

60. (a) I *think* it is not true.

(b) I *should think* it is not true.

贰 常易译错的文句

I 中译英

1. 中国的京戏你觉得怎样？

    How do you think of Chinese opera?（误）

    What do you think of Chinese opera?（正）

    How do you feel about Chinese opera?（正）

    How do you like Chinese opera?（正）

    注 How do you like it? = Do you like it much or little or dislike it?

2. 第二次世界大战是一九四五年八月十五日结束的。

    The World War II came to an end on August 15, 1945.（误）

    World War II came to an end on August 15th, 1945.（正）

    The Second World War ended on August 15th, 1945.（正）

3. 昨天晚上我们整晚在看电视。

    We spent last evening watching *the television*.（误）

    We spent last evening watching *television*.（正）

    注 television 是一个不可数的名词，不能加冠词，也不能变成复数，但加有 set 一字时则非加冠词不可，如 She won't leave *the* television set even though her husband is waiting for his supper.

4. 旅行社告诉了我们许多关于夏威夷的情形。

    The travel agency sent us *many informations* about the Hawaiian Islands.（误）

    The travel agency sent us *much information* about the Hawaiian Islands.（正）

    注 information 也是一个不可数的名词，不能说成复数。

5. 假期从明天开始。

    The vacation begins *from tomorrow*.（误）

    The vacation begins *tomorrow*.（正）

    注 中文的"从"字在这场合是不要译出的，其他场合也不要译成 from，例如"新学期从四月开始"。The new term begins *in* April. "新学期从四月五日开始。"The new term begins *on* the 5th of April. "茶会从六点开始。"The tea party begins *at* six o'clock. "教育从一个人出生开始。"Education begins *with* a man's birth. 例句中的 tomorrow，是一个副词，副词前是不可以用介词的。April, the 5th, six o'clock, birth 都是名词。

6. 这只表的价钱很贵。

    The price of the watch is *dear*.（误）

    The watch is *dear*.（正）

    The price of the watch is *high*.（正）

    注 以物品为主语时用 dear 或 cheap，以定价为主语时就说 high 或 low.

7. 我和他是好朋友。

   I am *a great friend* with him.（误）

   I am *great friends* with him.（正）

8. 旅行我总是坐三等。

   I *travel always by* the third class.（误）

   I *always travel* third class.（正）

   I *always take* a third-class car.（正）

   注 说坐几等时不要用介词，说坐船、坐车、坐飞机等才要，如 by boat, by train, by plane 之类。几等的等级前，不要用定冠词，但如不用 travel 而改用 take 时，则要在等级前加一个不定冠词，等级后加一个名词，如上译例。

9. 我不想去。——他也是。

   I don't wish to go.—*So* does he.（误）

   I don't wish to go.—*Nor* does he.（误）

   I don't wish to go.—*Neither* does he.（正）

   注 nor 在古文中虽可作副词用但现为连词，neither 古为连词，现为副词。

10. 我不喜欢喝酒。——我兄弟也是一样。

    I dislike to drink.—*Neither* does my brother.（误）

    I dislike to drink.—*So* does my brother.（正）

    注 dislike 一字虽有否定之意，但表面上并没有否定的字样，在使用时仍可看做是肯定的，故译文应将 neither 改为 so 才对。如说 I don't like to drink，虽意义相同，但字面上有否定（don't），所以后面可以接用 neither 一字。

11. 谁在敲门？

    Who is *knocking* the door?（误）

    Who is *knocking*?（正）

    Who is *at* the door?（正）

    Who is *knocking at* the door?（正）

12. 你什么时候到过伦敦的？

    When *have you been* to London?（误）

    When *did you go* to London?（正）

    When *were you* in London?（正）

13. 他没有告诉我说他什么时候回来。

    He *has* not *told* me *when* he *will* be back.（误）

    He *didn't tell* me *when* he *would* be back.（正）

14. 那一点你是错了。

    You *have mistaken in* that point.（误）

    You *are mistaken on* that point.（正）

15. 倘战争爆发我们会变得怎样呀？

    What shall *we become* if war breaks out?（误）

    What shall *become of us* if war breaks out?（正）

注　自动词的 become of = happen to，意为"降临"，"遭遇"，说时则为"怎样"。中国话是以"我们"为主语，但英文句中的主语则为 what。

16. 老张也没有来。

    Old Chang has not come *also* (or *too*). （误）

    Old Chang has not come *either*. （正）

    注　作"也"字解的 also 或是 too，只能与肯定连用，如果换上否定的句子，就得改用 either。

17. 昨天晚上我们玩得很愉快。

    We *played* very pleasantly last night. （误）

    We *enjoyed ourselves* very much last night. （正）

    We *had a good time* last night. （正）

    注　玩牌，打球，演戏之类就用 play，中国话这儿说的玩是指度过一个愉快的时候，最好译成 enjoy oneself 或 have a good time。

18. 如果他来，我愿尽力为他服务。

    If he comes, *I'm glad* to do anything I can for him. （误）

    If he comes, *I'll be glad* to do anything I can for him. （正）

    注　在副词子句中是用现在时态代替未来时态的。

19. 王君是一九六五年南洋大学毕业的。

    Mr. Wong *graduated* Nanyang University in 1965. （误）

    Mr. Wong *graduated at* Nanyang Univetsity in 1965. （正）

    Mr. Wong *was graduated from* Nanyang University in 1965. （正）

    注　英国人说 graduate at，美国人说 be graduated from，不过近来美国偶有略去 from 而说成 graduate college 的。

20. 他在那里专攻中文，荣誉毕业。

    There he *specialized* Chinese literature and graduated with *honour*. （误）

    There he *specialized in* Chinese literature and graduated with *honours*. （正）

    There he *took* Chinese literature and graduated with honours. （正）

    There he *majored in* Chinese literature and was graduated with honours. （正）

    注　"专攻"美国话说 major in，英国话单说 take 一字就行了。荣誉毕业即获得优等成绩，注意 honours 要用复数。

21. 上个礼拜我们班上讨论了关于男女同校的问题。

    Last week our class *discussed about* coeducation. （误）

    Last week our class *discussed* coeducation. （正）

22. 我惯于迟睡。

    I *am used to sit* up late at night. （误）

    I *am used to sitting* up late at night. （正）

    注　be used to = be accustomed to，"惯于"，后接名词或动名词，不可接不定词。如前无动词，单说 used to 时，则后接不定词，是指过去的习惯行为。参考：I used to sit up late at night. 意为"我以前常很迟睡觉"；现在睡得早了。

23. 你喜欢看看我搜集的邮票吗？

Do you like to see my stamp collection?（误）

Would you like to see my stamp collection?（正）

24. 他正忙着在写信。

    He is *busy to write* a letter.（误）

    He is *busy writing* a letter.（正）

25. 他们坐在小船上渡过河去了。

    They crossed the river *on a boat*.（误）

    They crossed the river *in a boat*.（正）

26. 她生于一九五零年。

    She was born *in the year of* 1950.（误）

    She was born *in the year* 1950.（正）

    She was born *in* 1950.（正）

27. 我在一九三九年夏天离开伦敦。

    I left London *in the summer 1939*.（误）

    I left London *in the summer of 1939*.（正）

28. 我想要一架电视机，但我没有钱买它。

    I want a TV set, but I can't afford to buy *it*.（误）

    I want a TV set, but I can't afford to buy *one*.（正）

    注 it 是代表前面用有定冠词（the）的名词，如前面的名词是冠有不定冠词（a）时，则须用 one 为代名词。

29. 他的情形跟我不同。

    His case is quite different from *me*.（误）

    His case is quite different from *mine*.（正）

30. 那地方像江南三月的温暖。

    The place is as warm as *March of Kiangnan*.（误）

    The place is as warm as *Kiangnan in March*.（正）

    注 place 不能与 March 比较，应以同类的名词"江南"来比。

31. 我跟叔父学英文。

    I *studied* English *from* my uncle.（误）

    I *studied* English *under* my uncle.（正）

    I *learned* English *from* my uncle.（正）

    I *was taught* English *by* my uncle.（正）

32. 他的职业是教师。

    His *profession* is a *teacher*.（误）

    He is a *teacher by profession*.（正）

33. 我的国籍是中国。

    My *nationality* is *China*.（误）

    My *nationality* is *Chinese*.（正）

34. 我的教授主张我去申请奖学金。

My professor *suggested me to apply* for a scholarship.（误）

My professor *suggested that I apply* for a scholarship.（正）

35. 请即回信。

    Please *reply this letter* early.（误）

    Please *answer this letter* early.（正）

    Please *reply to this letter* promptly.（正）

36. 那妇人跑到警察局去求救。

    The woman ran to the police *for getting help*.（误）

    The woman ran to the police *to get help*.（正）

    The woman ran to the police *for help*.（正）

37. 许多人在海上丧生。

    Many people lost *their life* at sea.（误）

    Many people lost *their lives* at sea.（正）

38. 听写我完全不错。

    I didn't *have mistakes* in *the* dictation.（误）

    I didn't *have any mistakes* in dictation.（正）

39. 他从来不撒谎。

    He always *says* the truth.（误）

    He always *speaks* the truth.（正）

    He always *tells* the truth.（正）

40. 他前妻生了两个孩子。

    He has two children *of* his former wife.（误）

    He has two children *by* his former wife.（正）

    注 by 有 born to him by 之意。

41. 我的见解和你相反。

    My views are *opposite from* yours.（误）

    My views are *opposite to* yours.（正）

    注 在 different 后才可接 from。

42. 他的意见和你的正相反。

    His opinion is the very *opposite to* yours.（误）

    His opinion is the very *opposite of* yours.（正）

43. 大多数的子女都想要自立，不愿依赖他们的父母。

    Most children want to be *independent on* their parents.（误）

    Most children want to be *independent of* their parents.（正）

    注 dependent 后接 on，而 independent 后接 of。

44. 我把窗子打开一下你不在乎吗？

    Do you mind if I *opened* the window?（误）

    Would you mind if I *opened* the window?（正）

    Do you mind if I *open* the window?（正）

45. 请你到这儿来一下好吗?

    Do you *mind to come* here for a moment?（误）

    Do you *mind coming* here for a moment?（正）

    Do you *care to come* here for a moment?（正）

46. 我开一下窗子你不在乎吗?

    Will you mind my opening the window?（误）

    Would you mind my opening the window?（正）

47. 他对中学教师讲授英语教授法?

    He lectured *teaching method of English* to high school teachers.（误）

    He lectured to high school teachers *on methods of teaching English*.（正）

48. 不久又有新的麻烦发生?

    It *didn't take long before* new troubles *arose*.（误）

    It *wasn't long before* new troubles *arose*.（正）

    It *didn't take long for* new troubles *to arise*.（正）

49. 旅行社宣布不再接受旅客前往开罗的订票。

    A travel agency *announced not to accept* any more bookings for tourist travel to Cairo.（误）

    A travel agency *announced that it would not accept* any more bookings for tourist travel to Cairo.（正）

50. 我很高兴接受你的邀请。

    It *gives me* much *pleasure in accepting* your invitation.（误）

    It *gives me* much *pleasure to accept* your invitation.（正）

    I *have* much *pleasure in accepting* your invitation.（正）

    I *take* great *pleasure in accepting* your invitation.（正）

    注　take great pleasure = greatly enjoy. 如说 have the pleasure 则后不接 in 而接 of, 如 I have the pleasure of accepting your invitation. 也是通的, 不过此种语法多用于下类句中: May I have the pleasure of taking a glass of wine with you? I once had the pleasure of being introduced to you. I am sorry I cannot have the pleasure of accompanying you today. I hope you will give me the pleasure of dining with me at 8 o'clock tomorrow evening at my place. There are many famous men whom I have not yet had the pleasure of meeting so far.

51. 这问题值得再讨论一下。

    It is *worth discussing* the question further.（误）

    It is *worth while* to discuss the question further.（正）

    The question is *worth discussing* further.（正）

    注　句中的 it 为形式上的主语, 真正的主语是 discussing the question further. 因此 worth 变成没有宾语了, 故第一句译文是不通的。第二句中的 it 仍为形式上的主语, 真正的主语为 to discuss the question further, 而 worth 另有 while 一个名词成为它的宾语, 所以就成为一个完善的句子了。注意 worth 这个形容词, 后面必须接用宾语。

52. 他给了我一张五百元的支票。

    He gave me a cheque *of* $500.（误）

    He gave me a cheque *for* $500.（正）

53. 他呼吸有大蒜味道。

    He breathes *with garlic smell*.（误）

    His breath *smells of garlic*.（正）

    注　他例如："这咖啡有点大蒜味道"，不可译为 This coffee has a garlic taste. 应译为 This coffee tastes of garlic.

54. 我最好来讲一个故事给你听。

    I can *do* no better than *to tell* you a story.（误）

    I can *do* no better than *tell* you a story.（正）

    注　在 than 后的字的形式应和 than 前的一致，句中前面是 can do，后面只能说（can）tell，不能说（can）to tell. 他例如 It is better *to win* than *to lose*. I'd rather *stay* at home than *go* for a walk.

55. 错误显然是在你那一边。

    The fault clearly *lies at* your side.（误）

    The fault clearly *lies with* your side.（正）

    注　在自动词 lie 后可接用各种各样的介词，惟含义各有不同，如 Sheets of paper lie *about* the room.（纸张散满一屋。）The village lie *across* the river.（村庄在河的对岸。）Accusation of theft lay *against* him.（控他以盗窃罪。）The path lies *along* a stream.（小路沿溪。）The hot springs lie *among* pretty scenery.（温泉在风光明媚之中。）The blame lies *at* his door.（错在他。）A happy future lies *before you*.（幸福就在你的前途。）What mystery lay *behind* the disappearance of the girl?（少女失踪的后面潜在着什么神秘?）The truth lies *between* extremes.（真理存于两个极端之间。）He has the manuscript lying *by* him for the next number.（下一期的原稿在他那里。）The charm of travel lies *in* its new experiences.（旅行的妙味在于新奇的经验。）The ship is lying *off* the mouth of the river.（船停在河口以外。）The book lies *on* the floor.（书在地上。）A white mist lay *over* London.（伦敦为白雾所笼罩。）The person lies *under* the suspicion of corruption.（那人有受贿的嫌疑。）The choice lies *with you*.（任你选择。）在 lie 字后接介词 with 时，意为"是……的义务"，"是……的责任"，他例如 It lies with you to decide.（决定的责任在你。你有义务来作决定。取决于你。）It lies with you to accept or reject the proposal.（接受或拒绝那个建议就全看你了。）The fault does not lie with the government officials.（责任不在政府官员。）

56. 那房间是用电力照明的。

    The room is lighted *with electricity*.（误）

    The room is lighted *by* [means of] *electricity*.（正）

    The room is lighted *with electric lamps*.（正）

    注　用于无形的手段时要用 by，所以与抽象名词连用，但用于有形的手段时则须用 with，所以与普通名词连用。electricity 为抽象名词，electric lamps 为普通名词。

57. 他觉得那杂碎是他从来没有尝过的美味，哪怕是在中国也没有。

    He thought the Chop Suey was more delicious than anything he had ever tasted before, *not even* in China.（误）

    He thought the Chop Suey was more delicious than anything he had ever tasted before, *even* in China.（正）

    He thought the Chop Suey was such a delicacy he had *never* before tasted anywhere, *not* even in China.（正）

58. 美国成为现今世界上最富有的国家。

    The United States *become* the richest country in the world.（误）

The United States *has become* the richest country in the world.（正）

注 The United States 要接单数动词。说"现在已经成为"应该用现在完成动词。

59. 我刚才把它写完了。

    I *have* written it *just now*.（误）

    I *have just* written it.（正）

    I *wrote* it *just now*.（正）

60. 他虽然生病但是仍去上学了。

    Though he was ill, *but* he went to school.（误）

    He was ill, *but* he went to school.（正）

    Though he was ill,〔yet〕he went to school.（正）

61. 我在下星期一去那里。

    I *will* go there *Sunday next*.（误）

    I *will* go there *next Sunday*.（正）

    I *will* go there *on Sunday next*.（正）

    注 凡 last, next 等字用于星期、年、月之前时，可将介词略去，用在那些字后面，就必须加上介词。

62. 你怎样认识他的呀？

    How you *come to know* him?（误）

    How *come* you *to know* him?（正）

    注 惯用法是 come to do 的问句中，要将 do, did 等发问的虚字略去，这是古来的传统。但在现今的口语中可说 How did you come to know him? 美口语还可以说 How come you didn't say anything?（你为何一言不发？）

63. 我从来没有听见讲过有这样的事。

    Never I have heard of such a thing.（误）

    Never have I heard of such a thing.（正）

64. 他称赞他妹妹的勤快。

    He *praised* his sister's *diligence*.（误）

    He *praised* his sister *for* her *diligence*.（正）

65. 有五百元一月就够生活了。

    Five hundred dollars a month is enough *to live*.（误）

    Five hundred dollars a month is enough *to live on*.（正）

    注 live 是自动词，故要加介词的 on.

66. 我从小孩子的时候起就认识他。

    I have known him *since* a child.（误）

    I have known him *from* a child.（正）

    I have known him *since* his childhood.（正）

    注 从过去某一时期到现在为止，英文要用现在完成时态，介词就用 since，但有时不说"迄"(till)也可以说"起"(from)的，即用"from + 普通名词"代替"since + 抽象名词"。但在 from 后也同样可接抽象名词，所以不说 He has been blind since childhood, 而说 He has been blind from childhood. 也是一样。

67. 我们登得越高,天气越冷。

    We ascended *the higher*, it became *the colder*. (误)

    The higher we ascended, *the colder* it became. (正)

68. 他既不会说华语,也不会说英语。

    He *neither* speaks Chinese *nor* English. (误)

    He speaks *neither* Chinese *nor* English. (正)

69. 消防队员死了不止一人。

    More than one firemen were killed. (误)

    More than one fireman was killed. (正)

70. 她打击了他的头,使他不省人事达一小时之久。

    When she struck his head, he remained unconscious for an hour. (误)

    After she struck him on the head, he remained unconscious for an hour. (正)

    He remained unconscious for an hour *after she struck him on the head*. (正)

71. 我正在听她唱歌。

    I *am hearing* her sweet song. (误)

    I *am listening to* her sweet song. (正)

72. 那便是我所收到的最后的消息。

    That is *the last news* I've received. (误)

    That is *the latest news* I've received. (正)

73. 双方的意见并没有什么不同。

    There is no difference *between both views*. (误)

    There is no difference *between their views*. (正)

    There is no difference *in their views*. (正)

74. 他有自己的一幢房子。

    He *has his own house*. (误)

    He *has a house of his own*. (正)

    注　英文的属格代名词(Possessive Pronouns)有两种形式,普通的形式为 my 等,后必须接名词如 my book,绝对的形式为 mine (＝my book)等,是为避免重复地来说那名词而采用的,例如 Your house is larger than mine (＝my house)。在属格代名词的前面如再加指示代名词时,即在 my book 前再加 this,that,a,some,any,no 等字样时,普通的形式便得改为绝对的形式,以避免指示代名词与属格代名词连在一起。三百年前的英文是可以连用的,即是可以说 this my book,而现代英文则必须改为 this book of mine 才行。反身属格(Reflexive Possessive)的 my own,your own,his own 等,也要采用绝对的形式,因为现代英文已不说 He has *that his* own house. 或 She has *some her* own reasons. 而必须改成 He has that house of his own. 或 She has some reasons of her own.

75. 他是我父亲的朋友。

    He is a friend of my *father*. (误)

    He is a friend of my *father's*. (正)

    注　名词前面的属格,可代定冠词用,如 my brother's wife ＝*the* wife of my brother. 又 my brother's friends ＝(all) *the* friends of my brother. 如果不是指某一个特定的人或几个人时,则须用不定冠词(a),那

是不能用属格来代替的,即是用了属格,还得有不定冠词,但我们又不能说 my brother's *a* friend. 或 *a* my brother's friend, 所以只好说 a friend of my brother's. 这种表现法所含有的意味是 a friend (that is) my brother's 或 one of my brother's friends. 这便是英文的两重属格的由来。

76. 我和王君久别重逢至为高兴。

   I am very glad to meet Mr. Wang again after a long *parting*. (误)

   I am very glad to meet Mr. Wang again after a long *separation*. (正)

   注 part 指离别的动作,如说离别的期间则用 separate.

77. 我在桥头和他分手。

   I *parted with* him on the bridge. (误)

   I *parted from* him on the bridge. (正)

   注 与人分离说 part from, 与物分离说 part with, 例如 He hates to part with his money. (他极舍不得用钱。)

78. 这学校有三千个学生。

   The school *has* three thousand students. (误)

   There are three thousand students in the school. (正)

   注 英文的动词 have 有三义:(1)物质上的所有,如 I have a lot of friends. (我有许多朋友。)(2)心身上的具有,如 I have a poor memory. (我的记性很坏。)(3)构成上的含有,如 A week has seven days. = There are seven days in a week. (一星期有七天。)例句中的 have 与(3)相似,但仍是似是而非,因学校是一个地点,不是机构,学校与学生的关系,不是不可分离的,不像星期少了一天就不成。还有 "there + be" 原意为"存在",存在于某处,因而变成"有"的意思。

79. 你方便的话,请在六点钟来。

   Please come at six if *you are convenient*. (误)

   Please come at six if *it is convenient to you*. (正)

80. 你有必要这样去做。

   It is *necessary of you* to do so. (误)

   It is *necessary for you* to do so. (正)

   注 一个形容词可以用来指"行为",又可以用来指"行为者",如 kind, good, foolish, nice, careful, careless 之类皆是。这种形容词可以接用 of 来造句,如 It is kind of you. (行为) = You are kind. (行为者)。另外有些形容词,只能用来指"行为",不能用来指"行为者",如 necessary, impossible, inconvenient, unbearable 之类皆是。这种形容词是不可以接用 of 来造句的,它只能接用 for, 例如 It is necessary for you to go. 而不能说 You are necessary to go.

81. 她父亲决不赞成她嫁给这样一个穷人。

   Her father will never *approve her marrying* such a poor man. (误)

   Her father will never *approve of her marrying* such a poor man. (正)

82. 由于整夜未睡,我们疲倦得要死。

   We were tired to death *through* having sat up all night. (误)

   We were tired to death *from* having sat up all night. (正)

   注 动名词前的 through 是表理由的,要 from 才能表原因。

83. 那囚犯的处死引起了很多的物议。

The prisoner's execution has caused a lot of public censure. (误)

The execution of the prisoner has caused a lot of public censure. (正)

 注 英文的属格有两种用法：一为主格作用(Subjective Possessive)。一为宾格作用(Objective Possessive)。例如 She has come to sing *his praise*.（她来赞美他。）是宾格作用。She doesn't want *his praise*.（她不要他赞美。）是主格作用。说 his praise(他的赞美)用作主格作用是不会有误解的，但说 his praise(赞美他)用作宾格作用，即属格变成了宾格，就令人费解了。这两种作用在文字上是没有分别的，读者要从意义上才能加以辨明。如上例句中所说的 the prisoner's execution,意为处死囚犯，当然是宾格作用，因为被人处死，是被动，决不可能变成囚犯自己处死的，所以不能说成 the prisoner's execution,只能改用 of 的造句而说成 the execution of the prisoner,因为用 of 的造句多是表宾格作用的，例如 the choice of him = the act of choosing him.（选择他）。如说 his choice = the preson or thing he has chosen(他所选定的人或物)，就是主格作用了。

84. 战争结束以后他就出洋去了。

 After the war being over, he went abroad. (误)

 The war being over, he went abroad. (正)

 注 在 Absolute Participle 的前面不要再加连词或介词。改正后的句子是属于 Written English 方面的，如改为 spoken English,则为 After the war was over,he went abroad.

85. 虽则他病过好几年,现在却完全好了。

 Though having been ill for years, he is now quite well. (误)

 After having been ill for years, he is now quite well. (正)

 Having been ill for years, he is now quite well. (正)

 注 though 是连词，只能用于连结两个子句(clause)。句中 having been ill for years,不是一个子句，至多前面只能用介词 after,或根本什么都不要。

86. 一到新加坡,我的朋友就在机场等我。

 On arriving at Singapore, *my friend* was waiting for me at the airport. (误)

 On arriving at Singapore, *I* found my friend waiting for me at the airport. (正)

 注 凡是带有介词的动名词，或是单独的分词，必须有一个意味上的主语，来配合这个动作。到达新加坡的是"我"，而主句中的主语却是"我的朋友"，动作不能配合，所以是错误的。介词 before 与 after 的情形和 on 一样，故下面的两句也是错的：After finishing his work,I paid him.（他把工作做完，我就付钱给他。）Before reading the text, the vocabulary should be learned.（在阅读课文之前应先学习生字。）

87. 他满足于默默无闻的生活。

 He is *content of living* in obscurity. (误)

 He is *content with living* in obscurity. (正)

 He is *content to live* in obscurity. (正)

88. 他禁止孩子们吸烟。

 He has *prohibited* the boys *to smoke*. (误)

 He has *prohibited* the boys *from smoking*. (正)

 注 古代英文原是可以接不定词的(如 God prohibited Adam to eat of the fruit of a certain tree.)但现代英文必须接"from + 动名词"。另一个同义字的 forbid,则可接不定词，如 I have forbidden the boys to smoke.

89. 我确信可以获得任命。

   I am *confident in getting* an appointment.（误）

   I am *confident of getting* an appointment.（正）

   注　confide 和 confidence 后皆接 in，如 He confided in your honesty.（他信任你的诚实。）She has great confidence in her success.（她自信她会成功。）但形容词的 confident 后却要接 of，他例如 We are confident of victory.（我们确信会胜利。）

90. 他后悔不该那样说的。

   He *repents to have* said so.（误）

   He *repents of having* said so.（正）

   He *repents his words*.（正）

91. 他坚持拒绝我的要求。

   He *persisted to refuse* my request.（误）

   He *persisted in refusing* my request.（正）

92. 总而言之，日本人在思想上有岛国根性。

   The Japanese people are insular in their thinking *to sum up*.（误）

   To sum up, the Japanese people are insular in their thinking.（正）

   注　独立片语，如 to sum up, to tell the truth, strictly speaking, taking everything into consideration, judging from…等等，都是应该放在句首的。

93. 日本的气候比英国温和。

   The *climate* of Japan is milder than *England*.（误）

   The *climate* of Japan is milder than *that* of England.（正）

   注　比较一定要同性质的才可以，例句中以气候比英国，故误。改正为 that 代表 climate，如前面名词为复数则用 those 代表。

94. 无知与疏忽是这错误的原因。

   Ignorance and negligence *have caused* this mistake.（误）

   Ignorance and negligence *has caused* this mistake.（正）

   注　两个以上的主语用 and 连起来表示一个单纯的目的或观念时，动词要用单数才对。他例如 Truth and honesty is always the best policy. Slow and steady wins the race. Bread and butter is his abomination.

95. 林博士代表新加坡大学出席会议。

   Dr. Lim, on behalf of the University of Singapore, *attended* the conference.（误）

   Dr. Lim attended the conference on behalf of the University of Singapore.（正）

   注　主语与述语务必放在一起，不要隔开。

96. 麦饼比米饼便宜。

   A *cake* made of wheat costs less than *that* made of rice.（误）

   A *cake* made of wheat costs less than *one* made of rice.（正）

   注　that 是从 the 变来的，属于定冠词的范围之内，所以它只能代表有定冠词的单数名词，如 The cost of oil is less than *that* of gas.（油价比煤气便宜。）但凡是有不定冠词的单数名词，就不能用 that 代表，只能用 one 代表，如上举的两个例句：one = a cake 而 that = the cost. 对于有定冠词的单数名词，也并不一定非用 that 代表不可,如 The step you have taken is *that* of much risk.(你所采取的步骤,是一个很危险的步骤。)一句中的 that 就错了,应改为 one 才对,因为在动词 is 后应接 a step,所以只能用 one 代表。

97. 他不但是一位作家,而且是一位画家。

   He *not only* is a writer,*but also* a painter.(误)

   He is *not only* a writer,*but also* a painter.(正)

98. 我住在离城一英里远的地方。

   I live *at a mile distant* from the town.(误)

   I live *at a mile's distance* from the town.(正)

   I live *a mile distant* from the town.(正)

   注　at 是介词,应置于名词前,不可置于形容词前,要用 at 则后必须接名词的 distance,不可接形容词的 distant,又 mile 既是名词,自应改为属格。

99. 黄君在台大读博士学位。

   Mr. Huang *studies the doctor's degree* at Taiwan University.(误)

   Mr. Huang *works for the doctor's degree* at Taiwan University.(正)

   Mr. Huang *is a doctoral student* at Taiwan University.(正)

100. 这些问题太难,我只能解答两个出来。

    The *questions* were so difficult that I could *solve* only two.(误)

    The *questions* were so difficult that I could *answer* only two.(正)

    注　solve a problem 和 answer a question 为一定的说法。

101. 彼德是一个十岁的男孩。

    Peter was *a boy of ten years old*.(误)

    Peter was *a boy of ten years of age*.(正)

    Peter was *a boy of ten*.(正)

    Peter was *a boy ten years old*.(正)

    Peter was *a ten-year old boy*.(正)

102. 学生们在星期六晚上要去参加一个舞会。

    The students are going to *a dance party* on Saturday night.(误)

    The students are going to *a dance* on Saturday night.(正)

    注　舞会应该说 dancing party,不要说 dance party,但一般只说 dance 也就够了。开舞会就说 give a dance,去参加舞会就说 go to a dance. 那旅馆每晚举行舞会:At the hotel dances are held nightly. 我第一次遇见她是在一个舞会上:She and I first met at a dance. 他们请我参加舞会:They asked me to a dance. 规模较大的舞会,英文又可说 ball,是从拉丁文来的。

103. 我很愿意帮你做任何事。

    I am willing to *assist you to do* anything.(误)

    I am willing to *assist you in doing* anything.(正)

    I am willing to *help you to do* anything.(正)

104. 辩论已近尾声。

    The debate was *drawing to an end*.(误)

The debate was *drawing to a close*. (正)

The debate was *coming to an end*. (正)

105. 他以儿子为荣。

    He is *proud in* his son. (误)

    He is *proud of* his son. (正)

    He *has a pride in* his son. (正)

    He *prides himself on* his son. (正)

    注　在形容词 proud 后要接 of, 在名词 pride 后则接 in, 在反身动词后则接 on。

106. 这章需要重新写过。

    This chapter *needs being rewritten*. (误)

    This chapter *needs rewriting*. (正)

    This chapter *needs to be rewritten*. (正)

    注　动词 need 后面接的动名词, 意思虽是被动, 但字面上一定要用自动。如不接动名词, 也可改接不定词, 不过形式便恰相反了, 这时的不定词, 一定要把被动表示出来, 不可用自动的 to rewrite, 要用被动的 to be rewritten. 他例如 This house needs repairing. = This house needs to be repaired. (这屋子要修理。)谚语有 The best horse needs breaking, and the aptest child needs teaching. (即使是最好的马也需要受驯, 即使是最聪明的孩子也需要受教。)如系人做主语则后可接自动的不定词, 例如 Each of us needs to master such a foolish fear. (我们每个人都需要克服那种愚蠢的恐怖。)

107. 这机器要修理。

    The machine *wants to repair*. (误)

    The machine *wants to be repaired*. (正)

    The machine *wants repairing*. (正)

    注　动词 want 也和动词 need 一样, 后接动名词时要用自动, 后接不定词时才可以用被动, 用自动便错了。如果以人做主语, 也就可以用自动的不定词了, 同时也可接被动的不定词, 例如 He wants to buy a watch. (他要买表。) He wants to be notified beforehand. (他要人事先通知他。)

108. 我现在到医院去看我兄弟的病。

    I'm *going to hospital* to see my brother. (误)

    I'm *going to the hospital* to see my brother. (正)

    注　到医院去求医是医院的本分, 不加冠词, 如 go to hospital (入院)。He is still in hospital. (他还在医院里。) He was taken to hospital. (他被送进医院去了。)反之, 则须加冠词, 如 My uncle lives near the hospital. (我叔叔住在医院附近。) Is it far from here to the hospital? (从这里去医院远不远?)

109. 那年我去了西贡, 而第二年我又去了河内。

    I went to Saigon that year, but *next year*, to Honoi. (误)

    I went to Saigon that year, but *the next year*, to Honoi. (正)

    注　我们现在说明年, 就用 next year, 如果是说过去的或未来的第二年, 就得加冠词说成 the next year. 如 The school year begins on the 1st of April and ends on the 31st of March of the next year. He started from here early the next morning. He arrived at New York on the 3rd of the next month.

110. 苹果坏了四分之三。

    Three-fourths of the apples *was* ruined. (误)

Three-fourths of the apples *were* ruined.（正）

注 英文以分数为主语时,由其后接的名词来决定动词的单复数,例句中 apples 为复数,故动词应改为复数的 were。但 Three-fourths of the crop was ruined.（四分之三的收成都毁了。）

111. 猫把家里的老鼠一扫而光。

    The cat *cleared off rats from* the house.（误）

    The cat *cleared the house of rats*.（正）

    The cat *swept rats out of the house*.（正）

    注 用动词 clear 时,其形式为"clear + 地点 + of + 物",如用 sweep 时,则为"sweep + 物 + out of + 地点"。

112. 昨夜他喝得大醉了。

    He *was* much *drunken* last night.（误）

    He *was* much *drunk* last night.（正）

    注 drunken 是一个限定形容词,只能用在名词前,如 a drunken man（醉人）,不能作叙述形容词用。

113. 笨人无药可医。

    There is no medicine *to cure* a fool.（误）

    There is no medicine *for curing* a fool.（正）

114. 昨晚我接到了他的电话。

    I *received a telephone* from him last night.（误）

    I *had*（or *received*）*a phone call* from him last night.（正）

    He *called me up* last night.（正）

115. 我觉得这样做是我的本分。

    I *think to do so* is my duty.（误）

    I think *it* my duty to do so.（正）

    注 英文惯用法是不用不定词作宾语的,故以 it 代替。

116. 峨眉山是中国的最高的山。

    Mt. Omei is the highest mountain *of* China.（误）

    Mt. Omei is the highest mountain *in* China.（正）

    Mt. Omei is *China's* highest mountain.（正）

117. 我打网球一年来大有进步。

    My tennis *has much progressed* in a year.（误）

    My tennis *has improved very much* in a year.（正）

    I have *made much progress* in tennis this past year.（正）

118. 日本好像以极大的速度富裕起来。

    Japan seems to be getting rich *at the tremendously speedy rate*.（误）

    Japan seems to be getting rich *at a tremendously speedy rate*.（正）

119. 去年我读了好些海明威的小说。

    Last year I read *many Hemingway's novels*.（误）

    Last year I read *many of Hemingway's novels*.（正）

    Last year I read *many Hemingway novels*.（正）

120. 名画落入了那人之手。

　　The famous painting *came into possession of* the man. (误)

　　The famous painting *came into the possession of* the man. (正)

　　The man *came into possession of* the famous painting. (正)

　　注　"物入人手"为 come into the possesion of, "人使物入手"即为 come into possession of, 因主语的不同, 影响名词前冠词的有无。

习　题

试改正下列错误的译文:

1. 到公园里去要怎样走?

　　How shall I go to the park?

2. 那讲演是在礼拜五从两点钟开始。

　　The lecture is from two o'clock on Friday.

3. 中国的风景很美。

　　The sceneries of China are very fine.

4. 他们没有房子住。

　　They have no houses to live.

5. 比起福克纳他更喜欢海明威。

　　He likes better Hemingway than Faulkner.

6. 这只表要修理。

　　This watch wants to mend.

7. 全家的人在九点钟上教堂去做礼拜。

　　The family go to the church at 9 o'clock.

8. 那年我身体很好, 但在那前一年我生了病。

　　I was quite well that year, but ill the last year.

9. 那条沉没的船不可能捞起来。

　　It is impossible to raise the sunk ship.

10. 你早上来吧, 不要晚上来。

　　Come in the morning instead of the evening.

11. 他的女儿嫁给一个阔人。

　　His daughter married to a rich man.

12. 这样一个好天气, 你为什么要呆在家里。

　　Why are you at home on such a fine weather?

13. 赶快, 再迟就赶不上了。

　　Make haste, and you will be behind time.

14. 日暮途穷。

　　The day is falling and the road is coming to an end.

15. 我从一星期前开始就生病了。

　　I have been ill since a week ago.

16. 你小时候读过的那些有趣味的故事你还记得吗?

    When you were a boy do you remember all the interesting stories you read?

17. 从汽车的遮风玻璃望过去,我们远远地就看见了那宝塔。

    Looking out of our windshield, the pagoda would be seen by us in the distance.

18. 兔子的耳朵比猫的长。

    The ears of a hare are longer than that of a cat.

19. 你去过美国吗?

    Have you gone to America?

20. 他来过此地一两次。

    He has come here once or twice.

21. 我昨天看见他。

    I have seen him yesterday.

22. 我觉得那菜很好,吃得很满意。

    I found the food very good, and enjoyed to eat it.

23. 我想很快就回家去。

    I think to go home very soon.

    I think going home very soon.

24. 一个普通信都不会写的人,对这样重要的职务是不能胜任的。

    A man who is unable to write a letter is incapable to hold an office of such importance.

25. 他好像很不喜欢说实话。

    He seems to have an aversion to speak the truth.

26. 中国人是刻苦耐劳的民族。

    The Chinese are hard-working and industrious people.

27. 我可以跟你借个电话吗?

    May I borrow your telephone?

28. 他被选为议员了。

    He was elected councilman.

29. 王先生昨天回返新加坡了。

    Mr. Wong returned back to Singapore yesterday.

30. 这报告必须在下月六日提出。

    This report must be presented by 6th next month.

31. 请你记得要我交还。

    Please remember me to give it back.

32. 我在纽约定购了十本书。

    I ordered ten books in New York.

33. 我确信我的英语可以使人听懂。

    I'm sure I can make myself understand in English.

34. 我确信我可以使你了解我的意味。

    I'm sure I can make you understood what I mean.

35. 汽车朝着公园的方向驶去了。

　　The motor car ran to the direction of the park.

36. 我对他的正直不能信赖。

　　I have no reliance in his honesty.

37. 他把大笔的钱交我代为保管。

　　He entrusted a large sum of money in me.

38. 小孩子总是这样那样顽皮的。

　　Children are always in some mischief or another.

39. 我对他的悲伤深表同情。

　　I sympathize him deeply on his sorrow.

40. 他向我道歉他所犯的过失。

　　He apologized me on his mistake.

41. 有人这样说，但我忘记是谁了。

　　Somebody said so, but I forget whom.

42. 他除了发财以外无他愿望。

　　He has no other desire but to make a fortune.

43. 她的服装不大入时。

　　Her dress does not conform to the fashion.

44. 如你所知道的，人生常比做航海。

　　As you know, life is often compared with a voyage.

45. 她入不敷出。

　　Her expenditures do not correspond with her income.

46. 我去吊慰了他父亲之死。

　　I condoled him about his father's death.

47. 学生到了多少？

　　How many students did come?

48. 这些就是他们说是傻瓜的人。

　　These are the people whom they say are fools.

49. 台湾比新加坡要大得多。

　　Taiwan is very larger than Singapore.

50. 我坐船回家要五天。

　　I take five days to return home by steamer.

51. 他是从后门进来的。

　　He entered from the back door.

52. 那个老人遭失明之痛。

　　The old man had his son died.

53. 这架缝衣机是中国制造的。

　　This sewing-machine is Chinese make.

54. 我从来没有见过这样高的人。

I never saw so a tall man before.

55. 他懂得知难而退。

He has good sense of quitting when he found the thing too difficult to do.

56. 马可·波罗以一二五四年生于威尼斯一个商人的家里。

Marco Polo was born in 1254 at a merchant's house in Venice.

57. 他从桌子上把花瓶拿去了。

He has taken the vase from the table.

58.《中国简史》的序文就是一部中国简史。

The preface of "A Short History of China" is a short history of China.

59. 我国的早期教育发展很快。

The early education of our country grows very rapidly.

60. 由于各学院中的教授皆一时之选，致使那间大学名扬遐迩。

It is due to the outstanding professors in the various faculties that the university has won a worldwide fame.

II 英译中

1. I am then never less alone than when alone. (W. Hazlitt)

   我出外旅行时决不比孤独时更少孤独。（误）

   我出外旅行时和一人在家时同样的寂寞。（正）

2. Nobody will be the wiser.

   谁也不会更为聪明。（误）

   谁也不懂得。（正）

   注 英文形容词 wise 有三个基本意思：(1)聪明的，如 You were wise not to go.（你不去是聪明的）。(2) 饱学的，如 He is wise in the law.（他精通法律）。(3) 知道的，如 We are none the wiser for his explanations.（听完他的解释，我们还是不明白）。上例便是第三义，等于说 Nobody will know it. 通常用比较级，意为"至今不知道的事，现在知道了"，所谓 none the wiser = no wiser than before = as wise as before，照旧。

3. The OED is the final court of appeal in all matters concerning English words.

   《牛津辞典》是有关英文一切问题的最后的申诉法院。（误）

   《牛津辞典》是有关英文一切问题的最高权威。（正）

4. Don't you see the writing on the wall?

   你不看见墙上的字吗？（误）

   难道你看不到灾难的迫切吗？（正）

   注 典出《旧约·但以理书》(Daniel 5: 5 – 25)。

5. Truth lies at the bottom of the decanter.

   真相从玻璃酒瓶底下看出来。（误）

   酒后出真言。（正）

6. Don't tell him home truths.

   不要告诉他家里的真相。（误）

不要对他讲逆耳的事实。(正)

7. This will go a long way in overcoming the difficulty.

    在克服困难上要走很远的路。(误)

    这在突破难关时是很有帮助的。(正)

    注 go a long way = will be helpful. 又 go a little way with a person,意为对那人一点效果也没有,对他影响很少。

8. He has a yellow streak in him.

    他身上有一条黄的纹路。(误)

    他有胆小的气质。(正)

9. One or two of the jewels would never be missed.

    一两粒宝石是决不会不见的。(误)

    失去一两粒宝石是决不会知道的。(正)

    注 作他动词用的 miss 有四义:(1)不中,不见,如 He hammered away,but half the time he missed the nail.(他不断地用钉锤在钉,但一半都未钉中钉子。)(2)略去,如 When we sing this hymn,miss out the second and fourth verses.(唱这首赞美歌时,略去第二第四两节不唱。)(3)逃避,避免,如 I missed the 7:30 train and so missed the accident.(我赶脱了七点半的车,所以未遇到那场车祸。)第一个 miss,是上述第一义。(4)觉察(什么)不在,因(某人)不在而想念。我们上面用来作例句的,正是这个意思。他例如 We shall miss you badly when you are away.(你走了我们一定会非常想念你的。)When did you miss your purse?(你何时才发觉你的钱包被扒去了?)Where did you miss your umbrella?(你到什么地方才想起你的伞来?)

10. I know he meant business.

    我知道他的用意在生意。(误)

    我知道他不是开玩笑的。(正)

    注 口语用法的 mean business = be serious;be earnest. 做生意的人是要认真的,讲求信用的,因此引申出上面这种意思来了。

11. This failure was the making of him.

    这次失败是他造成的。(误)

    这次失败实为他成功的基础。(正)

    注 动词 make 原是"造成"的意思,又可作"发展或发达的过程。成功的原因或手段"解,例句中所用的便是这个意思。making 还可以加复数,而构成"要素","素质"之意,例如 He has in him the makings of a poet.(他有诗人的素质。)

12. He has never recovered her loss.

    他永未能补偿她的损失。(误)

    他永含失恃之悲。(正)

    注 这是英文中最容易弄错意思的一种表现法。英文属格分主格作用和宾格作用两种。例句说的是宾格作用,所谓 her loss = the loss of his mother,而不是 his mother's loss,不是他母亲的损失,而是他失去母亲。如果说成 She has never recovered her loss. 就是主格作用,因为 she 和 her 是同一人,her loss 就是她的损失。从他动词变来的名词,就能有这两种作用。

13. I could do with more leisure time.

有更多的闲暇我就能做了。（误）

要再多有一些闲暇就好了呀。（正）

注　can do = be satisfied with; be content with, 满足, 忍受。在 do 之前用 can 的过去 could 时, 便有 "要能得到就好了", "想要" 的意思, 不过多出于戏言。That man could do with a shave.（那人要把胡子剃光就好了。）

14. She is now in a delicate condition.

她现在是在一种微妙的状态中。（误）

她现在是在怀孕中。（正）

注　分辨 a delicate condition 和 a delicate situation, 后者意为 "困难的局势"。

15. The lecturer carried his audience with him.

讲演者把他的听众带走了。（误）

讲演者博得全场喝彩。（正）

注　他动词 carry 除普通作 "搬运", "携带" 解外, 还有 "吸引（听众或观众）" 的意思, 如 His acting carried the house.（他的演技博得满场喝彩。）又有 "获胜"（在攻城略地, 选举, 提案等时）的意思, 如 Our troops carried the enemy's fort.（我军攻下了敌人的炮台。）He carried the election.（他当选了。）The proposal was carried with acclamation.（提案在大家鼓掌喝彩中通过了。）

16. General Smith and my father are on first name basis.

史将军和我父亲都是在第一名的基础上。（误）

史将军和我父亲是称呼名字的知交。（正）

注　on...basis 或 on the basis of; 意为 "在…原则上", "在…基础上"。on an equal basis（在平等的原则上）。I am on a fifty-fifty basis with him.（我和他平分。）

17. The grey mare is the better horse.

灰色的牝马是较好的马。（误）

牝鸡司晨。（正）

注　这是一句谚语, 意为丈夫受到妻子的支配。John Galsworthy 在他的名著 *The Man of Property* 中说："D'you think he knows his own mind? He seems to me a poor thing. I should say the grey mare was the better horse!"（你以为他有决心吗？我觉得他太可怜了。简直是牝鸡司晨呀！）

18. How much did you have to pay down on the car?

在那部车子上你一共花了多少钱？（误）

那部车子你第一次付出多少现钱？（正）

注　down = in cash, 在买东西时付出的现金, 如 You pay five thousand dollars down and the remainder in installments.（你付五千元现钱, 其余分期付款。）

19. Rich and poor were sitting cheek by jowl in the audience.

在听众中贫富分开坐着。（误）

穷人和阔人并肩坐在那里听讲。（正）

注　cheek by jowl 是一个成语, 意为 "极为接近", "密接", 因为 cheek 是脸颊, 而 jowl 是下颚, 二者原是紧接在一起的。胖人因有下颚的垂肉（jowl）, 而变成双下巴（double-chinned）。

20. Keep your chin up.

抬起头来。（误）

不要失去勇气。（正）

21. The wind blows south.

    风向南边吹去。（误）

    风从南边吹来。（正）

    注　凡表示方位的字，如东南西北，用作副词时，其意为"朝那方向去"，如 The river flows south. （河水向南流去。）唯有说到风的时候，就恰好相反，而指"从那方向来"。如赤壁之战那时正刮着东风，则说 At that time the wind blew east.

22. There was no living in the island.

    那岛上无生物。（误）

    那岛不能居住。（正）

    注　"There is no + 动名词" = "We cannot + 原形不定词" = "It is impossible + to-Infinitive".

23. A drowning man catches at a straw.

    一个落水的人抓住一根草。（误）

    一个将溺死的人哪怕是一根草也要去抓。（正）

    注　catch a straw 为实际抓住，catch at a straw 为还未抓到手，不过努力想去抓罢了。这个成语说的 catch at a straw 是指 an action of despair，表示绝望时的心情。

24. It was not that he had plenty of money.

    他并不是有很多的钱。（误）

    那并不是因为他有很多的钱。（正）

    注　这个 it 并不代表 that 以下的子句，而只是一个普通的代名词。在这种句式中常可将 it is 略去不说。这个 that = because，句首补上 it is，使成为一个完整的句子而已。说得更完全时，便是 It is not that... but it is... that...。代名词的 it 意为 the reason 或 what I mean。

25. The cavalry were well mounted.

    骑兵都已上马待发了。（误）

    骑兵都是骑的好马。（正）

    注　mount 在此不作"骑"解，而是指"供给马匹"，又 well 非"善于"骑马，而是指"好"马而言。他例如 The woman was well dressed. 不是说那妇人善于穿衣，而是说她的服装都漂亮。

26. He wanted to go to sea.

    他要到海边去。（误）

    他要去当水手。（正）

    注　want 作他动词用时，除"要"一个主要意思外，又还有"缺少"的意思，如 He wants judgment. （他缺少判断力。）作自动词用时则一定作"缺少"或"贫困"解，如 The house wants in height. （这房子不够高。）We mustn't let him want in his old age. （我们一定不要使他在老年贫困。）wanting 无论作形容词或介词用，都一定是作"缺少"解的，如 Many pages of this book are wanting. （这本书缺了很多页。）Wanting mutual trust, friendship is impossible. （无互信即无友谊。）

27. She is careless of her dress.

    她不注意她的衣服。（误）

    她不爱惜她的衣服。（正）

    注　careless of，意为"不重视"，若谓"不修边幅"则应说 careless about.

28. None is so deaf as those that won't hear.

   没有比听不见的人更聋的了。(误)

   没有比不要听的人更聋的了。(正)

   注 won't = will not,表示不要,不想要,含有意志在内,不是不能。

29. You must make good any loss.

   你必须转祸为福。(误)

   有任何损失你必须赔偿。(正)

   注 make good,有"赔偿"之意,如 Let me make good your loss.(让我赔偿你的损失。)又有"实践"之意,如 You must make good a promise.(你必须实践诺言。)

30. Those apples are good and ripe.

   那些苹果是优良且成熟的。(误)

   那些苹果是很成熟了的。(正)

   注 good and,当作一个副词用,意为"非常"(very),"完全"(thoroughly)。同类型的表现法还有 nice and (= nicely),rare and (= rarely)等,如 The car was going nice and fast. = The car was going satisfactorily fast.(车子跑得够快了。)

31. The smoke betrayed where the dwelling lay.

   烟将家屋毁坏了。(误)

   炊烟起处有人家。(正)

   注 动词 betray 有四义:(1)出卖。如 They betrayed their country.(他们出卖了自己的国家。)He was betrayed by his friend.(他为朋友所出卖。)(2)不忠,辜负。如 She betrayed her promise.(她不守诺言。)He will not betray our trust.(他不负我们所托。)(3)泄露。如 He betrayed his friend's secret.(泄友之秘密。)(4)无意中暴露,显示。如 His behaviour betrayed his intention.(他的行为显出企图。)His mistakes betrayed his lack of education.(错误显出他缺乏教育。)上面的例句正是这第四义,深山中的茅屋,为树木所遮蔽,外人看不出来,但有炊烟升起时,就显示出那里有人家了。

32. Curses come home to roost.

   诅咒回到老巢。(误)

   害人终害己。(正)

   注 roost 原意为巢,引申为安歇处,说 go to roost,即为上床睡觉。例句说诅咒回到原来出发的地方,即是反而害了自己。

33. He is brave like anything.

   他像任何东西一样的勇敢。(误)

   其勇无比。(正)

   注 like anything,意为拿任何东西来譬喻都不相称,引申而成"非常","不劣于任何东西"之意。

34. It is said that his days are numbered.

   据说他的日子都计算好了。(误)

   据说他的死期已近。(正)

   注 number 用作被动时,有"为数可数"之意,即"有限","无多","迫切"的意思。传说人寿有定,当生命将尽时,可以说 His hour has come. 或 His course is run.

35. It is time he began to work.

这时他已经开始工作了。（误）

现在是他应该开始工作的时候了。（正）

  注 "It is time + 主语 + 过去动词"，就和"It is time for + 宾语 + 不定词"一样的意思。句中的过去动词是一种假设语气的用法，他例如 It is time I was going.（我早应该告辞了。）

36. He was lost in admiration.

  他被人赞扬不置。（误）

  他不胜羡慕之至。（正）

  注 这句也可译为"他不胜赞赏"。be lost in，原意是隐匿在什么东西中间而看不见了，如山峰被云遮住，就说 The summit is lost in the clouds. 说某人走失在人群中看不见了，就是 He was lost (sight of) in the crowd. 所谓 be lost in，即从 be lost sight of in 而来，所以 He was lost in admiration. 原意是说在 admiration 中看不见自身，也就是进入忘我的境界，因羡慕或赞赏过甚，而忘其自身的存在了。中国话说的"发愤忘食"，"得意忘形"中的忘字，正是这种情形。

37. He was strong in his time.

  他在一生中都很强健。（误）

  他在年轻时身体强壮。（正）

  注 in one's time（或 days），意为 when he was young（或 at his best）。相反的说法则为 in one's age.（在老年）。

38. He may be drowned for all I care.

  不顾我怎样当心，他或许仍然会溺死的。（误）

  他也许会溺死，但我毫不介意。（正）

  注 for all I care = I don't care if. 英文说的 for all 或 with all，实有不顾（notwithstanding）之意，如 For all his wealth, he is unhappy.（他虽有那么多的钱还是不快乐。）

39. There is no love lost between them.

  他们之间并未失掉爱情。（误）

  我们非常不和。（正）

  注 这是委婉的说法，意为他们之间根本无爱情可言，换言之，There is hatred between them.（他们之间只有憎恨。）

40. He had words with her.

  他和她谈过话了。（误）

  他和她发生口角了。（正）

  注 have words with 或 exchange words with，为互相争论或口角之意。本例也可说成 They had words together. 英文的 words，常有吵嘴的意思，如 proceed from words to blows（由争论而至殴打。）

41. He was laid up for a few days.

  他被安插好几天了。（误）

  他病倒两三天了。（正）

  注 因病或伤睡在床上，英文说 lay up，如 be laid up with illness（卧病）；be laid up with a broken leg（因折腿不能起床）。

42. He took my advice in good part.

  他接受了我的忠告最好的部分。（误）

他嘉纳了我的忠言。（正）

> **注** take something in good part,意为"善意地接受"或"顺受"。相反的说法有 in bad（或 ill）part,则为"不悦"或"逆受"。A 教授请假一日后通知学生翌晨照常上课,在黑板上写道"Prof. A will meet his class tomorrow morning."有顽皮学生恶作剧,把 class 一字的第一个字母"c"擦去,变成了 lass（意为少女或情妇）,教授见到不以为忤(The professor took the practical joke in good part.)进而再擦去"l"那个字母,如是学生变成蠢材了。

43. It is a wise man that never makes mistakes.

聪明人从来不做错事。（误）

智者千虑必有一失。（正）

> **注** 此句照字面解释,似应照误句的译法,不过这是一句古来的谚语,凡"it is...that（who）"的构造,都含有"无论怎样……都不免"的意思。参考下列各句:It is an ill wind that blows nobody good.（害于此者利于彼。人病医生喜。人死和尚乐。)It is an ill bird that fouls its own nest.（自诽其家者未之有也。家丑不可外扬。)It is a good workman that never blunders.（无论怎样好的工人有时都不免做错。)It is a long lane that has no turning.（否极泰来。)It is a wise mother who knows her own child.（为母者不知其子之恶。)It is a good divine who follows his own instructions.（能说者不能行。）

44. We parted the best friends.

我们和最好的朋友离别了。（误）

我们在分别时是极好的朋友。（正）

> **注** part 是一个自动词,the best friends 为补语。

45. Twenty failed, myself among the rest.

有二十人落第,但我自己不在内。（误）

落第者二十名,我自己也是其中之一。（正）

> **注** the rest,原意为"其余",如 as for the rest(至于其他之点)。但 among the rest,则系一个成语,意为 among the number(就在那个数目之中)。

46. I am in his debt.

我是他的债主。（误）

我借了他的钱。（正）

> **注** be in one's debt,意为"有负于人","欠他的债",进而有"蒙恩"的意思。

47. He is dead, as I live.

他死了,我还活着。（误）

他的的确确是死了。（正）

> **注** as I live 在此意为 indeed(的确),是加重前面主句的。英文还有其他类似的说法,如 as I am here, as the sun shines, as you stand here, as my nose is on my face 等等。

48. She will make you a good wife.

她将使你做一个好妻子。（误）

她将成为你的好妻子。（正）

> **注** 这个 make 是完全他动词,采用了两个宾语,前面的 you 为间接宾语,后面的 good wife 为直接宾语。"母亲要替我买一只表"一语,如不译为 Mother will buy a watch for me. 时,也可译为 Mother will buy me a watch. 所以上举例句就是 She well make a good wife for you 的另一种说法。利用 make 这个他

动词,我们还可以造出这样的妙句:She made him a good husband because she made him a good wife. (因为她成为他的好妻子,所以也把他做成了一个好丈夫。)第一个 made 为不完全他动词;第二个 made 为完全他动词。

49. His picture does credit to a professional.

    他的画可增加专家的信用。(误)

    他的画较之专家所作亦无逊色。(正)

    注 does credit to = be worthy of,意为"有成为的价值","为之增光",如 She does credit to the educational system pursued here. (Thackeray)(她为这里所追求的教育制度增光不少。)

50. I am staying with a friend.

    我和一个朋友同住。(误)

    我现在住在一个朋友家里。(正)

    注 stay with = stay at — 's house. 用 with 时后接"人物",用 in 时后接"地方",用 at 时后接"房屋"。

51. They made an example of the boy.

    他们以此童为模范。(误)

    他们惩罚此童以儆其余。(正)

    注 make an example of one = punish one as an example to others. = make an example of the first offender as a warning to others. (惩初犯者以儆效尤)。注意:如说 set an example,就是"示范"了,如 He set an example to his inferiors. (他为晚辈示范。)You should set an example for the future. (你应以身作则,垂法于后。)

52. We found them at table.

    我发现他们在打牌。(误)

    我看见他们在用餐。(正)

    注 green table 是指赌博,普通单说 table 一字,多半是说用餐,如 lay the table 摆刀叉准备用餐。keep a good table 餐食丰美。keep an open table 广纳食客。

53. I will make myself obeyed.

    我要使自己服从。(误)

    我自己说的话必将恪守。(正)

    注 参考:I made myself understood in English. (我使别人能听懂我用英语说的话。)例句中的 obeyed 的用法,与上例中的 understood 相同。如说 I made you understand me. (我使你了解我。)则与说 I will make others obey me. (我要使别人服从我。)用法相同,understand 和 obey 二字,都是略去了 to 的不定词。

54. But for hope, life would be short.

    但是因为希望,人生是短促的。(误)

    如果没有希望,人生苦短。(正)

    注 but for = if it were not for 或 if it had not been for(如果没有),可作为过去或过去完成的省略。这个 but 有否定之意,后面如不接 for,而接 that 也是一样,如 Life could be short, but that hope prolongs it. (人生是短促的,若非希望去延长它的话。)

55. He is ignorant to a proverb.

    他不懂得这句谚语。(误)

他的无知是有名的。（正）

　　注　这句话又可说成 His ignorance is a proverb. 或 He is a proverb for ignorance. 所谓 proverb, 是指尽人皆知的事,故 to a proverb, 意即尽人皆知,达到尽人皆知的程度。参考：He is ignorant to a wonder.（他的无知令人吃惊。）改用形容词也是一样,如 His generosity is proverbial = He is proverbial for his generosity.（他的大量是人所共知的。）

56. The man was generous to a fault.

那人宽恕过失。（误）

他过于宽大。（正）

　　注　to a fault = to excess; excessively, 过度地, 极端地。他例如, He is kind to a fault.（他极端亲切。）用上 faut 一字,原意为即令有缺点也满不在乎。

57. I have no opinion of that sort of man.

我不赞成那种人的意见。（误）

我对于那种人毫无好感。（正）

　　注　句中的 opinion 一字,不是"意见",而是"评价"的意思,又可作"信用"解,如 I have no opinion of him.（我不相信其人。）他例如 I have a very high opinion of him.（我尊敬他。）

58. He will finish it in no time.

他将永远不能完成此事。（误）

他马上就会把这个做完。（正）

　　注　in no time = in a moment. 立刻。

59. I have a long letter in hand.

我手中拿着一封长信。（误）

我正在写着一封长信。（正）

　　注　如果是手中拿着的话,应说 I have a long letter in my hand, 单说 have in hand 意为 be engaged in（正进行中,担任着,制驭着）。他例如 He has a novel in hand.（他正在写一部长篇小说。）参考：at hand（近,在近边,在手边）, by hand（用手）, on hand（现存着,即来）, to hand（到手,收到）。

60. He thought all his own that she had.

他以为他自己所有的一切都是她的。（误）

他以为她所有的一切都是他自己的。（正）

　　注　all 是 that she had 的 antecedant（先行词）。

61. He is equal to any task whatever.

他对任何事情都是同等看待的。（误）

他对任何工作都可胜任愉快。（正）

　　注　be equal to the work = be able to do the work, 胜任愉快, 应付裕如。他例如 He was equal to the occasion.（他能应付那种局势。他能临机应变。）She is very weak and not equal to a long journey.（她身体很弱,不堪长途跋涉。）She does not feel equal to receiving so many visitors.（她觉得力有未逮,不能接待这么多的客人。）

62. He has to answer to me for the letter.

他必须回答我那封信。（误）

关于那封信他必须对我负责。（正）

注　answer for,有"负责"的意思,如 answer for a crime(对一种罪行负责。) answer for his safety. (负责他的安全。) You will have to answer for your wrongdoings one day. (将来有一天,你会自食其恶果的。) I can't answer for his honesty. (我不能保证他的诚实。)

63. They did not answer to your explanation.

　　他们对你的解释没有回答。(误)

　　那些和你的解释不相符合。(正)

　　注　"回答"只能用 answer 一字,不能加 to。英文说的 answer to = correspond,即"符合"之意。主语的 they,指事不指人。

64. The officer was broken for neglect of duty.

　　那军官破坏守则,忽视义务。(误)

　　那军官因玩忽职守而受降级处分。(正)

　　注　break = reduce in rank,是美国用法,说 break an officer,便是将他革职(dismiss),把他的官阶降级到士兵的地位。

65. They were killed to a man.

　　他们被杀得只剩下一个人了。(误)

　　他们被杀得片甲不留。(正)

　　注　(all) to a man = all without exception,(一个人都不留,全部),实连最后一人也包括在内,并无例外。他例如 Though we expected some absences, the staff were there to a man. (我们以为有人缺席,实则都到齐了。)

66. The village is on the side of the mountain.

　　那村庄在山旁。(误)

　　那村庄在山腰。(正)

　　注　山有阴阳两面(two sides),说在一面上,自然是在半山上,若说在旁边,则是指在山下的意思,英文为 by the side of.

67. He was at once a soldier and a writer.

　　他立刻成为一个军人和作家了。(误)

　　他是一个军人,同时又是一个作家。(正)

　　注　英文成语 at once,原有两个意思,即"立刻"和"同时",例句中后面跟了一个 and,说明是两件事,自然应作同时解。

68. She can play on the piano after a fashion.

　　她能随时俗的所尚弹奏钢琴。(误)

　　她能稍许弹弹钢琴。(正)

　　注　after a fashion = not satisfactorily but somehow or other,乃委婉的贬词,意为"稍许","略为"。他例如 She has a rough manner, but she is kind after a fashion. (她态度粗鲁,但人还和善。) 如把不定冠词改变为定冠词,就变成"追逐时髦"的意思了:after the fashion = in accordance with the prevailing style of dress, etc. 例如 This kind of hat is after the fashion。(这种帽子正在流行。)

69. He was worn out with company.

　　他已倦于交游了。(误)

　　来客太多使他疲于应接。(正)

注　company 在此作"客人"或"友伴"解,例如 He is fond of company.（他好客。）Will you favour me with your company at dinner?（敬备菲酌,恭候台光。）

70. Take this as an earnest of what is to come.
把这个当作未来热心从事的表示。（误）
拿这个去作为定金,以后再行付清。（正）

注　earnest 作形容词用时意为"热心"或"认真",但作名词用时,则意为"定金"、"保证"、"抵押"、"预兆"。

71. It is the man behind the gun that tells.
说话的是在大炮后面的人。（误）
胜败在人而不在武器。（正）

注　动词 tell = produce marked effect（见效,奏功）。例如 Money is bound to tell.（钱到效生。）Every shot tells.（百发百中。）Years begin to tell upon him.（年老使他开始显得虚弱起来。）

72. He never calls a spade a spade.
他从来不把锄头叫做锄头。（误）
他从来不说直话。（正）

注　call a spade a spade = speak quite plainly（直言无隐。）原是打桥牌的用法,因为玩牌时手上有什么牌常不直说,分明手上是一张 spade,却故意说成 club,或 heart,或 diamond,以乱视听。

73. The proper study of mankind is man.（A. Pope）
人类能正当学习的只有男人。（误）
要正当地研究人类,就应以人为对象。（正）

注　句尾的 man,无冠词,仍然是指 mankind.

74. The Child is father of the Man.（W. Wordsworth）
孩子是男人的父亲。（误）
成人是由幼儿长大的。（正）

注　意指从幼儿的心中产生出大人的思想感情来,俗语说的三岁儿童百岁魂,可知一粒小的种子可以长成一株参天乔木,现在倒过来说,成为 paradox（似非而是的隽语,如越帮越忙,越忙越慢之类）,倒是很有趣的。句中 Child 和 Man 都用大写,不但表示强调,而且含有抽象的意味。

75. Every time he snickers, he sprays his audience, like a Chinese laundryman.（Erle Stanley Gardner）
每次他用目光扫射他的听众时,他都不免暗笑,像一个中国洗衣匠烫衣服的样子。（误）
每次他笑时唾沫横飞到他的对谈者的身上,就好像中国人的洗衣工在烫衣时用口喷水一样。（正）

76. That picture flatters her.
那是逢迎她而画的。（误）
那画像美过她本人。（正）

77. He flatters himself that he speaks English as well as an Englishman.
他夸奖自己的英语说得和英国人一样好。（误）
他妄自以为他说英语跟英国人一样好。（正）

注　flatter oneself that = feel satisfaction with oneself,妄自以为,自鸣得意,私自窃喜。

78. It does not belong to me to dictate to my colleagues.
要同僚给我笔录的事是不属于我的。（误）

我无权对同僚下命令。(正)

注　自动词的 belong 有四种用法:(1)关系上的所属,如 He belongs to the Republican Party.(他是共和党。)(2)主权上的所属,如 This book belongs to me.(这本书是我的。)(3)配合上的所属,如 That cover belongs to this jar.(那盖是这个瓶子的。)(4)地位上的所属,如 This is a place where (= to which) he doesn't belong.(这是不合他身份的地方。)上例便是第四种用法。此字英国用法后常接介词 to,美国用法则可接 among, in, on, under, with 各样不同的介词。至于动词 dictate,也有二义:(1)口述令人笔录,如 I dictate letters to my clerk.(我令书记笔录信件。)(2)指示,命令,指定,如 The country that won the war dictated the terms of peace to the country that lost.(战胜国向战败国指令讲和的条件。)I cannot give order, nor will I be dictated to.(既不能令,又不受命。)It belongs to me to dictate to them.(我有权命令他们。)It is not for you to dictate to me.(你不可以向我下命令。)I will not be dictated to.(我不受命。)

79. Better not be at all than not be noble. (Tennyson)

与其不能高尚,不如完全不要。(误)

与其忍辱偷生,不如光荣而死。(正)

宁为玉碎,不为瓦全。(正)

注　句前省略了 It would be 三字,有时也可看作省略了 You had 二字,他例如 Better be a nettle in the side of your friend than his echo. (Emerson)(与其做朋友的应声虫,不如做他腰间的荨麻,即不能万事逢迎。)

80. Homekeeping youth have ever homely wits.

守在家里的青年总有家常的机智。(误)

足不出国门的年轻人,常是心智平庸的。(正)

老是呆在国内的年轻人,总是头脑呆板的。(正)

81. I will see you hanged first.

我要看你先吊死。(误)

那里有人肯做这样的事。(正)

注　see 字后面略去了 that 的连词。这个 see 即 see to it 之略,也就是 take care 的意思。他例如 I will see you avenged.(必定使你可以报仇。)

82. She's the sort of woman who likes to be very much in evidence.

她是那种喜欢求证的女人。(误)

她是属于爱出风头的女人。(正)

注　in evidence = conspicuous 显然可见。例如 Smith is nowhere in evidence.(史密斯不见了。)

83. He doesn't know any better.

他不知道任何更好的。(误)

他居然有这样笨。(正)

注　know better = be wiser.

84. He is one of the institutions of the place.

他是当地机构之一。(误)

他是当地知名人物之一。(正)

注　institution 俗语有名人之意。他例如 John W. Gardner 说的, Self-congratulation should be taken in small doses. It is habitforming, and most human institutions are far gone in addiction.（自歌自颂只可偶一为之，多必成瘾，而大多数的达官贵人都已成为瘾君子了。）

85. I'll eat my hat if I do.

    如果我做的话，我就要吃掉我的帽子。（误）

    我决不做。（正）

86. It is the watch I am anxious to have mended.

    这就是我系念着是否已修理好了的表。（误）

    这就是我渴望去把它修理好的表。（正）

    注　不可把 have mended 当作完成动词来看，须知 watch 才是 have 的宾语，全句用单句说时，则成 I am anxious to have the watch mended.

87. I can make nothing of what he says.

    我认为他说的话一文不值。（误）

    他说的话我一点也不懂得。（正）

    注　make...of, 普通是作 consider as（认为）解的，不过加上一个 can, 意思就大不相同了。can make... of = understand（了解）。

88. I did what I thought was wise.

    我做了我想做的事是聪明的。（误）

    我做了我以为是贤明的事。（正）

    注　句中有句，I thought 是插进去的另一个句子，was 的主语是 what. 主句是 I did what was wise. 不可把 what I thought 当作 was 的主语。

89. He talked himself hoarse.

    他用粗嘎的声音说说。（误）

    他说得声音都嘶哑了。（正）

    注　hoarse 是补语，不是表手段，而是表结果的。全文意为 He talked till he was hoarse. 类例如 She cried herself blind.（眼睛都哭瞎了。）

90. I went an enemy, and returned a friend.

    我去掉一个敌人，迎回一个朋友。（误）

    我去时是敌，归时为友。（正）

    注　enemy 和 friend 都是补语，与 I 一致。

91. He wants for something to read.

    他想要有点什么阅读的东西。（误）

    他没有东西阅读正感难过。（正）

    注　单说 want, 意为"要","需要","想得到", 是他动词，want for 意为"缺乏","短少", 是自动词。说 I do not want for a dictionary. 不是"不想要字典", 而是"不短少字典"。

92. She made light of her illness.

    她减轻了自己的病。（误）

    她轻视自己的病。（正）

    注　make light of, 轻视，瞧不起。

93. He looked thanks at her.

他看见她有感谢的样子。(误)

他以感谢的目光看着她。(正)

注　thanks 为 looked 的同系宾语,表现感激的是他,不是她。

94. There is nothing like home.

没有像家一样的东西。(误)

任何地方都没有家里好。(正)

注　There is nothing like,没有比这更好的,胜过这个的再没有了。

95. You have your own way to make.

你完全要照自己的意思去做。(误)

你非独力开拓你的前途不可。(正)

注　have one's own way,意为"随心所欲","为所欲为",但 make one's own way,则大不相同,意为"努力上进","独力奋斗"。

96. She is well-informed for a woman of the old school.

以一个古老学校出身的妇人来说,她是见闻广博的。(误)

以一个旧式的女人来说,她是见闻广博的。(正)

注　well-informed,见闻广博的,消息灵通的。old school,老派,旧式。

97. He will do for a teacher.

他努力想做个教师。(误)

他适宜于做个教师。(正)

注　do = suit,适合。

98. I am no man's man.

我不是谁何的人。(误)

我不是任何人的下走。(正)

注　等二个 man = servant.

99. He takes after his father more than his mother.

你从父亲遗传比从母亲更多。(误)

他比他的母亲更像他的父亲。(正)

注　take after,相貌相似。

100. I have next to nothing to say about my childhood.

其次关于我孩童时代的事我无话可说。(误)

关于我的孩童时代我几乎没有什么可说的。(正)

注　next to = almost,故 next to nothing,意为"几乎什么都没有";next to impossible,"几乎不可能"。

101. I shall leave here for good next year.

明年我将好好地离开这里。(误)

明年我离开这里不再回来。(正)

注　for good 或 for good and all,意为"永久地"。

102. He was caught red-handed.

他被红手抓住了。(误)

他在现行中被捕。(正)

103. Every man cannot be a poet.

 每个人都不能成为诗人。（误）

 人非尽可为诗人。（正）

 注 every 与否定连用时,也和 all,both 等一样,是部分否定而非全部否定。比较:部分否定说 Every couple is not a pair.（配合得宜的夫妇少有。）全部否定说 No couple is a pair.（配合得宜的夫妇没有。）又 All is not gold that glitters.（一切闪耀的东西,未必都是黄金。）

104. Don't cough more than you can help.

 不要多咳除非你能忍住的时候。（误）

 不要多咳除非你忍不住的时候。（正）

 注 这句极普通的英语,严格地说,是完全不合理的。合理的说法应该是 Don't cough more than you cannot help,因为固定的成语为 cannot help（不禁,不得不）,例如 I cannot help laughing.（我不禁发笑。）

105. You are not playing the game.

 你不是在竞技。（误）

 你不公平。（正）

 注 英国人讲究竞技精神(sportsmanship),在比赛时一定要 A fair field and no favour, may the best man win. 即所谓 fair play（公平）。这种精神运用到一般国民的日常生活上,凡事有不公平或不正直的地方,就说那不是竞技的办法。因此竞技一词就成为公平正直的代名词了。

106. The actress has her head turned.

 那女优回过她的头来。（误）

 那女优得意忘形。（正）

 注 have one's head turned,因不当的赞扬或意外的成功,使人改变常态,自以为了不起。

107. I'm a Dutchman if it is true.

 真的我就是一个荷兰人。（误）

 绝无其事。（正）

 注 在英荷战争时,"荷兰人"这个名词,就成为一切虚伪的事情或可恨的事物的同义字了。说 I would rather be a Dutchman,是表示极强硬的拒绝。I'm a Dutchman if I do.（我决不做。）至今英文中的 Dutch 或 Dutchman,总是含有不好的意思,如 Dutch courage（虚勇,酒后之勇）,Dutch defence（假防御）,Dutch feast（主人先客而醉的宴会）,Dutch treat（各自出钱的宴会）,Dutch widow（妓女）,Dutch wife（竹夫人）,Dutch auction（拍卖者自动落价,直到有人愿出钱购买的拍卖）。

108. There are friends and friends.

 那儿有许多朋友。（误）

 朋友有种种不同,有益友,有损友。（正）

 注 这表现法似乎是出自 Bacon 说的 There are dinners and dinners. 一语,现应用到其他一切事情上,如 There are shopkeepers and shopkeepers.（商人有好有坏。）

109. I wish peace could be saved at the eleventh hour.

 我希望在第十一点钟和平可以得救。（误）

 我希望在最后五分钟可以挽回和平。（正）

 注 at the eleventh hour = at the last possible moment,意为在最后一个可能的时机中。

110. I am now a little under the weather.

我现在有点像在露天之下。(误)

我现在有点不舒服。(正)

注　under the weather = unwell or depressed，意为受天气影响而患病。

111. Somebody will have to break the ice.

有人一定会把冰敲破的。(误)

总有人得先开口说话。(正)

注　break the ice = make a beginning, or break through reserve or stiffness. 打破僵局，打破冷场。When you have broken the ice (= When you know him better after the first formalities) with him, you will like him.（你跟他混熟一点，不受拘束自由言行时，你就会喜欢他的。）

112. The boy cried because his schoolfellows called him names.

因为同学叫了他的名字，那孩子哭了。(误)

那孩子哭了，因为他的同学骂了他。(正)

注　call names 即 call bad names such as "Fool" and "Dunce"，骂人。他例如 He called me all kinds of names.（他对我任意辱骂。）

113. If he has a hobby let him ride it.

如果他有一匹小马，让他去骑吧。(误)

如果他有什么得意的话题，让他发挥好了。(正)

注　hobby 在古文中或方言中，意为 pony（小马），故木马或竹马就说 hobbyhorse。成语有 side（或 mount）a hobby，意为叨叨不绝地谈论自己癖好的问题，使人听得厌倦。hobby 现为本职以外的癖好的事物或职业，如集邮、种花、养鸟之类。

114. Why should I quarrel with my bread and butter?

我为什么要和牛油面包发生口角呢？(误)

我为什么要和自己的生计作对呢？(正)

注　bread and butter，指我们所依靠的糊口之资，例如与衣食父母的老板吵架，结果不免打破饭碗。

115. He used to lay down the law in a teahouse.

他从前常在茶馆里无法无天的乱闹。(误)

他从前常在茶馆里大发议论武断一切。(正)

注　lay down the law = speak in tones of authority，在辩论时，说话独断，装做是权威一般地说话。此外还有斥责，下命令等义。

116. Most people have a daily fight to keep the wolf from the door.

许多人每天都在奋斗，以免引狼入室。(误)

许多人每天都在与饥饿奋斗。(正)

注　wolf 为贫苦与饥饿的象征。

117. There is no come and go with him.

与他毫无往来。(误)

他非常固执，怎也劝不动他。(正)

注　come and go，为复合名词，意为"往来"，尤指交通。又可作"星移物换"解，在本例中用在 no 字之后，则为"无可变动"之意。

118. He has come off second best.

　　他以第二名获得成功。(误)

　　他失败了。(正)

　　注　普通说 come off,为"成功"之意,second best 为"第二个最好的",但在本例中实为一种婉说法,意指在竞争中失败了。

119. He has got out of the bed on the wrong side today.

　　他今天是从床后面爬起来的。(误)

　　他今天很不高兴。(正)

　　注　这句又可说成 rise out of the wrong side of the bed. 一开头就错误,自然一天都不高兴。至于 wrong 一字,常指不正当的事,如说 He was born on the wrong side of the blanket. (私生子)。She laughs on the wrong side of the mouth. (哭)。

120. Go it while you are young.

　　去吧,当你正年轻的时候。(误)

　　青春不再,趁早努力。(正)

　　注　go 在此为他动词。go it = act with vigour and daring advocate or speak strongly, live freely, 故又可说 go it blind, (fast, strong, bald-headed, etc.) 例如 I don't like to go it blind. (毫不了解的事我不愿做。) come 也有同样的用法, 例如 He comes it strong. (过于夸大,恭维过度,行之过激等。) You can't come it = You cannot succeed. (你不会成功的。)

习　题

试改正下列错误的译文:

1. My shoes are the worse for wear.

　　我的皮鞋更加不好穿了。

2. Everybody bridled at his remarks.

　　人人都尽量控制自己说的话语。

3. Fight shy of the theoretical method of approach to the learning of English.

　　从理论上来讲,学英文的方法,就是要战胜害羞。

4. It is not women and Frenchmen only that would rather have their tongues bitten than bitted.

　　不只是妇女和法国人愿意用舌剑唇枪应付敌人。

5. He changed his condition only a week ago.

　　他的健康状态在一星期前改变了。

6. He got married accepting a leap-year proposal.

　　他在闰年接受提议而结婚了。

7. All my advice falls flat on him.

　　我的忠言使他平地跌倒。

8. You can always tell the somebodies from the nobodies at a cocktail party. The somebodies come late.

　　你可以报告鸡尾酒会有无人到或有人迟到。

9. The persons elected will sit till 31 Dec.,1973.

选出的人要坐到一九七三年底为止。

10. He is free with his money.

    他有钱很自由。

11. An airplane was ordered from France.

    从法国来定了一架飞机。

12. She has been a widow only six months.

    她只做了六个月的寡妇。

13. Your loss is nothing to mine.

    你的损失与我无关。

14. He started on New Year's Eve.

    他在新年的晚上出发了。

15. He left his watch with me.

    他丢下我和他的表走了。

16. He pretended not to be ill.

    他没有假装生病。

17. "I think not," said he.

    他说："我不以为然。"

18. It is two years come Christmas.

    耶诞日来过两年了。

19. Men of millions are possessed with the idea.

    几百万人都具有这种思想。

20. He is behind time.

    他已落伍。

21. He went up stairs.

    他上二楼去了。

22. One fine morning he found himself a ruined man.

    在一个晴天的早晨他发现自己衰颓了。

23. His English leaves nothing to be desired.

    他的英文毫无希望。

24. Take care that all is right.

    当心一切就好了。

25. He measured his length on the floor as soon as he entered the room.

    他一进房就在地板上测量了他的长度。

26. We searched him to no purpose.

    我们寻找他毫无目的。

27. I met a woman with child when I came home.

    我回家时遇见一个带着孩子的妇人。

28. He succeeded to a large property.

    他事业成功获得一笔大的财产。

29. He caught me by the hand.
    他用手抓住了我。
30. What shall I go in?
    我要加入什么?
31. He says what he does not mean.
    他说话毫无意思。
32. No alcohol this evening.
    今天晚上没有酒精了。
33. What does c-a-m-e-l spell?
    骆驼怎样拼的?
34. He is tired of the work.
    他工作得疲劳了。
35. Life is often compared to a voyage.
    生命好与航行比较。
36. Better to reign in hell than serve in heaven. (Milton)
    最好统治地狱,不要服事天堂。
37. Iowa's Governor Harold Hughes had withdrawn his favorite son candidacy 12 days ago and shortly afterwards announced his support for Senator Eugene J. McCarthy of Minnesota.
    爱荷华州州长休士已经把他宠爱的儿子的候补资格撤销,随后不久就宣布支持明尼苏达州的参议员麦卡席。
38. If the election were held today, we would not have a prayer.
    如果今天举行选举的话,我们就不去做祷告。
39. I would rather have his room than his company.
    我宁肯要他的房间,不要他的公司。
40. That women are bad drivers is open to question.
    说女人不会驾车是公开的问题。
41. The lost child was soon identified.
    那失去的孩子很快就认为系同一的了。
42. He begged to be remembered to you.
    他求你记得他。
43. I have seen nothing of him of late.
    我近来没有看见他的什么东西。
44. He shared the little he had with the poor.
    他把和穷人共有的少许东西全分配完了。
45. What you cannot afford to buy, do without.
    不能买到的东西,就不必去买了。
46. What is done cannot be undone.
    自己做了的事不能说未做。
47. She believed he said so honestly.

她相信他说得像真的一样。

48. They have been broken into a dozen pieces.
它们打碎成十二片了。

49. They that know nothing fear nothing.
可怕的事物他们全不知道。

50. The picture was painted after Wu Chang-shih.
这画是吴昌硕以后画的。

51. He knows what it is to have a boy idle.
他知道有一个懒惰的孩子是怎么一回事。

52. It is no proof that one cannot do a thing because one does not like it.
因为不喜欢就不能做，这是不能证明的。

53. I bought these books new.
我新近买了这些书。

54. He borrowed a horse of a friend.
他借了朋友的马。

55. He covered ten miles an hour.
他一点钟包括了十英里。

56. He helped himself to the wine.
他帮忙自己饮酒。

57. I believe in rough, manly sports.
我信仰激烈的男性的运动。

58. He did not see the movie out.
他没有看那电影演出。

59. Eighty poor fellows perished.
有八十个穷人死亡。

60. He said nothing to that effect.
他说的话一点效果也没有。

叁 翻译实例

I 中译英

(1) 郑燮致弟书

【原　文】

吾意欲筑一土墙院子,门内多栽竹、树、草花,用碎砖铺曲迳[1]一条,以达二门[2]。其内茅屋二间,一间坐客,一间作房,贮图书史籍,笔墨砚瓦[3],酒董[4]茶具其中,为良朋好友,后生小子论文赋诗之所。其后住家,主屋三间,厨房二间,奴子屋[5]一间,共八间,俱用草苫[6],如此足矣。或曰,此等宅居甚适,只是怕盗贼,不知盗贼亦穷民耳。开门延入,商量分惠,有什么便拿什么去。若一无所有,便王献之之青毡[7],亦可携取质[8]百钱救急也。吾弟当留心此地,为狂兄[9]娱老之资[10],不知可能遂愿否?

【译　文】

I am thinking of building a house enclosed with earthen walls, in which plenty of bamboos, trees and various flowers should be planted. There should be a curved path paved with broken bricks leading to the porch. There are two spacious rooms behind the porch, one used as drawing-room and the other as study. Books and paintings, records and documents, writing-brushes and ink-sticks as well as inkstones, wine utensils and tea-sets are to be put in these two rooms. My intimate friends and young people may come here to discuss literature and make poems. Behind these there is the residence consisting of three bedrooms for the family, two rooms as kitchen, and one as servant quarters, so the total number of rooms in this house is eight, under the same thatched roof. That will be quite enough for me. Some one says that such a house is comfortable to live in, but the trouble is that thieves might easily break in, too. But he doesn't realize that thieves are but poor people. If they should come, I would open the door and invite them to step in, so as to talk over the distribution of my belongings. They may take whatever I have. In case there is nothing at all worth taking, I would give them the hereditary blue blanket as what Wang Shien-tze had possessed, with which they may pawn for a hundred cashes to meet their urgent need. You must know, my dear brother, that this place will serve as the last resort to spend my peaceful latter years, but I wonder if I could be able to fulfill it or not.

【注　释】

(1) 碎砖铺曲迳(同径): crazy pavement。(2) 二门: 门廊, porch。(3) 砚瓦: 中国的书画家喜欢用汉瓦或汉砖作砚。inkstone。(4) 酒董: 酒器。wine utensils。(5) 奴子屋: 仆人住的地方。servant quarters. (6)草苫:thatched. (7)王献之之青毡:晋人王子敬被盗时,只说"那铺青毡是我家祖传的东西,请你特别给我留下,其余你要的东西,随便你拿去好了"。the hereditary blue blanket as Wang Shien-tze had possessed. (8)质:典当。pawn. (9)狂兄:板桥自称的谦词。Ⅰ. (10)娱老之资:娱老意为养老。资在此为凭借之物。last resort for my old age.

(2) 中国的山水画

【原　文】

要说明山水画[1]的布置,先得说明山水画的构图[2]原理。原来山水画的构图,不是对景写实,而是用鸟瞰[3]的方法,将真景缩小[4],然后加以描写的。眼睛[5]中所能看到的,只有一重[6]山或一重水,这样简单的景物,是不容易构成山水画面的。作画的人,得走入山水的深处,遍观所有的风景[7],回到家里,把所经历的地方,像画地图似的缩写出来,还得把自己放的很大[8],把风景缩的很小,好像看假山[9]似的,才能构成"咫尺千里"[10]的画面。

【译　文】

In order to explain the disposition of a landscape painting, we have to make clear at first the principle of its composition. Originally the composition of landscapes is not to paint a real picture as we see it, but to depict by means of a bird's eye view, namely, to diminish the subject matter in a nutshell. What we can see with our naked eyes is generally only a single layer of mountains or rivers. This of course is not enough for us to compose a scene of the landscape. The one who paints ought to go into the heart of mountains and rivers, inspecting all the scenery before he puts down from memory on returning home the whole scope of his travelled regions as a miniature as he draws a map. In doing so, he has to enlarge himself as big as possible and contract the scenery as small as a rock-work to look upon, then he can for the first time compose a picture of thousand miles represented on a few-foot piece of paper or the like.

【注　释】

(1)山水画:landscape painting. (2)构图:composition. (3)鸟瞰:a bird's eye view. (4)缩小:diminish. (5)眼睛:指肉眼。our naked eyes. (6)重:layer. (7)遍观所有的风景:inspect all the scenery. 注意 scenery 指一个地方或某一带的风景,不可写成复数如山景则说 mountain scenery,海岸风光则说 coast scenery, 风景如画则说 picturesque scenery. 又如 The scenery of West Lake is impressive. 西湖的山水留给游人深刻的印象。(8)放大:enlarge. (9)假山:rock-work. (10)咫尺千里:a picture of thousand miles represented on a small piece of paper.

(3) 为　学

【原　文】

天下事有难易乎[1]? 为之,则难者亦易矣;不为,则易者亦难矣。人之为学[2],有难易乎? 学之,则难者亦易矣;不学,则易者亦难矣。

蜀⁽³⁾之鄙⁽⁴⁾有二僧：其一贫，其一富。贫者语于富者曰："吾欲之⁽⁵⁾南海⁽⁶⁾，何如？"

富者曰："子⁽⁷⁾何恃⁽⁸⁾而往？"

曰："吾一瓶一钵⁽⁹⁾足矣。"

富者曰："吾数年来欲买舟⁽¹⁰⁾而下，犹未能也。子何恃而往！"

越明年⁽¹¹⁾，贫者自南海还，以告富者，富者有惭色⁽¹²⁾。

西蜀之去南海，不知几千里也⁽¹³⁾。僧富者不能至⁽¹⁴⁾，而贫者至焉。人之立志⁽¹⁵⁾，顾⁽¹⁶⁾不如蜀鄙之僧哉！（彭端淑）

【译 文】

There is nothing difficult for us to do in the world. If we do it, the difficult thing will be easy; if we don't, the easy thing will be difficult. There is nothing dificult for us to learn. If we learn it, the difficult thing will be easy; if we don't, the easy thing will be difficult.

There lived two monks in the western frontier of Szechuan, one poor and the other rich. One day the poor monk said to the rich one.

"I want to go to Nanhai, what do you think?"

"On what do you depend for going there?" asked the rich monk.

"A bottle and a basin will suffice me," answered the other.

"Well, I have been meaning to go there by boat for many years, but failed. How could you go without any support!"

After one year the poor monk returned from Nanhai, and told his story to the rich one, who was ashamed to hear it.

It is so many thousand miles from the western frontier of Szechuan to Nanhai. The rich monk failed to go, but the poor one went. Couldn't we make up our minds to do something as the poor monk of the western frontier of Szechuan did?

【注 释】

（1）因为一国有一国的特殊语法，翻译是决不能完全照字面直译的，例如本文第一句："天下事有难易乎？"用白话说，便是世界上的事有没有难和易的分别，如照此英译为 Is there a difference between difficulty and easiness in things of the world? 则不合英美语法的表现方法，所以应该意译，看英美人对于这样的意思是怎样表达的，我们就怎样来译，不必拘泥于原文字句。注意 nothing difficult，不能说成 difficult nothing，因为在 thing 字上已有一个形容词，就不能再加别的字。他例如 something Chinese（一点中国的东西）也是同样的用法。普通的情形，当然可以说 not a difficult thing（不是一件难事）。（2）为学：to learn. （3）蜀：古地名，即今四川省。（4）鄙：指边鄙地方，可译 the frontier districts，或简说 frontier. （5）之：去。（6）南海：不可译作 the South Seas（南半球的海洋；南太平洋），因为此处系指普陀山，南海观世音菩萨说法处，故音译为 Nanhai. （7）子：你。（8）恃：依赖，可译作 depend on. （9）钵：和尚盛饭的用具叫钵。用饭钵来化缘的和尚称托钵僧。（10）买舟：即买船票的意思，在此是指坐船。

(11)越明年:意即经过了一年,故译为 after one year. (12)惭色:意为惭愧之色,译为 to be ashamed 即可,色字不宜译出。(13)不知几千里也:意即有好几千里,故译为 many thousand miles. 文学作品对于距离不必太准确,否则应以 li(里)代 mile(英里)。(14)至:在此与其译成 reach,不如译为 go,更为适合说话的语气。(15)立志:下决心做事。to make up one's mind. (16)顾:反而。此处只好译成 Couldn't 的反问语气。

(4) 光与色

【原 文】

目⁽¹⁾睹物而知形⁽²⁾,然形非色⁽³⁾不见;色非光不见。故色必资乎⁽⁴⁾光;画资乎日,夜资乎月星与火。光盛则色显,光微则色隐。色依⁽⁵⁾光以现其形:色浓则明,色淡则藏;色立乎⁽⁶⁾异,则相得益彰⁽⁷⁾,色傍乎同,则若存若亡。(郑光复:《镜镜诒痴》)

【译 文】

We know the shape of a thing when we see it, but its shape will not be seen if it has no color. The color of a thing will not be seen if there is no light. So the color for us to see has to depend on light, just as the day on the sun; or the night on the moon and stars, and fire. When the light is strong, the color becomes apparent; and when the light is dim, the color becomes obscure. A thing shows its shape by its color: it is conspicuous when its color is deep; it is invisible when its color is light. There will be a striking contrast if the colors of the things are quite different while their existence will not be felt if their colors are almost the same.

【注 释】

(1)目:指我们的眼睛,英文要说"人"看,不要说"眼睛"看,故不可译成 the eye 或 our eyes. (2)形:外形,我们见到一件东西的样子。shape; form. (3)色:由一种特殊波长的光线所产生的效果。或是由于分解了的光线在我们眼睛上所产生的感觉。由此可知光与色的关系。(4)资乎:depend on; help. (5)依:by means of; by. (6)立乎:存在。be. (7)相得益彰:得到陪衬,愈为明显。help each other to become more conspicuous.

(5) 教学相长

【原 文】

虽⁽¹⁾有嘉肴⁽²⁾,弗食⁽³⁾,不知其旨也⁽⁴⁾;虽有至道⁽⁵⁾,弗学,不知其善也。是故学,然后知不足⁽⁶⁾;教,然后知困⁽⁷⁾。知不足,然后能自反⁽⁸⁾也,知困,然后能自强⁽⁹⁾也。故曰,教学相长⁽¹⁰⁾也。(《礼记》)

【译 文】

Even when there is good food, you will not know its deliciousness, if you don't taste it; even when there is a good doctrine, you will not know its virtue, if you don't learn it. Therefore, to learn makes us realize our deficiency, and to teach makes us know the difficulties. Having realized our deficiency, we may then come to reflect; having known the difficulties, we may be able to strengthen ourselves to overcome them. So, we say, to teach is to learn.

【注　释】

(1)虽:即使。even. 不是虽然,故不可译成 though. (2)嘉肴:table delicacy; viands. 简易地说 good food. (注意 food 不可用复数)。(3)弗食:弗,作"不"字解。食,作"品尝"解。这句翻译时,应加假设语气及主语上去。在这种副词子句中,要用现在动词以代未来动词。(4)不知其旨也:you will not know its deliciousness. 不可译成 delicacy 或 delicacies,因为此字意为"佳肴",而不是"美味"。(5)至道:good doctrine. (6)不足:deficiency. (7)困:difficulty. (8)自反:即反省。reflect. (9)自强:strengthen oneself. (10)相长:benefit each other.

(6)翻译文欠通顺

【原　文】

辜鸿铭著《张文襄幕府纪闻》有题为《不解》一则云:

昔年陈立秋侍郎⁽¹⁾兰彬,出使⁽²⁾美国,有随员⁽³⁾徐某⁽⁴⁾,夙不解西文⁽⁵⁾。一日,持西报展览⁽⁶⁾颇入神⁽⁷⁾。使馆译员⁽⁸⁾见之,讶然⁽⁹⁾曰:"君何时谙识⁽¹⁰⁾西文乎?"徐曰:"我固⁽¹¹⁾不谙。"译员曰:"君既不谙西文,阅此奚为⁽¹²⁾?"徐答曰:"余以为阅西文固不解,阅诸君之翻译文亦不解。同一不解⁽¹³⁾,固不如阅西文之为愈也。"至今传为笑柄⁽¹⁴⁾。

【译　文】

An Anecdote from Ku Hung-ming's "Hearsay Accounts at the Secretariate of Chang Tzu-tung."

Many years ago a Mr. Hsu was in the suite of Chen Lan-ping, who had been a vice minister at home and was then sent on a mission to the USA. Though quite ignorant of English, Mr. Hsu was seen one day holding in his hand an English newspaper, and reading it with absorbing interest. The interpreters of the Legation who had witnessed the scene asked him in surprise:

"When did you learn English?"

"I have not yet learned it," the other replied.

With great astonishment, the interpreters went on: "Since you don't know English, why on earth should you read the paper?"

"I cannot understand English," Mr. Hsu answered quietly, "nor can I understand your translation. So I think it's better to read the original than to read the translation of yours, because both are Greek to me."

This has been told as a laughng-stock since then.

【注　释】

(1)侍郎:官名。vice minister. (2)出使:be sent on a mission to. (3)随员:be in the suite of. (4)徐某:a Mr. Hsu. (5)夙不解西文:素来不懂得英文。quite ignorant of English. "夙"可

译作 from the first 或 originally,但不必译出。(6)展览:打开来看,但不是真的阅读,英文可说 pretend to read(佯装阅读),但仍以不如此明说为宜。(7)颇入神:对某事心醉神迷。with ecstasy;be in (go into) ecstasies over。(8)译员:interpreter;translator. (9)讶然:表示疑怪的样子。in surprise;in wonder. (10)谙识:懂得。understand. (11)固:surely;certainly;of course. (12)奚为:为什么。why. (13)同一不解:both are Greek to me. (14)笑柄:laughing-stock.

(7)学无所用

【原　文】

鲁人身(1)善织屦(2),妻善织缟(3),而欲徙(4)于越。或(5)谓之曰:"子必穷矣。"鲁人曰:"何也?"曰:"屦为履之(6)也,而越人跣行(7);缟为冠之(8)也,而越人被发(9)。以子之所长(10),游于不用之国,欲使无穷,其可得乎?"

【译　文】

A native of Lu was good at making hempen sandals and his wife at weaving silk taffeta; and they intended to move to the State of Yueh. Someone told them that they would become poor if they should do so. The native of Lu asked him, "Why do you think so?" The other said: "You know sandals are made for the feet, but the people of Yueh are barefooted. The silk taffeta is for the head, but the people of Yueh are bareheaded. Now you go to a country where your special skill is not wanted. How can it be that you will not become poor?"

【注　释】

(1)身:本身,本人。oneself. (2)屦:(音句)麻屦。hempen sandals. cf. 屩:草履。straw sandals. 履:皮履。leather shoes,即俗称革履。(3)缟:白色生绢。缟冠,a white silk cap. (4)徙:迁居。move. (5)或:有人。somebody. (6)履之:something for the feet to wear. (7)跣行:barefooted. (8)冠之:something for the head to wear. (9)被发:bareheaded. (10)子之所长:what you are skilled in;what you specialize in.

(8)画蛇添足

【原　文】

楚有祠(1)者,赐其舍人(2)卮酒(3)。舍人相谓曰:"数人饮之(4)不足,一人饮之有余。请画地为蛇,先成者(5)饮酒。"一人蛇先成,引酒且饮之(6),乃(7)左手持卮,右手画蛇,曰:"吾能为之足(8)!"未成!一人之蛇成,夺其卮,曰:"蛇固(9)无足,子(10)安能(11)为之足?"遂饮其酒。为蛇足者,终亡(12)其酒。(《战国策》)

【译　文】

A native of Chu after worshiping his ancestors gave his retainers a pot of wine. One of the retainers said, "It's insufficient for all of us, but too much for one of us. I suggest, therefore, that we draw snakes on the ground, and the one who first finishes drawing the snake will win the pot of wine." When one retainer had completed his drawing, he took the pot to drink. As he held it in his left hand, he continued to draw the snake with his right hand, saying: "I can add feet to it." While he was adding feet to his snake, another man who had then drawn his snake snatched the pot from his hand, protesting: "No snake has feet. How can you add feet to it?" Then he drank the wine. The man who added feet to the snake lost his prize at last.

【注　释】

(1)祠:春祭叫作祠。祠者即祭祖的人。(2)舍人:古时贵族家里的门客,侍从,家臣。(3)卮酒:即一卮酒。卮(goblet)为古时有足无柄的酒杯。(4)之:指卮酒。(5)先成者:先画好一条蛇的人。(6)引酒且饮之:拿起酒来打算要喝。引作取解。且作将解。(7)乃:竟然;居然。(8)为之足:给它添上脚。(9)固:本来,实在。(10)子:你。(11)安能:怎么能够。(12)亡:失去。

(9) 嗟来食

【原　文】

齐大饥,黔敖为食于路[1],以待饿者而食之[2]。有饿者蒙袂[3]辑屦[4],贸贸然[5]来,黔敖左[6]奉食,右[7]执饮[8]曰:"嗟! 来食[9]。"扬其目而视之曰:"予惟不食嗟来之食,以至于斯也。"从而谢焉[10],终不食而死[11]。曾子闻之曰:"微与[12],其嗟也可去,其谢也可食。"(《檀弓》)

【译　文】

There was a severe famine in Chi. Chien Ao had food ready at the roadside for the starvelings to eat. A famished man appeared staggeringly, covered his face with the sleeve because of shame, and his shoes in hand as he was too weak to wear them. He was halted by Chien Ao, who held food in his left hand and drink in the right, saying: "Holla, come, you." The man raised his eyes and looked at him. "I have become thus only because I don't want to eat anything given in such a manner," he said. So Chien Ao made an immediate apology to him for not being so polite at first, but still the man refused to take any food and died with hunger at last. On hearing this, Tseng Tzu said, "It's a pity for him to do so. He might have gone away when offered food as alms, but he should have eaten when apologized."

【注　释】

(1)为食于路:在路边上准备饮食。(2)食之:食为动词,之指饿者。(3)蒙袂:以衣袖蒙着面孔。(4)辑屦:用手提着鞋子。(5)贸贸然:好像瞎子一样。贸贸或写成眊眊。(6)左:左手。(7)右:右手。(8)执饮:拿着饮料。(9)嗟来食:嗟,即嗟乎,或咨嗟,指叹息的声音。嗟来食,意为喊他来吃,因哀悯贱视而施与食物,丝毫没有尊敬的意思,故使有自尊心的人,宁饿死也不吃这种嗟来食。(10)从而谢焉:因此便向他道歉。(11)不食而死:即饿死。die with hunger. 在 die 字后可接三个不同的介词,应加分别:1. die with hunger(fatigue, thirst, sword); 2. die from a disease(a wound, an accident, repletion, broken heart); 3. die of cancer (poison, an illness, old age, undernourishment, overwork, too much whisky)。(12)微与:不必啦。微作无或非字解。

(10) 老与少

【原　文】

老年为少年之过来人,少年为老年之候补者,老与少,只不过时间上之差别而已。然中国习惯,对老少之间,往往划有无形界限。在客观上,有时重老而轻少,有时重少而轻老。在主观上,老者自恃其老,少年自矜其少。几千年来,遂形成老者自以为持重(1)练达(2)而菲薄(3)少年为少不更事(4);而少年自以为新锐精进(5),而凌轹(6)老者为老朽昏庸(7)。此真所谓偏颇(8)两失之见也!

曩梁任公在其《少年中国》一文中,对老年人与少年人曾有一适当对比。其言曰:"老年人如夕照,少年人如朝阳;老年人如瘠(9)牛,少年人如乳虎;老年人如僧,少年人如侠;老年人如字典,少年人如戏文(10);老年人如鸦片烟,少年人如白兰地酒;老年人如别行星之陨石(11),少年人如大海洋之珊瑚岛;老年人如埃及沙漠之金字塔,少年人如西伯利亚之铁路;老年人如秋后之柳,少年人如春间之草;老年人如死海之潴为泽(12),少年人如长江之初发源……"

观此,则知老年与少年,各有所长,各有其用,如能祛除(13)成见,同为国家效力,则裨益民族,定非浅鲜。(血轮:《绮情楼杂记》之一)

【译　文】

The aged are the antecedents of the young, and the young are the candidates of the aged. The difference between age and youth is only a matter of time. But, according to the Chinese custom, there is always an invisible line of demarcation between them. Objectively speaking, sometimes the aged are held in esteem and the young are made light of; sometimes it is just the other way round. Subjectively speaking, the aged are self-conceited because of their good old age, while the young think no small beer of their own youth. For thousands of years it has been assumed that the aged, thinking themselves experienced and more skilful, look down upon the young for their greenness in worldly affairs, while the young, thinking themselves fresh in life and more energetic, call the aged old fogies. Either of these views, of course, is far from being impartial.

Liang Chi-chao in an article entitled "Young China" made a proper contrast between the aged and the young. He said: "The old man is like the setting sun; the young man, the morning sun. The old man is like a lean ox; the young man, a cub tiger. The old man is like a monk; the young man, a knight. The old man is like a dictionary; the young man, the text of a play. The old man is like opium; the young man, brandy. The old man is like a shooting star; the young man, a coral island. The old man is like the pyramid of Egypt; the young man, the Siberian railroad. The old man is like the willow after autumn; the young man, the grass in spring. The old man is like the dead sea that turns into a lake; the young man, the source of the Yangtze River……"

From this, we know that the aged and the young both have their own merits and uses. If they will cast away their prejudices and work together for the country, their services to the people shall be immense. (Hsueh Lun: *Old Age and Young*)

【注　释】

(1)持重:举止庄重的意思,成语有"老成持重"的说法。(2)练达:精熟通达。(3)菲薄:瞧不起;轻视。(4)少不更事:年少的人历事不多。更事当经历讲。(5)新锐精进:精明强干,活力充沛。(6)凌轹:原意为车轮辗过,引申为用权势压迫人的意思。成语有"仗势凌轹"一语。在此借用为欺侮轻蔑。(7)老朽昏庸:指因年老而糊涂无能。(8)偏颇:不正不平,侧重一方面。(9)癯:瘦。(10)戏文:戏剧的台词。(11)陨石:即流星。(12)潴为泽:成语潴为大泽,即积储许多水而成湖海。(13)祛除:除去。祛音驱,作除去解,如祛惑,祛弊等。

(11) 雕刻奇技

【原　文】

今日善雕刻者甚多,但重在神似,不在细巧。昔苏州有杜士元者,擅雕刻,号称鬼工,能将橄榄核或桃核雕刻成舟,作苏东坡游赤壁故事。舟虽小,而桅千两橹艄篷及舵篙帆樯毕具,两面窗槅,俱能移动开阖。舟中三人,东坡为长髯布袍,佛印则着禅衣对坐,几上纵横列骨牌三十二张,若将搜抹者然。旁有手持洞箫启窗外望者,则相从之客也。船头有童子持扇烹茶,旁置一小盘,陈茶杯三盏。舟师三人,两坐一卧,细逾毛发。

每一舟成,人争相购。然士元好饮,终年游宕,不轻易出手,惟贫困时,始能镂刻,否则虽千金不能致也。

清高宗南巡,于行宫见其作品,大加赞赏,因三召至启祥宫,赐金帛甚厚。顾士元处禁垣中,终日闷闷,欲出不可,因诈痴,始得放归。

按桃核不过两指头大耳,而能雕出如许人物,诚非气静神完者莫办,谁谓古人艺术,不逮今人!(血轮:《绮情楼杂记》之一)

【译　文】

Today there are many good engravers. But they lay emphasis on the very moral of what they engrave, and not on the fineness of it. Once, there lived in Soochow a man whose name was Tu Shih-yuan. He was so skilful at engraving that people called him supernatural craftsman. He could engrave on an olive or a peach stone the story of Su Tungpo making an excursion to the Red Cliff. Though the boat is very small, it has its mast and rigging, sculls, poles, and what not. The windows on either side of it are movable. Inside the cabin, there are three people. Su Tungpo with a long beard and in flowing robes, sits opposite to Fu Ying, the accomplished monk, who wears a Buddhist gown. Thirty-two pieces of dominos lying scattered on the desk show that a game is being played. By their side a man, flute in hand, opens the window to look out. He is their guest who joins them in the excursion. On her bow a boy with a fan in his hand is making tea near the stove, and by his side is a tray with three cups. Besides there are three boatmen, two sitting and one reclining—all life-like.

Every time he had finished a boat, people contended for buying it. When Tu Shih-yuan was indulging himself in wine, and idling away his time, you would find it no easy matter to have him cut such a boat. He would do the engraving only when he was hard up. If he was not short of money, he would refuse to do it for the wealth of a prince.

Kao Chung, the emperor of the Ching Dynasty, saw Tu Shih-yuan's skilled handiwork at travelling-lodges when he was touring south, and was very pleased with it. Then Shih-yuan was summoned to the palace, and the Emperor bestowed on him pots of money and silk. While living in the Forbidden City, Tu Shih-yuan was sad and depressed; for he was not allowed to wander beyond its walls. So he feigned to be mad until he was set free.

As you know a peach stone is no bigger than two of our fingers combined, but Tu Shih-yuan was able to engrave so many persons and things on it. It is indeed a piece of excellent workmanship. Who says the art of the ancients is inferior to that of the moderns? (Hsueh Lun: *The Ingenious Art of Engraving*)

(12) 狐　疑

【原　文】

我有一个漂亮的表姐,跟一个工程师结了婚,感情和好,生活美满。婚后三年,她突然变态:凭空指责她丈夫有外遇,日夜悲泣不已。任凭她的丈夫怎样解释,都无济于事。他只好寸步不离她,她的疑心犹不减,责备他每日死守家屋,意在追恋女佣。他换了一个女佣,她又说是他的新恋人。换上别个女佣,无论老妇童女,她无不怀疑。终于他的丈夫决心一个女佣都不用,她却乐得自己烧饭洗衣。

不久以后,她的疑心更多了。她认为妹妹、嫂嫂、姑姑,都是丈夫的恋人。于是,大家相信她发了狂,这才将她送进神经病院,施行电疗、打针,用尽百法,毫无效果。

在完全绝望的时候,我介绍一位心理学家去看她,单独与她密谈两小时后,他有了骇人的发现。

"夫人",心理学家诚恳地说:"我愿为你摘去内心的痛苦,但请坦白见告,你曾经有什么不可告人的遭遇吗?"

这一问,好像一股电流触及她的内心痛处,她惊跳一下,低头啜泣。

"愿向上苍指誓,为夫人严守秘密",专家继续说:"夫人,为了你的终身幸福,愿坦白见告。"

她终于说出了:半年前,她曾为一个青年而坠入情网,事后,荣誉心迫她回头改正,然而,她始终不敢正视自己既往的可耻事实,却在心里另觅一种自慰:那便是她的丈夫在外必定也有与她相似的不贞行为。久而久之,造成她反常的疑惧心理。

心理学家明白了她的病根所在,便轻易为她拔除掉了。使她逐渐领悟,她的不贞行为,乃属于她的偶然性错失,而非人人必然性的现象,更不能转移于丈夫身上。

过分多疑的心理,因素很是复杂,绝非单纯神经过敏可以解释。多疑往往由于自己的"内疚"反射于他人,在心理学上称之为"投射作用",我用最简单的一句中国俗语,可以说明"心理投射作用"的深奥原理。这句俗语是:"有此心,反疑心"。(林枕客:《狂人百相》之一)

【译　文】

　　After three happy years of conjugal life there came a sudden change in my pretty cousin's sensual nature. She suspected her husband, an engineer, to be unfaithful and reproved him for his disloyalty without any reason. Her husband tried in every way to explain but in vain. She was in so great a distress that she wept all the time. He had to stay at home with her in the hope that he might get rid of her doubt about him. But, to his amazement, this only led to her new suspicion. She thought that he remained at home all day because he was in love with the maid. He dismissed the maid and hired a new one whom his wife would call his new love. In short, she regarded any maid, irrespective of age, as the object her husband was in pursuit of. At last, her husband decided not to keep a servant in his house, leaving all the domestic work to his wife, which she undertook without a complaint.

　　Not many days had elapsed before she entertained more doubts about him. She suspected even her female relations, such as her sisters-in-law, being also in love with her husband. This made people think that she had gone out of her mind. She was then sent to a hospital where she was put under various medical treatments; but all of them had no effect upon her.

　　Such being her case, I recommended her to a psychologist. After two hours' tête-à-tête with her, the psychologist made a startling discovery.

　　"My dear madam," began the expert in a most sincere manner, "I should be able to remove all the worries from mind if you would tell me everything frankly. Have you anything to be kept secret?"

　　Thus asked, she started as if she were electric-stricken and began to weep.

　　"If you will let me into the secret, I promise to keep it from the knowledge of others," he continued. "For your own good, and for the happiness of your life, do tell me, madam!"

　　She sobbed bitterly and then gave the following account: It was about half a year ago when she met a young man with whom she fell in love. But before long, her sense of honor made her repent of her folly, and she came back to her husband again. What a shame it was to recall her past conduct, so she consoled herself by thinking that her husband must have done the same thing as she did. By and by this developed into an abnormal apprehension.

　　When the psychologist had found out the root of her disease, it was easy for him to uproot it. He told her that her disloyalty was due to her casual wrongdoing, not to the inevitable conduct of everybody. Nor could it be transferred to her husband.

　　That which gives one the feeling of distrust is rather complicated. It cannot be explained merely by nervousness. To have a suspicion against others usually comes of one's own sick conscience. Psychologically speaking, it is called the project action, that is the process of acting upon others. A Chinese proverb that presents fully the gist of this psychological action runs, "Suspicious are those who take an interest in the matter themselves."(Lin Chen-ko: *Smoke Without Fire*)

(13) 怕伞的姑娘

【原　文】

女孩子如有特癖,出嫁后非常痛苦。在家时,父母会容忍她的特癖,但婚后丈夫未必能谅解她,这里有一个悲剧为例证:

有个女人,名陈竹竹。她跟一个二十岁的青年吴铭结婚。过了一个秋天,生活都很愉快。入冬雨季却带来了悲剧:她上班去,穿雨衣走,吴铭要她再带把伞,她不肯,说她从来不用伞。他实在太爱她,便拿把美丽雨伞交给她,她一触到伞柄,状极惊恐,急推地上。吴铭大为骇异,便问:

"竹竹!你怎么啦……"

"我害怕……"竹竹说。

"雨伞有什么可怕呢?"吴铭问。

竹竹默然不答。青年人意气刚强,他的太太越怕伞,他越要给她伞,企图改变她的怪癖。竹竹在他的情感威严的压力下,不得不拿,可是,她每提起伞,都要惊哭一阵,昏厥过去为止。

这件事屡屡发生后,竹竹终于向法院请求离婚,理由是:不堪丈夫虐待,饱受强迫提伞的苦刑。当法官在庭上听吴铭申诉竹竹下雨不肯带伞的事,觉得很希奇。便问竹竹,她说生平怕伞,其夫偏用伞来恐吓她,不胜惊扰之苦,非离异不可。法官不信,令刑事取伞给她,果见她吓得脸色发青,掩面大哭。

法官认为她有神经病,吴铭加以否认说,她除怕雨伞之外,其他完全正常。这一对好夫妇终于双方同意地离婚了。离婚后,陈竹竹的生活正常,当然心情枯寂悲愁,幸而,嗣后,她遇见了救星,一个精神学家替她揭去内心之谜。

原来陈竹竹幼年失母,她的继母冷酷无情,竹竹在七岁时,每天上学,没有鞋穿,没有书包用,也没有一把伞,下大雨,就不上学。有一天适逢学校大考,偏偏天下大雨,她不能去,情急了,偷了继母的雨伞走。一撑开伞,她吓坏了,伞里爬出一条青蛇,立即昏迷过去。从此以后,有个恐怖的观念占据看她;至今长大,她仍怕伞,但已忘其所以然了。

心理学家用"联想法"使她回想起当年旧事,再以"提示法"剔除她内心所潜伏的顽固意识。最后,当她听见心理学家亲切的声音:"你也可以有一把伞,像任何人一样。"她何等惊喜!在医师协助下,她伸出发抖的手,握住伞,撑开来,她觉得那是多么新奇、安全,有趣的伞呀!她忽感到一阵害羞袭来,急把伞儿遮住脸。(林枕客:《狂人百相》之一)

【译　文】

A girl with idiosyncrasies often suffers greatly after getting married. While at home, She would not be unbearable, for all her personal peculiarities, to her parents. But it is not probable that her spouse would understand her. Here is a tragic case to illustrate the truth:

There was a girl whose name was Chen Chu-chu. She was married to Wu Ming, a young man twenty years old. Their married life was full of happiness during the first autumn. But the rainy season of winter brought them unexpected misfortunes. One day when she was setting out for her office, she put on her raincoat. Her husband asked her to take an umbrella along; but she refused, saying she had never used an umbrella. As he loved her very much, he handed her a beautiful umbrella. As soon as she touched its handle, she dazed with horror, threw it on the ground.

"What's up, my dear?" asked her husband, greatly perplexed.

"I'm afraid of……" said the wife.

"There's nothing to be afraid of in an umbrella, is there?" said Wu Ming.

Chu-chu remained silent. As young men are very obstinate, Wu Ming insisted upon his wife's taking with her umbrella, in order to do away with her peculiarity. Because of his affection for her and in deference to his wishes, Chu-chu had to take it. But every time she took the umbrella, she was horrified, burst into tears and fainted.

This happened so often that Chu-chu at last had to appeal to the court for a divorce. Her reason was that she could not stand the ill-treatment of her husband. He tortured her by forcing her to take an umbrella. On hearing the statement of the husband the judge felt it was rather odd. In answer to the judge's inquiry, Chu-chu said that as her husband terrified her with an umbrella and made her suffer a great deal, she had to divorce him. The judge did not believe it and ordered an umbrella to be brought to her, which indeed made her turn pale and weep bitterly.

The judge thought she was neurotic, but her husband denied it, saying that she was normal with everything except with the umbrella. Consequently the well-matched couple agreed to put an end to their marriage. After the separation Chen Chu-chu lived a normal life, though she felt very lonesome and miserable. Before long, to her relief, there came an alienist, who solved the riddle of her fear of umbrellas.

It was said that Chen Chu-chu lost her mother when she was only a few years old, and was brought up by her step-mother who was very severe to her. At seven, she went to school every day without shoes or bag. As no umbrella was given her, she was obliged to stay at home if it rained heavily. One day, it was raining cats and dogs. But she had to go to school for her final examinations. Under mental stress, she stole her step-mother's umbrella, and was ready to go. But alas! When she opened the umbrella, there crawled out a green snake which terrified her and made her faint on the spot. Since then, a certain terror had dominated her thoughts. She was now a grown-up woman, but she still feared the umbrella, though she could not tell why she was afraid of it.

The psychologist used the method of association to make her recollect the bygones, and then, by means of "suggestion", got rid of the obstinacy hidden in her mind. At length, she heard the psychologist say in a kind voice: "Like everyone else, you too may have an umbrella." How glad she was to hear this! With the help of the doctor, she held out her trembling hand and took the umbrella. Opening it, she felt it was so novel, interesting, and there was nothing treacherous in it. With shyness she hid her face behind the umbrella. (Lin Chen-ko: *The Girl Who Feared an Umbrella*)

(14) 偷窃狂

【原　文】

"十疯九偷",精神学家承认这句话。十个疯子有九个患"偷窃狂"。"偷窃狂"是精神病中最通常的病征,可怜他,起初都被人认为"道德堕落者",根本不把他当病人看待。直至其疯到不可救药,才认做疯子。"偷窃狂"和通常偷窃很易分别,窃贼偷东西是有目的的,偷窃狂则无目的不问其需要与否,常感觉有某些东西非偷不可,仿佛把"偷"当作一种享受。读者不难遇见一些人,经济颇有办法,对于有些他们家中决不缺乏的东西,也爱顺手窃取,或揩油带回家去。不论其需要与否,一拿到手满高兴。这实在是极可怜的心理病态。"偷窃狂"虽然多是精神病的病征,但也有是童年时期在不良家庭生活中所养成的习惯。

我在师范学校一年级读书时,发现一件怪事:大半同学的圆规、三角板、看地图用的放大镜都遗失了。我连续买过四次,也弄得没有一件器具用。校长据报后,请老师抽查学生箱箧,所注意的对象多是贫苦学生。查了一个月,不但毫无下落,而且这种窃案继续发生。我看见情形很严重,决心自己来捉贼。

那个星期天,我再买了一套新的,放在床前书桌上,躺在床上装做午睡。妙极了! 我从眼睛眯缝里,果然发现一个人影迫近桌前。我得意极了,我就要抓到贼了。

我高喊一声"嘿!"跳下床来,定睛一看,那一刹那间,我失望极了。而贼不是别人,居然是本级最富有人家的子弟吴津同学。他的学问品德都好,又乐于助人,决不至偷窃这些小东西的。然而,事实表现得太残酷了。他听见我"嘿"的一声,立即扑通一声跪下哀求着:

"老林! 我错得很,饶恕我吧!"

我仍半信半疑,老吴会做贼? 巧妙地笑着说:

"哈哈! 老吴! 够了吧,别再开我的玩笑,借去用吧!"

我放了他,可是没有救他。有一天,他终于被捕了,搜出百多套同样的用具。这件事,在别的学校,开除了事,幸好师范学校有教育心理学的老师,反对开除"问题学生",请求校长准予留校察看,以供研究,并加以感化。因此组织了"研究小组"研究吴津为什么会偷窃。

这问题终于在家庭访问时获得解答:吴津家富,兄弟姊妹共有七人,他居最小,最受父母溺爱,亦最缺乏教养,年幼时他喜爱哥哥姐姐们手上的东西就要,要不到就哭,母亲绝对他说:"等三姐不在时,我去偷来给你!"或是说:"等四哥出去了,我就拿来给你。"果然,兄姐们一走开,母亲便去拿给他,而且教他玩的时候,别让哥哥姐姐看见。他一拿到手,老是藏起来不玩。他从小便得到了这样的经验,要什么,只要在人家不在时去拿好了。这种拿的办法,在家庭里无所谓,在学校中或社会上,就成为"偷"了。他长大以后,也不自知其为偷,但那已经成为顽固的怪癖了。

(林枕客:《狂人百相》之一)

【译　文】

It is believed to be true by psychopathists that nine out of ten insane people have an inclination to steal. In fact, kleptomania is the commonest symptom of insanity. Poor souls! They are supposed to have morally degenerated and will never be treated as kleptomaniacs until their insanity is beyond cure. In that case, they are regarded as lunatics. The distinction between kleptomania and theft can easily be made. A theft is committed with an aim, while kleptomania without any object at all. A person suffering from kleptomania steals all sorts of things whether he needs them or not; he considers larceny a kind of enjoyment. You are apt to find some people who are rather well off, indulge in stealing from others things which they are never in want of. They would be very pleased with the thing they have stolen even if it is quite useless to them. This irresistible tendency to steal we may easily ascribe to the mental disease just mentioned. Although kleptomania is a symptom of mental weakness, the habit may be formed during one's childhood in a depraved family.

Something strange had come about while I was a first year student of the normal school. It occurred that my compasses, set-squares, magnifying glasses for reading maps were always missing. Though I had bought four sets of them, yet I could not find them when I wanted to use them. After being told of what had happened, the principal asked our teacher to search for them among the belongings of the students, especially the poor ones, in the school. The search continued for a month, but resulted in nothing. As the same thing happened again and again, I set to work to seek the mystery of the case myself.

I bought another new set of the above-mentioned instruments on a Sunday, and put it out on the desk just in front of my bed. Then I pretended to be asleep. Fancy! with half an eye, I saw a form moving stealthily towards my bed. I was so excited that I cried out "Hi!", and jumping up from my bed, ready to catch the thief on the spot, I found, to my disappointment, that he was no other than Wu Tsing, a classmate of mine, who was from one of the richest families, and who was very generous in helping others. It seemed improbable that he, who conducted himself well at school, would steal such trifles. But on hearing my voice, he dropped down on his knees in a panic, imploring:

"Forgive me, Old Lin, for Heaven's sake. I know it's very wicked of me to do so."

I was confounded and could not believe my eyes. It was beyond my comprehension that Wu Tsing should commit a larceny. In a moment I gathered my senses and answered:

"Ha, ha! Old Wu, that's enough. Don't make fun of me any more. You are welcome to use them."

I let him go, but I did not succour him. Some days later, he was caught at last. More than hundred sets of similar instruments were found in his suitcase. If it happened in other schools, he would be dismissed at once, but ours was a normal school, and the teacher of educational psychology objected to dismissing the student in question. He asked the principal to keep Wu Tsing in school for some time for investigation. A committee was formed to find out the reason why Wu Tsing should steal and how he could be "cured".

The answer to this problem was finally derived from a visit they paid to his family. As he was the youngest of seven children of a well-to-do family, his parents doted on him so much that they spoiled him. Whenever he saw anything interesting which his brother or sister had, he would cry for it if it was not given him. Having a weakness for the youngest, his mother would pacify him with these words: "Don' t cry, my boy, I'll steal it for you when your sister is not in," or "You can have it afterwards when your brother is out." Every time when his brother or sister was away from home, his mother would fetch him the thing he liked to have without fail. Moreover, he was told then not to play with it in his or her presence. Having had gained the experience that anything he wanted could be obtained during the absence of its owner, he did not realize that taking things away from others secretly was a crime. Of course, it would not be regarded as a theft by his brothers and sisters at home, but it was not so in the school or society. He came to know it was theft when he grew up, but the habit had been formed and could never be shaken off.

(15) 狐假虎威

【原　文】

虎求百兽[1]而食之,得狐。狐曰:"子无敢食我也! 天帝使我长百兽[2],今子食我,是逆[3]天帝命也。子以我为不信[4],吾为子先行[5],子随我后,观百兽之见我而敢不走乎?"虎以为然[6],故遂与之行,兽见之皆走,虎不知兽畏己而走也,以为畏狐也。(《战国策》)

【译　文】

A tiger went about in search of other weaker animals for food. Once in his hunting, he happened to find a fox. "You won't dare to eat me," said the fox, "as I am head of all animals appointed by God. It is against the will of God, if you eat me now. In case you don't believe what I say, let us go together. You just follow me as I go ahead to see if there is any animal that does not run away when I pass." The tiger agreed and went with the other. Certainly he saw all the animals run away on seeing the fox. He thought they were afraid of the fox without knowing it was he himself that they feared.

【注　释】

(1)百兽:各种动物,all kinds of beasts. (2)长百兽:为百兽之长。(3)逆:违反。(4)子以我为不信:你如果不相信我的话。又可译为 if you don't believe me. 英文说 believe me 是说"相信我说的话",如说 believe in me,则意为"信任我这个人"。(5)吾为子先行:让我走在你的前面。(6)虎以为然:老虎同意狐的建议。

(16) 习惯说

【原　文】

蓉[1]少时,读书养晦堂[2]之西偏一室。俛[3]而读,仰而思;思而弗[4]得,辄起,绕室一旋[5]。室有洼[6]径尺[7],浸淫[8]日广,每履之[9],足苦踬[10]焉;既久而遂安之。一日,父来室中,顾而笑曰:"一室之不治[11],何以天下国家为?"命童子取土平之。后蓉复履其地,蹴然[12]以惊,如土忽隆起者;俯视地,坦然[13]则既平矣。已而复然[14],又久而后安之。噫! 习[15]之中人[16]甚矣哉! 足利平地,不与洼适也;及其久而洼者若平;至使久而即乎其故[17],则反窒[18]焉而不宁[19]。故君子之学贵慎始。(刘蓉)

【译　文】

When I was young I studied in a western chamber of the Obscurity House. Sometimes I bent down to read; sometimes I looked up to think. When I could not, after much thinking, figure out the meaning of what I was reading, I rose to my feet and walked about the room. In the earthen floor of the room there was a hollow about one foot wide; and that grew larger day by day. Every time I walked over it, I stumbled; but by degrees, I got used to it. One day Father came into my study and saw the hollow. "How can you serve your country well," he said, smiling, "when you cannot keep such a little room tidy?" So he ordered a boy to fill it up with earth. Later when I walked over the spot again, I was surprised to find the earth there seemed swelling. I looked down, and found the hollow had already been filled up and the place was now as flat as a pancake. It was some time before I could get used to it again. Ah! how a habit works on man! You find it fit for your feet to walk on the level ground but not on places with holes. When you have, however, become accustomed to the sunken places in the floor, you will feel as if they were level. You will, on the contrary, stumble and feel uncomfortable when you walk on the spot newly leveled-up. Therefore the Superior Man is very cautious when he starts learning a thing.

【注　释】

(1)蓉是作者刘蓉的自称。(2)养晦堂为作者家中的斋名。(3)俛同俯。(4)弗当不字讲。(5)旋,转。(6)洼:低陷的地方。(7)径尺:直径有一尺的光景, it measures one foot in diameter. (8)浸淫:逐渐 gradually. (9)履之:走过那里, walk over it. (10)蹴:遇阻碍而颠跌, trip, stumble. (11)治:弄好, keep it tidy, make it in perfect trim. (12)蹴然:不安的样子, unsteady. (13)坦然:平坦的样子, as flat as a pancake. (14)复然:仍是这样。(15)习,即习惯, a habit. (16)中人:对人的影响, works on a person. (17)至使久而即乎其故:假使过了很久再恢复原状, if it is restored to its former condition after an elapse of time. (18)窒焉:受到阻碍, be obstructed. (19)不宁:不舒适, uncomfortable.

(17) 黔之驴

【原　文】

黔[1]无驴,有好事者[2],船载以入;至则无可用,放之山下。虎见之,庞[3]然大物也,以为神;蔽[4]林间窥之。稍出,近之,慭慭然[5]莫相知[6]。他日驴一鸣[7],虎大骇远遁,以为且噬[8]己也,甚恐。然往来[9]视之,觉无异能[10]者。益习其声[11]又近出前后,终不敢搏[12]。稍近益狎[13],荡倚冲冒[14];驴不胜怒,蹄之[15]。虎因喜,计之曰[16]:技止此耳[17]。因跳踉大㘎[18],断其喉,尽其肉,乃去。噫[19]:形之庞者,类有德[20],声之宏者,类有能[21]。向不出其技,虎虽猛,疑畏卒不敢取[22];今若是焉。悲夫[23]!(柳宗元)

【译　文】

There was no ass in Kweichow, and somebody brought in one by boat. But when it arrived, he found he could make no use of it, so he left it at the foot of a mountain. Seeing it, a tiger thought such a tremendous thing must be none other than a god. At first he peeped at it from behind the woods, and then moved timidly towards it; but still he dared not get in touch with it. One day the ass brayed, and the tiger was so frightened that he ran far away from it fearing it was going to eat him up. Later on he came back to look at it from all quarters, and found it possessing no particular ability. Though he, being more accustomed to its braying, was no longer afraid to come near it, yet he dared not attack it. He ventured to tease it more and more with a view to testing its abilities. Being greatly irritated, the ass gave him a kick. At this time the tiger was very glad as he found it was at its wit's end and had no other ability than this. Therefore he pounced upon it, first breaking its neck and then eating up all its flesh, and went away. Alas! those with a huge form appear to be powerful, and those with a loud voice appear to be capable. No matter how fierce the tiger was, he would not be bold enough to grapple the ass, so long as it did not show off its ability. What a pity that it should have done thus!

【注 释】

(1)黔即今贵州省。(2)好事者:喜欢兴造事端之人,如孟子说的"好事者为之也"。英译为 busy body,但在此译为 somebody 较好。(3)尨,通庞,巨大的意思,huge, tremendous. (4)蔽,藏匿的意思,hide. 译文中以 behind 表达出来。(5)慭慭然,谨敬的样子,timidly, cautiously 慭音㤑。(6)莫相知:不敢亲近,dared not get in touch with. (7)驴鸣,bray. (8)噬,吃掉的意思,eat up. (9)往来:应译 to and fro,译文中意译为 from all quarters(从各个角度)。(10)异能:特殊本领。(11)益习其声:更加习惯了驴的叫声 being more accustomed to its braying. (12)搏:攻击,attack. (13)狎:玩弄轻慢,to be intimate with. (14)荡倚冲冒:荡是动荡,倚为身体贴近,冲是冲过去,冒是追上前去。全句意为接近驴子而触怒它,来试试它的本领。(15)蹄之:用蹄去踢虎。(16)计之曰:估计着说,said in estimation. (17)技止此耳:只有这样一个本领,this is all it can do. 文中以 at its wit's end 表示。(18)跳踉大㘓:跳踉是脚乱动的样子。㘓同㘔或㘏,dancing and eating to his heart's content. (19)噫:叹息声,alas. (20)形之尨者,类有德:形体尨大,看去像是有德的。"德"字在此的用法,与《礼记·大学》上说的"富润屋,德润身,心广体胖"中用的"德"字意义相同,即显见于外者,实于内,那驴子外表看来,身体既那样尨大,则它的实力一定雄厚。"德"可译为 powerful. (21)声之宏者类有能:声音宏亮,好像有技能的样子。"能"可译为 capable. (22)疑畏卒不敢取:怀疑畏怯,终不敢去捕食,not be bold enough to grapple the ass. (23)悲夫:多么可悲,how sad.

(18) 少年孔融的机智

【原 文】

孔文举(1)年十岁,随父到洛。时李元礼(2)有盛名,为司隶校尉(3)。诣门者皆俊才清称(4),及中表亲戚乃通(5)。文举至门,谓吏曰:"我是李府君(6)亲。"既通,前坐,元礼问曰:"君与仆有何亲?"对曰:"昔先君(7)仲尼(8),与君先人伯阳(9),有师资之尊(10),是仆(11)与君奕世(12)为通好也。"元礼及宾客莫不奇之。太中大夫(13)陈韪后至,人以其语(14)语之(15)。韪曰:"小时了了(16),大未必佳。"文举曰:"想君小时,必当了了。"韪大踧踖(17)。(《世说新语》)

【译 文】

When Kung Yung went to Loyang, the then capital, with his father, he was only ten years old. At that time, Li Ying, the supreme official inspector, was a man of great reputation in the country. Nobody except his relatives and those who possessed distinct attainments and high commendation would be admitted to his presence.

"I'm a relative of your master." said the boy to the gate officer, who at once led him in. Sitting before the host, Kung Yung was questioned by Li Ying. "What relationship is there between you and me?" "In old times, my forefather Confucius had a teacher-pupil relationship with your ancestor Lao-tze," the boy guest replied, "and, therefore, our two families have been closely related for many generations." Li Ying and all his other guests present were greatly surprised at the answer.

Chen Wei, the counsellor, came later and was told what Kung Yung had said. "Being bright in early childhood does not necessarily mean that he will be clever when grown up," he observed. In response to this, Kung Yung said, "I guess you must have been very bright in your childhood," which made Chen Wei feel very much embarrassed.

【注　释】

(1)孔文举:孔融字文举,孔子后裔。(2)李元礼:李膺字元礼,有高名,被他接见的人即可身价百倍,称为登龙门。(3)司隶校尉:官名,掌纠察百官以下及近郡犯法者,东汉时并领有一州,权威极重。(4)俊才清称:超群的才学,清高的称誉。(5)通:通报,传达。(6)府君:郡守的称呼。(7)先君:今人称自已死去的父亲为先君,但古人对祖先亦称先君。(8)仲尼:孔子名丘字仲尼。(9)伯阳:老子姓李名耳字伯阳。今又有人考证老子姓老。(10)师资之尊:孔子适周,尝问礼于老子,故尊为师。(11)仆:孔融自称。(12)奕世:累世,累代。(13)太中大夫:官名,掌谏议,备咨询。(14)其语:孔融说的话。(15)语之:讲给他听。(16)了了:聪慧,晓解事理。(17)踧踖:不安的样子,音促籍。

(19) 绝妙好辞

【原　文】

魏武帝⁽¹⁾尝过曹娥碑⁽²⁾下,杨修⁽³⁾从。碑背上见题作黄绢幼妇外孙齑臼八字,魏武语修曰:"解不⁽⁴⁾?"答曰:"解。"魏武曰:"卿未可言,待我思之。"行三十里,魏武曰:"吾已得。"令修别记所知。修曰:"黄绢色丝也,于字为绝。幼妇少女也,于字为妙。外孙女子也,于字为好。齑臼受辛也,于字为辝。所记绝妙好辞也。"魏武亦记之与修同。乃叹曰:"我才不及卿⁽⁵⁾,乃觉⁽⁶⁾三十里。"(《世说新语》)

【译　文】

Emperor Wu Ti of Wei (in the Three Kingdoms) once went for an outing with Yant Hsiu, one of his officials. While riding by the foot of the stone tablet of Tsao É, they saw on its back an inscription consisting of eight characters: "Yellow lustring, young woman, external grandson, crushing mortar."

"Do you know," Wu Ti asked Yang Hsiu, "what they mean?"

"Yes, Sire," the other replied.

"Don't tell me now," Wu Ti said. "I'll think it over myself."

When they had gone for thirty *li*, Wu Ti exclaimed, "I've got it!" He told Yang Hsiu to write his explanation on a piece of paper, which read: "Yellow lustring" is coloured silk, which makes up the character "chüeh" meaning "extremely". "Young woman" is a little girl, which makes up the character "miao" meaning "admirable". "External grandson" is the son of a daughter, which makes up the character "hao" meaning "fine". "Crushing mortar" is the vessel in which pungent things are pounded, which makes up the character "tzu" meaning "expression". The whole inscription means "an extremely admirable fine expression".

On discovering what Yang Hsiu had written was just the same as his, Wu Ti heaved a deep sigh, saying: "I am far behind you in talent. There is, I find, a difference of thirty *li* between us".

【注　释】

(1)魏武帝:曹丕篡汉后追谥其父曹操为武帝。(2)曹娥碑:东汉时上虞女子曹娥,因父溺死,亦投江而死。经五日,抱父尸出。度尚使弟子邯郸淳为作诔辞,立石。蔡邕夜摸其文读之,题黄绢幼妇外孙齑臼八字,即绝妙好辞四字的隐语。(3)杨修:东汉人,字德祖,聪慧过人,为曹操主簿。后为曹操所杀。(4)解不?:懂得吗？(5)卿:秦汉以来君呼臣曰卿。后世夫妻间称卿。原来只有丈夫称妻子为卿,故世说《惑溺篇》中载:王安丰妇常称安丰为卿,安丰便对她说:"妇人卿婿,于礼为不敬,后勿复尔。"他的妻子反驳他说:"亲卿爱卿,是以卿卿,我不卿卿,谁当卿卿？"上述的"卿婿"及后面的"卿卿"的第一个卿字,都是作动词用的。(6)觉:相差的意思。

(20) 韩信忍受胯下辱

【原　文】

信⁽¹⁾钓于城下⁽²⁾,诸母⁽³⁾漂⁽⁴⁾,有一母见信饥,饭信⁽⁵⁾,竟漂数十日⁽⁶⁾。信喜,谓漂母曰:"吾必有以重报母⁽⁷⁾。"母怒曰:"大丈夫不能自食⁽⁸⁾,吾哀王孙⁽⁹⁾而进食,岂望报乎？"

淮阴屠中少年⁽¹⁰⁾,有侮信者,曰:"若⁽¹¹⁾虽长大,好带刀剑,中情怯⁽¹²⁾耳。"众辱之曰⁽¹³⁾:"信,能死,刺我⁽¹⁴⁾;不能死,出我胯下⁽¹⁵⁾。"于是信孰视之⁽¹⁶⁾,俛⁽¹⁷⁾出胯下,蒲伏⁽¹⁸⁾。一市人皆笑信,以为怯。(司马迁:《淮阴侯列传》)

【译　文】

Once Han Hsin was fishing on the outskirts of the city, where many a woman was bleaching silk. One of the women seeing him hunger-stricken offered him food out of her own lunch box, and continued to do so for scores of days till she had done all her bleaching. Han Hsin, quite gratified, said to the old woman: "I will pay you back much more for your kindness some day." Exasperated at this, she retorted, "Being a man, you cannot feed yourself. It is just out of pity that I share with you what I have, and not that I wish to have something in return!"

A youth among the butchers at Huai Yin once spat at Han Hsin, saying: "Though you grow so big and like to wear a sword, you are at heart a coward!" In presence of a large group of spectators, he went on with scorn: "Look here, Hsin, if you are not afraid of death, stab me; otherwise, go through under my legs." Thereupon, Han Hsin after staring at the youth for a while, crawled under his legs, face downwards on the ground. The whole town laughed at Hsin, thinking him a coward.

【注 释】

(1)信:韩信,汉兴三杰之一,灭项羽,使刘邦成帝业,封淮阴侯,后为刘邦所杀,夷三族。(2)钓于城下:在淮阴城下淮河边上钓鱼。(3)诸母:好些老大娘。(4)漂:洗丝绵。(5)饭信:把她自己的饭分给韩信吃。(6)竟漂数十日:一连几十天都分饭给韩信吃,直到漂完为止。(7)吾必有以重报母:我将来一定要厚厚地报答您老人家。(8)不能自食:不能够自己找到饭吃。(9)王孙:好像说公子一样,古代对青年人的敬称。(10)屠中少年:市上卖肉的少年们。(11)若:你。(12)中情怯:内心怯懦,即胆子小。整句意为"你虽然个子长得很高,又喜欢佩刀挂剑,其实是一个胆小鬼。"(13)众辱之曰:当众侮辱他说。(14)能死:你要不怕死的话。(15)出我袴下:从我的裤裆底下钻过去。(16)孰视之:仔细地打量他一番。"孰"即古写的熟字。(17)俛:同俯。(18)蒲伏:同匍匐,意为在地上爬行。

习 题

试将下列中文译成英文:

(1)"各人自扫门前雪,休管他人瓦上霜",是使世界达到和平幸福的最佳途径。一家如此,则一家和乐。一国如此,则一国安定。全世界如此,则天下太平。

(2)学问是自己的事,不能依靠别人的。环境好,图书设备充足,有良师益友指导启发,当然有很大的帮助,但是这些条件具备,也不一定能保证一个人在学问上就有成就。世间也有不少在学问上有成就的人,并不具备这些条件。最重要的因素,还是个人自己的努力。求学是一件艰苦的事,许多人不能忍受那必经的艰苦,所以不能得到成功。

(3)"我想认识伦敦,应该先到哪里去?巴力门,还是唐宁街?"我向寓所的女主人打听。那位老太太摇摇头说:"这种地方你去干什么?你得先上海德公园。在那公园里,你才能了解我们英国怎么会有巴力门和唐宁街的。"她的意思是说,造成英国政治的,是英国人民的精神,并不是有了议会和内阁,英国才得到民主的政治,而是人民有了民主的精神,才有英国的议会和内阁。海德公园正是民主精神表演的地方。

(4)善即是美。我们感到物事像理想一般的实现,我们就觉得是美。所谓理想一般的实现,就是说,那物事能把它的天性完全发挥出来。所以,如花在天性全露时最美一样,人在充分发挥他的天性时,也就达到美的极致了。

(5)道德非言语所能施教。凡未亲受仁爱待遇者毕生将不知仁爱为何物。故以仁爱待人,始能教人以仁爱。语云:"以言教者讼,以身教者从。"

(6)文学的工具是语言文字。我们第一须认识语言文字,其次须有运用语言文字的技巧。这事看来似很容易,因为一般人日常都在运用语言文字;但是实在极难,因为文学要用平常的语言文字产生不平常的效果。文学家对于语言文字的了解,必须比一般人都较精确,然后可以运用自如。他必须懂得字的形声义,字的组织以及音义与组织对于读者所生的影响。这要包涵语文学,逻辑学,文法,美学和心理各种知识。……一个人想做出第一流文学作品,别的条件不用说,单说语文研究一项,他必须有深厚的修养,他必须达到有话都可说出而且说得好的程度。

(7) 庄子与惠子游于濠梁之上,庄子曰:"儵鱼出游从容,是鱼之乐也。"惠子曰:"子非鱼,安知鱼之乐?"庄子曰:"子非我,安知我不知鱼之乐?"惠子曰:"我非子,固不知子矣。子固非鱼也,子之不知鱼之乐全矣。"

(8) 大家都知道下午四五点钟,在英国是喝茶的时间。首相也好,时装模特女郎也好,警察也好,甚至强盗也好,都是一定要喝下午茶的。

一杯茶,加上一点烤面包或饼干,再和朋友闲谈几句。这种光景在英国下午四五点钟的时候,是到处可以见到的,不问是在英王居处的白金汉宫,或是在寻常老百姓的家里,都是一样。对于在机关上做打字员一类工作的女性们,忙了一天而得到半小时的休息,去喝一杯茶,实在是一种最受欢迎的调剂了。甚至在前线的士兵们,如果情势允许的话,也要抽空去喝一杯茶。这原是英国牢不可破的传统。

(9) 人人都知道圣华伦泰节是景慕情人的一个爱情的节日。其起源可追溯到远古的罗马时代。当时的青年人以抽签的方式,取得住在附近女孩子的名字,而凭以决定他们的情人。在中世纪时,就把圣华伦泰节定在二月十四日,随后欧美的人们,又找出许多新花样来庆祝那一天。

一个青年男子不妨去吻他当日所遇到的第一个女人。这在东方人看来,也许是要觉得奇怪的。

到了十九世纪,人们开始寄赠美丽的辞句和专为当日设计的卡片,并进行交换礼物。

今天人们不但对情人寄赠卡片,而且对父母师长,也照样寄,成为很通行的习俗了。

(10) 在伊庸河附近我父母的产业,对我毫无吸引力。我常走下到河边去,偶然望望浮在河上的黄色的水藻,时而又拾起扁平的石块去打水漂,看它像燕子一般迅速地在水上掠过。

我父母的家屋是长形而灰色的。牧场一直伸展到像乳酪似的伊庸河边为止,燕子在空中飞翔着,河岸上的白杨树,长得枝叶互相连起来了。有一棵白杨树,我特别喜欢,常要躺在那树下。我发觉我自己在草中微笑着,我想要笑,可是不成。

II 英译中

(1) Too Clever Not to See

【原 文】

Elliott was too clever not to see[1] that many of the persons who accepted his invitations did so[2] only to get[3] a free meal and that[4] of these some[5] were stupid and some worthless[6]. (W. S. Maugham: *The Razor's Edge*)

【译 文】

艾略特是一个聪明的人,必然看得出来,大多数接受他邀请的人,只是为着要来吃一顿不花钱的饭。他知道他们当中有些是愚笨的,另外有些却是不足轻重的。

【注 释】

(1) too clever not to see = clever that he cannot but see, 以他的聪明岂有不知此事之理。他例如:He is too angry not to say that. 他那般愤怒而忍不住要说出那样的话来。(2) did so 即 accepted

his invitations. (3) to get = in order to get. (4) that 接前面 to see 说的。句子的构造是：to see that... and that... (5) of these some = some of these. (6) some worthless = some of these were worthless.

(2) The Busy Broker

【原　　文】

The broker's hour is not only crowded[1], but minutes and seconds are hanging to all the straps[2] and packing[3] both front and rear platforms[4]. (O. Henry)

【译　　文】

经纪人的时间不但是忙迫得像街车一样的拥挤，而且每分每秒车上所有的吊带都吊满了站立的乘客，在前后的站台上，也挤得水泄不通。

【注　　释】

(1) crowded：对个人的时间，只能说 fully occupied，意为很忙碌，完全被事情占有了，不能说 crowded，这是拥挤的意思。只有乘车等才可说拥挤，可知这是一种比喻的说法。作者把经纪人忙碌的时间，比做拥挤不堪的街车(street car，即英国人说的 tram car，或现通行的 bus)，所以才有拥挤及以下的种种说法。(2) straps：每部车子都有规定，可容坐客多少，站客多少，站立的乘客，车上悬有许多吊带，以便站着的人抓住，不至因车开动而跌倒，这种乘客就叫作 strap-hanger(挂在吊带上的人)。(3) packing：装载，塞满，挤紧，拥挤，例如 A hundred men were packed into a small room. (一百个人挤在一间小房子内。)(4) platforms：车子前后不设座位的空地，以便乘客上下的出入处所。这段文章的表现方法，是用的修辞学的一种，实为作家所不可少的技巧。比喻分明喻(simile)和隐喻(metaphor)两种，如《圣经》上说的(a) In the morning they are *like grass* which groweth up. (Psal. xc. 5) (早晨他们如生长的草。) (b) All flesh is *grass*. (Isa. xl. 6) (凡有血气的，尽都如草。) (a)句为明喻，而(b)句则为隐喻。上文没有说明像电车一样，所以是属于隐喻一类。

(3) Speculation on Important Subjects

【原　　文】

There[1] are few[2] circumstances among those[3] which make up the present condition of human knowledge, more significant[4] of the backward state[5] in which speculation[6] on the most important subjects[7] still lingers, than the little[8] progress which has been made in the decision of the controversy[9] respecting[10] the criterion[11] of right and wrong. (John Stuart Mill)

【译　　文】

就构成人的知识现状各种情形来说，没有什么比解决是非准绳的争论之罕有进展，更要表示吾人对最重要的问题的思索，是依然停滞在落后的状态中。

【注　　释】

(1) There 以下52字构成的一个句子，在动手翻译之前，必须提纲挈领，找出全文的骨干，才能把文法结构了然于心,译时便可把握正确的意义。全句的纲领如下:There are few circumstances... more significant of the state... than the progress. (2) few:几无。(3) those:即指 circumstances。(4) significant:意指,表示。例如 Smiles are usually significant of pleasure. (微笑通常是表示愉快。)原句可用动词 signify 来代此形容词的 significant,而改写为 few circumstances... which signify the backward state... more than the progress. (5) backward state:落后的情形;进步慢或发达迟的情形。(6) speculation:思索(thought),默想(meditation)。例如 He began to speculate on the origin of the universe. (他开始思索宇宙的起源。)She often speculates as to what sort of man she will marry. (关于她将来要嫁怎样的人她时常在想。)(7) subjects:问题,课题。(8) little:与前面的 few 同样是作几无解,little 指量,few 指数。(9) controversy:争论(discussion)。(10) respecting:关于。(11) criterion:准绳(a standard of judgment),例如 Money is only one criterion of success. (金钱只是成功的一种标志。)

(4) A Feeling of Eternity

【原　文】

No young man believes he shall⁽¹⁾ ever die. There is a feeling of Eternity in youth, which makes us amends for every thing. To be young is to be one of the Immortal Gods⁽²⁾. One half of time indeed is flown⁽³⁾—the other half remains in store for us with all its countless treasures; for there is no line drawn, and we see no limit to our hopes and wishes. We make the coming age our own⁽⁴⁾. "The vast, the unbounded prospect lies before us." We look round in a new world, full of life, and motion⁽⁵⁾, and ceaseless progress; and feel in ourselves all the vigour and spirit to keep pace with⁽⁶⁾ it, and do not foresee from any present symptoms how we shall be left behind⁽⁷⁾ in the natural course of things⁽⁸⁾, decline into old age, and drop into the grave.

【译　文】

没有一个年轻人相信他是要死的。在青春时有一种永恒的感觉,使人获得了一切的补偿。年轻人快乐似神仙。虽则半生一晃就过去了,还有下半生带着无限的宝藏,仍然给他储备着,因为前程远大,希望无穷。这个新的时代是属于年轻人的。一个广大无边的前景展开在他前面。他环顾周遭这个新的世界,充满着生命、活跃和不断的进步,他自身也感到元气旺盛,精神焕发,要来和它并驾齐驱。没有任何征候会使他预感到有朝一日,自己行将落伍,沦入老境,而终于要掉进墓穴中去的。

【注　释】

(1) he shall:第三人称不用 will 而用 shall,是表预言的,例如 East is East and West is West, and never the twain shall meet. (R. Kipling)(东是东,西是西,两者永远碰不到头。) (2) the Immortal Gods:神仙。单说 the Immortals 也是一样的意思。(3) flown:为 fly(飞)的过去分词。(4) our own:年轻人的。在本文中开端虽用的第三人称的 young man,但随即用 us 取代,通篇说的 we 或 us 都是指的年轻人。(5) motion:活跃。(6) keep pace with:与之并驾齐驱。(7) be left behind:落伍。(8) in the natural course of things:在万物的自然趋势中。

(5) The Spirit of Fair-Play

【原　文】

This spirit of fair-play, which in the public schools[1], at any rate, is absorbed[2] as the most inviolable[3] of traditions, has stood our race in good stead[4] in the professions, and especially in the administration of dependencies, where the obvious desire of the officials to deal justly and see fair-play in disputes between natives and Europeans has partly compensated for a want[5] of sympathetic understanding, which[6] has kept the English strangers in[7] lands of alien culture. (William Ralph Inge)

【译　文】

这种公正的精神，至少在私立公校中是当作最为神圣不可侵犯的传统而加以全神贯注的。这种精神在人们的供职上，尤其是在属地统治上，对于英国民族是很有用的。当统治属地时，英国的官员抱着一种显然的愿望，想要公正地处理土人与欧人间的争执，而冀得到公平的解决，使英国人处在海外的异族文化中，因缺乏同情的谅解而格格不入的情形，多少获得了一点补偿。

【注　释】

(1) public schools：英国为私立公校，为教育上层阶级子女的寄宿学校，如伊顿 (Eton) 等校。但在美国则为公立学校。(2) is absorbed：全神贯注，专心，神往。(3) inviolable：不可侵犯的，神圣的。(4) stand（或 serve）one in stead：于人有用，有好用处。(5) want：缺乏。(6) which：为 want 的关系代名词。(7) keep the English strangers in：使英国人在……始终陌生，不能融洽。

(6) On D. H. Lawrence

【原　文】

One of the great charms of Lawrence as a companion was that he could never be bored and so could never be boring. He was able to absorb himself completely in which he was doing at the moment; and he regarded no task as too humble for him to undertake, nor so trivial that it was not worth his while to do it well. He could cook, he could sew, he could darn a stocking and milk a cow, he was an efficient woodcutter and a good hand at embroidery, fires always burned when he had laid them and a floor, after Lawrence had scrubbed it, was thoroughly clean. Moreover, he possessed what is, for a highly strung and highly intelligent man, an even more remarkable accomplishment: he knew how to do nothing. He could just sit and be perfectly content. And his contentment, while one remained in his company, was infectious. (Aldous Huxley)

【译　文】

跟罗伦斯做朋友所感到的他的一种很可爱的地方，就是他从不讨人厌，因之，他也从不讨厌人。他在做着一件事的时候，总是专心致志，没有什么事他会觉得太卑屈而不屑于去做的，也没有一件小事他认为不值得他好好去做。他能烹调，他能缝纫他能编织袜子，还能挤榨牛奶。他是一个能干的樵夫，又是一个刺绣的好手。他生的火总是燃烧得很旺的。他洗擦过的地板，干净得一尘不染。此外，以他那样一个高度紧张和高度理智的人，更具有一种杰出的才能：那就是他知道无所为而为,他可以单只坐着什么事也不做而能心满意足。他这种满足,我们跟他一块儿坐着的话,也可以传染到的。

(7) On Books

【原　文】

　　Some books, like some persons, convey to us all that they will ever[1] have to give at a single sitting[2]. Others hold our attention profitably through two or three encounters……and the books to frequent, the books to be shipwrecked with[3], the great books into which rich and substantial lives have been distilled[4] and packed—the Dialogues of Plato, Montaigne's Essays, Boswell's Johnson, the Essays and Journals of Emerson—these are to be lived with and returned to[5] and made the companions of hours and days and moods as various as those in which they were written. (Stuart P. Sherman)

【译　文】

　　有些书也和有些人一样,大概都是把它们打算要传达给我们的东西一下子就完全倾吐出来。有些书则使我们要专心而获益地读上两三遍才能释手。……还有些是要再三反复去读的书,有些是在遭遇船只失事时也仍然要带着走的书,有些是从丰富而充实的人生中摘出而填入行间字里的伟大的书——柏拉图的语录,蒙田的随笔,鲍斯威尔的约翰生传,艾默逊的散文和日记——这些书是可以与之共同生活的,可以百读不厌的,也可以在不同的时日与心情中作为伴侣的,那种不同的时日与心情,也正和那些作品在写作时的情形一样。

【注　释】

　　(1) ever:在以 that 引导的关系子句中,前有最上级形容词或 all 或 the only 等字样时,则有 on any supposition, by any chance, at all(究竟,到底,的确)之意。(2) at a sitting:一口气(做完一件事,如读完一本书,写完一篇文章之类)。(3) be shipwrecked with:在船失事沉没时也要带着逃命的。(4) distill:精炼,摘出,精选。(5) returned to:重读。

(8) Arguments against Smoking

【原　文】

　　It is always inspiring to see a brave man fighting for a lost[1] cause, and I never cease to admire the Jacobitish[2] zeal with which year after year Mr. John Ervine[3] carries on a guerrilla warfare[4] against the ever-increasing power of tobacco. I admire it all the more because[5] I have fired a few shots in the war against tobacco myself, and have invariably retired defeated[6], with sign of defeat[7], a cigarette in my mouth. I can go on fighting for a week or a month, but there always comes a time when I strike my colours[8]—and a match. (Robert Lynd)

【译　文】

　　看到勇敢的人为着一种毫无成功希望的运动而奋斗的情形,是始终令人鼓舞的。年复一年地以斯图亚特王室拥护者的热诚,来对抗不断增长的烟草的势力,进行游击战的厄尔文,我一直都是衷心佩服的。我本人在对抗烟草的战争中,也曾开过几枪,而每次都败下阵来,口里衔着一支香烟,便是败北的标志,因此我对于他的热诚更加佩服。我能继续战斗一星期,或一个月,但最后总有一个时候要到来,那就是我挂降旗——刮火柴。

【注　释】

(1) lost:不作"失去的"解,应为"失败的","输了的"之意,如 a lost battle(败仗),故在上文中意为"一种完全没有成功希望的运动"。(2) Jacobitish:为 Jacobite 的形容词。Jacobite 为 1688 年被迫逊位的英王 James Ⅱ 的拥护者,即支持 House of Stuart(斯图亚特王室)者。(3) St. John Ervine 为英国爱尔兰出生的剧作家兼小说家。在第一次世界大战后渡美,成为百老汇的批评家。(4) guerrilla warfare:游击战。(5) all the more because:因此更加。(6) retired defeated:败下阵来。(7) the sign of defeat:与下面说的 a cigarette in my mouth 同格。(8) strike one's colours:投降。作者利用 strike a match 一语中的同一动词(strike)而作出此俏皮话语。

(9) The Definition of a Gentleman

【原　文】

It is almost a definition of a gentleman to say he is one who never inflicts pain. This description is both refined and, as far as it goes, accurate. He is mainly occupied in merely removing the obstacles which hinder the free and unembarrassed action of those about him; and he concurs with their movements rather than takes the initiative himself. His benefits may be considered as parallel to what are called comforts or conveniences in arrangements of a personal nature—like an easy chair or a good fire, which do their part in dispelling cold and fatigue, though Nature provides both means of rest and animal heat without them.

【译　文】

这差不多可以算是绅士的定义了:说一个人从来不使别人受苦。这个界说,就其本身而论,是既精到而又正确的。他主要是只忙着为他周围的人来消除那些阻止他们自由自在的行动上的障碍,他总是迎合别人的趋向,而自己是不肯发端的。他给人的恩惠,可认为就是那种为某一个人而安排的舒服与方便——好像一把安乐椅子或一盆炉火一样,在驱除寒冷和疲劳上尽其职责,虽则大自然也就准备好休息和体温两种办法,不要它们也行的。

(10) The Law of the Jungle

【原　文】

People in our culture[1] who like to think of themselves as tough-minded[2] and realistic, including influential political leaders and businessmen as well as go-getters[3] and hustlers[4] of smaller caliber[5], tend to take it for granted[6] that human nature is "selfish" and that life is a struggle in which only the fittest may survive. According to the philosophy[7], the basic law by which man must live[8], in spite of[9] his surface veneer[10] of civilization, is the law of the jungle[11]. The "fittest" are those who can bring to the struggle superior force, superior cunning, and superior ruthlessness[12].

The wide currency[13] of this philosophy of the "survival of the fittest" enables people who act ruthlessly and selfishly, whether in personal rivalries, business competition, or international relations, to allay[14] their consciences by telling themselves that they are only obeying a "law of nature". But a disinterested[15] observer is entitled to[16] ask whether the ruthlessness of the tiger, the cunning of the ape, and obedience to the "law of the jungle" are actually evidences of *human* fitness to survive. (S. I, Hayakawa)

【译 文】

在现代文化中,喜欢把自己看作是意志坚强而现实的人们,包括那些有势力的政治领袖和商界翘楚,以及才干较差的野心家和活动家在内,都想要把人性的自私,与人生是一场只有适者才能生存的奋斗,视为当然。由于这种人生观,人类为要生存而必须倚重的基本原则,就是弱肉强食,纵令他具有文明的外表。所谓适者就是那些能够以过人的力量,过人的狡猾和过人的残忍来奋斗的人。

由于这种"适者生存"的人生观广泛地流行着的缘故,不问是个人方面的敌对,事业上的竞争,或是国际间的关系,都要残忍而自私地来加以处理的人们,只消对自己说这样做只是服从大自然的法则而已,便可获得良心上的安慰。但是一个公正无私的观察者,有资格来问:老虎的残忍,猿猴的狡猾,以及服从弱肉强食的法则,是不是人类适者生存的实际证据呢?

【注 释】

(1) culture:文化(state of intellectual development among a people)。但常与 civilization(文明)混用。文明为人类社会开发的状态(与野蛮对称),而文化则为人类社会由野蛮进化为文明,其努力所得的成绩,表现于各方面的为科学、艺术、宗教、道德、法律、风俗、习惯等,其综合体则谓之文化。(2) tough-minded:意志坚强的。(3) go-getter:充满活力而有进取心的人(aggresive person who is full of vitality)。(4) hustler:非常活跃而机敏的人(very active, prompt, quick-moving person)。(5) caliber:才干,能力。(6) take it for granted:句中的 it 为下面 that 子句的代词。这成语的意思为"把它视为当然"。(7) philosophy:人生观。(8) live by:赖以为生。例如 He lives by teaching. (他以教书为生。)(9) in spite of:不顾。(10) veneer:虚饰,外表上的装饰。(11) the law of the jungle:弱肉强食。(12) ruthlessness:残忍。(13) currency:流通,流布。例如:The rumor gained currency. (谣言流布。)(14) enables people to allay:使人能够解忧。(15) disinterested:公正无私的。(16) is entitled to:有资格去做。

(11) Some well-informed People

【原 文】

We sometimes fall in with[1] persons who have seen much of the world[2], and of the man[3] who, in their day[4], have played a conspicuous part in it[5], but who generalize[6] nothing, and have no observation[7], in the true sense of the word[8]. They abound in[9] information in detail[10], curious and entertaining, about men and things; and, having lived[11] under the influence of no very clear or settled principles[12], religious or political, they speak of every one and everything, only as so many[13] phenomena, which are complete in themselves, and lead to nothing, not discussing any truth, or instructing the hearer, but simply talking[14]. No one would say that these persons, well informed as they are, had attained to any great culture or intellect or to philosophy. (Cardinal Newman)

【译　文】

我们有时邂逅一些熟悉世故的人，和一些曾经见过许多在其全盛时代，叱咤风云，世界安危所系的有名人物的人，但是他们却不能归纳出一点什么来，也毫无真正的观察力。我所遇见的那些人，对于人物和掌故，富有离奇有趣而又极为详尽的见闻。他们因为在宗教上和政治上，都无很明确的信念，而浑浑噩噩地度日，所以他们谈到一切的人物和一切的事情时，只是当作行云流水，映入他们眼帘的一些现象，把它说完即了，并未留有什么后果，也未讨论到任何真理，对听他说的人自然无所启发，只不过是一种闲谈而已。这样的人虽富有见闻，谁也不会认为他们在任何伟大的文化，知识，或哲理上有什么造诣的。

【注　释】

(1) fall in with：邂逅，偶然遇到。(2) see (or know) the world：阅历深的，世故深的(acquire or have experience)。see much of，看得多，世面见得多。(3) of the men：接前面的 have seen much 来解。(4) in one's day：在其全盛时代(in one's time of prosperity)。(5) played a part in it (i. e. the world)：与……有关。例如 Mencius's mother played a great part in his life and in his ultimate success. (孟母对孟子的一生和他的成就有很大的关系。) (6) generalize：归纳，做出结论(infer)。observation：观察力。(8) in the true sense of the word. (那字的)真义。(9) abound in：丰富。(10) in detail：详细地。修饰前面的 information (见闻知识) 的，与后面的 curious 和 entertaining 同为 information 的修饰语。(11) having lived：= as they have lived. (12) under the influence of no very clear or settled principles：= not influenced by very clear or settled principles. Cf. He uttered no word. = He didn't utter a word. (13) so many：同数的。例如 He looks upon his children as so many encumbrances. (他把他的孩子们看做许多累赘。) (14) not discussing any truth, ... but simply talking. 注意句中 not... but 在文法上的相连关系。

(12) The English Humour

【原　文】

Humour has been well[1] defined as "thinking in fun[2] while feeling[3] in earnest[4]". The English do not approach[5] life intellectually; they do not demand that it shall conform to[6] some rigid mental plan; they are not convinced[7] that the universe can be penetrated[8] by thought; they are willing to go to work, either in politics or art, without a theory to sustain them[9]; and when they are more practical than other races, it is not[10]—as those races frequently conclude—because they are coldly clear-sighted and unimaginative, but because they do not busy themselves[11] asking reason[12] to find a key when instinct has already shown them that the door is wide open. (J. B. Priestley)

【译　文】

幽默被人很巧妙地诠释说："一面认真地感觉一面滑稽地思考。"英国人是不肯聪明地去接触人生的。他们并不要求人生应与某种艰苦卓绝的，出自智力的计划一致。他们并不相信这个宇宙是可以用思想去突破的。即令没有支持他们自己的一种理论。他们也愿望去着手于政治上的或艺术上的工作。当他们比别的民族更要实际的时候(例如别的民族惯爱轻易下结论,所以不实际),那并不是因为他们只有冷静的明察力,却缺乏想像力,而是因为当直觉已经明示给他们看那门是打开着的时候,他们仍不肯忙着去讲理性找出一把钥匙来。

【注 释】

(1)well:巧妙地(skillfully)。(2)in fun:开玩笑的。(3)while feeling:= while one feels. (4)in earnest:认真的。(5)approach:接近(come or go near or nearer to)。(6)it shall conform to:句中的 it = life,而 shall 是表主句中主语(they)的意志。例如 I am determined she shall have no cause to complain. (Sheridan)(我决心不要让她有何抱怨。)conform to:使顺应,使一致,使相似。(7)they are not convinced:句中的 are convinced 在意义上几乎和 believe 相同。我们如将 are convinced 与一个他动词等量齐观的话,那么,其后的 that 子句,就可看做动词的宾语了。(8)penetrate:洞察,了解(fathom, comprehend)。I could not penetrate the mystery. (我无法了解这种神秘。)(9)sustain them:支持他们自己。(10)it is not:句中的 it 是指其前面的 they are more practical than other races. (11)busy oneself (in) doing:使自己忙于去做。(12)reason:在此不是"理由",而是"理知","理性"(intellectual faculty)。

(13) The Trouble with Translation

【原 文】

No one these days would, I suppose, maintain[1] that it is a bad thing to have so many translations of great books cheaply available[2]. But like most blessings, plentiful translations can be curses in disguise[3].

My feeling is that students, and readers generally[4], should as soon forgo the airplane and television as neglect the translations of Oriental and European literature[5] which are becoming so abundantly and cheaply available. But I also think that they should be constantly aware (and that publishers, editors, and teachers should constantly remind them) that what they are reading is someone's English version of a work[6] which, in its original language, had unique and untranslatable qualities[7]. Further, they should remember that the more the original work depended for its effect upon those qualities which make literature a fine art[8], the less is a translation able to provide equivalent effects[9] Baudelaire's[10] translations of Poe may be "better" poems than those Poe[11] wrote; but those who read them have read Baudelaire's version of Poe; not Poe. (John A. Kouwenhover)

【译 文】

我想现今没有一个人要坚持说,许多伟大的书的译本,数量繁多,售价低廉,是一件坏事。但是丰富的译本,也和大多数的幸福一样,到头来会变成不幸的。

我的感想是学生们和一般的读书人,都趋之若鹜,谁也不肯放弃数量如此繁多,价钱如此便宜的东洋文学和欧陆文学的译本,正如他们不肯放弃现代文明之赐的飞机与电视一样。但是我又觉得他们应经常留意(出版家,编辑者,及教师们也应经常提醒他们),他们听读着的译本,只是什么人英译出来的一部作品,在它原来的语文中,实具有不能翻译的独自的特质。此外还有一点,他们应该记住:要使原作成为文学上优美的艺术而产生效果,就得依靠那些特质,依靠的程度越深,译本所能给与的同等的效果越少。波德莱尔所译的爱伦·坡的诗,也许比爱伦·坡自己所写的更好;但读那些诗的人只是读了波德莱尔所译的爱伦·坡;而不是真正的爱伦·坡。

【注　释】

(1)maintain:主张,坚持。(2)cheaply available:廉价买到。(3)curses in disguise:化妆的祸根。前面说的 blessings 为 curse 的 antonym(反义字)。(4)readers generally:一般的读书人。(5)should as soon forgo the airplane...literature:如果把东洋文学和欧洲大陆文学的翻译本弃置不顾,就好像放弃飞机不坐,电视不看似的。(6)someone's English version of a work:什么人英译出来的一部作品。(7)which, in its original language, had unique and untranslatable qualities:在它原来的语文中,具有不能翻译的独自的特质。(8)the more the original work...a fine art:越是原作由于使文学成为一种优美的艺术,要靠那些特质才能产生效果。这句话的结构略异寻常,一般是说 depend upon A for B(由 A 而获得 B),现因 A 的修饰语句太长,故变更顺序而说成 depend for B upon A 了。(9)a translation able to provide equivalent effects:能产生同等效果的翻译。(10)Charles Baudelaire:法国诗人,代表作有《恶之花》诗集,以译介 Poe 的作品驰名于世,公认译得比原作更好。(11)Edgar Allen Poe:美国诗人兼短篇小说家。

(14) Too Distinguished to be a Personality

【原　文】

When the porter's wife (she used to answer the house-bell) announced "A gentleman—with a lady, sir," I had as I often had in those days, for the wish was father to the thought[1], an immediate vision of sitters[2]. Sitters my visitors in this case proved to be; but not in the sense I should have preferred[3]. However, there was nothing at first to indicate that they might not have come[4] for a portrait……It[5] was a truth of which I had for some time been conscious that a figure with a good deal of frontage[6] was, as one might say, almost never a public institution[7]. A glance at the lady helped to remind me of this paradoxical law[8]: She also looked too distinguished to be a "personality"[9]. Moreover one would scarcely come across two variations[10] together. (Henry James)

【译　文】

当守门人的妻子(她一向是在应门的)来通报说:"先生,有一位绅士带了一位女客来了。"因为愿望是思想的根源,正如我在当时所常有的情形一样,现在一听说有客人来,心里马上就想到是找我画像的人来了。这次来找我的人,果真是为画像而来的,不过却不是我所指望的对象。虽然如此,起初并没有一点什么迹象显示他们可能不是为画像而来的。……从不久以前起,我就留意到了一个事实,那就是一个风度翩翩的人物,我们不妨说,他差不多从来不会是一个社会上的名人。那个女客,一眼看去,就使我想起这种逆说的定则:她看去也是太杰出而不成其为一个名人呢。而且我们极少会同时遇到两个例外的。

【注　释】

(1) for the wish was father to the thought: 此为根据谚语 The wish is father to the thought. 说的。意为愿望是思想的根源。心有所欲，便有所思。在本文的场合，是正在期待要画像的人来，所以一听说有客，心里就想到是那样的人来了。(2) sitters: 被画像的人要坐着不动，故云。这字前说的 vision，不是指眼前所见到的，而是指当时心中所想像的。(3) not in the sense I should have preferred: 句中的 not in the sense，意为"不是那种意味的"，后半限定语中的 should，不可解释为"应该"，而是表示一种可能发生而实际并未发生的情形。如 I should have gone if you had asked me. (如果你要我去，我就去了。)(4) might not have come: 句中 might 的用法，是表示"推测"的，这句意思是"恐怕不是为……而来"。此句因前有 nothing 一字，致构成双重否定，若加以抵消的话，则意为"一开头就知道他们是为着求画像而来的呀"。(5) It: 这个代名词是代表 that a figure 等一个子句的。(6) a figure with a good deal of frontage: 风度翩翩的人物。一表人才。仪表漂亮的人。(7) public institution: 原意为"公共机关"，在此为"世间知名之士"，"名士"。institution 一字在口语中有 familiar object (有名的事物；熟悉的人物) 的意思，例如 He was one of the institutions of the place. (他是当地闻人之一。)(8) this paradoxical law: 这个逆说的定则，意指风度翩翩的人反而不成其为名士的那种现象。(9) too distinguished to be a "personality": 太杰出而不能成为名士。personality = personage 人物，名人。distinguished personage 有名望的人物，名人。(10) two variations. 指对上述法则的例外的人物。来客有两人，那女客即令是例外的存在，那绅士不可能也是，不至两个例外同时出现。

(15) Schadenfreude

【原　文】

If we contrast the resources of the United States and the resources of the Viet Cong[1], whatever we may think of the political morality of the activities of the Viet Cong, it does not seem to the outsider that the Viet Cong are inferior to the Americans in courage, resolution[2], or belief in their cause[3]. For this reason, the news that the Americans had dropped napalm[4] on their own troops was received with very mixed feelings[5] in Europe. There were, of course, professional and permanent anti-Americans[6] who had all the joys of Schadenfreude[7] at the news. For them, there is no folly and no crime of which the Americans are not intrinsically capable, and there is no folly and no crime which the enemies of the Americans are not justified in committing[8]. But many people who do not share these views[9] in the least[10] could not help reflecting that a fate[11] had befallen unfortunate young American soldiers that has frequently befallen even[12] more unfortunate Vietnamese children. (Sir Denis Brogan)

【译　文】

如果把美国的资源和越共的资源比较一下，无论我们对越共的所作所为在政治上的道德怎样想法，由局外人来看是不会认为越共在勇敢，决心，和忠于大义的信念上，有逊于美军的。由于这个原因，在欧洲听到美军把烧夷弹误投到他们自己的军队上的消息时，不免感到悲喜交集。当然，有些职业的，坚决永恒的反美主义者，听到这消息便要幸灾乐祸，感到高兴。他们认为美军在本质上是任何愚行,任何罪恶,都可以干得出来的,所以美军的敌人要干些愚行和罪恶,也是应该的。但即令许多决不同意这种见解的人,听到这消息时,也不得不有下面这样的想法:不幸的年轻美国兵曾经遭遇的悲惨的死,在更加不幸的越南儿童身上,到现在为止所遭遇到的同样的惨死,也不知有多少次了。

【注　释】

(1)Viet Cong:越共。(2)resolution:决心(firmness of purpose)。(3)belief in their cause:对于(民族解放的)大义的信念。普通说 one's cause 为人们所拼命支持的主义、主张、信仰、运动等。(4)napalm:燃烧弹。火焰喷射器等所用的胶状汽油。(5)mixed feelings:复杂的感情。(6)professional and permanent anti-Americans:职业的持久的反美主义者。(7)Schadenfreude (G.):幸灾乐祸(enjoyment obtained from the mishaps of others)。这是说对别人的不幸感到痛快。这是一个德文的字,英文无相当的字可以用的,故借用。(Schade = damage + freude = joy.) (8) there is no folly and no crime which the enemies of the Americans are not justified in committing:句中两重否定变成肯定,故可改写为肯定句 The enemies of the Americans are justified in committing any folly and crime. 即所谓"以牙还牙"的理论。(9)share these views:同意。(10)not…in the least: = not…at all 注意这个 in the least 与 at least 不同,不可混淆。(11)a fate:悲惨的运命,即死。(12)even: = still

(16) Aloneness is Worse than Failure

【原　文】

What is feared as failure in American society is, above all, aloneness. And aloneness is terrifying because it means that there is no one, no group, no approved cause to submit to. Even success often becomes impossible to bear when it is not socially approved or even known. This is perhaps why successful criminals often feel the need to confess, that is, to submit to the community's[1] judgment, represented in the person to whom the confession is made. They will confess even under circumstances where this will probably, if not certainly, endanger their previous success: proof, I think, that aloneness is more intolerable than mere failure. For mere failure, provided[2] it is found in company[3], can rather easily be borne; many ideologies have the function of making it possible for people to digest[4] the worst miseries and even death. Under the sway[5] of the ideology, they do not feel the impact[6] of their failure; they are in the grip of an authority, even if it lets them down[7]. On the other hand[8], one who is alone lacks this solace which can make even failure comfortable. (David Riesman)

【译　文】

在美国社会中作为失败而为人们所恐怖的,莫过于孤独了。而孤独之所以可怕,就因为那意味着没有一个可服从的人,没有一个可服从的团体,也没有一个可服从的公认的大义。即令获得成功,若不为社会所认可,或甚至不为世人所知道时,就是成功也常要变得使人不能忍受的。这也许就是成功的罪犯,时常觉得有必要去自首的原因,那就是,去服从那个听取自首的人所代表的公众的裁判。即令在如果不是一定的话,至少是可能危害他们前此的成功那种情形之下,他们仍然要去自首的。变成孤独比单纯的失败,更要难于忍受,我想这就足以证明了。因为单纯的失败,即令是与人共同遭受的,毋宁是能够容易忍受的。许多意识形态的作用,可使人能够忍受极大的不幸,甚至是死亡。人们在意识形态掩护之下,便不会感到自己失败的冲击。意识形态以一种权威的力量,掌握住他们,虽则在紧要关头也不免要把他们抛弃。在另一方面,孤独的人便缺乏那种甚至可以使失败也感到舒服的安慰。

【注　释】

(1)the community:公众(the public)。(2)provided:如果(if),即令(even if)。(3)in company:与人共同地。(4)digest:忍受(bear with patience;endure)。(5)sway:控制。(6)impact:冲击。(7)let them down:把他们抛弃(fail them at need)。(8)on the other hand:在另一方面。

(17) Being One's True Self

【原　文】

In literature, as in life, one of the fundamentals is to find, and be, one's true self. One's true self may indeed[1] be unpleasant; but a false self, sooner or later, becomes disgusting—just as a nice plain woman[2], painted to the eyebrows, can become horrid[3]. In writing, in the long run[4], pretense does not work. As the police put it[5], anything you say may be used as evidence against you. If handwriting reveals character, writing reveals it still more. You cannot fool your judges all the time[6].

Most style is not honest enough. Easy to say, but hard to practice. A writer may take to[7] long words, as young men to beards—to[8] impress. But long words like long beards, are often the badge of charlatans[9]. Or a writer may cultivate the obscure[10], to seem profound. But even carefully muddied puddles[11] are soon fathomed. Or he may cultivate eccentricity, to seem original. But really original people do not have to think[12] about being original—they can no more help it than[13] they can help[14] breathing. (Frank Laurence Lucas)

【译　文】

在文学中,也和在人生中一样,基本原理之一就是发现自我,乃至成为真正的自我。真正的自我诚然是令人不愉快的,但一个虚伪的自己迟早是会变得令人讨厌的——正好像一个丑陋的女人,涂脂抹粉,一直涂到眉毛以上去,也会变得可怕的一样。在写作中假装毕竟也是行不通的。正如警察所说的,你说的任何一句话,都可能要成为对你不利的证据。如果笔迹显示性格,写作显示的更多。你不能始终愚弄所有的评判人呀。

大多数的文体是不够诚实的。说时容易做时难。一个作家也许好用长字,正如年轻人好蓄胡须一样,目的无非是想使人留下深刻的印象。但是长字,有如长须,常成为骗子的标志。凡是一个作家想要显得高深,可能采用晦涩难解的文字。但是无论怎样细心弄得浑浊的水,也很快就可测出其深度的。或是有人想要显得独创,可能写出奇奇怪怪的文章。但是真正有独创力的人们无用乎去想怎样来独创,他们就像不得不呼吸一样,也不得不发挥出那种独创力来。

【注　释】

(1)indeed:与后面的but 呼应。(2)a nice plain woman:不说 ugly woman,而说 plain woman 或 homely woman,比较含蓄,是一种委婉的说法(Euphemism),其实这个 plain = ugly. 在男人方面说

plain man,意义就不同了,那是指率直的人,而所谓 plain people 便是指一般的人。形容词对男女意义有别,须加注意。他例如 an honest man 诚实的人;an honest woman 贞洁的女人(a chaste woman),成语有 make an honest woman of her,先奸后娶,使成正式妻子。nice 用在形容词前为副词,意为"十分地","怎样也是",如 It was nice cold weather. (天气很冷。)(3)painted to the eyebrows,can become horrid:涂到眉毛以上,意即浓妆艳抹。句中的 can 非指"能力",而指"可能性"。(4)in the long run:终久,毕竟。(5)put it:这个 put 有"表明"和"述说"的意思,如 To put it briefly.(简单地说。)Let me put it in another way. (换一个方式来说吧。)(6)all the time:一直,始终。(7)take to:喜欢,耽于。(8)to:即 in order to. (9)badge of charlatans:骗子的标志。charlatan 原为法文,有"走江湖者","骗子","冒充内行者"的意思。(10)the obscure:形容词前加定冠词即指名词,如 the beautiful = beauty;the poor = poor people. (11)muddied puddles:泥水潦。(12)do not have to think:意为 need not think. (13)no more...than:与……同样不。(14)help:避免(avoid)。

(18) Happiness Consists in Love

【原　　文】

Who can say⁽¹⁾ in what remoteness of time, in what difference of earthly shape, love first come to us as a stranger in the jungle? We, in our human family⁽²⁾, know him⁽³⁾ through dependence⁽⁴⁾ in childhood, through possession⁽⁵⁾ in youth, through sorrow and loss in their season⁽⁶⁾. In childhood we are happy to receive; it is the first opening of love. In youth we take and give, dedicate and possess—rapture and anguish are mingled, until parenthood brings a dedication⁽⁷⁾ that, to be happy, must ask for no return⁽⁸⁾. All these are new horizons of content⁽⁹⁾, which the lust of holding, the enemy of love⁽¹⁰⁾, slowly contaminates. Loss, sorrow and separation come, sickness and death; possession, that tormented us, is nothing in our hands; it vanishes. Love's elusive⁽¹¹⁾ enchantment, his ubiquitous⁽¹²⁾ presence, again become apparent; and in age we may reach a haven⁽¹³⁾ that asking for nothing knows how to enjoy. ⁽¹⁴⁾ (Freya Stark)

【译　　文】

爱这东西,不管是在多么远古的时代,不管是采取怎样现世的形态出现,总好像在森林中遇到的陌生人一样,是一个谁也不能了解的哑谜。属于人类的我们,在孩童时代,由于依赖爱自己的人而认识爱;在青年时代,由于占有所爱的人而认识爱,于是时候一到,由于失去了所爱的人感到悲伤而认识爱。在孩童时代我们很高兴来接受;这是爱的最早的端倪。在青年时代我们有取有予,有献身有占有——悲喜交集,直到做了父母时,对儿女那种献身的爱,心甘情愿,不望报答。这一切都是令人满足的爱的新境界,可惜不免要为与爱为敌的所有欲,慢慢地加以污损。失去了爱的痛苦,离别的悲哀,随即到来,还有疾病和死亡。以前那种使我们受苦的占有,已不在我们掌握之中,而早烟消云散了。爱的难于捉摸的魅力,它那不即不离的灵性,再度变得明显起来,及来到老年,我们就可能达到一个由于不求报答,故能体味到那种平静无波的爱的佳境。

【注　　释】

(1)say:(尤其是在否定和疑问句中)推测;评定;提出意见。(2)We, in our human family:等于说 We human beings. 人类。(3) know him：等于前面说的 love first comes to us 一样，将 he 作为 love 的代名词。这个 know，不是指状态，而是指"相知"。(4) dependence：依赖（父母）。(5) possession：占有（爱人）。(6) through sorrow and loss in their season：在人生的各个时期由于失去爱而感到悲伤。in their season 表示包括所有的时期，their 指 sorrow 与 loss 的，故译为"时候一到"。(7) until parenthood brings a dedication：直到做了父母，就献身地去爱儿女，天下父母心，莫不皆然。(8) must ask for no return：决不望报。(9) new horizons of content：令人满足的爱的新境界。(10) the lust of holding, the enemy of love：所有欲，也就是爱的大敌。(11) elusive：不可捉摸的，以为捉到了的东西又跑掉了，意指倏忽无常。(12) ubiquitous：原意为无所不在的，现译为不即不离的。以上两句并非同格的说法，由动词的复数便知。(13) haven：平静安乐的境界。(14) that asking for nothing knows how to enjoy：由于我们不求报答故能体味到那种……

(19) The Cosy Fire of Affection

【原　文】

You've been in love, of course!(1) If not you've got it to come. Love is like the measles; we all have to go through it. Also like the measles, we take it only once. One never need be afraid of catching it a second time. The man who has had it can go into the most dangerous places(2), and play the most foolhardy tricks(3) with perfect safety. He can, to see the last of a friend(4), venture into the very jaws of the marriage ceremony itself(5). He can keep his head through the whirl of a ravishing waltz(6), and rest afterwards in a dark conservatory(7), catching nothing more lasting than a cold.(8)

No, we never sicken with love twice. Cupid(9) spends no second arrow on the same heart. Love's handmaids(10) are our life-long friends. Respect, and Admiration, and Affection, our doors may always be left open for, but their great celestial master(11), in his royal progress, pays but one visit(12), and departs. Meteor-like, it blazes for a moment(13), and lights with its glory the whole world beneath. Happy those who(14), hastening down again e'er it dies out(15), can kindle their earthly altars at its flame. Love is too pure a light to burn(16) long among the noisome gases that we breathe, but before it is choked out(17) we may use it as a torch to ignite the cosy fire(18) of affection. (Jerome K. Jerome)

【译　文】

当然，你们都有过恋爱的经验！如果还没有的话，也就必然会要来的。恋爱好像麻疹一样，是每个人都要经历的。也好像麻疹一样，我们一生中只能罹上一次。谁也不用担心会再度罹上它的。凡是已经有过那种经历的人，可以深入最危险的地带，玩弄最鲁莽的勾当，逢场作戏，保证安全。他可以向独身生活告别，而大胆地走进结婚典礼的虎口。他可以满不在乎地从结婚晚会的狂欢圆舞的漩涡中安顿下来，然后进入幽暗的温室里去，从此相安无事，即令有平地波澜，也不过是像纠缠的伤风一样的小小毛病而已。

所以我们是不会再度罹上恋爱病的。爱神不会在同一颗心上射出第二支箭。爱的侍女们成为我们毕生的伴侣。尊敬，赞美，钟情，我们的心扉经常为她们开着，可是她们那伟大的天上的主子，在他的行幸中，只降临一次就离去了。像流星一般，它只燃烧一会儿，用它的荣光，照明下界整个的世界。趁着那光还未消失,再急忙地下降,能用它的火焰把他们地上的祭坛点燃的人们就有福了。爱是一种太纯洁的光,不能在我们呼吸的具有恶臭的气体中燃烧得太久,但是在它窒息之前,我们也许可用它作为火把,以点燃舒适的炉火,钟情的所在。

【注　释】

(1) You've been in love, of course!:作者认为男女之间总不免有相恋的事,但只有初恋才是真诚的,所以他把它比做每个人都要经历一次麻疹。确认了这种严肃的事实之后,他便达到了一个结论:正是王戎说的"情之所钟正在吾辈"。钟情才是最要紧的,维系男女的关系,家庭的存在,乃至快乐的婚后生活,或是避免离婚的悲剧,一切都有赖于此。(2) the most dangerous places:指男女间最容易出问题的情形。(3) play the most fool-hardy tricks:所谓 play a trick,意为开玩笑或诈骗,trick 是诡计或欺诈手段。fool-hardy 为有勇无谋的,鲁莽的。故全句译成玩弄鲁莽的勾当。(4) see the last of a friend:这里说的 a friend,是把 single-blessedness(独身生活)人格化了。所谓和那朋友见最后一面,就是和他告别的意思。(5) can venture into the very jaws of the marriage ceremony itself:句中动词的 venture,形容词的 very,乃至反身代名词的 itself,都是为加强语气而用的,全部总括在助动词的 can 之下。复数形的 jaws 有"峡谷"的意思,在此乃比喻的用法。(6) can keep his head through the whirl of a ravishing waltz:句中 keep his head 有 keep calm(沉着,满不在乎)之意。the whirl of a ravishing waltz,指结婚晚会的狂欢热舞的场面。(7) conservatory:温室,暖房(不可译作音乐学校),在此指家庭。因为人们说结婚是爱情的坟墓,现由结婚典礼来表示爱情的结束,晚会的狂欢敲响了葬送爱情的丧钟(funeral bell),而当事人在那个热闹的场面过后,能够安静下来(rest)的地方,便是可避风雨侵凌而由人工做出来的温室(家庭)了。(8) catching nothing more lasting than a cold:注意这儿说的 catching,与前面第五句说的 One never need be afraid of catching it a second time. 中的 catching 遥相呼应,而有对照的作用。全句意为延续的东西除伤风外就不会得到别的什么了。说结婚生活中即使有点平地波澜也不会大过伤风那样的小毛病。注意在 conservatory 前用了 dark 一个形容词,既系幽暗,自然难免伤风,而且这个 cold 还有对 love 已经冷却了的含义。(9) Cupid:罗马神话中的爱神,用箭射在男女的心上,他们就相爱起来。(10) Love's handmaids:指下面说的 Respect, Admiration, Affection. (11) their great celestial master:指 Love. (12) pays but one visit:只降临一次,与上段说的 Also like the measles, we take it only once. 遥相呼应。(13) it blazes for a moment:句中的 it 指 Love. 上句因有 master 的字样,故临时改用 his 为代名词。(14) Happy those who 即 Happy are those who 的省略说法。这使人不免要联想到新约圣经的 St. Matthew V 中的"The Sermon on the Mount"如 Blessed are the poor in spirit; for theirs is the kingdom of heaven 等句法。(15) hastening down again e'er it dies out:句中的 again 不是指 hastening down 的反复,而是指往返运动中返的意思,但不必译出,这原是说 Love 离开人间回到天上去,有时再来到人间。e'er 应写作 ere = before,这当然是作者的笔误(erroneous use)。全句意为趁着人们热恋的纯情还没有完全消失,再匆匆忙忙地从天上降下,用它的火焰点燃他们地上的祭坛上的火,能做到这点的人们便有福了。(16) too pure... to burn:太纯洁而不能燃烧。(17) it is choked out:窒息死去(指 love)。(18) the cosy fire:指家庭中的 hearth(火炉)而言。hearth 在英国因一年到头生火故为家庭的象征。最后说的 of affection 意指家庭有赖爱情的支持,故 the cosy fire 即为钟情的所在。

(20) Irrational Man

【原　文】

An observer from another planet might well be struck by[1] the disparity[2] between the enormous power which our age has concentrated in its external life and the inner poverty which our art seeks to expose to view. This is, after all, the age that has discovered and harnessed[3] atomic energy, and that will, in a few years (perhaps in a few months), have atomic-powered planes which can fly through outer space and not need to return to mother earth for weeks. What cannot man do[4]? But if an observer from Mars were to turn his attention from these external appurtenances[5] of power to the shape of man as revealed in our novels, plays, painting, and sculpture, he would find there a creature full of holes and gaps, faceless, riddled with doubts and negations[6].

This violent contrast between power and impoverishment[7] is frightening, for it represents a dangerous lagging of man behind his own works[8]; and in this lag lies the terror[9] of the atomic bomb which hangs over us like impending night. Here surely the ordinary man begins to catch a fleeting glimpse of that Nothingness[10] which both artist and philosopher have begun in our time to take seriously. (William Barrett)

【译　文】

现代的人在其外面的生活上集中巨大的力量，而现代艺术却企图把那内面的贫穷暴露出来让人们看，一个从别的星球来的观察者，看到这种悬殊的不同，要大吃一惊也是当然的。毕竟，现代是发现了原子能又加以利用的时代，在几年内，甚至几个月内，就会有原子动力的飞机，能够飞往外太空，好几个礼拜都无需回返地球。人类还有什么做不到的事呢？但是如果一个从火星来的观察者，把他的目光从这些人力发挥尽致的外表的工具，转移到现代小说，戏剧，绘画，雕刻，所显示的人的形状，他就会发觉那是为疑问和否定，弄得满目疮痍，面目全非的一个生物。

这种外表的威力和内在的脆弱，二者对照的激烈令人可怕，因为它表示人类落在他自己造出的强大工具的后面，已达到危险的程度。像迫近的黑夜一般悬在我们头上的原子弹的恐怖，就因为这种落后而将来临。那是一定的，原子战争的结果，一切归于毁灭。艺术家和哲学家早已在我们这个时代开始时，就认真地在考虑这"无"的世界，而一般的人也触目惊心，开始注意到这个问题了。

【注　释】

(1) might well be struck by：要为……而感到大为吃惊也是应该的。(2) disparity：不同，悬殊。(3) harnessed：利用。(4) What cannot man do?：人类还有什么不能做的？意即人类什么都能做（修辞疑问），是以否定加强肯定的。(5) appurtenances：*Random House Dictionary* 上解释说，something subordinate to another, more important thing, 更加重要的附属物，在此指原子弹及太空船一类的人力所造成的外表的工具。(6) a creature full of holes and gaps, faceless, riddled with doubts and negations：由于怀疑和否定使之伤痕累累，面目全非的生物。所谓 faceless 不是没有面孔，而是面

目不分明(unidentifiable),不能分辨是谁。这儿所描写的生物(人类)是指现代精神分裂的人,怀疑的人,虚无的人等形象化的东西。(7) power and impoverishment:外表的威力和内在的脆弱。(8) it represents a dangerous lagging of man behind his own works:这表示人类落在他自己的制作品的后面,达到危险的程度。lagging behind 的反意语为 catching up with。(9) in this lag lies the terror:恐怖就在这落后之中。这是一种倒装句法,意为因为这种落后而发生那种恐怖。(10) catch a fleeting glimpse of that Nothingness:一切皆空原是东方的思想,在西洋到了本世纪才有人提倡存在主义,于是也有了虚无思想,代表的有法国的卡缪著的《西奇斐的神话》(Albert Camus: *Le Mythe de Sisyphe*,1942),德国卡甫卡著的《奇妙之身》(Franz Kafka: *Die Verwandlung*,1916)等。Nothingness 指一切毁灭,是原子弹炸后的状态。catch a fleeting glimpse of,一瞬瞥见。指普通人也要骤然想到一切归于毁灭后的虚无状态。

习题

试将下列英文译成中文:

(1) You are a very strange creature by way of a friend! —always wanting me to play and sing before anybody and everybody! If my vanity had taken a musical turn, you would have been invaluable; but as it is, I would really rather not sit down before those who must be in the habit of hearing the very best performers.

(2) Twenty years had passed since then. He kept up a busy correspondence with various great ladies and his letters were amusing and chatty. He never lost his love for titled persons and paid no attention to the announcement in the Times of their comings and goings. He perused the column which records births, deaths, and marriages, and he was always ready with his letter of congratulation or condolence. (Maugham)

(3) The best of the communications an author has to make is to his own generation, and he is wise to let the generation that succeeds his choose its own exponents. They will do it whether he lets them or not. His language will be Greek to them. (Maugham)

(4) Often enough—and often justifiably—your ordinary lover of Nature has been accused of sentimentality. He prattles, so his condemners say, of the sweet twitter of birds and of the flowers that bloom in the spring. He disregards the seamy side of things and sees the world in greeting-card terms. (Joseph Wood Krutch)

(5) If to feel a false emotion based upon a deliberately incomplete view of the facts is to be guilty of sentimentalism, then the view that Nature is consistently violent and cruel is as sentimental as its opposite. She is no more characteristically red in tooth and claw than she is characteristically a kind mother. (Joseph Wood Krutch)

(6) Probably in nothing have man's inventive powers been so active as in his endeavour to triumph over the terrors of darkness. Light is among the first needs man has supplied for himself in his struggle against it. Yet darkness has its gracious gifts. As it descends upon the world nature prepares itself for rest

and sleep, and in the silence men recover strength of mind and body for the duties and burdens of the new day.

(7) Maybe the gradual actualization of this solidarity was the result of scientific and hence technological progress which caused distances to shrink and required ever expanding markets. But it is a preconceived and entirely unwarranted idea to believe this technological unification to have been a primary cause.

(8) A stout old lady was walking with her basket down the middle of a street in Petrograd to the great confusion of the traffic and with no small peril to herself. It was pointed out to her that the pavement was the place for foot-passengers, but she replied: "I'm going to walk where I like. We've got liberty now." It did not occur to the dear old lady that if liberty entitled the foot-passenger to walk down the middle of the road it also entitled the cab-driver to drive on the pavement, and that the end of such liberty would be universal chaos.

(9) Foolishly arrogant as I was, I used to judge the worth of a person by his intellectual power and attainment. I could see no good where there was no logic, no charm where there was no learning. Now I think that one has to distinguish between two forms of intelligence, that of the brain, and that of the heart, and I have come to regard the second as by far the more important.

(10) The educated man is presumed to know what is wrong in the world, and what should be done to rectify it. If his education has amounted to anything, it should have increased his ability to think clearly and scientifically, and thus to know how to get at the cause and effect of political, social, economic, industrial evils. No man has right to consider education as merely a personal benefit enabling him to be more prosperous and happy in the world. He must look upon it as imposing upon him a responsibility to increase the welfare of others. Too many regard it as their own possession, and do not realize that it is something to be shared with others, and to be used for good of society at large.

附录　当代英美名作摘译

小引

　　一般读书人都是陶渊明的信徒,读书不求甚解,明白了一点大意就满足了。因此一动手来翻译,立刻就露出马脚来,连大名鼎鼎的胡适博士亦在所不免。他所译的短篇小说和原文常有出入。日本人读书比较认真,所以他们的译文是不会有太离谱的。这并不太难,只要我们放弃不求甚解的习惯,仔细精读原文,自不难彻底理解。如果能把原文逐字逐句理解无遗,再运用中文的表现能力,自然就能很忠实而流利地翻译出来了。

(1)

　　Suppose you ignore the telephone when it rings, and suppose that, for once, somebody has an important message for you. I can assure you that if a message is really important it will reach you sooner or later. Think of the proverb: "Ill news travels apace." I must say good news seems to travel just as fast. And think of the saying: "The truth will out." It will. But suppose you answer the telephone when it rings. If, when you take off the receiver, you say "Hullo!" just think how absurd that is. Why, you might be saying "Hullo!" to a total stranger, a thing you would certainly think twice about before doing in public, if you were English.

　　But perhaps, when you take off the receiver, you give your number or your name. But you don't even know whom you are giving it to! Perhaps you have been indiscreet enough to have your name and number printed in the telephone directory, a book with a large circulation, a successful book so often reprinted as to make any author envious, a book more in evidence than Shakespeare or the Bible, and found in all sorts of private and public places. By your self-advertisement you have enabled any stranger, bore, intruder, or criminal to engage you in conversation at a moment's notice in what ought to be the privacy of your own home.

【解　说】

　　本文选自英国现代作家 William Plomer(1903—)写的 On Not Answering the Telephone 一篇随笔中的一节。文笔中讽刺与幽默并用,再加上日常说的谚语,写来极为生动有趣。作者生于非洲,虽曾回国入 Rugby 私立公校,因水土不合又回返他的出生地去了。他在非洲从商,又从事农业,后与诗人 Roy Campbell 合办一个文学杂志。第二次世界大战中从军,在海军部服务。作品涉及长篇小说,短篇小说,诗歌,传记各方面,以短篇小说最为有名。

【注　释】

　　(1)ignore 不理睬。(2)important message for you,有重要的消息告诉你。(3)sooner or later 迟早。(4)think of 想到,忆及。例如 I can't think of his name at the moment,我一时想不起他的名字。(5)"Ill news travels apace"恶事传千里。travels 一字,又常用 runs 或 flies 等字。apace 有 fast 的意思,如 The hours and days speed apace 时日飞逝。(6)The truth will out. 真相终将水落石出。will 表示习性。out 为 come out 的简略说法,单此一副词即可作自动词用。同样的俗语有 Murder will out，谋杀案隐藏不住，终将泄露出来。(7) receiver 电话的听筒。(8) total stranger 完全不认识的陌生人。(9) a thing 用作和上文同格的名词，这一件事即指对一个陌生人照呼。(10) think twice about 再思（而后行）的意思的陈句。(11) doing in public 公开的去做，在人前做。(12) if you were English 如果你是英国国民的话。the English 指英国全体的国民，单独的个体则说 an Englishman，复数为 three Englishmen，但普通说国籍时常把冠词略去，如 I am Chinese.（我是中国的国民）。比较：I am a Chinese.（我是中国人）。They are Italian.（他们都是意大利的国民）。比较：They are Italians.（他们是意大利人）。if you were English 的 English 是如上 Italian 同样的用法。(13) indiscreet 轻率的。(14) telephone directory 电话簿。(14) a book with a large circulation 一本销数很广大的书。(15) make any author envious 使任何作家妒羡。(16) in evidence 是一个有conspicuous（显著的）之意的成语，例如 She likes to be much in evidence 她很爱出风头。Smith was nowhere in evidence. 史密斯显然不见了。(17) self-advertisement 自作广告，自我宣传。指把自己的姓名住址登在电话簿上。一种讽刺的说法。(18) bore 令人讨厌的人。(19) intruder 闯入者。(20) criminal 罪犯。(21) engage you in conversation 来和你交谈。(22) at a moment's notice = immediately 在此场合的 notice 可作"预告"解。(23) in the privacy of your own home. 在你自己家里的私生活中。in privacy 秘密地，隐秘地。例如 He likes to live in privacy. 他喜欢与人无所接触的生活。他喜欢离群索居。I tell you this in strict privacy. 此事绝对秘密。in the privacy of one's thoughts 在心灵深处。

【译 例】

假定电话铃响你置之不理，又假定刚好这次那人有重要的消息要告诉你。我可以向你保证，如果那消息是真正重要的话，它迟早总会传达给你听的。想到那句谚语："恶事传千里"，我一定要说好的消息好像也同样地传达得很快的呀。再想想那句常言："真相总会水落石出的"，确是如此。但是假定你听到电话铃响，你就去接。当你拿起听筒，如果你说"哈罗！"的话，试想这是多么荒谬呀。哼，你也许正在对一个完全不相识的陌生人在说着"哈罗！"如果你是英国国民的话，这确实是一件在人前你要三思而后行的事。

但是当你拿起电话听筒的时候，也许你会把你的号码或是姓名告诉对方。你甚至还不知道你在告诉的人是谁呢！也许你太轻率把你的姓名号码，随便就印在电话簿上去了，那是一本销数极多的书，任何作家都要羡慕的一本再三重版的成功的书，一本比莎士比亚或是《圣经》更要引人注目的书，在各种各样的公私场所都可见到的。由于你的自我宣传，你使得任何陌生人，令人讨厌的家伙，闯入者，或是罪犯之流，都能够侵入你在自己家里的私生活，随时来和你交谈。

(2)

What is perhaps strangest today is the keen widespread interest displayed toward people who are, on the one hand, not real celebrities and, on the other, not personally known to one. Most gossip that doesn't concern one's friends and acquaintances has, classically, a certain snob appeal—has to do with people of great wealth or fame or beauty. But much that one reads today in the gossip columns has to do, it might almost be said, with people whose reputations are being made at the same time they're being unmade—people who only exist, as it were, in terms of the gossip. The who's-dating-whom, the rumors of divorce, the shifts of affection, the speculations as marriage, the pregnancies and births, are for the most part—in New York, at any rate—about people only marginally in the limelight and often actually on the side lines. That Sonny Tink, the underwear heir, is dating a starlet, or even a showgirl; that a TV scriptwriter is horning in on the happy home of a candy-bar maker; that it's a boy at the Gumbridges (his pajama company sponsors a minor radio program); that a dog-biscuit tycoon has taken to investing in Broadway shows—this is the run of such stuff; and in a city of 8,000,000 people—a city that teems with real celebrities—this would seem to me of a piece with the trailer items in an old-fashioned small-town society column.

【解　说】

本文采自美国作家 Louis Kronenberger(1904—) 的一篇文章 A Note on Privacy 中的一节。描写私生活日益遭受侵害,物议纷纭,人言可畏。行文故意规避平易的表现,而采用奇特的语法,点缀一些有趣的警句和新鲜的比喻,口语俗语自由使用,有时未免艰深难解,总之,不失为奔放不羁的文体。作者为德国系统犹太人的后裔,在出生地 Ohio 的 Cincinnati 大学毕业后,1924 年前往纽约,先在 Boni & Liveright 公司编辑部工作,后又改任 Knopf 出版公司编辑。发表了许多小说和评论,现为纽约《泰晤士报》写剧评,相当活跃。

【注　释】

(1) the keen widespread interest 热烈的普遍的兴趣。(2) displayed toward people who are 对那些人们展示的。(3) on the one hand... on the other (hand) 在一方面……在另一方面。(4) celebrities 名人,闻人。(5) personally known to 亲身认识。(6) gossip 街谈巷议;在人背后说人长短或是非闲谈。(7) that doesn't concern one's friends and acquaintances 无关他的朋友或相识的。(8) classically 原义为"正统地",在此用着"传统地"(traditionally)相近的意味。(9) snob appeal 意为 appeal to snobbery,以名词修饰名词,简洁有力,为现代英语中常见的用法。has a certain snob appeal 引起某种装模作样的兴趣。据 Random House Dictionary of the English Language 的解释说 snob = a person who pretends to have social importance, intellectual superiority, etc. 意为一个假装社会上重要的人物,或智力超人表示他什么事都知道的样子。snob 在此指 snobbish character 或 conduct. 即上述俗物的性格或行为。(10) has to do with 与……有关。(11) people of great wealth or fame or beauty 极为富有,极为有名,极为美貌的人。(12) much that one reads today in the gossip columns 今日我们在闲话栏中所读到的大部分的社会新闻。(13) reputations are being made at the same time they're being unmade. 由于声名狼藉而使声誉鹊起。意为以丑行而出名的。这种表现法很是有趣。(14) as it were 可谓。(15) in terms of 由于(by means of);从什么的观点(from the standpoint of). (16) The who's-dating-whom 谁在跟谁闹恋爱。这种随意加短划而把若干单字构成一语,也是新的表现法。(17) the shifts of affection 移情别恋。(18) speculations 臆测。(19) pregnancies 怀孕。(20) only marginally in the limelight 仅是略为靠近灰光灯所照射的部分。意指稍为世人所知的。(21) on the side lines 在界线外的地方。借用运动术语,以作比喻的表现。The spectators watched the game from the side lines. 观众站在线外看比赛。(22) Sonny Tink 捏造的名字,非实际的公司名。(23) underwear heir 内衣公司老板的继承人。是一种极为紧缩的表现法。(24) is dat-

ing a starlet 和一个小明星约会。(25)showgirl 在歌舞场献技的女郎。(26)a TV scriptwriter 电视脚本作者。(27)is horning in on the happy home 正在破坏一个幸福的家庭。horn in = intrude 闯入。为美国俗语。(28)candy-bar maker 糖果制造商。(29)it's a boy at the Gumbridges 在简家生了一个男孩。(30)his pajama company 简家经营的睡衣公司。(31)sponsor a minor radio program 赞助一个小型的广播节目。(32)a dog-biscuit tycoon 饲犬用的饼干业巨子。(33)take to 喜欢；耽于。(34)Broadway shows 百老汇上演的戏。(35)the run = the average kind 普通的种类。*cf.* the common run of men（普通人）。(36)teem with 充满着。(37)of a piece with = of the same kind 与……同一类。(38)the trailer items 附加的记事。trailer 原意为电影样片。

【译　例】

目下最奇怪的事，也许就是对于既非名人，又非熟识的人们所展示的一般热烈的兴趣。和自己的朋友或相识无关的大部分的闲谈，在传统上有一种诉诸俗物气质的魅力，而老是和富豪，名士或美人有关的。但是我们今日在闲话栏中所读到的多数的社会新闻，差不多可以说，都是有关以丑行而出名的人物的，以及有关那些可谓只存在于闲谈的世界中的人物的。谁又在跟谁闹恋爱，离婚的谣诼，移情别恋，关于结婚，怀孕及出生的臆测，大部分——至少是在纽约——都是关于一些不大出名的，而实际常是一些角落里的人的。说那个爽利丁克内衣公司的小开，正在爱上了一个小明星，甚至是一个歌女哪；又说一个写电视脚本的人，正在勾引着一个糖果制造商的妻子，而进行破坏他们的幸福家庭哪；又说赞助一个小型广播节目的，开睡衣公司的简家生了一个男孩哪；又说饲狗饼干业的大亨正有意投资于百老汇的戏剧哪，诸如此类，都是一般闲谈的材料：而在一个有八百万人口的，像纽约这样的大城市，其中充满着真正的名士，我觉得这些张家长李家短的玩意，就和旧式小镇上社交栏中所出现的附加的记事，没有什么两样呢。

(3)

Scobie is a sort of protozoic profile in fog and rain, for he carries with him a sort of English weather, and he is never happier than when he can sit over a microscopic wood-fire in winter and talk. One by one his memories leak through the faulty machinery of his mind until he no longer knows them for his own. Behind him I see the long grey rollers of the Atlantic at work, curling up over his memories, smothering them in spray, blinding him. When he speaks of the past it is in a series of short dim telegrams—as if already communications were poor, the weather inimical to transmission. In Dawson City the ten who went up the river were frozen to death. Winter came down like a hammer, beating them senseless: whisky, gold, murder—it was like a new crusade northward into the timberlands. At this time his brother fell over the falls in Uganda; in his dream he saw the tiny figure, like a fly, fall and at once get smoothed out by the yellow claw of water. No, that was later when he was already staring along the sights of a carbine into the very brainbox of a Boer. He tries to remember exactly *when* it must have been, dropping his polished head into his hands; but the grey rollers intervene, the long effortless tides patrol the barrier between himself and his memory.

【解　说】

本文作者 Lawrence George Durrel(1912—)是英国的诗人兼小说家，出生于印度，回国受教育。曾任海外各地的通讯员,甚至还做过夜总会的琴师。他有文学天赋,才气蓬勃,他的文章被誉为绣帷缀锦(tapestry)具有丰富的字汇和华丽的色彩。他以20世纪30年代的埃及亚历山大为背景,写成 The Alexandria Quartet 四部作,其第一部 Justine,成于1957年,第二部 Balthuzar 及第三部 Mountolive,均成于1958年,第四部 Clea 则成于1960年。各部的观点和写作手法都不同,具有立体的及其他多方面的效果。作者长于人物描写,即令是同一个人物,在各书中出现时,都是从不同的角度看去,而加以描写的。所以新的面影摧毁了旧的轮廓,但并未使之完全消失,仍在读者的心目中,留下一个残像,重重相叠,新像再印在旧像之上,就好像一张感光的底片,一次又一次把人相照上去,结果没有一个具有个性的特定的人物存在,只剩下一堆具有莫名其妙的侧面的人影,或是说得正确一点,像人一样的面影,浮现在读者的眼前。本文采自他的四部作的第一部 Justine 中的一段。我们且来欣赏一下作者的人物描写吧。Scobie 原服务海军中,经过长年的海上生活之后,现加入埃及警察部队,已经是一个快七十岁的老人了。这种喜剧的描写,隐喻叠出,有如用散文写出的一首诗。

【注　释】

(1) protozoic profile 原生动物的轮廓。Protozoa 原生动物,即单细胞的动物类,通常要用显微镜才可以看见的。(2) in fog and rain 在雾里和雨中。这表示更加模糊。(3) English weather 英国的天气,是以多雨多雾著称的。(4) microscopic woodfire 微微的炉火。microscopic = very small; tiny 极小的,微小的。wood-fire 英国家庭的火炉,讲究烧柴火,如云 Put some more wood on the fire. (在火炉上加点柴去。) (5) talk 接上面说的 can sit,即 can talk 之略。(6) his memories leak 他的记忆泄露出来。(7) through the faulty machinery of his mind 经由他心灵的破机器。意即从他那有毛病的头脑中。因人类的头脑构造复杂,故用机器的总称 machinery 一字,而不说单独一部机器的 machine. (8) Behind him I see the long grey rollers of the Atlantic at work 在他的背后我看见波澜起伏。roller 原意为滚动的东西,在此指"巨浪",如 Huge rollers broke on the beach. (巨浪冲上沙滩。)这是说 Scobie 的过去,令人联想到惊涛骇浪的海洋。现在人已经老了,过去的记忆,好像全埋没到海洋中去了似的。但并没有丧失。用波澜起伏的隐喻,至为生动。(9) curling up over his memories 蜷伏在他的记忆上。(10) smothering them in spray 用浪花把他的记忆全般掩蔽着。(11) blinding him 使他为之目盲。(12) a series of short dim telegrams 一连串短的意思不清楚的电报。(13) as if already communications were poor, the weather inimical to transmission 俨然是由于原来的通信联络已经不好,再加上气象条件不利,而传送大有困难似的。描写他说话如打电报,故云。inimical 不利的。(14) 从 In Dawson City 直到 into the very brain-box of a Boer 为止全用的过去动词,似乎是指 Scobie 断续的记忆,电报似的话语。(15) Dawson City 加拿大西北部森林地带的城市。the Yukon 河及 Klondike 河在此汇合。在1890年以后数年间在此曾发生淘金热。(16) like a new crusade 像一个新的十字军,指 whisky, gold, murder 连在一起而形成的。(17) timberlands 森林地带。(18) Uganda 乌干达,原为东非英国的保护国,位于刚果及肯雅之间。(19) get smoothed out 消失不见。(20) the yellow claw of water 黄色的水的魔爪,指人为水所吞没。(21) along the sights of a carbine 沿着一支卡宾枪的照准。意即瞄准射击。(22) into the very brain box of a Boer. 正射进一个波尔人的脑袋中去。Boer 波尔人为荷兰血统的南非人。the Boer War 发生于1899—1902

年。(23)polished head,光滑的头；油头。(24)the grey rollers intervene 波涛起伏遮断(他的记忆)。(25)the long effortless tides patrol the barrier 那长大的不需费力的浪潮巡逻守住界线(不让他的记忆突破)。

【译　例】

　　史可庇带有一种在雾里和雨中的原生动物的轮廓,因为他携带得有英国的天气,只要他在冬天能够坐在一个微微的炉火旁边,天南地北来闲聊的话,他就再快乐也没有了。一件一件的往事,从他那有毛病的头脑中泄漏出来,直到最后连他自己都不知道那些记忆的东西,是不是他自己的。在他的背后我看见大西洋上的灰色巨浪,汹涌起伏,蜷伏在他的记忆上,又用浪花把他的记忆掩蔽,使他再也看不见了。当他说到过去的时候,是用一连串短的意思不清的电报来说的——宛然是因为原来的通信联络已经不好,再加上气象条件不利,而使得传送大有困难似的。在道生市,那时有十个人走到河的上流去,全都冻死了。冬天像一把铁锤似的降下,把他们打得失去知觉了。威士忌酒,黄金,杀人——这些结合在一起,形成了一支向着北方森林地带而去的新十字军。正在这时,他的弟弟在乌干达坠下到瀑布里去了;他在梦中看见那像苍蝇一般的小小的人影落下去,而马上就被黄色的水的魔爪吞没得不见了。不对:那还在以后,那是他已经把一支卡宾枪正瞄准好,要射中一个波尔人的脑袋那个当儿呀。他很想正确地记忆出那到底是在什么时候,于是把他那油滑的头伏下在他的两手之中,可是那灰色的大波又出现了,那毫不费力的巨大的浪潮,守住了界限,不让他回复记忆。

(4)

　　He entered the penumbra of the storm slowly, marvelling at the light, at the horizon drawn back like a bow. Odd gleams of sunshine scattered rubies upon the battleships in the basin (squatting under their guns like horned toads). It was the ancient city again; he felt its pervading melancholy under the rain as he crossed it on his way to the Summer Residence. The brilliant unfamiliar lighting of the thunderstorm re-created it, giving it a spectral, story-book air—broken pavements made of tinfoil, snail-shells, cracked horn, mica; earth-brick buildings turned to the colour of ox-blood; the lovers wandering in Mohammed Ali Square, disoriented by the unfamiliar rain, disconsolate as untuned instruments; the clicking of violet trams along the sea-front among the tatting of palm-fronds. The desuetude of an ancient city whose streets were plastered with the wet blown dust of the surrounding desert. He felt it all anew, letting it extend panoramically in his consciousness—the moan of a liner edging out towards the sunset bar, or the trains which flowed like a torrent of diamonds towards the interior, their wheels chattering among the shingle ravines and the powder of temples long since abandoned and silted up……

【解　说】

　　本文采自 Durrell 作的四部作的第三部 Mountolive 中的一段。上一篇我们所精读的是 Durrell 的人物描写,现在我们再来看看他的景物描写。Mountolive 是英国驻埃大使,为着要去会晤他以前当秘书时代所爱的女子。遂从开罗出发。横渡沙漠,到亚历山大去。本文便是描写这旅途的情形。那是冬日的薄暮。作者对描写风景的特点,就是大用色彩的字眼和比喻,且都能诉诸感觉,鲜明如绘。不但是现实的外表,就连那些难于捉摸的内在的理性,都被作者描绘出来,使读者感觉得到,有如亲身的经历似的。所以在作者笔下所描绘出来的风景,对现实的轮廓很薄,而色彩浓厚,给人的印象极深。在本文中,那轮廓已经很薄了的风景,重重叠叠,印在读者的心上,使得海洋,城市,乃至沙漠混合起来,构成一幅镶嵌细工的图样,令人为之目迷。作者笔下的景物描写,与传统小说上的判然不同,反映出他特有的诗一般的美丽的文笔来,他的名文家的声誉是当之无愧的。

【注　释】

(1) penumbra (绘画)浓淡相交之处。原为天文上指日蚀,月蚀时部分入影的区域,即半阴影部分。复数为 penumbrae. (2) marvelling at 对于什么感到惊异。(3) drawn back like a bow 像被拉紧的弓一样。(4) Odd gleams of sunshine 夕阳的残照。(5) scattered rubies upon the battleships 把如红宝石一般的点点金光洒在战舰上。(6) basin 为陆地所包围的小海湾。(7) squatting under their guns like horned toads 像有角的蟾蜍一般蹲踞在突出的大炮之下。(8) its pervading melancholy 那城中弥漫的忧郁感。(9) Summer Residence 消夏的邸宅。驻在埃及的外交官入夏便从开罗迁居亚历山大。(10) The brilliant unfamiliar lighting of the thunderstorm re-created it, giving it a spectral, story-book air 那雷雨的不习见的闪电的光亮,把那城市重新造过,给了它一种非现实的童话一般的面貌。spectral 妖怪的;幽灵的。(11) tinfoil 锡箔。(12) snail-shells 贝壳。螺旋形的贝壳,蜗牛壳作螺旋形。(13) cracked horn 破碎的角。(14) mica 云母。(15) ox-blood 带黑的深红色。(16) Mohammed Ali Square 穆罕默德·阿里方场。以十九世纪初叶埃及太守名为纪念的地名。(17) disoriented = disorientated 对方向弄不清楚;迷失方向。(18) disconsolate as untuned instruments 像不合音调的乐器一样令人不快。形容爱侣的情绪不好。disconsolate 哀伤的,使人难过的。(19) clicking 金属物相碰的声音。(20) the tatting of palm-fronds 像梭织花边似的棕榈树叶。(21) desuetude 废止状态。作废,为 consuetude(惯例)之对。例如 Many words once commonly used have fallen into desuetude. (许多以往通用的字已废而不用了)。(22) were plastered with the wet blown dust of the surrounding desert 涂满了周围沙漠中吹来的湿的尘土。(23) 从 The brilliant unfamiliar lighting 起直到 the surrounding desert 为止都是描写 Mountolive 如梦如幻地所感到的亚历山大的情景。所以下面总结一句说 He felt it all anew. 更进一步地,让这个城市这种周围的景象,还栩栩如生之际,接着说 letting it extend (让它扩大下去)。(24) panoramically 全景在目地。(25) in his consciousness 在他的意识中。(26) the moan of a liner 一条定期船的呻吟。(27) edging out towards the sunset bar 向着落日的港口徐徐移动出去。(28) the trains which flowed like a torrent of diamonds towards the interior 像钻石的奔流一样向着内陆流去的火车。(29) ravines 由激流而构成的峡谷。(30) the powder of temples long since abandoned 早就被人遗弃了的庙宇的废墟。powder 腐朽而化成了灰。(31) silted up 为淤泥充塞。

【译　例】

　　蒙搭里夫慢慢地走进了那风暴的明暗相交的处所,惊奇地望着那拉紧像一把弓似的明亮的地平线。夕阳的残照有如红宝石的点点金光,洒向停泊在小海湾中的兵舰上(那些兵舰像有角的蟾蜍一般蹲踞在突出的大炮之下)。重又来到了这个古城。当他横过此城走向大使馆的消夏别墅去时,在大雨淋漓之下,他感觉到这城中弥漫着忧郁的感觉。大雷雨中那不习见的电光,使这城市面目一新,给了它一种非现实的童话一般的容貌。用锡箔、贝壳、碎角、云母铺成的破烂的铺道。土砖的房子变成了带黑的深红色。情侣们在穆罕默德·阿里方场散步,由于不习见的雨而使他们迷失方向,有如弹着走了调的乐器听来很不舒服一样,他们的情绪非常不好。沿着海岸线,在梭织花边似的棕榈叶的树荫下走着的紫色电车的轧轧声。这个古城好像要被废弃的样子,它的街道上涂满了从四周围沙漠中吹来的湿的尘土。这一切的情景他又重新充分地感到了,让那全景在目地在他心中扩展开去。——条定期轮船向着落日的港口徐徐移动出去的声音,或是像钻石的奔流一般向着内陆流去的火车,它们的车轮在满布鹅卵石的峡谷上,和很久已绝人烟,早为淤泥充塞的庙宇的废墟上辘辘地奔驰着。

(5)

Spearing wore his hair long even in Egypt. He had the kind of complexion the sun fired to a demonic redness and, in contrast, the hair looked whiter and silkier than it does today. Everybody knew him, by sight if not by name. He never wore a hat. You can imagine how he stood out in a crowd of Egyptians because of this flouncing mop of hair. He was a marked man. Perhaps he felt that the extravagance of his appearance had to be matched in some way by an extravagance of conduct. In England, where he is naturally less conspicuous, Spearing has never made a lot of trouble.

Both of us were teaching at the University but I saw more of him than the rest of my colleagues did because we put up at the same pension. Accordingly, When I heard him shouting abuse in Cairo Post Office one hot afternoon I went over to see what the trouble was this time.

We were in the Parcels Department, a long dark cavern equipped with an unusually wide counter, a number of scaler and a chute. Only one official seemed to be on duty that afternoon, a hard-faced little man with creased cheeks who closed his eyes when he spoke.

"If you don't put Alexandria," he said in English, "I won't take it."

Spearing was so angry that his hands visibly trembled when they gripped the edge of the counter. "Everybody knows where Sidi Gaber is, you coot! You know where Sidi Gaber is! I know where it is! He—"

【解　说】

作者为英国小说家 P. H. Newby(1918—),本文采自他的短篇小说 *A Parcel for Alexandria* 开端的一段,描写一个英国人在开罗邮局寄小包,因地址不全而被拒收的情形。文体如行云流水,明白通达,且多用单句,浅显易读。作者在大学毕业后从军,参加第二次世界大战,在埃及军中受命兼任大学讲师,任教至战后1946年止。1946年以后服务于 B.B.C. 常以近东及其他外国为背景来写小说,作风颇近似 E. M. Forster,自1945年 *A Journey to the Interior* 问世以来,差不多每年都有一部作品发表。

【注　释】

(1) complexion 面色。(2) the sun fired to a demonic redness 被太阳晒得变成魔鬼似的红色。这当然是修饰面色的。(3) in contrast 对照起来。(4) silkier 更为柔软发亮。(5) by sight if not by name. 即不知道他的姓名,也能认识他的面貌。这种表现法简洁有力。(6) stood out in a crowd 鹤

立鸡群。(7)this flouncing mop of hair 他这一头蓬松的头发。flounce 原意为女裙的荷叶边,在此无非形容多皱的头发。mop 拖把似的头发。(8)a marked man 引人注目的人。marked 显著的,明显的。(9)extravagance 过度;放纵。extravagance of appearance 他样子的放肆。extravagance of conduct 行为的放肆。(10)had to be matched by 相等,配合。(11)in some way 有些方面。(12)less conspicuous 不大引人注目。比较少人注意。(13)has never made a lot of trouble 从未惹起很多麻烦。(14)the University 用大写指当地唯一的大学。(15)put up at 住宿。(16)pension = boarding house 公寓,宿舍。原为法文,如 live en pension 住在宿舍里。(17)shouting abuse 大声辱骂。(18)the Parcels Department,邮局包裹部。(19)cavern 地下的大洞穴。在此指邮局下层包裹部黑暗得像地洞似的。(20)equipped with an unusually wide counter 装备得有一个异常宽大的柜台。(21)scales 天平(用复数)。(22)chute 使邮包自上滑下的装置,滑槽。(23)official 在此指邮局职员。(24)on duty 当值,值班。(25)hard-faced = hard-favoured 面貌严厉的;面色难看的。(26)little man 小个子;身材矮小的人。(27)creased cheeks 多皱的面颊。(28)I won't take it. 我不接受(这个邮包)。(29)when they gripped the edge of the counter 当他的两手紧抓着柜台边上的时候。(30)Sidi Gaber 为 Alexandria 的郊外地区。(31)Coot(俗语)愚人;笨东西。(32)He——实际是说的 I,如华语说的"人家"或"别人",有时也是指自己,例如:"人家(或别人)一番好意,你却这样不领情"。

【译　例】

　　史匹林的头发,哪怕是在埃及,都算是蓄得很长的。他的面孔被太阳晒得像魔鬼似的血红,与之成对照的,是他的头发却比现今更白,更为柔亮。人人都认得他,即令不晓得他的名字,也认识他的面貌。他从来不带帽子。你不难想像他那一头蓬松的头发,站在一群埃及人当中,简直是鹤立鸡群,非常突出。他成为一个引人注目的人了。也许他觉得他的放肆的样子,应该配上一些放肆的行为才对。在英国,那儿是本乡本土,他自然不会引人注目,史匹林也从未惹起过什么麻烦。

　　我们两人都是在大学教书,不过我比其余的同事和他见面的机会更多,因为我和他住在同一个宿舍的缘故。于是,在一个酷热的下午,当我听到他在开罗邮局大声辱骂的时候,我赶忙走过去看这次是发生了什么麻烦。

　　我们都在邮局的包裹部门,那是一间长形的黑暗洞穴似的屋子,设有一个非常宽大的柜台,里面有天平和滑槽。那天下午好像只有一个职员在值班似的,那是一个面色可怕,面颊多皱的小个子,他说话时总是把眼睛闭上。

　　"如果你不写上亚历山大的字样,"他用英语说,"我不接受。"

　　史匹林气得两手发抖,他的两手正紧握着那柜台的边缘。"人人都晓得西提加柏在什么地方,你这笨猪!你也知道西提加柏在什么地方!我也知道它在什么地方!人家——"

(6)

The gong was about to sound quite soon. Anne kicked her cigarette-stub into a dark corner. Greggie called over her shoulder, "Anne, here comes your boy-friend." "On time, for once," said Anne, with the same pretence of scorn that she had adopted when referring to her brother Geoffrey: "Geoffrey would be the last person I would consult." She moved, with her casual hips, towards the door. A squarebuilt high-coloured young man in the uniform of an English captain came smiling in. Anne stood regarding him as if he was the last person in the world she would consult. "Good evening," he said to Greggie as a well-brought-up man would naturally in the doorway. He made a vague nasal noise of recognition to Anne, which if properly pronounced would have been "Hallo". She said nothing at all by way of greeting. They were nearly engaged to be married. "Like to come in and see the drawing room wallpaper?" Anne said then. "No, let's get cracking." Anne went to get her coat off the banister where she had slung it. He was saying to Greggie, "Lovely evening, isn't it?" Anne returned with her coat slung over her shoulder. "Bye, Greggie," she said. "Goodbye," said the soldier. Anne took his arm. "Have a nice time," Greggie said. The dinner-gong sounded and there was a scuffle of feet departing from the notice-board and a scamper of feet from the floors above.

【解　说】

本文采自英国女作家 Muriel Spark(1918—) 所写的 *The Girls of Slender Means* 一篇小说,那是 1963 年的作品。作者生于 Edinburgh,旅居 Southern Rhodesia 达六年之久,于第二次世界大战中返国。此后近十年间专从事于诗作,似有"枉抛心力作诗人"的打算。直到 1951 年观察报悬赏征求小说,她应征写了一个短篇 *The Seraph and the Zambest* 寄去,居然获得首奖,而使她写小说的文名鹊起,这一来她也就放下诗作而转向于小说了。她以写诗的技巧和辞华来写小说,自然写来特别绚烂夺目。她的文章中常有对照的表现,如幻想与现实,讽刺与感伤,愤怒与欢笑等等,皆能有机地结合起来。在她的散文中洋溢着诗的影像和旋律,构成了她特殊的作风。

【注　释】

(1) gong (通知用餐时用的)碟形的铃,或称呼钟。此字又可作"铜锣"解。(2) kicked her cigarette-stub into a dark corner 把她的烟屁股丢向暗的角落上。kick 意为 send forcibly or angrily (ALD)用力掷去。(3) over her shoulder 回过头来。(4) on time 准时。(5) for once = as an exception 难得一次。(6) with a same pretence of scorn 带着同样假装的轻蔑(她内心对她的哥哥是很佩服的,但在人前却假装着瞧他不起的样子)。(7) Geoffrey would be the last person I would consult. 我绝对不会去和哥哥商量的。(8) She moved, with her casual hips, towards the door. 她移动了,无意识地扭着她的屁股,向门口走去了。这描写何等的具有诗的洗练,影像虽不显明,却能使人获得深的印象。这种 erotic (色情的)的描写正是作者的一种手法。(9) square-built 坚实的;粗壮的。(10) high-coloured 有朝气的,生龙活虎的。(11) in the uniform of an English captain 穿着英国陆军上尉的制服。(12) a well-brought-up man 一个有教义的人。(13) in the doorway 进门时。(14) made a vague nasal noise of recognition 发出含糊的鼻音来招呼一下。(15) properly pronounced 正规地发出音来。(16) by way of greeting 作为应酬的话。(17) nearly engaged 差不多算是订了婚。(18) the drawing room wallpaper 客厅里的糊壁纸。(19) let's get cracking = let's start. 俗语 get cracking = get busy (with work waiting to be done). (ALD) 马上就动身吧。(20) banister 栏干。(21) where she had slung it 她把上衣丢在那里。他动词 sling 意为抛掷。(22) Bye 为 bye-bye 的省略说法,原为儿语,现大人也说,表示亲密。(23) Have a nice time 希望你们玩的好。(24) The

dinner-gong sounded and there was a scuffle of feet departing from the notice-board and a scamper of feet from the floors above. 晚餐的铃声一响,就听见离开公告栏乱糟糟的脚步声,和楼上地板上急走的足音。从 sound 到 scuffle 最后及于 scamper 都是用齿音〔s〕作头韵。scuffle 混乱,乱做一团。scamper 疾走,急驰。

【译 例】

吃饭的铃子很快就要响了。安把她吸剩的香烟头,使劲地扔在那暗角上去。格雷琪回过头来叫道:"安,你的男朋友来了。""这次总算是准时来的,"安说,带着假装的轻蔑,正好像她提到她哥哥时所表示的一样:"我是决不会去找乔勿莱商量的。"她移动了,照常无意识地扭着屁股,向门口走去。一个穿着英国陆军上尉的制服,身体结实,活力充沛的青年,含笑走进来了。安站在那儿把他看做是这世界上她决不会去找他商量的人似的。"您晚上好。"他对格雷琪说,凡是一个有教养的人,一进门来,见到年长的人自然要这样说的。他发出含糊的鼻音来对安招呼了一下,如果要用正规的发言来说时,那便是"哈罗"了。作为应酬的话,她什么也没有说,他们快要订婚了。"你高兴进来看看客厅里的糊壁纸么?"安于是这样说。"不必啦,我们还是马上就走吧。"安走去栏干边取她的上衣,她早些时候把它掷在那上面的。那军人对格雷琪说:"真是一个可爱的夜晚呀。"安转来了,把她的上衣挂在肩上。"格雷琪,回头见。"她说。"再会。"那军人说,安挽着他的手走了。"希望你们玩得痛快。"格雷琪说。吃饭的铃子终于响了,只听见离开公告牌一阵混乱的脚步声,和从上面楼板上发出的疾走的足音。

(7)

Lois Taggett was graduated from Miss Hascomb's School, standing twenty-sixth in a class of fifty-eight, and the following autumn her parents thought it was time for her to come out, charge out, into what they called Society. So they gave her a five-figure, la-de-da Hotel Pierre affair, and save for a few horrible colds and Fred-hasn't-been-well-lately's, most of the preferred trade attended. Lois wore a white dress, an orchid corsage, and a rather lovely, awkward smile. The elderly gentlemen guests said, "she's a Taggett, all right"; the elderly ladies said, "She's a *very* sweet child"; the young ladies said, "Hey. Look at Lois. Not bad. What'd she do to her hair?"; and the young gentlemen said, "Where's the liquor?"

That winter Lois did her best to swish around Manhattan with the most photogenic of the young men who drank scotch-and-sodas in the God-and-Walter Winchell section of the Stork Club. She didn't do badly. She had a good figure, dressed expensively and in good taste, and was considered Intelligent. That was the first season when Intelligent was the thing to be.

【解 说】

这是美国现代作家 J. D. Salinger(1919—)的短篇小说 *The Long Debut of Lois Taggett* 的头上的一节。描写一个年轻姑娘初次进入社交界的情形。Salinger 在 1951 年发表长篇小说 *The Catcher in the Rye* 一举成名,在美国文坛获得崇高的地位,无论内容形式,都是最新颖的。研究这位作家的书,都出了好几本,如 Gwynn & Blotner 著的 *The Fiction of J. D. Salinger*(University of Pittsburgh Press,1958); H. A. Grunwald 著的 *Salinger*: *A Critical and Personal Portrait* (Harper & Brothers, 1962);Warren French 著的 *J. D. Salinger*(Twayne Publishers,1963). 此外还有 Laser & Fruman 编的 *Studies in J. D. Salinger*: *Reviews, Essays and Critiques of the Catcher in the Rye and Other Fiction*(Odyssey)及 James E. Miller 的 *J. D. Salinger*(Minnesota University Press),足见他的文学地位,我们要知道什么是美国最新的文体,最好阅读 Salinger 的作品。上面所选用的短文,便可看出作者的风格,不但文字洗练,而字句也十分新颖,读来真可一新耳目。

【注　释】

(1)standing twenty-six in a class of fifty-eight 一班五十八名中她名列第二十六。(2)come out = make a debut 开始进入社交界。(3)charge out 和 come out 同义,换一个说法重复一下,以加强语气。(4)Society 社交界。(5)gave her an affair 为她举办一个晚会。affair 在此作 party 解。(6)five-figure 五位数目的,不一定指万数,而是指大量的金钱。(7)la-de-da 或拼为 la-di-da,作形容词用时有 foppish(纨绔子的,适合于纨绔子的。空虚的,愚笨的,矫饰的),在此有 stylish(合乎时尚的,时髦的,漂亮的)的意思。(8)Hotel Pierre 是纽约 Manhattan 地区一流的旅馆。(9)save for = except for 除开。(10)a few horrible colds and Fred-hasn't-been-well-lately's 少数几个人因重伤风,以及胡来德近来健康欠佳。表示拒绝来参加晚会的理由,这种表现法颇为新奇有趣。(11)preferred trade 优先选定的客人。trade 原为 customers 的意思,作集合名词用。他例如 preferred stock(优先股),作者大概是想到这个而滑稽地使用的。(12)orchid corsage 胡姬花束。妇女胸前或肩上的饰物。(13)Not bad 很好,非常的好,这是一种 understate 的说法。(14)What'd = What did. (15)Where's = Where is. (16)did her best 尽力。(17)swish 瑟瑟声,表在冬天寒风中走动的神气。(18)photogenic 宜于艺术摄影的。the most photogenic of the young men 最会照艺术相的年轻人。(19)scotch-and-sodas 威士忌苏打 soda water 在美国叫 sodas. (20)God-and-Walter Winchell section 有名的新闻记者 Walter Winchell 等人常占用的席位。其中 God-and-无特殊意义,只是强调的说法。(21)Stork Club 鹳雀俱乐部。此为纽约 Manhattan 有名的夜总会。(22)figure 身材。(23)in good taste 有高尚的趣味。(24)Intelligent 有头脑的、有才智的、聪明的。(25)the thing to do 重要的事。

【译　例】

萝蕙·塔格特从赫斯康女士的学校毕业时,全班五十八人中她得到第二十六名。就在她毕业的第二年秋天,她的父母认为已经是她进入那个他们称为社交界的时候了。所以他们为她在匹尔亚大饭店举行了一个盛大的合乎时尚的晚会。除了几个说是因患了重伤风和近来健康欠佳的人以外,优先选定的客人们大部分都到了。萝蕙穿了一袭白色的衣服,胸前挂着一束胡姬花,面上浮着一片相当可爱而又笨拙的微笑。年长的先生们说:"她不愧是塔格特家的姑娘。"年长的太太们说:"她真是一位人见人爱的孩子呀。"年轻的妇女们说:"吓,看萝蕙。好漂亮呀。她的头发不晓得是怎样做的。"而年轻的男士们就说:"酒在哪儿?"

那年冬天萝蕙努力和那些在鹳雀俱乐部的瓦特温彻的座席上,喝威士忌苏打的青年人中最善于拍摄艺术照的人,一块儿在曼哈顿一带那瑟瑟的寒风中走来走去。她表现得很不错。她的身材既长得好,又穿上高价和趣味优雅的服装,被认为是有头脑的。在最初的时期,第一就是要有头脑。

(8)

It was too late to call up for a cab or anything, so I walked the whole way to the station. It wasn't too far, but it was cold as hell, and the snow made it hard for walking, and my Gladstones kept banging hell out of my legs. I sort of enjoyed the air and all, though. The only trouble was, the cold made my nose hurt, and right under my upper lip, where old Stradlater'd laid one on me. He'd smacked my lip right on my teeth, and it was pretty sore. My ears were nice and warm, though. That hat I bought had earlaps in it, and I put them on—I didn't give a damn how I looked. Nobody was around anyway. Everybody was in the sack.

Usually I like riding on trains, especially at night, with the lights on and the windows so black, and one of those guys coming up the aisle selling coffee and sandwiches and magazines. I usually buy a ham sandwich and about four magazines. If I'm on a train at night, I can usually even read one of those dumb stories in a magazine without puking. You know. One of those stories with a lot of phoney, lean-jawed guys named David in it, and a lot of phoney girls named Linda or Marcia that are always lighting all the goddam Davids' pipes for them.

【解 说】

如果要研读以俚俗语写的现代文学,最好还是读 J. D. Salinger 的长篇小说 *The Catcher in the Rye*. 这不但是他的代表作,也是现代俚俗语文学的代表。这部小说既无故事,也无结构,却能彻底地表现出作者的生活态度和真挚感情。全书描写一个阿飞学生在离校后回家前的三日间在外流浪的过程,全用极其正直的内心的独白表出,足见作者对个性的描写何等深入。这确是现代英文一种独特的文体,值得一读。

【注 释】

(1) too late to call up for a cab 太迟不能打电话去叫车。too...to do 意为"太……不能做"。cab = taxicab = taxi 出租汽车。(2) or anything 为 or something 的否定形,因前有 too……to 的否定。意为"还是什么",在此意为既不能去叫出租汽车,也不能去叫别的什么。此为口语中特有的表现法。(3) It wasn't too far. 并不太远。not too = not very 也是口语的说法。(4) cold as hell 冷得要死;非常的冷。(< as……as hell)这种 swearwords(咒骂语),是俚俗的(slangy)文体的特色。(5) the snow made it hard 中的 it 指 the way 而言。(6) Gladstones 英国十九世纪的政治家 William Ewart Gladstone(1809—1898),为自由党的党魁,曾四次任首相。由此而发生出两种东西,一为两人坐的四轮游览马车,一为由当中开口分为上下的旅行皮箱,二者都是用他的名字,叫作 Gladstone,这里是指后者。即又可称为 Gladstone bag 的。(7) banging hell out of my legs 重击在我的两条腿上。hell 一字为俚语表现法,在此除加强语气外别无他意。(8) I sort of enjoyed = I rather enjoyed. 我相当的喜欢。"sort of + 动词"的形式,也是美国口语的表现法。(9) and all 及其他。等等。(= and everything)也是口语特别的说法。(10) though 意为"可是"、"虽然",在口语中放在句尾是作副词用的。(11) old Stradlater'd = old Stradlater had. 这个 old 不作"老"解,而是指熟悉的朋友,一种亲

密的称呼,如我们同学间叫的老张,老李一样。(12)laid one on me 给我一拳。one = a blow。(13) He'd = He had。(14)smacked 捆;重击。(15)pretty sore 很痛。这个 pretty 为 understatement(说得较轻)。(16)nice and = quite satisfactorily,口语的表现法。(17)ear-laps = ear-flaps 耳罩。(18)in it 帽子上。(19)not give a damn 后可看作略去了一个 to 字,是 swearwords 的一种。意为"我一点也不在乎","管它个屁"。(20)around 附近。(21)anyway = anyhow 意为"左右","在任何情形下"(at any rate,in any case),"总之"。(22)sack = bed 作床解为美国俗语,hit the sack 就寝。(23)one of those guys 接前面的 with 说。美国语的 guy = fellow 并没有什么坏的意思,在此指小贩。(24)aisle 原为教堂中座位间的通道,美国用来指教室,戏院,火车上的通道(gangway)。(25)dumb stories = damn stories 低级的,或粗制滥造的小说。因避免用誓语的 damn 故以音近的字 dumb 来代替。(26)puking = vomiting 作呕的。(27)You know 是一句没有意思的口头禅。在对方多不知道时说的。(28)phoney = phony 美国俗语,意为 fraudulent(诈欺的,骗取的)。(29)lean-jawed guys 瘦尖下巴的人。(30)goddam = cursed,damned 一种咒语,并无特别的意思,只是为加强语气而说的。

【译 例】

那时已经太晚不能打电话去叫出租汽车什么的了,所以我便一直走路走到火车站去。那并不太远,不过却冷得要命,飞雪使步行增加困难,我手上所提的旅行皮箱老是在我腿上碰来碰去。可是我对于那空气等等倒是相当喜欢的。唯一的困难就是我的鼻子冷得发痛,还有正在我上嘴唇下面的部分也痛,因为老史重重的在那里打了我一下。他捆了我牙齿外面的嘴唇,那里痛的很。我的耳朵却很温暖,因为我买的那顶帽子是有耳罩的,我把那两个耳罩戴上了,——至于我变成一个什么怪相我一点也不管。好在附近也没有一个人。所有的人都睡到床上去了。

通常我是喜欢坐火车的,尤其是在夜里,电灯照着,窗外一片漆黑,还有那小贩来到通路上卖着咖啡,三明治,还有杂志。我总是要买一个火腿三明治,和差不多四种杂志。如果我是在夜间坐车,我通常都能读完一篇这种杂志上的低级故事而不作呕的。你知道的,这样的故事,有一篇其中出现不少名叫大卫的尖下巴的骗子,还有一些名叫苓达或玛琪的女骗子,她们老是要去替那些混帐东西的大卫们点燃他们的烟斗。

(9)

Then Dora noticed that there was a Red Admiral butterfly walking on the dusty floor underneath the seat opposite. Every other thought left her head. Anxiously she watched the butterfly. It fluttered a little, and began to move towards the window, dangerously close to the passengers' feet. Dora held her breath. She ought to do something. But what? She flushed with indecision and embarrassment. She could not lean forward in front of all those people and pick the butterfly up in her hand. They would think her silly. It was out of the question. The sunburnt man, evidently struck with the concentration of Dora's gaze, bent down and fumbled with his boot laces. Both seemed securely tied. He shifted his feet, narrowly missing the butterfly which was now walking into the open on the carriage floor.

"Excuse me," said Dora. She knelt down and gently scooped the creature into the palm of her hand, and covered it over with her other hand. she could feel it fluttering inside. Everyone stared. Dora blushed violently. Toby and his friend were looking at her in a friendly surprised way. Whatever should she do now? If she put the butterfly out of the window it would be sucked into the whirlwind of the train and killed. Yet she could not just go on holding it, it would look too idiotic. She bowed her head, pretending to examine her captive.

【解　说】

这是从英国现代女作家 Iris Murdoch(1919—)的小说 The Bell 中选出的头上的一段。作者生于爱尔兰的 Dublin,牛津大学毕业。1948 年以后在牛津教哲学。1956 年和同事 John O. Bayley 结婚。她和 John Wain 及 Kingsley Amis 诸人,代表第二次世界大战后英国的新文学。作者有象征主义的作家之称。她作品的标题多是象征的,以暗示作品的象征性。当然,称她的作品为象征主义,决不是由于使用直接的象征,而实另有其内容上的真正的魅力在,以及深入她文体中诗人的素质,一言以蔽之,是风格上的象征性。她自己说:"我们要用既非形而上学的,也非全体的,更非宗教的感觉,来描写现实的超绝性(transcendence of reality),实有必要。"以哲学的主题使之在小说中结晶,这便是这位闺秀作家对她写作的主张了。Tradition and Dream 一书的著者 Walter Allen 论英国现代小说到 Murdoch 时,说她的文体是"把诗完全融化在散文中了"。

【注　释】

(1) Red Admiral butterfly 红花蝴蝶。admiral 为各种彩色蝴蝶的俗称。(2) dusty floor 火车上肮脏的地板。(3) Every other thought left her. 把别的事全都忘了。所有的别种想法都从她的头脑中离开了。意即一心一意地想着那红花蝴蝶的事。(4) dangerously close to the passengers' feet 很危险地接近火车上来往旅客的脚,意即几乎要被人踏死。(5) held her breath 屏息;吓得不敢出气。(6) She ought to do something. 她应该有所作为。(7) But what? 但要做点什么呢? (8) flushed with 因……而脸发红。(9) indecision and embarrassment 犹豫不决和局促不安。(10) lean forward 弯下身去;倾身向前。(11) in front of 在……的眼前。(12) They would think her silly. 别人会以为她太孩子气了。(13) out of the question = impossible 不可能。(14) The sunburnt man 面孔被太阳晒黑了的人。(15) evidently struck with 显然是由……而想起。(16) fumbled with his boot laces 去摸索他的皮鞋带子。(17) securely tied 系得很紧。(18) shifted 移动了。(19) narrowly missing the butterfly 几乎踏到了那蝴蝶。miss 相差。逃过。(20) walking into the open 走到空敞的地方来。(21) gently scooped the creature into the palm of her hand 温柔地把那蝴蝶引到她的手板心里来了。scoop 汲取;舀取。(22) could feel it fluttering inside 可以感觉得到蝴蝶在她手中拍翅。(23) in a friendly surprised way 以友善的惊异态度。(24) whatever should she do now? 她现在到底要怎样办才好呢? (25) be sucked into the whirlwind of the train and killed 被火车开动时的旋风吸转进去而被压死。(26) it would look too idiotic 那看来太傻气了。(27) pretending to examine her captive 假装着来细看她手中的蝴蝶。captive 俘虏;捕获物。

【译　例】

正在那时,朵娜注意到了,一双红花蝴蝶,在对面座位底下积满灰尘的地板上走动着。她一意地想着那只蝴蝶,把别的事情全都忘了。她很担心地守望着它。它稍稍拍了一下翅膀,开始向着对面的窗口移动,很危险地靠近来往旅客们的脚下了。朵娜紧张得屏息望着。她真该想个办法去救救它才好。但要她想什么办法呢？她为了自己的犹豫不决和局促不安,而感到脸红了。她不能够在所有的乘客面前,弯下身去,拾起那只蝴蝶,放到她手上来的呀。她要那样做的话,别人就会认为她太孩子气了。这绝对办不到。那个面孔被太阳晒黑了的人,显然是由朵娜的集中凝视而想起,遂弯下腰去摸摸他的皮鞋带子。两脚好像都系得紧紧的。他移动了他的脚,险些儿把那只蝴蝶给踏死了,因为它正走向车厢地板上的空敞的地方来。

"对不起。"朵娜说。她随即跪了下去,轻轻地把那只蝴蝶舀入她的手板心来,然后又用另外一只手把它盖上了。她可以感觉得到蝴蝶在里面鼓翼。人人都在望着她。朵娜羞得满脸绯红。托比和他的朋友,用一种友好的惊奇态度,也在望着她。现在她到底要怎样办呢？如果她把它丢出车窗外面去,它便要被火车的旋风转入而压死的。可是她却不能老是用两手来捧着它呀。那看来未免太傻气了。她低下头去,假装着来细看她的捕获物似的。

(10)

Annette felt always that she was travelling at a speed which was not her own. Going to or from her parents on one of her innumerable journeys, her train would stop sometimes between stations, revealing suddenly the silence of the mountains. Then Annette would look at the grass beside the railway and see its green detail as it swayed in the breeze. In the silence the grass would seem very close to her; and she would stun herself with the thought that the grass was really there, a few feet away, and that it was possible for her to step out, and to lie down in it, and let the train go on without her. Or else, travelling towards evening, as the lights were coming on in the houses, she would see the cyclist at the level-crossing, his face preoccupied and remote, and think that when the train had passed and the gates opened he would go on his way and by the time he reached his house she would be passing another frontier. But she never got off the train to lie down in the grass, nor did she ever leave it, high up in the mountains, at the small station that was not mentioned in the time-table, where the train unexpectedly halted and where the little hotel, whose name she could read so plainly, waited with its doors open. She could not break the spell and cross the barrier into what seemed to her at such moments to be her own world. She stayed on the train until it reached the terminus, and the chauffeur came to take her luggage to the car and Nicholas came bounding into the carriage, filling her with both sadness and relief at the ending of the journey. But the world of the chambermaid and the cyclist and the little strange hotel continued to exist, haunting and puzzling her with a dream of something slow and quiet from which she was forever shut away.

【解　说】

这还是选的 Murdoch 的作品 *The Flight from the Enchanter* 中的一段,也和前一篇一样地是描写火车旅行的。不过是回想过去火车旅行的体验,富于哲学意味,且具象征的风格。

【注　释】

(1) always 通常放在 felt 的前面,在本句中放在后面是修饰往后的子句的。又 always 和进行式动词连用时,表示动作的反复。(2) at a speed 用一种速度。at a speed of 40 miles an hour 用每小时四十英里的速度。(3) which was not her own 不是她自己的；非她自己控制的。(4) Going to or from her parents 到父母家里去或从父母家里出来。(5) on one of her innumerable journeys 在她

数不清的旅途上,每次。(6)her train would stop sometimes between stations 她坐的火车有时总不免要在车站与车站的中间停下来。这个 would 是回想的,表过去的习惯。下同。(7)the silence of the mountains 有深山中那般寂静。(8)would look at the grass beside the railway 总要去看看铁路旁边的青草。(9)its green detail 绿的草尖(细小的部分)。(10)swayed 摇摆。(11)very close to = very near to 很靠近。(12)stun herself 使她自己昏晕;使目瞪口呆,如 We were stunned by the sudden news. 我们听到这突如其来的消息而为之目瞪口呆。stun = make senseless by a blow; confuse the mind of. (13)in it = in the grass. (14)let the train go on without her 她没有上车去,让火车开走。(15)towards evening 天将暮的时候。(16)the lights were coming on in the houses 万家灯火。(17)cyclist 坐脚踏车的人。(18)level-crossing 平面交叉,在此指铁路上的平交道。美国说 grade crossing. (19)preoccupied and remote 心不在焉的状态。(20)the gates 平交道因火车经过而关闭的栏栅。(21)he would go on his way 句中的 would 为普通的假定语气。下面的 she would be passing 的 would 用法同。(22)by the time 到那时。(23)another frontier 另外一个国境(因 Annette 现正在欧洲大陆旅行)。(24)got off 下(车)或下(马)。(25)nor did she ever leave it = and she never left it. (26)not mentioned in the time-table 火车时间表上没有载名的(小车站)。(27)halted 停下来。(28)whose name she could read so plainly 那小旅馆的名字很明显地她可以辨认得出来。(29)waited with its doors open 打开门在等待着她。(30)break the spell 破除符咒;突破魔力。spell 是作者喜欢用的字眼,尤其是在这部小说中,可说是表现主题的 key-word 呢。(31)cross the barrier 越过障碍。(32)at such moments 在这种时候。(33)to be her own world 完全属于自己的世界。(34)terminus 终站。在美国说 terminal. (35)the chauffeur 汽车夫。指私人雇用的司机。(36)luggage 行李。在美国说 baggage. (37)Nicholas 是 Annette 的哥哥。(38)came bounding into the carriage 跳进车厢里来。(39)filling her with 使她充满着……的感触。(40)both sadness and relief 既忧愁又安慰。(41)the chambermaid 在本节前所回想的人物。指儿时的女佣人。(42)haunting 时常浮现于脑海中。(43)puzzling her with 用……使她迷惑。(44)dream of something slow and quiet 悠然静止的梦。(45)from which she was forever shut away 她永远被关在梦的外面。

【译 例】

安呐特觉得她老是以非自己控制的速率在旅行着。从父母跟前出来,或回到父母跟前去,在数不清的旅程上,每次她坐的火车,有时总不免要在车站与车站的中途停下来,突然显示出有深山中一般的寂静。那时,安呐特总要去看看铁路旁边的青草,看那些绿的草尖在微风中摇摆的样子。在这种寂静中,那青草会变得好像很靠近她似的;她会使自己昏眩地以为那青草果真在那儿,离开她不过两三英尺远罢了。她又以为她是可以走出去的,走去躺下在青草中,让火车没有她坐在上面自个儿开走。要不然的话,当万家灯火近黄昏的时候坐在火车上,她就会看到在平交道上那骑脚踏车的人,面孔上显得心不在焉的样子,她想到当火车一经过,平交道的栅门打开时,那人就会继续上路,等到他回到家里的时候,她乘的火车恐怕又在经过欧洲的另外一个国境了。但是她实际并没有下车去躺下在青草中,哪怕是当火车走向高高的山路,在火车时间表上都没有名字的小站上意外地停下来,那儿的小旅馆,它的名字都看得清清楚楚,正敞开大门在等待着她,而她也从来没有离开过火车一步。她不能破除符咒,越过障碍进入在那种时候好像是她自己的世界里去。她只能留在火车上,直到它开到终站为止。于是汽车夫来替她把行李搬上汽车去,而她的哥哥尼可拉一下就跳进车厢里来了。到了旅程的终点,她满怀忧愁而又安慰,心绪颇为不宁。但是包含那个儿时的女仆,那个骑脚踏车的人,以及那个奇怪的小旅舍等等的世界,老是历历在目,不能忘怀,时常浮现于脑海中,变成一个悠然静止的梦境,使她永远被关在它的外面,深感迷惑。

(11)

I am always drawn back to places where I have lived, the houses and their neighbourhoods. For instance, there is a brownstone in the East Seventies where, during the early years of the war, I had my first New York apartment. It was one room crowded with attic furniture, a sofa and fat chairs upholstered in that itchy, particular red velvet that one associates with hot days on a train. The walls were stucco, and a colour rather like tobacco-spit. Everywhere, in the bathroom too, there were prints of Roman ruins freckled brown with age. The single window looked out on a fire escape. Even so, my spirits heightened whenever I felt in my pocket the key to this apartment; with all its gloom, it still was a place of my own, the first, and my books were there, and jars of pencils to sharpen, everything I needed, so I felt, to become the writer I wanted to be.

It never occurred to me in those days to write about Holly Golightly, and probably it would not now except for a conversation I had with Joe Bell that set the whole memory of her in motion again.

Holly Golightly had been a tenant in the old brownstone; she'd occupied the apartment below mine. As for Joe Bell, he ran a bar around the corner on Lexington Avenue; he still does. Both Holly and I used to go there six, seven times a day, not for a drink, not always, but to make telephone calls: during the war a private telephone was hard to come by. Moreover, Joe Bell was good about taking messages, which in Holly's case was no small favour, for she had a tremendous many.

【解　说】

美国现代小说家 Truman Capote(1924—)生于 New Orleans,因父母离婚的关系,少年时代在孤独中度过。受了中学程度的教育,十九岁时写的一个短篇,获得了欧·亨利文学奖金。二十三岁时发表 *Other Voices, Other Rooms*(1948),一举成名,而登上了美国的文坛。现在不过四十多岁的人,已成为美国文学界的大作家了。他所描写的感伤性和幻想界的异常的心理,正是第二次世界大战后这一代的特征。作品多以南部农村为背景,人物则为这时代的少年少女。本文采自他在1958年发表的短篇集 *Breakfast at Tiffany's*,主要是写 Manhattan 的妓女。

【注　释】

(1)drawn back 怀想;回想。(2)places where I have lived 我曾住过的地方。(3)the houses and their neighbourhoods 那些房屋和邻近的地区。上说住过的地方是一般的说法,现在具体地说出房屋来,下面还要更明确地说纽约的公寓。(4)a brownstone 一幢用红褐色沙岩造的房子。brownstone 为用于建筑的红褐色沙岩。(5)the East Seventies 东七十街一带地区。纽约以第五街为中心,分东西地区。(6)the war 指第二次世界大战。(7)my first New York apartment 我第一次住的纽约的公寓。(8)attic furniture 简单的家具。attic = simple. 据 *Random House Dictionary* 说 Attic (adj. often lower case)意为 displaying simple elegance. 这里只概说家具,下面便具体地细说 sofa, chair 的件名。(9)fat chair 臃肿、宽大的椅子。(10)upholster 为椅子装上椅套。(11)itchy 令人发痒的。(12)associate with 联想到。(13)stucco(粉饰墙壁的)灰泥。a stucco house 粉刷灰泥或水泥的房子。The walls were stucco 墙上涂的灰泥。(14)tobacco-spit 烟草的汁。(15)Everywhere in the bathroom too 先说"所有的地方"是概括的,随即又细别说"浴室",成为作者一贯的作风。(16)prints of Roman ruins 罗马废墟的版画。(17)freckled brown with age 因年深月久而生出褐色的斑点来了。(18)looked out on 开向。(19)fire escape 太平梯;避火梯。为发生火警时便于逃出屋子去的设备。(20)my spirits heightened 精神焕发。(21)gloom 阴郁;幽暗。(22)jars of pencils 插在铅笔筒中的铅笔。(23)It never occurred to me…to write about 我决没有想到要来写些关于……的事。(24)and probably it would not now 大概现在也不会想到要写的。(25)except for a conversation with 如果不是和……谈话。(26)that set the whole memory of her in motion again 那谈话使得我对她的记忆又重新活动起来。(27)tenant 房客。(28)ran a bar 经营一个酒吧。(29)Lexington Avenue 纽约第三街和 Park 街之间的一条大路。(30)still does 现在还经营着。(31)not for a drink 不是去喝酒。(32)not always(for a drink)并不一定(是去喝酒)。(33)make telephone calls 去打电话。(34)a private telephone was hard to come by 私人电话难于获得。come by 获得。例如 He seemed to have come by a large fund of knowledge. 他所获得的知识似乎很丰富。(35)taking messages 听取消息。(36)no small favour 大可感谢。(37)for she had a tremendous many 因为她的电话多得可怕。

【译 例】

  我老是要回想到我曾住过的地方,那些屋子和邻近一带。例如,在东七十街地区内的一幢用红褐色沙岩造的房子,在战争的初期,我第一次在纽约租下那公寓来住。那是一间房,里面塞满了简单的家具,一张沙发和一些臃肿的椅子,椅套是用令人发痒的特别红的天鹅绒做的,使人联想到暑天坐火车的味道。墙壁上是涂的灰泥,那颜色就像烟草的汁。屋子内到处,连浴室都不例外,挂着罗马废墟的版画,因年深月久都生出褐色的斑点来了。唯一的窗口是向一个太平梯子开着的。甚至如此,每次当我把手插进口袋去摸出我这公寓的开门钥匙时,我都感到非常高兴。哪怕是幽暗阴森,这总是我自己的家,第一,我的书都在这里,还有一筒子待削的铅笔,所以我觉得如我所指望的做一个作家,我所需要的一切,这儿都有了。

  在那些日子里,我从来没有想到要写点关于哈利·歌莱特里的事,大概我现在也不会想到要写的,如果不是和乔·白尔一席话,使我重又勾起了对她的记忆的话。

  哈利·歌莱特里也是那幢红褐色沙岩建造的公寓中的房客。她就住在我底下一层楼。至于谈到乔·白尔,他是在雷新顿大道的转角上开一家酒吧的,那店子现在还在。哈利和我两个人一天要到他那儿去上六七次,不是去喝酒,并不一定是去喝酒,而是去打电话。在战时私人是很难获得电话的呀。加之,乔·白尔很好,他不惮烦地替我们接电话,在哈利的场合十分可感,因为她的电话多得可怕呢。

(12)

That Monday in October 1943. A beautiful day with the buoyancy of a bird. To start, we had Manhattans at Joe Bell's. Later, we wandered towards Fifth Avenue, where there was a parade. We ate lunch at the cafeteria in the park. Afterwards, avoiding the zoo (Holly said she couldn't bear to see anything in a cage), we giggled, ran, sang along the paths towards the old wooden boathouse, now gone. Leaves floated on the lake; on the shore, a parkman was fanning a bonfire of them……

Passing a Woolworth's, she gripped my arm: "Let's steal something," she said, pulling me into the store, where at once there seemed a pressure of eyes, as though we were already under suspicion. "Come on. Don't be chicken." She scouted a counter piled with paper pumpkins and Hallowe'en masks. The saleslady was occupied with a group of nuns who were trying on masks. Holly picked up a mask and slipped it over her face; she chose another and put it on mine; then she took my hand and we walked away. It was as simple as that. Outside, we ran a few blocks, I think to make it more dramatic; but also because, as I'd discovered, successful theft exhilarates. I wondered if she'd often stolen. "I used to," she said, "I mean I had to. If I wanted anything. But I still do it every now and then, sort of to keep my hand in."

【解　说】

这篇还是从美国现代作家 Capote 的 *Breakfast at Tiffany's* 中选的。前面的文章是描写小说中的主人公,在纽约住公寓的情形。尾上点出小说中的女主人公,但没有对她加以描写。本文专写这位想当作家的主人公,和女主人公同游的一幕,并绘出下流社会女子的行为,被迫非盗窃不可,而且为要养成熟练的手法,对此勾当表示不敢荒废。

【注　释】

(1) with the buoyancy of a bird 具有小鸟的快乐(似的美丽的一日)。(2) To start 开始。(3) Manhattans 曼哈顿鸡尾酒(为威士忌和艾酒混合而成的)。(4) Fifth Avenue 纽约闹市中向南北伸展的大路。(5) parade 整队游行。(6) cafeteria 自助餐馆。(7) park 指纽约最大的 Central Park. (8) the zoo 中央公园中的小动物园。(9) couldn't bear to see 看了受不了;不忍看。(10) giggled 傻笑,格格地笑。(11) boathouse 船库;艇屋(原为贮藏小舟之屋,现多具有供人小憩的设备)。(12) now gone 现在早已不存在了。(13) bonfire of them 焚烧落叶。(14) Woolworth's 英美各地都开有的廉价商店。(15) pulling me into the store 把我拉到伍尔渥斯店里去。(16) pressure of eyes 人眼的压力,意即受人监视。(17) under suspicion 遭受嫌疑。(18) Don't be chicken 不要怕。chicken = (Slang) cowardly. (19) scout 侦察。(20) paper pumpkins 纸做的南瓜。为万圣节前夕的装饰用。(21) Hallowe'en masks 万圣节(All Saints' Day)前夕(十月三十一日)假装用的面具。(22) saleslady 女店员。(23) who were trying on masks 她们正在把面具试戴着看。(24) It was as simple as that. 就是那样简单的。(25) outside, we ran a few blocks. 从店子走出街上来,我们一气地跑了几条街。block 四围有街围住的一连房屋。(26) to make it more dramatic 使之更有戏剧性。(27) because successful theft exhilarates 因为盗窃成功,特别使人兴奋。exhilarates 使高兴;使快活;使兴奋。在此用的现在时态,表示一般的真相。(28) wonder if 急想知道是不是。(29) used to 表过去的习惯。(30) had to 表过去的必要。(31) now and then 时常。(32) sort of 稍稍地;有几分(= somewhat). (33) to keep my hand in 在干着;保持熟练。如 He plays his violin every day to keep

his hand in. 他每天拉小提琴以保持熟练。

【译 例】

一九四三年十月的那个礼拜一,是小鸟飞舞,风光明媚的一天。一开头我们就在乔·白尔的酒吧里,喝了曼哈顿鸡尾酒。随后,我们在第五街一带闲荡着,那儿正有人在列队游行。我们走到中央公园里的自助餐厅去吃了一顿午餐。后来,为避免动物园(哈利说她不能忍受看到任何东西被关在笼子里),我们格格地笑,又跑又唱,沿着小路,走向那现已不存在的古老的木造船库去。落叶漂满一湖;在湖畔有一个园丁正在焚烧落叶……

走过一家伍尔渥斯的百货商店,她紧抓住我的手臂:"我们去偷点什么吧。"她说着,就把我拉进那商店去了。一走进去我马上就感觉到众目睽睽好像都在监视着我们,俨然我们已经受到嫌疑了。"来呀。不要这样胆怯。"她侦察了一个堆满了纸做的南瓜和万圣节前夕用的假面具的柜台。那女店员正在忙着招待一群在试戴着假面具的尼姑顾主。哈利选了一个面具自己戴在面上;她又另外选了一个给我戴上;于是她牵了我的手,我们便走出那商店来了。那就是这样简单的呀。出了店门一走上街,我们一气跑了几条街,我认为这样可以使之更带戏剧性呢。可是,如我后来所发现的,也是为着盗窃的成功而特别高兴吧。我问她是不是常偷东西。她回答说:"我以前是常偷的,是迫不得已,非偷不可呀。当我想要点什么的时候。但是,现在我还是时常要这样来一下,为保持熟练起见。"

(13)

It must be remembered that the oppressed and the oppressor are bound together within the same society; they accept the same criteria, they share the same beliefs, they both alike depend on the same reality. Within this cage it is romantic, more meaningless, to speak of a "new" society as the desire of the oppressed, for that shivering dependence on the props of reality which he shares with the *Herrenvolk* makes a truly "new" society impossible to conceive. What is meant by a new society is one in which inequalities will disappear, in which vengeance will be exacted; either there will be no oppressed at all, or the oppressed and the oppressor will change places. But, finally, as it seems to me, what the rejected desire is, is an elevation of status, acceptance within the present community. Thus, the African, exile, pagan, hurried off the auction block and into the fields, fell on his knees before that God in Whom he must now believe; who had made him, but not in his image. This tableau, this impossibility, is the heritage of the Negro in America: *Wash me*, cried the slave to his Maker, *and I shall be whiter, whiter than snow*! For black is the color of evil; only the robes of the saved are white……

【解 说】

作者 James Baldwin(1924—)是美国现代黑人作家。本文采自他的散文集 Notes of a Native Son. 他的代表作为 Go Tell It on the Mountain 一部长篇小说。他生于纽约,曾往欧洲旅行,在法国住了一个时期,现住纽约有名的 Greenwich Village. 他写作的主题,无论是在小说或戏剧或评论或散文中都是一贯的为黑人请命。简单地说,就是"美国的黑人有何身份?"或"做美国的黑人有何意义?"他一直在探索美国黑人的真相,美国黑人的 specialness(特色)。他说美国的民主是只存在于白人社会的。这个社会和过去奴隶制社会并没有两样。要到真正的出现新的社会,奴隶才能翻身。现在美国黑人的祖先,为人奴役,不但失去自由,也忘记了故国的话语,失去了本来的姓名,肉体受到蹂躏,终至于丧失了自己,这便是美国黑人的历史。但有些自甘堕落的美国黑人,早丧失了他的人格,只希望他的皮肤能变白,头发能变直,这种人终将成为"看不见的人",既不能加入白人的队伍,又自动脱离了黑人的行列,早已无处可以存在了。

【注 释】

（1）the oppressed and the oppressor 受别人压迫的人和压迫别人的人。（2）criteria 判断的准绳。字尾的〔a〕表复数,单数为〔on〕（criterion）,此为希腊字的变化,他例如 phenomenon, phenomena（现象）。（3）cage 牢笼,指现实的社会。（4）romantic 空想的。（5）more meaningless 没有比这更无意义的了。（6）that shivering dependence 战战兢兢来依附的。（7）the props of reality 叫做现实的那个支柱。（8）Herrenvolk（德文）支配民族（纳粹主义的德国民族自夸之辞）。Herren 为 Herr（= lord, master）的复数形。volk = people.（9）inequalities 不平等。（10）vengeance 复仇;报仇。如向某人报仇则说 take vengeance upon a person.（11）exact 动词,意为坚持地要求;必要。（12）change places 调换地位。（13）the rejected desire 不被接受的要求;被拒绝的请求。（14）elevation of status, acceptance within the present community 身份地位的提高,被白人社会所接受。指现代美国黑人的公民权运动而言。（15）exile 被放逐的人;流亡者。（16）pagan 异教徒。非基督徒。（17）auction block 奴隶拍卖台。（18）fields 自由的原野。（19）that God 指基督教的上帝。（20）in Whom he must now believe 现在他必须信奉的,说黑人在他的故国非洲时,原是信的土族宗教,自从被卖为美国人的奴隶以后就被迫改信基督教。（21）who had made him but not in His image 上帝造人,但没有照着神的形像来造他。旧约全书《创世记》第一章第二十七节上说:"上帝就照着自己的形像造人,乃是照着他的形像造男造女。"（22）this tableau 这种光景。参考惊叹词的 Tableau! 试想那种光景!（23）this impossibility 这种不可能的事。人世间办不到的事。（24）heritage 祖先遗留下来的事物。（25）his Maker 他的造物主,即上帝。（26）black is the color of evil. 黑是罪恶的颜色。（27）the robes of the saved 被救者的外衣。

【译 例】

我们必须记住受压迫者和压迫者是在同一个社会中被束缚在一起的。他们接受同样的准绳;共有同样的信仰;他们彼此相像地都依赖同样的现实。在这种现实的樊笼中,作为受压迫者的要求,来说什么"新的"社会,简直是幻想,再没有什么比这更无意义的了。因为受压迫者和支配民族双方都要战战兢兢地依附在他们共有的现实支柱上,这就使人不可能去想像一个真正的"新的"社会了。新的社会的含义是其中不平等的现象完全消失,报仇的意义必须实现;要么是受压迫者已不存在,要么是受压迫者和压迫者调换地位。但是结局,我觉得那不能接受的要求,就是黑人身份地位的提高,被白人社会所接纳的那回事。这样一来,从奴隶拍卖台急急逃向自由的原野去的非洲人,流亡者,异教徒,就要跪下在他现在不得不信奉的上帝的前面去了。上帝造人,但没有照着他的形像来造他。试想这种光景,这种决办不到的事,正是在美国的黑人的祖先所遗留下来的奴性:洗净我吧,那奴隶对他的造物主叫出来,那样我就可以更白,比雪还要白呀!因为黑是罪恶的颜色;只有那些得救者的外衣才是白的……

(14)

I was naked, clean if sweating, just as I had come. Something seemed to hurry me through space. I heard that thunder again, on the remotest horizon, guns perhaps, something; above Java or palms on the Laccadives, in the profoundest sunlit sea. Something hurried me through memory, too, but I can't pause to remember, for a guilt past memory or dreaming, much darker, impels me on. I pray but my prayer climbs up like a broken wisp of smoke: *oh my Lord, I am dying*, is all I know, and *oh my father, oh my darling*, longingly, lonesomely, I fly into your arms! *Peyton you must be proper nice girls don't. Peyton.* Me? Myself all shattered, this lovely shell? Perhaps I shall rise at another time, though I lie down in darkness and have my light in ashes. I turn in the room, see them coming across the tiles, dimly prancing, fluffing up their wings. I think: my poor flightless birds, have you suffered without soaring on this earth? Come then and fly. And they move on past me through the darkening sands, awkward and gentle, rustling their feathers: come then and fly. And so it happens treading past to touch my boiling skin—one whisper of feathers is all —and so I see them go—oh my Christ! —one by one ascending my flightless birds through the suffocating night, toward paradise. I am dying. Bunny, dying.

【解　说】

本文作者 William Styron(1925—)为美国小说家,以巧于遣词用字著称,生于美国 Virginia 州的 Newport News,出身 Duke 大学,又在 New York's New School 学习文艺写作,受教于 H. Hyan 教授。1951 年发表 *Lie Down in Darkness* 一部小说,立刻引起文坛的注意。随又在 1953 年发表 *The Long March*,1960 年发表 *Set This House on Fire*,1967 年发表 *The Confessions of Nat Turner*,作品不多,但已足够表现作者的文才了。他的文笔,有时幽静,有时热情,有时素朴,颇多变化。总说起来,他不是一个惜墨如金的作家,他有丰富的想像力,笔下驱遣云烟,词汇多如潮涌。他把文字所有的象征的及比喻的机能,发挥到最高度,且能将字与字,句与句,人物与人物,形成微妙的对比,以浮雕出人心上的种种皱纹。他使用的词句虽很明朗,但决无地域的及时代的限制;他放眼乾坤,以整个的人生为对象,写出世间的混乱,不安,绝望,爱憎,伪善,复仇,背信,不平,犯罪,同情,怜悯种种现象。他的作风在表现上学 T. Wolfe,在主题上学 W. Faulkner,在手法上学 J. Joyce. 有人说艺术家是使得语言的绚烂幻影背后闪耀的真实,浮现出来的魔术师。本文作者就够得上称为这样的"语言的魔术师"了。他也算是当代一流的 storyteller,他的成功的作品,匠心独运,有如织锦,可算是高度的艺术品。本文采自 *Lie Down in Darkness* 第七部。他这部处女作《躺下在黑暗中》,在出版的第二年便获得美国艺术院的奖金。故事描述美国南部一个富人家的罪恶与堕落,以及衰败的悲剧。那个不能爱他妻子的丈夫米尔顿,不被丈夫所爱的孤独而严格的妻子海伦,生来残废但受母亲溺爱的白痴。长女莫蒂,恋父情结(Electra complex)的次女蓓顿,及其他米尔顿的情妇朵利,清教的神父凯亚里,和黑人的一家,这许多人物之间的爱与恨,同情与背信,报仇与死亡等等,都以次女蓓顿为中心而展开来。这部奇异的故事,展开的实际时间,不过五六小时的当中所发生的事情,作者用登场人物的回想方式,各人各样的意识流,把这一富人家三十多年的过去,全都表现出来了。

现在选用的这一段是最后的部分,即蓓顿从家庭中逃出来,大学也退学了,经过了许多的爱人之后,终于和一个犹太裔的无名画家哈利结了婚,得到了一个爱的家庭,可是她因 Electra Complex 的关系,仍然搞不好,她只要被爱,却不知什么是爱。丈夫无能为力,只好和她分居。蓓顿再三再四去恳求他回家,最后的希望落空之后,她已经酒精中毒,精神分裂,在神经失常之中,她从纽约的一座摩天楼的顶上跳下自杀了。现在采用的这一段,便是她自杀前的心理状态,实在描写得很巧妙,值得我们玩味。

【注 释】

(1) clean if sweating 即令满身的汗,也是很干净的。(2) had come = had come into the world = had been born. 出世。(3) guns perhaps, 也许不是雷声,而是炮声。(4) Java 爪哇。(5) the Laccadives 拉卡代夫群岛。此为阿拉伯海中的群岛名,位于印度西南海岸。(6) the profoundest sunlit sea 阳光灿烂的海域。(7) I can't pause to remember 我不能停下来从容回想。(8) a guilt 犯罪的意识。指蓓顿过去生活中种种行为而产生的心理状态,例如因对姊姊未细心照顾以致发生事故而使她送命,及对丈夫背信等等。(9) past memory or dreaming 越过记忆或梦想。(10) much darker 修饰前面 a guilt 的。(11) impels me on 将我向前推进。(12) a wisp of smoke 一缕烟。(13) oh my Lord 啊,主啊。呀,我的天呀。(14) oh my father, oh my darling. 啊,我的父亲,啊,我的爱人。因为蓓顿在家时曾无意识地对她父亲怀着异性的思慕。其说出自弗洛依德的精神分析学。儿子对母亲,便称 Oedipus complex. (15) Peyton you must be proper nice girls don't. Peyton. "蓓顿,你一定要学得高尚些,上等女孩子不是这样的,蓓顿。"蓓顿的母亲看见她的次女行为有欠检点,常是这样告诫她。蓓顿在酒精中毒以后,累累地和丈夫以外的男子乱来,现在心中不免发生犯罪的意识。(16) Me? Myself all shattered, this lovely shell? 是我吗?是完全被打得粉碎的这个我,这个可爱的贝壳?前后两句是同格的比喻。想到天真的儿童时代在海滨拾贝壳,童心与贝壳形成双重的影像,再拿来和现在的残花败柳,破碎之身对比。(17) Perhaps I shall rise at another time, though I lie down in darkness and have my light in ashes. 虽则我现在躺下在黑暗中,而到骨灰中去求我的光明,也许将来有一天我会苏醒过来的。作者在书前的题词(epigraph)中曾用了这样的词句。Sir Thomas Browne(1605—1682)曾著有《壶葬论》(*Urne-buriall*),对生死问题有所阐述,立论警策,作者即从该书引用了上述的文句,又拿来用作小说的题名。《壶葬论》中说到生死轮回的思想,darkness 和 light 即象征死生。(18) them 指小鸟。(19) coming across the tiles 从瓦上过来。(20) prancing 跳跃着。(21) fluffing up their wings 使翼翅松散。(22) my poor flightless birds 我可怜的不能飞的小鸟啊。蓓顿自喻的话,表示她不能自由地飞翔,加上烂饮与滥交的关系,而有犯罪之感,以及憧憬自由而不可得的焦躁之感,那种精神错乱的不安状态,用小鸟拍翅膀来形容,颇为巧妙传神。(23) darkening sands 逐渐变得黑暗了的沙滩。(24) treading past 走过。(25) my boiling skin 我那沸腾炽热的皮肤。(26) one whisper of feathers 羽毛一度作沙沙声。(27) suffocating night 闷热的夜晚。(28) Bunny 原来是对兔子或松鼠的爱称,在此为蓓顿叫她父亲时的爱称。

【译 例】

我全身赤裸,虽淌着汗,但很清洁,就像我刚生下来的时候一样。好像有什么东西,把我向太空推去。我再度听到遥远的地平线上的雷声,也许是炮声,或是别的什么声音。那是在阳光灿烂的海域中的爪哇上空呢,还是在拉卡代夫群岛的棕榈树的上空,不得而知。又有什么东西驱赶着我向记忆中去,但是我不能从容地来回想,因为超过记忆或梦想,一种更黑暗的犯罪意识驱使着我向前迈进。我祷告,但我的祷词,像一缕破碎的轻烟向天上升去:"啊,主呵,我要死了",这便是我所知道的一切。还有"啊,我的父亲;啊,我的爱人",满怀渴望,孑然一身,我要飞去投入你的怀抱!"蓓顿,你一定要检点些,好女孩子都不是这样的。蓓顿。"是我吗?是损毁不堪的这个我,这个可爱的贝壳?虽则我躺下在黑暗中,要到骨灰中去求取我的光明,也许有朝一日我会苏醒过来的。我在房间里回头一看,便看见一些小鸟松开着翅膀,糊里糊涂地在跳跃着,跳过花砖来了。我想:我可怜的不能飞的小鸟啊,你们不能高飞入云,在这地上很受了苦吧?那么,来起飞呀。于是小鸟们经过我的身边,羽毛沙沙作响,笨拙而又温柔地向前移动:来起飞呀。就是这样,小鸟们偶尔想要接触到我的滚烫的皮肤,而贴近我走将过来——羽毛一度发出小声,如是而已——随即我看见它们飞走——啊,我的救主!——一只一只地我那些不能飞的小鸟,突破窒息的夜晚,向天国飞升而去。我要死了,朋宜,就要死了。

(15)

I seemed to be walking alone at the edge of a swamp at nightfall, the light around me glimmering, crepuscular, touched with the greenish hue presaging the onslaught of a summer storm. The air was windless, still, but high in the heavens beyond the swamp thunder grumbled and heaved, and heat lightning at somber intervals blossomed against the sky. Filled with panic, I seemed to be searching for my Bible, which strangely, unaccountably I had left there, somewhere in the depths and murk of the swamp; in fear and despair I pressed my search into the oncoming night, pushing now deeper and deeper into the gloomy marshland, haunted by the ominous, stormy light and by a far-off pandemonium of thunder. Try desperately as I might, I could not find my Bible. Suddenly another sound came to my ears, this time the frightened outcry of voices. They were the voices of boys, hoarse and half grown and seized with terror, and now instantly I saw them: half a dozen black boys trapped neck-deep in a bog of quicksand, crying aloud for rescue as their arms waved frantically in the dim light and as they sank deeper and deeper into the mire. I seemed to stand helpless at the edge of the bog, unable to move or to speak, and while I stood there a voice echoed out of the sky, itself partaking of that remote sound of thunder.

【解 说】

本文采自美国作家 William Styron 在 1967 年发表的 *The Confessions of Nat Turner* 一书的 *Judging Day* 第一部。《挪特·颓累的忏悔》获得 1968 年度的普立策奖(Pulitzer Prize)。故事说到 1831 年 8 月某日,在维吉尼亚州的东南部地方,突然发生了美国黑奴历史上唯一的,持续很久,颇有效果的黑人暴动。为首的挪特·颓累,是这反叛的计划人兼指导者。他是为黑人所尊敬的传教师,通文墨的黑奴,受到神的指示,要把当地的白人全都杀死,可说是一个对宗教着了魔的人。于是他便带着好几十个黑人暴动起来,用斧头和枪把那地方的农场主人及其家族等近六十人完全残杀了。几天之后暴动被镇压下来,挪特被捕。作者以挪特在狱中向律师的自白为题材,再加上丰富的想像力,而创造出一篇优美的小说来了。

现在这个断片是指挪特被带入法庭,在开庭的几分钟之间,叙述他所经历的白日梦的一段。沼泽地的暮色,和黑人们的悲惨,以及挪特的心境等等,作者以巧妙而朴素的文笔,象征地描绘出来,实不愧为"语言的魔术师"。

【注　释】

(1) swamp 沼泽。浸有水的低湿地带,与后面出现的 marsh 同义,至于最后说的 bog 也是沼池,但无水。(2) glimmering 发微光的,例如 lights glimmering in the distance 远处微弱的灯光。(3) crepuscular 晨光熹微的,黄昏的。crepuscular birds or insects 在晨暮之际活动的鸟或昆虫。a crepuscular period 初期,蒙昧未开的时期。(4) touched with = being touched with 染得有(那种色彩)。(5) the greenish hue 略带青色。(6) presage 预示,前兆。Some people think that a circle around the moon presages a storm. 有些人以为月晕预示有暴风雨。(7) onslaught 猛攻。(8) heavens = sky. 散文中通例用复数,如 the starry heavens. (星空),大约是因为古代的天文学认为天有七重,上帝和天使们住在最上一重。(9) grumbled and heaved 隆隆作响,有起有伏。(10) at somber intervals 此为作者所特有的修辞法。我们应把 at intervals (= now and then 时时)和 somber(阴沉的,幽暗的)分开来看。(11) blossomed 形容闪电有如开花。(12) Filled with panic = Being filled with panic 凡是过去分词开头的句子,都可以加上 being 来解释。(13) I seemed to be……of the swamp. 描写挪特在暴动失败后一时找不到神的焦躁状态,这也是象征的表现法。(14) depths and murk 在黑暗的深处。(15) press = hasten, urge on 加速,赶快。(16) oncoming 即将来临的。(17) haunted by 萦绕于怀;为……所困扰。A wrongdoer is constantly haunted by the fear of discovery. 作恶者心中经常害怕被人发觉。I am haunted by regrets. 我悔恨无已。(18) pandemonium = perfect confusion 骚乱,喧嚣。大混乱的场所。原出 Milton 著 *Paradise Lost*,指群鬼的宫殿。(19) Try desperately as I might. 普通"形容词 + as" = though(虽则),但此句为"动词 + as",用法完全不同,应译作"尽管",上句可译为"尽管我拼命去找,(我也找不到我的《圣经》)"。(20) outcry of voice 人声的叫喊。(21) half grown 还没有变成大人的声音,还带得有儿童的声音。(22) seized with terror 为恐怖所侵袭,大为恐怖。(23) trapped neck-deep in a bog of quicksand 陷于沼地的流沙中,深入齐颈。(24) mire 泥淖,泥泞。(25) itself partaking of 和那声音相伴。itself 是接前面的 a voice 说的。

【译　例】

我好像是在暮色中独自一人在沼泽岸边走着似的。那包围着我的薄暮的微光,染得有带青的颜色,预示着一个夏天的暴风雨就要袭来。微风不动,静寂寂的,但在沼泽那边高高的天上,却雷声隆隆,由小而大,而闪电时时在阴沉的天上开出花来。我充满着恐怖,好像是在寻找我的《圣经》似的,很奇怪而无法说明地,我把《圣经》放在沼泽的黑暗深渊中的什么地方忘记了。在恐惧和绝望中,我加快在即将来临的夜色中寻找,受着那恶兆的暴风雨的电光,和辽远的吵闹的雷声所困扰,我现在向着阴郁的沼泽地越来越深入地推进了。尽管我拼命地寻找,但怎也找不到我的《圣经》。突然间另外一个声音来到我的耳中,这次却是人们恐慌的叫喊声。那原是一群男孩子的声音,嘶嘎而未成年的声音,为恐怖所袭时的声音。现在一瞬间,我看明白他们了:那原是五六个黑孩子陷在沼地的流沙中,深及颈部,当初他们越来越深地沉下到那泥淖中去时,他们在幽暗的夜色中,疯狂地舞动手臂,高声呼喊救命。我好像是站在那沼地的岸边一点办法也没有的样子,既不能移动,也不能说话,而当我站在那里的时候,突然从天上传来一个声音,听去却和远处的雷声混在一起了。

(16)

Scurridge reached for the morning newspaper and turned to the sports page. "I fancy a bit o'bacon an'egg," he said, and sat down beside the fire and placed his pointed elbows in the centres of the two threadbare patches on the arms of his chair.

His wife threw a surly glance at the upraised newspaper. "There is no eggs," she said, and Scurridge's pale, watery blue eyes fixed on her for the first time as he lowered the paper.

"What y'mean 'there is no eggs'?"

"I mean what I say; I didn't get any." She added with sullen defiance. "I couldn't afford'em this week. They're five-an'-six a dozen. Something's got to go—I can't buy all I should as it is."

Scurridge smacked his lips peevishly. "God! Oh! God. Are we at it again? It's one bloody thing after the other. I don't know what you do with your brass."

"I spend it on keeping you," she said. "God knows *I* get precious little out of it. Always a good table, you must have. Never anything short. Anybody'ud think you'd never heard of the cost of living. I've told you time an'again'at it isn't enough, but it makes no difference."

【解　说】

本文作者是英国劳动阶级出身的作家 Stan Barstow(1928—).这是他的作品 *Gamblers Never Win* 当中的一节。描写一个沉溺于赌博中的矿坑夫,在早餐时和老婆口角的情景。用活生生的现代英语表出,平易可读。下层阶级的口吻,连他们说话的声音,都被刻画出来。

【注　释】

(1)reach for 伸手去取。(2)turn 翻动,转向,如 The car turned to the left.(汽车向左转去了)。在自动词 turn 后接介词 to 时,可作"查阅"解,如 turn to a dictionary for guidance(参考类书)。又可作"开始工作"解,如 He turned to stamp-collecting again.(他又开始集邮了)。此外还可以作"求助于"解,如 I have no one but you to turn to.(我可以求助的人只有你呀)。如果把 to 作副词用时,则可说 It's time to turn to.(是开始工作的时候了)。(3)fancy = would like to have(想吃)。这个动词的 fancy,原有 take a fancy to(爱好)的意思,如对病人等说 Don't you fancy anything?(你想吃点什么吗?)(4)of,and 等字说得很轻的时候,便成为 o'和 an'了,即是不把 f 和 d 的音说出来。(5)bacon and eggs 英国人一般做早餐吃的。(6)the fire 炉火(无论贫富英国家庭终年都生火)。(7)his pointed elbows 他的尖肘(形容工人的消瘦)。(8)the two threadbare patches 椅子扶手因用久破烂而加上的补丁(形容主人的穷相)。(9)a surly glance 不高兴的一瞥。(10)the upraised newspaper 双手拿起在看的报纸。(丈夫的面孔被报纸遮住了,她只好对那报纸投以不高兴的一瞥。)(11)There is no eggs. 没有鸡蛋了。(在口语中不管主语是单数或复数,一概用 there is.)(12)pale,watery blue eyes 无神的浅蓝色的眼睛。pale = feeble 缺乏健康的气色。watery 不是修饰 eyes 的(watery eyes 泪汪汪的眼睛),而是修饰 blue 的。watery blue 浅蓝色。(13)for the first time 第一次(说那赌徒的丈夫那天起身以后还是第一次来凝视他的老婆)。(14)What y'mean = What do you mean? 你是什么意思?(15)I mean what I say. 就是我说的意思。不是和你开玩笑的,我是认真说的。mean 意谓,如 What do you mean by saying that? 你那样说是什么意思?(16)get 买。

(17)with sullen defiance 带着愠怒的反抗。(18)They're five-an'-six a dozen. 鸡蛋卖到五先令六便士一打。five-and-six = five shillings and six pence 口语都不说出先令和便士的字眼来。(19)Something's got to go. = something has to go. 有些事情一定得废止才好。句中的 go 有 be abolished（废止）之意，例如 Drink must go.（酒必须废止）。口语常以 have got to 代 have to 用。(20)as it is 照现在这个样子。(21)smack one's lips 咂唇作响。(22)peevishly 气恼地。(23)Are we at it again? 难道我们又要斗嘴了吗？at it 进行某事和进行口角等。(24)bloody 他妈的。在英国卑语中用的颇多，只是表示强烈的感情无特殊意义。如强调否定时说的 not a bloody one（连一个都没有）。(25)brass 口语中指 money 说的。(26)God knows I get precious little out of it. 天晓得我为自己用的极少。句中 I 用斜体是加重语气说的。God knows 后接有子句时，表发誓的意思，即"皇天在上，我绝对没有为自己花掉多少钱"。如后面不接 that, 而接 why, where, when, what 等时，God knows 意为 Nobody knows. 又口语中将 precious 作副词用, precious little = very little 极少。他例如 It is precious cold.（冷极了。）(27)a good table 餐食丰盛。(28)Never anything short. 从未缺少一点什么。(不用主语和动词, 简明有力。)(29)'ud = would. (30)you'd = you had. (31)the cost of living 生活费。(32)time and again 再三再四。(33)'at = that. (34)it makes no difference 没有什么不同, 毫无效果。

【译 例】

　　史卡力支伸手去拿了早报，翻开运动栏来看。"我想吃点腊肉鸡蛋。"他说着在火炉旁边坐下来，把他的两只尖肘搁在他坐椅扶手上那两块破补丁的中央。

　　他的老婆对那举起的报纸投以不高兴的一瞥。"没有鸡蛋了。"她说，而史卡力支放下报纸，把他那无神的浅蓝眼睛第一次瞪着他老婆望了。

　　"你说没有鸡蛋了是什么意思？"

　　"就是我说的意思，我一个蛋也没有买呀。"她带着愠怒的反抗补充着说了。"这个礼拜我买不起鸡蛋。一打涨到五个六了。有些事情一定得停止才好。——照现在这个样子，我想要买的东西都不能买呀。"

　　史卡力支气恼地咂唇作响。"天啦！啊！天。难道我们又要斗嘴了吗？一个问题刚解决，第二个又来了。我不晓得你的钱，是怎样用的。"

　　"我用来维持你的生活呀！"她说。"天老爷明白，我为自己用的极少。你一定要吃得好，不能短缺一点什么。人家以为你从来不知道生活费要多少呀。我再三告诉过你说这点子钱是不够的，但你老是把它当作耳边风。"

习题解答

第一编 汉译英与英文句型

壹 由要素来分的造句

习题 1

1. A sound thought dwells in a sound personality.
2. We do not live in order to eat, but we eat in order to live.
3. Stay if the work fits well, or you go away.
4. Don't falter when you speak.
5. The school year in China begins on the 1st of August and ends on the 31st of July.
6. My brother started from here the day before yesterday, and will arrive at London towards (or about) the middle of next month.
7. He may return very soon, but I cannot say for certain.
8. The cat can see in the dark.
9. The knife cuts well.
10. The work does not pay.
11. These hens have begun to lay.
12. My friend has stood by me.
13. The sun appears to move round the earth.
14. I could not see distinctly owing to the darkness.
15. Having walked about an hour, we arrived at the place.
16. When industry comes in at the window, poverty goes out of the window.
17. I do not sleep soundly, eat heartily, and my heart leaps all the time.
18. He descends from the lofty tree and goes into the dark valley.
19. The snow melts away in spring.
20. I could not have lived till today without my grandmother, and she would not survive in her later days without me. Both my grandmother and I rely on each other so as to exist in this world.

习题 2

1. We must be very careful in picking our company. One must be very careful in the choice of one's friends.
2. The Americans are fond of activity and rich in the spirit of independence. The American people are a nation that likes an active life and is full of the spirit of independence.

3. The examination questions of that university are very difficult, and it is doubtful whether I shall succeed in the entrance examination. As the examination questions of that university are very difficult, I doubt if (it is uncertain that) I shall pass the entrance examination (or not).

4. She felt a little awkward and was quite at a loss to know what to do.

5. Good medicine tastes bitter (to the mouth), but is good for a disease.

6. He stands firm in his purpose.

7. He has kept attentive through the lecture.

8. The rule does not always hold good.

9. True worth often goes unrecognized.

10. It remains to be proved.

11. He continued sullen, without speaking a word.

12. She sat thoughtful for a few minutes.

13. He appears to be aware of the fact.

14. After that they rested content.

15. The Chinese attitude is a reaction to the behaviour of the West.

16. The regions lying at the furthest extremes of the world remained entirely or virtually unknown to each other for centuries.

17. The account of his journey is an extraordinarily interesting document.

18. Few of the accounts of other travelers are as lively and informative as Marco Polo's.

19. A few words of explanation appear necessary.

20. No student who keeps abreast of the times can afford to ignore the publications of the day.

习题 3

1. Did you attend the welcome meeting yesterday?

2. Mr. Su has successfully entered Oxford University.

3. Mr. Wang has passed the Civil Service Examination with honours.

4. If we must fight, we must fight it out.

5. They have stripped the Chinese of all their wealth in Indonesia.

6. He has provided me with everything I need.

7. He seized me by the hand and would not let me go.

8. She affected to talk to my friend, but she was really speaking at me.

9. Diligence makes up the deficiency in ability.

10. I insist that you shall come.

11. He did not work hard, and played away another year at school.

12. When I make a journey, I always take third class.

13. The audience shouted applause at the end of his speech.

14. He breathed his last at 11:10 p.m.

15. Can you swim it across the Yangtze River as that old man did?

16. I gave the poor little boy some money to buy food with.

17. She wrote me a long letter about her future.

18. We discussed the problem far into the night.

19. He admitted to her that she was right.

20. She suggested to us that we should do the whole thing over again.

习题 4

1. Heaven has given man only the gift of speech.

2. He offered her his seat.

3. His father left him a large fortune.

4. I paid him the money.

5. I will read you the letter.

6. Will you sing me a Chinese song?

7. I envy you your good fortune.

8. I paid him a high compliment.

9. I wish you joy of your success.

10. I am sorry to give you so much trouble.

11. They grudged me even my pittance.

12. I hope you will not refuse me the favour.

13. Passengers are allowed 30 lbs of luggage.

14. An old Chinese proverb says that too much learning does not become a woman.

15. They have no sense of the duty which they owe their country.

16. She would be glad to die, but for the love she bears her child.

17. I do not envy the rich their wealth which causes them so much anxiety.

18. To do him justice, he has always been a good husband and a good father.

19. The rascal has at last been caught, after long giving the police the slip.

20. I beg you will do me the honour of accepting the trifling present.

习题 5

1. The people of the U.S.A. would never elect a colored man president.

2. They elected Mr. Wang a councilman.

3. Outdoor exercise makes us strong in mind and body.

4. People think him honest, but he is really an impostor.

5. I make it a rule to take an hour's walk after supper.

6. He left the room unobserved.

7. I had my license renewed for another three years.

8. We found him lying on the pavement.

9. I caught them stealing fruit from my garden.

10. We should keep our bodies and clothes clean not to be attacked by illness.

11. I call that answer impertinent.

12. I consider what he said irrelevant.

13. I found it difficult to solve that problem.

14. I deemed it prudent to keep the thing a secret.

15. Hsün Shuan esteemed it an honour to be the driver of Li Ying.

16. I look upon him as my benefactor.

17. He represents the state of the country as deplorable.

18. They describe her as a fairylike beautiful woman.

19. His knowledge of English leaves nothing to be desired.

20. Learning has always been held in high esteem in our country.

贰　由构造来分的造句

习题 6

1. The sun having set, we went home.

2. In haste, there is error.

3. I got acquainted with him two years ago.

4. Return him my best thanks for the present.

5. To return to the subject, they got married the very day.

6. Judging from appearance you will lose the man of Tsu Yu.

7. The love of money is the root of all evil.

8. He came to see me for the purpose of borrowing some money from me.

9. The allied countries are suspicious of one another.

10. Fame has nothing to do with money.

11. To the joy of his mother, he won a lot of money.

12. Having written a letter, I went out for a walk.

13. He is content with very little.

14. To get up early for three mornings is equal to one day of time.

15. Diseases enter by the mouth.

16. An inch of gold will not buy an inch of time.

17. We know men's faces, not their minds.

18. There is many a good man to be found under a shabby hat.

19. Intelligence consists in recognizing opportunity.

20. Among men who is faultless?

习题 7

1. It is getting dark and we are still a long way off our destination.

2. Give me liberty or give me death.

3. An intelligent man studies for knowledge, but a foolish man just for a diploma.

4. It is going to rain, for the barometer is falling.

5. Some families are making merry while others are suffering from poverty.

6. He comes to help me when he has plenty to do at home.

7. How can I convince him when he will not listen?

8. He kept on talking when he knew it annoyed us.

9. He paid me only two thousand dollars when he owed me five thousand.

10. Please be quiet while I am talking to you.

11. He has nothing to spend his money on, while I have no money to spend.

12. He was the only candidate; therefore, he was elected.

13. He is a most popular candidate; consequently, he will be elected.

14. I hate, whereas you merely dislike, him.

15. A man does not live a hundred years, yet he worries enough for a thousand.

16. I must give him his share, for I have promised to go halves.

17. The train started before I had got to the station.

18. He talked about peace but he brought us war.

19. I accepted his well-meant advice, and now I do not feel futile in my new life.

20. Such work may do with others, but it won't do with me.

习题 8

1. We all know that time is money.

2. I do not know whether it is true or not.

3. This is the dog that barked at me wildly yesterday.

4. I wonder if he is at home at this time of day.

5. I have not seen him since he left here last year.

6. He speaks as if he understood everything.

7. The harder you work, the sooner you will improve.

8. Since you say so, I must believe it.

9. We study in order that we may gain knowledge.

10. I open the window that I may let the moon come in.

11. He is so cunning that nobody wants to make friends with him.

12. When the leopard dies, he leaves his skin; a man, his reputation.

13. I will undertake the work, if it pays.

14. None are so deaf as those who will not listen.

15. If you are a gentleman, you must show yourself as such.

16. Strange as it may sound, I am too rich to afford it.

17. I do not envy him his wealth, which causes him so much anxiety.

18. Grief has made him what he is.

19. Time passes quickly when we are engaged in the pursuit of pleasure.

20. There can be no friendship where mutual respect is wanting.

叁 由内容来分的造句

习题 9

1. There is no art that can make a fool wise.

2. She writes home once a week.

3. He spent all his money on books (= in buying books).

4. The rich have their troubles as well as the poor.

5. There has been a lot of rain this week.

6. Now was the time for thought.

7. Here stood her sewing machine.

8. Behind him came a long stream of horse and foot.

9. Immediately the button is pressed, the mine explodes.

10. Typical is the regiment at the pigeon loft of the Army Signal Corps at Fort Monmouth.

11. Fame and wealth people like best.

12. Nothing but a little water was in the cup.

13. Seldom has there been more fuss.

14. Should he meet me, he would know me at once.

15. Hardly had he began to speak when the audience interrupted him.

16. Here we differ about this matter.

17. They had to take care of their sick and wounded.

18. He will not succeed, try he (= though he try) never so hard.

19. Happy is the man who is contented with his lot.

20. Thus spoke the orator.

习题 10

1. What does it matter?
2. Where did you buy that stick of yours?
3. Aren't you proud of your son?
4. What is he? (= What is his occupation?)
5. What (= How much) did this book cost you?
6. Which man are you going to employ?
7. Is there anything you want which I can get for you?
8. Who is there but commits (= that does not commit) errors? (= Who is infallible?)
9. Can any ladies swim well?
10. Has anything happened?
11. Will you have some beer? (= Please have some beer.)
12. Have you not some English books? (= You have some English books, haven't you?)
13. Can I have some wine? (= Please give me some wine.)
14. Who do you say Sally is going to be married to? (Thomas Hardy)
15. Do you know what sort of thing a castle in the air is?
16. What sort of speech shall I make tomorrow?
17. Is there a bus close by?
18. What time do you expect her back?
19. He cannot understand English while living in England for ten years?
20. Shall I get there in time if I take the 3:30 p.m. train?

习题 11

1. Let us not do what is dishonest.
2. Let me not hear of it any more.
3. Be diligent!
4. Don't be idle!
5. Don't go away so soon.
6. Bring a chair for your uncle to sit on.
7. You let that cat alone!
8. Now, Franz, you read.
9. Do come!
10. Take it easy.
11. Do not neglect your lessons.

12. Do not rely much on the help of others.

13. Tell him it's urgent.

14. Don't talk nonsense.

15. Please come to order.

16. Don't worry.

17. Give up drinking, and your health will improve.

18. Never speak ill of others.

19. Do not read for mere pleasure as many people do.

20. Wait a moment please. I'll come at once.

习题 12

1. How spotless the snow is!

2. What a glorious sunset this is!

3. What a pretty flower this is!

4. How late you are!

5. What a noise the engine makes!

6. What a time we have had!

7. What an ass he is!

8. What a strange thing is our brain!

9. What an impudent rascal (he is)!

10. May he have good luck!

11. What a vast number of pilgrims go to Jerusalem every year!

12. If I could only go to the concert!

13. How he snores!

14. How eloquent (he is)!

15. How happy I am to meet you here!

16. May she be happy after getting married!

17. Good-bye, my friends!

18. Hurrah! she's come.

19. Alas! I am ruined!

20. May those who love each other get married!

第二编　英文惯用法及其翻译

习题 1

1. 由正义而获得一个名位是光荣的,不过宁取正义而牺牲名位,则更加光荣。
2. 关于学习语言,我有我自己的想法。我认为只要学到足够我们自由阅读,自由谈论日常生活的情形就行了,研求再多的语言知识,简直是时间的浪费。
3. 纸牌在此可能很帮了他一点忙是很难说的。

习题 2

1. 要一个病人不成为凶恶的人是非常困难的。
2. 大家认为要妇女的见解高到可以对任何要求行动的事,采取广大自由的观点,是很不容易的。
3. 他真是愚笨,让自己去做那不可能的事。
4. 一个男子老是单身是不好的。
5. 不得他的允许就骑走他的脚踏车,原是你不对。
6. 不接受他们的提议,他是聪明的。

习题 3

1. 空谈我们的伟大是没有用的,除非我们致力使它伟大。
2. 他们的成功得力于教育的地方到底有多大是值得查究的。
3. 你独自一人住在这里,一定很无聊吧。

习题 4

1. 确实的,中国人的态度大半是对西方行为的一种反感,所以西方必须自我检讨,而经常接受批评。
2. 希望人是正直的,但这不是因为正直是最好的政策,而是由于更高的动机。
3. 凡是印象深刻的东西,就应该趁那最初的印象记忆犹新的时候,加以描写,这是必须记住的一条法则。
4. 我曾听到一个有名望的政治家说过,大部分的伟人都是因为吃得太多而送命的。

习题 5

1. 人病医生喜。

2. 引吭高歌,最爱诙谐笑谑的人,并不是心情最轻松的。
3. 使我们大部分的人活跃的,是因为没有钱和需要钱。
4. 读书只能供给心灵以知识的材料,思想才能把我们所读的变成自己的东西。
5. 多数大公司都训练得有叫做人事经理的专家,他们的任务就是接见可能聘雇的人员,决定取舍。
6. 他是一个翻译者,其任务就是做一架桥梁或一条通路,以沟通作者和读者的心灵。

习题 6

1. 很奇怪他总是犯同样数目的错误。
2. 她的父母几乎是同时死去;那是很可怕的。
3. 他亟想知道麦伯尔说的是真是假。

习题 7

1. 纳尔逊说:"当我想到我们所成就的事,不禁惊叹不止。"
2. 华盛顿对于措辞非常谨慎,在辩论中他从来不欺骗他的对手,或是争取暂时的胜利。
3. 当她非常神经过敏地在等待着铃子响的时候,他突然一下站到她的眼前来了。

习题 8

1. 竹是最美丽又最奇特的热带产物之一。
2. 他让做法官的正义压倒做父亲的慈爱,宣布了自己的儿子有罪。

习题 9

1. 他因工作关系,只能隔周在周末回家一次。
2. 因为机械的关系,工厂的出品比以前便宜多了。
3. 感到肚子的饥饿,和看到日影的倾斜,使我知道我睡着了以后,太阳走过很远的路程了。

习题 10

1. 当瓦丁顿离去之后,琪娣把他刚才信口随便说的话细细想了一下。那是听来很不舒服的,她费了多少的气力才忍住没把她内心的伤痛表现出来。
2. 这是那孩子生平第一次听到的亲切的话语;那温柔的音调和态度,奇怪地感动了那狂暴而粗野的心,一滴眼泪似的东西像一点火花在那锐利圆圆的发亮的眼睛中照耀了。
3. 他没有一点学生的样子,但很有矿工的神气。(全不像学生,倒像是矿工。)
4. 戈登,你知道的,我真算不得是一个会侍候女性的人。

习题 11

1. 他因受失母的惨痛而促短了他的天年。
2. 母爱与其他的爱情在本质上是大有分别的。
3. 后代的人会追慕他。
4. 没有法律上的任何理由可以将他除名的。
5. 毫不顾到在储蓄上付出多大牺牲的那种小钱的储蓄是不科学的,也是不实际的节俭之道。
6. 他的伟大就在他致力实行他的计划时那种毅力上可以看得出来。
7. 失去这些审美的趣味,就等于失去幸福。

习题 12

1. 无论你怎样称赞他,他仍不免是一个残暴的人。
2. 打倒布尔朋皇族,和那个大肥猪路易十八!
3. 他们给莎莉一条扭动屁股的蓝色短裙来穿。

习题 13

1. 这只表的价钱决不便宜,对我这种一个没有钱的人来说,确是太贵了;不过照它的定价看来,也算是便宜的,因为在效能上它是无比的。
2. 据我看来,他努力想要比平常更甚地来炫耀他的口才,无非是打算侮慢我的沉默,和在亚丽达那样具有风趣而又聪悟的女人前面显露头角而已。

习题 14

1. 在敌人的炸弹密如雨下的当中,这位军官所表现的英勇是最高级的。
2. 那些塔的高度完全是一样的。
3. 当我第一次见到他时,他一定是差不多跟我父亲同样的年纪。
4. 落选者约五倍于当选的人。

习题 15

1. 他自己做饭。
2. 通常一个人所说的命运,原是一张他用自己纺的纱而自己织成的网。
3. 她违背父母的意思,嫁给自己选择的男人。

习题 16

1. 那孩子来回地扇着,以驱逐那些嗡嗡飞舞,随时无礼地飞近婴孩的面孔的苍蝇。

2. 他有投保火险的先见。

习题 17

1. 米尔顿有属于最高天才的普遍性。
2. 在质上最优,在量上无限,能够引导我们走向快乐的惟有教育。

习题 18

1. 在一个人的面前是一套,在他的背后又是一套,这种作法再危险也没有了。
2. 别的人认为艺术的本质与其形式是两回事。

习题 19

1. 他和他的表兄弟同年。
2. 他既残酷又贪婪。
3. 达宾看去面色苍白,态度庄严,而他的同志就是面孔发红,心情愉快。

习题 20

1. 他的小说比一百年来文人所写的小说,更有传诸后世的可能性。
2. 那不但是真的,而且在大小那一点说起来,是我至今所见到的一串最好的珍珠。

习题 21

1. "我的朋友,你错了,"哈尔王说:"错得不能再错了。"
2. 父老们欢迎我,亲切得无以复加。
3. 自从我进入监狱以来,他常来看我,有时他和我谈话,亲切得不得了。

习题 22

1. 正如没有两个字是完全同义的一样,也没有两种表现法能够正确地表示同一件事。
2. 正如化学家从实验的结果获得论断一样,学习语文的人也必须从观察语文的实况而获得论断。

习题 23

1. 人的情形和土地一样,有什么潜在的能力自己也不知道,正像地主有时并不知道他那土地上蕴藏着有黄金的矿苗。
2. 言语犹如阳光,越凝缩越强烈。

习题 24

1. "不对,我早已和你这样说过了。"布隆特说。
2. 那墙约有十五英尺高,十五英尺厚。
3. 我们所有的街道上,两旁都种有树木,当街灯照耀时,就好像那么多的星星,从枝叶间发出光来。
4. 我召集了许多玩耍的伴侣,就像一群那样多的蚂蚁一样勤快地工作了。

习题 25

1. 八个在战斗中倒下的人,只有三个还未断气,而其中两个却像死了一样。
2. 男人应该是既勇敢而又温柔,女人则要既温柔而又勇敢。
3. 我因为肚子饿了非进食不可的缘故,便回到洞穴中去做饭,同时也得去照顾一下我的马,整个上午都没有去理会它了。
4. 美国的名歌手朵莉戴的音乐背景,是渊源于她那教风琴、钢琴和声乐的父亲维廉的。

习题 26

1. 人类的痛苦是不会减轻的,除非我们具有正确的思想行为,并以坚定的决心去面对现实的世界。
2. 假如我更为结实的话,我就早已跟随他从窗口跳出去了。实际上,我只是按铃把全家的人叫醒来。

习题 27

1. 难得的是在这样一个时期出版,他的书引起了很大的注意。
2. 因为这运动是发生于穷人本身之间的,很可能比来自上流社会的更有力量。
3. 因为这事发生在特殊沉闷的时候,所以它比应有的更吸引了人们的注意。

习题 28

1. 他虽则年轻,他虽则贫穷,但没有一个国王或爵爷的儿子,在学问上及得他的。
2. 尽管我们奋斗,我们是决不能完全满足的。
3. 即令学生很笨,功课起初看去很难,如果他能坚忍不拔,努力做去的话,他就会感到那研究越来越容易,至少也不会那样难了。

习题 29

1. 关于气候,日本在本质上与英国无异,所以在这一点上,说日本是太平洋上的英国,确是很有理由的。

2. 这个善良的妇人喜不自胜。她要以自己的儿子为荣也是应当的。
3. 在这期间中我遇见了一些人,凭他们的身份、名誉或地位,是很可以自命要注定成为历史上的有名人物的。

习题 30

1. 友情好像花瓶一样,只要偶然发生裂痕,就很可能马上破碎的。
2. 你想要我改变意见,就和想要太阳从西边升起一样。
3. 当这妇人看见杂志没有增加销路,她对那编辑就有点讨厌起来了,而决心要趁着还有什么可加利用的时候,把凡是可以入手的东西最好全部捞过来。

习题 31

1. 科学的目的就在把一些事实汇集拢来,以便从而引出一般的法则与结论来。
2. 学生们一见到鸟巢,就要极为小心地不去惊动它,生怕母鸟受惊而弃之他去。

习题 32

1. 她对于每个弱小无助的东西都不禁对之发生同情;遇到受伤的小鸟或小兽,她总要为之痛心。
2. 想到他日后成就的伟业,我便记忆到在我叔叔家的食桌上,大家谈论他的那种样子,我不禁为之莞尔不已。

习题 33

1. 任何人想要理解这一对要靠法律来医治他们的创伤的,不和夫妇的心情,就非得密切注视过他们结婚生活的数十万个小时不可。
2. 有些人是生来就伟大的,有些人则独力完成伟大的事业,而另外还有些人就是被人把伟大加诸其身的。
3. 为要发觉自由是值得渴望的东西,我们首先有被剥夺自由的必要。
4. 我计划了各种策略,以便获得机会,使那曾经冤枉过我的人,了解他因从前所犯的罪过而受到了惩罚。

习题 34

1. 他的天性是想要别人怎样对他,他就怎样对待别人。
2. 因为我们住在路边,所以常有旅人为试饮我们的醋栗酒而过访。
3. 与其有这样的事发生,我宁愿加倍地遗失金币。
4. 一个很有教养的英国人问我,美国黑人是否不能和美国白人同在一条人行道上走路。

习题 35

1. 下个月我们就请室内装饰师来家装饰。
2. 那个他受不了吧。他打算在星期二要把你赶出去,所以你还是作个准备的好。

习题 36

1. 我看见楼下的那个女人居然搞了两个水手坐在那里。我不晓得她是怎样认识他们的。
2. 什么都不要你做,我很大方吧。
3. 我不想听到你在孩子们前面说些下流话。

习题 37

1. 有天早晨我一醒来,就发觉我已成名了。
2. 时间一刻一刻地流去了,而他注意一看,自己正凝视着那支小蜡烛。烛光与晨光争辉中越来越微弱了。
3. 不到一分钟我发觉我跟那有同情心的秘书又进入了那间等待室,他要我签定了更多的文件。

习题 38

1. 许多的人发了财的时候,始知财富并不能从罪恶逃避,反而是一种新的更坏的形式的罪恶。
2. 格兰斯顿才是一个高洁的人,也就是终生献身于运用崇高的主义于国事的人。他是这样一个完美的典型,是很容易知道的。

习题 39

1. 我在什么地方看见有人说过,我们要像蜜蜂利用鲜花一样来利用书本,它盗取花的甜蜜,而并不伤害花朵。
2. 假如你想到一个什么重要的观念,如果你不能把它记录下来,你的观念就会要随着你的死亡而消逝。即令你把它记录下来了,也不免有虫伤鼠患之灾,常常很快就被它啮光了。

习题 40

1. 一个人必须养成一种习惯,在穷困的时候,依靠自己的能力,信赖自己的勇气。
2. 没有几个人知道人生的幸福和性格的形成,大半是靠我们所读的精选的书籍。
3. 我深为相信我们心灵的和平及有生的快乐,并不是看我们的地位,我们的财产,或是我们的身份而定,而是完全以我们的精神的态度为转移的。外界的条件和它差不多没有关系。

习题 41

1. 逢迎者和真朋友是很难辨别明白的,因为好像狼和狗的相似一样,逢迎者和真朋友也是很相似的。
2. 绵羊看去都是一样的,不过它们之间仍然是有差别的,约翰就能够辨别得出来。

习题 42

1. 如果你交的朋友对你无益,你也不能对他有所帮助,你就得马上离开他。
2. 青年朋友,我不是当面奉承,我实在宁肯对你们聊天,而不愿对成年人讲话。

习题 43

1. 在某种范围之内艺术家是可以随心所欲地把他的生活做成一个什么样子的。在别的职业上,如医生的或律师的,你要不要去就那种职业,是可以自由选择的,不过,一度选定了,你便再没有自由了。
2. 成就大事业的人,是要把他们的失败作为阶梯的。(意即以失败为基础而达到成功的地步。)

习题 44

1. 你要不是一个有用的人,忠实而诚笃的话,你就不能希望在这世间获得成功。
2. 他努力奋斗一步一步地做到总统的高位。
3. 在面临反对声中而获得社会承认,无需要奋斗的那种伟大的真理是很少有的。

习题 45

1. 他通知我那个消息,所以我能及时准备。(so that 表结果)
2. 一种愚笨的想法,认为坐马车比骑马要威严些,使得法国的贵族都停止去骑马了。
3. 我很幸运作为一个剧作家突然一下声望鹊起,这样一来我就用不着要每年写一个长篇小说来维持我的生活了。

习题 46

1. 不要抓住别人,要他听完你想说的话。
2. 如果那个女人走进我的屋子,我就要打她的耳光。
3. 那医生愤怒地抓住那少年的领子,问他为什么要这样顽皮。

习题 47

1. 世间有许多人不肯让他们的主张在别人心中生根,而要像孩子们的揠苗助长一样,时常把他们种的花拔出来看是不是长大了。

2. 如果一个船长真个爱他的船的话,他就会对于船上极小的毛病都不忽视。他一定要报告这种毛病出来,并留意使它修理完好。

3. 当霍乱流行的时候,我仍然呆在这里,满不在乎。最要紧的就是不要吃没有煮熟的东西,不要吃生的水果和蔬菜,或是这类的任何东西,还有要注意的事,就是饮水必须煮沸。

习题 48

1. 他对于英国的乡村生活一无所知;他竟认为所有生活在乡下的人,当然都是愚笨和悲惨的。

2. 我认为善人的善良是当然的,当我发现善人的缺点和败德时,我感到很有趣;当我看到恶人的善良时,我就为之感动,而很愿意对于他们的邪恶一耸我宽大的肩膀。

3. 我是在小孩子的时候到那里去的,一直在那里长大。所以那里的人并不怎样重视我的存在。

习题 49

1. 他说:"我对这世界什么都不在乎,既不在乎将来的事,也不在乎人们的批评,更不在乎任何种类的确立的地位,或者甚至是文学家的声名,那是我早年许多的夜里睡不着觉所梦想的。"

2. 当然他曾提议要送她回家,起初她是不肯接纳的——她说那确是没有需要,因为从车站回到她父母家里去,不过几分钟的路程,她独自一人已经走惯了。

3. 我们岛上的空气曾是那般纯洁芳香,我们用不着要什么遮盖也能露宿得很舒服的,但是我们不惯在露天底下睡觉,所以我们并未能十分欣赏头上毫无遮盖而躺下睡觉的那种想法。

习题 50

1. 客人都到齐了,马上可以开饭了。

2. 今天早上我们大家聚集一堂来毫无偏见地讨论时下的问题。

3. 我的工作大体上都做完了,只剩下一些零星的事。

习题 51

1. 谁都必然会看得出来,他们现在正遭遇到国家发展上的危机。

2. 如果我们照应当做的一样爱我们同类的话,我们就一定要殷勤有礼地对待他们。

习题 52

1. 你去看看那棵树,看是不是树上有果子成熟了。

2. 如果你不喜欢我写的东西,你不妨去读别人的。

习题 53

1. 把这种讨厌的歧见去掉之后,这两个共和国之间的友好关系,便将变得毫无遗憾了,甚至当其中一个还是帝国时代就很友善的。
2. 如果你把它放在手上衡量一下,你就会感觉到这是够重量的,至于说到它的完美,那更是无懈可击。

习题 54

1. 如果你想要了解这个奇怪,而有几分悲惨的故事的话,你至少对那背景得有一个印象——由四大强国来瓜分为四的维也纳,那个被破坏的可怕的都市。
2. 预定大学校长将在恳亲会上致辞。
3. "我真个吓倒了。她被你看中有多久了?请你告诉我,什么时候我可以庆贺你们的订婚呢?"

习题 55

1. 有些作家提笔写作,是因为他们不得不说出一个故事,而不是因为他们已有一个故事要说。
2. 我因生病游荡了一个月,所以我必得加倍努力,以补足失去的时间。
3. 她从来不表示意见,据推测是她无意见可表示。
4. 即使从这个小车站去,也非驱车跑上好几英里路不可。

习题 56

1. 社会在任何时代都不会阻止一个人的成就的。
2. 如果你把能率的原理应用到你的事业上,没有任何事物能阻止你去实现你的抱负。

习题 57

1. 威胁利诱都不能使之作恶的人我是尊敬的。
2. 文学帮助在挣扎中的人们,来说服那叫做宇宙的怪物,要它提出一个较为易解的哑谜。

习题 58

1. 他们看到钟索的情形大吃一惊。
2. 我是来埋葬凯撒的,不是来赞美他的。
3. 他并没有看到他事业的成果就死去了。
4. 我们匆匆走过那里,结果却是又回到原来的监狱里了。
5. 如果现代的个人或现代的国民,不顾人类的尊严,再度追求这些疯狂的竞赛,那么我们活着时还可以看到对战争中每死一百万人,就有一千万人会要因此而死亡。

6. 许多年轻人在一度失恋之后,就感觉到人生是不值得活下去了,结果他们发现不到几年之后,毕竟幸福是在等待着。

习题 59

1. 在我们开始调查那个之前,让我们努力来理解我们所知道的事,以便充分加以利用,而分别主要的部分与附属的部分。

2. 蔬菜生产不足,难以应付全国的需求。

习题 60

1. 相信他们自己的思想太过深奥,而不能明白易解地表现出来,这说法未免美过其实。这些作家不会想到原只怪他们自己的心灵未具正确的思想能力,这也是很自然的。

2. 只要我们不太傲慢而不肯自己说明或请求别人解释,人生大部分的误会就都会消除了。

3. 我读过非常多的小说,在学校里也学了不少的东西,所以对于恋爱的事懂得相当的多,但我想这只是年轻人的玩意。我以为儿子有我这样大的一个有胡子的人,是不会有那种情感的。

习题 61

1. 我很快就注意到了,在她以外我所认识的人们的性质,她一人兼而有之,我很高兴那些性质在她一个人身上都能发现出来。

2. 哲学家太爱作此假定,认为事实的问题是可以用言辞上的考虑来解决的。

习题 62

1. 那样地来偷窃东西,真使我吓倒了。

2. 愚笨的家伙,居然以为他是可以被赦的。

3. 别人犹可,你也这样说真是太出意外了。

习题 63

1. 如果运输频繁,铁路就能使运费更为经济,至于其火车的有规律,舒适和迅速,犹其余事。

2. 事实上,所有值得称为大发现家的人,都曾一度被人看作梦想者,不被当作狂人看待已经很好了。

习题 64

1. 在这种场合不晓得他要怎样办。

2. 一个人的家屋在何时会从他的头上倾倒下来,是未可逆料的。

3. 他过去老是很容易兴奋的,可是现在他简直神经错乱了;没有法子再去说服他。

习题 65

1. 如果有人不满足他的职业或他的薪水的话,他只消去申请,就可以得到一块农场,用来开始一种生产的新生活。
2. 谁会满足于只要想望就可以得到的成功呢?

习题 66

1. 想要由经验而获得利益的人,是决不认为求助是可耻的。
2. 国魂应该高升到使强国以欺凌弱小为耻。

习题 67

1. 凡是具有价值的东西都不是可以不劳而获的。
2. 去做好一件很值得做的小事,就比发一笔大财好多了。

习题 68

1. 他不但不后悔他的过错,反而感到得意。
2. 诚然,贫穷决非不幸,由于孜孜不息的自助,贫穷也许可能变成一种幸福的。

习题 69

1. 他那时为处理桌上堆积如山的工作非常忙碌。
2. 他忙于保守党候补的竞选。

习题 70

1. 我们不应太快来责难说一切的妥协都是败坏的道德。
2. 到家一看,我们发觉她只找了我们一会儿就放弃不再找,而独自回家了。

习题 71

1. 但裴蒂并不要,也不想忘记约翰。想到要跟另外一个人结婚,就和接受一个突然向她推挤过来的异教的新神一样是决不可能的。
2. 陶乐斯不能说美,她的鼻子太高,身体矮胖;所以贾斯丁夫人除了指望她嫁给一个富裕而有适当职业的青年以外,更无奢望了。
3. 约翰比她要大八岁,多年来他很少把她放在心上,虽则他认为当然他们毕竟是要结婚的;订婚的证书当他还是一个小孩子,裴蒂还在襁褓的时候就签定了。

习题 72

1. 因为缺乏细心使得放荡的人为之身败名裂,好人亦复如此。
2. 写作的技巧和其他艺术的技巧是同样困难的,不过因为谁都能读懂或写出一封信,使人想到任何人也能够好好地写出一本书来。

习题 73

1. 毁灭人的与其说是他们所犯的过错,毋宁说是他们在犯过后的行为举止,即持身之道。
2. 那警察左右双方都没有顾盼地从群众中走过去了。
3. 发生影响的与其说是时间,不如说是我们使用时间的方法。

习题 74

1. 像我们的小岛一样如此小的范围而能有这样多的变化,是世界上任何地方所没有的。
2. 在电车里吸烟的习惯是最无礼貌的了。
3. 对于爱好文学的学生,最重要的是和批评家多多接近。

习题 75

1. 得到别人恩惠的人是无论怎样感谢也不为过的。
2. 高声朗诵与再三易稿的重要性,是无论怎样评价也不为过的。
3. 一本书可以比做邻居;如果是好的,结识越久越好;如果是坏的,分手越早越好。

习题 76

1. 正好像我们没有经典的知识就不能了解中国文学一样,所有学习英文的人,都应该懂得一点《圣经》。
2. 我们哪怕是拿起一本普通的书,一份杂志,或一张报纸,都会发现有提到《圣经》的地方,或引用它的字句的。

习题 77

1. 有名的政治家没有一个不是勤励的人。
2. 没有一个人家不是至少有一个亲人受伤的。
3. 两个人只要有半个钟头在一起的话,就一定有其中一个要显明地凌驾另外一个的。
4. 在一年当中没有任何一周,在世界上某个地方,不是为英国市场而在收割小麦的。

习题 78

1. 有少数的人要等到钱用完了才考虑到钱的事,而大多数的人,对于时间也是这样。

2. 真正的友谊就像健康一样,其价值要到失去之后才知道的。

3. 生物学上主要事实的进化论,直到近代科学产生二百多年以后才建立起来。

习题 79

1. 任何强大的东西,都不免有受到弱小侵害的危险。

2. 战争在物质上的破坏,无论怎样的大,到现在也可以修复了,只要无延误地恢复了和平。

习题 80

1. 法律的目的不是要废止或抑制自由,而是要保护和扩大自由。

2. 他们感到无聊的主要原因,是精神的单调,而不是环境的单调。

习题 81

1. 他没有理由要瞧不起自己,虽则他的服装不够富丽时髦。

2. 一个青年偶因身体有欠强壮,并不一定就是说他不适于过海上生活。

习题 82

1. 他的好处不是因为有任何美德,而是因为他太懦弱不敢作恶。

2. 你的奖金不及别人的多,不是因为你做事欠缺效率,而是因为你缺勤太久。

习题 83

1. 我们所夸耀的,不是因为我们有更多的想法,而是因为我们的想法比较更为健全。

2. 我们之所以想要进入上流社会,并不是因为我们想要占有它,只是因为想要让人看见我们置身其间而已,我们对于上流的想法,原来也只在它的发放异彩一点上。

3. 如果我偶然注意到一个别的孩子比我知道得少,我就会推断那并不是因为我知道的多,而是因为某种理由他不知道罢了。

习题 84

1. 伟大的真理都是明白的真理。但不见得所有明白的真理都是伟大的真理。

2. 礼拜天禁止游玩,我觉得这不失为一个勉强可以忍受的消磨时间的方法。

习题 85

1. 人的贫富不在他的财产而在他的品德。重视名誉过于黄金的人就是富人。

2. 这个世界上一半的不幸是由于羡慕别人,想要获得别人的财富,而失去由享受自己现有财富的乐趣所产生的幸福而引起的。

习题 86

1. 在长期干旱中未死去的作物，却在接踵而来的洪水中淹没了。
2. 我要讲给你们听，我在那种环境中怎样获得了大家认为我在那方面所有的一点点能力。
3. 最可悲痛的光景之一，就是为着大学课程而牺牲了仅有的健康和身体的一个青年的光景。

习题 87

1. 不到一分钟风暴就向我们袭来了——不到两分钟天完全黑了，因为这个以及迎面而来的水沫飞溅，突然变得黑暗不堪，我们同在一个渔船上都彼此看不见人了。
2. 一方面用威胁，一方面用恳求，他终于达到了他的目的。
3. 既要看护伤病的人，又要缝制沙包，有时一天缝好四打之多，她的时间便完全占去了。

习题 88

1. 还有，勤勉有着不但是可使身体休息，而且更重要的，是有可使心灵平安的倾向。
2. 这样那个前途有望的青年，不但是违背了对他自己和对别人一切的诺言，而且最糟糕的是又伤透了他老父的心。

习题 89

1. 弗洛依德对于心理学的关系，正像牛顿对于力学，达尔文对于生物学的关系一样。
2. 他为着安抚那狗下巴下面的神经，弯曲了他的一只膝头。这种鼓励对于那狗，就像一支好的雪茄对于男人一样。

习题 90

1. 谁愿雇用一个没有自尊心的人？
2. 能够得到这样一头牛，我什么都愿给。
3. 去年的雪而今安在？

习题 91

1. 走过一条大路时，不意遇到了你最初给我介绍了的我们那位表兄。
2. 今天他一大早起身，预备做点什么呢？突然想到要去洗楼梯。

习题 92

1. 我们也说不定会要和这个有趣的家庭愉快地结交的。

2. 他大概已尽了全力。

习题 93

1. 如果他的能力可与他的脾气相埒,他就成为一个很好的国王了。
2. 许多成功的人如果当初他们能自由选择职业的话,他们也许会选择和现在使之赢得极好的地位的这种职业完全不同的另外一种职业。

习题 94

1. 鸟是人类的好朋友。如果没有鸟,这个世界就会被昆虫所占领了。
2. 如果没有甘地的话,印度的自由就要来得更迟,而且形式也要两样了。
3. 有愉快家庭的人们,如果不是天雨的话,他们决不会想到他们所有的室内的乐趣。
4. 如果不是他来救援,我一定早已死去了。

习题 95

1. 一个人尽可能及早地坦白承认他的无知,他便要终将由此获益不浅。
2. 把莎翁所有的自然描写部分,以及偶然触及的田园的生活和外观,完全去掉的话,将是一个何等大的损失。
3. 不要太接近他,否则他就会找你的岔子的。

习题 96

1. 从那路上一转弯进去,我们便到了一个仙境,只消离开那里一百码的地方,就没有一个人会想到有那样一个仙境存在的。
2. 子弹射入我的左肩——只要再下去一点,我就早已进了天国。

习题 97

1. 不管怎样死法,我都要死得像勇士之子一样。
2. 想要立身处世的青年,不管遭遇什么困难,都要抱定决心,非达到成功不止。
3. 不管你怎么说,你之有今日,完全是你父亲之赐。

习题 98

1. 不管那些青年人是体重一百零五磅,还是二百零五磅,他都把他们看作轻乙级(指体重在一百二十六磅与一百一十八磅之间的拳击家)的人而教他们拳术。
2. 不管你怎样富有经验,怎样能干,你也决不能完全克服写作技巧上的困难,等到你学会了写作时,很可能你已经没有东西可写了。

习题 99

1. 无论选择哪条路,都走不到我的目的地。
2. 无论她怎样去想,她绝对想不起来他所说的一个字。

习题 100

1. 虽则在划船和帆行上,法国人并不弱于英国人,但他们对这些运动的趣味就很有限了。
2. 如果世上果真有什么使青年人比别的更要感激的事物,那就是在非常恶劣的环境下,来开始谋生时所必要的贫穷。

习题 101

1. 无论是怎样普通的动植物,都有研究的价值,如果理智地观察的话,也会提供一个很有兴趣的故事。
2. 不问是什么职业,如果要想成功的话,就必须以献身的精神去干。

习题 102

1. 他们要是冷淡的话,就会招致跟他们所想望的完全相反的结果也未可知,因为等到危险来临的时候,国内的事情就真个要完全被压倒了。
2. 一度你结了婚,你除了规规矩矩以外,你什么自由也没有了,甚至连自杀都不允许的。

习题 103

1. 如果太阳消灭了的话,全世界就要很快地为坚冰所封,可怕得令一切死尽灭绝。
2. 如果我们觉得吉拉德夫人的想法是对的,那么,我亲爱的法官,我们就得停止你对他们的裁判,我也得停止我对他们的分析,而去追随吉拉德夫人才对。

习题 104

1. 如果是一个漂亮姑娘的话,他就会更加注意了。
2. 若是没有历史的话,作为国民或是作为个人,我们就无法了解我们在这世界上的存在了。
3. 他若拒绝前往就不对了。
4. 听他说话,我们就会把他当作一个傻子。
5. 同样的事情如果是发生在战时,就会要造成很大的灾难。
6. 如果他是生在太平盛世,他就早在文学界建立声望了。

习题 105

1. 一般都是懒惰的人抱怨他们没有时间去做想做的事。

2. 从庄严到滑稽只有一步之差。

习题 106

1. 依照大自然的法则,溪流是要朝下面流去的,任何强而有力的人,也不可能加以阻止。
2. 工艺是必须有的技术,无论怎样未开化的野蛮民族,也不得不学习手艺,无论怎样文明的天才人物也不能放弃它。

习题 107

1. 躺在草上,他一直遥望天空。天色青青,他望得越久,天就显得越高。
2. 我们一生的大部分都为空想所占据,我们越富想象力,这种空想也越加多彩多姿,越为生动。

习题 108

1. 过度的耽溺,读书也要变成一种恶习的——因为不被一般人所确认,所以是一种更危险的恶习。
2. 我想我至今所发现的最有用的一件事,就是多么容易说一声"我不知道"。我从来没有注意过这居然使得别人因此而瞧不起我。

习题 109

1. 他决不是一个看到自己的权力被人蔑视而一声不响的人。
2. 哈斯丁好像是决不需要有何借口的。

习题 110

1. 我觉得任何人不从华勒的辞典多多学习,是不能写出很好的文章来的。
2. 许多食物因价钱不太便宜,穷人无法买来吃。
3. 愿我们的生活能够垂范后昆。

习题 111

1. 为着使他避免危险,我警告过他了。
2. 只要社会认为你是大丈夫的话,不管你怎样做,它也就不会对你怎样吹求了。
3. 他只要能把钱索回,犯罪者是谁,他都漠不关心。

习题 112

1. 那是非常凶猛而狂暴的——使土人们畏之过于狮子。

2. 但是人的怕死是当然的。在人的一生中,随时都不可避免地要想到死那回事,也是当然的。

习题 113

1. 我父亲去了巴黎,成为英国驻法大使馆中的律师,我真不明白他为什么要去,除非是为着追求未知的事物那也使他的儿子的我,将心身消耗殆尽的那种不安的情绪所吸引。

2. 书籍并没有怎样地使他着魔。每当他打开一本书时,他一定会遇到什么东西,要控制他的思想,刺激他的想象,使他沉迷于幻想之中的,于是那天他就不再阅读了。

习题 114

1. 史买克在与其说是活着不如说是死了的状态中,被抬进去,锁在地窖中了。

2. 毕竟他并没有传染到那种热病;他只是吓坏了,并未怎样受到伤害。(意为受惊较受伤更甚,等于说 He was frightened rather than hurt.)

3. 我注意到每当有人打电话找你,听说你不在家时,他就要留下口信,说你一回家,就要你立刻打电话给他,因为有要紧的事情,其实事情常是对他要紧,而不是对你要紧。

习题 115

1. 许许多多的父母死去,留下来的孤儿,多得使孤儿院都照顾不了。

2. 我们大家都抱怨时间的短少,可是却又有许多时间我们不晓得要怎样处理才好。

习题 116

1. 他岂特是微笑,简直是大笑了。

2. 他对于那结果满意之至。

习题 117

1. 一个没有那船长一般钝感的人,即令听到尼尔逊的话而感到迷惑,也许是会被宽恕的。

2. 学问在太多的场合只是普通常识的陪衬物,真知灼见的代用品。书籍被当作观看大自然的眼镜时,常加以利用的时候较少,反而被当作从视力微弱及气质懒惰的人们,遮断大自然那种强烈的光线和不断变化的光景的目障,加以利用的时候较多。

习题 118

1. 谁也不想在冬天去游白峰,更没有人愿意在那种季节中去住在那里。

2. 如果崇拜一颗星也有什么意义的话,那么,崇拜英雄的意义就大得多了。

习题 119

1. 我问她要不要叫一部计程车。她回答说:"不要,我宁肯走路,天气太好了。"
2. 与其劝你把爱给与那个男人,我宁肯在冬天把那小金丝雀放到公园里去。

习题 120

1. 小偷一看到那个,马上跳起来逃走了。
2. 他刚动身天就变得阴暗了,随即又下起雨来了。
3. 门开处狗就冲向箱子那地方去了。
4. 一个人一旦开始爱他的工作,便是他进步的开端。

习题 121

1. 他心情一点也不沉着地在人群中来去地走着。
2. 我相信科学不过是有训练和有组织的常识罢了。
3. 超过一定程度的体力劳动,是痛苦得可怕的,而体力劳动经常是使人生几乎不能忍受地在过度地进行着。

习题 122

1. 在这个场合名声不如实际。(名不副实)
2. 睡眠是不可能的。因为即令他们斗胆留宿,他们也知道睡在地上,差不多一定会死的。
3. 把一种新的文明加在一种旧的文化之上,自然是一种艰巨的事业,而日本从事于此是可佩服的。要实现这个成就而不损失任何一种文明的优点,那简直是奇迹。

习题 123

1. 他在那里听到很多的人声,比平常更为吵闹。
2. 如果我所经历的世路是一条达到成功的坦途,我也就无异议;如果是一条艰难的路,无论怎样险阻,我都要使它化为平易而达到我的目的。
3. 他无论怎样聪明,都不免有错。(智者千虑必有一失。)

习题 124

1. 那汽车跑得很快。
2. 我希望你的眼睛永远是那样炯炯有光,因为那有男子气概。

习题 125

1. 使他大惊和悲伤的,是他看见他那亲爱的老母病重在床,面色苍白,几乎没有知觉了。

2. 写作的通病之一,是短简的字一样行的时候,偏要用长的多音节的字。即使是最伟大的作家,也常犯这毛病,使之蒙羞。

习题 126

1. 看踢足球而感到高兴的人,单这一点就比不看的人高出一等。
2. 自有历史以来,人们常常对大自然的现象具有一些知识;像埃及人和中国人很久以前就有高度的文化,学得了很多的东西,西方人至今还不知道的他们大概早知道了。
3. 就那些对音乐没有欣赏能力的人们来说,要他们学习音乐,简直是浪费时间与金钱。
4. 正如历史要能在现代的舞台上投以一线光明才有用处一样,过去的文学也只当它对今日有意义的时候才有价值。

习题 127

1. 只有他们有权改变这个,而且只能用一种特殊的方法。
2. 德国学者虽具有饮食和怠惰的恶习,却能长时间从事研究工作,而且直到高龄不衰,我尽力想要找出一个理由来,可是徒劳无功。

习题 128

1. 几乎没有人要怀疑科学使现代对一般教育的要求加速了,同时使得教育本身更有效果。
2. 在高贵的社交界中做惯了当主人的角色,他接触到的所有的人都为他所吸引而受其支配;他待人接物的态度,既有魅力,而又威严;而他那种异常的冷静,在这个半疯狂的社会中,给了他另外一种特征。

习题 129

1. 他们做的有些事情,是因为他们是人,有些事情是因为他们是被误导的人,由错误而不辨是非的人。
2. 这个方案和说明我们感情的起源的普通方法有所不同,因为它把我们感情中的个人的乃至自私的东西,看做时间与习惯的产物,在这一点上是有不同的。

习题 130

1. 诚然古代陆路旅行是困难的,既无聊而又不舒服,不过却比较安全。
2. 生在贵族之家的人们,诚然有许多利益,不过为那些利益所付出的代价也很高。

习题 131

1. 他没有被培养成为军人,也没有想做军人的倾向。
2. 新年立下的决心,就决心而论当然是很好的,单是明白写在纸上,如果不是铭刻在心,付诸实行的话也是没有用的。

3. 机智的人易于想象作为一个机智的人是令人愉快的。

习题 132

1. 藏书万卷是一回事,能够贤明地加以利用又是另外一回事。
2. 在人前是一套,在他背后又是一套,这种作法再危险也没有了。

习题 133

1. 如果你想要有一个朋友,礼查·史狄尔就正好做你的朋友。
2. 杀死那怪物的人就是我呀。
3. 我认出那个剧界明星,原来是我的一个老朋友。

习题 134

1. 他走了很远才想起那本书来。
2. 他们没有走到好远,就看到了一条大熊愤怒地朝向他们而来。(make toward 朝向)

第三编　疑难句法及文章译例

壹　英文类似句辨异

1. （a）我在街上遇到一个年轻的男人。

    （b）我在街上遇到一个年轻的女人。

    注　（b）句中说的 a young person，普通的意思多指年轻的女性而言，如 There's a young person to see you.（有一个年轻的女人要会你。）

2. （a）他来到这城里了。

    （b）他回到这城里了。

    注　（a）句中的"他"对这城是一个陌生人，而（b）句中的"他"，原是这城里的人，或是对这城非常熟悉的人。

3. （a）等我们吃饭的时候，我才来听取你的意见吧。

    （b）现在我们一面吃饭，我一面就来听取你的意见吧。

    注　（a）句是在开始吃饭以前说的。

4. （a）他们要来。

    （b）他们就要来了。

    注　（b）是表示时间的迫切。

5. （a）他似乎颇为迟钝。

    （b）他也许像是有一点儿迟钝的样子。

    注　（b）句说得婉曲多了。

6. （a）他们一直住在星洲。

    （b）他们眼下住在星洲。

    注　（a）表示经常的居住，（b）则有暂时的感觉，或根本是暂时性的，如我们从外地到星洲观光，住在旅馆中，则说 I am living in the hotel. 又 live 一个动词有"居住"和"生活"二义，如云 Are your parents living?（你父母都健在吗?）便是"生活"的意思，这句话一定要用现在分词，不可说成 Do your parents live?

7. （a）他推开了门。

    （b）他试图把门推开。

    注　英文动词有他动与自动之分，同一动词由他动变成自动时，意义常有改变，多是变得空虚而不实在了。如他动词说 A cat *catches* mice.（猫抓老鼠。）自动词说 A drowning man will *catch at* a straw.（将溺的人哪怕是一根草也要去抓住求救。）

8. （a）在一个晴天他出门了。

    （b）有一天他出门了。

    注　（b）句中的 fine 是一个虚字，没有什么意思的。说 one fine day 或 one fine morning 等句，多半用作一种意外事件或毋安之灾时的前奏,可能由法文 un beau jour 及 un beau matin (= in opinement 即英文说的 unexpectedly 意外地)直接译成英文的。

9. (a)她彻夜不睡坐待她丈夫回家。

   (b)她彻夜不睡来看护她的丈夫。

   注 (a)句的 sit up for,意为"不睡来等待",(b)句的 sit up with,意为"不睡来看护"。

10. (a)我们确知人是要死的。

    (b)我们确知那人是死了。

    注 (a)句中的 that 是连词,man 是指人类,而(b)句中的 that 是形容词。

11. (a)约翰不安的原因是考试落第。

    (b)约翰的不安考试落第也是原因之一。

    注 (a)意为 His failure was the specific case. (b)意为 His failure was one of the causes—there are others. His poor health might be another.

12. (a)首相在电视上出现。

    (b)首相的演词由电视加以广播。

    注 参考:The symphony was broadcast on (or over) the radio. (交响乐由无线电广播。)注意:在 television 前不要冠词。

13. (a)这是一个可信的故事。

    (b)这是一回可称赞的成就。

    注 credible = believable. creditable = praiseworthy.

14. (a)他不是一个教师。

    (b)他不是一个好教师。

    注 not a 比 no 的意义要重些,(a)句意为"他不是以教书为业的,也许是商人,也许是公务员,总之是做别的事情的人。"(b)句意为"纵然他现在以授徒为业,可是他学问不好,教授无方,或是品行欠佳,不配做人师表。"类例如 He is not a businessman. (= a statement of fact;the man's profession is not business). He is no businessman. (= an ironical statement. The man may or may not be a businessman. Whether he is or not,he certainly is unskillful in business matters)。同样 He is not a gentleman. (= He is a workman 他是工人或是下等人)。He is no gentleman. (= He has bad manners. 他的举止粗鄙不像上等人)。He is not a lawyer. (= that is,not his profession. 他的职业不是律师)。He is no lawyer. (= not an efficient lawyer. 他不是能干的律师)。

15. (a)你想向我要求什么?

    (b)你想和我接洽什么?

    注 (a)want something from somebody,欲从某人得到某物。(b)want something with somebody,欲向某人接洽某事。

16. (a)他的书至多只有十本。

    (b)他的书不少于十本。

    注 no less than = as many as(至多,刚够)。not less than = as many more(不少或多过)。同样的还有 no better than = as bad as,例如 He is no better than a beggar. (他和乞丐一样),not better than = perhaps worse than,例如 He is not better than a beggar. (他不比乞丐好,也许比之更坏)。

17. (a)家里有电报来给我了。

(b)家里有电报来要我回去。

注 如果换成 active voice,则(a)便成 wire to me(打电报给我),而(b)便成 wire for me(电促我归)。for = to get.

18. (a)这是远胜过林语堂的一种幽默。
    (b)这是及不上林语堂的一种幽默。

19. (a)他自信一定成功。
    (b)我想他一定成功。

20. (a)我们中间没有几个人知道那真相的。
    (b)我们中间只有几个人知道那真相的。
    (c)我们中间知道那真相的人不少。

    注 few 意为"差不多没有",无的成分多于有的成分。a few 意为"只有二三人",有的成分多于无的成分。not a few 意为"不少",即有很多。以上均系表数的,如表量则用 little, a little, not a little. 义与上同。

21. (a)反之,他什么也没有说。
    (b)反对的话他一句也没有说。

    注 on the contrary 意为"反之",副词片语。to the contrary 意为"与之相反的",形容词片语。

22. (a)可惜你没有去。
    (b)幸亏你没有去。

    注 It is a pity = I regret. 遗憾。It is a mercy = I rejoice. 幸喜。

23. (a)事竟如此使我觉得惊愕。
    (b)我亟欲知道事情何以会这样。

    注 wonder that = be amazed at,觉得惊愕,感到骇异。wonder + 疑问词 = be curious about; be anxious to learn,亟想知道。

24. (a)那也许可以做。
    (b)那不一定不能做。

    注 (a)含有 It is possible,(b)含有 It is not impossible 的意味。might 是假想。

25. (a)我希望我有他那样富有。
    (b)我希望成为他那样的富人。

    注 (a)在 wish 后接假设语气,这是对现在的事实相反的假设,无法办到的事。(b)表示未来的愿望,并不一定是做不到的事。

26. (a)让我们修理家园。
    (b)让我们回家去吧。

    注 repair 作他动词用时,意为"修理",作自动词用时,意为"往(某处)","赴" = go.

27. (a)他写了一封信给我。
    (b)他替我写了一封信。

    注 for = in place of,代为。

28. (a)他投骨于犬。
    (b)他投犬以骨。

    注 (a)是好意,以骨头给狗吃。(b)是敌意,以骨头来打狗。

29. (a)灯放在桌子上面。

(b)灯悬在桌子上空。
30. (a)他拥有大宗财产。
   (b)他抱有危险思想。
   注 is possessed of = has,拥有。is possessed with = is controlled by.受迷住,为其所乘。
31. (a)我想他不会有罪。
   (b)我觉得他好像有罪。
   注 doubt if,意为"难信","好像没有"。suspect that,意为"可疑","好像有"。suspect = imagine to be.
32. (a)他老是来干涉我的事。
   (b)他老是来妨碍我的事。
   注 interfere in,干涉。interfere with,妨害。
33. (a)他以学者之名混过去了。
   (b)人皆视彼为学者。
   注 pass by = be currently known by a name of,以……之名混过。pass for = be accepted as;be thought of,被认为,被视为。他例如 His name is Wang but he passes by the name of Li.(人皆知其姓李,其实他是姓王。)Many a coward passed for a hero.(懦夫而充作勇士者比比皆是。)
34. (a)空气由氧和氮组成。
   (b)幸福存于满足之中。
   (c)他的言行一致。
   注 consist of = be composed of 由……而组成。consist in = lie in = is in,在,存于……之中。consist with = be in accordance with,与……一致。
35. (a)他打算说什么?
   (b)他预定要说的是什么?
   注 be about to = be going to,为较文言的说法。be to,表示预定。
36. (a)我看见那里有很多的人。
   (b)我看见那里有很多大人物。
   注 a great many 后接复数名词。many a great 后接单数名词。
37. (a)我没有听见她歌唱过。
   (b)她作的歌我没有听见人唱过。
   注 (a)句中的 her 为宾语,sing 为原形不定词所构成的宾格补语。(b)句中的 her 为所有格,song 为名词,her 的宾语。
38. (a)我们租的船以时间计算。
   (b)我们只租了一小时的船。
39. (a)谁的兄弟带你去游公园的?
   (b)你带谁的兄弟去游公园的?
   注 (a)句的主语为 brothers,(b)句的主语为 you.
40. (a)那些宝石有许多被盗。
   (b)那些宝石的大部分被盗。
41. (a)他被视为天才。
   (b)他被崇为天才。

注　look upon as = regard as,视为。look up to as = respect as,作为……而崇仰。

42. (a)我必得注意那件事。
    (b)我必得调查那件事。

    注　look to = attend to,注意,照顾。look into = investigate,调查。

43. (a)我并不想出洋。
    (b)我不反对出洋。

    注　"not care + to-Infinitive" = not like + to-Infinitive,不想做。"not mind + Gerund" = have no objection to + Gerund,不反对。

44. (a)明天会有一些客人来。
    (b)明天我要请一些客人来。

    注　(a)是无意志的,(b)是有意志的。

45. (a)那岛周围五英里。
    (b)那岛直径五英里。

    注　around = in circumference,周围。across = in diameter,直径。

46. (a)我学过五年的英文。
    (b)我从五年前起开始学英文。

    注　(a)意为到现在为止我一共学了五年。(b)意为从五年前开始学起,至今未停,一直在学。

47. (a)他到过纽约。
    (b)他去了纽约。

    注　(a) have been = have gone somewhere and come back 或 have come and gone away again,例如 I have been to (= visited) Paris three times.(我到过巴黎三次。)(b) = he is now in New York or on the way there. 他已去了或正在去的途中。

48. (a)他们在花园里玩耍。
    (b)他们说这话只是戏言。

    注　at play,游戏,嬉戏。in play,玩笑,戏谑。

49. (a)他至急地做了那个。
    (b)他慌忙地做了那个。

    注　in haste,迅速,赶忙,急遽。in a hurry,匆匆,仓促,慌忙。英文的 in a hurry 另外还有两种惯用的说法(collq.):(1) = easily(容易地),例如:You won't find a better specimen than that in a hurry.(你一下子不容易找到更好的标本。)(2) = willingly(愿意地),例如:I shan't ask him to dinner again in a hurry.(我不会愿意再请他吃饭的。)

50. (a)我没有什么可写的。
    (b)我没有笔写。
    (c)我没有纸写。

    注　(a)write 为他动词,nothing 为其宾语。(b)(c)write 为自动词,nothing 仍为宾语。

51. (a)没有什么可看的。
    (b)看不见什么。

    注　(a)意为 nothing worth seeing.(b)意为 nothing visible.

52. (a)这样的人很难得寻获。

(b)这样的人差不多不能够找到。
53. (a)我悬念其结果。
    (b)我亟欲知其结果。
    注 anxious about"悬念","忧虑"。anxious + Infinitive,意为"切望","渴望"。
54. (a)我未尝注意到他。
    (b)我并未把他放在眼下。
    注 (a)是无意的,(b)是有意的。
55. (a)她在街上遇见了一个朋友。
    (b)她在街上遇见一桩事故。
    注 meet with = come across;experience,是一个自动词,所以附有介词,普通对遇见事物而言,即遭遇,如云 meet with fortune. (success,failure,obstruction,kindness,rebuff,etc.)。但对人则通常是用他动词,所以不要附加介词,即可直接接宾语,除非意外地遇见什么人时才用自动词,如 Such a man is rarely to be met with. (这样的人真是少见。)
56. (a)此中有无困难呢?
    (b)此中有点困难吧?
    注 (a)是在完全不知有无困难时问的。(b)是在认为有点困难时问的。
57. (a)我和他一样很钦佩她。
    (b)我很钦佩她,也很钦佩他。
58. (a)我想在这个月底付款。
    (b)我想经过一个月再付款。
59. (a)我到达时还未开会。(正要开会)
    (b)我到达时正开会。(刚刚开会)
    注 in time,意为"及时",时间比规定的略早,on time,意为"准时",再迟则来不及了。如火车准时开行,则说 The train leaves exactly on time. 还有 in time 除 not late; early enough 的含义外,又有 sooner or later; after the passing of an indefinite period of time,例如 You will learn how to do it in time. (你慢慢就会知道做的。)
60. (a)我想这不会是真的。
    (b)我看这恐怕不会是真的。

贰 常易译错的文句

Ⅰ. 中译英

1. What way shall I take to get to the park?
   注 How shall I go 是问怎样去法,如坐计程汽车去,坐公共汽车去,或坐三轮车去之类。问路应说 What way 才得。
2. The lecture begins at two o'clock on Friday.
   The lecture starts at two o'clock on Friday.
3. The scenery of China is very fine.

注　scenery 是集合名词,不可用复数。

4. They have no houses to live in.

5. He likes Hemingway better than Faulkner.

6. This watch wants repairing.

7. The family goes to church at 9 o'clock.

　　注　把全家的人看做一个整体,即一家人,应该接用单数动词。"去做礼拜",英文应说 go to church,如果加了冠词说成 go to the church,便不是去做礼拜,而只是去参观礼拜堂的建筑。同样"上学读书"是 go to school,如说 go to the school,便是指校舍而言,与读书无关。

8. I was quite well that year, but ill the year before.

9. It is impossible to raise the sunken ship.

　　注　sunk 只能作叙述用法,要 sunken 才可作限定用法。

10. Come in the morning instead of in the evening.

11. His daughter married a rich man.

　　His daughter was married to a rich man.

　　注　中国语的"嫁"或"娶",英文都是 marry。此外"主婚"也是 marry,例如 She is married to a foreigner.（她嫁给一个外国人。）He married a wife last year.（他在去年娶了妻。）He has been married two years.（他结婚两年了。）He wished to marry his daughter to a peer.（他希望把女儿嫁一个贵族。）The clergyman married Mary Jones to John Smith.（牧师主持玛利和约翰的婚礼。）

12. Why are you at home on such a fine day?

　　Why are you at home in such fine weather?

13. Make haste, or you will be behind time.

　　注　命令句接顺意的说法用 and,接逆意的说法用 or。

14. The night is falling and the road is coming to an end.

　　注　我们说的"日"英文应译作"夜"。中文的"日暮"除译作 The night is falling 外,又可译成 the night is closing in,或 night is coming [on],或 it is getting dark。中文的"途穷",除如上照字面译出的以外,又可译为 no road ahead,或意译为 straitened, in poor circumstances 等。

15. I have been ill for a week.

　　I have been ill since last Monday.

　　注　ago 只能用于有过去动词的句中,它不能与现在完成时态同用。

16. Do you remember all the interesting stories you read when you were a boy?

　　注　副词子句应置于它所修饰的动词附近。这句中的副词子句 when you were a boy,是修饰动词 read 的,所以应紧接在 read 之后。

17. Looking out of our windshield, we could see the pagoda in the distance.

18. The ears of a hare are longer than those of a cat.

19. Have you been to America?

　　注　have gone 不能用于第一人称和第二人称,只能用于第三人称,意为"去了"。

20. He has been here once or twice.

21. I saw him yesterday.

　　注　现在完成时态不能与表过去的字连用。

22. I found the food very good, and enjoyed eating it.
23. I think of going home very soon.

    I think I will go home very soon.
24. A man who is unable to write a letter, is incapable of holding an office of such importance.
25. He seems to have an aversion to speaking the truth.
26. The Chinese are a hard-working and industrious people.
27. May I use your telephone?
28. He was elected a councilman.

    注　总统,市长,主席等独一无二的职位,不用冠词,其他如议员等,同样的职位有许多名存在,故必须加不定冠词,以示其中之一。
29. Mr. Wong returned to Singapore.

    Mr. Wong went back to Singapore.
30. This report must be presented by the 6th of next month.
31. Please remind me to give it back.

    Please remind me to return it.
32. I ordered ten books from New York.
33. I'm sure I can make myself understood in English.
34. I'm sure I can make you understand what I mean.
35. The motor car ran in the direction of the park.

    The motor car ran towards the park.
36. I place no reliance upon his honesty.

    I have no confidence in his honesty.
37. He entrusted a large sum of money to me.

    He entrusted me with a large sum of money.

    注　"entrust + 物 + to + 人"或"entrust + 人 + with + 物"。
38. Children are always in some mischief or other.

    Children are always in one mischief or another.
39. I sympathize deeply with him in his sorrow.

    注　"sympathize + with + 人 + in + 事"。
40. He apologized to me for his mistake.

    注　"apologize + to + 人 + for + 事"。
41. Somebody said so, but I forgot who it was.
42. He has no other desire than to make a fortune.

    He has no desire but to make a fortune.
43. Her dress does not conform with the fashion.

    注　conform to (custom),从(俗),依照(习惯),是有意志的,至于 conform with (custom),(与习惯)相合,是无意志的。例如 Conform to the custom of the land,入国从俗。Your conduct does not conform with the custom. 你的行为不合习惯。
44. As you know, life is often compared to a voyage.

注　同种类的东西相比用 compare with,不同种类的东西相比,则要用 compare to,例句中 life 与 voyage 完全不同种类,故用 compare to 方合,再看下例 Famous as she is, she cannot be compared with him as a writer of tragedies.(她虽有名,但作为一个悲剧作者是不能和他相比的。)

45. Her expenditures do not correspond to her income.

    注　correspond to (something),相当,相称,相配。correspond with (each other),一致,符合。例如 The punishment should correspond to the offence.(刑罚应与犯罪相当。)This house exactly corresponds with my needs.(这房子正符合我的需要。)又 correspond with,可作通信解,如 We have corresponded with each other for several years.(我们通信有好几年了。)

46. I condoled with him on his father's death.

    注　"condole + with + 人 + on + 事"。

47. How many students came?

    注　问句中有了疑问词时,就不要再加 do 了。

48. These are the people who, they say, are fools.

    These are the people whom they call fools.

49. Taiwan is much larger than Singapore.

    注　very 只能用于形容词的原级,如系比较级则要用 much, far, by far the 等字样。

50. It takes me five days to return home by steamer.

51. He entered at the back door.

    He came in at the back door.

    注　"出去"也要说 go out at the door.

52. The old man had his son die.

    注　"have + 物 + 过去分词",如 have the box removed. 又"have + 人 + 原形不定词",如 have the servant remove the box.

53. This sewing machine is of Chinese make.

    注　说何国制造而用 make 时,必须带有 of 的字样,如 of Chinese (English, American, Japanese) make,但如用 made 时则说 Chinese made 或 made in China,不要再加 of,如说 manufacture 也是要有 of 的,如 of Chinese manufacture(中国制造)。

54. I never saw so tall a man before.

    I never saw such a tall man before.

    注　用 so 或 such 时冠词的位置不同,应加注意。

55. He has the good sense to quit when he found the thing too difficult to do.

    注　用 ability 也是一样,如 He has the ability to speak English clearly.

56. Marco Polo was born in 1254 into a Venetian merchant family.

    注　说生于什么人家,即俗称投生于某家,故英文要用 into,不用 at。他例如 No man is born into this world whose work is not born with him. (James Russel Lowell)。如果是指由什么人即父母而生,则要用 of,例如 He was born of Chinese parents (of humble parentage, of poor fisherfolk in Holland 等)。但家庭在这种意义之下即可用 of,例如 He was born of a wealthy (noble, good) family. 又 But in every child born of man lurks some of greatness—waiting for the food. (H. G. Wells)(但是每个孩子都潜伏着有将来伟大的种子只等待加以培养。)生于什么人家,有时又可译成 to 字,例如 She was born to the purple;diamonds suited her.(她生于贵族之家,所以钻石是适合她的。)这个 to 是指的对象,如 Two children were born to them.(他们生有两个孩子。)Mark Twain was born to Samuel Langhorne Clemens, in Florida,Mo. November 30,1835.(马克·吐温以 1835 年 11 月 30 日,于密苏里州佛罗里达市,作为桑米·郎洪·克来门斯的儿子而出生的。)

57. He has taken the vase off the table.
58. The preface to "A Short History of China" is a short history of China.
59. The early education in our country grows very rapidly.
60. It is due to the outstanding professors on the various faculties that the University has won a worldwide fame.

Ⅱ. 英译中

1. 我的皮鞋穿破了。

   注 这句话的意思是"因为穿得太久的结果,破烂不堪"。(My shoes are badly worn as the result of long wear.)他例如 He was plainly the worse for drink.(显明地他是喝醉了酒。)I am none the worse for a single failure.(一度失败我并不灰心。)

2. 大家听了他说的话都感愤怒。

   注 原意为马缰的 bridle 一字,虽引申可作"控制"解,如 Try to bridle your temper.(设法控制你的脾气。)但用作自动词时,就作"昂首"(表示愤怒、傲慢或轻视)解,如 bridle up,bridle with anger,bridle at somebody's remarks 等。例如 She bridles at the least slight.(她略为受到一点藐视就要昂首发怒。)

3. 学英文要尽力避免讲理论而不务实际。

   注 形容词的 shy 普通作"羞怯的"解,如 I am shy of doing it.(我怕作此事。)又可作"畏缩的"解,如 The boatmen were shy of the rapids.(船夫畏惧险滩。)但此字因在动词 fight 后,就有"避开","敬远"(avoid,keep aloof from)之意。

4. 宁肯割断舌不愿塞住口的不止是妇女与法国人而已。

   注 作"咬"字解的 bite,过去式为 bit,过去分词为 bitten,但作"装马口铁","抑制","约束"解的 bit. 过去和过去分词都是 bitted。这个 bit = mouth piece(metal bar),原是名词,由"马嚼口"引申为"拘束物","控制物"之意。再用作动词时,便意为"约束","控制",例如 Tell him to put a bridle on his tongue.(告诉他说话要谨慎。)又可说 Curb your tongue.(少说话。)因为 bridle(马勒;缰辔)实包括全套马头上的配备:马嚼铁(metal bit),皮带(straps)及缰(reins),在马嚼铁外有马衔(curb),在皮带靠近两眼处又有遮眼革(blinkers),这一切总称为 bridle. 参看上面第二例。

5. 他刚在一星期前结了婚。

   注 句中的 change 改为 alter 也是一样,condition 普通指健康状态,此处指生活状态。

6. 他接受女方提出的求婚而结婚了。

   注 闰年不比常年,闰年提出的求婚,当然也是不平常的,普通总是男方向女方提出求婚,现反过来由女方提出,故云。

7. 他把我的忠告当作耳边风。

   注 fall flat 这个成语有二义:(1)直挺地跌倒(be prostrate),如 The wounded man staggered,and fell flat on the floor.(伤者蹒跚了几步,使直挺地倒在地上。)(2)终于完全失败,毫无反应,一点效力也没有,如 His best jokes fell flat.(他最好的笑话也未能使人发笑。)现将此成语译成中国成语的耳边风(preaching to the wind)似乎是再恰当也没有了。

8. 在鸡尾酒会上你常可看出大人物和无名小卒来。那些迟到的人就是大人物。

   注 作名词用的 somebody 是与 nobody 对称的,前者为大人物,后者为微不足道的人。He thinks himself to be somebody.(他自以为了不得。)In a small village you are somebody, but you become nobody when you come to a big city.(你在小村庄很了不起,到大城市就变得微不足道了。)

9. 当选的职员任期至一九七三年年底为止。

   注 sit = occupy a seat,就某种职位,成为议员、委员或职员。注意后面接的介词,sit in Parliament(做议员),sit on a committee(当委员),sit for a constituency(在议会中成为某选区的代表)。

10. 他用钱豪爽。

    注 这个 with 不作"持有"解,而作"关于"解。free with,意为"大方的","不吝啬的"(lavish)。例如 He is very free with his advice. = He gives plenty of advice.(他给与很多的忠告。)如说 make free with = use another person's things as if they were one's own,当作自己的一样随便使用别人的东西。例如 They entered the house and made free with whatever they could lay their hands on.(他们一进屋内,随意取用所有的东西。)

11. 向法国去定了一架飞机。

    注 普通作"从"解的 from,与 order 连用时,就有"向"的意,不是"从法国来定",而是"向法国去定"。

12. 她的丈夫死了至今不过半年。

    注 这句英文意为 It is only six months since she became a widow. 若译成"只做了六个月的寡妇",则不免有很快再嫁之嫌。

13. 你的损失和我的比较起来真算不了什么。

    注 nothing to mine 中的 to,有比较的意思。

14. 他在除夕出发了。

    注 eve 和 evening 二字虽是同根生,然其含义则大不相同。eve 为节日等的前夜或前日,如 Christmas Eve(耶诞的前夜),on the eve of victory(胜利的前夜),故 New Year's Eve 为除夕,而非元旦(New Year's Day)的夜晚。

15. 他将表托我保管。

    注 "leave + 宾语 + 介词 + 人",意为"将某物(事)托付某人"。I'll leave the matter to him.(这事我交给他去处理。)I left a message with your servant.(我留言要你的佣人转告你。)

16. 他假装没有生病。

    注 not 是否定 to be 一个不定词的。He did not pretend to be ill,才是"没有假装生病"。

17. 他说:"我以为不然。"

    注 这个 not 不是修饰 think 的,而是后面接着的否定句所留下的代表,意为 I think it is not so. 如果照误译句的意思,英文是说 I do not think so. 比较:I am afraid not.(我恐怕不是那样。)I am not afraid.(我不怕。)

18. 到今年耶诞时就是两年了。

    注 come Christmas 的说法,据《牛津简明辞典》的解释是 including the time from now to Christmas(包括从现在到耶诞日的时间)。come Christmas = if Christmas comes(如果到了耶诞日的话),是假设的用法(suppositional use)。命令句是有这种假设用法的,如 Give me good fortune (= if good fortune is given me),I will strike him dead. (Tennyson)(时运来时,我就要将他打死。)莎剧 *Romeo and Juliet* 中有句:Come Lammas-eve at night shall she be fourteen.(到收获节的前夕,她就有十四岁了。)

19. 百万富翁都具有这种思想。

    注　men of millions 不可与 millions of men 混同。

20. 他迟到了。

    注　behind time＝late,迟到。behind the times,时代落伍。

21. 他上楼去了。

    注　普通说"上楼",多半是指"到二楼去",英文说,He went upstairs. 句中的 upstairs 为副词,是修饰动词 went 的。若分开写成二字的 up stairs,则不论二楼也好,四楼也好,无论哪一层楼去就是了。

22. 一朝醒来,自己已经成为一个破产的人了。

    注　one fine morning 中的 fine 一字,实无意义,可以不译,其用法与 one of these fine days(不久总有一天)相同。find oneself,不知不觉间,而自己已变成了。他例如 She found herself a mother at fifteen.（她刚十五岁不知不觉之中做了母亲。）

23. 他的英文毫无遗憾。

    注　nothing to be desired,不能指望更好。至于婉言某人对于某事不好,还应多多努力,也可用此表现法：In her English there is still much to be desired.（她的英文实尚未能副我们的期望。）

24. 注意使一切平善。

    注　take care that＝see (to it) that,当心,注意。他例如 Take care that the quality is satisfactory.（注意要使品质满意。）Take care that you don't get knocked down when you cross the road.（小心过街以免撞倒。）

25. 他一进房就跌倒在地板上。

26. 我们搜查过了他的身上,但毫无所得。

    注　寻找一个人的踪迹,是 search for a person,单说 search a person,意为搜查一个人的身上看有无违禁品之类。to no purpose＝with no result. 无结果。

27. 我回家时遇见一个孕妇。

    注　with child 怀着孩子,with a child 携着孩子。

28. 他承继了一笔大的财产。

    注　succeed in,成功。succeed to,承继,如 Who will succeed to his office when he resigned?（他辞职后谁来继任?）

29. 他抓住了我的手。

    注　他例如 He pulled me by the sleeve.（他拉住我的衣袖。）He struck me on the head.（他打了我的头。）

30. 我穿什么出去呢?

    注　这个 in 意为 dressed in(穿衣)。他例如 I have nothing to go in.（我没有衣服穿着出去。）普通说 She is in red.（她穿的红衣。）

31. 他说话无心。

    注　mean 除"意义"外,还有"意谓",have in mind(心有成竹)的意思。I mean what I say. 说话作数,决非口是心非。What do you mean by saying that?（你说那话是什么意思?）

32. 今晚不要喝酒。

    注　alcohol 原意为酒精引申为酒,如 His doctor told him not to touch alcohol.（医生要他不要喝酒。）由 no 开头的句子有禁止意。

33. c-a-m-e-l 拼成一个什么字?

    注　spell 除作"拼"解外,还有"拼成一字"(make up a word)的意思。如照误句的意思应说 How do you spell camel?

34. 他对那工作已厌倦了。

    注　"疲劳"为 tired with,"厌倦"为 tired of = sick of.

35. 人生常常譬作航海。

    注　compare to (for dissimilar things),是"譬喻"的意思, compare with (for similar things)是"比较"。Some people have compared books to friends.(有人以书喻友。)Artificial light cannot compare with day light for general use.(在一般的用途上,人造光是不能与日光比较的。)

36. 宁为鸡先,勿为牛后。

    注　在 than 后省去了不定词的 to。

37. 爱荷华州州长休士,已经把他自己被州内一致推举出来提名竞选总统的候补资格撤销,而随后不久就宣布他支持明尼苏达州的参议员麦卡席竞选。

    注　favorite son = a candidate favored by the political leaders of his own State, city, etc. for nomination to a high office, especially the presidency. 由其州内的政治领袖们所推举出来的总统候选人。

38. 如果今天举行选举的话,我们就用不着要感谢上帝了。

    注　既然失败,自然不必感谢上帝了。have a prayer = offer a prayer of thankfulness 或 a prayer of thanks to God.

39. 我宁愿他不在此。

    注　句中 room 作"余地"解,company 作"伴侣"解。his room 指"他的余地"或"他的空间",即空了他,也就是说他不在。例句全文意为"与其跟他同席,宁愿他不在场的好",简译成"我宁愿他不在此"。

40. 说女人不会驾车实有疑问的余地。

    注　在 open 后无 to 者,如 an open question(尚未解决的问题),但有 to 时,如 open to = not protected 易受……的,招致……的。His conduct is open to grave objections.(他的行为易受严重的反对。)The evidence is open to doubt.(证据有可疑的余地。)

41. 那迷失的孩子很快就认明身份了。

42. 他致意你。

    注　remember A to B,意为 A 向 B 致意。

43. 我近来简直没有看见他。

    注　nothing of 为副词用法,意为"一点也没有"。

44. 他把他所有的少许东西,也分配给穷人了。

    注　with the poor 是接 shared 说的,不是接 had 的。

45. 无钱购买的东西,只好不要。

    注　what you cannot afford to buy 是 do without 宾语。

46. 做了的事不能取消。

    注　这句话用主动语态说便是 we cannot undo what we do.

47. 她相信他诚实地这样说了。

    注　so 是修饰 said 的,不是修饰 honestly.

48. 它们打成碎片了。

注　a dozen 不一定是说十二,在此只是表示多数。
49. 新生之犊不畏虎。
　　注　意为什么都不懂的人什么都不怕。
50. 这画是模仿吴昌硕画的。
51. 他知道让孩子游荡下去是很不好的。
　　注　have a boy idle(让孩子游荡)和 have an idle boy(有懒惰的孩子)大不相同,前者的 idle 为 have 的补语。
52. 不喜欢做并不是不能做的证明。
　　注　it 的真正的主语,不是 that 以下的文句,而是 because 以下的文句。
53. 那些是我买的新书。
　　注　new 是补语。
54. 他从朋友处借了马来。
　　注　of = from,用法与 buy of 或 receive of 中的 of 相同。
55. 他一点钟走了十英里。
　　注　cover 与距离连用时,意为"通过","走过",如:These cars cover 200 miles a day.(这些车一天能走二百英里。)
56. 他随意自斟自酌。
　　注　help oneself to,自己取用。
57. 我认为激烈的男性的运动是好的。
　　注　believe in,一般都作"相信"解,但在此意为"相信有效","相信是好的","信以为真"。
58. 他没有看完那部影片。
　　注　see……out,看到最后为止。
59. 不幸有八十人死亡。
　　注　poor = unfortunate,可怜,不幸。
60. 他没有说一点含有那种意思的话。
　　注　to that effect 中的 effect = meaning. 他例如 He wrote to that effect. (他写的大意如此。)The letter is to the effect that……(那信的大意为……)

叁　翻译实例

Ⅰ. 中译英

(1)(a)One of the best ways to make the world peaceful and happy is for every individual to keep within his own province, refraining from encroaching upon others'. If a family follows this way, that family will be free from worry; if a nation follows this way, that nation will be at peace; and if the entire world follows this way, it will find itself in perfect peace.

(b)In order to secure (or bring about) a happy and peaceful world, we must first of all, limit our activity within our own spheres, strictly refraining from trespassing upon others'. Suppose that this rule is observed in all families, countries of the world, surely there will be no trouble in them all.

(c) "Just sweep away the snow in front of your own house, and never mind the frost on other people's roof," as the Chinese proverb says, may be the best way to bring about a happy and peaceful world. So long as we limit our activity within our own spheres, strictly refraining from trespassing upon others', we can surely win peace in the family, in the country as well as in the world.

(2) Learning is one's own business, which cannot rely upon others. It will certainly be of great help, if there are good environment, sufficient books and equipment, as well as instructions and enlightenments from scholarly mentors and benefitial friends. But even if you have got all these favorable conditions, you cannot be sure to succeed in learning, for not a few people who have successful in learning are not armed with all these things. The most impottant factor consists in one's own effort. To learn is rather a painstaking and persevering business. Many a man is a failure because he cannot bear such indispensable hardships.

(3) "As I want to know more of London, will you please tell me where shall I go first, Parliament or Downing Street?" I once asked the advice of my landlady. The old woman shook her head and replied, "Why should you go to those places? You had better go to Hyde Park first. You will understand from there how our England has got Parliament and Downing Street." Of course, she meant to say it is the spirit of the English people that has made the English politics, in other words, it is not because of Parliament and the Cabinet that England has got its democratic politics, but because of the people with their democratic spirit that there comes to be the English Parliament as well as the English Cabinet. Hyde Park is the very place where democratic spirit is fully demonstrated.

(4) Virtuousness is synonymous with beauty. We feel the beauty of a thing when it has come to realization ideally. By ideal realization we mean that a thing has displayed fully its true nature. Therefore, as a flower is at its best when it has revealed its natural character, a man may be said to have reached the zenith of his beauty when he has made the fullest use of human nature.

(5) Morals cannot be inculcated by means of spoken or written words. Those who have never been treated kindly must end their days without realizing what kindness is. To treat others with kindness, therefore, is to teach them what this virtue is. As the saying goes: Those who teach in word will be criticized, and those who teach in deed will have their followers.

(6) The implement of literature is the language. First we have to know the language, and then we must be armed with the craft of using it. The thing looks easy, as all of us are using the language every day, but it is really difficult, because literature is something that is expressed by ordinary language to produce an extraordinary effect. A man of letters must apprehend the language more precisely and thoroughly than the ordinary people, so that he can use it at his will. He must understand the form, the sound, and the meaning of a word, as well as the effects of the arrangements of words in connexion with the sound and meaning to be felt by the reader. This will involve such knowledge as philology, logic, grammar, aesthetics, and psychology……If a man is to create some literature of the first class, he must,

besides other conditions, have profound knowledge of the language, so as to be able to express any idea and express it effectively.

(7) Chuang-tzu went out for pleasure with his friend Hui-tzu on the bridge over River Hao.

"How happily those little silver fish are swimming in the water! I wish I were a fish, too," said Chuang-tzu.

At this Hui-tzn said, "You aren't a fish, are you? How can you know whether the fish are happy or not?"

"You aren't me," retorted the other, "how do you know that I do not know the happiness of the fish?"

"Quite so," Hui-tzu said, taking advantage of what the other had said. "It is true that I don't know your happiness because I am not you, and for the same reason, you don't know the happiness of the fish, because you are not a fish. Isn't it clear enough?"

(8) As everyone knows, four or five o'clock is tea time in England. The Prime Minister, fashion models, policemen—very likely even robbers too—must have their afternoon tea.

A cup of tea, with toast or biscuit, with a bit of conversation. This is the scene to be witnessed everywhere in England at four or in the average home. For women office workers, the "tea break" is a welcome relief from the day's busy work. Even soldiers at the battlefront will take time out for tea, if circumstances permit. It is a firm British tradition.

(9)(a) Everybody knows of St. Valentine's Day, a "love day" to admire sweethearts. Its origin is rather old and goes back to the Roman times. Young men chose their sweethearts by picking from a lottery box the names of girls who lived nearby. In the Middle Ages St. Valentine's Day came to be held on February 14th, and people in Europe and America developed a variety of new ways to celebrate the day.

Although it may seem odd to oriental people, a young man would kiss the first girl whom he met on that day.

In the 19th century people began sending beautiful verses and cards particular to that day, and exchanging gifts.

Today it is a popular custom from people to send cards not only to their sweethearts but to their parents and teachers as well.

(b) St. Valentine's Day is known as a "love day" honoring sweethearts. Its origin goes back to the Roman times. In those days young men picked their own sweethearts by drawing from a lottery box the names of young girls living in the same towns and villages. During the Middle Ages, the date of the St. Valentine's festival is supposed to have been fixed on February 14th, and people in Europe and America found new ways to celebrate the day. Strange as it may seem to some orientals, young men would kiss the first lady whom they happened to meet on that day. In the 19th century young people started sending beautifully decorated verses and cards specially designed for this day, and also began exchanging gifts. Today not only to particular persons like sweethearts, but also to parents and teachers as well, people often send cards on this day.

(10)(a) My parents' property on the River Yonne offered few distractions. I would go down to the river bank, occasionally look for a moment at the weeds floating yellow on the surface, then choose little flattened stones to send skimming over the water like darting swallows.

The house where we lived was long and grey. A field stretched down from it to the River Yonne full of foam, which was girdled by flights of swallows in the sky and poplars on the field. One in particular I loved to lie under. I was surprised to see myself smile in the grass. I did not stop myself from smiling, nor could I. (in British English)

(b) My parents' place on the Yonne River offered little to do. I used to go down to the bank of the stream, now and then look for a while at the formations of yellow algae on the surface and then skip flat stones across the water, which moved as swiftly as swallows.

Our house was long and gray. A meadow ran down to the foamflecked Yonne River, with swallows soaring overhead and poplar trees on the ground bordering each side. There was one poplar, in particular, in whose shade I liked to lie. I saw myself smile. I did try to prevent it, could not even if I had tried. (in American English)

注 本文是从现代法国女作家沙冈的小说《微笑》(*Un Certain Sourire*)中取出来的,用英国话和美国话分别加以译出。英语译文由英国人罗爵斯执笔,美语译文由美国人加查林女士执笔。

Ⅱ.英译中

(1)当作一个朋友你是一个非常奇怪的人! 常常要我在任何人的面前来弹唱! 如果我的虚荣心转向音乐方面的话,那你对我倒是很有价值的鼓励;可惜像我现在这样,我真是不愿坐在那些必然是便于听最好的演奏的人们面前来献丑。

注 1. by way of:"作为","当作"。例如 He said something by way of an apology. (他说了一点道歉的话。)2. take a musical turn:这个 turn 的意思是"转机","改变","变化"的意思。例如 The sick person has taken a turn for the better. (病人情形有了好转。)

(2)从那以来已经有二十年了。他一直在忙着和一些贵妇们通信,而他写的信是很有趣而健谈的。对于那些有爵位的人,他从来没有失去爱好的心情,在《泰晤士报》上所刊登的人物往来的报导,他都要很注意地来看的。他对于通知诞生,死亡,结婚的一栏,也看得很仔细,随时都准备好,要去信道贺或是悼唁。

(3)一个作家必须尽力来给它传达思想的,原只限于他自己的一代,而他要让后继的一代去选择他们自己的代言人,实为明智的办法。不管他要不要这样做,他们终归是会这样做的。他所说的这一套,他们是不会懂得的。

注 1. exponent:代言人,代表者(= representative)。例如 This form of discontent found its exponent in Mr. A. (对于这种不满,A 氏以代表人物的姿态出现。)

(4)世间一般认作爱好自然的人,屡屡地常被指责为多情善感,而这种指责常是颇为中肯的。照那些指责者的说法,他只是一味花香鸟语,说个不停而已。他忽视了事物的黑暗面,拿庆贺佳节时的祝颂语句的词意来看这个世界。

(5)基于对事实的一种故意使之不完全的想法,而具有错误的感情,也被谴责为伤感的话,那么,说大自然经常是狂暴而残酷的那种想法,也和反对论调同样是感情用事。大自然的特质,既不是慈爱的母性,也不是血染的爪牙。

注　1. be guilty of：犯（commit）。例如 You have been guilty of a serious blunder.（你犯过一个大错。）又有"有……缺点"的意思，例如 be guilty of breach of good manners.（违反礼节。）be guilty of bad taste（低级趣味。）I was guilty of great impoliteness.（我大为失礼。）2. red in tooth and claw. 爪牙染血。（见 Tennyson 的名作：*In Memoriam*, LV.）

（6）人类的创造力，在征服黑暗的努力上，大概是比在其他任何方面，都要来得活跃。在人类与黑暗奋斗的当中，灯光是人类自力供给的最初的必需品之一。虽然，黑暗也有它的好处，当夜幕下降，大自然便准备着来休息和睡眠，而在那种夜的寂静之中，人类便得为第二天的职责及任务，而恢复心身的力量。

注　1. in nothing have……powers been so active as in his. = powers have been so active in nothing as in his. 2. triumph over：征服，胜过。3. is among：= is one of. 例如 Light is among the first needs. = Light is one of the first things that were needed.（光明是首要的必需品之一。）4. in his struggle against it：= when he was struggling against darkness. 5. burden：重荷，费力的任务。6. nature prepares itself for：便进入……的状态。

（7）这种团结的逐渐实现，也许是由于科学进步所促成的工艺进步的结果。那种进步使得各大城市间的距离缩短，市场不断扩大。但是若把这种工艺上的统一当作主要的原因，就不免带有成见，而完全是一种不当的想法。

注　1. unwarranted：不当的。动词 warrant，有"证明……为正当"的意思。2. preconceive：预想，例如 a preconceived idea（或 notion）（成见，偏见，先入为主的意见）。3. solidarity：团结。*Cf*. solidity：团体性，充实，坚固，坚实，体积。

（8）一个肥胖的老妇人，手上提着一个篮子，在彼得堡的马路当中走着。一时使得交通大为混乱，她自己也冒上很大的危险。有人向她指明，走路的人应该在人行道上走，她却回答说："现在革过命了，我们获得了自由。我喜欢在哪里走，就可以在哪里走呀。"那个老妇人却有所不知，如果允许走路的人走到马路当中去，那么也要让开车的人把车子开到人行道上来，这样自由的结果，会要造成普遍的混乱是无疑的。

注　1. Petrograd：为 1914 到 1924 年苏联的首都，后改名为 Leningrad. 2. no small：= great. 3. occur to：心中想到。4. entitle：使有资格，使有权。例如　This ticket entitles you to a free lunch.（凭此券可免费午餐一次。）You are not entitled to sit here.（你没有资格坐在此地。）

（9）因为愚笨地妄自尊大，我尝拿一个人的智力和学识来判断他的真价：认为不合逻辑的就不好，没有学问的就不美。现在我以为我们必须把两种不同的智力分别一下才是。知识的智力和感情的智力，而我觉得后者比前者重要得多。

注　logic：与前面说的 intellectual power 相呼应。2. learning 与前面说的 attainment 相呼应。3. the brain：理智。4. the heart：感情。

（10）受过教育的人，是被认为知道什么是人间不正的行为，及应该怎样去加以纠正的。如果他的教育达到某种程度的话，那便能促进他明确的思考能力——找出事物的因果关系，进而明悉政治上，社会上，经济上，和工业上的病根。谁也无权认定教育只是为个人的利益的，使他能够更加飞黄腾达。他必须把教育视为加诸其身的一种责任，用来造福人群才对。但大多数的人都把教育认为是他们所私有，而不了解那是应与他人分享的，应该用来增进社会一般福利的。

注　1. amount to anything：达到某种程度。2. clearly and scientifically：明确地。3. be more prosperous and happy in the world：更加飞黄腾达。4. at large：一般的。例如 Did the people at large approve of the war?（一般的人都赞成打仗吗？）

出版后记

在钱歌川先生编写的大量英语教学资料中，《翻译的技巧》是最富盛名的。

能让那么多的读者从中获益，端赖于这本书是在他数十年从事翻译教学工作的基础上，花费十年的工夫，反复修订校改，于七十岁高龄才付梓出版，可谓浓缩了钱先生英语知识的精华，供读者学习汲取。

钱先生长期身处教学第一线，最明白不过所谓技巧，无非是尊重学习的规律，由点滴积累的量变促成质变的飞升，这是他在《翻译的基本知识》一书中反复强调的。是以这本书的编排，并非是零碎技巧的补丁集合，也没有什么一招鲜的秘诀，而是从英语语法的梳理开始，经由对12项134条语法知识点的讲解，再上升到段落篇章的翻译。这样的科学的系统化的编排方式，使得无论是想提升自己的英语翻译水平还是希望夯实自己的英语知识的读者，都可以依照本书，循序渐进地学习下去。是以，钱先生在序言中所言，"像本书这样有系统，有方法，来研究翻译的书，似乎还不多见，也可说是破天荒之举"，绝非自夸之词。

钱先生不仅熟习英语，中文的功底也是相当了得。书中中文段落，有些选自中国的古书和明清小品，翻译文言文的过程，最能体现钱先生在《翻译的基本知识》中强调的"首先要了解原文"，读者在对文言原文字句意思的推敲琢磨中，自觉地锻炼严复强调的信达雅的原则。

本书的附录选取了16篇当时欧美文学名著中的段落进行摘译。我们从钱先生对名家名作的解说中可以看到，钱先生非常熟悉欧美文坛的动态，其阅读量之大，评论之中允深刻才情横溢，提醒了我们学习英语一定要建立在大量的阅读和思考之上，非一朝一夕之功可成。

本书简体版曾与1981年由商务印书馆精装出版，市面上早已难以买到。鉴于当今中国与世界接轨的步伐越来越快，英语学习的热潮前所未有的高涨，我们认为这样一本扎实丰厚的英语教本可以让读者少走很多弯路，进行有效的学习，重新出版是非常必要的，希望这本书的再版能够为读者答疑解惑。

在此感谢帮助我们联系版权的张兆龙先生，他的热心帮助促成了钱歌川先生的作品在大陆的出版。我社也相继推出了钱先生的《翻译的基本知识》《英文疑难详解》《英文疑难详解续篇》《英文语法作文大全》，以进一步满足读者的英语学习需求。

服务热线：133-6631-2326　188-1142-1266
服务信箱：reader@hinabook.com

后浪出版公司
2015年6月

图书在版编目（CIP）数据

翻译的技巧 / 钱歌川著. -- 北京：北京联合出版公司，2015.8（2023.4重印）
ISBN 978-7-5502-5435-0

Ⅰ.①翻… Ⅱ.①钱… Ⅲ.①英语—翻译 Ⅳ.①H315.9
中国版本图书馆CIP数据核字（2015）第113477号

Simplified Chinese edition

Copyright © 2015 POST WAVE PUBLISHING CONSULTING (Beijing) Co., Ltd.
本书中文简体版权归属于后浪出版咨询(北京)有限责任公司

翻译的技巧

著　　者：钱歌川
出 品 人：赵红仕
选题策划：后浪出版公司
出版统筹：吴兴元
特约编辑：张　鹏
责任编辑：刘　凯
封面设计：周伟伟
营销推广：ONEBOOK
装帧制造：墨白空间

北京联合出版公司出版
（北京市西城区德外大街83号楼9层　100088）
北京天宇万达印刷有限公司印刷　新华书店经销
字数700千字　787×1092毫米　1/16　26印张　插页4
2015年8月第1版　2023年4月第11次印刷
ISBN 978-7-5502-5435-0
定价：60.00元

后浪出版咨询(北京)有限责任公司　版权所有，侵权必究
投诉信箱：copyright@hinabook.com　fawu@hinabook.com
未经许可，不得以任何方式复制或抄袭本书部分或全部内容
本书若有印、装质量问题，请与本公司联系调换，电话010-64072833

小说鉴赏
（双语修订第3版）

著　者：（美）克林斯·布鲁克斯　罗伯特·潘·沃伦
译　者：主　万　冯亦代　草　婴　丰子恺　汝　龙　等
书　号：978-7-5062-5475-5
出版时间：2012.10
定　价：78.00元

**美国新批评里程碑性质著作　全世界大学的经典文学教科书
真正意义上的双语全版　中文版英文版尽入囊中**

经典著作　美国新批评派里程碑性质的著作，全世界大学都在使用的经典文学教科书，同时也被认为是最好的文学自修读物。两位作者站在世界文学的前沿，从内部到外部对小说进行研究，突破传统意义上的小说审美，是新批评理论观点和方法在小说批评与理论领域的全新体现。

双语呈现　既可欣赏信达雅致的中文译文，又能品尝原汁原味的英文文献，使本书既是一部绝妙的小说读本，同时又是一部难得的英语学习素材。

权威著者　本书作者布鲁克斯和沃伦同为新批评派的领军人物，耶鲁大学教授，著名文学评论家，享有世界声誉。沃伦曾两获普利策奖，是美国第一位桂冠诗人。二人共同创办了当时美国最有影响力的文学杂志《南方评论》。

超强阵容　我国著名翻译家草婴、主万、汝龙、冯亦代、丰子恺、雨宁等联手献上绝佳译文。著名作家、小说理论家、北京大学中文系曹文轩教授，著名翻译家《世界文学》主编李文俊审阅；海外著名华人女作家聂华苓女士倾力推荐。

这是美国新批评派学者布鲁克斯和沃伦合编的一部短篇小说鉴赏集，是新批评理论观点和方法在小说批评与理论领域的体现。作者选用各种题材和多种风格的短篇小说，加以分析讨论和互相比较，提出鉴别好小说的一些原则，阐述小说的形成与发展过程，为我们提供了小说批评与赏析的范例；目的是为了加深读者对作品的理解和提高他们的鉴赏力，使读者更接近于成功小说的真谛。

作为新批评派细读式批评和理论阐述的名著，本书帮助新批评派在美国大学的文学讲坛中确立了"文学批评"的地位，对文学教学与批评实践影响深远。它既是一本文学教科书，也是文学爱好者的自修读物。本书采用中英文对照模式，对于广大具有一定英语基础的文学爱好者和英文专业的师生来讲，它又是一部难得的英语阅读材料。

翻译的基本知识
（修订版）

著　　者：钱歌川
书　　号：978-7-5502-5092-5
出版时间：2015.07
定　　价：26.00 元

流行华语世界四十载的翻译知识入门书
民国英语教育泰斗一生翻译经验之菁华

　　大家小书　作者钱歌川有丰富的翻译教学和亲手翻译经验，《翻译的基本知识》以短小的篇幅，凝聚了翻译理论与实践的菁华，适合所有对翻译问题感兴趣的人阅读。

　　面向新手　本书前半部介绍了翻译的历史、语言学基础、规则和标准，后半部手把手地教授翻译的具体步骤，以点带面，涵括了翻译领域的基本问题，引领读者轻松步入翻译的殿堂。

　　风味隽永　钱歌川为海派散文名家，具有高超的字句锤炼功夫和卓然的语言感悟能力。本书虽为学术著作，却如英国散文一般耐读。

　　名句为例　书中的英译中举例皆选自莎士比亚、欧·亨利、海明威等名家名作，中译英则多出于《论语》、《左传》、李白、苏轼名篇佳句，读者在学习翻译的过程中可随之提高文学修养。

作者简介：

　　钱歌川（1903—1990），原名慕祖，笔名歌川、味橄等。湖南湘潭人。著名的散文家、翻译家、英语学者。1920年赴日留学。1930年进上海中华书局做编辑，曾参与创办《新中华》杂志，并担任《中华英语半月刊》主编，在此期间，将大量精力放在英语读物的翻译、编写、出版方面。1936年入英国伦敦大学研究英美语言文学。1939年回国后，先后在武汉大学、东吴大学等处任教。曾与鲁迅、茅盾、田汉、郭沫若、郁达夫等文化名人交往，参与文化运动。1947年春，前往台北创办台湾大学文学院并任院长。20世纪60年代赴新加坡，先后任义安学院、新加坡大学和南洋大学中文系教授。1972年底，以70岁高龄退出讲台，后移居美国纽约。

　　钱歌川一生发表了大量散文与英语教学资料，包括《翻译的基本知识》《翻译的技巧》《英文疑难详解》《英文疑难详解续篇》《英文语法作文大全》《论翻译》《简易英文文法》《简易英文动词》《美国日用英语》《英语造句例解》等，影响深远。

韦洛克拉丁语教程
（插图修订第7版）

著　　者：（美）弗雷德里克·M·韦洛克
修 订 者：（美）理查德·拉弗勒
译　　者：张卜天
推 荐 者：雷立柏　彭小瑜　沈弘
书　　号：978-7-5502-9681-7
出版时间：2017.05
定　　价：118.00 元

学习拉丁语，人必称韦洛克

《韦洛克拉丁语教程》是20世纪后半期以来英语世界最受欢迎的拉丁语教材，初版于1956年，很快就因其严密的组织结构、清晰的叙述讲解、循序渐进的设计安排、适中的难易程度，以及其中收录的丰富的古代文献而被誉为"拉丁语学习的标准著作"，其"拉丁语学习首选教材"的地位无可撼动。

全书共分四十课，以简洁而不学究气的语言，系统讲解了拉丁语的基本词形、句法，并通过丰富的词汇学习、众多的英语词源研究、英拉句子互译和古典拉丁语作家原文赏读，来锻炼拉丁语学习者使用单词的灵活性和精确性，培养其观察、分析、判断和评价的能力，加强对语言形式、清晰性和美的感受；并通过探讨战争、友谊、未来、生老病死等发人深省的主题来学习古典作家的思想和技艺，分享他们的人文主义传统。

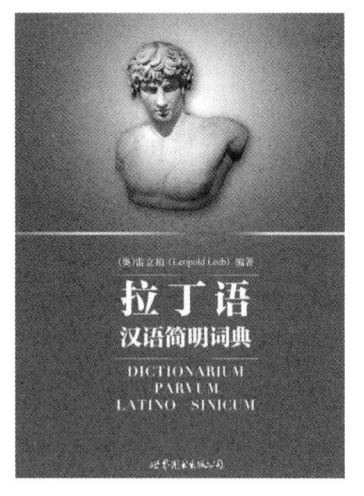

拉丁语汉语简明词典

著　　者：（奥）雷立柏
书　　号：978-7-5100-3172-4
出版时间：2011.01
定　　价：49.80 元

21 世纪中国首部综合性拉丁语汉语词典
语文为主，兼顾百科，收录常用常见拉丁词汇 15000 余条
释义准确，简明精当，标注详尽
条目编排清晰醒目，便于读者查询